that may give you some ideas. It suggests ways to combine the chapters in Part I with the reading selections in Part II and the added reading materials in Part III.

4. Use a workshop approach. Just as students benefit from varied exercises, they profit from varied approaches to a skill. One way to cover a skill is to work through a chapter page by page, alternating between putting some of the material on the board and explaining or reading some of it aloud. When you get to a practice in a chapter, give students a couple of minutes to do the practice. When a majority of the class has finished the practice, call on someone to read the first question and answer it. If the answer is right, say "Good job," and call on someone else to read the next question. If the answer is wrong, say something like "Does anyone have a different answer?" This can lead to a discussion where you can see if students are catching on, and you can find a way to move them in the right direction.

You should feel confident about having students read a sentence or so out loud. Even if they have limited reading skills, a sentence or two will not cause them undue anxiety or embarrassment. On the other hand, reading an entire paragraph may be too much for some students. It is best to call on volunteers for paragraphs or to read them aloud yourself. Or, if there are time constraints, have students read the paragraph silently and then ask them to read aloud the questions that follow the paragraph.

5. Use a small-group approach at times. When you get to a review test, you may want to divide the class into groups of four and ask them to work together to do the answers for the test. Tell them that when they are done and everyone in the group agrees on the answers, a representative from the group should go to the board and write down the group's answers. Say, "Let's see which group is first to answer all the questions correctly."

Put a grid such as this one on the board:

	1	2	3	4	5
Kim's Group					
Robert's Group					
Nelson's Group					
Nina's Group					

Students will enjoy the competition, and peer pressure will keep everyone attentive and involved. When all of the groups have finished, you and the class can look at the board together to see just where the groups agree and disagree. You can then focus discussion on answers where there is disagreement.

6. Use a pairs approach at times. Having two students work together on questions is another way to energize students and help them teach one another. When an exercise has been completed by the majority of the class, one way to go over the material is to have one student in each pair read a question and the other student read the answer.

FOURTH EDITION

TEN STEPS
to
IMPROVING
COLLEGE
READING SKILLS

John Langan
ATLANTIC CAPE COMMUNITY COLLEGE

INSTRUCTOR'S EDITION

Books in the Townsend Press Reading Series:

Groundwork for College Reading
Ten Steps to Building College Reading Skills
Ten Steps to Improving College Reading Skills
Ten Steps to Advancing College Reading Skills

Books in the Townsend Press Vocabulary Series:

Vocabulary Basics
Groundwork for a Better Vocabulary
Building Vocabulary Skills
Building Vocabulary Skills, Short Version
Improving Vocabulary Skills
Improving Vocabulary Skills, Short Version
Advancing Vocabulary Skills
Advancing Vocabulary Skills, Short Version
Advanced Word Power

Supplements Available for Most Books:

Instructor's Edition
Instructor's Manual and Test Bank
Computer Software (Windows or Macintosh)

Copyright © 2003 by Townsend Press, Inc.
Printed in the United States of America
ISBN 1-59194-004-4
9 8 7 6 5 4 3 2 1

Send book orders and requests for desk copies or supplements to:
Townsend Press Book Center
1038 Industrial Drive
West Berlin, New Jersey 08091

For even faster service, contact us in any of the following ways:
By telephone: 1-800-772-6410
By fax: 1-800-225-8894
By e-mail: TownsendCS@aol.com
Through our website: www.townsendpress.com

Contents

Preface:
To the Instructor

We all know that many students entering college today do not have the reading skills needed to do effective work in their courses. A related problem, apparent even in class discussions, is that students often lack the skills required to think in a clear and logical way.

The purpose of *Ten Steps to Improving College Reading Skills, Fourth Edition*, is to develop effective reading and clear thinking. To do so, **Part I** presents a sequence of ten reading skills that are widely recognized as essential for basic and advanced comprehension. The first six skills concern the more literal levels of comprehension:

- Understanding vocabulary in context
- Recognizing main ideas
- Identifying supporting details
- Recognizing implied main ideas and the central point
- Understanding relationships that involve addition and time
- Understanding relationships that involve examples, comparison and/or contrast, and cause and effect

The remaining skills cover the more advanced, critical levels of comprehension:

- Distinguishing between facts and opinions
- Making inferences
- Identifying an author's purpose and tone
- Evaluating arguments

In every chapter in Part I, the key aspects of a skill are explained and illustrated clearly and simply. Explanations are accompanied by a series of practices, and each chapter ends with four review tests. The last review test consists of a reading selection so that students can apply the skill just learned to real-world reading materials, including newspaper and magazine articles and textbook selections. Together, the ten chapters provide students with the skills needed for both basic and more advanced reading comprehension.

Following each chapter in Part I are **at least six mastery tests for the skill in question.** The tests progress in difficulty, giving students the additional practice and challenge they may need for the solid learning of each skill. While designed for quick grading, the tests also require students to think carefully before answering each question.

Part II is made up of ten additional readings that will improve both reading and thinking skills. Each reading is followed by *Basic Skill Questions* and *Advanced Skill Questions* so that students can practice all ten skills presented in Part I. In addition, an *Outlining, Mapping, or Summarizing* activity after each reading helps students think carefully about the basic content and organization of a selection. *Discussion Questions* then afford instructors a final opportunity to engage students in a variety of reading and thinking skills and thus deepen their understanding of a selection.

Part III serves a variety of purposes. Fifteen combined-skills passages and tests review the skills taught in Part I and help students prepare for the standardized reading test that is often a requirement at the end of a semester. A section on propaganda techniques offers instruction and practice in a reading skill that some (but probably not all) instructors will have time to address. Next, there is a section on logical fallacies that can be covered depending on student needs and course requirements. Finally, there are writing assignments for all twenty readings in the text. When time permits, asking students to write about a selection will help reinforce the reading and thinking skills they have practiced in the book.

Important Features of the Book

- **Focus on the basics.** The book is designed to explain in a clear, step-by-step way the essential elements of each skill. Many examples are provided to ensure that students understand each point. In general, the focus is on teaching the skills—not just on explaining or testing them.

- **Frequent practice and feedback.** Because abundant practice and careful feedback are essential to learning, this book includes numerous activities. Students can get immediate feedback on the practice exercises in Part I by turning to the limited answer key at the back of the book. The answers to the review and mastery tests in Part I, the reading questions in Part II, and the combined-skills tests in Part III are in the *Instructor's Manual.*

The limited answer key increases the active role that students take in their own learning. They are likely to use the answer key in an honest and positive way if they know they will be tested on the many activities and selections for which answers are not provided. (Answers not in the book can be easily copied from the *Instructor's Edition* or the *Instructor's Manual* and passed out at the teacher's discretion.)

- **High interest level.** Dull and unvaried readings and exercises work against learning. Students need to experience genuine interest and enjoyment in what they read. Teachers as well should be able to take pleasure in the selections, for their own good feeling can carry over favorably into class work. The readings in the book, then, have been chosen not only for the appropriateness of their reading level but also for their compelling content. They should engage teachers and students alike.

- **Ease of use.** The logical sequence in each chapter—from explanation to example to practice to review test to mastery test—helps make the skills easy to teach. The book's organization into distinct parts also makes for ease of use. Within a single class, for instance, teachers can work on a new skill in Part I, review other skills with one or more mastery tests, and provide variety by having students read one of the selections in Part II. The limited answer key at the back of the text also makes for versatility: the teacher can assign some chapters for self-teaching. Finally, the mastery tests—each on its own tear-out page— and the combined-skills tests make it a simple matter for teachers to test and evaluate student progress.

- **Integration of skills.** Students do more than learn the skills individually in Part I. They also learn to apply the skills together through the reading selections in Parts I and II as well as the combined-skills tests in Part III. They become effective readers and thinkers through repeated practice in applying a combination of skills.

- **Online exercises.** As they complete each of the ten chapters, students are invited to go online to the Townsend Press website to work on two additional practice exercises for each skill—exercises that reinforce the skill taught in the chapter.

- **Thinking activities.** Thinking activities—in the form of outlining, mapping, and summarizing—are a distinctive feature of the book. While educators agree that such organizational abilities are important, these skills are all too seldom taught. From a practical standpoint, it is almost impossible for a teacher to respond in detail to entire collections of class outlines or summaries. This book then, presents activities that truly involve students in outlining, mapping, and summarizing—in other words, that truly make students *think*—and yet enable a teacher to give immediate feedback. Again, it is through continued practice *and* feedback on challenging material that a student becomes a more effective reader and thinker.

- **Supplementary materials.** The three helpful supplements listed below are available at no charge to instructors who have adopted the text. Any or all can be obtained quickly by writing or calling Townsend Press (1038 Industrial Drive, West Berlin, New Jersey 08091; 1-800-772-6410), by sending a fax to 1-800-225-8894, or by e-mailing Customer Service at **<townsendcs@aol.com>**.

  1 An *Instructor's Edition*—chances are that you are holding it in your hand—is identical to the student book except that it also provides hints for teachers (see the front of the book), answers to all the practices and tests, and comments on selected items.

  2 A combined *Instructor's Manual and Test Bank* includes suggestions for teaching the course, a model syllabus, and readability levels for the text and the reading selections. The test bank contains four additional mastery tests for each of the ten skills and four additional combined-skills tests— all on letter-sized sheets so they can be copied easily for use with students.

  3 *Computer software* (in Windows and Macintosh formats) provides two additional mastery tests for each of the ten skill chapters in the book. The software contains a number of user- and instructor-friendly features: brief explanations of answers, a sound option, frequent mention of the user's first name, a running score, and a record-keeping score file.

- **One of a sequence of books.** This is the intermediate text in a series that includes three other books. The first book in the series, *Groundwork for College Reading,* is suited for ESL students and basic adult learners. The second book, *Ten Steps to Building College Reading Skills,* is often the choice for a first college reading course. The *Improving* book is appropriate for the core developmental reading course offered at most colleges. *Ten Steps to Advancing College Reading Skills* is a higher developmental text than the *Improving* book. It can be used as the core book for a more advanced class, as a sequel to the intermediate book, or as a second-semester alternative to it.

  A companion set of vocabulary books, listed on the copyright page, has been designed to go with the *Ten Steps* books. Recommended to accompany this book is *Improving Vocabulary Skills* (300 words and word parts) or *Improving Vocabulary Skills, Short Version* (200 words).

  Together, the books and all their supplements form a sequence that should be ideal for any college reading program.

To summarize, *Ten Steps to Improving College Reading Skills, Fourth Edition,* provides ten key reading skills to help developmental college students become independent readers and thinkers. Through an appealing collection of readings and a carefully designed series of activities and tests, students receive extensive guided practice in the skills. The result is an integrated approach to learning that will, by the end of the course, produce better readers and stronger thinkers.

Changes in the Fourth Edition

Teacher suggestions and class use of the text have led to a number of major changes in the book:

- **Online exercises for each of the ten chapters in the book.** These are signaled at the end of each chapter with the following icon: 🖥. Students can go to the Townsend Press website (**www.townsendpress.com**) to do two additional practice exercises for each skill. Each exercise consists of ten items, and as students answer the items, they are provided with both a running score and explanations of each answer. The exercises, in other words, teach as well as offer practice, and they should serve as an excellent supplement to the activities and tests in each chapter of the book.

- **New teaching features within the chapters.** Three new features—Study Hints and Tips, "Check Your Understanding" exercises, and Chapter Reviews—make the book even easier to use. In addition, a new format for practice and test questions makes them even simpler to grade. If you were happy before with the notably clear format of the book, you'll be even more pleased with the Fourth Edition.

- **A completely revised chapter on main ideas.** No skill is more important to good comprehension, so a great deal of time and class testing went into developing a fresh approach to teaching main ideas. The result is a chapter that, in an exceptionally clear, step-by-step way, shows students three specific ways to locate main ideas. This central skill will now be even more accessible to students.

- **New sections on reading tables and graphs and on figurative language.** The chapter on inferences has been expanded to include the reading of visual materials—tables and graphs. Students also learn to infer the meanings of similes and metaphors that are so often a part of literary writing.

- **New introductory chapters.** The Introduction has been expanded to include three separate chapters. One of the added chapters will help motivate students to read regularly—the most essential step to sustained reading growth; another chapter presents some quick study tips every student should know.

- **Greater visual appeal.** Additional photographs and cartoons in this edition create visual appeal and also help teach key skills. Boxes, rules, and screens set off patterns of organization, chapter reviews, and important points. The book is more visually friendly without becoming visually cluttered.

- **Many new models and practice materials and four new readings.** One reading is particularly noteworthy: "The Real Story of Flight 93" celebrates the heroic passengers who thwarted the terrorist plan to fly a hijacked plane into a second Washington, D.C. government building.

Acknowledgments

I am grateful for the many helpful suggestions provided by the following reviewers: Glenda Bell, University of Arkansas Community College at Batesville; Gwendolyne Bunch, Midlands Technical College; Donna Clack, Schoolcraft College; Kay Fell, Tarrant County College; Linda Gilmore, Carroll Community College; Belinda C. Hauenstein, Burlington County College; Nancy Joseph, Southeast Community College; Ellen Kaiden, Ramapo College; Miriam Kinard, Trident Technical College; Jerre J. Kennedy, Brevard Community College; Jackie Lumsden, Greenville Technical College; Vashti Musc, Hinds Community College; Helen Sabin, El Camino College; Eileen Suruda, Essex Community College; Mary Temerson, Richmond Community College; José Rafael Trevino, Laredo Community College; B. Jean Van Meter, Montgomery College; Paula Wimbish, Hinds Community College; and Leta Wium, Florida Community College at Jacksonville. In addition, Joanne Ernst of Manatee Community College provided helpful feedback on the prepublication copy of this edition. And I particularly appreciate the invaluable comments and suggestions made by Iris Hill, a reading instructor at Wake Technical Community College. Her insights led to changes in both the content and the format of the Fourth Edition and were pivotal to the new approach taken in the chapter on main ideas.

At Townsend Press, I thank Eliza Comodromos, Beth Johnson, Paul Langan, Carole Mohr, and Barbara Solot for the help they provided along the way. And I owe special thanks to editor extraordinaire Janet Goldstein. Because of her superb design and editing skills, the book enjoys an even more clear and "user-friendly" format than the previous edition. Her talents have also made possible the creation of the *Instructor's Edition*, complete with answers and marginal comments, that accompanies the book. It is always a special pleasure to work with people who aspire toward excellence. With help from my colleagues in the teaching profession and at Townsend Press, I have been able to create a much better book than I could have managed on my own.

John Langan

INTRODUCTION

1

How to Become a Better Reader and Thinker

The chances are that you are not as good a reader as you should be to do well in college. If so, it's not surprising. You live in a culture where people watch an average of *over seven hours of television every day!!!* All that passive viewing does not allow much time for reading. Reading is a skill that must be actively practiced. The simple fact is that people who do not read very often are not likely to be strong readers. *Answers will vary.*

- How much TV do you guess you watch on an average day? _____

Another reason besides TV for not reading much is that you may have a lot of responsibilities. You may be going to school and working at the same time, and you may have a lot of family duties as well. Given a hectic schedule, you're not going to have much time to read. When you have free time, you're exhausted, and it's easier to turn on the TV than to open up a book.

- Do you do any regular reading (for example, a daily newspaper, weekly magazines, occasional novels)? _____

- When are you most likely to do your reading? _____

A third reason for not reading is that school may have caused you to associate reading with worksheets and drills and book reports and test scores. Experts agree that many schools have not done a good job of helping students discover the pleasures and rewards of reading. If reading was an unpleasant experience in school, you may have concluded that reading in general is not for you.

- Do you think that school made you dislike reading, rather than enjoy it?

_____

Here are three final questions to ask yourself:

- Do you feel that perhaps you don't need a reading course, since you "already know how to read"? _____
- If you had a choice, would you be taking a reading course? (It's okay to be honest.) _____
- Do you think that a bit of speed reading may be all you need? _____

Chances are that you don't need to read *faster* as much as you need to read *smarter*. And it's a safe bet that if you don't read much, you can benefit enormously from the reading course in which you are using this book.

One goal of the book is to help you become a better reader. You will learn and practice ten key reading comprehension skills. As a result, you'll be better able to read and understand the many materials in your other college courses. The skills in this book have direct and practical value: they can help you perform better and more quickly—giving you an edge for success—in all of your college work.

The book is also concerned with helping you become a stronger thinker, a person able not just to understand what is read but to analyze and evaluate it as well. In fact, reading and thinking are closely related skills, and practice in thoughtful reading will also strengthen your ability to think clearly and logically. To find out just how the book will help you achieve these goals, read the next several pages and do the brief activities as well. The activities are easily completed and will give you a quick, helpful overview of the book.

HOW THE BOOK IS ORGANIZED

The book is organized into four main parts:

Introduction (pages 1–18)

In addition to this chapter, which will give you a good sense of the book, there are two other parts to the introduction. "Reading for Pleasure and Power" is a personal essay that describes my own experience in becoming a reader and suggests ways for you to develop the reading habit. Turn to page 13 and write, on the line below, the first of the suggestions:

Create a half hour or hour of reading in your daily schedule.

"Learning Some Quick Study Tips" presents four hints that can make you a better student. If I had time to say just four things to an incoming college students based on my thirty years of teaching experience, these are the things I would say. Turn to page 17 and write, in the space below, the first of these tips:

Go to every class and take a lot of notes.

Part I: Ten Steps to Improving College Reading Skills (pages 19–414)

To help you become a more effective reader and thinker, this book presents a series of ten key reading skills. They are listed in the table of contents on page v. Turn to that page to fill in the skills missing below:

1 Vocabulary in Context
2 *Main Ideas* _____
3 *Supporting Details* _____
4 Implied Main Ideas and the Central Point
5 Relationships I
6 Relationships II
7 *Fact and Opinion* _____
8 Inferences
9 *Purpose and Tone* _____
10 Argument

Each chapter is developed in the same way.

First of all, clear explanations and examples help you *understand* each skill. Practices then give you the "hands-on" experience needed to *learn* the skill.

• How many practices are there for the second chapter, "Main Ideas" (pages 53–94)? ___*Eight*___

Closing each chapter are four review tests. The first review test provides a check of the information presented in the chapter.

• On which page is the first review test for "Main Ideas"? ___*74*___

The second and third review tests consist of activities that help you practice the skill learned in the chapter.

• On which pages are Review Tests 2 and 3 for "Main Ideas"? ___*74–77*___

The fourth review test consists of a story, essay, or textbook selection that both gets you reading and gives you practice in the skill learned in the chapter as well as skills learned in previous chapters.

• What is the title of the reading selection in the "Main Ideas" chapter?
___*"Here's to Your Health"*___

Following each chapter are six mastery tests which gradually increase in difficulty.

• On what pages are the mastery tests for the "Main Ideas" chapter? ___*83–94*___

The tests are on tear-out pages and so can be easily removed and handed in to your instructor. So that you can track your progress, there is a score box at the top of each test. Your score can also be entered into the "Reading Performance Chart" on the inside back cover of the book.

Part II: Ten Reading Selections (pages 415–510)

The ten reading selections that make up Part II are followed by activities that give you practice in all of the skills studied in Part I. Each reading begins in the same way. Look, for example, at "The Yellow Ribbon," which starts on page 417. What are the headings of the two sections that come before the reading itself?

- _____ *Preview* _____

- _____ *Words to Watch* _____

Note that the vocabulary words in "Words to Watch" are followed by the numbers of the paragraphs in which the words appear. Look at the first page of "The Yellow Ribbon" and explain how each vocabulary word is marked in the reading itself.

- _____ *It has a small circle after it.* _____

Activities Following Each Reading Selection

After each selection, there are four kinds of activities to improve the reading and thinking skills you learned in Part I of the book.

1 The first activity consists of **basic skill questions**—questions involving vocabulary in context, main ideas (including implied main ideas and the central point), supporting details, and relationships.

- Look at the basic skill questions for "The Yellow Ribbon" on pages 419–420. Note that the questions are labeled so you know what skill you are practicing in each case. How many questions deal with understanding vocabulary in context? _____ *Two* _____

2 The second activity is made up of **advanced skill questions**—ones involving fact and opinion, inferences, purpose and tone, and argument.

- Look at the advanced skill questions on pages 421–422. How many questions deal with making inferences? _____ *Four* _____

3 The third activity involves **outlining**, **mapping**, or **summarizing**. Each of these activities will sharpen your ability to get to the heart of a piece and to think logically and clearly about what you read.

- What kind of activity is provided for "The Yellow Ribbon" on page 423? _____ *Summarizing* _____

- What kind of activity is provided for the reading titled "Urban Legends" on page 432? _____ *Mapping* _____

Note that a **map**, or diagram, is a highly visual way of organizing material. Like an outline, it shows at a glance the main parts of a selection.

4 The fourth activity consists of **discussion questions**. These questions provide a chance for you to deepen your understanding of each selection.

- How many discussion questions are there for "Urban Legends" (page 433)—and indeed for every other reading? _____ *Four* _____

Part III: For Further Study (pages 511–596)

This part of the book contains additional materials that can help improve your reading.

1 The first section, "Combined-Skills Tests," on pages 513–544, is made up of short passages that give you practice in all ten of the skills in the book.

- How many such tests are there in all? _____ *Fifteen* _____

2 The second section, "Propaganda," discusses techniques that your instructor may choose to cover, depending on the needs of the class.

- How many kinds of propaganda techniques are explained? _____ *Seven* _____

3 The third section, "More About Argument: Errors in Reasoning," explains a number of logical fallacies.

- How many fallacies are treated on pages 571–582? _____ *Six* _____

4 The fourth section, "Writing Assignments," presents writing assignments for all twenty of the reading selections in the book. Reading and writing are closely connected skills, and writing practice will improve your ability to read closely and to think carefully.

- How many assignments are offered for each reading? _____ *Three* _____

HELPFUL FEATURES OF THE BOOK

1 The book centers on *what you really need to know* to become a better reader and thinker. It presents ten key comprehension skills and explains the most important points about each one.

2 The book gives you *lots of practice*. We seldom learn a skill only by hearing or reading about it; we make it part of us by repeated practice. There are, then, numerous activities in the text. They are not "busywork" but carefully designed materials that should help you truly learn each skill.

Notice that after you learn each skill in Part I, you progress to review tests and mastery tests that enable you to apply the skill. And as you move from one skill to the next, the reading selections help you practice and reinforce the skills already learned.

3   The selections throughout the book are *lively and appealing.* Dull and unvaried readings work against learning, so subjects have been carefully chosen for their high interest level. Almost all of the selections here are good examples of how what we read can capture our attention. For instance, begin "The Yellow Ribbon," which is about a repentant man just released from prison who is wondering if his wife will allow him to return home—and try to stop reading. Or look at the textbook selection on pages 483–492, which considers the question of whether Lizzie Borden really was an ax-murderer. Or read the textbook selection "Preindustrial Cities," which, despite its unexciting title, is full of fascinating details about city life before modern food distribution and sanitary facilities.

4   The readings include *eight selections from college textbooks.* Therefore, you will be practicing on materials very much like the ones in your other courses. Doing so will increase your chances of transferring what you learn in your reading class to your other college courses.

HOW TO USE THE BOOK

1   A good way to proceed is to read and review the explanations and examples in a given chapter in Part I until you feel you understand the ideas presented. Then carefully work through the practices. As you finish each one, check your answers with the "Limited Answer Key" that starts on page 599.

For your own sake, *don't just copy in the answers without trying to do the practices!* The only way to learn a skill is to practice it first and then use the answer key to give yourself feedback. Also, take whatever time is needed to figure out just why you got some answers wrong. By using the answer key to help teach yourself the skills, you will prepare yourself for the review and mastery tests at the end of each chapter as well as the other reading tests in the book. Your instructor can supply you with answers to those tests.

If you have trouble catching on to a particular skill, stick with it. In time, you will learn each of the ten skills.

2   Read the selections first with the intent of simply enjoying them. There will be time afterward for rereading each selection and using it to develop your comprehension skills.

3   Keep track of your progress. Fill in the charts at the end of each chapter in Part I and each reading in Part II. And in the "Reading Performance Chart" on the inside back cover, enter your scores for all of the review and mastery tests as well as the reading selections. These scores can give you a good view of your overall performance as you work through the book.

In summary, *Ten Steps to Improving College Reading Skills* has been designed to interest and benefit you as much as possible. Its format is straightforward, its explanations are clear, its readings are appealing, and its many practices will help you learn through doing. *It is a book that has been created to reward effort*, and if you provide that effort, you will make yourself a better reader and a stronger thinker. I wish you success.

John Langan

2

Reading for Pleasure and Power

WHY READ?

Recently I was at a conference where a panel of first-year college students were asked, "If you could give just one bit of advice to high-school kids, what would it be?" One student answered, "I can answer that in one word: **Read.** Read everything you can. The more you read, the better off you're going to be." Up and down the panel, heads nodded. No one disagreed with this advice.

All these students agreed because they had learned the truth about reading—that it is the very heart of education. They had been in college long enough to realize that the habit of regular reading is the best possible preparation for college and for success in life. Here are four specific reasons why you should become a regular reader:

1 **Real Pleasure.** Chances are that you have done little reading for pleasure in your life. You may be an unpracticed reader who has never gotten into the habit of regular reading.

Perhaps you grew up in a home like mine where a television set dominated the household. Perhaps you got off to a bad start in reading class and never seemed to catch up. Or maybe you were eager to learn about reading when you began school but then soured on it. If you were given uninteresting and irrelevant material to read in school, you may have decided (mistakenly) that reading cannot be rewarding for you.

The truth is that reading can open the door to a lifetime of pleasure and adventure. If you take the time to walk through that door, chances are you will learn that one of the great experiences of life is the joy of reading for its own sake.

2 **Language Power.** Research has shown beyond any question that frequent reading improves vocabulary, spelling, and reading speed and comprehension, as well as grammar and writing style. If you become a regular reader, all of these language and thinking abilities develop almost automatically!

3 **Job Power.** Regular reading will increase your chances for job success. In today's world more than ever before, jobs involve the processing of information, with words being the tools of the trade. Studies have found that the better your command of words, the more success you are likely to have. *Nothing will give you a command of words like regular reading.*

4 **Human Power.** Reading enlarges the mind and the heart. It frees us from the narrow confines of our own experience. Knowing how other people view important matters helps us decide what we ourselves think and feel. Reading also helps us connect with others and realize our shared humanity. Someone once wrote, "We read in order to know that we are not alone." We become less isolated as we share the common experiences, emotions, and thoughts that make us human. We grow more sympathetic and understanding because we realize that others are like us.

A Personal Story about the Value of Reading

I did little reading as a boy, with one notable exception: I loved comic books. In particular, I can remember reading comics at lunch time. Since I attended a grade school that was only several blocks away, I could walk home at noon. There I would drink chocolate milk and eat my favorite sandwich—baloney, mustard, and potato chips layered between two pieces of white bread. I would sit at the kitchen table with my two sisters, home from the same school, as well as my father, home for lunch from his job with a local insurance company. The four of us sat silently because we were all reading. My sisters and I read mostly Donald Duck, Scrooge McDuck, and Mickey Mouse comic books, while my father read *Reader's Digest, Life* magazine, or the morning newspaper. Coffee cup in hand, my mother hovered nearby, always a bit frustrated, I suspect. She was in the mood for conversation, but her family was too busy reading.

Even when I went on to high school, I was more likely to read a comic book than anything else. Each year my English teachers typically assigned two books for students to read and report on—books such as Sir Walter Scott's *Ivanhoe* and Charles Dickens's *A Tale of Two Cities*. I had no interest in reading such books, especially ones that seemed to be about, as I remember saying at the time, "old dead stuff." How then did I deal with these assignments? I was rescued by a series of comics called classic comic books, which were illustrated stories of famous novels. Classic comics helped me pass tests and do book reports. They also kept me from actually having to sit down and read a book—an activity that I never imagined could be a source of enjoyment.

What did give me pleasure was watching television. I developed a routine after school: get my homework done, do any household chores, eat dinner, and then spend the whole evening watching the tube.

Fortunately, something happened in the summer before my junior year that changed my life. The country was in the middle of a recession, so I was not able to get a job. I felt too old to spend the summer playing back-alley baseball with neighborhood buddies, and there was not enough on daytime TV (this was before cable) to hold my interest. Except for a once-a-week job of cutting my aunt's grass, I had nothing to do and felt restless and empty.

Then, sitting on my front porch one day in early June, I saw a public service message on the side of a bus that was rumbling noisily down the street. I remember the exact words: "Open your mind—read a book." Such messages had always annoyed me. On general principle I never liked being told what I should do. I also resented the implication that my mind was closed just because I didn't read books. I thought to myself, "For the heck of it, I'm going to read a book just so I know for sure there's nothing there."

That afternoon I walked to the one bookstore in town, browsed around, and picked out a paperback book—*The Swiss Family Robinson*—about a family that had been shipwrecked on an island and had to find a way to survive until rescue came. I spent a couple of days reading the story. When I was done, I had to admit that I had enjoyed it and that I was proud of myself for actually having read an entire book.

But in the perverse frame of mind that was typical of me at age 15, I thought to myself, "I just happened to pick out the one story in the world that is actually interesting. Chances are there aren't any more." But the more reasonable part of me wondered, "What if there are other books that wouldn't waste my time?"

I remembered that upstairs in my closet were some books that my aunt had once given me but I had never read. I selected one that I had heard of and that seemed to have some promise. It was *The Adventures of Tom Sawyer*, by Mark Twain, and it was a hardbound book now so old that its binding cracked when I opened it up. I began reading, and while the activities of Tom were interesting enough, it was his girlfriend Becky Thatcher who soon captured my complete attention. My adolescent heart raced when I thought of her, and for a while I thought about her night and day. For the first time in my life, I had fallen in love—incredibly enough, with a character in a book! The character of Becky helped show me what power a book can have.

Tom had a friend named Huck Finn, about whom Mark Twain had written another book. So when I finished Tom's story, I went to the library, got a library card, and checked out *The Adventures of Huckleberry Finn*. I figured this book might tell me more about Becky. As it turned out, it didn't, but by pure chance I wound up reading one of the great novels of American literature.

If Becky had made my blood race, the story of Huck Finn and the trip that he and his friend Jim took on a raft down the Mississippi River caught me up in a different but equally compelling way. While I could not express what happened at the time, the book made me look at people in a new light. I saw a whole stage of characters who felt very human and whose stories seemed very real. Some of these characters were mean and stupid and cowardly and hateful, others were loyal and courageous and dignified and loving, and a few were a blend of good and bad. By the time I finished Huck's story, I knew that books could be a source of pleasure, and I sensed also that they could be a source of power—that they could help me learn important things about the world and the people around me. I was now hooked on books. By the end of the summer, I had read over twenty novels, and I have been reading ever since.

HOW TO BECOME A REGULAR READER

How, you might be wondering, does one become a regular reader? The key, as simple as it might sound, is to do a great deal of reading. The truth of the matter is that reading is like any other skill. The more you practice, the better you get. In his book *The Power of Reading: Insights from the Research*, the reading scholar Stephen Krashen surveys an extensive number of studies and concludes that reading itself is the "way that we become good readers." The value of regular reading is a point about which common sense and research are in complete agreement.

The following suggestions will help you make reading a part of your life. Remember, though: These suggestions are only words on a page. You must decide to become a regular reader, and you must follow through on that decision. Only then will reading become a source of pleasure and power.

- Create a half hour or hour of reading in your daily schedule. That time might be during your lunch hour, or late afternoon before dinner, or the half hour or so before you turn off your light at night. Find a time that is possible for you and make reading then a habit. The result will be both recreation time and personal growth.

- Subscribe to a daily newspaper and read the sections that interest you. Keep in mind that it is not what you read that matters—for example, you should not feel obliged to read the editorial section if opinion columns are not your interest. What does matter is the very fact that you read. Feel perfectly free to read whatever you like: the sports page, the fashion section, movie reviews, front-page stories—even the comics.

- Subscribe to one or more magazines. Browse in the magazine section of your library or a local bookstore; chances are you'll find some magazines that interest you. You may want to consider a weekly news magazine, such as *Newsweek* or *Time*; a weekly general-interest magazine such as *People*; or any number of special-interest monthly magazines such as *Glamour, Sports Illustrated, Essence,* or *Health and Fitness.*

You'll find subscription cards within most magazines; and on many college bulletin boards, you'll see display cards offering a wide variety of magazines at discount rates for students.

• Read aloud to children in your family, whether younger brothers or sisters or sons or daughters or nephews or nieces. Alternatively, have a family reading time when you and the children take turns reading.

• Read books on your own. This is the most important step on the road to becoming a regular reader. Reading is most enjoyable when you get drawn into the special world created by a given book. You can travel in that world for hours, unmindful for a while of everyday concerns. In that timeless zone, you will come to experience the joy of reading. Too many people are addicted to smoking or drugs or television; you should try, instead, to get hooked on books.

What should you read? Select anything that interests you. That might be comic books, fantasies or science fiction, horror and mystery stories, romances, adventure and sports stories, biographies and autobiographies, or how-to books. To select a book, browse in a bookstore, library, or reading center. Find something you like and begin reading. If you stick to it and become a regular reader, you may find that you have done nothing less than change your life.

Questions

1. Was reading a priority in the home where you grew up? If so, tell how reading was emphasized? If not, describe what seemed to be the attitude towards reading in your home. How did your family's attitude (positive or negative) about reading affect your development as a reader?

2. When you were growing up, what role did school play in encouraging or discouraging you to read? Describe experiences in school that made you feel positive or negative about reading.

3. What do you think that parents and schools could do to make reading a source of pleasure for children? Suggest some specific ideas that would have worked for you as child.

4. Of the five suggestions that appear in the section in this chapter titled "How to Become a Regular Reader," which one or two are the most appealing and realistic to you?

5. Read one of the books recommended on the Townsend Press website. Go to **www.townsendpress.com** and click on the line that says, "A booklet titled *40 Good Books to Read*. To see it, click here." You'll then be shown a list of forty books, along with detailed descriptions of each book so you can pick out a book that seems promising to you.

A SPECIAL OFFER

To promote your reading growth, Townsend Press will send you three books at no charge except for postage and handling. Here are the three books:

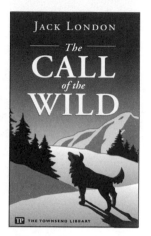

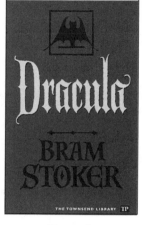

Great Stories of Suspense and Adventure

The Call of the Wild

Dracula

Use the order form below, enclosing five dollars to cover the cost of shipping and handling. You'll then be sent these three very readable books plus your own copy of the booklet mentioned on the previous page, *40 Good Books to Read*.

ORDER FORM

YES! Please send me copies of the three books listed. Enclosed is five dollars to cover the shipping and handling of the books.

Please PRINT the following very clearly. It will be your shipping label.

Name _____

Address _____

City _____ *State* _____ *Zip* _____

MAIL TO: TP Book Center, 1038 Industrial Drive, West Berlin, NJ 08091.

3

Some Quick Study Tips

While it's not my purpose in this book to teach study skills, I do want to give you four quick hints that can make you a better student. The hints are based on my thirty years of experience working with first-year college students and teaching reading and study skills.

 Tip 1 The most important steps you can take to succeed in school are to go to every class and take a lot of notes. If you don't go to class, or you go but just sit there without taking notes, chances are you're heading for a heap of trouble.

 Tip 2 Let me ask you a question: Which is more important—learning how to read a textbook or learning how to read your professor? Write your answer here:

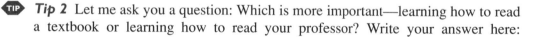

You may be surprised at the answer: What is far more important is learning how to read your professor—to understand what he or she expects you to learn in the course and to know for tests.

I remember becoming a good student in college only after I learned the truth of this statement. And I have interviewed hundreds of today's students who have said the same thing. Let me quote just one of them:

> *You absolutely have to be in class. Then you learn how to read the teacher and to know what he or she is going to want on tests. You could read an entire textbook, but that wouldn't be as good as being in class and writing down a teacher's understanding of ideas.*

 Tip 3 Many teachers base their tests mainly on the ideas they present in class. But when you have to learn a textbook chapter, do the following.

First, read the first and last few paragraphs of the chapter; they may give you a good overview of what the chapter is about.

Second, as you read the chapter, look for and mark off definitions of key terms and examples of those definitions.

Third, as you read the chapter, number any lists of items; if there are series of points and you number them *1, 2, 3,* and so on, it will be easier to understand and remember them.

Fourth, after you've read the chapter, take notes on the most important material and test yourself on those notes until you can say them to yourself without looking at them.

TIP ▸ *Tip 4* Here's another question: Are you an organized person? Do you get out of bed on time, do you get to places on time, do you keep up with school work, do you allow time to study for tests and write papers?

If you are *not* an organized person, you're going to have trouble in school. Here are three steps to take to control your time:

First, pay close attention to the course outline, or *syllabus,* your instructors will probably pass out at the start of a semester. Chances are that syllabus will give you the dates of exams and tell you when papers or reports are due.

Second, move all those dates onto a *large monthly calendar*—a calendar that has a good-sized block of white space for each date. Hang the calendar in a place where you'll be sure to see it every day—perhaps above your desk or on a bedroom wall.

Third, buy a small notebook and write down every day a *"to do"* list of things that need to get done that day. Decide which items are most important and focus on them first. (If you have classes that day, going to those classes will be "A" priority items.) Carry your list with you during the day, referring to it every so often and checking off items as you complete them.

Questions

1. Of the four hints listed above, which is the most important one for you? Why?

2. Which hint is the second most important for you, and why?

3. A graph later in this book makes clear just how quickly we forget new material. For example, how much class material do you think most people forget in just two weeks? Check (✓) the answer you think is correct.

   _____ 20 percent is forgotten within two weeks

   _____ 40 percent is forgotten within two weeks

   _____ 60 percent is forgotten within two weeks

   __✓__ 80 percent is forgotten within two weeks

   The truth is that within two weeks most people forget almost 80% of what they have heard! Given that fact, what should you be sure to do in all your classes?

Part I

TEN STEPS TO IMPROVING COLLEGE READING SKILLS

1

Vocabulary in Context

If you were asked to define the words *ambivalent*, *ascertain*, and *incessant*, you might have some difficulty. On the other hand, if you saw these words in sentences, chances are you could come up with fairly accurate definitions. For example, see if you can define the words in italics in the three sentences below. Then, using a capital letter, write the letter of your choice on the answer line.

Do not use a dictionary for this work. Instead, in each sentence, try the word you think is the answer. For example, put *mixed* or *critical* or *approving* into the sentence in place of *ambivalent* to see which one makes the best sense.

_A_ Many of us have *ambivalent* (ăm-bĭv′ə-lənt) feelings about our politicians, admiring but also distrusting them.

Ambivalent means

A. mixed.   B. critical.   C. approving.

_C_ The officer tried to *ascertain* (ăs′ər-tān′) the truth about the accident by questioning each witness separately.

Ascertain means
A. create.   B. avoid.   C. find out.

_C_ I prefer the occasional disturbance of ear-splitting thunder to the *incessant* (ĭn-sĕs′ənt) dripping of our kitchen sink.

Incessant means
A. harmless.   B. exciting.   C. nonstop.

In each sentence above, the **context**—the words surrounding the unfamiliar word—provides clues to the word's meaning. You may have guessed from the context that *ambivalent* means "mixed," that *ascertain* means "find out," and that *incessant* is "nonstop."

Using context clues to understand the meaning of unfamiliar words will help you in several ways:

- It will save you time when reading. You will not have to stop to look up words in the dictionary. (Of course, you won't always be able to understand a word from its context, so you should always have a dictionary nearby as you read.)

- After you figure out the meaning of the same word more than once through its context, it may become a part of your working vocabulary. You will therefore add to your vocabulary simply by reading thoughtfully.

- You will get a good sense of how a word is actually used, including any shades of meaning it might have.

TYPES OF CONTEXT CLUES

There are four common types of context clues:

1 Examples

2 Synonyms

3 Antonyms

4 General Sense of the Sentence or Passage

In the following sections, you will read about and practice using each type. The practices will sharpen your skills in recognizing and using context clues. They will also help you add new words to your vocabulary.

Remember not to use a dictionary for these practices. Their purpose is to help you develop the skill of figuring out what words mean without using a dictionary. Pronunciations are provided in parentheses for the words, and a brief guide to pronunciation is on pages 597–598.

1 Examples

Examples may suggest the meaning of an unknown word. To understand how this type of clue works, read the sentences below. An *italicized* word in each sentence is followed by examples that serve as context clues for that word. These examples, in **boldfaced** type, will help you figure out the meaning of each word. On the answer line, write the letter of each meaning you think is correct.

Note that examples are often introduced with signal words and phrases like *for example, for instance, including,* and *such as*.

_C_ 1. *Nocturnal* creatures, such as **bats and owls**, have highly developed senses that enable them to function in the dark.

    Nocturnal (nŏk-tûr′nəl) means
    A. feathery.   B. living.   C. active at night.

_B_ 2. The *adverse* effects of this drug, including **dizziness, nausea, and headaches,** have caused it to be withdrawn from the market.

    Adverse (ăd-vûrs′) means
    A. deadly.   B. harmful.   C. expensive.

_C_ 3. Instances of common *euphemisms* include **"final resting place"** (for *grave*), **"intoxicated"** (for *drunk*), and **"restroom"** (for *toilet*).

    Euphemisms (yōō′fə-mĭz′əmz) means
    A. unpleasant   B. answers.   C. substitutes for
       reactions.   offensive terms.

    In the first sentence, the examples given of nocturnal creatures—bats and owls—may have helped you to guess that *nocturnal* creatures are those that are "active at night," since bats and owls do come out at night. In the second sentence, the unpleasant side effects mentioned are clues to the meaning of *adverse*, which is "harmful." Finally, as the examples in sentence three indicate, *euphemisms* means "substitutes for offensive terms."

➤ Practice 1: Examples

For each item below, underline the examples that suggest the meaning of the italicized term. Then write the letter of the meaning of that term on the answer line. Note that the last five sentences have been taken from college textbooks.

_B_ 1. Even presidents must perform such *mundane* activities as brushing their teeth and washing their hands and faces.

    Mundane (mŭn-dān′) means
    A. pleasant.   B. ordinary.   C. expensive.

    Hint: For this and all the exercises in this chapter, actually insert into the sentence the word you think is the answer. For example, substitute *pleasant* or *commonplace* or *expensive* into the sentence in place of *mundane* to see which one fits.

_B_ 2. Today was a day of *turmoil* at work. The phones were constantly ringing, people were running back and forth, and several offices were being painted.

    Turmoil (tûr′moil′) means
    A. discussion.   B. confusion.   C. harmony.

_B_ 3. Some animals have remarkable *longevity*. For example, the giant land tortoise can live several hundred years.

Longevity (lŏn-jĕv′ĭ-tē) means
A. appearances.   B. length of life.   C. habits.

_A_ 4. Before the invention of television, people spent more time on *diversions* such as going to town concerts and ball games, visiting neighborhood friends, and playing board games.

Diversions (dĭ-vûr′zhənz) means
A. amusements.   B. differences.   C. chores.

_A_ 5. Since my grandfather retired, he has developed several new *avocations*. For instance, he now enjoys gardening and long-distance bike riding.

Avocations (ăv′ō-kā′shənz) means
A. hobbies.   B. vacations.   C. jobs.

_A_ 6. Children who move to a foreign country *adapt* much more easily than their parents, soon picking up the language and customs of their new home.

Adapt (ə-dăpt′) means
A. adjust.   B. struggle.   C. become bored.

_C_ 7. The Chinese government provides *incentives* for married couples to have only one child. For example, couples with one child get financial help and free medical care.

Incentives (ĭn-sĕn′tĭvz) means
A. warnings.   B. penalties.   C. encouragements.

_B_ 8. Changes in such abilities as learning, reasoning, thinking, and language are aspects of *cognitive* development.

Cognitive (kŏg′nĭ-tĭv) means
A. physical.   B. mental.   C. spiritual.

_C_ 9. Some mentally ill people have *bizarre* ideas. For instance, they may think the TV is talking to them or that others can steal their thoughts.

Bizarre (bĭ-zär′) means
A. limited.   B. ordinary.   C. odd.

_C_ 10. *White-collar crime*—for example, accepting a bribe from a customer or stealing from an employer—is more costly than "common" crime.

White-collar crime (hwīt-kŏl′ər krīm) means crime committed by
A. gang members.   B. strangers.   C. people in the workplace.

2   Synonyms

A context clue is often available in the form of a **synonym**: a word that means the same or almost the same as the unknown word. A synonym may appear anywhere in a passage to provide the same meaning as the unknown word.

In each of the following items, the word to be defined is italicized. Underline the synonym for the italicized word in each sentence.

1. Fresh garlic may not *enhance* (ĕn-hăns′) the breath, but it certainly does improve spaghetti sauce.

2. As soon as I made a *flippant* (flĭp′ənt) remark to my boss, I regretted sounding so disrespectful.

3. Although the salesperson tried to *assuage* (ə-swāj′) the angry customer, there was no way to soothe her.

In each sentence, the synonym given should have helped you understand the meaning of the word in italics:

- *Enhance* means "improve."
- *Flippant* means " disrespectful."
- *Assuage* means " soothe."

> The parallel structure in items 1 and 3 points to the synonyms: may not **enhance** . . . does **improve** tried to **assuage** . . . no way to **soothe**

➤ Practice 2: Synonyms

Each item below includes a word that is a synonym of the italicized word. Write the synonym of the italicized word in the space provided. Note that the last five sentences have been taken from college textbooks.

__*embarrasses*__ 1. Speaking in front of a group *disconcerts* (dĭs′kən-sûrtz′) Alan. Even answering a question in class embarrasses him.

    Hint: How does Alan react when he has to speak in public?

__*examine*__ 2. Because my friends had advised me to *scrutinize* (skro͞ot′n-īz′) the lease, I took time to examine all the fine print.

__*practical*__ 3. The presidential candidate vowed to discuss *pragmatic* (prăg-măt′ĭk) solutions. He said the American people want practical answers, not empty theory.

__*confusing*__ 4. I asked the instructor to explain a confusing passage in the textbook. She said, "I wish I could, but it's *obscure* (ŏb-skyo͝or′) to me, too."

Comment: Item 1— Parallel structure points to the synonym: **Speaking** in front of a group *disconcerts* . . . **answering** a question in class *embarrasses*

_____ *overlook* _____ 5. Teachers may overlook it when a student is two minutes late. But they are not going to *condone* (kən-dōn′) someone's walking into class a half hour late.

_____ *necessary* _____ 6. When people are broke, they find that many things which seem *indispensable* (ĭn′dĭ-spĕn′sə-bəl) are not so necessary after all.

_____ *opponents* _____ 7. Managers should beware of having *adversaries* (ăd′vər-sĕr′ēz) work together; opponents often do not cooperate well.

_____ *arrival* _____ 8. In the same way that the arrival of mechanical equipment meant fewer farm jobs, the *advent* (ăd′vĕnt′) of the computer has led to fewer manufacturing jobs.

_____ *charitable* _____ 9. Many corporations like to be seen as *benevolent* (bə-nĕv′ə-lənt) and will actively seek publicity for their charitable donations.

_____ *customary* _____ 10. Throughout history, the *prevalent* (prĕv′ə-lənt) authority pattern in families has been patriarchy, in which males are in control. In only a few societies has matriarchy been the customary authority pattern.

> Item 10: Parallel structure points to the synonym:
> *Prevalent* authority pattern . . . **customary** authority pattern

3 Antonyms

An **antonym**—a word that means the opposite of another word—is also a useful context clue. Antonyms are often signaled by words and phrases such as *however, but, yet, on the other hand*, and *in contrast*.

In each sentence below, underline the word that means the opposite of the italicized word. Then, on the answer line, write the letter of the meaning of the italicized word.

_____ *B* _____ 1. Many people have pointed out the <u>harmful</u> effects that a working mother may have on the family, yet there are many *salutary* effects as well.

Salutary (săl′yə-tĕr′ē) means
A. well-known.   B. beneficial.   C. hurtful.

> Parallel structure points to the antonym:
> **harmful** effects . . . *salutary* effects

_A_ 2. Trying to control everything your teens do can *impede* their growth. To <u>advance</u> their development, allow them to make some decisions on their own.

Impede (ĭm-pēd′) means

A. block.   B. predict.   C. improve.

_A_ 3. During their training, police officers must respond to *simulated* emergencies in preparation for dealing with <u>real</u> ones.

Simulated (sĭm′yə-lā′tĭd) means

A. made-up.   B. mild.   C. actual.

In the first sentence, salutary effects are the opposite of "harmful effects, " so *salutary* means "beneficial." In the second sentence, *impede* is the opposite of "advance," so *impede* means "block." Last, the opposite of "real" is "simulated"; *simulated* means "made-up."

➤ Practice 3: Antonyms

Each item below includes a word that is an antonym of the italicized word. Underline the antonym of each italicized word. Then, on the answer line, write the letter of the meaning of the italicized word. Note that the last five sentences have been taken from college textbooks.

_A_ 1. Many politicians do not give *succinct* answers. They prefer <u>long</u> ones that help them avoid the point.

Hint: If politicians prefer to give long answers, what kind of answer do they usually *not* give?

Succinct (sək-sĭngkt′) means

A. brief.   B. accurate.   C. complete.

_B_ 2. Although investments in the stock market can be *lucrative,* they can also result in great <u>financial loss.</u>

Lucrative (lōō′krə-tĭv) means

A. required.   B. financially rewarding.   C. risky.

_B_ 3. "I've seen students *surreptitiously* check answer sheets during exams," said the professor. "However, until today I never saw one <u>openly</u> lay out a cheat sheet on his desk."

Surreptitiously (sûr′əp-tĭsh′əs-lē) means

A. legally.   B. secretly.   C. loudly.

Items 1 and 3: Parallel structure points to the antonyms:
do not give **succinct** answers . . . prefer **long** ones
surreptitiously check . . . **openly** lay out

___B___ 4. While Melba's apartment is decorated <u>plainly</u>, her clothing is very *flamboyant*.

  Flamboyant (flăm-boi′ənt) means
  A. inexpensive.   B. flashy.   C. washable.

___A___ 5. To keep healthy, older people need to stay <u>active</u>. Remaining *stagnant* results in loss of strength and health.

  Stagnant (stăg′nənt) means
  A. inactive.   B. lively.   C. unhealthy.

___C___ 6. In formal communication, be sure to avoid *ambiguous* language. <u>Clear</u> language prevents confusion.

  Ambiguous (ăm-bĭg′yōo-əs) means
  A. wordy.   B. ineffective.   C. unclear.

___B___ 7. Being raised with conflicting values can be a *detriment* to boys' and girls' relationships with each other. In contrast, shared values can be a <u>benefit</u>.

  Detriment (dĕt′rə-mənt) means
  A. improvement.   B. harm.   C. relationship.

___B___ 8. While houses and antiques often <u>increase in value</u>, most things, such as cars and TV's, *depreciate*.

  Depreciate (dĭ-prē′shē-āt′) means
  A. remain useful.   B. lose value.   C. break.

___C___ 9. Reliable scientific theories are based not upon <u>careless</u> work, but rather upon *meticulous* research and experimentation.

  Meticulous (mĭ-tĭk′yə-ləs) means
  A. hasty.   B. expensive.   C. careful.

___C__ 10. In the early days of automobile manufacturing, *stringent* laws controlled motorists' speed. In contrast, the laws designed to protect consumers from faulty products were extremely <u>weak</u>.

  Stringent (strĭn′jənt) means
  A. informal.   B. not effective.   C. strict.

Comments: Parallel structure points to the antonyms:
  Item 4 — apartment . . . **plainly** . . . clothing . . . *flamboyant*
  Item 6 — *ambiguous* language . . . **clear** language
  Item 7 — can be a *detriment* . . . can be a **benefit**
  Item 8 — houses and antiques often **increase** in value . . . cars and TV's *depreciate* in value
  Item 9 — not upon **careless** work, but . . . upon *meticulous* research

4 General Sense of the Sentence or Passage

Sometimes it takes a bit more detective work to puzzle out the meaning of an unfamiliar word. In such cases, you must draw conclusions based on the information given with the word. Asking yourself questions about the passage may help you make a fairly accurate guess about the meaning of the unfamiliar word.

Each of the sentences below is followed by a question. Think about each question; then, on the answer line, write the letter of the answer you think is the correct meaning of the italicized word.

_B_ 1. A former employee, *irate* over having been fired, broke into the plant and deliberately wrecked several machines.

(What would be the employee's state of mind?)

Irate (ī-rāt′) means

A. relieved.   B. very angry.   C. undecided.

_B_ 2. Despite the *proximity* of Ron's house to his sister's, he rarely sees her.

(What about Ron's house would make it surprising that he didn't see his sister more often?

Proximity (prŏk-sĭm′ĭ-tē) means

A. similarity.   B. nearness.   C. superiority.

_C_ 3. The car wash we organized to raise funds was a *fiasco*—it rained all day.

(How successful would a car wash be on a rainy day?)

Fiasco (fē-ăs′kō) means

A. great financial   B. welcome surprise.   C. complete disaster.
   success.

The first sentence provides enough evidence for you to guess that *irate* means "very angry." *Proximity* in the second sentence means "nearness." And a *fiasco* is a "complete disaster." (You may not hit on the exact dictionary definition of a word by using context clues, but you will often be accurate enough to make good sense of what you are reading.)

➤ *Practice 4: General Sense of the Sentence or Passage*

Try to answer the question that follows each item below. Then use the logic of each answer to help you write the letter of the meaning you think is correct. Note that the last five sentences have been taken from college textbooks.

   B   1. The lizard was so *lethargic* that I wasn't sure if it was alive or dead. It didn't even blink.

      (Would an animal that seemed dead be green, inactive, or big?)

      Lethargic (lə-thär′jĭk) means
      A. green.   B. inactive.   C. big.

   C   2. Jamal didn't want to tell Tina the entire plot of the movie, so he just gave her the *gist* of the story.

      (What kind of information would Jamal have given Tina?)

      Gist (jĭst) means
      A. ending.   B. title.   C. main idea.

   A   3. After the accident, I was angered when the other driver told the police officer a complete *fabrication* about what happened. He claimed that I was the person at fault.

      (How truthful was the other driver's information?)

      Fabrication (făb′rĭ-kā′shən) means
      A. lie.   B. description.   C. confession.

   B   4. The public knows very little about the *covert* activities of CIA spies.

      (What kind of activities would the CIA spies be involved in that the public wouldn't know much about?)

      Covert (kŭv′ərt *or* kōv′ərt *or* kō-vûrt′) means
      A. public.   B. secret.   C. family.

   C   5. Whether or not there is life in outer space is an *enigma*. We may never know for sure until we are capable of space travel or aliens actually land on our planet.

      (What would we call something to which we have no answer?)

      Enigma (ĭ-nĭg′mə) means
      A. reason.   B. certainty.   C. mystery.

_A_   6. Suicide rates tend to *fluctuate* with the seasons, with much higher rates in the winter than in the summer.

(What happens to the suicide rate from season to season?)

Fluctuate (flŭk′chōō-āt′) means
A. go up and down.   B. disappear.   C. stay the same.

_C_   7. Human beings are *resilient* creatures—they can often bounce back from negative experiences and adjust well to life.

(What point is the author making about the nature of human beings?)

Resilient (rĭ-zĭl′yənt) means
A. not flexible.   B. living.   C. able to recover.

_B_   8. A major accomplishment of sociology is *dispelling* the myths and prejudices that groups of people have about each other.

(What would a profession do to "myths and prejudices" that could be considered a "major accomplishment"?)

Dispelling (dĭ-spĕl′ĭng) means
A. ignoring.   B. making vanish.   C. creating again.

_C_   9. Ten years of research *culminated* in a report explaining the mysterious behavior of the praying mantis, a large green or brownish insect.

(What would be the relationship of the report to the research?)

Culminated (kŭl′mə-nāt′ĭd) means
A. failed.   B. began.   C. concluded.

_B_ 10. Despite complaints from parents, educators, and government officials, violence and sex on television seem to go on *unabated*.

(In spite of the complaints, does anything happen?)

Unabated (ŭn′ə-bā′tĭd) means
A. more slowly.   B. unstopped.   C. at great expense.

An Important Point about Textbook Definitions

You don't always have to use context clues or the dictionary to find definitions. Very often, textbook authors define important terms. Also, after giving a definition, authors usually follow it with one or more examples to ensure that you understand the new term. For instance, here is a short textbook passage that includes a definition and an example:

> [1]People do not always satisfy their needs directly; sometimes they use a substitute object. [2]Use of a substitute is known as **displacement**. [3]This is the process that takes place, for instance, when you control your impulse to yell at your boss and then go home and yell at the first member of your family who is unlucky enough to cross your path.

Textbook authors, then, often do more than provide context clues: they define a word, set it off in *italic* or **boldface** type, and provide examples as well. When they take the time to define and illustrate a word, you should assume that the term is important enough to learn.

More about textbook definitions and examples appears on pages 213–214 in the "Relationships II" chapter.

CHAPTER REVIEW

In this chapter, you learned the following:

- To save time when reading, you should try to figure out the meanings of unfamiliar words. You can do so by looking at their *context*—the words surrounding them.

- There are four kinds of context clues: **examples** (marked by words like *for example, for instance, including,* and *such as*); **synonyms** (words that mean the same as unknown words); **antonyms** (words that mean the opposite of unknown words); and **general sense of the sentence** (clues in the sentence or surrounding sentences about what words might mean).

- Textbook authors typically set off important words in *italic* or **boldface** and define those words for you, often providing examples as well.

The next chapter—Chapter 2—will introduce you to the most important of all comprehension skills, finding the main idea.

On the Web: If you are using this book in class, you can visit our website for additional practice in understanding vocabulary in context. Go to **www.townsendpress.com** and click on "Online Exercises."

➤ Review Test 1

To review what you've learned in this chapter, answer the following questions by filling in the blank or writing the letter of the correct answer.

    1. Often, a reader can figure out the meaning of a new word without using the dictionary—by paying attention to the word's _____*context*_____.

<u> A </u> 2. In the sentence below, which type of context clue is used for the italicized word?

    A. example   B. synonym   C. antonym

    You can't take certain courses unless you've taken a *prerequisite* (prĕ-rĕk′wĭ-zĭt); for instance, you can't take Spanish Literature I unless you've taken Spanish III.

<u> C </u> 3. In the sentence below, which type of context clue is used for the italicized word?

    A. example   B. synonym   C. antonym

    There are thick pine forests at the foot of the mountain, but higher up, the trees become *sparse* (spärs).

<u> B </u> 4. In the sentences below, which type of context clue is used for the italicized word?

    A. example   B. synonym   C. antonym

    Talent may take years to surface. When Beethoven was a young child, his great *aptitude* (ăp′tĭ-tōōd′) in music was not at all apparent to his teachers.

    5. Often when textbook authors introduce a new word, they provide you with a _____*definition*_____ and follow it with _____*examples*_____ that help make the meaning of the word clear.

➤ Review Test 2

A. Using context clues for help, write, on the answer line, the letter of the best meaning for each italicized word.

___B___ 1. *Nepotism* (nĕp′ə-tĭz′əm) is commonplace where I work: the boss's daughter is vice-president of the company, her husband runs the order department, and their son has just started working in the warehouse.
A. good managerial practice   C. arguments among employees
B. favoritism to relatives   D. confusion among management

Three examples of nepotism are given.

___A___ 2. Because the professor's explanation was *nebulous* (nĕb′yə-ləs), several of the students asked him to make himself clear.
A. vague   C. fascinating
B. boring   D. brief

Students needed clarifi-
cation because the
explanation was vague.
Antonym clue: *clear*

___B___ 3. The bank robber was apparently *nondescript* (nŏn′dĭ-skrĭpt′)—none of the witnesses could think of any special characteristics that might identify him.
A. poorly disguised   C. memorable
B. lacking distinctive qualities   D. cruel

Antonym-like clue for *nondescript*: "special
characteristics"

___C___ 4. The lake water was so *murky* (mûr′kē) that my hand seemed to vanish when I dipped it only a few inches below the surface.
A. cold   C. dark
B. dangerous   D. inviting

General-sense-of-
the-sentence clue:
What would be a
characteristic of water that makes a hand seem to vanish?

___A___ 5. During the Revolutionary War, the English paid German *mercenaries* (mûr′sə-nĕr′ēz) to help fight the Americans.
A. hired soldiers   C. rebels
B. traitors   D. recent immigrants

Hired soldiers are ones
who are paid to fight.

B. Using context clues for help, write the definition for each italicized word. Then write the letter of the definition in the space provided. Choose from the definitions in the box below. Each definition will be used once.

A. provided	B. doubtful	C. discouraged
D. overjoyed	E. nag	

___D___ 6. I would not just be glad if I won the lottery; I'd be *ecstatic*.
Ecstatic (ĕk-stăt′ĭk) means _____ overjoyed _____ .

___A___ 7. Nature has *endowed* hummingbirds with the ability to fly backward.
Endowed (ĕn-doud′) means _____ provided _____ .

Comment: Items 6–10: General sense of the sentence.

_C___ 8. Opponents of the death penalty say it has never actually *deterred* anyone from committing murder.

Deterred (dǐ-tûrd′) means _____ *discouraged* _____.

_E___ 9. Around the age of two or three, small children like to *badger* their parents with endless questions beginning with the word "why."

Badger (băj′ər) means _____ *nag* _____.

_B___ 10. While four-year-old Mattie claimed she was going to stay up until midnight on New Year's Eve, her parents were *dubious* of her ability to remain awake that late.

Dubious (dōō′bē-əs) means _____ *doubtful* _____.

➤ **Review Test 3**   *Wording of answers may vary.*

A. Use context clues to figure out the meaning of the italicized word in each of the following sentences, and write your definition in the space provided.

1. While it's often not *feasible* to work full-time while going to school, it may be practical to hold down a part-time job.

    Feasible (fē′zə-bəl) means _____ *practical* _____
                                    Synonym clue: *practical*

2. It's amazing that my neighbors always appear *immaculate*, yet their apartment is often quite dirty.

    Immaculate (ĭ-măk′yə-lĭt) means _____ *clean* _____.
                                    Antonym clue: *dirty*

3. It's against the law to ask people to *divulge* their ages at job interviews.

    Divulge (dĭ-vŭlj′) means _____ *reveal* _____.

4. Doctors should *alleviate* the pain of terminally ill patients so that their final days are as comfortable as possible.

    Alleviate (ə-lē′vē-āt′) means _____ *relieve* _____.

5. When rain and sunshine are *simultaneous*, the rain is often described as a sun shower.

    Simultaneous (sī′məl-tā′nē-əs) means _____ *at the same time* _____.

Comments: Items 3–10: General sense of the sentence. To find the meaning of *alleviate* in item 4, for example, one could ask, "What would a doctor do to pain to make patients comfortable?"

B. Use context clues to figure out the meanings of the italicized words in the following textbook passages. Write your definitions in the spaces provided.

> [1]Although mysteries and science fiction may seem like very different kinds of writing, the two forms share some basic similarities. [2]First of all, both are action-directed, emphasizing plot at the expense of character development. [3]Possibly for this reason, both types of literature have been *scorned* by critics as being merely "entertainment" rather than "literature." [4]But this attack is unjustified, for both mysteries and science fiction share a concern with moral issues. [5]Science fiction often raises the question of whether or not scientific advances are of benefit to humanity. [6]And a mystery story rarely ends without the *culpable* person being brought to justice.

    6. *Scorned* (skôrnd) means   *looked down upon*   .

    7. *Culpable* (kŭl′pə-bəl) means   *guilty*   .

> [1]Why did people begin to live in cities? [2]To answer this question, we must start by looking back some ten thousand years ago. [3]In certain parts of the world (probably those where the natural food supply was fairly unreliable), people *endeavored* to tame nature for their own purposes. [4]They began weeding and watering groups of edible plants, adding organic matter to help fertilize the soil, and saving the seeds from the strongest, most desirable plants to sow the next spring. [5]At the same time, they began protecting herds of small wild animals that were often hunted by larger animals. [6]They would move them to more plentiful pastures during the dry months of summer. [7]During the harshest periods of winter, they would *supplement* whatever fresh food was available with stored food. [8]These changes, *coupled* with a few simple techniques for storing grain and meat, enabled people to abandon a wandering lifestyle in favor of settlement in small villages. [9]These villages were the basic form of human social organization for the next several thousand years.

    8. *Endeavored* (ĕn-dĕv′ər) means   *tried*   .

    9. *Supplement* (sŭp′lə-mənt) means   *add to*   .

    10. *Coupled* (kŭp′əld) means   *joined*   .

> ## Review Test 4

Here is a chance to apply the skill of understanding vocabulary in context to a full-length selection. Read the story below, a version of which appeared in *Reader's Digest*, and then answer the questions that follow.

Words to Watch

Below are some words in the reading that do not have strong context support. Each word is followed by the number of the paragraph in which it appears and its meaning there. These words are indicated in the article by a small circle (°).

smudged (2): dirty with streaks or stains
boondocks (3): a rural region
maneuvers (3): military exercises

NIGHT WATCH

Roy Popkin

1   The story began on a downtown Brooklyn street corner. An elderly man had collapsed while crossing the street, and an ambulance rushed him to Kings County Hospital. There, during his few returns to consciousness, the man repeatedly called for his son.

2   From a smudged°, often-read letter, an emergency-room nurse learned that the son was a Marine stationed in North Carolina. Apparently, there were no other relatives.

3   Someone at the hospital called the Red Cross office in Brooklyn, and a request for the boy to rush to Brooklyn was relayed to the Red Cross director of the North Carolina Marine Corps camp. Because time was short—the patient was dying— the Red Cross man and an officer set out in a jeep. They located the sought-after young man wading through marshy boondocks° on maneuvers°. He was rushed to the airport in time to catch the one plane that might enable him to reach his dying father.

4   It was mid-evening when the young Marine walked into the entrance lobby of Kings County Hospital. A nurse took the tired, anxious serviceman to the bedside.

5   "Your son is here," she said to the old man. She had to repeat the words several times before the patient's eyes opened. Heavily sedated because of the pain of his heart attack, he dimly saw the young man in the Marine Corps uniform standing outside the oxygen tent. He reached out his hand. The Marine wrapped his toughened fingers around the old man's limp ones, squeezing a message of love and encouragement. The nurse brought a chair, so the Marine could sit alongside the bed.

6   Nights are long in hospitals, but all through the night the young Marine sat there in the poorly lighted ward, holding the old man's hand and offering words of hope and strength. Occasionally, the nurse suggested that the Marine move away and rest a while. He refused.

7   Whenever the nurse came into the ward, the Marine was there. His full attention was on the dying man, and he was oblivious of her and of the night noises of the hospital—the clanking of an oxygen tank, the laughter of night-staff members exchanging greetings, the cries and moans and snores of other patients. Now and then she heard him say a few gentle words. The dying man said nothing, only held tightly to his son through most of the night.

8   Along toward dawn, the patient died. The Marine placed on the bed the lifeless hand he had been holding, and went to tell the nurse. While she did what she had to do, he relaxed—for the first time since he got to the hospital.

9   Finally, she returned to the nurse's station, where he was waiting. She started to offer words of condolence for his loss, but the Marine interrupted her. "Who was that man?" he asked.

10   "He was your father," she answered, startled.

11   "No, he wasn't," the Marine replied.

"I never saw him before in my life."

12   "Why didn't you say something when I took you to him?" the nurse asked.

13   "I knew right off there'd been a mistake, but I also knew he needed his son, and his son just wasn't here. When I realized he was too sick to tell whether or not I was his son, I figured he really needed me. So I stayed."

14   With that, the Marine turned and left the hospital. Two days later a routine message came in from the North Carolina Marine Corps base informing the Brooklyn Red Cross that the real son was on his way to Brooklyn for his father's funeral. It turned out there had been two Marines with the same name and similar serial numbers in the camp. Someone in the personnel office had pulled out the wrong record.

15   But the wrong Marine had become the right son at the right time. And he proved, in a uniquely human way, that there are people who care what happens to their fellow human beings.

Vocabulary Questions

Use context clues to help you decide on the best definition for each italicized word. Then, on the answer line, write the letter of each choice.

___B___ 1. In the sentence below, the word *relayed* (rē′lād) means
    A. hidden.   C. made a gift.
    B. passed along.   D. ignored.

    "Someone at the hospital called the Red Cross office in Brooklyn, and a request for the boy to rush to Brooklyn was relayed to the Red Cross director of the North Carolina Marine Corps camp." (Paragraph 3)   To find the meaning of *relayed,* one might ask, "What could be done with a request to get it from one person to another?"

___D___ 2. In the sentence below, the words *enable him* (ĕ-nā′bəl hǐm) mean
    A. stop him.   C. know him.
    B. encourage him.   D. make him able.

    "He was rushed to the airport in time to catch the one plane that might enable him to reach his dying father." (Paragraph 3)

_D_ 3. In the excerpt below, the word *sedated* (sĭ-dāt′ĭd) means
A. spoken loudly.   C. armed.
B. wide awake.   D. drugged with a pain reliever.

"'Your son is here,' she said to the old man. She had to repeat the words several times before the patient's eyes opened. Heavily sedated because of the pain of his heart attack, he dimly saw the young man . . . " (Paragraph 5)

_B_ 4. In the excerpt below, the word *dimly* (dĭm′lē) means
A. clearly.   C. rarely.
B. unclearly.   D. often.

"She had to repeat the words several times before the patient's eyes opened. Heavily sedated because of the pain of his heart attack, he dimly saw the young man . . . " (Paragraph 5)

_A_ 5. In the sentence below, the word *limp* (lĭmp) means
A. lacking firmness and strength.   C. long.
B. equally tough.   D. bleeding.

"The Marine wrapped his toughened fingers around the old man's limp ones, squeezing a message of love and encouragement." (Paragraph 5)

_A_ 6. A clue to the meaning of *limp* in the sentence above is the antonym
A. toughened.   C. message.
B. old.   D. love.

_C_ 7. In the excerpt below, the word *oblivious* (ə-blĭv′ē-əs) means
A. mindful.   C. unaware.
B. bothered.   D. informed.

"Whenever the nurse came into the ward, the Marine was there. His full attention was on the dying man, and he was oblivious of her and of the night noises of the hospital . . . " (Paragraph 7)

_D_ 8. In the excerpt below, the word *condolence* (kən-dŏ′ləns) means
A. excuse.   C. surprise.
B. bitterness.   D. sympathy.

"She started to offer words of condolence for his loss . . ." (Paragraph 9)

_D_ 9. In the excerpt below, the word *startled* (stär′tld) means
A. very pleased.   C. angry.
B. with admiration.   D. surprised.

"'Who was that man?' he asked. 'He was your father,' she answered, startled." (Paragraphs 9–10)

Comment: Most of the context clues in these items are general-sense-of-the-passage clues.

_C_ 10. In the sentence below, the words *uniquely human* (yōō-nĕk′lē hyōō′mən) mean

    A. impossible for humans.   C. done only by humans.

    B. scary to humans.   D. sudden by human standards.

"And he proved, in a uniquely human way, that there are people who care what happens to their fellow human beings." (Paragraph 15)

Discussion Questions

1. When do you think the Marine realized that calling him to the hospital was a mistake? Was it when he first saw the old man or before? What parts of the reading support your conclusion?

2. How do you think the dead man's real son felt about the other Marine being with his dying father? How would you feel?

3. The incident in the reading took place because of some surprising coincidences. What were they? Has a surprising or interesting coincidence ever taken place in your life? If so, what was it, and how did it affect you?

4. By going out of his way for a stranger, the Marine showed "in a uniquely human way that there are people who care what happens to others." Have you ever gone out of your way to help a stranger? Or have you seen someone else do so? Tell what the situation was and what happened.

Note: Writing assignments for this selection appear on page 585.

Check Your Performance	**VOCABULARY IN CONTEXT**		
Activity	*Number Right*	*Points*	*Score*
Review Test 1 (5 items)	_____	× 2 =	_____
Review Test 2 (10 items)	_____	× 3 =	_____
Review Test 3 (10 items)	_____	× 3 =	_____
Review Test 4 (10 items)	_____	× 3 =	_____
	TOTAL SCORE	=	_____%

Enter your total score into the **Reading Performance Chart: Review Tests** on the inside back cover.

VOCABULARY IN CONTEXT: Mastery Test 1

A. For each item below, underline the **examples** that suggest the meaning of the italicized word. Then, on the answer line, write the letter of the meaning of that word.

    _D_   1. When I finally get around to cleaning out my refrigerator, I always find something *vile* (vīl) at the back of a shelf, such as <u>moldy fruit</u> or <u>old smelly beans</u>.

            A. tempting   C. false

            B. recent   D. disgusting

    _B_   2. The Easter egg hunt featured *cryptic* (krĭp′tĭk) clues such as, <u>"You'll find a prize somewhere narrow"</u> and <u>"Look for the pink."</u>

            A. rhyming   C. clear

            B. puzzling   D. overused

    _C_   3. *Verbose* (vər′bōs) writing can be hard to follow. For instance, <u>"At this point in time, we have an urgently felt need for more and greater financial resources"</u> is less clear than "We need money now."

            A. realistic   C. wordy

            B. informal   D. ungrammatical

B. Each item below includes a word or words that are a **synonym** of the italicized word. Write the synonym of the italicized word in the space provided.

     risk   4. "I'll try any ride in this amusement park except the Twister," said Nick. "I'll *venture* (vĕn′chər) getting sick to my stomach, but I won't risk my life."

     search   5. Americans spend millions each year on a *quest* (kwĕst) for the perfect weight-loss plan. Their search is for a pill or diet that will allow them to eat much and exercise little.

   false name   6. Samuel Langhorne Clemens wasn't the first author to use the *pseudonym* (sōōd′n-ĭm′) Mark Twain. A newspaper writer of the time used the same false name.

Comments: Item 4 — Parallel structure points to the synonym: I'll **venture** . . . , but I won't **risk**.

              Item 6 — Parallel structure points to the synonym: use the **pseudonym** . . . used the same **false name**.

(Continues on next page)

C. Each item below includes a word or words that are an **antonym** of the italicized word. Underline the antonym of each italicized word. Then, on the answer line, write the letter of the meaning of the italicized word.

___C___ 7. Computer manuals are often very hard to understand, so I was surprised to discover how *lucid* (lōō′sĭd) this one is.

 A. long   C. clear
 B. expensive   D. new

___B___ 8. When my sister first got her job at the recording studio, she was excited to go to work each day. Now after ten years, she's *blasé* (blä-zā′) about her work and wants to change jobs.

 A. tardy   C. thrilled
 B. bored   D. curious

To determine the meaning of *blasé*, one could ask: "How is she different now from what she was then? How was she then?"

D. Use the **general sense of each sentence** to figure out the meaning of each italicized word. Then, on the answer line, write the letter of the meaning of the italicized word.

___A___ 9. A person can be very intelligent and yet be *deficient* (dĭ-fĭsh′ənt) in common sense.

 A. lacking   C. overqualified
 B. well supplied   D. lucky

___B___ 10. The store detective faced the *dilemma* (dĭ-lĕm′ə) of either having an elderly, needy man arrested or ignoring store rules about shoplifters.

 A. memory   C. proof
 B. difficult choice   D. reason

To determine the meaning of *dilemma*, one could ask: "How would you feel about having this needy man arrested?"

VOCABULARY IN CONTEXT: Mastery Test 2

A. For each item below, underline the **examples** that suggest the meaning of the italicized word. Then, on the answer line, write the letter of the meaning of that word.

___B___ 1. Every *habitat* (hăb′ĭ-tăt′) in the world, from <u>volcano tops</u> to <u>icebergs</u>, can support some sort of life.
- A. country
- B. environment
- C. food source
- D. practice

___A___ 2. Common *redundant* (rĭ-dŭn′dənt) phrases include <u>"cooperate together"</u> (instead of simply "cooperate") and <u>"postponed until later"</u> (instead of "postponed").
- A. repetitious
- B. descriptive
- C. difficult
- D. useful

B. Each textbook item below includes a word that is a **synonym** of the italicized word. Write the synonym of the italicized word in the space provided.

_____*plain*_____ 3. The Amish people prefer *austere* (ô-stîr′) styles—their clothing and homes are plain.

_____*conduct*_____ 4. Airport security guards must observe people's *demeanor* (dĭ-mē′nər) so as to notice any suspicious conduct.

_____*modest*_____ 5. In business, it can be harmful to be too *unassuming* (ŭn′ə-sōō′mĭng). If you're overly modest about your achievements, for example, you may be passed up for a promotion.

C. Each textbook item below includes a word that is an **antonym** of the italicized word. Underline the antonym of each italicized word. Then, on the answer line, write the letter of the meaning of the italicized word.

___C___ 6. Even when textbooks are *standardized* (stăn′dər-dīzd′) throughout a school system, methods of teaching with them may be greatly <u>varied</u>.
- A. different
- B. expensive
- C. made the same
- D. lacking

___C___ 7. During the Middle Ages, everyone—from the <u>rich</u> landowner down to the most *impoverished* (ĭm-pŏv′ər-ĭsht) peasant—had a clear place in society.
- A. weak
- B. common
- C. poor
- D. decent

(Continues on next page)

D. Use the **general sense of each sentence** to figure out the meaning of each italicized word. Then, on the answer line, write the letter of the meaning of the italicized word.

_D_ 8. America has often been called a "melting pot" into which people of many different cultures *assimilate* (ə-sĭm′ə-lāt′). Question: "What would
   A. learn
   B. leave
   C. avoid each other
   D. blend
   happen to things put in a pot to melt?"

_D_ 9. It is odd how often public figures who loudly *espouse* (ĭ-spouz′) "traditional family values" are later caught in some scandal concerning their own private lives. Question: "What is odd about these public figures
   A. recognize
   B. remember
   C. reject
   D. argue for
   who have been caught in personal scandals?"

_B_ 10. It is widely believed that Columbus sailed westward to *validate* (văl′ĭ-dāt′) the theory that the world is round. In fact, it was already well known at that time that the world is round.
   A. think up
   B. prove
   C. contradict
   D. foresee

VOCABULARY IN CONTEXT: Mastery Test 3

Using context clues for help, write, in the space provided, the letter of the best meaning for each italicized word.

_____A_____ 1. It's a good idea for married couples to discuss their plans in case of each other's *demise* (dĭ-mīz'). For example, do they wish to be buried or cremated?
- A. death
- B. success
- C. desire to divorce
- D. concern

Question: "What would a couple be discussing if they talked about being buried or cremated?"

_____C_____ 2. The press *assailed* (ə-sāld') the mayor for giving large city construction jobs to his brother-in-law's firm.
- A. searched for
- B. paid
- C. attacked
- D. fined

Question: "What would the press do to cause the company to increase its cleanup efforts?"

_____C_____ 3. One *tenet* (tĕn'ĭt) of Islam is that its followers should not drink alcohol.
- A. answer
- B. prediction
- C. teaching
- D. guarantee

Example of a *tenet* of Islam: "followers should not drink alcohol."

_____C_____ 4. Toddlers are naturally *inquisitive* (ĭn-kwĭz'ĭ-tĭv). Because they are so curious about their surroundings, they are eager to explore everything.
- A. unreliable
- B. clumsy
- C. curious
- D. tired

Question: "Why are toddlers eager to explore everything?"

_____B_____ 5. After x-rays were discovered in 1895, there were some *preposterous* (prĭ-pŏs'tər-əs) reactions. For example, London merchants sold x-ray-proof underwear.
- A. logical
- B. ridiculous
- C. dangerous
- D. delayed

Question: "When you think of 'x-ray-proof underwear,' what word comes to your mind to describe such a notion?"

_____D_____ 6. The foolish defendant *waived* (wāvd) his right to an attorney and instead spoke for himself in court.
- A. depended upon
- B. greeted
- C. wrote
- D. gave up

General sense of the sentence.

_____D_____ 7. Sexual standards in England during the 1800s were so strict that it was considered *sordid* (sôr'dĭd) for women to reveal their legs in public.
- A. proper
- B. impossible
- C. popular
- D. indecent

General sense of the sentence.

(Continues on next page)

_C_ 8. Young children believe their parents are perfect, until they become teen-
agers, when their parents suddenly become quite *fallible* (făl′ə-bəl).
A. unhealthy   C. imperfect   Antonym of *fallible*:
B. dangerous   D. skilled   "perfect."

_A_ 9. At the company where Gerry works, people who are laid off during a
brief *recession* (rĭ-sĕsh′ən) are often rehired when there's a business
upturn.   Antonym of *recession*:
A. business decline   C. holiday   "a business upturn."
B. bankruptcy   D. war

_B_ 10. The Englishman John Merrick's illness gave him such a *grotesque*
(grō-tĕsk′) appearance that he was called "The Elephant Man." Despite
people's reactions to his misshapen head and body, Merrick remained
affectionate and gentle.   Question: "How would
A. strong   C. gray   you describe a misshapen
B. deformed   D. childlike   head and body?"

VOCABULARY IN CONTEXT: Mastery Test 4

Using context clues for help, write, in the space provided, the letter of the best meaning for each italicized word or words. Note that all of the sentences have been taken from college textbooks.

_C_ 1. After the Civil War, trolleys and streetcars greatly expanded workers' *mobility* (mō-bĭl'ĭ-tē), permitting them to move beyond walking distance from factories.
Question: "What would trolleys and streetcars expand for workers that would permit them to move beyond walking distance from factories?"
A. pay
B. skills
C. ability to move
D. interests

_C_ 2. What people say may not reflect accurately what they are actually feeling. It is sometimes necessary to *resort to* (rĭ-zôrt' tōō) clues other than their spoken words to understand them fully.
General sense of the sentence.
A. remove from
B. make light of
C. make use of
D. ignore

_A_ 3. Individual political organizations often join together to form *coalitions* (kō'ə-lĭsh'ənz) to increase the support for their issues.
A. partnerships
B. lines
C. contests
D. questions
Question: "What would help an organization get more support for its issues?"

_B_ 4. Surveys about people's sexual habits are often inaccurate because people may lie, and there is no way to *corroborate* (kə-rŏb'ə-rāt') what they say.
General sense of the sentence.
A. forget
B. prove the truth of
C. change
D. recall

_D_ 5. Everyone at the party was shocked by how *blatantly* (blāt'nt-lē) the woman insulted her former boss. She refused to shake his hand, saying, "I don't want to get my hand dirty." Examples of "acts that *blatantly* violate American norms": "burning the flag," "damaging a church."
A. secretly
B. accidentally
C. barely
D. obviously

_C_ 6. Following the English principle that voters had to have a *stake* (stāk) in the community, the colonies generally required citizens to own a certain minimum amount of land in order to vote.
Example of having "a *stake* in the community": owning "a certain minimum amount of land."
A. job
B. relative
C. investment
D. employee

(Continues on next page)

_A_ 7. William Henry Harrison's 1840 campaign brought many *innovations* (ĭn′ə-vā′shənz) to the art of electioneering. For example, for the first time, a presidential candidate spoke out on his own behalf.

    A. new things   C. crimes

    B. people   D. financial skills

> Example of an *innovation* "to the art of electioneering": "for the first time, a presidential candidate spoke out on his own behalf."

_D_ 8. To fully *assess* (ə-sĕs′) patients in order to place them in appropriate programs, mental health professionals need information on emotional adjustment and physical health.

    A. find   C. hide

    B. recognize   D. evaluate

> General sense of the sentence.

_B_ 9. In the eating disorder bulimia nervosa, a person will go on huge eating binges and then will try to *nullify* (nŭl′ə-fī′) the outrageous food intake by purposely vomiting or strictly dieting.

    A. increase   C. forget

    B. undo   D. delay

> Examples of ways "to nullify the outrageous food intake": "vomiting or strictly dieting."

_C_ 10. Adults who have both children of their own and elderly parents need to balance their commitments. They must look after their children and also *allocate* (ăl′ə-kāt′) time and energy to care for their parents.

    A. recall   C. set aside

    B. pay for   D. view

> General sense of the sentence.

Comment: Item 8 — Question: "What would professionals have to do before putting a patient in a program suited to the patient's needs?"

VOCABULARY IN CONTEXT: Mastery Test 5

A. Using context clues for help, write, in the space provided, the letter of the best meaning for each italicized word. Note that all of the sentences have been taken from college textbooks.

___C___ 1. The possibility of developing a top seller is so *alluring* (ə-loŏr′ĭng) that American companies spend billions of dollars a year trying to create new products or improve old ones.
    A. dangerous   C. attractive   Question: "How
    B. final   D. unreasonable   would American
                   companies view the possibility of developing a top seller?"

___D___ 2. Using sign language, chimpanzees can *convey* (kən-vā′) such ideas as "Candy sweet" and "Give me hug."
    A. reject   C. think of
    B. accept   D. communicate

___C___ 3. Smoking or chewing tobacco, wrote King James I, was "*loathsome* (lōth′səm) to the eye, hateful to the nose, harmful to the brain, and dangerous to the lungs."
    A. appealing   C. disgusting
    B. hidden   D. healthy

___A___ 4. The death of a spouse can cause *profound* (prə-found′) depression that, in some cases, can even lead to the death of the partner.
    A. deep   C. occasional
    B. accidental   D. mild   Question: "What kind
                 of depression might be so severe as to lead to death?"

___C___ 5. The healthiest type of parents are those who guide and instruct their children, but also grant them a degree of *autonomy* (ô-tŏn′ə-mē), encouraging the children to make their own decisions and form their own opinions.
    A. financing   C. independence
    B. knowledge   D. guidance

Comment: Items with general-sense-of-the-sentence context clues: 1, 2, 3, 4, 8, 10.

(Continues on next page)

B. Use context clues to figure out the meaning of the italicized word in each of the following items. Then write your definition in the space provided.

Wording of answers may vary.

6. A person giving first aid needs to make sure a body part that has been completely *severed* is sent to the hospital with the victim. Surgeons can often reattach the body part with microsurgery.

    Severed (sĕv′ərd) means _____ *cut off* _____

    Question: "Under what condition would a surgeon reattach a body part?"

7. Tabloid newspapers often *distort* the news by reporting rumors as if they were true.

    Distort (dĭ-stôrt′) means ___ *give a false account of; misrepresent; twist* ___

    Example of distorting the news: "reporting rumors as if they were true."

8. It's not always necessary for adults to *intervene* in children's fights; sometimes it's best to let children handle quarrels themselves.

    Intervene (ĭn′tər-vēn′) means _____ *come between; get involved* _____

9. Many companies once had retirement policies that made it *mandatory* for people to quit working as soon as they turned a certain age.

    Mandatory (măn′də-tôr′ē) means _____ *required* _____

10. After a heavy public relations campaign against the union, the hospital finally *relented* and allowed its workers to join.

    Relented (rĭ-lĕnt′ĭd) means _____ *became more forgiving; gave in* _____

VOCABULARY IN CONTEXT: Mastery Test 6

A. Five words are italicized in the textbook passage below. Write the definition for each italicized word, choosing from the definitions in the box. Then write the letter of the definition in the space provided.

  Be sure to read the entire passage before making your choices. Note that five definitions will be left over.

A. colorful	D. delayed	G. disappeared	I. increased
B. passed	E. most common	H. pray	J. punished
C. stir up interest	F. uncontrolled		

¹A century ago, the *prevailing* view among industrialists was that business had only one responsibility: to make a profit. ²By and large those were not good times to be a low-level worker or an incautious consumer. ³People worked sixty-hour weeks under harsh conditions for a dollar or two a day. ⁴The few people who tried to fight the system faced violence and unemployment. ⁵Consumers were not much better off. ⁶If you bought a product, you paid the price and took the consequences. ⁷There were no consumer groups or government agencies to come to your defense if the product was defective or caused harm. ⁸If you tried to sue the company, chances were you would lose.

⁹These conditions caught the attention of a few crusading journalists and novelists known as muckrakers. ¹⁰They used the power of the pen to create public anger and *agitate* for reform. ¹¹Largely through their efforts, a number of laws were passed to limit the power of monopolies and to establish safety standards for food and drugs.

¹²Despite these reforms, business continued to pursue profits above all else until the Great Depression. ¹³When the economic system collapsed in 1929 and 25 percent of the work force was unemployed, people lost their faith in *unbridled* capitalism. ¹⁴Pressure *mounted* for government to fix the system.

¹⁵At the urging of President Franklin Roosevelt, Congress voted in laws to protect workers, consumers, and investors. ¹⁶The Social Security system was set up, employees were given the right to join unions and bargain collectively, the minimum wage was established, and the length of the workweek was limited. ¹⁷Legislation was also *enacted* to prevent unfair competition and false advertising.

___E___ 1. In sentence 1, *prevailing* (prĭ-vā′lĭng) means _____*most common*_____.

___C___ 2. In sentence 10, *agitate* (ăj′ĭ-tāt′) means _____*stir up interest*_____.

___F___ 3. In sentence 13, *unbridled* (ŭn-brīd′ld) means _____*uncontrolled*_____.

___I___ 4. In sentence 14, *mounted* (mount′ĭd) means _____*increased*_____.

___B___ 5. In sentence 17, *enacted* (ĕn-ăkt′ĭd) means _____*passed*_____.

(Continues on next page)

B. Five words are italicized in the textbook passage below. Write the definition for each italicized word, choosing from the definitions in the box. Also, write the letter of the definition in the space provided.

Be sure to read the entire passage before making your choices. Note that five definitions will be left over.

A. causing	D. deadly	G. delay	I. die
B. enjoyable	E. give credit for	H. helpful	J. reducing
C. pay for	F. be forced to experience		

¹In the early days of medicine, there were few drugs or treatments that gave any real physical benefit. ²As a result, patients were treated in a variety of strange, largely ineffective ways. ³For instance, Egyptian patients were medicated with "lizard's blood, crocodile dung, the teeth of a swine, the hoof of an ass, rotten meat, and fly specks." ⁴If the disease itself didn't cause the patient to *succumb*, he or she had a good chance of dying instead from the treatment. ⁵Medical treatments of the Middle Ages were somewhat less *lethal*, but not much more effective. ⁶And as late as the eighteenth century, patients were *subjected to* bloodletting, freezing, and repeatedly induced vomiting to bring about a cure.

⁷Amazingly, people often seemed to get relief from such treatments. ⁸Physicians have, for centuries, been objects of great respect, and this was no less true when few remedies were actually effective. ⁹To what can one *attribute* the fair level of success that these treatments provided and the widespread faith in the effectiveness of physicians? ¹⁰The most likely answer is that these are examples of the tremendous power of the placebo effect—"any medical procedure that produces an effect in a patient because of its therapeutic intent and not its specific nature, whether chemical or physical." ¹¹Even today, the role of placebos in *curtailing* pain and discomfort is substantial. ¹²Many patients who swallow useless substances or who undergo useless procedures find that, as a result, their symptoms disappear and their health improves.

___I___ 6. In sentence 4, *succumb* (sə-kŭm′) means _____*die*_____.

___D___ 7. In sentence 5, *lethal* (lē′thəl) means _____*deadly*_____.

___F___ 8. In sentence 6, *subjected to* (səb-jĕkt′ĭd tōo) means ___*be forced to experience*___.

___E___ 9. In sentence 9, *attribute* (ə-trĭb′yōot) means _____*give credit for*_____.

___J___ 10. In sentence 11, *curtailing* (kər-tāl′ĭng) means _____*reducing*_____.

Comment: All items have general-sense-of-the-passage clues.

2

Main Ideas

WHAT IS THE MAIN IDEA?

"What's the point?" You've probably heard these words before. It's a question people ask when they want to know, in a nutshell, what someone is trying to express. The same question can guide you as you read. Recognizing the **main idea**, or point, is the most important key to good comprehension. To find it in a reading selection, ask yourself, "What's the main point the author is trying to make?" For instance, read the following paragraph, asking yourself as you do, "What is the author's point?"

> ¹School bullies have been around as long as there have been schools. ²Studies reveal several reasons why some children become bullies. ³Research shows that a certain combination of size and personality may be one factor. ⁴Bigger, more aggressive children are more likely to try to dominate their smaller, quieter peers. ⁵Another factor linked to bullying is overexposure to violent TV programs. ⁶By the time the average American child is ten years old, he or she has watched thousands of acts of violence, including assault and murder. ⁷Such exposure can lead to aggression and violence. ⁸Finally, exposure to *real* violence is a factor in bullying. ⁹Studies indicate that victims of bullies often turn into bullies themselves. ¹⁰Whether abused by family members or tormented by other kids, bullies typically learn their behavior from others. ¹¹Look closely into the eyes of a bully, and you may be looking into the eyes of a former victim.

A good way to find an author's point, or main idea, is to look for a general statement. Then decide if that statement is supported by most of the other material in the paragraph. If it is, you have found the main idea.

On the next page are four statements from the passage. Pick out the one that is both a general statement *and* that is supported by the other material in the passage. Write the letter of that statement in the space provided. Then read the explanation that follows.

Four statements from the passage:

    A. School bullies have been around as long as there have been schools.

    B. Studies reveal several reasons why some children become bullies.

    C. Research shows that a certain combination of size and personality may be one factor.

    D. Studies indicate that victims of bullies often turn into bullies themselves.

    The general statement that expresses the main idea of the passage is   *B* .

Explanation:

Sentence A: While this *is* a general statement, the paragraph does not go on to show how bullying has been a problem from when schools first began to the present day. Sentence A, then, is not the main idea.

Sentence B: The phrase "several reasons" is a general one. And in fact the rest of the passage goes on to describe a series of three supporting reasons why some children become bullies. Sentence B, then, is the sentence that expresses the main idea of the passage.

Sentence C: This sentence is about only one reason. It is not general enough to include the other reasons for bullying.

Sentence D: This sentence provides detailed support for the third reason for bullying—"exposure to *real* violence." It does not cover the other material in the paragraph.

The Main Idea as an "Umbrella" Idea

Think of the main idea as an "umbrella" idea. The **main idea** is the author's general point; under it fits all the other material of the paragraph. That other material is made up of **supporting details**—specific evidence such as examples, causes, reasons, or facts. The diagram below shows the relationship.

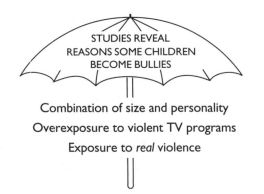

STUDIES REVEAL
REASONS SOME CHILDREN
BECOME BULLIES

Combination of size and personality

Overexposure to violent TV programs

Exposure to *real* violence

The explanations and activities on the following pages will deepen your understanding of the main idea.

RECOGNIZING A MAIN IDEA

As you read through a passage, you must **think as you read**. If you merely take in words, you will come to the end of the passage without understanding much of what you have read. Reading is an active process as opposed to watching television, which is passive. You must actively engage your mind, and, as you read, keep asking yourself, "What's the point?" Here are three strategies that will help you find the main idea.

1 Look for general versus specific ideas.
2 Use the topic to lead you to the main idea.
3 Use clue words to lead you to the main idea.

Each strategy is explained on the following pages.

1 Look for General versus Specific Ideas

You saw with the bullying paragraph that the main idea is a *general* idea supported by *specific* ideas. The following practices will improve your skill at separating general from specific ideas. Learning how to tell the difference between general and specific ideas will help you locate the main idea.

➤ Practice 1

Each group of words below has one general idea and three specific ideas. The general idea includes all the specific ideas. Identify each general idea with a **G** and the specific ideas with an **S**. Look first at the example.

Example

1. _S_ dogs
   _S_ goldfish
   _S_ hamsters
   _G_ pets

(*Pets* is the general idea which includes three specific types of pets: dogs, hamsters, and goldfish.)

1. _S_ home cooking
    _S_ take-out
    _G_ ways to eat dinner
    _S_ frozen foods

2. _S_ hot and humid
    _S_ cold and rainy
    _S_ cloudy with scattered showers
    _G_ weather forecasts

3. _S_ oversleeping
    _G_ bad habits
    _S_ overeating
    _S_ smoking

4. _S_ traffic delays
    _S_ head cold
    _S_ bad coffee
    _G_ minor problems

5. _G_ communicating
    _S_ writing
    _S_ reading
    _S_ speaking

6. _S_ deadbolt locks
    _S_ alarm system
    _S_ barking dog
    _G_ kinds of security

7. _S_ divorce
    _S_ failing grades
    _G_ major problems
    _S_ eviction

8. _S_ not taking notes in class
    _G_ poor study habits
    _S_ missing classes
    _S_ cramming for exams

9. _S_ surprised
    _G_ tone of voice
    _S_ enthusiastic
    _S_ humorous

10. _S_ hurry up
    _S_ get to bed
    _G_ commands
    _S_ clean up this mess

➤ **Practice 2**   *Answers will vary.*

1. Let's say you are describing a good friend. That he or she is a good friend is a general idea. List three *specific* reasons why he or she is a good friend.

    _____   _____   _____

2. All of us have certain valued material possessions in our lives. What are three *specific* objects that are very important to you?

    _____   _____   _____

3. Everyone has goals. What are three of the *specific* goals in your life?

    _____

    _____

    _____

4. Most students have had teachers whom they admire. Name one such teacher and three *specific* qualities or behaviors that made you like or respect that teacher.

Name of teacher: _____

Specific qualities or behaviors: _____

Answers will vary. Among qualities students might name: fair, enthusiastic, caring,

appreciative, humorous, respectful.

5. At one time or another you had to do a really unpleasant chore or job. Write three *specific* reasons why that chore or job was so unpleasant.

Answers will vary. Among reasons students might list: poor pay, inconsiderate

boss, long hours, few breaks, noisy or dirty or stressful environment, etc.

_____

➤ Practice 3

In the following groups, one statement is the general point and the other statements are specific support for the point. Identify each point with a P and each statement of support with an S.

1. _P_ My family has real problems.

    _S_ My mother has cancer.

    _S_ My sister is pregnant.

    _S_ I lost my job.

    Three problems shown.

2. _S_ Iris has a great smile.

    _S_ Iris asks you questions about yourself.

    _P_ Iris is a pleasure to be around.

    _S_ Iris really listens when you talk.

    Three specific reasons why Iris is a pleasure to be around.

3. _S_ I feel short of breath.

    _S_ I'm getting dizzy and sweating.

    _S_ There is a pain in my chest.

    _P_ I may be having a heart attack.

    Three symptoms of a heart attack.

4. _P_ My boss is hard to work for.

    _S_ He lacks a sense of humor.

    _S_ He never gives praise.

    _S_ He times all our breaks to the second.

    Three specific reasons why the boss is hard to work for.

5. _S_ We had different political beliefs.

    _P_ The date was a nightmare.

    _S_ We were dressed completely differently.

    _S_ Both of us were too nervous to say much.

    Three specific reasons why the date was a nightmare.

➤ *Practice 4*

In each of the following groups, one statement is the general point, and the other statements are specific support for the point. Identify each point with a **P** and each statement of support with an **S**.

1. _S_ A. Last night we could hear and smell a large animal prowling outside our tent.

   _S_ B. Green flies with stinging bites are in abundance around our campsite.

   _P_ C. The time has come to find a new campsite.   Three reasons for finding a new campsite.

   _S_ D. Nearby we came upon a nest of baby rattlesnakes.

2. _P_ A. Children are at risk at the school.

   _S_ B. There are two active gangs in the school.   Three reasons why children are at risk at the school.

   _S_ C. Knives and guns have been found in lockers.

   _S_ D. Drug busts have been made at the school.

3. _S_ A. Cats are clean and do not require much attention.   "Definite advantages" is a clue to the point.

   _P_ B. There are definite advantages to having a cat as a pet.

   _S_ C. Cats like living indoors and are safe to have around children.

   _S_ D. Cats are inexpensive to feed and easy to keep healthy.

4. _S_ A. Many credit card companies charge people annual fees of $25 to $50.

   _P_ B. Credit card companies make money from their customers in several ways.   "Several ways" is a clue to the point.

   _S_ C. Nearly all credit-card companies charge people high interest rates, up to 20% or more.

   _S_ D. Most credit card companies sell their customers' names and addresses to other companies.

5. _S_ A. Communicating with family and friends using computer e-mail takes very little effort or time.

   _S_ B. Finding information is as easy as typing several key words.

   _S_ C. Shopping can be quickly handled online with a few clicks of the mouse and the use of a credit card.

   _P_ D. Computers make everyday matters much easier.

   Three examples of the "everyday matters" that computers make much easier are given in items A, B, and C.

➤ *Practice 5*   *Comment:* Clue words to the points are underlined.
                                  Note that clue words often end in *s*.

In each of the following groups—all based on textbook selections—one statement
is the general point, and the other statements are specific support for the point.
Identify each point with a **P** and each statement of support with an **S**.

1. _S_ A. Teenagers gather at malls to meet friends, eat fast food, and socialize.

   _S_ B. Elderly people often walk at malls for exercise.

   _P_ C. Malls have <u>many uses</u> in American society.

   _S_ D. Malls provide space for community groups to stage events.

2. _S_ A. Instead of working full-time, many of today's employees work part-
          time with little job security and few benefits.

   _P_ B. Job security and our ideas about work have <u>changed dramatically</u> in
          recent years.

   _S_ C. Unlike in years past, most people entering the workforce today will
          change jobs several times during their careers.

   _S_ D. Rather than work for someone else, many of today's workers hope to
          start their own businesses.

3. _P_ A. The American food industry is serving ever <u>larger portions of food</u> to
          American consumers.

   _S_ B. Fast food restaurants including Burger King, McDonald's and Taco
          Bell now offer extra "super-sized" meals to customers.

   _S_ C. Many chain restaurants in the U.S. today offer "all you can eat" buffets.

   _S_ D. Supermarkets now feature oversized or "family size" portions of many
          foods.

4. _S_ A. By decreasing the production of certain hormones, exercise lessens the
          risk of certain cancers.

   _S_ B. Regular exercise strengthens the immune system, promotes mental
          health, and generates feelings of well-being.

   _S_ C. People who exercise regularly have stronger bones, more limber joints,
          and a healthier heart.

   _P_ D. Regular exercise four to five days a week has <u>significant health benefits.</u>

5. _P_ A. When toddlers play, they are having fun, but they are also developing
          in <u>important ways.</u>

   _S_ B. During play, young children are learning to use their muscles and
          becoming more coordinated.

   _S_ C. Children pretending to be other people are exploring their identities and
          "trying on" other ones.

   _S_ D. By making up stories and acting them out, children are learning about
          emotions and feelings.

2   Use the Topic to Lead You to the Main Idea

You already know that to find the main idea of a selection, you look first for a general statement, which is often at the beginning of a selection. You then check to see if that statement is supported by most of the other material in the paragraph. If it is, you've found the main idea. Another approach that can help you find the main idea is to decide on the topic of a given selection.

The **topic** is the general subject of a selection. It can often be expressed in one or more words. Knowing the topic can help you find a writer's main point about that topic. Paying close attention to the topic of a selection can lead you to the main idea.

Textbook authors use the title of each chapter to state the overall topic of that chapter. They also provide many topics and subtopics in boldface headings within the chapter. For example, here is the title of a chapter in a sociology textbook:

Aggression: Hurting Others (a 38-page chapter)

And here are the subtopics:

Theories of Aggression (a 12-page section)

Influences on Aggression (a 20-page section)

Reducing Aggression (a 6-page section)

If you were studying the above chapter, you could use the topics to help find the main ideas. (Pages 17–18 explain just how to do so, as well as other textbook study tips.)

But there many times when you are not given topics—with standardized reading tests, for example, or with individual paragraphs in articles or textbooks. To find the topic of a selection when the topic is not given, ask this simple question:

Who or what is the selection about?

For example, look again at the beginning of the paragraph that started this chapter:

School bullies have been around as long as there have been schools. Studies reveal several reasons why some children become bullies.

What, in a single word, is the above paragraph about? On the line below, write what you think is the topic.

Topic: _____ *Bullying* _____

You probably answered that the topic is "Bullying." As you reread the paragraph, you saw that, in fact, every sentence in it is about bullying.

The next step after finding the topic is to decide what main point the author is making about the topic. Authors often present their main idea in a single sentence. (This sentence is also known as the **main-idea sentence** or the **topic sentence**.) As we have already seen, the main point that is made about bullying is that "Studies reveal several reasons why some children become bullies."

☑ *Check Your Understanding*

Let's look now at another paragraph. Read it and then see if you can answer the questions that follow.

> [1]Though fun to watch, chimpanzees should not be kept as pets. [2]They are dangerously stronger than any NFL lineman. [3]Adult chimps weigh only 100 to 160 pounds, but have been measured pulling six to nine times their own weight—*with one hand.* [4]Thus, to match the strength of an average chimp, a human being would have to be able to register a two-handed pull of about a ton; it takes a very strong man to pull a quarter of that. [5]Combined with this strength is the fact that a chimp is capable of losing its temper—for reasons known only to the chimp. [6]Chimps signal their feelings with subtle cues of behavior that aren't apparent to most humans. [7]It's quite possible for a chimp to be on the verge of violence while its owner sits unaware or even unknowingly continues to provoke it. [8]Furthermore, it's not wise to keep a cute young chimp and release it into the wild when it becomes dangerous. [9]Wild-raised chimps will routinely gang up on and kill those raised in captivity.

1. What is the *topic* of the paragraph? In other words, what is the paragraph about? _____ *Chimpanzees* _____

   Hint: It often helps to look for (and even circle) a word or idea that is repeated in the paragraph.

2. What is the *main idea* of the paragraph? In other words, what is the main idea the author is stating about the topic? (Remember that the main idea will be supported by the other material in the paragraph.)

   _____ *Chimpanzees should not be kept as pets.* _____

Explanation:

As the first sentence of the paragraph suggests, the topic is "chimpanzees." Reading the paragraph, you see that, in fact, everything in it is about chimpanzees. And the main idea is clearly that "chimpanzees should not be kept as pets." This idea is a general one that sums up what the entire paragraph is about. It is an "umbrella" statement under which all the other material in the paragraph fits. The parts of the paragraph could be shown as follows:

Topic: Chimpanzees

Main idea: Chimpanzees should not be kept as pets.

Supporting details:
1. Dangerously strong
2. Capable of losing temper
3. Liable to be attacked if released in the wild

The following practices will sharpen your sense of the difference between a topic, the point about the topic (the main idea), and supporting details.

➤ Practice 6

Below are groups of four items, In each case, one item is the topic, one is the main idea, and two are details that support and develop the main idea. Label each item with one of the following:

    T — for the **topic** of the paragraph
    MI — for the **main idea**
    SD — for the **supporting details**

Note that an explanation is provided for the first group; reading it will help you do this practice.

Group 1

    _SD_   A. The creakings of a house settling may sound like a monster coming out of a grave.

    _SD_   B. Gusts of wind rattling a bedroom window can sound like invaders about to break in.

    _MI_   C. Nighttime noises can be frightening to children.

    _T_   D. Noises at night.

> The topics are easy to spot because they are short phrases— not full sentences.

Explanation:

All of the statements in Group 1 are about noises at night, so item D must be the topic. Statements A and B each describe specific nighttime noises. Statement C, however, presents the general idea that nighttime noises can be frightening to children. It is the main idea about the topic "noises at night," and statements A and B are supporting details that illustrate that main idea.

Group 2

    _MI_   A. People vary in the amount of daydreaming they do.

    _SD_   B. Around 2 to 4 percent of the population spend at least half their free time fantasizing.

    _SD_   C. Almost everyone daydreams about 10 percent of the time.

    _T_   D. Daydreaming.

> Statements B and C are specific examples of how people vary in their daydreaming.

Group 3

_T_   A. Global warming.

_SD_   B. Melting ice caps will raise ocean water levels and flood coastal areas.

_SD_   C. A warmer atmosphere may cause droughts that will turn farmlands to deserts.

_MI_   D. Global warming may cause destructive changes to life on Earth.

> The words "destructive changes" are a clue to the main idea.

Group 4

_MI_   A. There are ways to remain healthy in old age.

_SD_   B. One way for people to remain healthy as they age is to continue to find mental challenges.

_SD_   C. Sticking to a balanced, low-cholesterol diet and a reasonable exercise program helps keep people in good shape throughout their lives.

_T_   D. Health in old age.

> The words "ways to remain healthy" point to the main idea.

Group 5

_MI_   A. Love at first sight is a poor basis for a happy marriage, according to a study of one thousand married and divorced couples.

_SD_   B. Couples who knew each other only slightly but fell instantly in love found that their feelings for each other grew weaker instead of stronger.

_T_   C. Love at first sight.

> Identifying the topic—"love at first sight"—helps lead to the main idea.

_SD_   D. The couples who considered themselves happily married reported that they were not powerfully attracted to their partners when they first met, but that they gradually found each other more attractive as they grew to know and understand each other.

➤ Practice 7

Following are five paragraphs. Read each paragraph and do the following:

1 Ask yourself, "What seems to be the topic of the paragraph?" (It often helps to look for and even circle a word or idea that is repeated in the paragraph.)

2 Next, ask yourself, "What is the writer's main point about this topic?" This will be the main idea. It is stated in one of the sentences in the paragraph.

3 Then test what you think is the main idea sentence by asking, "Is this statement supported by most of the other material in the paragraph?"

Hint: When looking for the topic, make sure you do not pick one that is either **too broad** (covering a great deal more than is in the selection) or **too narrow** (covering only part of the selection). The topic and the main idea of a selection must include everything in that selection—no more and no less.

For example, in Group 1 on page 62, the topic is "noises at night." "Noises" would be too broad, since there are many other types of noises that are not mentioned. "The creakings of a house" would be too narrow, since this is only one type of nighttime noise mentioned.

Paragraph 1

[1]Stories have the magic to focus our attention and maintain our interest. [2]The politician or preacher who says, "That reminds me of a story . . . " has an audience's attention immediately. [3]Consider the success of television's *60 Minutes,* the longest-running and most profitable prime-time show in the history of television. [4]The person behind its success, producer Don Hewitt, says, "The secret of our show is so simple I can't believe the formula hasn't been followed by others. [5]It's four words that every kid knows: 'Tell me a story.' [6]I look at things in screening rooms and I say, 'That's an interesting guy and those are some great scenes you've got, but what's the story?'" [7]Without the "story," Hewitt knows the audience is leaving.

1. What is the *topic* of the paragraph? In other words, what (in one or more words) is the paragraph about? _____ *Stories* _____

_____1_____ 2. What point is the writer making about this topic? In other words, what is the *main idea* of the paragraph? In the space provided, write the number of the sentence containing the main idea. (Remember that the main idea will be supported by the other material in the paragraph.)

The word *story* (or *stories*) appears five times in the paragraph. The example in sentence 2 and the long example starting in sentence 3 provide support for the main idea in sentence 1.

Paragraph 2

[1]Extrasensory perception, or ESP, is an area that fascinates people. [2]However, ESP is not documented by any convincing evidence. [3]For instance, it would seem that ESP would be an excellent way of winning at games of chance, such as are played at gambling casinos. [4]But casino owners in Las Vegas and Atlantic City report no problem with "psychics" winning great sums of money. [5]Also, although great publicity is generated when a psychic seems to help police solve a crime, the value of such help has never been scientifically proven. [6]Psychics' tips are usually worthless, and a case is solved through traditional police work. [7]And while audiences may be amazed at the feats of "mind readers," the fact is that mind readers use simple psychological tricks to exploit their audiences' willingness to believe.

1. What is the *topic* of the paragraph? _____*ESP*_____

_2_ 2. What point is the writer making about this topic? In other words, what is the *main idea* of the paragraph? In the space provided, write the number of the sentence containing the main idea.   Sentences 3–9 *are examples of the lack of convincing evidence for ESP. Sentence 1 merely introduces the topic.*

Paragraph 3

[1]Hospices are a special type of health-care institution. [2]Hospices differ from hospitals and nursing homes in several ways. [3]First of all, they treat patients suffering from incurable diseases who are not expected to live for more than a year. [4]Hospitals, however, aim to help patients recover from disease, and nursing homes provide long-term care for the disabled and elderly. [5]Also, the hospice's purpose is to help the dying and their families. [6]In contrast, hospitals and nursing homes have limited resources for helping patients' families.

1. What is the *topic* of the paragraph? _____*Hospices vs. hospitals*_____

_2_ 2. What point is the writer making about this topic? In other words, what is the *main idea* of the paragraph? In the space provided, write the number of the sentence containing the main idea.   *Several ways (note the s word) is a clue to the main idea.*

Paragraph 4

[1]Some people persist in believing that they can drink and be alert drivers. [2]Yet alcohol is estimated to be a factor in at least half of all fatal highway accidents. [3]Another poor attitude about driving is the refusal to wear seat belts. [4]Statistics show that the chances of being seriously hurt or dying in a car accident are greater when a seat belt is not worn. [5]Also potentially deadly is the view that the best driving is fast driving. [6]Again, statistics contradict this attitude—fast driving is more likely to be deadly driving. [7]After speed limits are lowered, traffic fatalities fall significantly. [8]A final mistaken attitude is that speaking on a cell phone will not detract from a driver's attention and response time to unexpected traffic conditions. [9]Studies prove otherwise, with the result that many have called for a ban on cell phones while driving. [10]There is simply no question that poor attitudes about driving contribute to the high rate of traffic accidents and their brutal effects.

1. What is the *topic* of the paragraph? *Driving (or Poor attitudes about driving)*

_10_ 2. What point is the writer making about this topic? In other words, what is the *main idea* of the paragraph? In the space provided, write the number of the sentence containing the main idea.   *The word attitude appears four times in the paragraph, and the word driving appears even more. They are clues to the topic—poor attitudes about driving—and to the main idea in the last sentence.*

Paragraph 5

> [1]Our behavior is strongly influenced by our environment. [2]Consider a newborn baby. [3]If we were to take the baby away from its U.S. parents and place it with a Yanomamo Indian tribe in the jungles of South America, you can make predictions about the child's behavior. [4]You know that when the child begins to speak, his or her words will not be in English. [5]You also know that a child living in this tribe environment will not behave like an American. [6]He or she will not grow up wanting credit cards, for example, or designer jeans, a new car, and the latest video game. [7]Equally, the child will unquestioningly take his or her place in Yanomamo society—perhaps as a food gatherer, a hunter, or a warrior—and he or she will not even know about the world left behind at birth. [8]And in this environment, the child will grow up assuming that it is natural to want many children, not debating how many children to have.

1. What is the *topic* of the paragraph? _____*Environment and behavior*_____

__1__ 2. What point is the writer making about this topic? In other words, what is the *main idea* of the paragraph? In the space provided, write the number of the sentence containing the main idea.   Sentence 2 begins an extended example that supports the main idea in sentence 1.

3 Find and Use Clue Words to Lead You to the Main Idea

Sometimes authors make it fairly easy to find their main idea. They announce it using **clue words or phrases** that are easy to recognize. One type of clue word is a **list word**, which tells you a list of items is to follow. For example, the main idea in the paragraph about bullies was stated like this: *Studies reveal several reasons why some children become bullies.* The expression *several reasons* helps you zero in on your target: the main idea. You realize that the paragraph is going to be about specific reasons why some children become bullies.

Here are some common words that often announce a main idea. Note that all of them end in **s**.

List Words

several kinds (or ways) of	several causes of	some factors in
three advantages of	five steps	among the results
various reasons for	a number of effects	a series of

When expressions like these appear in a sentence, look carefully to see if that sentence might be the main idea. Chances are a sentence with such clue words will be followed by a list of major supporting details.

☑ Check Your Understanding

Underline the list words in the following sentences.

Hint: Remember that list words usually end in **s**.

List words have been underlined in color in the Instructor's Edition.

Example   Certain kinds of behavior can quickly get you fired from a job.

1. American workers can be said to earn several types of income.

2. Water pollution takes two forms.

3. The purchase price of a house is only one of various costs that buyers must consider.

4. Problem solving usually involves a series of four steps.

5. The increasing flow of women into the labor force was caused by a number of economic factors.

Explanation:

You should have underlined the following groups of words: *several types, two forms, various costs, a series of four steps,* and *a number of economic factors.* Each of these phrases tells you that a list of details will follow.

There is another type of clue word that can alert you to the main idea. This type of clue word, called an **addition word**, is used right before a supporting detail. When you see this type of clue word, you can assume that the main idea of the paragraph will be the general statement that includes this detail.

Here is a box of words that often introduce major supporting details and help you discover the main idea.

Addition Words

one	to begin with	in addition	last
first	another	next	last of all
first of all	second	moreover	finally
for one thing	also	furthermore	

☑ *Check Your Understanding*

Reread the paragraph about bullies, underlining the addition words that alert you to supporting details.

> [1]School bullies have been around as long as there have been schools. [2]Studies reveal several reasons why some children become bullies. [3]Research shows that a certain combination of size and personality may be <u>one</u> factor. [4]Bigger, more aggressive children are more likely to try to dominate their smaller, quieter peers. [5]<u>Another</u> factor linked to bullying is overexposure to violent TV programs. [6]By the time the average American child is ten years old, he or she has watched thousands of acts of violence, including assault and murder. [7]Such exposure can lead to aggression and violence. [8]<u>Finally,</u> exposure to *real* violence is a factor in bullying. [9]Studies indicate that victims of bullies often turn into bullies themselves. [10]Whether abused by family members or tormented by other kids, bullies typically learn their behavior from others. [11]Look closely into the eyes of a bully, and you may be looking into the eyes of a former victim.

List words have been underlined in color in the *Instructor's Edition*.

Explanation:

The words that introduce each new supporting detail for the main idea are *one, another*, and *finally*. As soon as you see the words *another factor* in the paragraph, you realize that one factor has already been mentioned and that the paragraph must be about factors. Noticing the words that introduce the supporting details suggests the main idea: several reasons (or factors) that cause children to become bullies.

The following chapter, "Supporting Details," includes much practice in the words and phrases that alert you to the main idea and supporting details. But what you have already learned here will help you find main ideas.

LOCATIONS OF THE MAIN IDEA

Now you know how to recognize a main idea by 1) distinguishing between the general and the specific, 2) identifying the topic of a passage, and 3) using clue words. You are ready to find the main idea no matter where it is located in a paragraph.

A main idea may appear at any point within a paragraph. Very commonly, it shows up at the beginning, as either the first or the second sentence. However, main ideas may also appear further within a paragraph or even at the very end.

Main Idea at the Beginning

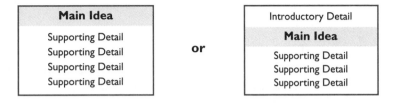

In textbooks, it is very common for the main idea to be either the first or the second sentence. See if you can underline the main idea in the following paragraph.

[1]Spanking is a poor way to shape a child's behavior. [2]For one thing, spanking will result in feelings of anger and frustration. [3]The child, then, will not learn anything positive from the punishment. [4]In addition, spanking may actually lead to more bad behavior. [5]Having learned that hitting is okay, the child may attack smaller children. [6]Finally, spanking teaches children to hide certain actions from their parents. [7]Once out of their parents' sight, however, children may feel they can get away with the bad behavior.

In this paragraph, the main idea is in the *first* sentence. All the following sentences in the paragraph provide details about the negative effects of spanking.

Addition words include *for one thing, in addition,* and *finally.*

☑ *Check Your Understanding*

Now read the following paragraph and see if you can underline its main idea:

[1]Tailgating—following too closely behind another vehicle—is a common cause of accidents. [2]Yet tailgating accidents could be avoided if drivers followed some clear-cut guidelines. [3]Any car that is less than two seconds behind the one ahead is definitely too close. [4]Two car lengths is a safe following distance to maintain in local driving. [5]Two-car accidents often become chain-reaction pileups when a number of drivers are all tailgating in a line. [6]At freeway speeds, or in snowy, icy or foggy conditions, people should increase following distance well beyond what is normally safe. [7]Finally, drivers who are impatient or aggressive need to develop the self-control not to express those feelings through dangerous behaviors like tailgating.

Comment: Main ideas in the paragraphs on this page and page 70 have been underlined.

Explanation:

In the preceding paragraph, the main idea is stated in the *second* sentence. The first sentence introduces the topic, but it is the idea in the second sentence—tailgating can be avoided by following clear-cut guidelines—that is supported in the rest of the paragraph. So keep in mind that the first sentence may simply introduce or lead into the main idea of a paragraph. Very often, a contrast word like *yet, but,* or *however* signals the main idea, as in the paragraph you have just read:

> Tailgating—following too closely behind another vehicle—is a common cause of accidents. **Yet** tailgating accidents could be avoided if drivers followed some clear-cut guidelines.

Main Idea in the Middle

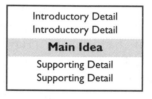

The main idea at times appears in the middle of a paragraph. Here is an example of a paragraph in which the main idea is somewhere in the middle. Try to find it and underline it. Then read the explanation that follows.

> [1]Many of us are annoyed by telemarketers who call us day and night, trying to sell us everything from magazine subscriptions to vacation homes. [2]These electronic intruders don't seem to care how much they are inconveniencing us and refuse to take "no" for an answer. [3]However, nuisance callers can be stopped if we take charge of the conversation. [4]As soon as one of them asks if we are Mr. or Ms. X, we should respond, "Yes, and are you a telephone solicitor?" [5]This technique puts them on the defensive. [6]We then have an opening to say that we don't accept solicitations over the phone, only through the mail. [7]This puts a quick end to the conversation.

If you thought the third sentence states the main idea, you were correct. The two sentences before the main idea introduce the topic: the problem of annoying telemarketers. Then the writer presents the main idea, which is that we can stop telemarketers from going on by taking charge of the conversation. The rest of the paragraph develops that idea by telling us how we can take charge of the conversation.

Main Idea at the End

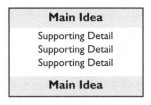

Sometimes all the sentences in a paragraph will lead up to the main idea, which is presented at the end. Here is an example of such a paragraph.

> [1]A study at one prison showed that owning a pet can change a hardened prison inmate into a more caring person. [2]Another study discovered that senior citizens, both those living alone and those in nursing homes, became more interested in life when they were given pets to care for. [3]Even emotionally disturbed children have been observed to smile and react with interest if there is a cuddly kitten or puppy to hold. [4]**Animals, then, can be a means of therapy for many kinds of individuals.**

Main Idea at the Beginning and End

At times an author may choose to state the main idea near the beginning of the paragraph and then emphasize it by restating it later in the paragraph. In such cases, the main idea is both at the beginning and the end. Such is the case in the following paragraph.

> [1]**Many "modern" advances have their origins in ancient times.** [2]For example, ancient Babylon, Assyria and Egypt all had postal systems. [3]By the ninth century B.C.E., "banks" in Baghdad not only accepted checks, but had branches as far away as China. [4]An electric battery featuring a copper cylinder, an asphalt stopper, and an iron rod was discovered in a 2000-year-old tomb in Iraq. [5]The ancient Etruscans made false teeth and dental bridgework while Rome was still a small town. [6]Ancient India had specialized surgical tools such as scalpels, needles, forceps, and syringes. [7]Two thousand years ago, the Chinese were using bamboo to pipe in natural gas for light, heat and cooking. [8]The ancient Egyptians used lightning rods to protect their temples. [9]Indoor toilets with sewage-disposal systems date back nearly five thousand years in several cultures. [10]**The lesson to be learned is clear: many "modern" inventions are, in fact, quite ancient.**

➤ *Practice 8*

The main ideas of the following paragraphs appear at different locations—the beginning, somewhere in the middle, or at the end. Identify each main idea by filling in its sentence number in the space provided.

_____1_____ 1. [1]The American badger is an especially tough, resourceful resident of the prairie. [2]The badger is about two feet long, with a low silhouette and dusty brown coloring that enable it to blend into its surroundings well. [3]Fierce and stubborn, the badger knows no fear and will fight anyone or anything if provoked. [4]Dog owners have a dread of their pets tangling with a badger, which can inflict terrible wounds. [5]A badger is nearly immune to rattlesnakes because of the thick layer of fat under its skin and will, in fact, happily eat the rattler as a tasty snack. [6]Badgers are the champion diggers of the prairie, using their powerful one-inch claws to tunnel quickly through any type of soil. [7]They hunt at night with the help of these powerful claws and will eat nearly any type of animal or plant. [8]The badger's primary meal is rodents, but if it discovers a chicken coop, it will quickly develop a taste for poultry.

> The details support the idea that the badger is tough and resourceful.

_____4_____ 2. [1]Before the early 1800s, most Americans did not know how to tell time. [2]Most, in fact, did not even own clocks. [3]The seasons and the rising and setting of the sun were their time guidelines. [4]But Americans' relationship with time changed greatly in the mid-1800s as many New Englanders shifted from farming to factory work. [5]Hundreds of thousands of factory workers had to adjust to a new sense of time. [6]Bells signaled the beginning and end of work shifts and mealtimes. [7]The first dawn bell might begin their days at 4:30 a.m. [8]They were expected to go to bed when a curfew bell sounded.

> Sentences 1–3 lead up to the main idea in sentence 4, signaled by the contrast word *but*.

_____2_____ 3. [1]Caffeine is a natural ingredient in coffee, tea, colas, cocoa, and chocolate, and is added to some prescription and non-prescription drugs. [2]Despite being "natural," caffeine is also a powerful drug, which greatly affects the body. [3]In healthy, rested people, a dose of 100 milligrams (about one cup of coffee) increases alertness, banishes drowsiness, quickens reaction time, enhances intellectual and muscular effort, and increases heart and respiratory rates. [4]Drinking one to two cups of coffee an hour before exercise encourages the body to preserve glycogen and burn fat—something that results in greater endurance. [5]In addition, caffeine masks fatigue. [6]In doses above 300 milligrams, caffeine can produce sleeplessness, nervousness, irritability, headaches, heart palpitations, and muscle twitches. [7]Caffeine is also habit-forming, and those who try to suddenly stop after heavy use may experience such withdrawal symptoms as headaches, lethargy, irritability, and difficulty in concentrating.

> The details in sentences 3–7 support the main idea in sentence 2.

<u>5</u>   4. [1]Queen Isabella of Spain, who died in 1504, boasted that she'd had only two baths in her life—at birth and before her marriage. [2]In colonial America, leaders frowned on bathing, because it involved nudity, which, they feared, could lead to loose morals. [3]Indeed, laws in Virginia and Pennsylvania either limited or outright banned bathing—and for a time in Philadelphia, anyone who bathed more than once a month faced jail. [4]Furthermore, some of the early Christian churches discouraged sudsing up because of its association with the immorality common in the Roman baths. [5]Clearly, the notion that cleanliness is next to godliness has not always been a popular one.

The details in sentences 1–4 all support the main idea in sentence 5.

<u>1</u>   5. [1]Research has demonstrated our self-centered tendency to rate ourselves more favorably than others rate us. [2]In one study, members of a random sample of men were asked to rank themselves on their ability to get along with others. [3]Defying mathematical laws, all subjects—every last one—put themselves in the top half of the population. [4]Sixty percent rated themselves in the top 10 percent of the population, and an amazing 25 percent rated themselves in the top 1 percent. [5]In the same study, 70 percent of the men ranked their leadership in the top quarter of the population, whereas only 2 percent ranked their leadership as below average. [6]Sixty percent said they were in the top quarter in athletic abilities, whereas only 6 percent said they were below average.

The details of the study (sentences 2–6) support the main idea in sentence 1.

CHAPTER REVIEW

In this chapter, you learned the following:

- Recognizing the main idea is the most important key to good comprehension. The main idea is a general "umbrella" idea under which fits all the specific supporting material of the passage.

- Three stategies that will help you find the main idea are to 1) look for general versus specific ideas; 2) use the topic (the general subject of a selection) to lead you to the main idea; 3) use clue words to lead you to the main idea.

- The main idea often appears at the beginning of a paragraph, though it may appear elsewhere in a paragraph.

The next chapter—Chapter 3—will sharpen your understanding of the specific details that authors use to support and develop their main ideas.

On the Web: If you are using this book in class, you can visit our website for additional practice in recognizing main ideas. Go to **www.townsendpress.com** and click on "Online Exercises."

➤ Review Test 1

To review what you've learned in this chapter, answer the following questions by filling in the blank or writing the letter of the correct answer.

_B_ 1. The umbrella statement that covers all of the material in a paragraph is called the

A. topic.   B. main idea.   C. supporting details.

_B_ 2. Supporting details are always more (A. general; B. specific) than the main idea.

_A_ 3. To locate the main idea of a selection, you may find it helpful to first decide on its

A. topic.   B. structure.   C. length.

_A_ 4. While a main idea may appear anywhere within a paragraph, in textbooks it very commonly appears

A. at the beginning.   B. in the middle.   C. at the end.

5. To help you decide if a certain sentence is the main idea, ask yourself, "Is this statement supported by all or most of the _____

other sentences in the paragraph _____?"

➤ Review Test 2

A. In each of the following groups, one statement is the general point, and the other statements are specific support for the point. Identify each point with a **P** and each statement of support with an **S**.

1. _S_ A. Executives kept fake accounting records to hide the fact that the company was losing money.

_S_ B. Employees were strongly encouraged to buy company stock, which is now worthless.

_S_ C. Top company executives made millions of dollars while the company was failing.

_P_ D. Officers of that failed energy company should be put in jail for a long time.   Sentences A, B, and C are all specific reasons why the officers should go to jail.

2. _S_ A. Traditional Japanese culture emphasizes self-discipline and respect for authority.

   _S_ B. No one in Japan, including police officers, may keep a handgun at home.

   _P_ C. The crime rate in Tokyo is the lowest of any major city in the world for a number of reasons.

   _S_ D. At least once a year, police officers visit every home in Japan to discuss neighborhood conditions.   Sentences A, B, and D are all specific reasons for the low crime rate in Tokyo.

B. Each group of statements below includes one topic, one main idea, and two supporting details. In the space provided, label each item with one of the following:

> **T** — for the **topic** of the paragraph
> **MI** — for the **main idea**
> **SD** — for the **supporting details**

Group 1

   _SD_ A. Staying in the sun too long can cause sunstroke.

   _SD_ B. People develop skin cancer after years of working in direct sunlight or "working in the sun" or after years of exposure to direct sunlight.   Details in items A and B support the point in D.

   _T_ C. Time in the sun.

   _MI_ D. Spending time in the sun can be dangerous.

Group 2

   _SD_ A. Rubbing one's nose and eyes transfers viruses to the hands, which then contaminate whatever they touch, such as a doorknob, serving spoon, or telephone.

   _SD_ B. Because the dried cold virus can live as long as three hours, you can pick it up from an object after the person with a cold is gone.

   _T_ C. Getting a cold.

   _MI_ D. The most likely way to catch a cold is by touching an object that someone suffering from a cold has handled.

   Details in items A and B explain
   and support the point in D.

➤ *Review Test 3*

The main idea appears at various places in the following paragraphs. Write the number of each main idea in the space provided.

___3___ 1. ¹Criticism is a valuable means of helping ourselves and others achieve personal growth. ²However, because it is often done carelessly or cruelly, criticism has a bad reputation. ³Here are some guidelines for offering criticism constructively. ⁴First, wait until the person asks for feedback on his or her performance or actions. ⁵Unasked-for criticism is not usually valuable. ⁶Second, describe the person's behavior as specifically as possible before you criticize it. ⁷Instead of just saying, "You were awful," tell the person exactly what you observed. ⁸And finally, try to balance your criticism with positive statements. ⁹Look for significant points in the other person's performance that you can honestly praise.

___1___ 2. ¹Leroy "Satchel" Paige was one of baseball's unforgettable characters. ²He spent most of his playing years dominating the Negro Leagues' best hitters before Jackie Robinson broke the color line with Brooklyn in 1947. ³By the time "Satch" got the opportunity to pitch in the newly integrated major leagues, he was supposedly 41 (Paige never revealed his true age), but he pitched so well that his name was seriously proposed for Rookie of the Year. ⁴He had an array of weird pitches that most batters had never seen before, combined with a confusing pitching motion and pinpoint accuracy. ⁵His combination of competitiveness, baseball knowledge and wondrous storytelling made him so popular with teammates that several notoriously prejudiced white players became his friends. ⁶In 1965, Paige, probably in his late 50s, pitched his last game: three scoreless innings for the Kansas City A's. ⁷Satch was elected to the Hall of Fame six years later.

___9___ 3. ¹In Bulgaria, one nods one's head for "no" and shakes it back and forth for "yes." ²If you make the "A-OK" sign in Brazil, with the index finger and thumb making a circle, it's not only *not* okay, it's very impolite. ³To show the bottom of one's feet to a Turk is a serious insult, implying that "you are lower than the ground I walk on." ⁴Throughout the Middle East, to offer the left hand in a handshake—or to wave it at someone—will give deep offense. ⁵The Japanese consider it polite to bow to varying levels, depending on the message one is trying to convey. ⁶When a Frenchman wants to make a strong point, he waves his upraised index finger from side to side. ⁷In many Mediterranean cultures, men who are

Comments: Paragraph 1—The **s** word *guidelines* is a clue to the main idea.

Paragraph 2—Sentences 2–7 all support the main idea in sentence 1.

Paragraph 3—Sentence 1–8 all provide details that support the main idea in sentence 9.

nonromantic friends walk hand in hand. [8]And in America—especially out West—a firm handshake and a direct look in the eye are expected when men meet one another; in many cultures, this would be considered very rude. [9]Clearly, body language that is perfectly normal or meaningless in one culture may mean something quite different in another.

    _2_   4. [1]Some Americans believe that colonials cleverly won the Revolutionary War by hiding behind rocks and trees and sniping at the British, who marched and fought in bright red rows and didn't even aim their muskets. [2]In fact, the British were worn down in the American colonies by a combination of factors. [3]While the colonies never had a powerful army, they had a steady source of plentiful manpower and could easily replace their losses. [4]The British regular soldier (or German soldiers for hire), by contrast, took more time to train and generally had to be shipped across the Atlantic Ocean. [5]Also, the colonies were not Britain's only worry; a much greater concern was France, with which the British were consistently at odds. [6]If too much energy had been spent holding the colonies, France might well have invaded and conquered Britain. [7]France was well aware of this, so it began sending supplies to the colonials early in the war and soon sent a fleet and an army. [8]The French contributions proved decisive at Yorktown in 1781, where the French and American armies held Lord Cornwallis's army at bay in Virginia while the French fleet turned back the Royal Navy's rescue effort.

    _2_   5. [1]People often think of shame as a strong form of embarrassment. [2]A psychological study of 104 persons, however, suggests that shame and embarrassment are quite different experiences. [3]In general, embarrassment results from a relatively minor event that occurs while others are around. [4]It is more likely to cause a person to blush. [5]Also, an embarrassing event is likely to include an element of surprise and to be remembered with smiles or jokes. [6]Embarrassment generally does not lead to a feeling that one must correct a situation. [7]Shame is felt when people reveal a personal flaw to themselves and perhaps to others. [8]Unlike embarrassment, it is likely to make one feel that a situation needs repairing. [9]In addition, while embarrassment is strongly related to how we believe others view us, shame is often felt when one is alone. [10]And it is not generally looked upon later as humorous.

Comments: Paragraph 4—The phrase "combination of factors" in sentence 2 is a clue to the main idea.
                Paragraph 5—If sentence 1 were the main idea, there would be supporting examples of how shame is a strong form of embarrassment. The details in the paragraph all support the point in sentence 2.

➤ *Review Test 4*

Here is a chance to apply your understanding of main ideas to a full-length selection. Read the article below, and then answer the questions on main ideas that follow. There are also questions to help you continue practicing the skill of understanding vocabulary in context.

Words to Watch

Below are some words in the reading that do not have strong context support. Each word is followed by the number of the paragraph in which it appears and its meaning there. These words are indicated in the article by a small circle (°).

tequila (1): a strong liquor made from a Mexican plant
myth (3): a false belief
illusion (8): false impression
irony (12): a meaning that is the opposite of what is actually said

HERE'S TO YOUR HEALTH

Joan Dunayer

1   As the only freshman on his high school's varsity wrestling team, Tod was anxious to fit in with his older teammates. One night after a match, he was offered a tequila° bottle on the ride home. Tod felt he had to accept, or he would seem like a sissy. He took a swallow, and every time the bottle was passed back to him, he took another swallow. After seven swallows, he passed out. His terrified teammates carried him into his home, and his mother then rushed him to the hospital. After his stomach was pumped, Tod learned that his blood alcohol level had been so high that he was lucky not to be in a coma or dead.

2   Unfortunately, drinking is not unusual among high-school students or, for that matter, in any other segment of our society. And that's no accident. There are numerous influences in our society urging people to drink, not the least of which is advertising. Who can recall a televised baseball or basketball game without a beer commercial? Furthermore, alcohol ads appear with pounding frequency in magazines, on billboards, and in college newspapers. According to industry estimates, brewers spend more than $600 million a year on radio and TV commercials and another $90 million on print ads. In addition, the liquor industry spends about $230 million a year on print advertising, and since 1966 it has greatly expanded its presence on cable and independent broadcast stations. Just recently, NBC became the first network station to accept hard liquor ads for broadcast.

3   To top it all off, this aggressive advertising of alcohol promotes a harmful myth° about drinking.

4   Part of the myth is that liquor signals professional success. In a slick men's magazine, one full-page ad for

Scotch whiskey shows two men seated in an elegant restaurant. Both are in their thirties, perfectly groomed, and wearing expensive-looking gray suits. The windows are draped with velvet, the table with spotless white linen. Each place-setting consists of a long-stemmed water goblet, silver utensils, and thick silver plates. On each plate is a half-empty cocktail glass. The two men are grinning and shaking hands, as if they've just concluded a business deal. The caption reads, "The taste of success."

5   Contrary to what the liquor company would have us believe, drinking is more closely related to lack of success than to achievement. Among students, the heaviest drinkers have the lowest grades. In the work force, alcoholics are frequently late or absent, tend to perform poorly, and often get fired. Although alcohol abuse occurs in all economic classes, it remains most prevalent among the poor.

6   Another part of the alcohol myth is that drinking makes you more attractive to the opposite sex. "Hot, hot, hot," one commercial's soundtrack begins, as the camera scans a crowd of college-age beachgoers. Next it follows the curve of a woman's leg up to her bare hip and lingers there. She is young, beautiful, wearing a bikini. A young guy, carrying an ice chest, positions himself near to where she sits. He is tan, muscular. She doesn't show much interest—until he opens the chest and takes out a beer. Now she smiles over at him. He raises his eyebrows and, invitingly, holds up another can. She joins him. This beer, the song concludes, "attracts like no other."

7   Beer doesn't make anyone sexier. Like all alcohol, it lowers the levels of male hormones in men and of female hormones in women—even when taken in small amounts. In substantial amounts, alcohol can cause infertility in women and impotence in men. Some alcoholic men even develop enlarged breasts.

8   The alcohol myth also creates the illusion° that beer and athletics are a perfect combination. One billboard features three high-action images: a sprinter running at top speed, a surfer riding a wave, and a basketball player leaping to make a dunk shot. A particular light beer, the billboard promises, "won't slow you down."

9   "Slow you down" is exactly what alcohol does. Drinking plays a role in over six million injuries each year—not counting automobile accidents. Even in small amounts, alcohol dulls the brain, reducing muscle coordination and slowing reaction time. It also interferes with the ability to focus the eyes and adjust to a sudden change in brightness —such as the flash of a car's headlights. Drinking and driving, responsible for over half of all automobile deaths, is the leading cause of death among teenagers. Continued alcohol abuse can physically change the brain, permanently impairing learning and memory. Long-term drinking is related to malnutrition, weakening of the bones, and ulcers. It increases the risk of liver failure, heart disease, and stomach cancer.

10   Finally, according to the myth, alcohol is the magic ingredient for social success. Hundreds of TV and radio ads have echoed this message in recent years. In one commercial, for instance, an overweight man sits alone in his drab living room. He reaches into a cooler, pulls out a bottle of beer, and twists off the bottle cap. Instantly dance music erupts, and dozens of attractive young adults appear in a shower of party streamers and confetti. "Where the party

begins," a voice says. The once lonely man, now a popular guy with lots of male and female friends, has found the answer to his social problems—beer.

11   Relationships based on alcohol are unlikely to lead to social success and true friendships. Indeed, studies show that when alcohol becomes the center of a social gathering, it may lead to public drunkenness and violence. The ad's image of the man's new friends ignores an undeniable reality: that alcohol ruins—not creates—relationships. In addition to fighting and simple assault, drinking is linked to two-thirds of domestic violence incidents. Rather than leading to healthy social connections, alcohol leads to loneliness, despair, and mental illness. Over a fourth of the patients in state and county mental hospitals have alcohol problems; more than half of all violent crimes are alcohol-related; the rate of suicide among alcoholics is fifteen times higher than among the general population.

12   Advertisers would have us believe the myth that alcohol is part of being successful, sexy, healthy, and happy; but those who have suffered from it—directly or indirectly—know otherwise. For alcohol's victims, "Here's to your health" rings with a terrible irony° when it is accompanied by the clink of liquor glasses.

Reading Comprehension Questions

Vocabulary in Context

___D___ 1. In the excerpt below, the word *caption* (kăp′shən) means
   A. man.
   B. menu.
   C. contract that seals the business deal.
   D. words accompanying the picture.

   "In a slick men's magazine, one full-page ad for Scotch whiskey shows two men seated in an elegant restaurant. . . . The caption reads, 'The taste of success.'" (Paragraph 4)

___C___ 2. In the sentence below, the word *prevalent* (prĕv′ə-lənt) means
   A. weak.
   B. colorful.
   C. widespread.
   D. inexpensive.

   "Although alcohol abuse occurs in all economic classes, it remains most prevalent among the poor." (Paragraph 5)

___A___ 3. In the excerpt on the next page, the word *substantial* (səb-stăn′shəl) means
   A. large.
   B. reasonable.
   C. weak.
   D. pleasing.

   The word *small* is an antonym clue.

"Beer . . . lowers the levels of male hormones in men and of female hormones in women—even when taken in small amounts. In substantial amounts, alcohol can cause infertility in women and impotence in men." (Paragraph 7)

_A_ 4. In the sentence below, the word *impairing* (ĭm-pâr'ĭng) means
    A. damaging.
    B. doubling.
    C. postponing.
    D. teaching.

"Continued alcohol abuse can physically change the brain, permanently impairing learning and memory." (Paragraph 9)

_C_ 5. In the sentence below, the word *generates* (jĕn'ə-rātz') means
    A. removes.
    B. hides.
    C. produces.
    D. follows.

Items 1, 2, 4, and 5 have general-sense-of-the-sentence context clues.

"Finally, according to the myth, alcohol is the magic ingredient for social success." (Paragraph 10)

Main Ideas

_C_ 6. The main idea of paragraph 2 is its
    A. first sentence.
    B. second sentence.
    C. third sentence.
    D. last sentence.

_A_ 7. The main idea of paragraph 4 is its
    A. first sentence.
    B. second sentence.
    C. third sentence.
    D. last sentence.

The main idea is supported by one extended example.

_D_ 8. The topic of paragraph 5 is drinking and
    A. grades.
    B. work.
    C. the poor.
    D. lack of success.

_A_ 9. The main idea of paragraph 5 is its
    A. first sentence.
    B. second sentence.
    C. third sentence.
    D. fourth sentence.

_A_ 10. The main idea of paragraph 10 is its
    A. first sentence.
    B. second sentence.
    C. next-to-last sentence.
    D. last sentence.

Discussion Questions

1. Unfortunately, Tod's experience with alcohol is not so rare. Do you know anyone who has had a negative experience because of drinking or because of drinking and driving? Where was that person drinking, and how much did he or she have? Explain what eventually happened.

2. If it's true that "beer doesn't make anyone sexier," why do you think so many young people drink so much beer in social situations?

3. Think about a wine, beer, or liquor ad you have seen in a magazine, in a newspaper, or on television. What part of the alcohol myth described in "Here's to Your Health" does that ad promote? What details of the ad contribute to that element of the myth?

4. Cigarette advertising is no longer allowed on television. Do you think beer ads should also be outlawed on TV? In college newspapers? Explain your answers.

Note: Writing assignments for this selection appear on pages 585–586.

Check Your Performance   **MAIN IDEAS**

Activity	Number Right	Points	Score
Review Test 1 (5 items)	_____	× 2 =	_____
Review Test 2 (16 items)	_____	× 2.5 =	_____
Review Test 3 (5 items)	_____	× 4 =	_____
Review Test 4 (10 items)	_____	× 3 =	_____
		TOTAL SCORE =	_____%

Enter your total score into the **Reading Performance Chart: Review Tests** on the inside back cover.

MAIN IDEAS: Mastery Test 1

A. In each of the following groups, one statement is the general point, and the other statements are specific support for the point. Identify each point with a **P** and each statement of support with an **S**.

1. _S_ A. Hungry bears searching for food often threaten hikers.

   _P_ B. Hiking on that mountain trail can be very dangerous.

   _S_ C. Severe weather develops quickly, leaving hikers exposed to storms and cold.

   _S_ D. When it rains, the trail—which is very steep at some points—becomes slippery.

2. _P_ A. Even after he became deaf, the musical genius Beethoven did not stop composing.

   _S_ B. He sometimes tried out passages at the piano to make sure they could be played, even though he could not hear his playing.

   _S_ C. Every day at dawn, Beethoven began working at his desk, writing down the music he heard only in his head.

   _S_ D. While deaf he created chamber music, his famous Ninth Symphony, and many other works.

3. _S_ A. Terrorists hijacked and flew jetliners into the World Trade Center and the Pentagon, both on the same day.

   _S_ B. Suicide bombers have killed themselves and dozens of others in the Middle East.

   _S_ C. One hundred sixty-eight people died when an American terrorist blew up the federal building in Oklahoma City.

   _P_ D. Children have had to deal with the knowledge of many horrible acts of terrorism.

Comments: Group 1—The clue word is *dangerous* in item B. Items A, C, and D are specific supporting examples of how hiking the trail can be dangerous.

Group 2—Items B, C, and D are examples that support the point in A.

Group 3—Items A, B, and C are examples of the "horrible acts of terrorism" in D.

(Continues on next page)

B. Each group of statements below includes one topic, one main idea, and two supporting details. In the space provided, label each item with one of the following:

> **T** — for the **topic** of the paragraph
> **MI** — for the **main idea**
> **SD** — for the **supporting details**

Group 1

  SD A. Some people knock on wood when talking about good luck.

  T B. Everyday superstitions.

  SD C. Some people believe they should leave a house through the same door they entered.

  MI D. There are many superstitions that are practiced in everyday life.

Group 2

  MI A. Desert plants have various features that make them highly tolerant of long dry spells.

  SD B. Many desert plants have waxy leaves, stems, or branches that reduce water loss.

  T C. Features of desert plants.

  SD D. The roots of some desert plants often extend to great depths to tap the moisture there.

Comments: Group 1—Items A and C are examples of the "superstitions . . . practiced in everyday life" referred to in D.

Group 2—The phrase "various features" includes an **s** word that signals the main idea. Items B and C describe specific features that make desert plants tolerant of dry spells.

MAIN IDEAS: Mastery Test 2

A. In each of the following groups—all based on textbook selections—one statement is the general point, and the other statements are specific support for the point. Identify each point with a **P** and each statement of support with an **S**.

1. _S_ A. The pessimistic view of human nature holds that people are basically lazy and have to be forced to work.

   _P_ B. Political and business leaders often base their policies on one of several assumptions about people.

   _S_ C. The optimistic view presumes people are interested in doing a job well and are capable of directing themselves.

   _S_ D. A middle-of-the-road theory is that while people do not dislike work, they do not work efficiently without appropriate direction.

2. _S_ A. African-American and Hispanic children have the highest rates of diabetes and obesity in the country.

   _S_ B. Hispanics in the United States are four times more likely than whites to contract tuberculosis.

   _P_ C. Health profiles in the United States reveal differences between racial and ethnic groups.

   _S_ D. Native Americans have a rate of infant mortality that is higher than that of whites, but lower than that of African-Americans.

3. _P_ A. Anxiety disorders, in which normal anxieties have become exaggerated or unrealistic, take several forms.

   _S_ B. A phobia is an anxiety disorder in which an unrealistic fear interferes with a person's normal life.

   _S_ C. Eating disorders such as anorexia nervosa (refusing to eat) and bulimia (bingeing followed by purging) are thought to be anxiety disorders.

   _S_ D. Obsessive-compulsive behavior is an anxiety disorder characterized by persistent, unrealistic ideas (such as contamination by germs) that lead to meaningless behaviors (such as constant hand-washing).

Comments: Group 1—The phrase "several assumptions" in item B includes an s word that signals the main idea.

Group 2—The phrase "differences between racial and ethnic groups" in item C signals the three examples of differences in items A, B, and D.

Group 3—The phrase "several forms" in item A signals the main idea. Items B, C, and D are specific examples of anxiety disorders.

(Continues on next page)

B. Each group of statements below includes one topic, one main idea, and two supporting details. In the space provided, label each item with one of the following:

> **T** — for the **topic** of the paragraph
> **MI** — for the **main idea**
> **SD** — for the **supporting details**

Group 1

_SD_ A. School officials complain that students damage school property, and parents complain their children can't read or do math.

_SD_ B. Teachers complain about the low salaries they get for their difficult and important jobs.

_T_ C. Problems in our schools.

_MI_ D. The problems within our school systems are varied and affect almost everyone involved.

Group 2

_MI_ A. Self-help groups based on the Alcoholics Anonymous model exist to serve people with a variety of problems.

_T_ B. Self-help groups.

_SD_ C. Narcotics Anonymous sponsors meetings where drug abusers and their loved ones can get support.

_SD_ D. Overeaters Anonymous assists people whose eating has gotten out of their control.

Comments: Group 1—Items A and B are examples of the "problems within our school systems" cited in D.

Group 2—The phrase "variety of problems" is a clue that item A is the main idea. Items C and D are specific examples of the variety of problems addressed by self-help groups.

MAIN IDEAS: Mastery Test 3

Note: These paragraphs are on a basic level of difficulty.

The main idea may appear at any place within each of the five paragraphs that follow. Write the number of each main idea sentence in the space provided.

___1___ 1. ¹Creatures that are very sensitive to the changes in the air before a storm can "predict" a change in the weather. ²Birds, for example, sense the pressure change and fly lower. ³Low-flying birds, then, indicate that rain is coming. ⁴Similarly, houseflies detect this change and move indoors to avoid the downpour. ⁵And cats are known to groom themselves just before a storm. ⁶In doing so, they are reacting to the static electricity that enters the air before a thunderstorm. ⁷The electricity separates their fur and makes them feel dirty, so they lick themselves to make the fur smooth and "clean" again.

___2___ 2. ¹Men, we are reminded over and over, are the stronger sex. ²Yet men are more likely than women to have a number of health problems at every age. ³More males than females are miscarried, are stillborn, or die in their first year of life. ⁴In all societies, men die earlier than women do. ⁵American men are more likely than women to die from heart disease, lung disease, and cirrhosis of the liver. ⁶They are more likely to suffer from stress-related diseases, such as hypertension, ulcers, and asthma. ⁷They are hospitalized for mental illness more frequently. ⁸Women attempt suicide more often than men, but men succeed in killing themselves three times as often (largely because they use violent means—guns rather than sleeping pills).

___6___ 3. ¹The eruption of volcanoes has caused death and misery throughout the centuries. ²But in parts of Italy, Iceland, Chile, and Bolivia, volcanic steam is used to run heat and power plants. ³Pumice, which is made from volcanic lava, is used as a grinder and polisher. ⁴Sulfur produced by volcanoes is useful to the chemical industry. ⁵Hawaiian farmers grow crops on land made rich by decayed volcanic material. ⁶Clearly, in spite of all the damage they cause, volcanoes do benefit us in various ways.

Comments: Paragraph 1—Sentence 1 is a general statement and the main idea. Sentences 2–7 then provide and explain specific supporting examples of the main idea.

Paragraph 2—After an introductory first sentence, the main idea is presented in sentence 2. The phrase "number of health problems" (note the **s** word!) is a clue to the main idea.

Paragraph 3—The first sentence cannot be the topic sentence, since if it were, the paragraph would have to be about the death and misery caused by the eruption of volcanoes. Instead, the paragraph lists the ways in which volcanoes benefit us. The phrase "various ways" (again, note the **s** word!) signals the main idea in the last sentence.

(Continues on next page)

_1_   4. [1]Adult children who move back home can avoid family conflicts by following some helpful tips. [2]First, they should contribute what they can—and it doesn't necessarily have to be in terms of money. [3]Being productive family members will help them earn their keep. [4]This can involve tutoring or coaching younger sisters or brothers, or helping Mom and Dad with household chores and errands. [5]Second, grown children at home should not expect their parents to rescue them from difficulties. [6]As adults, they are responsible for getting out of their own scrapes—and for trying to avoid scrapes in the first place. [7]Last, they must respect their parents' lifestyles and own needs for independence. [8]It is unrealistic to expect parents' lives to revolve around the needs of a grown child, as they may have when the child was younger.

_2_   5. [1]Police estimate that only 1 to 2 percent of hitchhiking crimes are reported, so there are no accurate statistics on such events. [2]But frequent horror stories indicate that hitchhiking can be dangerous to both hitchhiker and driver. [3]There was the nineteen-year-old woman who accepted a lift from three young men in New Jersey, expecting a ride across the bridge to New York City. [4]Instead they drove to a motel, where they repeatedly raped her. [5]Luckily, she escaped with her life. [6]Less fortunate was the eighteen-year-old woman student who disappeared from campus after accepting a ride with a stranger and whose decomposed body was found in a suburban sewage plant two years later. [7]Male hitchhikers are less open to assault, but a number of incidents show that they are far from immune. [8]Hitchhikers also face the hazards of riding with an intoxicated or stoned driver, not the least of which is an accident. [9]They also risk assault or robbery by other hitchhikers and being stranded in out-of-the-way places. [10]Drivers, too, are subject to assault and robbery. [11]And they risk accident by stopping on a busy highway, or arrest if their passengers happen to be carrying drugs. [12]Some male drivers have picked up young girls who threatened to call the police and cry rape unless the men handed over all their money.

Comments: Paragraph 4—The phrase "helpful tips" (note the **s** word) signals the main idea. Sentences 2–7 then provide and explain examples of the main idea.

Paragraph 5—Sentence 1 introduces the topic of hitchhiking. The phrase "frequent horror stories" (again, note the **s** word) signals the main idea. The specific horror stories are the supporting details that make up the rest of the paragraph.

MAIN IDEAS: Mastery Test 4

Note: These paragraphs are on a slightly higher level of difficulty.

The main idea may appear at any place within each of the five paragraphs that follow. Write the number of each main idea sentence in the space provided.

___3___ 1. ¹Fire extended humans' geographical boundaries by allowing them to travel into regions that were previously too cold to explore. ²It also kept predators away, allowing early humans to sleep securely. ³Fire, in fact, has been a significant factor in human development and progress in many ways. ⁴Other obvious benefits of fire are its uses in cooking and in hunting. ⁵Probably even more important, however, is that learning to control fire allowed people to change the very rhythm of their lives. ⁶Before fire, the human daily cycle coincided with the rising and setting of the sun. ⁷With fire, though, humans gained time to think and talk about the day's events and to prepare strategies for coping with tomorrow.

___2___ 2. ¹The stages of life, from birth to death, may seem controlled by biology. ²However, the way we think about life's stages is shaped by society. ³During the Middle Ages, for example, children dressed—and were expected to act—just like little adults. ⁴Adolescence became a distinct stage of life only fairly recently, when a separate teenage subculture began to appear. ⁵But in the Middle Ages, young people were "children" until about age 16. ⁶Then they went to work, married, and had their own children. ⁷Today, "young adulthood" has become a new stage of life, stretching from about age 20 to 30. ⁸As life expectancy becomes longer and people spend years in active retirement, older adulthood has also become a distinct life stage.

___1___ 3. ¹New technology often creates unanticipated problems. ²Automobiles, for example, provide numerous benefits, but they also pollute the air and kill about fifty thousand Americans each year. ³It is difficult to imagine life without electricity, but the generation of electricity pollutes the air and causes the thermal pollution of rivers. ⁴Insecticides and chemical fertilizers have performed miracles in agriculture but have polluted food and streams (and even "killed" some lakes). ⁵Jet planes, while helping us in many ways, cause air pollution (one jet taking off emits the same amount of hydrocarbon as the exhausts from ten thousand automobiles) and noise pollution near busy airports.

Comments: Paragraph 1—Some of the "many ways" referred to in sentence 3 are listed in the other sentences.

Paragraph 2—The first sentence introduces the topic of the stages of life.

Paragraph 3—Sentence 1 is a general statement and the main idea. Specific examples of "unanticipated problems" then follow.

(Continues on next page)

____7____ 4. ¹By the end of the first series of Sherlock Holmes stories, the author, Sir Arthur Conan Doyle, had become tired of writing detective stories. ²So at the end of his second book of Holmes stories, he decided to have the detective die. ³The book ends with Holmes and his archenemy, Moriarty, plunging to their deaths from a high cliff overlooking a waterfall. ⁴After that, hundreds of letters poured in to Conan Doyle, begging him to bring Holmes back. ⁵Also, magazines offered him huge sums of money for additional Sherlock Holmes adventures. ⁶Finally, after nine years, Conan Doyle wrote a new story in which Holmes reappears and tells Dr. Watson that he did not die after all. ⁷Sometimes it is the reader, not the author, who determines how long fictional heroes will live.

____2____ 5. ¹With so many young, single people having babies, the question arises as to how happy they are being young parents. ²A national survey of young, single mothers and fathers reveals that most were happier before they became parents. ³Sixty-seven percent of the nine thousand new parents who responded to the survey said having a baby presented more problems than they envisioned. ⁴Fifty-six percent of the respondents said they had to drop out of school, despite their hopes that they could manage schoolwork plus rearing a baby. ⁵A majority (73 percent) said they were forced to seek financial help from family, friends and/or government agencies, and 37 percent said they accepted low-paying, unsatisfying jobs out of necessity. ⁶Also, 70 percent said they missed the "good times" with friends that they enjoyed before their babies were born.

Comments: Paragraph 4—The main idea in the last sentence is a general conclusion supported by the story about Conan Doyle and Sherlock Holmes.

Paragraph 5—Sentence 1 introduces the topic: just how happy are young, single people who become parents? Sentence 2 then presents the main idea: they were happier before they became parents. Sentence 3–6 then provide specific supporting details for this idea.

MAIN IDEAS: Mastery Test 5

Note: These paragraphs are more challenging than those in Mastery Tests 3 and 4.

The five paragraphs that follow are all taken from college textbooks. The main idea may appear at any place within each paragraph. Write the number of each main idea sentence in the space provided.

__6__ 1. [1]An author doing research for a book asked thousands of Americans what made them happy. [2]Among the popular responses she received were: eating ice-cream sandwiches and candy, being offered a football ticket, and visiting city parks. [3]Other specific responses included eating ravioli, feeling the cool underside of a pillow, and rereading old love letters. [4]The most frequently cited response was simply spending time with family. [5]Almost no one gave the answer of owning flashy jewelry, showy cars, or other fancy things. [6]The author concluded that most of the things that put a smile on our face are simple and free or inexpensive.

__4__ 2. [1]To erase or not to erase? [2]That is the question in many students' minds after they've penciled in one of those small circles in multiple-choice tests. [3]Folk wisdom has long held that when answering questions on such tests—or on any test—you should trust your first instincts. [4]However, a research instructor has found that students who change answers they're unsure of usually improve their scores. [5]The instructor spent three years compiling and analyzing college students' tests, watching for telltale erasure marks, which would indicate that the student had, indeed, revised his or her answer. [6]What the instructor found was that revised answers were two-and-a-half times as likely to go from wrong to right as vice-versa. [7]This statistic held up even across such variables as sex, age, and race; the subject matter of the tests studied also proved not to be a factor.

__2__ 3. [1]Finding a good way to get rid of garbage is a problem that faces many municipalities today. [2]It may be of some consolation for them to know that getting rid of garbage has almost always involved problems. [3]When settlements were very small, garbage was simply thrown outdoors, where it eventually decomposed. [4]But as communities grew, pigs and other animals helped clear away garbage by eating it; of course, the animals, in turn, recycled that garbage and thus created an even less appealing garbage problem. [5]The first municipal effort to deal with garbage was begun in Philadelphia by Benjamin Franklin, whose solution was to have it dumped into the Delaware River. [6]A century later, municipal incinerators, generally located in the most crowded part of town, burned garbage and produced the worst of odors as a by-product.

Comments:

Paragraph 1 — Sentence 1 introduces the topic; sentences 2–4 provide examples; sentence 6 is a general statement and the main idea.

Paragraph 2 — Sentences 1–3 introduce the topic. Sentence 4 (note the contrast word *however*) then presents the main idea, supported by sentences 5–7.

Paragraph 3 — Sentences 3–6 provide supporting examples of the "problems" referred to in sentence 2.

(Continues on next page)

___1___ 4. ¹In both Canada and the United States, many people arrested for a crime never receive appropriate punishment. ²Prosecutors often drop charges because of flaws in the arrest procedures—officers didn't follow the rules with sufficient care or file their paperwork properly. ³In many other cases, the charges are dismissed at preliminary hearings because of problems of evidence, such as key witnesses failing to appear. ⁴Of cases surviving these barriers, many are resolved by a plea bargain. ⁵That is, the charges are reduced in exchange for a plea of guilty. ⁶This spares the government the expense of a trial, but it also makes punishment less severe. ⁷And of those who do go to prison, very few will serve their full sentence. ⁸Time off for good behavior often equals 25 percent of one's sentence, so most will be out on parole well before their time is up.

___2___ 5. ¹If we compressed the entire history of life on the planet into a single year, the first modern human would not appear until December 31 at about 11:53 p.m., and the first civilizations would emerge only about a minute before the end of the year. ²Yet humanity's achievements in its brief history on Earth have been remarkable. ³Some 15,000 years ago, our ancestors practiced religious rituals and painted superb pictures on the walls of their caves. ⁴Around 11,000 years ago, some human groups began to domesticate animals and plants, thereby freeing themselves from total dependence on hunting and gathering food. ⁵About 6,000 years ago, people began to live in cities, to specialize in different forms of labor, to divide into social classes, and to create distinct political and economic institutions. ⁶Within a few thousand years empires were created, linking isolated groups and bringing millions under centralized rule. ⁷Advanced agricultural practices improved farming, resulting in growing populations and the emergence of large nation-states. ⁸A mere 250 years ago the Industrial Revolution began, thrusting us into the modern world of factories and computers, jets and nuclear reactors, instantaneous global communications, and terrifying military technologies.

Comments: Paragraph 4—Sentence 1 is a general statement and the main idea; sentences 2–8 are about specific ways the author feels people receive too little punishment for their crimes.

Paragraph 5—Sentences 3–8 describe some of the remarkable "achievements" (note the **s** word) referred to in sentence 2.

MAIN IDEAS: Mastery Test 6

Note: These paragraphs are more challenging than those in Mastery Test 5.

The five paragraphs that follow are all taken from college textbooks. The main idea may appear at any place within each paragraph. Write the number of each main idea sentence in the space provided.

___2___ 1. ¹People may think that love and romantic feelings are enough of a basis for choosing a spouse. ²The chances of a marriage surviving, however, would improve if prospective marriage partners considered a few unromantic questions before deciding on matrimony. ³For example, do the two individuals involved share a common socioeconomic background? ⁴The more similar they are in their social, economic, religious, and cultural backgrounds, the more similar their expectations about married life will be. ⁵In addition, what are their goals? ⁶It's a big advantage to the marriage if they know and share one another's goals concerning career, lifestyle, and family. ⁷Finally, and maybe most important, how does the prospective spouse treat others in his or her life? ⁸During the courtship, the boyfriend or girlfriend may get special consideration, but in the long run, spouses will probably treat each other about the same way they treat their own family members.

The phrase "few unromantic questions" signals the main idea.

___1___ 2. ¹There is a tendency in our society to turn important decisions over to groups. ²In the business world, most important decisions are made around a conference table rather than behind one person's desk. ³In politics, major policy decisions are seldom made by just one person. ⁴Groups of advisers, cabinet officers, committee members, or aides meet to deliberate and decide. ⁵In the courts, a defendant may request a trial by jury, and for some serious crimes, a jury trial is required by law. ⁶And of course, the U.S. Supreme Court renders group decisions on issues of major importance.

Sentences 2–6 are examples that support the general idea in sentence 1.

___2___ 3. ¹The American ideal of a lush green lawn is borrowed from England, where the cool, misty climate makes it easy to grow grass. ²In America, however, lawns are an energy-intensive, wasteful, and nonproductive form of landscaping. ³To begin with, achieving a picture-perfect lawn requires gallons of expensive fertilizer and hazardous pesticides that pollute groundwater and run off into lakes and rivers. ⁴In addition, lawn owners often exterminate the insects, moles, and gophers that play a part in the balance of nature. ⁵Equally destructive is the constant watering lawns require, often where water is a limited resource. ⁶Finally, the lawn must be mowed on a regular basis to give it that green carpet effect, requiring endless output of human and mechanical energy. ⁷After all the labor and expense, the final result is a flat carpet that lacks interesting features, wildlife, or edible produce.

Sentences 3–7 are reasons that support the general idea in sentence 2.

(Continues on next page)

_3_   4. [1]Propaganda is information that is methodically spread in order to persuade audiences to adopt a certain opinion. [2]Advertising is an ever-present form of propaganda in our lives. [3]Four common propaganda techniques are present in the advertising we see and hear every day. [4]One technique, the testimonial, involves having a well-known person appear on behalf of the product being sold. [5]Advertisers assume, for example, that if we admire a sports star, we'll want to eat the cereal he or she endorses. [6]Another common propaganda technique, the bandwagon, makes us want to be "one of the gang." [7]"Everybody's switching to . . . " "Don't be left out . . . " and "All across America, people are discovering . . . " are phrases that signal a bandwagon approach. [8]The plain-folks propaganda technique is especially popular on TV. [9]In plain-folks commercials, we see and hear "regular" consumers talk about their experience using a certain phone company, headache remedy, or brand of coffee. [10]The fourth common propaganda technique, the transfer, encourages us to link two unrelated objects in our mind. [11]When a powerful cougar prowls around a shiny new car, for example, advertisers hope we will transfer our sense of the wild cat's speed, strength, and beauty to our vision of their product.

_11_   5. [1]Stories of the mythical Camelot, the location in England of King Arthur's court, depict a world of dashing knights in shining armor and beautiful damsels in distress. [2]In actuality, the real world of that time probably consisted of smelly men in rusty tin suits and damsels in a certain kind of distress—the distress of being constantly pregnant and of having no rights in a male-dominated society. [3]Those same stories often glorified the brave men who fought to the death for king and country. [4]However, most battle fatalities of the time resulted from medieval medicine. [5]Letting the "bad blood" out of a sick person was a common medical practice, and cleanliness was not. [6]Other stories of the fabled Camelot housed royalty in glittering palaces, clothed them in silks, and covered them in mystery and awe. [7]But what is awesome about living in a cold, stone, rat-infested fortress with poor ventilation? [8]As for silks, war-indebted kings could rarely afford such foreign commodities. [9]Wool from home usually did the trick. [10]And there's certainly nothing silky about the discomfort caused by coarse woolen undergarments. [11]It is obvious that the Camelot myth ignores the harsh realities of life in the Middle Ages in favor of a fantastic, unrealistic view of history.

Comments: Paragraph 4—The phrase "four common propaganda techniques" in sentence 3 signals the main idea.

Paragraph 5—The topic is "Stories of the mythical Camelot versus the real Camelot." A series of specific examples of the imagined Camelot versus the real Camelot then follow. The final sentence states the general point of all of the examples: that "harsh realities" have been overlooked and people have created "fantastic and unrealistic images" of history.

3

Supporting Details

In Chapter 2 you worked on the most important reading skill—finding the main idea. A closely related reading skill is locating *supporting details*. Supporting details provide the added information that is needed for you to make sense of a main idea.

This chapter describes supporting details and presents three techniques that will help you take study notes on main ideas and their supporting details: outlining, mapping, and summarizing.

WHAT ARE SUPPORTING DETAILS?

Supporting details are reasons, examples, facts, steps, or other kinds of evidence that explain a main idea. In the paragraph below, three major details support the main idea that many people are strangely passive when they visit a doctor. As you read the paragraph, try to identify and check (✓) the three major details.

> ¹Many people are strangely passive when they visit a doctor. ²First of all,✓they often fail to provide the doctor with complete information about their medical problem. ³They may barely describe their symptoms, believing that a skilled doctor—like a master car mechanic—will somehow easily be able to diagnose what is wrong with them. ⁴Secondly,✓many people fail to ask their doctors for a full and clear explanation of their condition. ⁵They don't want to appear ignorant in front of their "all-knowing" doctor, and they don't want to take up too much of this Important Person's time, so they say little and ask almost nothing. ⁶Last of all,✓they often fail to understand a doctor's orders. ⁷Studies show that many patients don't understand why they should take a certain medication or for how long they should take it. ⁸Incredibly enough, some patients are not even sure, as they are about to be rolled into an operating room, why they are having surgery!

Now see if you can complete the basic outline below that shows the three major details supporting the main idea. *Wording of answers may vary.*

Main idea: Many people are strangely passive when they visit a doctor.

Supporting detail 1: <u>*Don't provide enough information about their problem*</u>

Supporting detail 2: <u>*Don't get a full explanation of their problem*</u>

Supporting detail 3: <u>*Don't understand a doctor's orders*</u>

Explanation:

You should have added that patients fail to 1) provide enough information about their problem, 2) get a full explanation of their problem, and 3) understand a doctor's orders. These major supporting details help you fully understand the main idea. To read effectively, you must often learn to recognize main ideas *and* the details that support those ideas.

Understanding Major and Minor Details

There are often two levels of supporting details—major and minor. The **major details** explain and develop the main idea. In turn, the **minor details** help fill out and make clear the major details.

In the paragraph below, the main idea is stated in the first sentence. Read the paragraph and put a check (✓) by the two major details that support the main idea. The major details are in turn supported by minor details, which are examples in this case. The first major detail is followed by three examples, and the second major detail is followed by one long example.

¹There are two ways to relate to people in our lives. ²One way is to see them as *objects*: we get something from them, but we are not concerned with how they feel. ³They are there only for our use. ⁴For example, we might treat as an object the person who sells us items in a convenience store or waits on us in a restaurant or even teaches a class we are taking. ⁵The second way we can see people is as *subjects,* letting ourselves be aware that they have feelings just as we do. ⁶There is a story about a British woman who was expecting important guests for tea one afternoon. ⁷She looked out from her front porch after lunch and was horrified to see that her gardener had not shown up for work. ⁸When he finally arrived, she tore into him. ⁹"Do you know who is coming here in an hour? ¹⁰I ought to fire you!" ¹¹Without looking up, the man quietly said, "I'm sorry. ¹²My little girl died during the night, and we had to bury her today." ¹³For the first time, the woman saw the man as a human being, not simply as a device for keeping her lawn attractive. ¹⁴He stopped being an object and became a subject, a possessor of feelings, needs, pains, and relationships to which she had never given a thought.

Explanation:

The major details are the "two ways to relate to people in our lives" mentioned in the main idea. The first major detail is to see people as objects, and the second detail is to see them as subjects. The minor details are the examples the author has used to make those two major details clear. The relationships between the main idea and its major and minor details can be seen at a glance in this brief, informal outline:

Main idea: Two ways to relate to people in our lives

1. See them as objects
    Examples: convenience-store salesperson, waiter, teacher
2. See them as subjects
    Example: British woman and her gardener

Notice that just as the main idea is more general than its supporting details, the major details are more general than the minor ones. For example, to see people as subjects is more general than the specific example of the British woman and her gardener.

The purpose of the rest of this chapter is to sharpen your sense of the relationships between main ideas and their major and minor supporting details. You will practice three note-taking techniques that will make you a better reader: outlining, mapping, and summarizing.

OUTLINING

Preparing an outline of a passage will help you understand and see clearly the relationship between a main idea and its supporting details. Outlines start with a main idea (or a heading that summarizes the main idea) followed by major supporting details. Sometimes there will be a level of minor details as well.

Suppose you wanted to outline the paragraph on bullying that appeared in Chapter 2. Reread the paragraph, trying to identify and check (✓) the three major supporting details.

¹ School bullies have been around as long as there have been schools. ²Studies reveal several reasons why some children become bullies. ³Research shows that a certain combination of size and personality may be one factor. ⁴Bigger, more aggressive children are more likely to try to dominate their smaller, quieter peers. ⁵Another factor linked to bullying is overexposure to violent TV programs. ⁶By the time the average American child is ten years old, he or she has watched thousands of acts of violence, including assault and murder. ⁷Such exposure can lead to aggression and violence. ⁸Finally, exposure to *real* violence is a factor in bullying. ⁹Studies indicate that

victims of bullies often turn into bullies themselves. [10]Whether abused by family members or tormented by other kids, bullies typically learn their behavior from others. [11]Look closely into the eyes of a bully, and you may be looking into the eyes of a former victim.

☑ Check Your Understanding

Now see if you can fill in the missing items in the following outline of the paragraph, which shows both major and minor details.

Main idea: Studies reveal several reasons why some children become bullies.

Major detail: **1.** A certain combination of size and personality

   Minor details: Bigger, more aggressive children may dominate their smaller, quieter peers.

Major detail: **2.** *Overexposure to violent TV programs* _____

   Minor details: *By age 10, a child has watched thousands of acts of violence*

on TV, including assaults and murders.

Major detail: **3.** *Exposure to real violence* _____

   Minor details: Kids abused by family members or bullied by other kids often become bullies.

Explanation:

You should have added two major supporting details: (2) overexposure to violent TV programs; (3) exposure to real violence. And to the second major supporting detail you should have added the minor detail that the average American ten-year-old has watched thousands of acts of violence on television.

Notice that just as the main idea is more general than its supporting details, so major details are more general than minor ones. For instance, the major detail that "overexposure to violent TV programs" is a factor in bullying is more general than the minor detail that "the average American child of ten has watched thousands of acts of violence."

Outlining Tips

The following tips will help you prepare outlines:

 Tip 1 **Look for words that tell you a list of details is coming.** Here are some common list words:

List Words

several kinds of	various causes	a few reasons
a number of	a series of	three factors
four steps	among the results	several advantages

For example, look again at the main ideas in two paragraphs already discussed and circle the list words:

- Studies reveal several reasons why some children become bullies.
- There are two ways to relate to people in our lives.

Here the words *several reasons* and *two ways* tell us that a list of major details is coming. You will not always be given such helpful signals that a list of details will follow. For example, there are no list words in the paragraph with this main idea, "Though fun to watch, chimpanzees should not be kept as pets." However, you want to note such words when they are present. *Such list words help you to understand quickly the basic organization of a passage.*

 Tip 2 **Look for words that signal major details.** Such words are called **addition words**, and they will be explained further on page 174. Here are some common addition words:

Addition Words

one	first of all	in addition	furthermore
first	also	next	last of all
second	another	moreover	finally

 Check Your Understanding

Now look again at the selection on bullying on pages 97–98:

1. The word *one* (in *one factor*) signals the first major supporting detail.
2. What addition word introduces the second major supporting detail?

   another

3. What addition word introduces the third major supporting detail?

   finally

And look again at the selection on two ways of relating to people on page 96:

1. What word introduces the first major detail? _____*one*_____
2. What word introduces the second major detail? _____*second*_____

Explanation:

In the selection on bullying, the second major detail is introduced by the word *another (factor)* and the third by the word *finally.* In the selection on relating to people, the first major detail is introduced by the word *one* and the second by the word *second.*

 Tip 3 When making an outline, put all supporting details of equal importance at the same distance from the margin. In the outline on bullying on page 98, the three major supporting details are all placed at the same point on the margin. Likewise, all of the minor supporting details are placed at their own fixed point from the margin. You can therefore see at a glance the main idea, the major details, and the minor details.

☑ Check Your Understanding

Put appropriate numbers *(1, 2, 3)* and letters *(a, b)* in front of the items in the following outline.

    Main idea
    _*1*_ Major detail
      _*a*_ Minor detail
      _*b*_ Minor detail
    _*2*_ Major detail
      _*a*_ Minor detail
      _*b*_ Minor detail
    _*3*_ Major detail

Explanation:

You should have put a *1, 2,* and *3* in front of the major details and an *a* and *b* in front of the minor details. Note that an outline proceeds from the most general to the most specific, from main idea to major details to minor details.

The practice that follows will give you experience in finding major details, in separating major details from minor details, and in preparing outlines.

➤ Practice 1

Read and then outline each passage. Begin by writing in the main idea, and then fill in the supporting details. The first outline requires only major details; the second calls for you to add minor details as well.   *Wording of answers may vary.*

1. ¹Parents can take several steps to discourage TV watching and encourage reading. ²For one thing, have only one television set, and place it in the family room. ³Then if your child wants privacy, he or she will have to go elsewhere, away from the TV. ⁴Secondly, connect reading with eating. ⁵Put a bookcase rather than a television in the kitchen and make sure it is filled with comics, magazines, local newspapers, and so on. ⁶Explain that all snacks have to be eaten in the kitchen. ⁷Given the fact that most kids can go only a short time without putting food in their mouths, your kids should get a lot of reading done while they're snacking. ⁸Last of all, don't even dream of putting a television set in a child's bedroom. ⁹You want your kids to fall asleep over books, not glued to a flickering screen.

Main idea: *Parents can take several steps to discourage TV watching and encourage reading.*

Major detail: 1. *Have only one TV set, and place it in the family room.*

Major detail: 2. *Connect reading with eating.*

Major detail: 3. *Don't put a TV set in a child's bedroom.*

2. ¹Colleges of the early nineteenth century had distinct differences from today's schools. ²First, the student body during this time was almost entirely white males. ³Higher education was considered a final polishing for upper-class gentlemen—a privilege unnecessary for those who had lower social status. ⁴In addition, no matter what their interests were, all students had to take the same courses. ⁵They were required to study the ancient languages

Comments: Paragraph 1 — The three major supporting details are introduced with the addition words *for one thing*, *secondly*, and *last of all*.

Paragraph 2 — The four major supporting details are introduced with the addition words *first*, *in addition*, *third*, and *final*.

(Latin, Greek, sometimes Hebrew), literature, natural science, mathematics, and political and moral philosophy. [6]A third feature of nineteenth-century colleges was their small size. [7]Except for a few of the very oldest institutions, most colleges had a student body of only a few dozen students. [8]The typical faculty consisted of just three or four professors and an equal number of tutors. [9]A final difference was that student life in the early 1800s was much more regulated than today. [10]Strict curfews determined what times students had to turn the lamps out in their rooms, and most schools required students to attend religious services on campus.

Note: Don't write in *all* the minor details, but try to summarize them in a few words.

Wording of answers may vary.

Main idea: *Colleges of the early nineteenth century were distinctly different from today's schools.*

Major detail: 1. *Students were mostly white males.*

    Minor details: *College was considered a final polishing for upper-class gentlemen.*

Major detail: 2. *All students had to take the same courses.*

    Minor details: *They studied ancient languages, literature, natural science, mathematics, and political and moral philosophy.*

Major detail: 3. *Colleges were small.*

    Minor details: *Most had only a few dozen students, three or four professors, and three or four tutors.*

Major detail: 4. *Student life was more regulated.*

    Minor details: *Strict curfews determined when students had to turn off lights, and attendance at religious services was required.*

Study Hint: At times you will want to include minor details in your study notes; at other times, it may not be necessary to do so. If you are taking notes on one or more textbook chapters, use your judgment. It is often best to be aware of minor details but to concentrate on writing down the main ideas and major details.

MAPPING

Students sometimes find it helpful to use maps rather than outlines. **Maps,** or diagrams, are highly visual outlines in which circles, boxes, or other shapes show the relationships between main ideas and supporting details. Each major detail is connected to the main idea. If minor details are included, each is connected to the major detail it explains.

☑ *Check Your Understanding*

Read the following passage and then see if you can complete the map and the questions that follow.

[1]Several factors can interfere with having a good memory. [2]One such factor is a lack of motivation. [3]Without a real desire to learn or remember something, you probably won't. [4]Another cause is a lack of practice. [5]To stay sharp, memory skills, like any other skill, must be used on a regular basis. [6]A third factor that can hurt memory is self-doubt. [7]If you're convinced you won't remember something, you probably won't. [8]A person with a positive attitude will do much better on a test than someone who is sure he or she won't remember the material. [9]Last, distraction can interfere with memory. [10]If you are being distracted by the sound of a television or a conversation nearby, try to find a quiet environment before you attempt to commit something to memory.

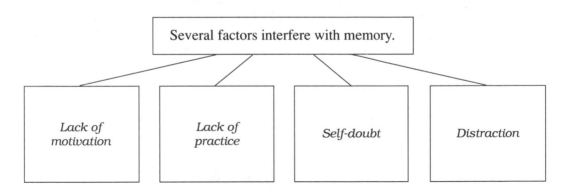

What words introduce:

1. The first major detail? _____ *one*
2. The second major detail? _____ *another*
3. The third major detail? _____ *a third [factor]*
4. The last major detail? _____ *last*

Explanation:

> The map sets off the major details in a very visual way. You see at a glance the four factors that can interfere with memory: lack of motivation, lack of practice, self-doubt, and distraction. The words that introduce the major details are *one, another, a third,* and *last.*

➤ Practice 2

Read each passage, and then complete the maps that follow. The main ideas are given so that you can focus on finding the supporting details. The first passage requires only major details. The second passage calls for you to add both major and minor details.

1. ¹Many people become nearly tongue-tied when they want to meet other people. ²For those of us who find starting conversations with strangers difficult, the following four strategies may be useful. ³Notice that each is developed in question form, inviting the other person to respond. ⁴One approach is to introduce yourself, giving your name and asking the name of the other person. ⁵"Hi, I'm Shelby. And who are you?" ⁶A second approach is to refer to the physical setting in a question. ⁷You might, for example, make such a comment as, "This is awful weather for a game, isn't it?" ⁸Another approach is to give the other person a compliment and ask a question related to it. ⁹You might say, for instance, "Your braid looks great. Did it take long to do?" ¹⁰Finally, you can seek direct information from the other person. ¹¹At a work gathering, you can ask such a question as, "Which department do you work in?" ¹²At a party, you might say, "Walt and Jan give a really nice party. ¹³How do you happen to know them?"

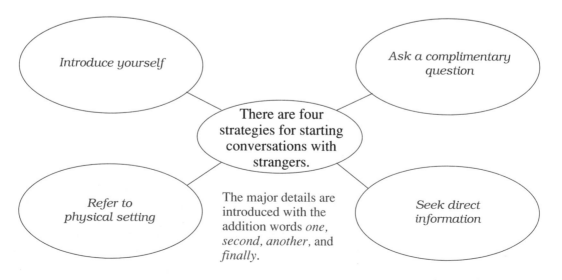

2. ¹Industrialized dairy farming differs from old-fashioned dairy farming in two basic respects. ²First of all, there is an immense saving of labor in industrial farming. ³Industrial farms have milking machines installed on a huge carousel, and each revolution allows sufficient time for a cow to be milked. ⁴Consequently, it takes only one operator to place and release cows as each milking station comes by the gateway. ⁵In contrast, in many nations milking still is done by hand and takes about 10 minutes per cow. ⁶The second major difference is the higher milk output per cow on industrial farms. ⁷The average American cow gives 7.5 times more milk than does the average cow in Brazil, where farms are old-fashioned. ⁸The productivity differences are so great that milk is far cheaper in the United States than in Brazil.

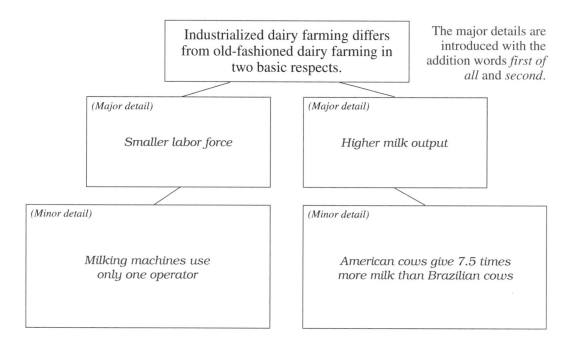

SUMMARIZING

A **summary** is the reduction of a large amount of information to its most important points. The length and kind of summary will depend upon one's purpose as well as on the material in question. Often, a summary will consist of a main idea and its major supporting details. As a general guideline, a paragraph might be reduced to a sentence or two, an article might be reduced to a paragraph, and a textbook chapter might be reduced to about three pages of notes.

One of the most common types of summarizing occurs when you are taking study notes on textbook material. Very often you will find it helpful to summarize examples of key terms. For instance, look at the textbook passage on the next page and the summary that follows.

[1]In some circumstances, the most effective way of coping with stress is **withdrawal**—avoiding the situation. [2]A person at an amusement park who is overcome by anxiety when just looking at a roller coaster can walk on to a less threatening ride or even leave the park entirely. [3]A woman whose promotion depends on temporarily relocating might simply quit her job and join another company. [4]Or she might withdraw emotionally from the stressful situation by deciding that promotion no longer matters to her and that she has already advanced in her career as far as she wants to go.

Summary:

Withdrawal—coping with stress by avoiding the situation. For example, a person made anxious by being near a roller coaster may walk elsewhere.

Note that a textbook definition of a key term (such as *withdrawal*) should generally not be summarized, but should be worded in the language chosen by the author. On the other hand, it usually makes sense to summarize the supporting information. Summarizing often involves two steps:

1   *Select* one example from several that might be given. Which example you select is up to you, as long as it makes the term clear for you. In the summary above, the example about the roller coaster has been chosen to illustrate withdrawal.

2   *Condense* the example if it's not already very brief. Notice that the example about the roller coaster has been condensed from a very long sentence to a short one.

A definition of a key term followed by one condensed example is a very useful way to take notes—especially in introductory college courses, where many terms are defined and illustrated.

> *Study Hint:* If you have a textbook chapter to learn, very often you can get what you need by doing two things: 1) writing down the definitions in the chapter and summarized examples of the definitions, and 2) writing down lists of major supporting details and any minor details that you think are important.

Summarizing a Passage

Read the selection on the next page, taken from an introductory textbook for a college social science course. As is often the case in such introductory texts, a new term is presented and then followed by an extended example. Complete the study notes by circling the letter of the answer choice that best summarizes that example.

[1]Bureaucracies have become a part of modern life because they are a powerful form of social organization. [2]Once in existence, however, they tend to take on a life of their own. [3]In a process called **goal displacement**, an organization continues even after it achieves its goal and no longer has a reason to go on. [4]A classic example is the National Foundation for the March of Dimes, organized in the 1930s to fight polio. [5]At that time, the origin of polio was a mystery. [6]Parents lived in fear because no one knew whose child might be stricken next with this crippling disease. [7]To raise money to discover the cause and a cure, the March of Dimes placed posters of children on crutches near cash registers in almost every store in the United States. [8]The U.S. public took the campaign to heart and contributed heavily. [9]The organization raised money beyond its wildest dreams. [10]During the 1950s, Dr. Jonas Salk developed a vaccine for polio, and this threat was wiped out almost overnight.

[11]What then? [12]Did the organization fold? [13]After all, its purpose had been fulfilled. [14]But, of course, the March of Dimes is still around. [15]Faced with the loss of their jobs, the professional staff that ran the organization quickly found a way to keep its bureaucracy intact by pursuing a new enemy—birth defects. [16]Their choice of enemy is striking, for it is doubtful that we will ever run out of birth defects—and thus unlikely that these people will ever run out of jobs.

Study notes:

Goal displacement—An organization finds a way to continue even after it achieves its goal and no longer has a reason to go on.

Example—

A. A classic example is the National Foundation for the March of Dimes, organized in the 1930s to fight polio.
B. After the March of Dimes achieved its goal of wiping out polio, it found a way to continue by taking on a new enemy, birth defects.
C. The March of Dimes successfully raised money to discover a cause and cure for polio, and when Dr. Jonas Salk developed a vaccine for polio, the threat was wiped out almost overnight.

Explanation:

Useful study notes should clearly show how an example illustrates a new term. In the case of the paragraph above, the notes should include the key point that an organization finds a way to continue even after reaching its goal. Neither answer A nor answer C explains how the organization in question, the March of Dimes, found a way to continue. Answer B does and is the correct answer. Remember, the purpose of an example is to make a definition clear.

➤ *Practice 3*

Read each textbook selection below. Then complete the study notes by circling the letter of the answer that best summarizes an example of the term being defined.

1. ¹People deceive themselves in various ways to cope better with problems. ²One such way is **denial**, the unconscious refusal to recognize a painful or threatening reality. ³One researcher cites the example of a woman who was near death from severe burns. ⁴At first, she was depressed and frightened, but after a few days she began to feel sure that she would soon be able to return home and care for her children, although all her medical indications were to the contrary. ⁵By denying the extent of her injuries, this woman was able to stay calm and cheerful. ⁶She was not merely putting on an act for her relatives and friends; she believed she would recover. ⁷In another situation, researchers interviewed the parents of children who were dying of leukemia. ⁸Some parents denied their children's condition; others accepted it. ⁹Physical examinations revealed that those who denied the illness did not have the physiological symptoms of stress, such as excessive stomach acid, found in those who accepted their children's illness.

Study notes: Neither answer A nor answer B includes the "refusal to recognize a painful or threatening reality."

Denial—the unconscious refusal to recognize a painful or threatening reality.

Example—

A. Being near death from extreme burns depressed and frightened a woman.

B. According to all the medical indications, the woman who had suffered severe burns was near death.

C. By refusing to believe her burn injuries were deadly, a woman near death was able to stay calm and cheerful.

2. ¹Imagine a ball lying on a level table. ²Left alone, the ball stays where it is. ³Given a gentle push, the ball rolls a short way and then comes to a stop. ⁴The smoother the ball and the tabletop, the farther the ball rolls before stopping. ⁵Suppose that we have a perfectly round ball and a perfectly smooth and level tabletop, and that no air is present to slow down the ball. ⁶If the table is infinitely long and we give the ball a push, will it ever stop rolling? ⁷In fact, we can reasonably expect that under ideal conditions the ball would keep rolling forever. ⁸This conclusion was first reached by Galileo and later stated by Newton as the first law of motion: An object will continue in its state of rest or of motion in a straight line at constant speed if the object does not interact with anything else.

Study notes:

Newton's first law of motion—an object will continue in its state of rest or of motion in a straight line at constant speed if the object does not interact with anything else.

Example—

A. If a ball lying on a level table is given a gentle push, it won't roll too far.
(B.) A perfectly round ball on an endless table won't move if left alone, but can roll forever if pushed.
C. Galileo first came to a conclusion which Newton later stated as his first law of motion.

➤ Practice 4

Read each textbook selection below. Then take study notes by 1) writing down the key term and its definition, 2) selecting an example that makes the definition clear, and 3) writing that example in your notes, condensing it if possible.

1. [1]**Passive listening** occurs when a listener tries to make sense out of a speaker's remarks without being able to interact with the speaker. [2]Probably the most familiar example of passive listening would be students hearing an instructor's lecture without having the opportunity to ask questions or otherwise interact with the speaker. [3]Passive listening also takes place in interpersonal settings, as when one person dominates a conversation while the others fall into the role of audience members, or when some parents lecture their children without allowing them to respond.

Study notes:

Passive listening ——— *trying to make sense out of a speaker's remarks without being able to interact with the speaker*

Example— *Students listen to an instructor's lecture without having the chance to ask questions.*

2. [1]In an attempt to convince ourselves and others that the positive face we show to the world is true, we tend to judge ourselves in the most generous terms possible. [2]Social scientists have labeled this tendency the **self-serving bias**. [3]On one hand, when others suffer, we often blame the problem on their personal qualities. [4]On the other hand, when we suffer, we blame the problem on forces outside ourselves. [5]Consider a few examples. [6]When *they* botch a job, we might think they were not listening well or trying hard enough; when *we* botch a job, the problem was unclear directions or not enough time. [7]When *he* lashes out angrily, we say he's being moody; when *we* lash out angrily, it's

because of the pressure we've been under. [8]When *she* gets caught speeding, we say she should have been more careful; when *we* get caught speeding, we deny that we were driving too fast, or we say, "Everybody does it."

Study notes:

Self-serving bias _____ — *the practice of judging ourselves*

leniently

Example— *When he lashes out angrily, we say he's moody. When we lash*

out angrily, we say we're under pressure.

A Final Note

This chapter has centered on supporting details as they appear in well-organized paragraphs. But keep in mind that supporting details are part of readings of any length, including selections that may not have an easy-to-follow list of one major detail after another. Starting with the reading at the end of this chapter (page 116), you will be given practice in answering all kinds of questions about key supporting details. These questions will develop your ability to pay close attention to what you are reading.

CHAPTER REVIEW

In this chapter, you learned the following:

- Major and minor details provide the added information you need to make sense of a main idea.
- List words and addition words can help you to find major and minor supporting details.
- Outlining, mapping, and summarizing are useful note-taking strategies.
- Outlines show the relationship between the main idea, major details, and minor details of a passage.
- Maps are very visual outlines.
- Writing a definition and summarizing an example is a good way to take notes on a new term.

The next chapter—Chapter 4—will show you how to find implied main ideas and central points.

On the Web: If you are using this book in class, you can visit our website for additional practice in identifying supporting details. Go to **www.townsendpress.com** and click on "Online Exercises."

➤ *Review Test 1*

To review what you've learned in this chapter, answer each of these questions about supporting details.

1. *Fill in the blanks:* Major supporting details are more *(general, specific)* _____*specific*_____ than main ideas. Minor supporting details are more *(general, specific)* _____*specific*_____ than major details.

2. ___*T*___ TRUE OR FALSE? Supporting details can be reasons, examples, facts, or other specific information.

3. Outlining is a way to show at a glance the relationship between a main idea and its _____*supporting details*_____.

4. In _____*mapping*_____, you create a visual outline using circles, boxes, and other shapes to set off main ideas and supporting details.

5. When taking notes on textbook material, you will often find it useful to write out each definition in full and then select and _____*condense*_____ one example of that definition.

➤ **Review Test 2**   *Wording of answers in outlines and maps may vary.*

A. (1–7.) Complete the outline of the following paragraph by adding words to the main idea and filling in the missing major and minor details. Note that addition words introduce the major details and some of the minor details as well.

> ¹Several factors influence the justice system's treatment of criminals. ²For one thing, the sex of offenders affects the severity of sentences. ³A woman is less likely to receive the death penalty than a man. ⁴Also, the court is more reluctant to send a mother to prison than a father. ⁵Another factor in the treatment of offenders is their race. ⁶Nonwhites are awarded parole and probation less often. ⁷In addition, blacks are executed more often for capital crimes. ⁸Finally, the age of offenders is considered in sentencing. ⁹Young offenders are given special treatment. ¹⁰And the elderly are given more lenient sentences.

Main idea: _____*Several factors*_____ influence the justice system's treatment of criminals.

Major detail: **1.** _*Sex of offender affects severity of sentence*_

Minor details: a. Woman less likely to receive death penalty than a man

                        b. _*Court more reluctant to send mother to prison than father*_

Major detail: **2.** _*Race is another factor*_

Minor details: a. _*Nonwhites get parole and probation less often*_

                        b. _*Blacks executed more often for capital crimes*_

Major detail: **3.** Age of offenders considered in sentencing

Minor details: a. _*Young offenders given special treatment*_

                        b. More lenient sentences for the elderly

The major details are introduced with the addition words *for one thing, another,* and *finally.*

B. (8–10.) Answer the questions about supporting details that follow the passage. Note that the main idea is boldfaced.

> ¹More than one anthropologist has taken the time to explore old cemeteries in New England and look at the gravestones there. ²**The anthropologists discovered that over different time periods there were three different types of images carved on the gravestones.** ³The first, which appears on the oldest stones (from the 1600s into the mid-1700s), is the death's head: a grinning skull. ⁴The death's head corresponds with the pessimistic view of life and death held by the Puritans that populated New England at that time. ⁵But as more liberal thought took hold in New England in the mid-1700s, another image began to be seen on headstones. ⁶This was a

cherub—a smiling, baby-faced angel. ⁷The cherub seemed to represent a more hopeful view of death and a happy afterlife in heaven. ⁸In the late 1700s, there was a preference for the classic-looking urn and willow. ⁹This image indicates a turn to a more intellectual and less emotional attitude toward death.

___C___ 8. The addition word that signals the second major detail is
    A. *one.*
    B. *first.*
    C. *another.*
    D. *this.*

___C___ 9. The list words that tell what types of details will follow are
    A. "more than one anthropologist."
    B. "old cemeteries."
    C. "three different types of images."

___B___ 10. How many major supporting details are in the paragraph?
    A. Two
    B. Three
    C. Four

> The major details are the "different time periods." Two of these are introduced with the addition words *first* and *another*. The third time period is introduced with the phrase "In the late 1700s."

➤ Review Test 3

A. (1–5.) Outline the following passage by completing the main idea and filling in the major supporting details.

¹Serious depression, as opposed to the fleeting kind we all feel at times, has definite warning signs. ²Some or all of these signs may be present within the affected individual. ³One symptom of depression is a change in sleep patterns—either sleeplessness or sleeping too much. ⁴Another sign is abnormal eating patterns, either eating too much or loss of appetite. ⁵A third sign is trouble in thinking or concentrating—even to the point of finding it difficult to read a magazine or newspaper. ⁶Finally, a general feeling of hopelessness may signal depression. ⁷People feel indifferent to their families and jobs and may begin to think that life is not worth living.

Main idea: Serious depression has _____*definite warning signs.*_____ .

    1. *Change in sleep patterns* _____

    2. *Abnormal eating patterns* _____

    3. *Trouble in thinking or concentrating* _____

    4. *General feeling of hopelessness* _____

B. (6–9.) Map the following paragraph by filling in the main idea and the major supporting details.

> [1]There are three common ways that people deal with their feelings. [2]One way is to withhold them—to keep them inside without giving any verbal or nonverbal clues to their existence. [3]Such people use "poker faces" in relationships, so that others have to guess about whether they are happy or sad inside. [4]A second and often more appropriate way to deal with feelings is to display them—expressing them verbally or through facial or body language. [5]For example, a person who displays feelings would cheer at a sporting event, laugh or cry at a moving scene in a movie, or openly admire an unexpected act of kindness. [6]Displays must always be handled carefully if the feelings are negative. [7]Often the best method of dealing with feelings is to describe them—put them into words in a calm, nonjudgmental way. [8]If someone borrows one of your books without asking or otherwise takes advantage of you, tell him or her that makes you feel angry. [9]If someone does you a favor, let him or her know how much you appreciate it. [10]Describing feelings helps you keep open clear lines of communication with other people.

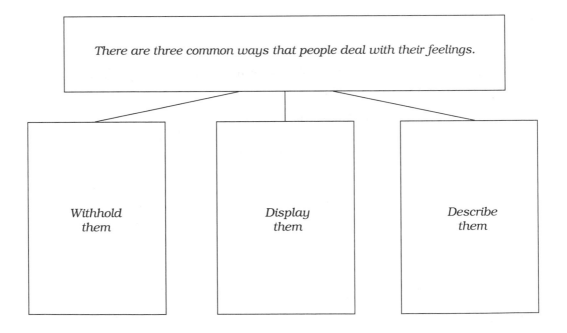

There are three common ways that people deal with their feelings.

| Withhold them | Display them | Describe them |

The three major details are introduced with the addition words *one, second,* and *best.*

C. (10.) Read the textbook selection below. Then complete the study notes by circling the letter of the answer choice that best summarizes the example of the term being defined.

[1]**Cultural lag** refers to a practice or belief that once made sense and still persists even though it is no longer useful. [2]You can see an example of cultural lag every time that you eat. [3]Americans, after they cut their meat, put down the knife and switch the fork from the left hand to the right. [4]Only then do they put the food in their mouths. [5]This differs from the European practice of simply raising the food to the mouth with the fork in the left hand after cutting the meat. [6]Why did Americans develop this habit? [7]Some experts guess that in the old days of the American frontier, Americans needed to keep a hand free in case they had to grab a weapon to fight an intruder. [8]Today the frontier is gone, and putting down the knife and switching the fork to the other hand is no longer of practical use. [9]Americans continue to do it anyway, and to eat in the European style is considered to be "bad manners."

Study notes:

Cultural lag—a practice or belief that once made sense and still persists even though it is no longer useful.

Example—

A. Europeans eat with a fork in the left hand, but Americans put the knife down after cutting and switch the fork to the right hand.
B. Americans consider the European style of eating with a fork in the left hand to be bad manners even though that method is more practical than switching the fork to the right hand.
C. Americans consider it correct to switch the fork to the right hand after cutting even though the supposed purpose—keeping the left hand free for a weapon—no longer exists.

Only answer C includes the idea,
cited in the definition, of a practice continuing
even after its original purpose is gone.

➤ *Review Test 4*

Here is a chance to apply your understanding of supporting details to a passage from a college textbook: *Psychology,* Second Edition, by Diane E. Papalia and Sally Wendkos Olds (McGraw-Hill). Read the passage and then answer the questions that follow.

To help you continue to strengthen your work on the skills taught in previous chapters, there are also questions on vocabulary in context and main ideas.

Words to Watch

Below are some words in the reading that do not have strong context support. Each word is followed by the number of the paragraph in which it appears and its meaning there. These words are indicated in the article by a small circle (°).

provocation (1): annoyance
loath (1): reluctant
temperament (1): emotional makeup
competence (2): skill
thrive (3): grow well
self-reliant (3): independent
assertive (3): positive and confident
detached (4): emotionally apart from others
withdrawn (4): shy

CHILD-REARING STYLES

Diane E. Papalia and Sally Wendkos Olds

1   What makes Mary burst into tears of frustration when she can't finish a jigsaw puzzle, while Gary will shrug and walk away from it, and Cary will sit with it for hours until he finishes? What makes Polly independent and Molly a clinger? What makes Tim ready to hit out at the slightest provocation° and Jim loath° to fight? One answer lies in the basic temperament° children are born with. A second very important influence on behavioral styles is the early emotional environment—how children are treated by their parents.

2   The psychologist Diana Baumrind set out to discover relationships between different styles of child rearing and the social competence° of children. She reviewed the research literature and conducted her own studies with ninety-five families of children in nursery school. Using a combination of long interviews, standardized testing, and observations at school and home, she identified three categories of parenting styles and linked them to children's behavior.

3   *Authoritative* parents exert firm control when necessary, but they explain

why they take a stand and encourage children to express their opinions. They feel confident in their ability to guide their children, while respecting the children's interests, opinions, and unique personalities. They combine firm control with encouragement and love. Their children know that they are expected to perform well, fulfill commitments, and carry out duties in the family. They know when they are meeting expectations and when it is worth risking their parents' displeasure to pursue some other goal. They seem to thrive° on their parents' reasonable expectations and realistic standards, and they are most self-reliant°, self-controlled, assertive°, exploratory, and content.

4   *Authoritarian* parents value unquestioning obedience and punish their children forcibly for not conforming to set and quite absolute standards. They are somewhat detached°, controlling, and distant. Their children tend to be discontented, withdrawn°, and distrustful of others.

5   *Permissive* parents make few demands on their children, set few rules, and hardly ever punish. As preschoolers, their children are immature—the least self-reliant, the least self-controlled, the least exploratory.

6   On the basis of her research, Baumrind has recommended that parents who want to raise competent, socially responsible, independent children should do several things:

- Teach by example; that is, behave the way you want your children to behave.
- Reward behaviors you want to encourage and punish behaviors you want to discourage, giving explanations in both cases.
- Show interest in children.
- Bestow approval only when the child has earned it.
- Demand achievement and the meeting of standards, while being open to hearing the child's point of view.
- Encourage original thinking.

7   Baumrind's work raises important issues about child-rearing practices, but before we conclude that parenting is all that matters, we have to remember what children bring to the family. Through their own inborn temperaments, children influence their parents. It is possible, for example, that "easy" children will elicit an authoritative attitude from their parents, while "difficult" children may make tyrants out of theirs.

Reading Comprehension Questions

Vocabulary in Context

___B___ 1. In the sentence below, the word *bestow* (bĭ-stō′) means
     A. deny.
     B. give.   *Context clue:* Approval is
     C. accept.   given to someone.
     D. risk.

       "Bestow approval only when the child has earned it." (Paragraph 6)

___A___ 2. In the excerpt below, the word *elicit* (ĭ-lĭs′ĭt) means
     A. draw out.
     B. dislike.   *Context clue:* A child might draw out a
     C. imitate.   particular attitude from parents.
     D. abuse.

       "Through their own inborn temperaments, children influence their parents. It is possible, for example, that 'easy' children will elicit an authoritative attitude from their parents, while 'difficult' children may make tyrants out of theirs." (Paragraph 7)

Main Ideas

___D___ 3. The topic of paragraph 6 is
     A. Diana Baumrind.
     B. teaching by example.
     C. giving approval.
     D. raising children.

___A___ 4. Which sentence best expresses the main idea of paragraph 6?
     A. "On the basis of her research, Baumrind has recommended that parents who want to raise competent, socially responsible, independent children should do several things:"
     B. "Teach by example, that is, behave the way you want your children to behave."
     C. "Reward behaviors you want to encourage and punish behaviors you want to discourage, giving explanations in both cases."
     D. "Demand achievement and the meeting of standards, while being open to hearing the child's point of view."

       The phrase "several things" signals the main idea.
       A list of specific things to do then follows.

Supporting Details

5. *Complete the sentence:* To study the ninety-five families of children in nursery school, Baumrind used standardized tests, observations at school and at home, and _____*long interviews*_____.

6–10. Complete the following outline of parts of the reading by filling in the blanks.

A. Two influences on how a child behaves

   1. _*Basic temperament the child is born with*_

   2. _*Early emotional environment*_

B. Three parenting styles

   1. _*Authoritative*_

   2. _*Authoritarian*_

   3. _*Permissive*_

Discussion Questions

1. What type of parenting style did you grow up with? Would you say this style was effective? Why or why not?

2. Why do you think Diana Baumrind feels that teaching by example is useful?

3. Baumrind encourages parents to show interest in children. What are some ways in which parents can show interest in children?

4. The authors feel that children are born with "their own inborn temperaments." Has your experience with children confirmed or contradicted their idea that children have different temperaments from the time they are born? Give some examples.

Note: Writing assignments for this selection appear on page 586.

Comments: Item 5—See paragraph 2.

      Items 6–10— A. The two minor details under A in the outline are stated in paragraph 1 of the selection. They are introduced with the addition words *one* and *second.*

             B. Note how the authors use *italic type* to set off the three kinds of parenting styles. The italic type makes the list so clear that there is no need to use addition words or numbers to set off the three items. Pay close attention to the use of *italic* and **boldface** type, which help authors present ideas in a clear and organized manner.

Check Your Performance   SUPPORTING DETAILS

Activity	Number Right	Points		Score
Review Test 1 (5 items)	_____	× 2	=	_____
Review Test 2 (10 items)	_____	× 3	=	_____
Review Test 3 (10 items)	_____	× 3	=	_____
Review Test 4 (10 items)	_____	× 3	=	_____
		TOTAL SCORE	=	_____%

Enter your total score into the **Reading Performance Chart: Review Tests** on the inside back cover.

SUPPORTING DETAILS: Mastery Test 1

A. (1–6.) Complete the outline of the following textbook passage by adding the main idea and the missing major or minor details.

> [1]Divorce has serious negative consequences. [2]First, social adjustment after the divorce is a troublesome time. [3]The former couple often finds that starting to date again can be nerve-racking. [4]Also, married friends may exclude singles from social plans. [5]Secondly, emotional difficulties among the original family members are common. [6]Feelings of guilt and resentment may persist between the former husband and wife. [7]At the same time children may be confused and hurt; many also feel guilty, imagining that they were somehow to blame for the divorce. [8]A third consequence is that financial adjustments are necessary. [9]Alimony, child support, and property dispersal must be dealt with. [10]Also, the high fees that lawyers charge can be a burden.
>
> *Wording of answers may vary.*

Main idea: *Divorce has serious negative consequences.* _____ .

Major detail: 1. Social adjustment is troublesome.

Minor details: a. *Starting to date again can be nerve-racking.* _____

       b. Married friends may exclude singles from social plans.

Major detail: 2. *Emotional difficulties among original family members* _____

                are common. _____

Minor details: a. *Husband and wife feel guilt and resentment.* _____

       b. Children may be confused and hurt and feel guilty.

Major detail: 3. *Financial adjustments are necessary.* _____

Minor details: a. *Alimony, child support, and property disposal* _____

                must be dealt with. _____

       b. High fees charged by lawyers can be a burden.

Comments: In this test and the five supporting-details mastery tests that follow, the main ideas are underlined in color in this *Instructor's Edition.*

The three major details in the passage above are introduced with the addition words *first*, *secondly*, and *third*.

(Continues on next page)

B. (7–10.) Answer the questions about supporting details that follow the passage.

> ¹When we call someone "pig" or "swine," we do not mean it as a compliment. ²But pigs do not deserve to be used as a symbol for an insult. ³They are probably not as dirty as they are made out to be. ⁴According to one pig keeper, swine are very clean when allowed to live in a clean environment. ⁵He feels that pigs are usually dirty simply because their keepers don't clean their pens. ⁶In any case, no one has proven that the pig that wallows in mud prefers that to a cool bath. ⁷Furthermore, pigs are smarter than most people think. ⁸Many farmers, for example, have observed that pigs frequently undo complicated bolts on gates in search of adventure or romance. ⁹So the next time you call someone a pig, perhaps he or she ought to be someone you wish to praise.

_B_ 7. In general, the major details of this passage are
     A. reasons why pigs are dirty.
     B. reasons why pigs should not be used as symbols for insults.
     C. ways to insult or compliment people.

_A_ 8. Specifically, the major details are
     A. Pigs are probably not as dirty as people think; pigs are smarter than most people think.
     B. Pigs may be dirty because their pens are dirty; it hasn't been proved that pigs prefer mud to a cool bath; pigs have been seen undoing complicated bolts.
     C. People use "pig" and "swine" as insults; "pig" and "swine" should be considered praise.

_C_ 9. One pig keeper feels that pigs will stay clean if they are
     A. given baths.
     B. praised.
     C. kept in a clean environment.

  10. What example is used to show that pigs are smarter than they are often thought to be?   _They can undo complicated bolts on gates._

Comment: The first sentence introduces the topic of calling someone "pig" or "swine."

SUPPORTING DETAILS: Mastery Test 2

A. Answer the questions about supporting details that follow the textbook passage.

> ¹The climate becomes colder when the amount of dust at high altitudes in the atmosphere increases. ²There are several ways that dust may get into the atmosphere. ³Volcanic eruptions can add so much dust that sunlight is scattered back to outer space. ⁴Chimneys, especially industrial smokestacks, also throw large amounts of dust into the atmosphere. ⁵The burning of tropical forests to clear land for farming is another way the amount of airborne dust is increased. ⁶Finally, should a nuclear war ever occur, it might add so much dust to the atmosphere that it could cause a new ice age—a nuclear winter in which the climate becomes so cold that no new crops can be grown.

___B___ 1. In general, the major details of this paragraph are
- A. reasons why dust in the atmosphere makes the climate colder.
- B. ways that dust may get into the atmosphere.
- C. natural causes of dust getting into the atmosphere.
- D. ways that industry puts dust into the atmosphere.

___D___ 2. How many major details are in this paragraph?
- A. One
- B. Two
- C. Three
- D. Four

___C___ 3. One source of dust in the atmosphere is
- A. sunlight.
- B. farming.
- C. chimneys.
- D. cold weather.

___D___ 4. An enormous amount of dust in the atmosphere could lead to
- A. warmer weather.
- B. burning of tropical forests.
- C. volcanic eruptions.
- D. a new ice age.

___C___ 5. The last major detail is introduced with the addition word
- A. *several.*
- B. *add.*
- C. *finally.*
- D. *another.*

(Continues on next page)

_B_   6. Which is the best outline of the paragraph?
   A. Ways the climate can become colder
      1. Dust getting into the atmosphere
      2. Scattering sunlight to outer space
      3. Clearing land for farming
      4. A nuclear winter

   B. Ways dust can get into the atmosphere and make climate colder
      1. Volcanic eruptions
      2. Chimneys
      3. Burning of tropical forests
      4. Nuclear war

   C. Effects of a colder climate
      1. Additional dust in the atmosphere
      2. New ice age
      3. No new crops

B. (7–10.) Outline the following textbook passage by filling in the main idea and the major supporting details. Condense the major details.

> [1]Chimpanzees, skillful tool-users, use several objects found in their environment as tools. [2]First of all, they use sticks. [3]They have been seen inserting carefully trimmed sticks into termite mounds and then withdrawing the sticks and eating the termites that cling to them; they also are known to use sticks to steal honey from beehives. [4]In addition, chimps use leaves in a variety of ingenious ways. [5]For example, they have been seen rolling leaves into cones to use as drinking cups, dampening them and using them to clean their bodies, and chewing them until they can serve as sponges. [6]Finally, chimpanzees have been observed using stones to crack open nuts.

Wording of answers may vary.

Main idea: *Chimpanzees use objects in their environment as tools.*

_____.

   1. *Sticks to catch termites and steal honey*

   2. *Leaves as drinking cups, for cleaning, and as sponges*

   3. *Stones to crack open nuts*

Comment: The three types of tools chimpanzees use are introduced with the addition words *first of all*, *in addition*, and *finally*.

SUPPORTING DETAILS: Mastery Test 3

A. Answer the questions about supporting details that follow the textbook passage.

[1]A **social dilemma** is a situation in which the most rewarding short-term choice for an individual will ultimately lead to negative outcomes for all concerned. [2]For example, as you hike along a beautiful mountain trail, you stop for a snack. [3]You are tempted to throw away your empty water containers and granola bar wrappers, knowing that your backpack will be lighter if you don't have to carry your trash to the top of the mountain and back. [4]But you hesitate, knowing that if all hikers litter the trail, it will soon be unpleasant for all who use it. [5]Or consider the situation of many communities in the Southwest that have suffered severe drought for years, so that water conservation is essential. [6]Individuals living in such drought-stricken areas face personal decisions. [7]For instance, should I forgo the pleasure of a long shower today so that there will be more water for all in the future?

A 1. The main idea is expressed in sentence
   A. 1.
   B. 2.
   C. 4.
   D. 7.

B 2. In general, the major supporting details of this paragraph are
   A. rewarding short-term choices.
   B. examples of social dilemmas.
   C. examples of negative outcomes.
   D. common rewarding experiences.

A 3. How many major details are in this paragraph?
   A. Two
   B. Three
   C. Four
   D. Five

D 4. The second major detail of the paragraph begins in sentence
   A. 1.
   B. 2.
   C. 4.
   D. 5.

(Continues on next page)

_B_   5. In the Southwest, the desire to take a long shower presents a social dilemma because
   A. cleanliness and neatness are important there.
   B. a pleasant long shower could mean less water for others.
   C. the water is polluted.
   D. water costs more there, so long showers are expensive.

_A_   6. Which summary best completes the study notes of the paragraph?

Social dilemma—a situation in which the most rewarding short-term choice for an individual will ultimately lead to negative outcomes for all concerned.

Example—
   A. Littering a beautiful trail is tempting, but would soon make for an unpleasant trail for all.
   B. Littering a beautiful trail is convenient because then you wouldn't have to carry trash to the top of the mountain and back.
   C. To avoid littering when hiking in public places, carry empty containers and wrappers until you get to a trash can.

B. (7–10.) Complete the outline of the textbook passage by filling in the missing main idea and major details, including a brief explanation of each. One explanation has been done for you.

[1]The three types of human memory allow a person to remove or retain information, as needed. [2]Everything that we notice—see, smell, hear, or touch—forms a brief mental impression called a sensory memory. [3]Information is stored in this sensory memory for only a few tenths of a second before it disappears forever. [4]Information that is retained for slightly longer enters what's called short-term memory. [5]This form of memory can store about seven items for about thirty seconds—about enough information to dial a telephone number. [6]In order to be remembered for a long period, information must pass into long-term memory. [7]No one knows just how much information can be stored in a person's long-term memory, but the capacity seems enormous.

Wording of answers may vary.

Main idea: _Three types of human memory allow us to remove or keep_

information as needed.

1. _Sensory memory_ —stores memory for a few tenths of a second.

2. _Short-term memory—stores about 7 items for about 30 seconds._

3. _Long-term memory—stores enormous number of items for a long period._

Comment: Item 6 — Answer A includes both the rewarding short-term choice and the negative outcome mentioned in the definition.

SUPPORTING DETAILS: Mastery Test 4

A. (1–5.) Outline the following textbook passage by filling in the main idea and a brief statement of each major supporting detail.

> [1]After studying all night for an important exam, most college students find themselves wishing for one thing after their big test: sleep. [2]Although the exact reasons why people sleep are still being debated, researchers have come up with a number of theories to explain the functions of sleep. [3]First of all, sleep is believed to give the body time to repair burned-out brain cells and make more of the special chemical that makes it possible for the brain to think. [4]Another theory holds that sleep enables the body to save energy because when we sleep, the body temperature is lower, so less energy is needed to create heat. [5]This method of energy conservation may have helped people survive thousands of years ago when food was hard to find. [6]Sleep may also have helped humanity survive by keeping people out of trouble. [7]In prehistoric times, when many large predators like the saber-toothed tiger hunted in darkness, the habit of sleeping at night helped prevent people from being an animal's dinner. [8]Scientists also believe that sleep, in addition to being a survival tactic, is used to reduce memory. [9]It allows the brain to forget or unlearn things that are not necessary. [10]Otherwise, the mind would become cluttered and overwhelmed with unneeded information. *Wording of answers may vary.*

Main idea: *Researchers have created a number of theories to explain the*

*functions of sleep.*_____.

1. *Gives body time to repair brain cells and create chemical that makes*

brain think

2. *Enables body to save energy*

3. *Keeps people out of trouble*

4. *Reduces memory*

Note the addition words: *first of all, another, also, also.*

B. (6.) Read the textbook excerpt below. Then complete the study notes on the next page by circling the letter of the best summary of the supporting details.

> [1]The **multiplier effect** refers to any change in one part of our economic system that creates changes elsewhere. [2]For example, if a university decides to build a new dormitory, some construction workers will have more income. [3]If some of these workers decide to spend the extra income on new boats, boat-builders will have more income. [4]The boat-builders, in turn, might spend this income in neighborhood restaurants, and the restaurant owners might spend it on cars. [5]Money never stays in one place, and every market decision has an impact on other markets.

(Continues on next page)

Study notes:

Multiplier effect—Any change in one part of our economic system that creates changes elsewhere.   Answer C shows how work for construction workers "creates changes elsewhere."

Example—

A. The decision to build a new university dormitory will lead to work for some construction workers.

B. Our economic system is very complicated.

C. Building a dorm allows construction workers to buy boats, giving boat-builders money for restaurants, and so on.

C. Answer the questions about supporting details that follow the textbook passage.

[1]Studies done in the 1930s in New Guinea by the social scientist Margaret Mead show that not all cultures share our views of the differences between the sexes. [2]The mountain people called the Arapesh, for example, do not think men and women are different in temperament. [3]They expect both sexes to be equally gentle, home-loving, and what we would call "maternal" in their relations with others. [4]The neighboring Mundugumor people, by contrast, are as fierce as the Arapesh are gentle. [5]Men and women are equally "macho," paying less attention to their children than to plotting for power and position. [6]A third tribe, the Tchambuli, do believe the sexes are different in temperament, but their sex roles are the reverse of ours. [7]Tchambuli women are the practical, hard-headed providers, while the men of the tribe spend their days beautifying themselves and looking for approval from the women.

_A_ 7. Sentence 1 provides

A. the main idea.

B. a major supporting detail.

C. a minor supporting detail.

_B_ 8. In general, the major supporting details of this paragraph are

A. differences between the sexes.

B. examples of differing cultural views of the sexes.

C. studies of the Arapesh.

D. a series of stereotypes about Western culture.

_B_ 9. How many major details are in this paragraph?

A. Two

B. Three

C. Four

D. Five

_D_ 10. The Arapesh do not think that men and women are

A. equally gentle.

B. "maternal."

C. alike in temperament.

D. different in temperament.

SUPPORTING DETAILS: Mastery Test 5

A. Answer the questions that follow the textbook passage.

¹Suburbs arose out of a complex set of social factors. ²One factor was the economic and technological developments that made it possible for people to live far from where they worked. ³Early in this century, most people were limited in where they could live by the need to find transportation to work. ⁴This meant that most had to live in the cities near where the jobs were. ⁵Because there were relatively few automobiles and highways, people walked or used public transportation to get to work and go shopping. ⁶This encouraged the concentration of population, and central cities served as the commercial and cultural core of urban areas. ⁷By the 1940s and 1950s, the increasing prosperity of many Americans, along with the automobile, made it possible for them to live farther from work and opened up suburban life to middle-class Americans.

⁸In addition, government policy was also a factor contributing to suburbanization. ⁹First of all, the government paid 80 percent of the cost of developing the interstate highway system. ¹⁰With cars and high-speed highways, people can now live far from where they work and shop. ¹¹In sprawling cities such as Los Angeles, for example, it is common to live fifty or more miles from where you work. ¹²Also, government agencies made available federally guaranteed mortgage loans for the purchase of new homes. ¹³Because land outside of the cities was both inexpensive and available, this is where much of the construction took place.

___B___ 1. In general, the major details of this passage are
    A. economic developments that led to the growth of suburbs.
    B. factors that contributed to suburbanization.
    C. ways the government helped suburbs to develop.
    D. early roles of our cities.

___D___ 2. Specifically, the major details of the passage are
    A. suburbs; cities.
    B. central cities; federally guaranteed mortgage loans for new homes.
    C. where people live; where people work.
    D. economic and technological developments; government policy.

___A___ 3. Sentence 1 provides
    A. the main idea of the passage.
    B. a major detail of the passage.
    C. a minor detail of the passage.

Economic and technological developments are discussed in the first paragraph (and introduced in sentence 2). Government policy is discussed in the second paragraph (and introduced in sentence 8).

___B___ 4. Sentence 8 provides
    A. the main idea of the passage.
    B. a major detail of the passage.
    C. a minor detail of the passage.

(Continues on next page)

_C_   5. Sentence 12 provides
   A. the main idea of the passage.
   B. a major detail of the passage.
   C. a minor detail of the passage.

B. (6–10.) Complete the map of the following textbook passage by filling in the main idea and the four major supporting details.

¹Through the years, experts in our country have suggested various purposes of imprisonment. ²Prior to 1800 it was widely assumed that the punishment of those who did not follow society's rules was necessary if the community was to feel morally satisfied. ³In recent years there has been a renewed interest in punishment—not for the sake of vengeance, but to restore a sense of moral order. ⁴During the last century and a half, a second purpose of imprisonment has been rehabilitation. ⁵In this view, crime resembles "disease," something foreign and abnormal to most people. ⁶It is presumed that individuals are not to blame for the disease, and that we should focus on curing them. ⁷Another purpose of imprisonment has been to deter crime. ⁸Some studies suggest that the certainty of arrest and punishment does tend to lower crime rates. ⁹Last, some argue that neither rehabilitation nor deterrence really works, so that it is useless to send people to prison with these goals in mind. ¹⁰Instead, imprisonment should be used as selective confinement, reducing crime rates by keeping "hard-core" criminals off the streets. ¹¹One study of young men in Philadelphia showed that 6 percent of the men were responsible for over half the crimes committed by the entire group.

Wording of answers may vary.

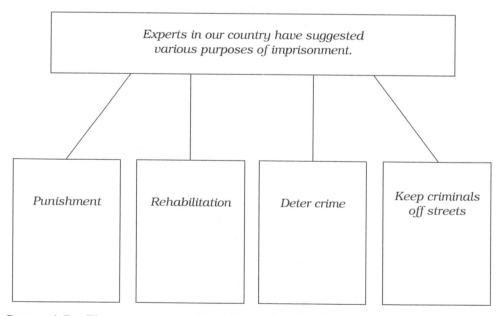

Experts in our country have suggested
various purposes of imprisonment.

| Punishment | Rehabilitation | Deter crime | Keep criminals off streets |

Comment: Paragraph B—The paragraph lists the "purposes of imprisonment" mentioned in the topic sentence.

SUPPORTING DETAILS: Mastery Test 6

A. (1–6.) Outline the following textbook passage by filling in the missing major and minor details.

> ¹Certain significant differences exist between the House and the Senate. ²The most obvious difference, of course, is size—the House has 435 members and the Senate 100. ³This factor leads to differences in style. ⁴Perhaps, as one author has stated, "the most striking difference noticed by most visitors to the Capitol is the apparent formality and impersonality in the House chamber as contrasted to the relatively informal and friendly atmosphere in the Senate." ⁵Size also influences the procedures followed by the House and the Senate. ⁶House rules are many and complex; Senate rules are short and relatively simple. ⁷House rules, for example, sharply limit the time in which a member may speak during a debate, whereas senators are subject to few limits.
>
> ⁸Another difference between the two houses of Congress is the political outlook of their members. ⁹Most representatives have smaller constituencies; each speaks for the residents of a particular district. ¹⁰The representative's concerns, therefore, are often limited to local issues that are of interest to fewer groups. ¹¹Senators have statewide constituencies. ¹²As a result, they must keep in mind the interests of a variety of groups.
>
> ¹³A further major difference between the two houses of Congress derives from the different terms of office of their members (two years in the House, six years in the Senate). ¹⁴This means that most representatives are campaigning almost all the time, whereas senators have more time before they must seek reelection. ¹⁵As a result, senators can pay more attention to aspects of legislation that do not directly affect their chances of winning or losing voters' support.　　　　　*Wording of answers may vary.*

Main idea: Significant differences exist between the House and the Senate.

1. Differences in size: 435 in House vs. 100 in Senate
   a. Style differences
      1) Formal style in the House
      2) *Informal and friendly atmosphere in the Senate*
   b. *Procedural differences*
      1) *House rules—many and complex*
      2) *Senate rules—short and simple*
2. *Political outlook of members*
   a. *Representatives concerned with local issues*
   b. Statewide outlook of senators

(Continues on next page)

3. Differences in terms of office: 2 years in House vs. 6 years in Senate
   a. Constant campaigning of representatives
   b. More time for senators to spend on legislation not affecting their campaigns

B. (7–10.) Complete the map of the following textbook passage by filling in the main idea and the missing major supporting details.

¹To a greater or lesser extent, all of us have learned aggressive responses. ²We are each a potential aggressor. ³A number of conditions have been found to stimulate aggression. ⁴For one thing, pain—both mental and physical— heightens aggressiveness. ⁵Any decidedly hurtful event, whether a big disappointment, a personal insult, or a physical pain, can incite an emotional outburst. ⁶Environmental irritants can also stimulate aggression. ⁷The most-studied is heat. ⁸Studies have found that, compared with students who answered questionnaires in a room with a normal temperature, those who did so in an uncomfortably hot room (over 90° F) reported feeling more tired and aggressive and expressed more hostility toward a stranger they were asked to rate. ⁹A third condition, one that especially provokes aggression, is attacks by another. ¹⁰Experiments confirm that attacks bring counterattacks, especially when the victim perceives the attack as intentional. ¹¹Finally, crowding—the feeling of not having enough space— can be stressful. ¹²The stress experienced by animals allowed to overpopulate a confined environment produces heightened aggressiveness. ¹³And it is undeniably true that dense urban areas suffer higher rates of crime and emotional distress.

Wording of answers may vary.

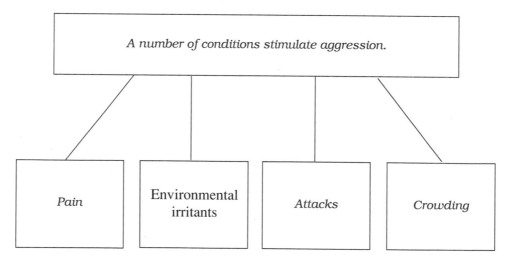

| A number of conditions stimulate aggression. |
| Pain | Environmental irritants | Attacks | Crowding |

Comment: The conditions referred to in the topic sentence are introduced with the addition transitions *for one thing*, *also*, *third*, and *finally*.

4

Implied Main Ideas and the Central Point

In Chapters 2 and 3 you learned the two basic parts of anything you read: a **main idea** and the **supporting details** that explain and develop that idea. A main idea may be clearly stated in one sentence of a paragraph.

This chapter explains and offers practice in two more advanced ways of finding a main idea:

- **Figuring out implied main ideas.** At times authors **imply**, or suggest, a main idea without stating it clearly in one sentence. In such cases, the reader must figure out that main idea by considering the supporting details.

- **Finding central points.** A selection consisting of several paragraphs or more has an overall main idea called the **central point**, or **thesis**. The paragraphs that make up the selection provide the supporting details for that central point. As with the main idea of a paragraph, the central point may be either clearly stated or implied.

IMPLIED MAIN IDEAS

Sometimes a selection lacks a sentence that directly states the main idea. In such cases, the author has simply decided to let the details of the selection suggest the main idea. You must figure out what that implied idea is by deciding upon the point all the details support. For example, read the following paragraph.

[1]All people are concerned about a few great questions: the existence of God, the purpose of life, the existence of an afterlife, and morality. [2]About the first, science has nothing to say: no test tube has either proved or disproved God's existence. [3]As to the purpose of life, although science can provide a definition of life and describe the characteristics of living organisms, it has nothing to say about ultimate purpose. [4]Regarding an afterlife, science can offer no information, for it has no tests that it can use to detect a "hereafter." [5]As for the question of morality, science can demonstrate the consequences of behavior but not the *moral* superiority of one action compared with another. [6]Science cannot even prove that loving your family and neighbor is superior to hurting and killing them.

You can see that no sentence in the paragraph is a good "umbrella" statement that covers all of the other sentences. To decide on the main idea, we must ask the same three questions we've already used to find main ideas:

- "Who or what is this paragraph about?"
- "What is the main point the author is trying to make about that topic?"
- And when we think we know the main point, we can test it by asking, "Does *all or most* of the material in the paragraph support this idea?"

In the paragraph above, all of the details are about science and great human concerns, so that must be the topic. Which of the following statements expresses the general point that the author is trying to make about the topic? Check (✓) the answer you think is correct.

_✓_ A. Science alone cannot tell us about the four main concerns that all people have.

_____ B. Science alone has not contributed any answer to the question of whether God exists.

_____ C. There is no scientific data on whether there is life after death.

_____ D. Science alone cannot provide us with any guidance on whether we should love our neighbor as ourselves.

The details reveal the author's general point to be answer A: science alone cannot tell us about the four main concerns that all people have. All the other statements above are supporting details for this main idea. Although the main idea is not directly stated, it is clearly implied by all the material in the paragraph.

Recognizing Implied Main Ideas

To find implied main ideas, it often helps to decide on the topic first. Do so by asking yourself, "Who or what is the selection about?" After you find the topic, then ask yourself, "What is the author's main point about the topic?"

☑ *Check Your Understanding*

Read the following selection and try to answer the questions that follow.

[1]The original intention of a school worksheet was intelligent: to discover which students didn't understand the reading lesson, so the teacher could work with them individually. [2]Unfortunately, the teacher had to keep the rest of the class busy while doing that, so more worksheets were passed out. [3]The assessment tool soon turned into a crowd control device. [4]To make matters worse, the worksheets multiplied faster than the loaves and fishes, often reaching 1,000 per child per school year. [5]But research shows no connection between the number of worksheets a student does and how good a reader the child eventually becomes. [6]If you're fed reading as six worksheets a day, 1,000 sheets a year, under the pronouncement, "Boys and girls, it's time for reading," by the time you reach fourth grade you think worksheets *are* reading, and you mistakenly think you hate reading.

_A_ 1. What is the topic of the above paragraph?
  A. School worksheets
  B. Books
  C. Teaching tools
  D. Crowd control device

_A_ 2. Which statement best expresses the unstated main idea of these sentences?
  A. School worksheets may do more harm than good.
  B. Reading is one of the most difficult skills for teachers to teach and students to learn.
  C. Over the years, school worksheets have served as both an assessment tool and a crowd control device.
  D. Teachers have a variety of teaching tools to choose from.

Explanation:

The topic, referred to in a number of sentences in the paragraph, is school worksheets. The implied main idea about worksheets is that they may do more harm than good.

When you think you have determined an implied main idea, test yourself by asking, "Does all or most of the material in the paragraph support this idea?" In this paragraph, the author (Jim Trelease, in his book *The Read-Aloud Handbook*) describes how worksheets turned into a student control device and multiplied out of control. He also notes that research has showed no benefit from worksheets and that students given too many worksheets may wind up thinking they "hate reading." So the paragraph clearly supports the idea that worksheets may do more harm than good.

> ### Practice 1

Read each paragraph and then answer the questions that follow. Remember to find a topic by asking "Who or what is the selection about?" and to find an implied main idea by asking "What is the author's point about the topic?"

Hint: Noticing addition words (such as *first, another, also, moreover,* and *finally*) will help you identify the major supporting details that can suggest the main idea.

Comment: In the comments that follow, the terms "too broad" and "too narrow" explain why certain answers are incorrect. Remind students that the topic and the main idea of a selection must include *everything* in that selection—no more and no less.

Paragraph 1

[1]Mining coal is dangerous to the miner and usually leaves large areas of land unfit for further use. [2]Acid rain from the burning of coal harms plant and animal life on a large scale. [3]Also, the air pollution from the same source damages the health of millions of people. [4]Moreover, coal-burning power plants expose the people living around them to more radioactivity, from traces of uranium, thorium, and radon in their smoke, than do nuclear plants. [5]Most estimates put the number of deaths in the United States from cancer and respiratory diseases caused by burning coal at over ten thousand per year.

__D__ 1. What is the topic of the above paragraph? Too narrow (C covers only
    A. Air pollution   Too broad.   C. Effects of acid rain one detail).
    B. Mining (A and B cover more   D. Drawbacks of coal
    than the content of the paragraph).

__A__ 2. Which statement best expresses the unstated main idea?
    A. Coal is far from being a desirable fuel.
    B. Acid rain is a major environmental problem.
    C. More people are dying from cancer and respiratory diseases than at any time in the past.
    D. Air pollution has become our largest single environmental problem today. *Also* and *moreover* are addition words that introduce supporting details, hinting at the main idea.

Paragraph 2

[1]One myth about exercise is that if a woman lifts weights, she will develop muscles as large as a man's. [2]Without male hormones, however, a woman cannot increase her muscle bulk as much as a man's. [3]Another misconception about exercise is that it increases the appetite. [4]Actually, regular exercise stabilizes the blood-sugar level, which prevents hunger pains. [5]Some people also think that a few minutes of exercise a day or one session a week is enough, but at least three solid workouts a week are needed for muscular and cardiovascular fitness. *One, another,* and *also* are addition words that introduce supporting details, hinting at the main idea.

__C__ 3. What is the topic of the above paragraph?
    A. Women and exercise   C. Myths about exercise
    B. Blood-sugar levels   D. Three workouts a week

_____B_____ 4. Which statement best expresses the unstated main idea?
        A. Women who lift weights cannot become as muscular as men.
        B. There are several myths about exercise.
        C. Exercise is beneficial to everyone.
        D. People use many different excuses to avoid exercising.

Paragraph 3

[1]Scientists count such animals as elephants, timber wolves, ducks, and whistling swans by flying over them and counting them. [2]Small animals such as field mice are counted by trapping every single one in a given area and then counting them. [3]Microscopic creatures are gathered in a sample and counted little by little under a microscope. [4]Songbirds are counted by people walking through every part of a certain area at the same time, with each person counting every single songbird seen in his or her assigned space.

_____C_____ 5. What is the topic of the above paragraph?
        A. Counting microscopic creatures   Too narrow (covers only one detail).
        B. Counting   Too broad (covers more than the content of the paragraph).
        C. Methods of counting animals
        D. Scientists who count animals The focus of the paragraph is on counting,
                                   not on scientists.

_____B_____ 6. Which statement best expresses the unstated main idea?
        A. There are various reasons for counting the population of certain types of animals.
        B. The methods scientists use to count animals vary according to the species.
        C. The microscope is one of the tools used by biologists in counting the populations of species.
        D. Biologists face many difficult tasks in studying the large variety of animal life on Earth.

Paragraph 4

[1]Are you one of the millions of people who are terrified of going to the dentist? [2]You should know that some dentists actually specialize in treating people who are very fearful of dental work. [3]These dentists encourage patients to discuss their fears and will answer questions in an honest, understanding manner. [4]Even if your dentist does not have such a specialty, you can arrange with him or her to use a signal, such as raising your right hand, if you experience too much pain. [5]This will give you a feeling of control and the assurance that the pain—if any—will not go beyond what you can tolerate. [6]You can also try the relaxation technique of breathing deeply, before and during appointments. [7]A last good idea is to bring

headphones and listen to your favorite music in the dental chair. [8]It's hard for the brain to register pain when your favorite rap group, or classical musician, is filling your head.

___D___ 7. What is the topic of the above paragraph?
    A. Dentists   Too broad.
    B. Ways to relax   Too broad.
    C. Better communication with your dentist   Too broad.
    D. Less scary dental visits

___B___ 8. Which statement best expresses the unstated main idea?   Introductory
    A. Millions of people are frightened of visits to the dentist.   detail.
    B. There are ways to make visits to the dentist less painful and frightening.
    C. There are dentists who specialize in treating patients who are very fearful of dental work.   Too narrow.
    D. If you are frightened of going to the dentist, try the relaxation technique of breathing deeply before and during appointments. Too narrow.

➤ *Practice 2*

The main idea of each of the following paragraphs is unstated, and each paragraph is followed by four sentences. In the space provided, write the letter of the sentence that best expresses each unstated main idea.

Remember to consider carefully all of the information given and to ask yourself the following two questions:

- Who or what is the selection about? In other words, what is the topic?

- What is the author's main point about that topic? In other words, what is the implied main idea?

Then test your answer by asking:

- Does *all or most* of the material in the paragraph support this idea?

Paragraph 1

[1]Albanian legend adheres to the traditional method for killing a vampire—a stake through the heart as the proper method. [2]According to legend, the Hungarian method of killing a vampire advises a stake through the heart, but insists that a nail be driven through the temples as well. [3]The Irish way is less colorful; one must simply pile rocks on the vampire's grave. [4]Macedonians are supposed to pour boiling oil on the vampire and then

hammer a nail through its navel. [5]Their neighbors, the Serbs, held to a variant of that method: they proposed cutting off the undead creature's toes and pounding a nail through its neck. [6]Saxon legend says that a lemon in the mouth will do the trick, but in Prussian legend, you should instead put poppy seeds in the grave. [7]In Poland, it was believed that just burying the vampire face downward would kill it. [8]And from Romania itself—the home of the original Dracula—comes one of the most complicated methods: cut out the heart and slice it in two, put garlic in the monster's mouth, and pound a nail into its head.

_D_ Which statement best expresses the unstated main idea of the paragraph?
- A. Nails play an important role in many European legends about killing vampires.
- B. Macedonia and Serbia, two neighboring nations, share similar legends about how to kill vampires.
- C. Vampires are popular legendary creatures in many European countries.
- D. Although many European countries have legends about vampires, those countries vary wildly on the best way to kill a vampire.

Paragraph 2

[1]During the Civil War, soldiers first gathered into companies of a hundred men and then formed into regiments (ten companies). [2]When two or three regiments were assembled—2,000 to 3,000 men—they were called a brigade and then sent off to battle. [3]Under the command of a brigadier general, the soldiers formed double lines that advanced over a front of a thousand yards. [4]From there, junior officers led the army's charge through clouds of grapeshot, bullets, and thick black gunpowder smoke. [5]Men who panicked or broke from ranks were often shot by their own officers, who remained behind the advancing line. [6]Once the advancing army neared the enemy, they had to scramble through fortifications of earth and timber. [7]Finally, if they made it this far, the soldiers had to engage in hand-to-hand combat. [8]The attackers and defenders fought until everyone was killed or wounded or one side gave up and ran away.

_B_ Which statement best expresses the unstated main idea of the paragraph?
- A. Hand-to-hand combat played an important role in most Civil War battles.
- B. A battle during the Civil War followed a clear plan.
- C. Officers in the Civil War had no sympathy for frightened soldiers.
- D. Earth and timber fortifications were easy to defend and difficult to attack.

Paragraph 3

¹The work homemakers do is essential to the economy. ²The estimated value of the cleaning, cooking, nursing, shopping, child care, home maintenance, money management, errands, entertaining, and other services homemakers perform has been estimated at equal to roughly one-fourth of the gross national product. ³In fact, the Commerce Department's Bureau of Economic Analysis has proposed a revision of the gross national product that would take into account the value of the homemaker's services. ⁴But homemaking is not formal employment that brings money or prestige. ⁵No financial compensation is associated with this position, and the *Dictionary of Occupational Titles* places mothering and homemaking skills in the lowest category of skills, lower than the occupation of "dog trainer."

_C_ Which statement best expresses the unstated main idea of the paragraph?
  A. We no longer value the work done by homemakers.
  B. Homemakers should receive salaries for their work.
  C. Although homemaking is essential to the economy, it brings no money or prestige.
  D. It's better to be a dog trainer than a homemaker.

Paragraph 4

¹It is against the law for competing companies to agree on set prices, rather than pricing their products or services competitively. ²Yet corporate executives convicted of price fixing often argue that their unlawful price-fixing schemes are far from being criminal. ³They claim they have really served a worthwhile purpose for the nation's economy by "stabilizing prices." ⁴They congratulate themselves for having effectively helped their companies by "recovering costs." ⁵Another kind of white-collar criminal, company embezzlers, tend to define their stealing as only "borrowing," insisting that they truly intended to pay the money back. ⁶White-collar employees who steal supplies from their companies feel that they are not actually stealing because the companies can make up the losses by using them as tax deductions and charging customers higher prices. ⁷Finally, tax return cheaters tend to see themselves as victims, rather than offenders. ⁸They argue that they were just unlucky enough to get caught for doing something that can hardly be regarded as wrong "because everybody does it."

_C_ Which statement best expresses the unstated main idea of the paragraph?
  A. White-collar crimes often result in increased costs for customers.
  B. Tax return cheaters are a common type of white-collar criminal.
  C. White-collar criminals tend to see themselves as respectable individuals rather than common criminals.
  D. White-collar crimes are less harmful to society as a whole than other kinds of crimes.   *Another (kind)* and *finally* are addition words that introduce supporting details, hinting at the main idea.

Putting Implied Main Ideas into Your Own Words

When you read, you often have to **infer**—figure out on your own—an author's unstated main idea. The implied main idea that you come up with should cover all or most of the details in the paragraph.

See if you can find and write the topic of the paragraph below. Then write the implied main idea in your own words. Finally, read the explanation that follows.

> **Hints:**   Remember that you can help yourself identify the topic and main idea if you 1) look for repeated words as you read and 2) try to mark major supporting details. Major details are often signaled by such common addition words as the following:

Addition Words

one	to begin with	in addition	last
first	another	next	last of all
first of all	second	moreover	finally
for one thing	also	furthermore	

¹A mistaken belief about sleepwalking is that sleepwalkers drift about in a ghost-like way, with arms extended. ²The fact is most sleepwalkers walk around quite normally, though their eyes are usually closed or glazed. ³It is also commonly believed that one should never wake a sleepwalker. ⁴But it is advisable to do so if the walker seems in immediate danger—for example, if he or she is going toward an open window or handling a sharp object. ⁵Another popular misconception is that sleepwalkers are not "really" sleeping or are only half-asleep. ⁶In fact, they are in a very deep state of sleep. ⁷A last commonly held belief is that sleepwalkers are easy to spot because they're in nighties or pajamas. ⁸Often this isn't true because sleepwalkers can do routine tasks, including getting completely dressed.

What is the topic of this paragraph?   *Beliefs about sleepwalkers*

What is the implied main idea of this paragraph?

   There are several mistaken beliefs about sleepwalkers.

Explanation:

One key to the topic here is the word *sleepwalkers*, which is repeated through the paragraph. The other key to the topic is major details in the paragraph. Two of the details are signaled by addition words (*another* in "Another popular misconception" and *last* in "A last commonly held belief"). Here are the three major details in the paragraph:

- Sleepwalkers drift in a ghost-like way.
- Sleepwalkers are not really sleeping.
- Sleepwalkers are easy to spot.

What do those three major details have in common? They're all *beliefs about sleepwalkers,* so that phrase can be considered the topic. And the author's main point about the topic could be stated like this: *There are several mistaken beliefs about sleepwalkers.*

➤ Practice 3

In the spaces provided, fill in the topic of each paragraph. Then write the implied main ideas of the paragraphs in your own words.

Hints: *Wording of answers may vary.*

1. Remember that to find the topic, it often helps to look for repeated words in a paragraph.

2. Remember that you can help yourself identify the topic and main idea if you mark major supporting details as you read. These major details are often signaled by such common addition words as the ones shown in the box on the previous page.

1. ¹One of the reasons for lying is to save face. ²For example, you might pretend to remember someone at a party in order to save that person from the embarrassment of being forgotten. ³A second reason for lying is to avoid tension or conflict. ⁴You might, for instance, say you really like a friend's new hairstyle or a new outfit in order to prevent the hassle that would result if you expressed your real feelings. ⁵Lies are also told in order to make everyday relationships run smoothly. ⁶You might pretend to be glad to see someone you dislike, or you might fake interest in a person's boring stories just to make a social event pass quickly. ⁷An additional reason for lying is to expand or reduce relationships. ⁸In one study, a majority of college students willingly lied to improve their chances of getting a date with an attractive partner. ⁹Sometimes people lie to reduce interaction with others: "I really have to go. ¹⁰I should be studying for a test tomorrow." ¹¹A final reason for lying is to gain power. ¹²A person might turn down a last-minute request for a date by claiming to be busy, saying in effect, "Don't expect me to sit around waiting for you to call."

Topic: _____ *Reasons for lying* _____

Implied main idea: _____ *People tell lies for several reasons.* _____

_____ Note the five addition words: *one, second, also, additional, final.*

2. ¹Many people think that children without brothers or sisters are lucky because of the material goods and attention they receive. ²But consider that an only child has no privacy—parents always feel entitled to know everything that's going on in his or her life. ³A second drawback of being an

only child is the lack of certain advantages that children with brothers and sisters have. [4]An only child can never blame a sibling for something that goes wrong or ask for a privilege that an older brother or sister was given earlier. [5]In addition, only children miss the companionship of siblings. [6]The result can be loneliness as well as trouble making friends later in life because they never learned to get along with a brother or sister.

Topic: _____ *Being an only child* _____

Implied main idea: ___ *Being an only child has its drawbacks.* _____

_____ Addition words: *second, in addition*
_____

3. [1]Some people have opposed the death penalty for religious reasons. [2]The Quakers, for instance, were the first to institute prison sentences in an effort to eliminate torture and execution. [3]Others have opposed capital punishment on grounds of racism because African Americans were executed more often than whites. [4]Some have even argued that executions actually increase murders by brutalizing the public sense of the value of life. [5]Still others point to social-science research that seems to show capital punishment does not deter murder. [6]If that's true, they say, there is no good reason for risking the execution of an innocent person.

Topic: _____ *Opposition to capital punishment* _____

Implied main idea: ____ *People have opposed the death penalty for different*

_____ *reasons.* _____

4. [1]If you fear growing older, keep in mind that Sigmund Freud published his first important work, on dream interpretation, at age 44; Henry Kissinger was appointed Secretary of State at 50; and Rachel Carson completed her classic book on environmental damage, *Silent Spring*, at 55. [2]"If you continue reading, thinking and creating all of your life, your intelligence increases," says one medical researcher. [3]The mental health of many people also tends to improve as they grow older. [4]Young people often protect their feelings with such defenses as denial and impulsive actions. [5]By middle age, we are more likely to use such constructive defenses as humor, altruism, and creativity. [6]Finally, growing older will make you more "yourself," as new or previously unexplored aspects of your personality emerge. [7]As the actress Candice Bergen wrote in her autobiography, "It takes a long time to become a person."

Topic: _____ *Growing older* _____

Implied main idea: ___ *Growing older can make us better in many ways.* ___
_____

CENTRAL POINTS

Just as a paragraph has a main idea, so a longer selection has a **central idea**, also known as a **central point** or **thesis**. The longer selection may be an essay, an article, or even a section within a textbook chapter. The central point may be clearly stated, or it may be implied. You can find a central point in the same way that you find a main idea—by looking for a topic (which is often suggested by the title of a longer selection) and considering the supporting material. The paragraphs within the longer reading will provide supporting details for the central point.

In the following essay, the central point is stated. See if you can find and underline it. Then, in the space provided, write the number of the sentence that contains the central point.

Disappointment

¹Ben Franklin said that the only sure things in life are death and taxes. ²He left something out, however: disappointment. ³No one gets through life without experiencing many disappointments. ⁴But many people seem unprepared for disappointment and react to it with depression or escape, rather than using it as an opportunity for growth.

⁵Depression is a common negative response to disappointment. ⁶Yvonne, for example, works hard for over a year in her department, trying to win a promotion. ⁷She is so sure she will get it, in fact, that she has already picked out the car she will buy when her salary increase comes through. ⁸However, the boss names one of her coworkers to the spot. ⁹The fact that all the other department employees tell Yvonne she really deserved the promotion doesn't help her deal with the crushing disappointment. ¹⁰Deeply depressed, Yvonne decides that all her goals are doomed to defeat. ¹¹She loses her enthusiasm for her job and can barely force herself to show up every day. ¹²She tells herself that she is a failure and that doing a good job just isn't worth the work.

¹³Another negative reaction to disappointment is escape. ¹⁴Kevin fails to get into the college his brother is attending, the college that was the focus of all his dreams, and reacts to his disappointment by escaping his circumstances. ¹⁵Why worry about college at all? ¹⁶Instead, he covers up his real feelings by giving up on his schoolwork and getting completely involved with friends, parties, and "good times." ¹⁷Or Linda doesn't make the varsity basketball team—something she wanted very badly—and so refuses to play sports at all. ¹⁸She decides to hang around with a new set of friends who get high every day; then she won't have to confront her disappointment and learn to live with it.

¹⁹The positive way to react to disappointment is to use it as a chance for growth. ²⁰This isn't easy, but it's the only useful way to deal with an inevitable part of life. ²¹Yvonne, the woman who wasn't promoted, could

have handled her disappointment by looking at other options. [22]If her boss doesn't recognize talent and hard work, perhaps she could transfer to another department. [23]Or she could ask the boss how to improve her performance so that she would be a shoo-in for the next promotion. [24]Kevin, the young man who didn't get into the college of his choice, should look into other schools. [25]Going to another college may encourage him to be his own person, step out of his brother's shadow, and realize that being turned down by one college isn't a final judgment on his abilities or potential. [26]Rather than escape into drugs, Linda could improve her basketball skills for a year or pick up another sport, like swimming or tennis, that might turn out to be more useful to her as an adult.

[27]Disappointments are unwelcome but regular visitors to everyone's life. [28]The best response is to step over the unwelcome visitor on the doorstep and get on with life.

   _4_   is the number of the sentence that states the central point.

Explanation:

The central point is a general statement that covers all or most of the details in a reading. To find the central point of the essay above, look first for its topic. Since the title is "Disappointment," and every paragraph is about that subject, we can say "disappointment" is the topic. Then decide on what point is being made about the topic by looking at the major details of the essay. The first major detail, presented in paragraph 2, is about a negative response to disappointment: depression. The second major detail, discussed in paragraph 3, is about another negative response to disappointment: the desire to escape. Paragraph 4 then explains a positive reaction to disappointment— using it as a chance for growth.

The central point, then, will be a statement that covers the two negative responses and the one positive response to disappointment. As is often the case, the central point is stated near the start of the essay, in the first paragraph. The last sentence in that paragraph, sentence 4, mentions reacting to disappointment with depression or escape, or using it as an opportunity for growth, so that sentence is the central point.

➤ *Practice 4*

Read the following selection from a history textbook. See if you can find and underline the clearly stated central point that covers most of the supporting details. Then, in the space provided, write the number of the sentence that contains the central point.

Housewives in Nineteenth-Century America

[1]For many people, the image of the woman in movies about the old West is a gentle one of a mother quietly tending to her kitchen, shopping at the general store, and raising her children. [2]In fact, the days of a housewife in nineteenth-century America were spent in harsh physical labor.

[3]Preparing even a simple meal was a time- and energy-consuming chore. [4]Prior to the twentieth century, cooking was performed on a coal- or wood-burning stove. [5]Unlike an electric or a gas range, which can be turned on with the flick of a single switch, cast-iron and steel stoves were especially difficult to use. [6]Housewives would first have to clean out the ashes left from previous fires. [7]Then, paper and kindling had to be set inside the stove, dampers and flues had to be carefully adjusted, and a fire had to be lit. [8]Since there were no thermostats to regulate the stove's temperature, a woman had to keep an eye on the contraption all day long. [9]Any time the fire slackened, she had to adjust a flue or add more fuel. [10]All day long, the stove had to be fed with new supplies of coal or wood—an average of fifty pounds or more. [11]At least twice a day, the ash box under the fire had to be emptied. [12]All together, a housewife spent four hours every day rubbing the stove with thick black wax to keep it from rusting, lighting the fire, adjusting dampers, sifting ashes, and carrying wood or coal.

[13]It was not enough for a housewife to know how to use a cast-iron stove. [14]She also had to know how to prepare unprocessed foods for consumption. [15]Prior to the 1890s, there were few factory-prepared foods. [16]Shoppers bought poultry that was still alive and then had to kill and pluck the birds. [17]Fish had to have scales removed. [18]Green coffee had to be roasted and ground. [19]Loaves of sugar had to be pounded, flour sifted, nuts shelled, and raisins seeded.

[20]Cleaning was an even more arduous task than cooking. [21]The soot and smoke from coal- and wood-burning stoves blackened walls and dirtied drapes and carpets. [22]Gas and kerosene lamps left smelly deposits of black soot on furniture and curtains. [23]Each day, the lamps' glass chimneys had to be wiped and the wicks trimmed or replaced. [24]And periodically floors had to be scrubbed, rugs beaten, and windows washed.

[25]Since indoor plumbing was available only to the wealthy, chores that involved the use of water were especially demanding. [26]The mere job of bringing water into the house was a challenge. [27]According to calculations

made in 1886, a typical North Carolina housewife had to carry water from a pump or well or a spring eight to ten times each day. [28]Washing, boiling, and rinsing a single load of laundry used about fifty gallons of water. [29]Over the course of a year, she walked 148 miles toting over 36 tons of water! [30]Homes without running water also lacked the simplest way to dispose of dirty water: sinks with drains. [31]That meant that women had to remove dirty dishwater, kitchen slops, and, worst of all, the contents of chamber pots from their house by hand.

All the details in the passage support "harsh physical labor" in sentence 2.

___2___   is the number of the sentence that states the central point.

> ## Practice 5

Read the following selection from a sociology textbook. Find and underline the clearly stated central point that covers most of the supporting details. Then, in the space provided, write the number of the sentence that contains the central point.

Excessive Use of Alcohol

[1]Moderate drinking can bring social benefits, such as relaxation and recreation with others. [2]However, excessive use of alcohol contributes to a number of negative social consequences. [3]One is a relatively high rate of *automobile accidents*, the leading cause of death among young people in the United States. [4]Over half of each year's automobile deaths and injuries can be traced to excessive drinking. [5]As the National Institute on Alcohol Abuse and Alcoholism has found, "Most people killed in traffic accidents after drinking . . . have very high blood-alcohol concentration, averaging twice the level of alcohol considered legally impairing." [6]Those young people most likely to have auto accidents, including deadly ones, are more likely to drink excessively, use illicit drugs, violate various traffic laws, enjoy taking risks, and exhibit aggressiveness or hostility toward others.

[7]Excessive drinking also leads to a high rate of *other criminal offenses*. [8]The offenses include public drunkenness, disorderly conduct, and vagrancy. [9]Such crimes result in so many arrests that they put a severe strain on the operation of the criminal justice system. [10]Since 1970 many treatment programs for problem drinkers have helped reduce the number of arrests for alcohol-related offenses, but they still constitute the largest arrest category today. [11]The majority (over 90 percent) of the crimes committed by students on college campuses are also alcohol-related. [12]The perpetrators usually commit multiple crimes, including vandalism, fighting, theft, and alcohol violations.

[13]Heavy drinking further plays a significant part, albeit indirectly, in the commission of more serious, *violent crimes*, such as homicide, aggravated

assault, and forcible rape. [14]In fact, alcohol is implicated in 42 percent of all violent crimes in the United States. [15]Those who commit these crimes seem to use alcohol as an excuse for expressing their aggression. [16]Alcohol can thus become dynamite in the hands of an aggressive person. [17]According to one study, subjects with a history of arguments and other aggressive acts were more likely to get involved in interpersonal aggression after they had done some heavy drinking.

___2___ is the number of the sentence that states the central point.

The phrase "a number of negative social consequences" signals the central point. Addition words *(one, also,* and *further)* and *italics* signal the supporting points.

CHAPTER REVIEW

In this chapter, you learned the following:

- At times authors imply, or suggest, a main idea without stating it clearly in one sentence. In such cases, you must figure out that main idea by considering the supporting details.

- To find central points—which may be stated or implied—in longer reading selections, you must again look closely at the supporting material.

The next chapters—Chapters 5 and 6—will explain common ways that authors organize their material.

On the Web: If you are using this book in class, you can visit our website for additional practice in recognizing implied main ideas and the central point. Go to **www.townsendpress.com** and click on "Online Exercises."

➤ Review Test 1

To review what you've learned in this chapter, complete each of the following sentences.

1. When a paragraph has no sentence that states the main idea, we say the main idea is *(central, general, implied)* _____*implied*_____.

2. If you have trouble finding an implied main idea, it may help to first determine the *(topic, central point)* _____*topic*_____ of the paragraph.

3. After you figure out what you think is the implied main idea of a paragraph, test yourself by asking, "Does all or most of the material in the paragraph _____*support*_____ this idea?"

4. The "main idea" of a selection that is longer than several paragraphs is called the *(topic, central point)* _____*central point*_____.

5. The central point is *(never, sometimes, always)* _____*sometimes*_____ implied.

➤ Review Test 2

A. In the space provided, write the letter of the sentence that best expresses the implied main idea of each of the following paragraphs.

___*B*___ 1. ¹Lean against a tree almost anywhere, and the first creature that crawls on you will probably be an ant. ²Stroll down a suburban sidewalk—or anywhere else—with your eyes fixed on the ground, counting the different kinds of animals you see. ³The ants will win hands down. ⁴The British entomologist C. B. Williams once calculated that the number of insects alive on Earth at a given moment is one million trillion. ⁵If, to take a conservative figure, 1 percent of those insects are ants, their total population is ten thousand trillion. ⁶Individual workers weigh on average between one and five milligrams, according to the species. ⁷When combined, all ants in the world taken together weigh about as much as all human beings.

    A. Ants are commonplace in the suburbs.   Too narrow.
    B. There are huge numbers of ants on Earth.
    C. There are too many ants in the world.   Unproved opinion.
    D. C. B. Williams, the British entomologist, calculated the number of insects alive on Earth at any one time.   Too narrow.

_A_   2. ¹Some actors and rock stars are paid more than a hundred times as much per year as schoolteachers are. ²We enjoy such performers, but certainly they do not do work that is many times more important than those who teach and guide our nation's students. ³Indeed, the reverse is true. Also, professional athletes earn vastly more than firefighters. ⁴The first group may bring enjoyable diversion to our lives, but the latter literally save lives. ⁵Again, there can be little doubt that the lower-paid group, firefighters, makes the more important, indeed essential, contribution to society. ⁶Similarly, most high-fashion designers, who can make up to $50,000 for a single gown, far outearn police officers. ⁷Now, we can easily live without sophisticated clothes (and probably about 99.9 percent of us do), but a society without law-enforcement officers would be unlivable for all of us.

A. Workers in our society are not necessarily paid according to how important their work is.   Examples: firefighters, police officers.
B. Teachers deserve to be paid as much as actors and rock stars.
C. High-fashion designers should be paid less money for their work.
D. Entertainment is a valuable and needed diversion in our society—one which commands a high salary.

B. Write out the implied main idea of the following paragraphs.

3. ¹TV is our favorite way of relaxing. ²After a stressful day it's restful to just put our feet up and enjoy a favorite program. ³And, of course, TV is entertaining for all ages. ⁴Movies, video games, and special cable offerings, as well as regular network programming, provide a choice of amusements for the whole family. ⁵TV is also deservedly popular for being informative. ⁶When history is being made—for example, during the terrorist attacks on September 11, 2001—we are often there, thanks to TV. ⁷Perhaps the most important benefit of television is that it is a real educational tool. From *Sesame Street* to public television's nature programs, it teaches in a colorful and interesting fashion.

Implied main idea: _____ *Watching television has several benefits.* _____

List of benefits of TV: relaxing, entertaining, informative, educational

4. ¹Lower-class criminals are more likely to be caught than wealthy criminals. ²And once caught, they are less likely to be able to afford highly skilled legal representation. ³When they appear in court, their life history—which often includes quitting school, unemployment, divorce, and an apparent lack of responsibility when judged by middle-class standards—may work against them. ⁴As a result, lower-income

criminals are likely to receive heavier penalties than higher-income criminals for the same crime. ⁵And because they often cannot afford bail, lower-income criminals often have to wait for trial in jail cells rather than in the comfort of their own homes.

Implied main idea: _____ *Lower-class criminals are not treated as well as*

higher-class criminals. _____

> The passage contrasts ways that lower- and higher-class criminals are treated.

➤ **Review Test 3**

A. In the space provided, write the letter of the sentence that best expresses the implied main idea of each of the following paragraphs.

___B___ 1. ¹When anti-smoking campaigns made teens aware of the risks of smoking, the percentage of teens smoking dropped from 28 to 20 percent over the last ten years. ²Additionally, in schools where students have access to health clinics which provide birth control information and devices, pregnancy rates have declined by 30 percent. ³Furthermore, another study demonstrated that students in schools with comprehensive health education were less likely to use alcohol, to try drugs, or to attempt suicide.   Addition words (*additionally* and *furthermore*) signal the major details.

   A. If more schools would conduct anti-smoking campaigns, the number of teens who smoke would greatly decline.

   B. Evidence suggests that health education programs have a favorable effect on teenagers' behavior.

   C. Health education clinics are a positive influence on how people of all ages take care of themselves.

   D. One study found that students in schools with comprehensive health education were less likely to use drugs or to attempt suicide.

___D___ 2. ¹President John Adams's wife, Abigail, helped him with speeches, public relations, and policy decisions. ²Abraham Lincoln's wife, Mary, and Ulysses S. Grant's wife, Julia, both advised their husbands on political appointments. ³When Woodrow Wilson suffered a paralyzing stroke, his wife, Edith, became his intermediary; she determined what papers he saw and when, kept high officials out of his bedroom, and relayed his instructions. ⁴Eleanor Roosevelt actively advised her husband, Franklin, on the New Deal and championed the cause of black people at a time when it was politically inconvenient for him to do so. ⁵With her husband confined to a wheelchair, she traveled widely to observe and report back to him on social and economic conditions and New Deal projects. ⁶Nancy Reagan protected her husband, Ronald, from those advisors she judged unfit, pushed him hard toward arms control talks, and rewrote his speeches. [7]More recently, Hillary Clinton acted as one of her husband Bill's chief advisors. [8]Her strong behind-the-scenes role led to her own successful campaign for political office.

A. Presidents' wives have played a major role in shaping U.S. political appointments.
B. Many presidential wives have served as champions for important social causes.
C. Certain presidential wives have had great political power—especially when their husbands were ill.
D. Many presidential wives have been quite influential in government during their husbands' administrations.

B. Write out the implied main idea of the following paragraph.

3. [1]If you have trouble getting a good night's sleep, don't have an alcoholic drink before bedtime. [2]While alcohol can certainly knock you out, it also damages the quality of sleep you'll get. [3]That's because it chemically interferes with dreaming, an important part of restful sleep. [4]Also, avoid beverages and foods that contain caffeine, such as coffee, most teas, colas, and chocolate. [5]Caffeine can stimulate you, making sleep difficult or impossible. [6]A better before-bed choice is milk, which contains a mild, sleep-inducing type of protein. [7]Another piece of good advice is to exercise during the day; this can leave you tuckered out enough at night to fall promptly and soundly asleep. [8]But do avoid exercise right before bedtime, as its immediate effects are more stimulating than relaxing. [9]Last, try to get up at about the same time every day; this practice will help your body establish a solid sleep and wake cycle. [10]Varying your hours too much can confuse your body's "inner clock."

Implied main idea: Several techniques can help you get a good night's sleep.

Addition words (*also, another,* and *last*)
signal the major details.

C. Read the following selection from a sociology textbook. Find and underline the clearly stated central point that covers most of the supporting details. Then, in the space provided, write the number of the sentence that contains the central point.

Living in Poverty

¹Compared to middle-income people, the poor are ill more often, receive poorer and more limited medical care, and live shorter lives. ²In fact, in virtually every way imaginable, life is more difficult for people living in poverty. ³The poor have a higher rate of mental illness, particularly for the more serious illnesses such as depression, schizophrenia, and personality disorders. ⁴They also report lower levels of personal happiness than the nonpoor.

⁵The children of the poor are at greater risk of dying in infancy, and if they survive, they have a greater risk than nonpoor children of getting into trouble with the law or becoming pregnant as teenagers. ⁶Their education is inferior to that of nonpoor children, and they are far less likely to complete high school. ⁷One study showed that in Chicago's public schools, where a large proportion of the students are from poverty-stricken families, fewer than half graduated on time, and of those who did graduate, only one out of three could read at a twelfth-grade level.

⁸Poor people spend more of their income on food and housing than the nonpoor, but they are still worse fed and worse housed. ⁹A study of housing in southern Illinois revealed that poor people were several times as likely as the general public to live in overcrowded housing, yet 80 to 90 percent of these poor people were paying more than the government standard of 25 percent of their incomes for rent.

¹⁰Poor people are more likely to commit street crimes and to be the victims of such crimes. ¹¹Crime rates are highest in poor neighborhoods, for criminals tend to victimize those who are close by and available. ¹²As a result, a highly disproportionate number of victims of robbery, assault, and homicide are poor. ¹³So high is the incidence of crimes in some poor neighborhoods that poor people are afraid to venture outside their homes. ¹⁴Summer after summer in major cities, elderly poor people have died from heat-related illnesses because they could not afford air conditioning and were afraid to open their windows because of crime.

___2___ is the number of the sentence that states the central point.

> The passage lists numerous ways in which life is more difficult for poor people.

➤ *Review Test 4*

Here is a chance to apply your understanding of implied and central ideas to a reading about childhood cruelty.

To help you continue to strengthen your skills, the reading is followed by questions not only on what you've learned in this chapter but also on what you've learned in previous chapters.

Words to Watch

Below are some words in the reading that do not have strong context support. Each word is followed by the number of the paragraph in which it appears and its meaning there. These words are indicated in the article by a small circle (°).

simulate (1): imitate
musty (3): stale or moldy in odor
trudge (5): walk in a heavy, tired way
brunt (6): greatest part
taunted (6): mocked and insulted
gait (7): manner of moving
sinister (7): evil
distracted (9): interested in something else
stoic (13): emotionless
vulnerable (25): defenseless

ROWING THE BUS

Paul Logan

1   When I was in elementary school, some older kids made me row the bus. Rowing meant that on the way to school I had to sit in the dirty bus aisle littered with paper, gum wads, and spitballs. Then I had to simulate° the motion of rowing while the kids around me laughed and chanted, "Row, row, row the bus." I was forced to do this by a group of bullies who spent most of their time picking on me.

2   I was the perfect target for them. I was small. I had no father. And my mother, though she worked hard to support me, was unable to afford clothes and sneakers that were "cool." Instead she dressed me in outfits that we got from "the bags"—hand-me-downs given as donations to a local church.

3   Each Wednesday, she'd bring several bags of clothes to the house and pull out musty°, wrinkled shirts and worn bell-bottom pants that other families no longer wanted. I knew that people were kind to give things to us, but I hated wearing clothes that might have been donated by my classmates. Each time I wore something from the bags, I feared that the other kids might recognize something that was once theirs.

4   Besides my outdated clothes, I wore thick glasses, had crossed eyes, and spoke with a persistent lisp. For whatever reason, I had never learned to say the "s" sound properly, and I pronounced words that began with "th" as if they began with a "d." In addition, because of my severely crossed eyes, I lacked the hand and eye coordination necessary to hit or catch flying objects.

5   As a result, footballs, baseballs, soccer balls and basketballs became my enemies. I knew, before I stepped on the field or court, that I would do something clumsy or foolish and that everyone would laugh at me. I feared humiliation so much that I became skillful at feigning illnesses to get out of gym class. Eventually I learned how to give myself low-grade fevers so the nurse would write me an excuse. It worked for a while, until the gym teachers caught on. When I did have to play, I was always the last one chosen to be on any team. In fact, team captains did everything in their power to make their opponents get stuck with me. When the unlucky team captain was forced to call my name, I would trudge° over to the team, knowing that no one there liked or wanted me. For four years, from second through fifth grade, I prayed nightly for God to give me school days in which I would not be insulted, embarrassed, or made to feel ashamed.

6   I thought my prayers were answered when my mother decided to move during the summer before sixth grade. The move meant that I got to start sixth grade in a different school, a place where I had no reputation. Although the older kids laughed and snorted at me as soon as I got on my new bus—they couldn't miss my thick glasses and strange clothes—I soon discovered that there was another kid who received the brunt° of their insults. His name was George, and everyone made fun of him. The kids taunted° him because he was skinny; they belittled him because he had acne that pocked and blotched his face, and they teased him because his voice was squeaky. During my first gym class at my new school, I wasn't the last one chosen for kickball; George was.

7   George tried hard to be friends with me, coming up to me in the cafeteria on the first day of school. "Hi. My name's George. Can I sit with you?" he asked with a peculiar squeakiness that made each word high-pitched and raspy. As I nodded for him to sit down, I noticed an uncomfortable silence in the cafeteria as many of the students who had mocked George's clumsy gait° during gym class began watching the two of us and whispering among themselves. By letting him sit with me, I had violated an unspoken law of school, a sinister° code of childhood that demands there must always be someone to pick on. I began to realize two things. If I befriended George, I would soon receive the same treatment that I had gotten at my old school. If I stayed away from him, I might actually have a chance to escape being at the bottom.

8   Within days, the kids started taunting us whenever we were together. "Who's your new little buddy, Georgie?" In the hallways, groups of students began mumbling about me just loud enough for me to hear, "Look, it's George's ugly boyfriend." On the bus rides to and from school, wads of paper and wet chewing gum were tossed at me by the bigger, older kids in the back of the bus.

9   It became clear that my friendship with George was going to cause me several more years of misery at my new school. I decided to stop being friends

with George. In class and at lunch, I spent less and less time with him. Sometimes I told him I was too busy to talk; other times I acted distracted° and gave one-word responses to whatever he said. Our classmates, sensing that they had created a rift between George and me, intensified their attacks on him. Each day, George grew more desperate as he realized that the one person who could prevent him from being completely isolated was closing him off. I knew that I shouldn't avoid him, that he was feeling the same way I felt for so long, but I was so afraid that my life would become the hell it had been in my old school that I continued to ignore him.

10   Then, at recess one day, the meanest kid in the school, Chris, decided he had had enough of George. He vowed that he was going to beat up George and anyone else who claimed to be his friend. A mob of kids formed and came after me. Chris led the way and cornered me near our school's swing sets. He grabbed me by my shirt and raised his fist over my head. A huge gathering of kids surrounded us, urging him to beat me up, chanting "Go, Chris, go!"

11   "You're Georgie's new little boyfriend, aren't you?" he yelled. The hot blast of his breath carried droplets of his spit into my face. In a complete betrayal of the only kid who was nice to me, I denied George's friendship.

12   "No, I'm not George's friend. I don't like him. He's stupid," I blurted out. Several kids snickered and mumbled under their breath. Chris stared at me for a few seconds and then threw me to the ground.

13   "Wimp. Where's George?" he demanded, standing over me. Someone pointed to George sitting alone on top of the monkey bars about thirty yards from where we were. He was watching me. Chris and his followers sprinted over to George and yanked him off the bars to the ground. Although the mob quickly encircled them, I could still see the two of them at the center of the crowd, looking at each other. George seemed stoic°, staring straight through Chris. I heard the familiar chant of "Go, Chris, go!" and watched as his fists began slamming into George's head and body. His face bloodied and his nose broken, George crumpled to the ground and sobbed without even throwing a punch. The mob cheered with pleasure and darted off into the playground to avoid an approaching teacher.

14   Chris was suspended, and after a few days, George came back to school. I wanted to talk to him, to ask him how he was, to apologize for leaving him alone and for not trying to stop him from getting hurt. But I couldn't go near him. Filled with shame for denying George and angered by my own cowardice, I never spoke to him again.

15   Several months later, without telling any students, George transferred to another school. Once in a while, in those last weeks before he left, I caught him watching me as I sat with the rest of the kids in the cafeteria. He never yelled at me or expressed anger, disappointment, or even sadness. Instead he just looked at me.

16   In the years that followed, George's silent stare remained with me. It was there in eighth grade when I saw a gang of popular kids beat up a sixth-grader because, they said, he was "ugly and stupid." It was there my first year in high school, when I saw a group of older kids steal another freshman's clothes and

throw them into the showers. It was there a year later, when I watched several seniors press a wad of chewing gum into the hair of a new girl on the bus. Each time that I witnessed another awkward, uncomfortable, scared kid being tormented, I thought of George, and gradually his haunting stare began to speak to me. No longer silent, it told me that every child who is picked on and taunted deserves better, that no one—no matter how big, strong, attractive or popular—has the right to abuse another person.

17   Finally, in my junior year when a loudmouthed, pink-skinned bully named Donald began picking on two freshmen on the bus, I could no longer deny George. Donald was crumpling a large wad of paper and preparing to bounce it off the back of the head of one of the young students when I interrupted him.

18   "Leave them alone, Don," I said. By then I was six inches taller and, after two years of high-school wrestling, thirty pounds heavier than I had been in my freshman year. Though Donald was still two years older than me, he wasn't much bigger. He stopped what he was doing, squinted and stared at me.

19   "What's your problem, Paul?"

20   I felt the way I had many years earlier on the playground when I watched the mob of kids begin to surround George.

21   "Just leave them alone. They aren't bothering you," I responded quietly.

22   "What's it to you?" he challenged. A glimpse of my own past, of rowing the bus, of being mocked for my clothes, my lisp, my glasses, and my absent father flashed in my mind.

23   "Just don't mess with them. That's all I am saying, Don." My fingertips were tingling. The bus was silent. He got up from his seat and leaned over me, and I rose from my seat to face him. For a minute, both of us just stood there, without a word, staring.

24   "I'm just playing with them, Paul," he said, chuckling. "You don't have to go psycho on me or anything." Then he shook his head, slapped me firmly on the chest with the back of his hand, and sat down. But he never threw that wad of paper. For the rest of the year, whenever I was on the bus, Don and the other troublemakers were noticeably quiet.

25   Although it has been years since my days on the playground and the school bus, George's look still haunts me. Today, I see it on the faces of a few scared kids at my sister's school—she is in fifth grade. Or once in a while I'll catch a glimpse of someone like George on the evening news, in a story about a child who brought a gun to school to stop the kids from picking on him, or in a feature about a teenager who killed herself because everyone teased her. In each school, in almost every classroom, there is a George with a stricken face, hoping that someone nearby will be strong enough to be kind—despite what the crowd says—and brave enough to stand up against people who attack, tease or hurt those who are vulnerable°.

26   If asked about their behavior, I'm sure the bullies would say, "What's it to you? It's just a joke. It's nothing." But to George and me, and everyone else who has been humiliated or laughed at or spat on, it is everything. No one should have to row the bus.

Reading Comprehension Questions

Vocabulary in Context

___B___ 1. In the sentence below, the word *feigning* (fān'ĭng) means
   A. escaping.
   B. faking.
   C. recognizing.
   D. curing.

> "I feared humiliation so much that I became skillful at feigning illnesses to get out of gym class." (Paragraph 5)

___C___ 2. In the excerpt below, the word *rift* (rĭft) means
   A. friendship.
   B. agreement.
   C. break.
   D. joke.

> "I decided to stop being friends with George. . . . Our classmates, sensing that they had created a rift between George and me, intensified their attacks on him." (Paragraph 9)

Main Ideas

___A___ 3. At times, a main idea may cover more than one paragraph. Which sentence best expresses the main idea of paragraphs 2–4?
   A. The first sentence of paragraph 2
   B. The first sentence of paragraph 3
   C. The first sentence of paragraph 4
   D. The first sentence of paragraph 5

> Paragraphs 3 and 4 discuss ways in which the author "was the perfect target." Paragraph 5 begins a new topic.

___A___ 4. The topic sentence of paragraph 8 is its
   A. first sentence.
   B. second sentence.
   C. third sentence.
   D. final sentence.

Supporting Details

___D___ 5. When Chris attacked George, George reacted by
   A. fighting back hard.
   B. shouting for Logan to help him.
   C. running away.
   D. accepting the beating.

> See paragraph 13.

_A_   6. Logan finally found the courage to stand up for abused students when
he saw   See paragraph 17.
   A. Donald throwing paper at a younger student.
   B. older kids throwing a freshman's clothes into the showers.
   C. seniors putting bubble gum in a new student's hair.
   D. a gang beating up a sixth-grader whom they disliked.

Central Point

_C_   7. Which sentence best expresses the central point of the selection?
   A. Although Paul Logan was a target of other students' abuse when he
      was a young boy, their attacks stopped as he grew taller and stronger.
   B. When Logan moved to a different school, he discovered that another
      student, George, was the target of more bullying than he was.
   C. Logan's experience of being bullied and his shame at how he
      treated George eventually made him speak up for someone else who
      was teased.
   D. Logan is ashamed that he did not stand up for George when George
      was being attacked by a bully on the playground.

Implied Main Ideas

_A_   8. Which sentence best expresses the implied main idea of paragraph 5?
   A. Because of Logan's clumsiness, gym was a miserable experience
      for him in elementary school.
   B. Because Logan hated gym so much, he made up excuses to avoid it.
   C. The gym teacher caught on to Logan's excuses.
   D. Logan knew that other students did not want him to be a member of
      their team when games were played.   The details in paragraph 5
                                         support "miserable experience."

_D_   9. Which sentence best expresses the implied main idea of paragraph 6?
   A. Logan's mother moved so that Logan could get a fresh start in a
      new school.
   B. Even at the new school, students laughed at Logan's appearance.
   C. Riding on the bus was the worst part of Logan's school experience.
   D. When Logan started at his new school, he realized that a student
      named George was more unpopular than he was.   Answer D
                                    summarizes the important parts of paragraph 6.

_B_   10. Which sentence best expresses the implied main idea of paragraph 16?
   A. Older kids were often cruel to younger students at Logan's schools.
   B. Because of what happened to George, Logan became increasingly
      bothered by students' picking on others.
   C. In Logan's first year in high school, some students threw a
      freshman's clothes into the showers.
   D. In school, Logan learned a great deal about how people behave in
      various situations throughout life.   Answers A and C are too narrow.
                                    Answer D is too broad—the paragraph focuses
                                    only on bullying, not on "various situations."

Discussion Questions

1. Paul Logan titled his selection "Rowing the Bus." Yet very little of the essay actually deals with the incident the title describes—only the first and last paragraphs. Why do you think Logan chose that title?

2. Logan wanted to be kind to George, but he wanted even more to be accepted by the other students. Have you ever found yourself in a similar situation—where you wanted to do the right thing but felt that it had too high a price? Explain what happened.

3. Logan refers to "a sinister code of childhood that demands there must always be someone to pick on." Why do children need someone to pick on?

4. The novelist Henry James once said, "Three things in human life are important. The first is to be kind. The second is to be kind. And the third is to be kind." What do you think schools or concerned adults could do to encourage young people to treat one another with kindness, rather than with cruelty?

Note: Writing assignments for this selection appear on page 587.

Check Your Performance	IMPLIED MAIN IDEAS / CENTRAL POINT		
Activity	*Number Right*	*Points*	*Score*
Review Test 1 (5 items)	_____	× 2 =	_____
Review Test 2 (4 items)	_____	× 7.5 =	_____
Review Test 3 (4 items)	_____	× 7.5 =	_____
Review Test 4 (10 items)	_____	× 3 =	_____
		TOTAL SCORE =	_____%

Enter your total score into the **Reading Performance Chart: Review Tests** on the inside back cover.

IMPLIED MAIN IDEAS AND THE CENTRAL POINT: Mastery Test 1

A. In the space provided, write the letter of the sentence that best expresses the implied main idea of each of the following paragraphs.

___C___ 1. ¹Many people think there is no difference between an alligator and a crocodile. ²However, the alligator's snout is shorter and broader than that of a crocodile. ³A more dramatic difference between the two creatures lies in how dangerous they are to humans. ⁴There are very few documented instances in which alligators have killed a person. ⁵On the other hand, crocodiles, particularly those along the Nile River, are quite dangerous to humans. ⁶It is said, in fact, that as far as killing people is concerned, crocodiles are second only to poisonous snakes.

   A. Poisonous snakes are more dangerous to humans than crocodiles.
   B. Many people believe that alligators and crocodiles are the same.
   C. There are clear differences between alligators and crocodiles.
   D. Alligators aren't particularly dangerous to humans.

___A___ 2. ¹Intellectual curiosity is a desire for knowledge simply for its own sake—not to get a good grade, pass a test, get a diploma, or get a job. ²Intellectual curiosity prevents boredom and apathy—and bored, apathetic people are dreary people, to themselves and to others. ³Such curiosity also broadens our horizons. ⁴If we pursue only the knowledge that we think we need for "success," our possibilities will be limited. ⁵Moreover, curiosity of the mind makes us versatile. ⁶People with broad knowledge and wide interests can change the course of their work and activities if they need to—as they well might, given the rapid pace of change in our world—or simply if they want to. ⁷Last, although practicality is not its aim, intellectual curiosity can have practical advantages; at any time, any kind of knowledge may turn out to be useful to our happiness and growth in life.

   Addition words: also, moreover, last. Answers B, C, and D are too narrow.

   A. Intellectual curiosity has many benefits.
   B. Intellectual curiosity prevents boredom and apathy.
   C. People with intellectual curiosity can change their jobs if they want or need to.
   D. Intellectual curiosity has practical advantages.

___D___ 3. ¹Children in Finland are the highest-scoring young readers in the world, but they also spend more time watching TV than reading. ²A Finnish national research coordinator has pointed out a key relationship between reading and Finnish TV: "Many programs have subtitles, and watching these programs seems to motivate and enhance reading among young students." ³In fact, almost 50 percent of Finnish

(Continues on next page)

television consists of foreign TV programs and movies whose subtitles must be read—and read quickly—for the shows to be understood. [4]Finnish nine-year-olds want to learn to read in order to understand TV and therefore watch a moderately heavy amount.

A. Children in Finland are the best young readers in the world.
B. Finnish television is very different from television in the United States.
C. Finnish teenagers watch less TV than younger children do.
D. Captioned television appears to help children learn to read.

B. (4.) The author has stated the central point of the following textbook selection in one sentence. Find and underline that sentence. Then, in the space provided, write the number of the sentence that contains the central point.

An Endangered Way of Life

[1]<u>Small towns across America are in crisis, and the quality of life for their citizens is declining.</u> [2]In 1950, about 36 percent of Americans lived in small towns and rural areas; by 1990, only 25 percent did. [3]Young people (especially those with higher education) are moving away, often leaving their parents behind. [4]As a result, rural America is aging.

[5]Also, the economic life of rural America is discouraging. [6]Because many small towns depend on a single employer, their economies are fragile. [7]Moreover, with more people than jobs, employers are able to pay just the minimum wage. [8]The poverty rate for young people in rural areas has more than doubled in the past twenty years, and the unemployment rate is twice the national average.

[9]Health care in rural America is deteriorating. [10]Of the three hundred hospitals that closed in recent years, more than half were in small towns. [11]The country doctor is also disappearing. [12]Many small towns have only a part-time physician who serves several communities, and some have no doctor at all.

[13]Small-town schools are also in trouble. [14]With dwindling numbers of students, the cost of educating a single student often becomes prohibitive, and many small districts have been forced to merge. [15]In consolidated school districts, students may be forced to travel fifty miles back and forth to school each day.

[16]The crisis in rural America is taking its toll on the mental health of its residents. [17]A recent study of Iowa farmers found that one in three suffered symptoms of depression. [18]Another study, of rural adolescents, found that they are far more prone to depression and suicidal thoughts than are their urban counterparts.

___1___   is the number of the sentence that states the central point.

IMPLIED MAIN IDEAS AND THE CENTRAL POINT: Mastery Test 2

A. In the space provided, write the letter of the sentence that best expresses the implied main idea of each of the following paragraphs.

___C___ 1. [1]As you speak with someone, you can easily gather clues about how much he or she understands or agrees with you and adjust your conversation accordingly. [2]But when you write, you must try to anticipate the reader's reactions without such clues. [3]You also have to provide stronger evidence in writing than in conversation. [4]A friend may accept an unsupported statement such as "He's a lousy boss." [5]But in writing, the reader expects you to back up such a statement with proof.

    A. There are special techniques to communicating verbally with others.

    B. Speaking and writing are both challenging ways of communicating.

    C. Communicating effectively in writing is more demanding than communicating verbally.

    D. When speaking, you get feedback about a person's reaction that helps you to make your conversation more effective.

___B___ 2. [1]Many people dream of being celebrities, but do they consider what celebrities' lives are really like? [2]For one thing, celebrities have to look perfect all the time. [3]There's always a photographer ready to take an unflattering picture of a famous person looking dumpy in old clothes. [4]Celebrities also sacrifice their private lives. [5]Their personal struggles, divorces, or family tragedies all end up as front-page news. [6]Most frighteningly, celebrities are in constant danger of the wrong kind of attention. [7]Threatening letters and even physical attacks from crazy fans are things the celebrity must contend with.

    A. Many people dream of being celebrities.   Addition words: *for one thing,*

    B. Being a celebrity is often difficult.   *also, most frighteningly.*

    C. Being a celebrity means having to look good all the time.

    D. Celebrities face dangers.   Answer A is an introductory detail; answers C and D are too narrow.

___D___ 3. [1]In murders investigated by the FBI, more than one-third have been committed by one family member against another. [2]Three percent of them involve the murder of a child by a parent. [3]Aggression by parents toward children also takes a less drastic form. [4]Each year two million children are kicked, beaten, or punched by their parents. [5]Aggression is evident in marriages as well. [6]Each year, four million husbands and wives violently attack each other. [7]These attacks result in severe injuries in a quarter of a million cases.

    A. Abuse of children by parents is widespread in the United States.

    B. Aggression is part of many marriages in this country.

    C. In the United States, family violence is increasing steadily.

    D. In the United States, aggression is often directed toward members of one's own family.   Answers A and B are too narrow; answer C is not supported in the paragraph.

(Continues on next page)

B. (4.) The author has stated the central point of the following psychology article in one sentence. Find and underline that sentence. Then, in the space provided, write the number of the sentence that contains the central point.

Missing Persons

[1]Many of the world's girls and women are missing from schools. [2]In sub-Saharan Africa, for every ten boys, only six girls are enrolled in secondary school, and in southern Asia, only four. [3]In these regions, three-quarters of women aged 25 and over are still illiterate. [4]A major reason why girls leave school is that they are married off, often to older men, and begin bearing children in their teens. [5]Some are sold by their parents to prostitution rings, where young girls are in demand because they are considered less likely to carry the AIDS virus.

[6]Women are missing from the paid labor force. [7]Women work as hard as or harder than men (on average, thirteen more hours a week worldwide). [8]But the work women do—caring for children; providing food and health care to their families; tending gardens and livestock; processing crops; gathering firewood and hauling water; weaving cloth, carpets, and baskets; and selling home-grown food and home-made crafts at local markets—is not considered "real" work. [9]When women do work for wages, they are usually employed in clerical, sales, and service occupations, and they are excluded from higher-paying jobs in manufacturing, transportation, and management. [10]Even when women do the same work as men, they earn—on average worldwide—30 to 40 percent less.

[11]Women are missing in the halls of power, policy, and decision making. [12]Although women make up more than half the world's population, less than 5 percent of heads of state, heads of corporations, and directors of international organizations are female.

[13]Women are missing from the battlefield, but tragically not from the ranks of the dead and wounded. [14]In the many ethnic and civil wars in the world today, hostile groups are fighting for towns and cities, and civilians are caught in the crossfire. [15]Hundreds of thousands of women and children have become widows, orphans, and refugees.

[16]War or not, women the world over are regularly abused sexually, physically injured, and even killed simply because they are women. [17]In 1987 in India, 1,786 "dowry deaths"—in which the husband and/or his family kill a woman because her dowry was insufficient—were recorded. [18]In Thailand, more than 50 percent of married women living in Bangkok's largest squatter settlement said they were regularly beaten by their husbands. [19]Not until 1991 did the Brazilian Supreme Court outlaw the "honor" defense, which excused a man who murdered an adulterous wife on the grounds that he was defending his honor.

[20]<u>Throughout the world, females are clearly second-class citizens, and worse.</u>

_20_   is the number of the sentence that states the central point.

IMPLIED MAIN IDEAS AND THE CENTRAL POINT: Mastery Test 3

A. In the space provided, write the letter of the sentence that best expresses the implied main idea of each of the following paragraphs.

___A___ 1. [1]A baby's most basic cry consists of a rhythmic pattern which begins with a cry followed by a brief silence and then a shorter higher-pitched whistling sound. [2]Experts believe the basic cry is triggered by hunger, tiredness, or mild discomfort. [3]Researchers have also identified an anger cry. [4]A bit more forceful than the basic cry, the anger cry involves larger volumes of air passing over the baby's vocal chords. [5]Such a sound might be made when a baby wants to be picked up and is not, or when a baby is put in a crib when it wants to be held. [6]A third type of cry that babies use is the pain cry. [7]A sudden loud wail followed by an extended period of breath holding, the pain cry is the loudest sound a baby can make.

    A. Babies have three distinct cries to communicate what they are feeling.
    B. The pain cry is the loudest sound a baby can make.
    C. Babies communicate differently at different ages.
    D. Experts believe that hunger, tiredness, or mild discomfort may cause the basic cry.   *Addition words: also, third.*
                  Answers B, C, and D are too narrow.

___A___ 2. [1]The earliest humans probably used the lengthening and shortening of shadows on the ground to measure the passage of time. [2]Later, the sundial was invented to tell time more precisely, but still by using the shadow principle. [3]The hourglass, a slightly more recent invention, measured time by allowing grains of sand to fall from one container to another. [4]In about the year 1300, a primitive clock was invented. [5]It had only an hour hand, but it became the most exact way yet to tell the time. [6]Since then, clocks have been so improved technically that today's clocks and watches can be depended upon to be quite precise.

    A. Throughout history, people have found better and better ways to measure the passing of time.
    B. The hourglass is a slightly more recent invention than the sundial.
    C. The first methods of measuring the passing of time took advantage of the changing shadows cast by the sun throughout a day.
    D. A primitive clock invented in about 1300 was the most exact way to tell time up to that point.   Answers B, C, and D are too narrow.

___D___ 3. [1]Adolescents and old people are both often segregated from the rest of society: young people are isolated in schools, and many old people in retirement communities, assisted-living facilities, and nursing homes. [2]Also, both groups tend to be poorer than young adults or middle-aged people: adolescents because they do not yet have the education or experience to command high salaries, and old people because they are retired and living on their savings and social security. [3]Third, independence is important for both groups—they are conscious of wanting it, whereas young adults and middle-aged people take it for granted. [4]Adolescents want to become independent of their parents; old people want to

(Continues on next page)

keep their independence and not have to rely on their children or on social institutions. [5]Fourth, they both tend to have a relatively large amount of leisure time or, at least, time that they can choose or not choose to fill with study or work. [6]By contrast, young and middle-aged adults typically spend most of their time at their jobs or taking care of home duties such as child-rearing.

A. Adolescents and old people, more than other social groups, strongly value their independence.

B. Both adolescents and old people have different economic conditions from young and middle-aged adults.

C. Young and middle-aged adults spend much of their time taking care of home duties such as child-rearing.   Addition words: *also, third, fourth.*

D. Adolescents and old people, as groups in our culture, are very similar in certain ways.   Answers A, B, and C are too narrow.

B. (4.) The author has stated the central point of the following textbook selection in one sentence. Find and underline that sentence. Then, in the space provided, write the number of the sentence that contains the central point.

Learned Helplessness

[1]A researcher at Johns Hopkins University has repeatedly done a simple experiment with two rats. [2]He holds one rat firmly in hand so that, no matter how much the rat struggles, he cannot escape. [3]The rat will finally give up. [4]The researcher then throws that unmoving rat into a tank of warm water, and the rat sinks, not swims. [5]He has "learned" that there is nothing he can do, that there is no point in struggling. [6]The researcher then throws another rat into the water—one that doesn't "know" that his situation is hopeless and that he is therefore helpless. [7]This rat will swim to safety.

[8]A comparable experiment involving people has been conducted by Martin E. P. Seligman of the University of Pennsylvania. [9]Two groups of college students are put in rooms where they are blasted with noise turned up to almost intolerable levels. [10]In one room there is a button that turns off the noise. [11]The students quickly notice it, push it, and are rewarded with blissful silence. [12]In the other room, however, there is no turn-off button. [13]The students look for one, find nothing, and finally give up. [14]There is no way to escape the noise (except to leave the room before a previously agreed-upon time period has elapsed), so they simply endure the noise.

[15]Later, the same two groups are put in two other rooms. [16]This time, both rooms contain a switch-off mechanism—though not a simple button this time and not as easy to find. [17]Nevertheless, the group that found the button the first time succeeds in finding the "off" switch the second time, too. [18]But the second group, already schooled in the hopelessness of their circumstances, doesn't even search. Its members just sit it out again.

[19]Both experiments suggest that past failures can teach one to feel helpless and, as a result, to give up trying. [20]Being aware of this possibility may give people the courage to persist despite previous disappointments.

The words "both experiments" in the last paragraph are a clue that the author is about to summarize what's said about the experiments in the first three paragraphs.

_____19_____ is the number of the sentence that states the central point.

IMPLIED MAIN IDEAS AND THE CENTRAL POINT: Mastery Test 4

A. In the space provided, write the letter of the sentence that best expresses the implied main idea of each of the following paragraphs.

_____D_____ 1. ¹Earth is surrounded by a thick gaseous envelope called the atmosphere. ²The atmosphere provides the air that we breathe and protects us from the sun's intense heat and dangerous radiation. ³The energy exchanges that continually occur between the atmosphere and space produce the effects we call weather. ⁴If, like the moon, Earth had no atmosphere, our planet would be lifeless, and many of the processes and interactions that make the surface such an energetic place could not operate. ⁵Without weathering and friction, the face of our planet might more closely resemble the lunar surface, which has not changed much in nearly three billion years.

    A. The atmosphere is a thick gaseous layer covering the entire Earth.

    B. The moon, unlike Earth, has no atmosphere and has therefore not changed much in almost three billion years.

    C. There are many influences on Earth's development.

    D. The atmosphere is a key part of our environment and of Earth's processes.

_____B_____ 2. ¹Baby mammals are born nearly helpless. ²They cannot survive if they are not cared for, usually by older members of their species. ³Food and shelter are the most obvious needs of a baby animal. ⁴But scientists have also observed another, less obvious need of baby mammals. ⁵Monkeys who are raised alone, with no physical contact with other animals, develop strange habits such as constantly rocking or moving in circles. ⁶In addition, they cannot relate normally to other monkeys. ⁷The males can rarely breed with females. ⁸The females who do bear young ignore or abuse their babies. ⁹When monkeys who were raised alone are put in contact with friendly, "motherly" monkeys who touch and cuddle them, they eventually develop normal monkey behaviors.

    A. Baby mammals need to be given food and shelter.

    B. Studies suggest that touching, like food and shelter, is key to normal mammal development.

    C. All animals who are raised without physical contact with other animals develop strange habits.

    D. Scientists have done studies of monkeys raised without physical contact with other animals.

(Continues on next page)

B. Write out the implied main idea of the following paragraph.

> 3. ¹You don't have to scare your family with statistics about heart attacks. ²To get them to exercise more often, emphasize instead how good they'll feel and how much better they'll look if they work out daily. ³Another method you can use is to set an example. ⁴If they see you walking to the convenience store instead of driving, they might be encouraged to do likewise the next time they have errands in the neighborhood. ⁵Finally, make exercise a family activity. ⁶Suggest that the whole family go swimming together, take up early morning jogging, or join the Y at the group rate.

> *Implied main idea:*   There are several positive ways to encourage your family

> to exercise more often.   Addition words: *another, finally.*

>   The phrase "to get them to exercise more often" is one clue to the main idea.

C. (4.) The author has stated the central point of the following textbook passage in one sentence. Find and underline that sentence. Then, in the space provided, write the number of the sentence that contains the central point.

Teenagers and Jobs

¹Today's world puts a lot of pressure on teenagers to work. ²By working, they gain more independence from their families, and they also get the spending money needed to keep up with their peers. ³Many people argue that working can be a valuable experience for the young.

⁴However, schoolwork and the benefits of extracurricular activities tend to go by the wayside when adolescents work more than fifteen hours a week. ⁵Teachers are then faced with the problems of keeping the attention of tired pupils and of giving homework to students who simply don't have the time to do it. ⁶In addition, educators have noticed less involvement in the extracurricular events many consider healthy influences on young people. ⁷School bands and athletic teams are losing players to work, and sports events are poorly attended by working students. ⁸Those teenagers who try to do it all—homework, extracurricular activities, and work—may find themselves exhausted and prone to illness.

⁹Another drawback of too much work is that it may promote materialism and an unrealistic lifestyle. ¹⁰Some parents say that work teaches adolescents the value of a dollar. ¹¹Undoubtedly, it can, and it's true that some teenagers work to help out with the family budget or save for college. ¹²But surveys have shown that the majority of working teens use their earnings to buy luxuries—stereos, tape decks, clothing, even cars. ¹³These young people, some of whom earn $300 and more a month, don't worry about spending wisely—they can just about have it all. ¹⁴In many cases, experts point out, they are becoming accustomed to a lifestyle they won't be able to afford several years down the road, when they'll no longer have parents to pay for car insurance, food and lodging, and so on. ¹⁵At that point, they'll be hard pressed to pay for necessities as well as luxuries.

¹⁶<u>Teens can benefit from both work *and* school—and avoid the pitfalls of materialism—simply by working no more than fifteen hours a week.</u> ¹⁷As is often the case, a moderate approach is likely to be the most healthy and rewarding one.

_16_   is the number of the sentence that states the central point.

IMPLIED MAIN IDEAS AND THE CENTRAL POINT: Mastery Test 5

A. In the space provided, write the letter of the sentence that best expresses the implied main idea of each of the following paragraphs.

___D___ 1. [1]There is no doubt that businesses can improve their productivity. [2]If every person and machine did things right the first time, the same number of people could handle much larger volumes of work. [3]High costs of inspection could be channeled into productive activities, and managers could take all the time they spend checking and devote it to productive tasks. [4]Wasted materials would become a thing of the past. [5]In fact, it's been estimated that attention to quality can reduce the total cost of operations anywhere from 10 to 50 percent. [6]As Philip Crosby said: "Quality is free. What costs money are the unquality things—all the actions that involve not doing jobs right the first time."

    A. Philip Crosby is an expert in quality in business.
    B. It is wasteful to spend so much money on plant inspections.
    C. Businesses can improve their sales in several ways.
    D. If quality is improved, productivity improves.

___D___ 2. [1]In nineteenth-century America, people shared beds, both at homes with relatives and in hotels with strangers, without inquiring about their bed partner's health. [2]They exchanged combs, hairbrushes, and even toothbrushes, and they fed babies from their mouths and spoons, with no sense of danger. [3]They coughed, sneezed, and spat without concern for their own health or the health of those around them. [4]They cooked and stored their meals with little worry about food-borne illness. [5]They drank unfiltered water from wells and streams, often using a common dipper or drinking cup. [6]Last but not least, they used chamber pots and outhouses with little regard for where the contents ended up in relation to the community water supply.

    A. Nineteenth-century Americans were friendlier than modern Americans.
    B. There was less water pollution in nineteenth-century America than there is today.
    C. In nineteenth-century America, people were probably as concerned about health as they were about survival.
    D. Nineteenth-century Americans engaged in behaviors that could easily spread disease.

B. Write out the implied main idea of the following paragraph.

3. [1]According to study experts, one tip for exam success is regular daily and weekly study. [2]Another tip is to focus on, in your study sessions, ideas that the instructor has emphasized in class. [3]In addition, use the night before an exam for a careful review rather than a stressful cramming. [4]Then get up a bit early the next morning and review your notes one more time. [5]Arriving early for an exam is another helpful tip that experts suggest. [6]Sit in a quiet spot and go through a final reading of notes. [7]Last, once the test begins, the advice of experts is to answer the easier questions first; then go back and tackle the hard

(Continues on next page)

ones. [8]And on essay questions, it's most productive to think a few minutes and make a brief outline before beginning to write.

Implied main idea: <u>You can improve your success on exams by using</u>

<u>several tips.</u>   Addition words: *one, another, in addition, another, last.*

C. (4.) The author has stated the central point of the following essay in one sentence. Find and underline that sentence. Then, in the space provided, write the number of the sentence that contains the central point.

Alcohol Reform

[1]In the nineteenth century, reformers wanted to persuade Americans to adopt more godly personal habits. [2]They set up associations to battle profanity and Sabbath breaking, to place a Bible in every American home, and to provide religious education for the children of the poor. [3]And beginning early in the 1800s, an <u>extensive moral reform campaign was conducted against liquor.</u>

[4]At the start of the century, heavy drinking was an integral part of American life. [5]Many people believed that downing a glass of whiskey before breakfast was healthful. [6]Instead of taking coffee breaks, people took a dram of liquor at eleven and again at four o'clock as well as drinks after meals "to aid digestion" and a nightcap before going to sleep. [7]Campaigning politicians offered voters generous amounts of liquor during campaigns and as rewards for "voting right" on Election Day. [8]On the frontier, one evangelist noted, "A house could not be raised, a field of wheat cut down, nor could there be a log rolling, a husking, a quilting, a wedding, or a funeral without the aid of alcohol."

[9]By 1820 the typical adult American consumed more than 7 gallons of absolute alcohol a year (compared with 2.6 gallons today). [10]Consumption had risen markedly in two decades, fueled by the growing amounts of corn distilled by farmers into cheap whiskey, which could be transported more easily than bulk corn. [11]In the 1820s, a gallon of whiskey cost just a quarter.

[12]In their campaign, reformers identified liquor as the cause of a wide range of social, family, and personal problems. [13]Alcohol was blamed for the abuse of wives and children and the squandering of family resources. [14]Many businesspeople linked drinking with crime, poverty, and inefficient and unproductive employees.

The introductory paragraph begins by discussing various reform movements, then narrows its focus to the reform movement discussed in the rest of the passage.

[15]The stage was clearly set for the appearance of an organized movement against liquor. [16]In 1826 the nation's first formal national temperance organization was born: the American Society for the Promotion of Temperance. [17]Led by socially prominent clergy and laypeople, the new organization called for total abstinence from distilled liquor. [18]Within three years, 222 state and local anti-liquor groups were laboring to spread this message.

[19]By 1835, membership in temperance organizations had climbed to 1.5 million, and an estimated 2 million Americans had taken the "pledge" to abstain from hard liquor. [20]Reformers helped reduce annual per capita consumption of alcohol from seven gallons in 1830 to just three gallons a decade later, forcing four thousand distilleries to close. [21]Fewer employers provided workers with eleven o'clock or four o'clock drams, and some businesses began to fire employees who drank on the job.

_____3_____   is the number of the sentence that states the central point.

IMPLIED MAIN IDEAS AND THE CENTRAL POINT: Mastery Test 6

A. In the space provided, write the letter of the sentence that best expresses the implied main idea of each of the following paragraphs.

_D_ 1. [1]Salespeople who want to increase their sales may make promises which the company's production and accounting departments find difficult to support. [2]Production, for example, may not be able to meet the sales department's schedule because purchasing didn't get raw materials in time. [3]While salespeople might like to have large inventories available, production and finance are likely to resist building up stocks because of the high cost of storing and/or owning unsold goods. [4]Also, if production is in the middle of union negotiations, it is likely to feel they are more important than anything else. [5]At the same time, however, salespeople may feel that nothing is more urgent than increasing sales.

    A. In a company, the demands of the sales department should be given priority.
    B. Union demands can slow up production.
    C. Businesses tend to be disorganized because of lack of communication.
    D. Different parts of a business may have competing needs.

_B_ 2. [1]A Senate committee estimates the loss of earnings of men ages 25 to 34 who have less than high school-level skills at $236 billion. [2]Half of the heads of households classified below the federal poverty line cannot read an eighth-grade book. [3]More than a third of mothers on welfare are also functionally illiterate. [4](Functional illiteracy is the inability to read and write well enough for everyday practical needs.) [5]So are 60 percent of the adult prison population and 84 percent of juveniles who come before the courts. [6]Businesses have difficulty filling such entry-level jobs as clerk, bank teller, and paralegal assistant. [7]A major insurance firm reports that 70 percent of dictated letters must be retyped "at least once" because secretaries cannot spell and punctuate correctly. [8]The military, too, pays a price for functional illiteracy. [9]The navy has stated that 30 percent of new recruits are "a danger to themselves and costly to naval equipment" because they cannot read very well or understand simple instructions.

    A. Americans are among the most poorly educated people in the world.
    B. Functional illiteracy, widespread among Americans, is costly for individuals and society.
    C. Businesses must face the problem of poorly prepared workers.
    D. Our prisons and courts are filled with adults and juveniles who are functionally illiterate.

B. Write out the implied main idea of the following paragraph.

3. [1]There are plenty of jokes about the trials of being married. [2]And we all know that being married doesn't necessarily mean living happily ever after. [3]But did you know that married people live longer and suffer fewer chronic illnesses than single people do? [4]In contrast, divorced people have a greater risk of dying early than people in any other category. [5]Widowed people, too, tend to die younger than married folks. [6]In addition, single men are much more likely than married men to experience serious emotional breakdowns.

(Continues on next page)

171

Implied main idea: <u>Marriage is good for people's physical and mental</u>

<u>health.</u>

C. (4.) The author has stated the central point of the following textbook selection in one sentence. Find and underline that sentence. Then, in the space provided, write the number of the sentence that contains the central point.

Marriage Contracts

¹Every year, thousands of couples marry unwisely. ²Their decision to wed is based on the great rush of emotion that comes along with falling in love. ³"We love each other!" they proclaim. ⁴"Of course our marriage will work!" ⁵Unfortunately, the rosy glow that accompanies romantic love doesn't last forever. ⁶Couples who promise "Till death do us part" often regret that vow a few months or years later. ⁷They may feel that their decision was made hastily, that they didn't know each other well enough, that their ideas about marriage are too different. ⁸And then they are faced with two unhappy options. ⁹They can stay in a disappointing marriage, or they can start proceedings for an unpleasant, expensive, time-consuming divorce.

¹⁰<u>Another approach is needed here: People who want to marry should sign renewable marriage contracts.</u> ¹¹Such a marriage contract could be valid for three years, at which time the partners would decide whether or not to renew the agreement. ¹²If they did not choose to stay together, no divorce would be necessary. ¹³They would simply file a paper stating that they would not be renewing their contract.

¹⁴One advantage of the marriage contract system is that it would force couples to think in concrete terms about their marriages. ¹⁵They would have to talk ahead of time about some essential questions. ¹⁶How will our money be handled? ¹⁷How will household chores be divided? ¹⁸Will we have children? ¹⁹How will they be raised? ²⁰Will we have a religious life? ²¹How often will our in-laws visit? ²²These are the kinds of questions that most couples who are wildly in love would otherwise never face.

²³It would not be surprising if many couples in the process of working on a contract decided that they shouldn't get married after all. ²⁴And that would be a good thing. ²⁵They are the couples whose marriages probably wouldn't survive the first clash with reality.

²⁶In addition, a contract would encourage couples to work harder at their marriages. ²⁷They couldn't afford to let problems simmer under the surface, assuming that they had unlimited years to fix them. ²⁸If they knew that their contract was coming up for renewal every few years, people would give as much attention to their marriages as they do to their careers or relationships with friends.

²⁹Finally, a renewable marriage contract would make ending a marriage far easier than it is today. ³⁰No longer would both partners have to hire expensive lawyers and endure long waits in the divorce courts. ³¹Their marriage contract would spell out the terms of a split. ³²It would say how property would be divided and how custody of children would be handled. ³³The simple filing of a paper in the courthouse would end a marriage. ³⁴The man and woman would then go their own ways, sadder perhaps, but wiser about what it takes to make a marriage work.

<u> 10 </u> is the number of the sentence that states the central point. The first paragraph states the problem; sentence 10 in the second paragraph proposes a solution to the problem. The remaining paragraphs explain the advantages of this solution.

5

Relationships I

Authors use two common methods to show relationships and make their ideas clear. The two methods—**transitions** and **patterns of organization**—are explained in turn in this chapter. The chapter also explains two common types of relationships:

- Relationships that involve **addition**
- Relationships that involve **time**

TRANSITIONS

Look at the following items and put a check (✓) by the one that is easier to read and understand:

____ One way to lose friends is to always talk and never listen. A way to end friendships is to borrow money and never pay it back.

✓ One way to lose friends is to always talk and never listen. Another way to end friendships is to borrow money and never pay it back.

You probably found the second item easier to understand. The word *another* makes it clear that the writer is adding a second way to lose friends. **Transitions** are words or phrases (like *another*) that show the relationships between ideas. They are like signs on the road that guide travelers.

Two major types of transitions are words that show addition and words that show time.

Words That Show Addition

Once again, put a check (✓) beside the item that is easier to read and understand.

___ Many people rent videos because rental is cheaper than tickets to a movie theater. Videos are now available almost everywhere.

_✓_ Many people rent videos because rental is cheaper than tickets to a movie theater. Also, videos are now available almost everywhere.

The word *also* in the second item makes the relationship between the sentences **clearer**. The author is providing reasons why renting movies is popular. The first reason is that renting videos is cheaper than buying tickets to the movies. A *second* reason is that the movies are so readily available. The word *also* makes it clear that another reason is being given. *Also* is an addition word.

Addition words signal added ideas. These words tell you a writer is presenting one or more ideas that continue along the same line of thought as a previous idea. Like all transitions, addition words help writers organize their information and present it clearly to readers. Here are some common words that show addition:

Addition Words

one	to begin with	in addition	last
first	another	next	last of all
first of all	second	moreover	finally
for one thing	also	furthermore	

Examples:

The following examples contain addition words. Notice how these words introduce ideas that *add to* what has already been said.

Garlic improves the flavor of many dishes. *In addition*, it lowers cholesterol, fights heart disease, and kills certain viruses.

Rivers serve as highways for migrating birds. *Also*, the nearby wetlands provide the birds with places in which to rest and refuel.

My neighbors are so safety-conscious that they had the wooden front door of their apartment replaced with a steel one. *Moreover*, they had iron bars installed on all their apartment windows.

> *Practice 1*

Complete each sentence with a suitable addition word from the box on the previous page. Try to use a variety of transitions.   *Answers may vary.*

> **Hint:** Make sure that each addition word or phrase that you choose fits smoothly into the flow of the sentence. Test each choice by reading the sentence aloud. (Be sure to use this hint when doing Practice 2.)

1. This old computer has a slow, sticky keyboard. It _____*also*_____ crashes at least once a day.

2. There are several ways to use old jeans. _____*For one thing*_____, you can use them for patching other jeans.

3. One million stray dogs live in the New York City metropolitan area. _____*In addition*_____, there are more than 500,000 stray cats in the same area.

4. "_____*First*_____, and most important," said my adviser, "you've got to complete that term paper or you won't graduate on time."

5. Part-time workers have second-class status. For one thing, they are easily laid off. Second, they get no fringe benefits. _____*Finally*_____, they are often paid less than half the hourly rate of a full-timer.

Words That Show Time

Put a check (✓) beside the item that is easier to read and understand:

___ The two neighboring families got along well. They are not on speaking terms.

✓ Previously, the two neighboring families got along well. Now they are not on speaking terms.

The words *previously* and *now* in the second item clarify the relationship between the sentences: *Before*, the families got along well; and *now* they don't speak to each other. *Previously* and *now* and words like them are time words.

These transitions indicate a time relationship. **Time words** tell us *when* something happened in relation to when something else happened. On the next page are some common words that show time:

Time Words

before	during	while	later
previously	now	next	eventually
first	as	soon	finally
then	when	after	last
following			

Examples:

The following examples contain time words. Notice how these words show us *when* something takes place.

While the nurse prepared the needle, I rolled up my sleeve. *Then* I looked away.

Many people get sleepy *after* eating a heavy meal.

During my last semester in college, I spent more time job hunting than I did studying.

Helpful Tips About Transitions

Here are two points to keep in mind about transitions.

 Tip 1 Some transition words have the same meaning. For example, *also, moreover,* and *furthermore* all mean "in addition." Authors typically use a variety of transitions to avoid repetition.

 Tip 2 In some cases the same word can serve as two different types of transitions, depending on how it is used. For example, the word *first* may be used as an addition word to show that the author is presenting a series of points, as in the following sentences:

> For many athletes, life after a sports career is a letdown. *First,* they are often not prepared for nonathletic careers. In addition, they . . .

First may also may be used to signal a time sequence, as in these sentences:

> A trip to a giant supermarket can be quite frustrating. *First,* you have trouble finding a parking space close to the store. Then, . . .

> ## Practice 2

Complete each sentence with a suitable time word from the box on the previous page. Try to use a variety of transitions.   *Answers may vary.*

> **Hint:** Make sure that each time word or phrase that you choose
> fits smoothly into the flow of the sentence. Test each choice by
> reading the sentence aloud.

1. _____*After*_____ my cousin took a long shower, there was no hot water left for anyone else in the house.

2. To make chicken stock, begin by putting a pot of water on the stove to boil. _____*Then*_____ drop in a chicken and some diced celery and onions.

3. Gerald waited impatiently all day for the Monday night football game to begin on TV, but _____*during*_____ the first half, he fell asleep.

4. Recent advances in medicine make it possible to treat babies even _____*before*_____ they are born.

5. Some students listen to a CD, eat snacks, and talk on the phone _____*while*_____ doing their homework.

PATTERNS OF ORGANIZATION

You have learned that transitions show the relationships between ideas in sentences. In the same way, **patterns of organization** show the relationships between supporting details in paragraphs, essays, and chapters. It helps to recognize the common patterns in which authors arrange information. You will then be better able to understand and remember what you read.

The rest of this chapter discusses two major patterns of organization:

- The **list of items pattern**
  (Addition words are often used in this pattern of organization.)

- The **time order pattern**
  (Time words are often used in this pattern of organization.)

Noticing the transitions in a passage can often help you become aware of its pattern of organization. Transitions can also help you locate the major supporting details.

1   THE LIST OF ITEMS PATTERN

List of Items
Item 1
Item 2
Item 3

To get a sense of the list of items pattern, try to arrange the following sentences in a logical order. Put a *1* in front of the sentence that should come first, a *2* in front of the sentence that comes next, a *3* in front of the third sentence, and a *4* in front of the sentence that should come last. The result will be a short paragraph. Use the addition words as a guide.

  2   One common strategy is to consume massive quantities of junk food, which is easily done thanks to all the ever-present convenience stores and fast-food restaurants.

  1   There are some widely popular, inappropriate methods that people use to combat stress.

  4   Finally, watching hours of nonstop TV can put people in a stupor that helps them forget the problems of everyday life.

  3   Another way to deal with stress is to doze or sleep for hours and hours, even during the day.

This paragraph begins with the main idea: "There are some widely popular, inappropriate methods that people have to combat stress." The next three sentences go on to list three of those methods, resulting in the pattern of organization known as a list of items. The transitions *one, another,* and *finally* introduce the points being listed and indicate their order:

> [1]There are some widely popular, inappropriate methods that people use to combat stress. [2]One common strategy is to consume massive quantities of junk food, which is easily done thanks to all the ever-present convenience stores and fast-food restaurants. [3]Another way to deal with stress is to doze or sleep for hours and hours, even during the day. [4]Finally, watching hours of nonstop TV can put people in a stupor that helps them forget the problems of everyday life.

A **list of items** refers to a series of reasons, examples, or other points that support an idea. The items have no time order, but are listed in whatever order the author prefers. Addition words are often used in a list of items to tell us that other supporting points are being added to a point already mentioned. (A list of addition words appears on page 174.) Textbook authors frequently organize material into lists of items, such as a list of types of economic systems, symptoms of heart disease, or reasons for teenage drinking.

☑ *Check Your Understanding*

The paragraph below is organized as a list of items. Complete the outline of the list by first filling in the missing part of the main idea. Then add to the outline the three major details listed in the paragraph.

To help you find the major details, do two things:

• Underline the addition words that introduce the major details in the list;

• Number (1, 2, . . .) each item in the list.

> [1]Like all social institutions, sports serve various purposes. [2]First,[1] they provide the leisure-time exercise so necessary in a society in which most jobs provide little or no physical activity. [3]Second,[2] sports supply an outlet for energies that might otherwise strain the social order. [4]Emotions such as anger and frustration can be expressed in ways that are acceptable to society—through both watching and participating in sports. [5]Finally,[3] sports give society role models. [6]At their best, athletes, especially famous ones, are examples of dedication, hard work, and conduct for others to imitate.

Main idea: Sports serve   *various purposes*   .

1. *They provide leisure-time exercise.*

2. *They provide an outlet for energies that might strain the social order.*

3. *They give society role models.*

Explanation:

The main idea is that sports serve several purposes. (You may also express main ideas at times in a short heading; the heading here could be "Purposes of sports.") Following are the three purposes you should have added to the outline:

1. They provide leisure-time exercise. (This point is signaled with the addition transition *first*.)

2. They supply an outlet for energies that might otherwise strain the social order. (This point is signaled with the addition transition *second*.)

3. They give society role models. (This point is signaled with the addition transition *finally*.)

➢ *Practice 3*

A. The following passage uses a listing pattern. Outline the passage by filling in the main idea and the major details.   *Wording of answers may vary.*

> **Hint:** Underline the addition words that introduce the items in the list and number the items.

> ¹Today, beef is America's favorite meat. ²But, for several reasons, America's most popular meat a hundred years ago was pork. ³First of all, ¹pigs grew quickly. ⁴They could multiply their weight 150 times in just eight months by eating nuts, roots, fallen orchard fruit, spoiled food, and garbage. ⁵Another reason for the popularity of pork was that ²pigs required almost no attention. ⁶In a nation with lots of land and not enough workers, pigs were perfect because they could take care of themselves. ⁷Indeed, wild pigs, such as the American razorback, were so fierce that they didn't need a farmer's protection. ⁸A third reason for the preference for pigs was that ³they could be cheaply preserved. ⁹A butchered pig could be packed into barrels filled with heavily salted water and saved for up to a year. ¹⁰Indeed, it was salted pork— not hamburger—that fed most people in the first century and a half of the growing United States.

Main idea: *For several reasons, pork was America's most popular meat a hundred years ago.*

1. *Pigs grew quickly.*
2. *Pigs required little attention.*
3. *Pigs could be preserved cheaply.*

Addition words: *first of all, another, third.*

B. The following passage uses a listing pattern. Complete the map of the passage by completing the main idea and filling in the missing major details.

> ¹Various theories explain the aging process. ²The most obvious is that our bodies simply wear out. ³Yet since many bodily systems are able to replace or repair their worn components (wounds heal, for example, and skin cells are constantly being generated), this version cannot be the whole story. ⁴A related theory is that as cells repeatedly divide, more and more contain genetic errors and stop working properly. ⁵A third theory holds that our body chemistry loses its delicate balance over the years. ⁶For example, our excretory system, after years of filtering pollutants from our bloodstream, becomes less efficient. ⁷The resulting change in our blood chemistry can produce a variety of other malfunctions. ⁸Finally, according to another theory, our bodies tend with age to reject some of their own tissues.

The phrase "various theories" (ending in **s**) and the addition words *third* and *finally* are clues to the main idea and major details.

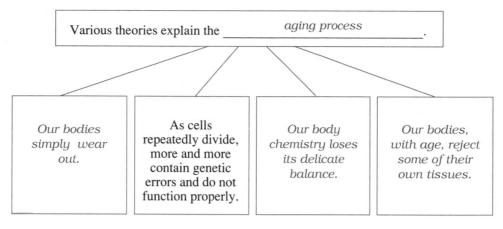

Various theories explain the _____ *aging process* _____.

| Our bodies simply wear out. | As cells repeatedly divide, more and more contain genetic errors and do not function properly. | Our body chemistry loses its delicate balance. | Our bodies, with age, reject some of their own tissues. |

Wording of answers may vary.

2 THE TIME ORDER PATTERN

To get a sense of the time order pattern, try to arrange the following sentences in a logical order. Put a *1* in front of the sentence that should come first, a *2* in front of the sentence that comes next, a *3* in front of the third sentence, and a *4* in front of the sentence that should come last. The result will be a short paragraph. Use the time words as a guide.

__2__ Before he was a teenager, he was charging admission to his home movies.

__1__ Famed director Steven Spielberg was born in Cincinnati, Ohio, in 1946.

__4__ After *Duel,* he went on to make *Jaws, Indiana Jones, E.T., Jurassic Park, Saving Private Ryan,* and many more.

__3__ His big break came in 1973 when he directed *Duel,* a made-for-television movie.

Authors usually present events in the order in which they happen, resulting in the time order pattern of organization. Clues to the order of the above sentences are time transitions (*before, when,* and *after*) and dates. The paragraph should read as follows:

> [1]Famed director Steven Spielberg was born in Cincinnati, Ohio, in 1946. [2]Before he was a teenager, he was charging admission to his home movies. [3]His big break came in 1973 when he directed *Duel,* a made-for-television movie. [4]After *Duel,* he went on to make *Jaws, Indiana Jones, E.T., Jurassic Park, Saving Private Ryan,* and many more.

As a student, you will see time order used frequently. Textbooks in all fields describe events and processes, such as the events leading to the Boston Tea Party, the important incidents in Abraham Lincoln's life, the steps involved for a bill to travel through Congress, the process involved in writing a paper, or the stages in the development of a cell.

In addition to the time transitions listed on page 176, signals for the time order pattern include dates, times, and such words as stages, series, steps, and process.

The two most common kinds of time order are 1) a series of events or stages and 2) a series of steps (directions in how to do something). Each is discussed below and on the following pages.

Series of Events or Stages

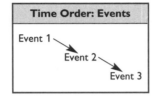

☑ *Check Your Understanding*

Following is a paragraph that is organized according to time order. Complete the outline of the paragraph by listing the missing stages in the order in which they happen.

To help you find the stages, do two things:

- Underline the words that introduce each stage;
- Number (1, 2, . . .) each stage.

[1]Children master language in predictable stages. [2]First, at about six months,[1] babies start to repeat simple sounds, such as "ma-ma-me-me." [3]About three or four months later,[2] they can repeat sounds that others make and carry on little conversations. [4]These interchanges are rich in emotional meaning, although the sounds themselves are meaningless. [5]At the next stage,[3] toddlers learn the meanings of many words, but they cannot yet talk. [6]A toddler might understand a sentence such as "Bring me your sock" but be unable to say any of the words. [7]Finally,[4] the child begins to talk in single words and in two-word sentences.

Main idea: Children master language in predictable stages.

1. *At about six months, babies begin to repeat simple sounds.*

   _____

2. Three or four months later, babies can repeat sounds and carry on little "conversations."

3. *Toddlers understand many words but cannot talk.*

   _____

4. *Finally, the child talks in single words and two-word sentences.*

   _____

Explanation:

You should have added these points to the outline:

1. At about six months, babies begin to repeat simple sounds. (The author signals this stage with the time transition *first* and the mention of age: "at about six months.")

3. Toddlers understand many words but cannot talk. (The author signals this stage with the time word *next:* "At the next stage. . . .")

4. Finally, the child talks in single words and two-word sentences. (The author signals this stage with the time word *finally*.)

As emphasized by the transitions used, the relationship between the points is one of time: The second stage happens *after* the first, and so on.

➤ Practice 4

The following passage describes a sequence of events. Outline the paragraph by filling in the main idea and major details. Note that the major details are signaled by time words and dates.

> **Hint:** Underline the time word or words that introduce each major detail, and number each major detail.

[1]The 1960s were a time of profound events in America. [2]The <u>first</u> thunderclap occurred in 1963, with[1] the bullets that assassinated President John Kennedy, depressing the spirit of the country. [3]<u>Then</u> in 1965,[2] urban riots moved the long-simmering issue of racial equality onto center stage. [4]A minor summer incident involving police in Watts, a black section of Los

Angeles, set off five days of looting and rioting that left thirty-four people dead. ⁵Over a hundred major urban riots, all centered in black ghettos in cities like Newark and Detroit, were to follow. ⁶The <u>next</u> profound explosion was³ a series of protests against the increasing American presence in Vietnam. ⁷The protests began in 1968 and spread across the country, centering on college campuses. ⁸Soon almost every major campus in the United States was torn by rallies, teach-ins, and riots.   *Wording of answers may vary.*

Main idea: *The 1960s were a time of profound events in America.*   .

1. *1963—assassination of President John Kennedy*

2. *1965—urban riots in black ghettos*

3. *1968—protests against increasing American presence in Vietnam*

The phrase "profound events" (note the **s** word) and the time transitions (*first, then, next*) signal the main idea and major details.

 **Practice 5**

The following passage describes a series of stages. Complete the map by writing the main idea in the top box and filling in the three major details (the stages).

The events below happen in a particular time order. The second stage must happen before the third stage can happen. Note the time words: first, second, third.

¹Many people pass through three stages in reacting to their unemployment. ²At first they experience shock followed by relief. ³In many cases they had anticipated that they were about to lose their jobs, so when the dismissal comes, they may feel a sense of relief that at last the suspense is over. ⁴On the whole they remain confident and hopeful that they will find a new job when they are ready. ⁵During this time, they maintain normal relationships with their family and friends. ⁶The first stage lasts for about a month or two. ⁷The second stage centers on a strong effort to find a new job. ⁸If workers have been upset or angry about losing their jobs, the feeling tends to evaporate as they marshal their resources and concentrate on finding a new job. ⁹This stage may last for up to four months. ¹⁰But if another job is not found during this time, people move into a third stage, one of self-doubt and anxiety, which lasts about six weeks. ¹¹They must struggle to maintain their self-esteem as they question their own personal power and worth.

Wording of answers may vary.

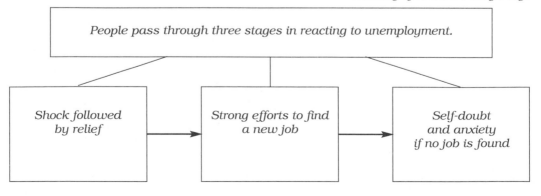

Series of Steps (Directions)

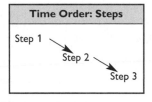

When authors give directions, they use time order. They explain step 1, then step 2, and so on through the entire steps of steps that must be taken toward a specific goal.

☑ Check Your Understanding

Below is a paragraph that gives directions. Complete the outline of the paragraph by listing the missing steps in the correct sequence. To help yourself identify each step, do two things:

- Underline the time words that introduce each item in the sequence;
- Number (1, 2, . . .) each step in the sequence.

      [1]Here is a six-step technique that will help you relax quickly. [2]First,[1] lie down with your arms at your sides and your fingers open. [3]When you are comfortable,[2] close your eyes and put all distracting thoughts out of your mind. [4]Next,[3] tighten all the muscles of your body at once. [5]Do this by pushing your toes together, tightening your buttocks and abdomen, clenching your fists, and squeezing your eyes shut. [6]Then,[4] let everything relax, and feel the tension flow out of your body. [7]After that,[5] take a deep breath through your mouth, hold it for twenty seconds, and then let it out slowly, breathing slowly and easily, as you do when you are sleeping. [8]Finally,[6] think of a pleasant scene as you feel your whole body becoming calm and relaxed.

Main idea: Here is a six-step technique that will help you relax quickly.

1. _Lie down, arms at your sides and fingers open._

2. _When you are comfortable, close your eyes and clear your mind._

3. Tighten all muscles at once.

4. _Let everything relax, and feel the tension flow out of your body._

5. _Take a deep breath, hold it, let it out, and breathe slowly and easily._

6. _Think of a pleasant scene as you feel yourself relax._

Explanation:

You should have added these steps to the outline:

1. Lie down, arms at your sides and fingers open. (The author signals this stage with the time word *first*.)

2. When you are comfortable, close your eyes and clear your mind. (The author signals this stage with the time word *when*.)

4. Let everything relax, and feel the tension flow out of your body. (The author signals this stage with the time word *then*.)

5. Take a deep breath through your mouth, hold it for twenty seconds, let it out, and breathe slowly and easily. (The author's signal is the time word *after*.)

6. Think of a pleasant scene as you feel yourself relax. (The author signals this last step with the time word *finally*.)

As indicated by the transitions used, the relationship between the steps is one of time: The second step happens *after* the first, and so on.

➤ Practice 6

The following passage gives directions involving several steps that must be done in order. Complete the map on the next page by writing the main idea in the top box and filling in the three missing steps. To help yourself identify each step, you may want to underline the time words.

> **Hint:** Underline the time words that introduce each step in the sequence and number each step.

[1]There are several steps to remembering your dreams. [2]To begin with, you must make up your mind to do so, for consciously deciding that you want to remember increases the likelihood that it will happen. [3]Then put a pen and a notebook near your bed, so that you can write down what you remember as soon as you wake up. [4]When possible, turn off your alarm before you go to sleep so that you can wake up gradually; this will increase the likelihood of remembering your dreams. [5]Finally, when you wake up in the morning and remember a dream, write it down immediately, even before getting out of bed.

The steps must occur in a particular order. Note the time words: *to begin with, then, when, finally.*

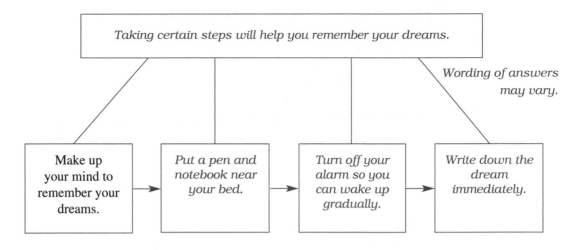

A Note on Main Ideas and Patterns of Organization

A paragraph's main idea often indicates its pattern of organization. For example, here's the main idea of the paragraph you just read: "There are several steps to remembering your dreams." The words *several steps* suggest that this paragraph will be organized according to time order. Another good example is the main idea of the earlier paragraph on aging: "Various theories explain the aging process." The words *various theories* suggest that this paragraph will be a list of items.

Paying close attention to the main idea, then, can give you a quick sense of a paragraph's pattern of organization. Try, for instance, to guess the pattern of the paragraph with this main idea:

While there are thousands of self-help groups, they all fall into three basic categories.

The phrase "three basic categories" is a strong indication that the paragraph will list those categories. The main idea helps us guess that the paragraph will be a list of three items.

➤ Practice 7

Most of the main ideas below have been taken from college textbooks. In the space provided, write the letter of the pattern of organization that each main idea suggests.

   _B_   1. The process of digestion can be divided into four stages.
            A. List of items   B. Time order

   _A_   2. A federal form of government has advantages and disadvantages.
            A. List of items   B. Time order

_A_   3. The stock market crash resulted from a number of basic weaknesses in the economy.
    A. List of items   B. Time order

_B_   4. Serious relationships in our lives often evolve gradually, going through several phases.
    A. List of items   B. Time order

_B_   5. Law enforcement officers are taught a series of steps to follow upon arriving at the scene of a violent crime.
    A. List of items   B. Time order

_A_   6. There are several search aids that can be of great help when you are looking for information online.
    A. List of items   B. Time order

_A_   7. Educational opportunities vary greatly in different regions of the United States.
    A. List of items   B. Time order

_B_   8. Treating the allergic patient often involves a three-stage process.
    A. List of items   B. Time order

_A_   9. Convenience products can be subdivided into four groups on the basis of how people buy them.
    A. List of items   B. Time order

_B_ 10. The worldwide fall of communism was marked by a series of dramatic events.
    A. List of items   B. Time order

Three Final Points

1 While many passages have just one pattern of organization, often the patterns are mixed. For example, you may find that part of a passage uses a list of items pattern, and another part of the same passage uses a time pattern.

2 You may have noted that when an author presents a series of events or stages or steps, that series is itself a list of items. For example, here's a time order passage:

> [1]To read and study a textbook more effectively, follow a few helpful steps. [2]**First**, preview the reading, taking a couple of minutes to get a quick sense of what the selection is about. [3]**Next**, read and mark the selection, using a highlighter pen to set off important points. [4]**Then**

write up a set of study notes that summarize the most important ideas in the selection. [5]**Last**, go over and over the ideas in your notes until you know the material.

The above passage is indeed made up of a list of items. But what makes it a time order passage is that the list of items appears not at random but in a *time sequence*. Realizing that there is a time sequence will help you achieve your study purpose, which is probably to take effective notes on the material.

3   Remember that not all relationships between ideas are signaled by transitions. An author may present a list of items, for example, without using addition words. So as you read, watch for the relationships themselves, not just the transitions.

CHAPTER REVIEW

In this chapter, you learned how authors use transitions and patterns of organization to make their ideas clear. Just as transitions show relationships between ideas in sentences, patterns of organization show relationships between supporting details in paragraphs and longer pieces of writing.

You also learned two common kinds of relationships that authors use to make their ideas clear:

- **Addition relationships**

  — Authors often present a list or series of reasons, examples, or other details that support an idea. The items have no time order, but are listed in whatever order the author prefers.

  — Transition words that signal such addition relationships include *for one thing, second, also, in addition,* and *finally*.

- **Time relationships**

  — Authors usually discuss a series of events or steps in the order in which they happen, resulting in a time order.

  — Transition words that signal such time relationships include *first, next, then, after,* and *last*.

The next chapter—Chapter 6—will help you learn three other important kinds of relationships: definition-example, comparison and/or contrast, and cause-effect.

On the Web: If you are using this book in class, you can visit our website for additional practice in understanding relationships that involve addition and time. Go to **www.townsendpress.com** and click on "Online Exercises."

➤ Review Test 1

To review what you've learned in this chapter, fill in the blanks in the following items.

1. Transitions are words that signal *(parts of, the relationships between, the importance of)* ____*the relationships between*____ ideas.

2. A(n) *(addition, time)* ____*addition*____ transition signals that the writer is adding to an idea or ideas already mentioned.

3. When a passage provides a series of directions or steps, or a series of events, it is likely to use *(addition, time)* ____*time*____ transitions.

4. __*T*__ TRUE OR FALSE? A main idea often suggests a paragraph's pattern of organization.

5. A passage's pattern of organization is the pattern in which its *(supporting details, main ideas, causes and effects)* ____*supporting details*____ are organized.

➤ Review Test 2

A. Fill in each blank with one of the words in the box. Use each word once. Then write the letter of the word in the space provided.

| A. then | B. second | C. also |
| D. one | E. before | F. final |

__*E*__ 1. Rubber tires were invented in 1845, ____*before*____ cars existed. At that time, the tires were meant for bicycles.

__*C*__ 2. The average square inch of human skin includes 19 million cells. It ____*also*____ includes 625 sweat glands and 60 hairs.

__*D*__ 3. There are two main kinds of fats: ____*one*____ is saturated fats; the other is unsaturated fats.

_A_   4. Read the paragraph carefully and _____*then*_____ answer the questions that follow.

_F_   5. First dig a hole and work peat moss into the soil. Then put the plant in and pile in enough dirt to refill the hole. The _____*final*_____ step is to water the plant liberally.

_B_   6. The first type of small business is often called the "mom-and-pop operation." The majority of small businesses fall into this category. The _____*second*_____ type is the high-growth enterprise. This type of business aims to outgrow its small-business status as quickly as possible.

B. Read the textbook paragraph below, and then answer the questions that follow.

> [1]The first professional baseball team, the Cincinnati Red Stockings, was founded in 1869. [2]After only a short time, there were teams in all the major Eastern and Midwestern cities. [3]The ballpark brought together crowds of strangers who could experience a sense of community within the big city as they watched a baseball game. [4]Immigrants were able to shake loose their ethnic ties and become absorbed in the new national game. [5]The green fields and fresh air of the ballpark were a welcome change from the sea of bricks and stone that dominated the city scene. [6]Workers could temporarily escape the routine of their daily lives. [7]They loved indirectly participating in the competition and accomplishment that baseball games symbolized. [8]The ballpark also provided a means for spectators to release their frustrations against authority figures. [9]The umpire became a symbol of scorn, and frequent cries of "kill the umpire" were heard.

_B_   7. The relationship of sentence 2 to the sentence before it is one of
   A. addition.   B. time.

       8. The key transition word in sentence 2 is _____*after*_____.

_A_   9. Sentences 3–9 present a
   A. list of benefits people found in attending baseball games.
   B. series of events in baseball's history.
   C. series of stages in the history of baseball.

      10. The relationship of sentence 8 to the sentences before it is signaled by the transition _____*also*_____.

➤ *Review Test 3*

A. Fill in each blank with the appropriate transition from the box. Use each transition once.

A. after	B. as	C. then
D. later	E. first	

> [1]In one of the most terrifying scenes in all of literature, George Orwell in his classic novel *1984* describes how a government known as Big Brother destroys a couple's love. [2]The couple, Winston and Julia, fall in love and meet secretly, knowing the government would not approve. [3](1) _____*After*_____ informers turn them in, a government agent named O'Brien takes steps to end their love. [4](2) _____*First*_____ he straps Winston down and explains that he has discovered Winston's worst fear. [5](3) _____*Then*_____ he sets a cage with two giant, starving sewer rats on the table next to Winston. [6]He says that when he presses a lever, the door of the cage will slide up, and the rats will shoot out like bullets and bore straight into Winston's face. [7](4) _____*As*_____ Winston's eyes dart back and forth, revealing his terror, O'Brien places his hand on the lever. [8]Winston realizes that the only way out is for Julia to take his place. [9]Suddenly, he hears his own voice screaming, "Do it to Julia! Not me! Julia!" [10]Orwell does not describe Julia's interrogation, but (5) _____*later*_____, when Julia and Winston see each other, they realize that each has betrayed the other. [11]Their love is gone. [12]Big Brother has won.

_____*B*_____ 6. The pattern of organization for the above selection is
      A. list of items.   B. time order.

This scene tells a story in time order, with time words.

B. Below are the beginnings of four passages. Label each one with the letter of its pattern of organization. (You may find it helpful to underline the transition or transitions in each item.)

     A   List of items
     B   Time order

_____*B*_____ 7. [1]The process of labor during childbirth takes place in three overlapping phases. [2]The first stage is the longest, lasting an average twelve to twenty-four hours for a woman having her first child. [3]The second stage typically lasts about one and a half hours. . . .

_____*A*_____ 8. [1]There are various ways to combat fatigue. [2]One excellent way is exercise—walking, running, or lifting weights several times a week. [3]Another useful strategy is to take a daily nap of twenty minutes or less, preferably around mid-afternoon, a low-energy period for many people. . . .

___B___ 9. ¹Even before he meets the three witches, Macbeth dreams of becoming king of Scotland. ²Then the witches predict he will be king, intensifying his ambition. ³Finally, his wife persuades him to murder King Duncan and take over the country. . . .

___A___ 10. ¹Today's cell phones offer many convenient features. ²Voice mail allows you to leave and receive messages, taking the place of old-fashioned answering machines. ³Another convenient feature is automatic dialing, which allows you to make a call by pressing just one or two buttons. . . .

➤ Review Test 4

Here is a chance to apply your understanding of addition and time relationships to a full-length reading—an article about stress in college. To help you continue to strengthen your skills, the reading is followed by questions not only on what you've learned in this chapter but also on what you've learned in previous chapters.

Words to Watch

Below are some words in the reading that do not have strong context support. Each word is followed by the number of the paragraph in which it appears and its meaning there. These words are indicated in the article by a small circle (°).

aptitude (4): natural ability
anorexia (6): an abnormal lack of appetite which can result in serious
         illness or death
bulimia (6): an abnormal craving for food that leads to heavy eating and
         then intentional vomiting
stability (9): steadiness
bombarded (9): attacked
devastating (9): very destructive
magnitude (11): great importance
meditation (13): a relaxation technique involving mental concentration
relevant (14): related to the issue at hand

STUDENTS IN SHOCK

John Kellmayer

1   If you feel overwhelmed by your college experiences, you are not alone—many of today's college students are suffering from a form of shock. Going to college has always had its ups and downs, but today the "downs" of the college experience are more numerous and difficult, a fact that the schools are responding to with increased support services.

2   Lisa is a good example of a student in shock. She is an attractive, intelligent twenty-year-old college junior at a state university. Having been a straight-A student in high school and a member of the basketball and softball teams there, she remembers her high school days with fondness. Lisa was popular then and had a steady boyfriend for the last two years of school.

3   Now, only three years later, Lisa is miserable. She has changed her major four times already and is forced to hold down two part-time jobs in order to pay her tuition. She suffers from sleeping and eating disorders and believes she has no close friends. Sometimes she bursts out crying for no apparent reason. On more than one occasion, she has considered taking her own life.

4   Dan, too, suffers from student shock. He is nineteen and a freshman at a local community college. He began college as an accounting major but hated that field. So he switched to computer programming because he heard the job prospects were excellent in that area. Unfortunately, he discovered that he had little aptitude° for programming and changed majors again, this time to psychology. He likes psychology but has heard horror stories about the difficulty of finding a job in that field without a graduate degree. Now he's considering switching majors again. To help pay for school, Dan works nights and weekends as a sales clerk at K-Mart. He doesn't get along with his boss, but since he needs the money, Dan feels he has no choice except to stay on the job. A few months ago, his girlfriend of a year and a half broke up with him.

5   Not surprisingly, Dan has started to suffer from depression and migraine headaches. He believes that in spite of all his hard work, he just isn't getting anywhere. He can't remember ever being this unhappy. A few times he considered talking to somebody in the college psychological counseling center. He rejected that idea, though, because he doesn't want people to think there's something wrong with him.

6   What is happening to Lisa and Dan happens to millions of college students each year. That means roughly one-quarter of the student population at any time will suffer from symptoms of student shock. Of that group, almost half will experience depression intense enough to warrant professional help. At schools across the country, psychological counselors are booked up months in advance. Stress-related problems such as anxiety, migraine headaches, insomnia, anorexia°, and bulimia° are epidemic on college campuses.

7   Suicide rates and self-inflicted injuries among college students are higher now than at any other time in history. The suicide rate among college youth is 50 percent higher than among nonstudents of the same age. It is estimated that each year more than 500 college students take their own lives.

8   College health officials believe that these reported problems represent only the tip of the iceberg. They fear that most students, like Lisa and Dan, suffer in silence.

9   There are three reasons today's college students are suffering more than those in earlier generations. First is a weakening family support structure. The transition from high school to college has always been difficult, but in the past there was more family support to help students get through it. Today, with

divorce rates at a historical high and many parents experiencing their own psychological difficulties, the traditional family is not always available for guidance and support. And when students who do not find stability° at home are bombarded° with numerous new and stressful experiences, the results can be devastating°.

10   Another problem college students face is financial pressure. In the last decade tuition costs have skyrocketed—up about 66 percent at public colleges and 90 percent at private schools. For students living away from home, costs range from eight thousand dollars to as much as twenty thousand a year and more. And at the same time that tuition costs have been rising dramatically, there has been a cutback in federal aid to students. College loans are now much harder to obtain and are available only at near-market interest rates. Consequently, most college students must work at least part-time. And for some students, the pressure to do well in school while holding down a job is too much to handle.

11   A final cause of student shock is the large selection of majors available. Because of the magnitude° and difficulty of choosing a major, college can prove a time of great indecision. Many students switch majors, some a number of times. As a result, it is becoming commonplace to take five or six years to get a degree. It can be depressing to students not only to have taken courses that don't count toward a degree but also to be faced with the added tuition costs. In some cases these costs become so high that they force students to drop out of college.

12   While there is no magic cure-all for student shock, colleges have begun to recognize the problem and are trying in a number of ways to help students cope with the pressures they face. For one thing, many colleges are upgrading their psychological counseling centers to handle the greater demand for services. Additional staff is being hired, and experts are doing research to learn more about the psychological problems of college students. Some schools even advertise these services in student newspapers and on campus radio stations. Also, juniors and seniors are being trained as peer counselors. These peer counselors may be able to act as a first line of defense in the battle for students' well-being by spotting and helping to solve problems before they become too big for students to handle.

13   In addition, stress-management workshops have become common on college campuses. At these workshops, instructors teach students various techniques they can use to deal with stress, including biofeedback, meditation°, and exercise.

14   Finally, many schools are improving their vocational counseling services. By giving students more relevant° information about possible majors and career choices, colleges can lessen the anxiety and indecision often associated with choosing a major.

15   If you ever feel that you're "in shock," remember that your experience is not unique. Try to put things in perspective. Certainly, the end of a romance or failing an exam is not an event to look forward to. But realize that rejection and failure happen to everyone sooner or later. And don't be reluctant to talk to somebody about your problems. The useful services available on campus won't help you if you don't take advantage of them.

Reading Comprehension Questions

Vocabulary in Context

   B   1. In the sentence below, the word *prospects* (prŏs′pĕkts′) means
   - A. failures.
   - B. possibilities.
   - C. candidates.
   - D. limitations.

> "So he switched to computer programming because he heard the job prospects were excellent in that area." (Paragraph 4)

   D   2. In the excerpt below, the word *warrant* (wôr′ənt) means
   - A. fight.
   - B. have no need for.
   - C. get degrees in.
   - D. justify.

> "Of that group, almost half will experience depressions intense enough to warrant professional help. At schools across the country, psychological counselors are booked up months in advance." (Paragraph 6)

Central Point and Main Ideas

   B   3. Which sentence best expresses the central point of the selection?
   - A. Going to college is a depressing experience for many students.
   - B. College life has become more stressful, so schools are increasing support services.
   - C. Lisa and Dan have experienced too much stress at school to enjoy college life.
   - D. Colleges should increase their counseling services.

   A   4. At times, a main idea may cover more than one paragraph. The main idea of paragraphs 2 and 3 is stated in the
   - A. first sentence of paragraph 2.
   - B. second sentence of paragraph 2.
   - C. first sentence of paragraph 3.
   - D. last sentence of paragraph 3.

Comments: Item 3 — The central point is stated in paragraph 1. Paragraphs 2–11 contain examples of symptoms of and reasons for increased numbers of students in shock. Paragraphs 12–14 present ways schools are trying to help students in shock.

Item 4 — Paragraphs 2 and 3 provide details about why Lisa is a student in shock.

_A_ 5. The main idea of paragraphs 9, 10, and 11 is
      A. stated in the first sentence of paragraph 9.   See item 7 below.
      B. stated in the first sentence of paragraph 10.
      C. stated in the first sentence of paragraph 11.
      D. unstated.

Supporting Details

_C_ 6. According to the author, the large selection of majors now available
      A. makes for less stability in students' home lives.   See paragraph 11.
      B. helps students get through school more quickly.
      C. makes many students' career choices more difficult.
      D. allows students to end up in careers for which they are especially well suited.

Transitions

7. The first sentence of paragraph 9 states, "There are three reasons today's college students are suffering more than those in earlier generations." The reasons are then introduced in paragraphs 9, 10, and 11 by what three transitions?

    Transition introducing first reason for student shock: _____*first*_____

    Transition introducing the second reason for student shock: _*another*_

    Transition introducing the third reason for student shock: _*final*_

_A_ 8. The transitions that introduce the major details of paragraphs 9, 10, and 11 signal
      A. addition.
      B. time.

9. The major details of paragraphs 12–14 are introduced with the transitions *for one thing, also, in addition,* and _____*finally*_____.

Patterns of Organization

_B_ 10. Paragraphs 12–14
      A. describe a series of school events in their order in time.
      B. list ways to help students cope.

Discussion Questions

1. If you were a peer counselor for Lisa or Dan, what advice might you give her or him?

2. What were—or are—the most stressful parts of college life for you? Explain why. What ways have you found for dealing with that stress?

3. Kellmayer writes that "colleges . . . are trying in a number of ways to help students cope with the pressures they face." What resources does your college offer? Have you tried any? How do you think your school could improve the services it offers to help students deal with "student shock"?

4. On the basis of your college experience so far, what one piece of advice would you give to an incoming freshman?

Note: Writing assignments for this selection appear on pages 587–588.

Check Your Performance			RELATIONSHIPS I
Activity	*Number Right*	*Points*	*Score*
Review Test 1 (5 items)	_____	× 2 =	_____
Review Test 2 (10 items)	_____	× 3 =	_____
Review Test 3 (10 items)	_____	× 3 =	_____
Review Test 4 (10 items)	_____	× 3 =	_____
		TOTAL SCORE =	_____ %

Enter your total score into the **Reading Performance Chart: Review Tests** on the inside back cover.

RELATIONSHIPS I: Mastery Test 1

A. Fill in each blank with an appropriate transition from the box. Use each transition once. Then, in the spaces provided, write the letter of the transition you have chosen.

A. another	B. then	C. also
D. next	E. when	

> *Hint:* Make sure that each word or phrase that you choose fits smoothly into the flow of the sentence. Test your choices by reading each sentence to yourself.

_A_ 1. ¹I have a limited interest in people whose main topic of conversation is themselves and who never show any interest in what is happening to me. ²_____Another_____ group I avoid is people who never allow facts to interfere with their opinions.

_E_ 2. ¹To train a puppy, first buy some small dog biscuits or other small dog treats. ²Then teach the puppy one short command, such as "Sit!"—speaking the word loudly and firmly until he or she obeys. ³_____When_____ you get a correct response, give the dog a treat and praise him or her loudly.

_C_ 3. ¹The world of business is one area in which technology has isolated us. ²Many people now work alone at a display terminal that connects to a large central computer. ³Personal banking has _____also_____ become a detached process. ⁴To deposit or withdraw money from their accounts, customers often interact with machines rather than people.

_B_ 4. ¹For much of my life, I have been haunted by dreams of falling. ²In a typical dream, I have fallen off a tall building or over the edge of a cliff or out of a plane, and I am plunging at a breathtaking speed toward the ground. ³_____Then_____, just as I am about to crash into the ground, I wake up in a cold sweat, my heart racing.

_D_ 5. ¹Many television ads proceed in three stages: the problem, the advice, and the resolution. ²For example, a mouthwash commercial will first establish the problem—that someone has bad breath. ³_____Next_____ it will suggest that the person try the advertised mouthwash. ⁴This is followed by an obvious resolution of the problem: the person's being chased by attractive members of the opposite sex.

Comment: Remind students that sentence structure and punctuation are useful in placing the transition words.

(Continues on next page)

B. (6–9.) Fill in each blank with an appropriate transition word from the box. Use each transition once.

A. then	B. next	C. after
D. last		

¹Two Minnesota brothers, Ed and Norman, are engaged in a war. ²It all started (6)_____*after*_____ Ed's wife gave him a pair of pants that didn't fit. ³Ed wrapped up the pants and put them under Norman's Christmas tree. ⁴As soon as Norman opened the box, he recognized the unwanted pants. ⁵The (7)_____*next*_____ year, he gave them back to Ed, sealed in a heavy carton tied with knotted ropes. ⁶The War of the Pants was on. ⁷Each year, on one of the brothers' birthdays, or on Christmas, the dreaded pants reappear. ⁸Two years ago, Norman bought an old safe, put the pants in it, welded it shut, and delivered it to Ed's house. ⁹Somehow, Ed retrieved the pants. ¹⁰(One of the rules of the war is that the pants must not be damaged.) ¹¹(8)_____*Last*_____ year Ed took the pants to an auto junkyard. ¹²The pants were placed in an ancient Ford's backseat, and the car (9)_____*then*_____ went through the auto crusher. ¹³On his birthday, Norman found a four-foot square of smashed metal on his doorstep. ¹⁴He knew it could only be Ed's doing and the pants must be inside. ¹⁵Norman is still trying to get at the pants and prepare next year's "topper."

___*B*___ 10. The pattern of organization of the above selection is
      A. list of items.
      B. time order.

The story of the War of the Pants is told from its beginning to the present time.

RELATIONSHIPS I: Mastery Test 2

A. Fill in each blank with an appropriate transition from the box. Use each transition once. Then, in the spaces provided, write the letter of the transition you have chosen.

A. when	B. moreover	C. before
D. first	E. also	

___A___ 1. ¹Big snapping turtles don't get to weigh so much without eating a lot of food. ²Here's how they do it: ³Most snapping turtles float, or lie motionless on the bottom of a pond or river. ⁴___When___ a fish, frog, or other prey swims close enough, the turtle snaps very fast with powerful jaws.

___D___ 2. ¹Experts cite several reasons for Japan's low crime rate. ²___First___, Japan has had strict gun control for four hundred years. ³In addition, the country relies on some fifteen thousand small neighborhood police stations known as *koban*. ⁴Police officers and their families actually live as part of the neighborhood, helping prevent the growth of conditions that might lead to crime.

___B___ 3. ¹By today's standards, early automobiles were difficult to operate and uncomfortable to drive. ²A driver had to start the car's engine by cranking it by hand, and the crank sometimes sprang back and broke the driver's thumb. ³___Moreover___, early cars were open on top, so driving on unpaved roads left riders choking on dust and dirt.

___C___ 4. ¹After resting for 1,500 years, Italy's Mount Vesuvius woke up to do enormous damage. ²The volcano erupted in the early afternoon of August 24, A.D. 79, and the residents of Pompeii, four miles away, were able to see and hear the explosion, which sent a huge black cloud into the sky. ³___Before___ a day had passed, Pompeii and its inhabitants were buried under thirty to fifty feet of stones and ash.

___E___ 5. ¹Whoever you are, whatever you look like, chances are you're not happy with your appearance. ²Our culture constantly sends out the message that you're not attractive enough. ³Television is one of the most powerful message-carriers, showing you an endless parade of impossibly thin, beautiful people. ⁴Magazines are ___also___ designed to make you feel ugly, with glossy airbrushed models on every page providing an impossible ideal of thin, ageless beauty.

(Continues on next page)

B. Read the passage and answer the question that follows.

[1]Probably every child remembers digging a hole in his or her back yard and being told, "If you dig deep enough, you'll go to China." [2]What would really happen if a man dug a hole through the center of the Earth and then jumped into it? [3]The traveler entering the tunnel would first fall rapidly under the force of gravity. [4]Eventually, as he approached the Earth's center, the jumper's weight would decrease. [5]By the time he reached the center of the Earth, he would be weightless. [6]An equal amount of the Earth's mass on all sides of him would cancel out the forces of gravity. [7]Still, the traveler's original momentum would carry him past the center toward the opening on the far side of the world. [8]After almost reaching that point, he would fall back up the hole toward his starting point. [9]Back and forth he would then go, like a yo-yo, gradually slowing down until coming to a stop at the very center of the Earth.

_B_   6. The main pattern of organization of the passage is
   A. list of items.
   B. time order.

> This passage is a sequence of events as they would occur.

C. (7–10.) Fill in each blank with an appropriate transition word from the box. Use each transition once. Then answer the question that follows.

A. also	B. finally	C. first

[1]The microbes that cause infection are transmitted to people in several ways. [2](7)_____First_____, there is direct transmission, which involves bodily contact with an infected person. [3]Examples are passing along a cold through handshaking or herpes through sexual relations. [4]There is (8)_____also_____ indirect transmission, which occurs when microbes are passed from an infected person to an individual via airborne particles, water, food, or anything else the infected person touches. [5]For example, someone might catch the flu by drinking from a glass that has been used by a person with the flu. [6](9)_____Finally_____, animals and insects can transmit microbes. [7]Flies, for instance, carry harmful microbes on their feet, and can transmit them to people by landing on their food.

_A_ 10. The pattern of organization of the above selection is
   A. list of items.
   B. time order.

> The phrase "several ways" suggests a list pattern.

RELATIONSHIPS I: Mastery Test 3

A. (1–5.) Arrange the scrambled sentences below into a logical paragraph by numbering them *1, 2, 3,* and *4* in an order that makes sense. Then, in the space provided, write the letter of the pattern of organization used.

     Note that transitions will help you by clarifying the relationships between sentences.

  3 In addition, check the puppy's personality by watching how it plays with other puppies.

  1 There are some important points to keep in mind when choosing a puppy.

  4 Last, since curiosity is a sign of intelligence, clap your hands to see if the puppy is curious and interested.

  2 For one thing, look for signs of good health, including clear, bright eyes and firm, pink gums.

  A 5. The pattern of organization of the above selection is
   A. list of items.
   B. time order.

B. Read the passage and answer the question that follows. You may find it helpful to underline transitions as you read.

[1]In January of 1954, Ernest and Mary Hemingway left Nairobi on a vacation trip on which they flew over grazing elephants, hippos bathing in the lakes, and huge flocks of feeding flamingos. [2]As they were circling a spectacular waterfall, a flock of ibises flew in front of the plane. [3]When the pilot dived to avoid the birds, he struck an abandoned telegraph wire that crossed the gorge. [4]In the crash that followed, Ernest sprained his shoulder; Mary was only slightly injured. [5]Luckily, a boat came down the river the next morning, and its crew rescued them. [6]By that evening, they were on board a small plane bound for Entebbe. [7]The plane lifted from the plowed field that served as a runway, then crashed and burst into flames. [8]Ernest escaped by breaking through a window with his head and injured shoulder, and Mary got out through another window. [9]Twice in two days they had crashed and come out alive, but Ernest had injured his head, his backbone, and a kidney. [10]After this, even writing a letter was difficult for him.

  B 6. The pattern of organization of the above selection is
   A. list of items.
   B. time order.   This paragraph tells what happened in the order that the events happened.

(Continues on next page)

C. (7–10.) Read the textbook passage below, and then answer the question and complete the outline.

> ¹Prevention against injury involves a combination of two types of preventive measures. ²First is active prevention, which refers to methods that require people to do something to reduce the risk of being injured. ³Examples include the use of nonautomatic seat belts, the use of bicycle and motorcycle helmets, following drunk driving laws, and obeying gun laws. ⁴The second type of preventive measure is passive prevention. ⁵Passive prevention refers to methods requiring little or no action on the part of those being protected. ⁶These measures include seat belts that automatically engage when a person enters a car, automobile air bags, better street lighting, and built-in safety switches on power tools and electrical equipment.

___A___ 7. The pattern of organization of the above selection is
   A. list of items.
   B. time order.   *Wording of answers may vary.*

8–10. Complete the outline of the passage.

Main idea: _Prevention against injury involves a combination of two_
types of preventive measures.

Major supporting details:
1. _Active prevention—methods that require people to do something_
   to reduce the risk of injury

   Example—use of nonautomatic seat belts; bike helmets.
2. _Passive prevention—methods requiring little or no action on the part_
   of those being protected

   Example—automatic seat belts; air bags.

The phrase "two types" suggests a list pattern. Note the addition transitions *first* and *second*.

RELATIONSHIPS I: Mastery Test 4

A. (1–4.) Arrange the scrambled sentences below into a logical paragraph by numbering them *1, 2, 3,* and *4* in an order that makes sense. Then, in the space provided, write the letter of the pattern of organization used.

Note that transitions will help you by clarifying the relationships between sentences.

_4_ When you have chosen your apartment, have a lawyer or another person knowledgeable about leases examine your lease before you sign it.

_1_ If you're looking for an apartment, begin by making a list of promising openings. Check the classified ads and two or three real estate offices for apartments within your price range and desired locale.

_3_ As you inspect each apartment, make sure that faucets, toilets, stoves, and electrical wiring and outlets are functioning efficiently and safely.

_2_ After you have made a solid list, visit at least five of the most promising available apartments.

___B___ 5. The pattern of organization of the above selection is
    A. list of items.
    B. time order.

B. Read the textbook passage below and answer the question that follows.

¹Did you ever wonder how trainers get porpoises to do all those tricks, like leaping over a high bar or jumping through a hoop? ²Wild porpoises are first taught to eat fish from their trainer's hand. ³When the animal accepts a fish, the trainer blows a whistle. ⁴The porpoise associates the whistle with "correct" behavior. ⁵Once the porpoise touches a human hand to get a fish, it will touch other things, like a red target ball. ⁶For example, the trainer will hold the ball high above the water while leaning over a kind of pulpit. ⁷Seeing the ball, the porpoise leaps out of the water; it knows it will be rewarded with a fish. ⁸A hoop can then be substituted for a ball, and the porpoise's behavior can be "shaped" so it will jump through the hoop. ⁹If the porpoise misses by jumping too low, the fish reward is withheld. ¹⁰The intelligent mammal will associate "no fish" with "wrong" behavior; very quickly, the porpoise will be leaping gracefully through the center of the hoop.

This passage presents a logical sequence of steps that must be followed to teach porpoises to do tricks. Note the time words: *first, when, then.*

___B___ 6. The pattern of organization of the above selection is
    A. list of items.
    B. time order.

(Continues on next page)

C. (7–10.) Complete the map of the following textbook passage.

¹Work shapes human lives in fundamental ways. ²First, work consumes enormous amounts of people's time. ³Most people spend about one-third of their adult lives working. ⁴According to a recent survey, almost half of all employed people spend 40 hours or more per week at work; only 10 percent work less than 30 hours a week. ⁵Work also gives life a structure and rhythm. ⁶The traditional eight-hour "shift" allows people to balance their days with productive time and recreational time. ⁷This daily pattern promotes mental health. ⁸In fact, many studies show that when people are unable to work, they experience emotional distress and low self-esteem. ⁹A third way work shapes life is that it causes stress. ¹⁰For some this stress can be positive—resulting in increased performance and professional success. ¹¹For others, however, the stress can be extreme and lead to health problems and illness.

Wording of answers may vary.

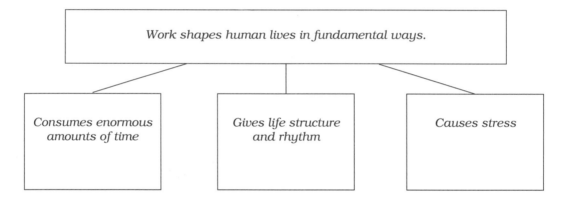

The phrase "fundamental ways" suggests a list pattern.
Note the list words: *first, also, third.*

RELATIONSHIPS I: Mastery Test 5

Read each textbook passage and answer the questions or follow the directions provided.

A. [1]Many couples go through a predictable sequence of events moving toward greater commitment. [2]Events that usually occur early in the development of a relationship include spending a whole day together and calling the partner by an affectionate name. [3]At a later stage, partners start referring to each other as "boyfriend" and "girlfriend," and receive invitations to do things together as a couple. [4]Eventually, the couple may begin to say "I love you" and to date each other exclusively. [5]Common next steps are taking a vacation together and discussing living together and marriage. [6]Events indicating great progress toward commitment include living together or becoming engaged.

_____B_____ 1. The pattern of organization of the above selection is
  A. list of items.
  B. time order.

Note the time words: early, later, eventually, next.

2. A transition that introduces one of the major details of the paragraph is
  Any of the following: early, later, eventually, next
  _____.

B. [1]Many food products are stamped with dates that tell consumers when the product is still fresh. [2]Products are dated in one of three ways. [3]Some food products contain the date following the words "sell by." [4]These foods remain fresh for about one week after the date on the label. [5]Other foods list the date after the words "best if used by." [6]Products with this label can still be used for a few weeks after the date on the label, but they might not have the same quality. [7]_____, certain products, such as baby formulas, have an expiration date. [8]These products should not be used after the date on the label.

The phrase "three ways" suggests a list pattern.

_____A_____ 3. The paragraph
  A. lists ways in which food products are dated.
  B. describes stages in dating food products.

_____C_____ 4. The transition that would best fit the blank space is
  A. *After.*
  B. *Eventually.*
  C. *Third.*

(Continues on next page)

C. [1]Dr. Elisabeth Kübler-Ross has identified five stages in the reactions of dying patients. [2]The first stage, she says, is denial. [3]Patients will at first deny the seriousness of their illness, claiming that some error has been made. [4]Then patients become angry. [5]They ask, "Why me?" [6]Their anger may be directed against God, fate, or even their doctors. [7]Next comes depression. [8]During this stage, patients feel hopeless and lose interest in life. [9]After depression comes bargaining—patients try to bargain for their lives. [10]They may promise God or their doctors that they'll be good, stop smoking, give up alcohol, or do whatever is necessary if only they can survive. [11]The fifth stage is that of acceptance. [12]Patients finally resign themselves to the inevitable. [13]They are not joyful, but they gain a sense of inner peace. [14]While there has been some criticism of Kübler-Ross's stages, her work has contributed much to making death a more comfortable and better-understood subject.

_B_ 5. The pattern of organization of the above selection is
A. list of items.
B. time order.

6–10. Complete the map of the paragraph.

The phrase "five stages" clearly suggests a time pattern. Note the time words marking each stage: *first, then, next, after,* and *fifth.*

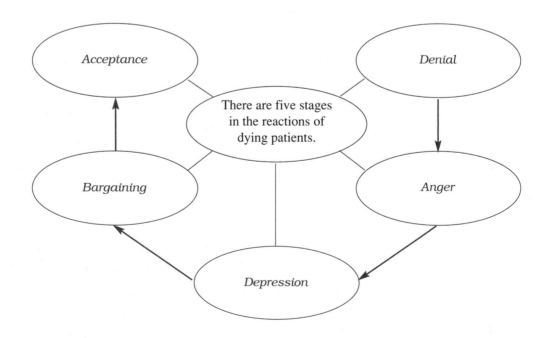

RELATIONSHIPS I: Mastery Test 6

Read each textbook passage and answer the questions or follow the directions provided.

A. [1]According to the National Institute on Drug Abuse, thirty million Americans—one out of eight people—suffer from a drug or alcohol dependency. [2]The development of an addiction typically unfolds in four stages. [3]First, some stimulus—drugs, alcohol, sex, chocolate—holds out the promise of short-lived pleasure or excitement. [4]Next, a person discovers that indulging in one of these activities temporarily satisfies some psychological need, making him or her feel good, if only for a short time. [5]Third, certain recurring situations start to trigger the addictive behavior, and the pattern repeats itself. [6]Finally, the habit takes control, and the individual loses self-control. [7]Often, by this stage a physical dependency will have been added to a psychological one, thereby making the addictive behavior pattern even more difficult to break.

____B____ 1. The pattern of organization of the above selection is
   A. list of items.
   B. time order.

> The phrase "four stages" suggests a time pattern.

   2–3. Two of the transitions that introduce the major details of the paragraph are

   _____   _____
   Any two of the following: first, next, third, finally

B. [1]After World War II began, women's roles changed. [2]The most visible change was the sudden appearance of large numbers of women in uniform. [3]The military organized them into auxiliary units with special uniforms, their own officers, and, amazingly, equal pay. [4]Most either filled traditional women's roles, such as nursing, or replaced men in noncombat situations.
     [5]Women also substituted for men on the home front. [6]During the war 6.3 million women entered the labor force, and for the first time in history married working women outnumbered single working women. [7]The war challenged the public's image of proper female behavior, as "Rosie the Riveter" became the popular symbol of women who abandoned traditional jobs as domestic servants and store clerks to work in construction and heavy industry.

____A____ 4. The pattern of organization of the above selection is
   A. list of items.
   B. time order.

   5. The second major detail is signaled with the transition _____*also*_____.

____A____ 6. The total number of major details is
   A. two.
   B. three.
   C. four.

(Continues on next page)

209

C.   ¹There are three main ways that children learn their gender roles. ²One is conditioning through rewards and punishments. ³For example, boys who play with model airplanes and girls who play with dolls will usually be encouraged by their parents. ⁴On the other hand, boys who prefer dolls and girls who prefer airplanes will often be criticized or even punished. ⁵Another element is imitation. ⁶Young children will usually imitate adults who they think are like themselves. ⁷This means that boys will usually imitate their fathers and girls their mothers. ⁸The third and perhaps most important element is self-definition. ⁹Children quickly learn that all people are either male or female and define themselves as belonging to one sex rather than the other. ¹⁰They then use this self-definition to choose their future interests and to develop their personalities and social roles.

_A_   7. The pattern of organization of the above selection is
   A. list of items.   The phrase "three main ways"
   B. time order.   suggests a list pattern. Note the
                                              list words: *one, another, third.*
8–10. Complete the outline of the paragraph.

   Main idea: _Children learn their gender roles in three main ways._

   Major supporting details:

   1. Conditioning through rewards and punishments
   2. _Imitation_
   3. _Self-definition_

                                    Wording of answers may vary.

6

Relationships II

In the previous chapter, you learned how authors use transitions and patterns of organization to show relationships and make their ideas clear. You also learned about two common types of relationships:

- Relationships that involve **addition**
- Relationships that involve **time**

In this chapter you will learn about three other types of relationships:

- Relationships that involve **illustration**
- Relationships that involve **comparison and contrast**
- Relationships that involve **cause and effect**

1 ILLUSTRATION

Words That Show Illustration

Put a check (✓) beside the item that is easier to understand:

_____ I've become very absent-minded. Last week I went to work on my day off.

_✓_ I've become very absent-minded. Last week, for instance, I went to work on my day off.

The second item is easier to understand. The words *for instance* make it clear that what happened on that day off is just one example of the absent-mindedness. *For instance* and other words and phrases like it are illustration words.

Illustration words indicate that an author will provide one or more *examples* to develop and clarify a given idea. Here are some common words that introduce examples:

Illustration Words

(for) example	(for) instance	illustration
including	such as	once

Examples:

The following items contain illustration words. Notice how these words signal that one or more *examples* are coming.

Certain colors are associated with particular emotions. *For instance,* green represents jealousy, red stands for anger, and blue means "gloomy."

My grandmother doesn't hear well anymore. *For example,* whenever I say, "Hi, Granny," she answers, "Fine, just fine."

A cat's curiosity can get it into ridiculous situations. *Once,* a neighbor's cat got its head stuck in the garbage disposal.

➤ Practice 1

Complete each item with a suitable illustration word or phrase from the above box. Try to use a variety of transitions.

> **Hint:** Make sure that each word or phrase that you choose fits smoothly into the flow of the sentence. Test each choice by reading the sentence aloud. (Be sure to use this hint when doing Practices 3, 4, and 6.)

Answers may vary.

1. Animals were once tried for crimes. ____*For instance*____, in 1740 a cow convicted of witchcraft was hanged by the neck until dead.

2. Some soap opera fans take the shows too seriously. There are viewers, ____*for example*____, who actually send threats to soap opera "villains."

3. My mother believes in various superstitions, ____*such as*____ the idea that if you drop a fork, it means company's coming.

4. When a couple divorces, the partners often experience a wide range of emotions, ____*including*____ anger, regret, depression, and relief.

5. People have chosen to end their lives in a variety of unusual ways. As an ____*illustration*____, in ancient China, people committed suicide by eating a pound of salt.

Illustration words are common in all types of writing. In textbooks, they are often used in paragraphs organized in the definition and example pattern.

The Definition and Example Pattern

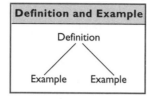

To get a sense of the definition and example pattern, try to arrange the following sentences in an order that makes sense. Put a *1* in front of the sentence that should come first, a *2* in front of the sentence that comes next, and a *3* in front of the sentence that should be last. The result will be a short paragraph.

   _2_   Someone might, for instance, sit calmly through a friend's criticism and act as if it didn't bother him or her.

   _1_   Apathy is an avoidance response in which a person acknowledges unpleasant information but pretends he or she does not care about it.

   _3_   Another example is responding to the loss of a job by acting indifferent: "Who cares? It was a dumb job anyhow."

This paragraph begins with a definition: "Apathy is an avoidance response in which a person acknowledges unpleasant information but pretends he or she does not care about it." The second sentence makes clear this special meaning of apathy with an example: "Someone might, for instance, sit calmly through a friend's criticism and act as if it didn't bother him or her." The third sentence then provides an added example: "Another example is responding to the loss of a job by acting indifferent: 'Who cares? It was a dumb job anyhow.'" The second and third sentences include the illustration words *for instance* and *example*. As you can see, the definition and example pattern of organization includes just what its name suggests: a definition and one or more examples.

An Important Study Hint: Good textbook authors want to help readers understand the important ideas and terms in a subject— whether it is psychology, sociology, business, biology, or any other field. Such authors often take time, then, to include key definitions. These definitions are usually set off in *italic* or **boldface** print, and they are signaled by such words as *is, are, is called, termed*, and *refers to*. Here are some definitions from a variety of textbooks:

* An **instinct** is a form of behavior that occurs in all normal members of a species without having been learned.

- **Phobias** are fears that are out of proportion to the actual danger involved in a situation.

- **Divergent thinking** refers to the ability to generate unusual, yet nonetheless appropriate, responses to problems or questions.

- Once a tumor has been detected, cells can be removed from it in a procedure called a **biopsy**; the cells are then examined under the microscope by a pathologist.

- Party funding, along with the money a candidate receives from individual contributors and interest groups, is termed **hard money** since it goes directly to the candidate and can be spent as he or she chooses.

Comment: Sometimes a dash is used to signal a definition.

- Both rapidly growing countries and slowly growing countries can have a problem with their **dependency ratio**—the number of nonworking compared to working individuals in a population.

If an author defines a term, you can assume that it is important enough to learn. So when reading and taking notes on a textbook, always do two things:

1) Write down key definitions.

2) Write down helpful examples of definitions. When definitions are general and abstract, examples are often essential to help make an idea clear.

☑ Check Your Understanding

The following paragraph defines a word, explains it a bit, and then gives an example of it. After reading the paragraph, see if you can answer the questions that follow.

[1]Acrophobia is an intense, unreasonable fear of high places. [2]People with acrophobia exhibit emotional and physical symptoms in response to being at great heights. [3]For instance, one sufferer of extreme acrophobia, Sally Maxwell, is unable to go above the third floor of any building without feeling enormous anxiety. [4]Her acrophobia began one evening when she was working alone in her office on the eighth floor of a large building. [5]Suddenly she was struck with terror by the idea that she might jump or fall out the open window. [6]She crouched behind a steel filing cabinet, trembling, unable to move. [7]When she finally gathered her belongings and left the building, she was sweating, her breathing was rapid, and her heart was pounding. [8]Yet she had no rational explanation for her fears.

What word is being defined? _____*acrophobia*_____

What is the definition? _____*An intense, unreasonable fear of high places*_____

_____

Which sentence explains more about the word? _____*Sentence 2*_____

In which sentence does the example begin? _____*Sentence 3*_____

Explanation:

The word *acrophobia* is defined in the first sentence—"an intense, unreasonable fear of high places." The second sentence explains a bit more about acrophobia. The story about Sally Maxwell, which begins in the third sentence, provides an example of how acrophobia affects one sufferer. The example helps make the new term clear to the reader. The author introduces that illustration with the transition *for instance*.

➤ Practice 2

A. The following passage includes a definition and two examples. Underline the term being defined. Then, in the spaces provided, write the number of the definition sentence and the number of the sentence where each example begins.

> [1]Shaping is a way to teach a new behavior by encouraging a series of small bits of the whole behavior. [2]This approach, for instance, was used to teach a disturbed little boy named Dickey to wear eyeglasses after cataract surgery. [3]His physician feared that without glasses, his vision would deteriorate permanently. [4]At the mere mention of eyeglasses, however, Dickey threw terrible temper tantrums. [5]So researchers used shaping to ease him into the idea of wearing his glasses. [6]Dickey was deprived of his breakfast so that food could be used as a reward. [7]He received a bit of food each time he picked up some glass frames. [8]Later in the procedure, he had to put glasses on in order to receive a reward. [9]Within eighteen days, Dickey had learned through gradual steps to wear his glasses for twelve hours a day.
>
> [10]Another example is teaching a circus tiger to jump through a flaming hoop. [11]The tiger might first be rewarded for jumping up on a pedestal and then for leaping from that pedestal to another. [12]Eventually, the hoop would be set on fire, and the tiger would have to leap through the burning hoop to be rewarded.

Definition ___1___   *Example 1* ___2___   *Example 2* ___10___

B. The following passage includes a definition and one example. Underline the term being defined. Then outline the selection by doing two things: 1) filling in the word being defined and its definition; 2) in a few words, summarizing the example.

Wording of answer may vary.

[1]Jonathan Swift (1667–1745), author of *Gulliver's Travels,* often used irony—saying one thing but meaning another—in his writing. [2]For instance, in his famous essay "A Modest Proposal," he makes this suggestion for ending the famine in Ireland: the Irish should raise babies to be eaten. [3]Swift did not mean his suggestion to be taken seriously. [4]His actual goal was to shock his British audience into facing the mass starvation and misery in Ireland that British policies had produced at that time.

_____*Irony*_____ — ____*saying one thing but meaning another*____
_____

Example—____*To end the famine in Ireland, Swift suggests the Irish should*____

____*raise babies to be eaten.*_____

2 COMPARISON AND CONTRAST

Words That Show Comparison

Put a check (✓) beside the item that is easier to understand:

____ Driving a car is a skill that we learn through practice. Writing a paper is a skill that we learn through hands-on experience.

_✓_ Driving a car is a skill that we learn through practice. Similarly, writing a paper is a skill that we learn through hands-on experience.

The first item makes us wonder, "What has learning to drive a car got to do with writing a paper?" The word *similarly* makes it clear that the author intends to compare learning to write a paper with learning to drive a car. *Similarly* and words like it are comparison words.

Comparison words signal similarities. Authors use a comparison transition to show that a second idea is *like* the first one in some way. Here are some common words that show comparison:

Comparison Words

(just) as	likewise	in a similar manner
(just) like	in like manner	in the same way
alike	similar(ly)	resemble

Examples:

The sentences below contain comparison words. Notice how these words show that things are *alike* in some way.

> When buying milk, my mother always takes a bottle from the back of the shelf. *Similarly,* when my father buys a newspaper, he usually grabs one from the middle of the pile.

> Moviemakers with a big hit tend to repeat the winning idea in their next film, *just like* authors who use a successful plot over and over.

> The printing press greatly changed the way people learned news and ideas. *In a similar manner,* the Internet has revolutionized the way in which people obtain information.

➤ *Practice 3*

Comment: Remind students to use the hint on page 212 as they complete these sentences.

Complete each sentence with a suitable comparison word or phrase from the box on the previous page. Try to use a variety of transitions. *Answers may vary.*

1. Lighting a cigarette in a darkened theater will not win you any friends. _____*Similarly*_____, talking out loud with your movie partner will soon make people scowl in your direction.

2. _____*Just like*_____ an athlete in training, the mind of a reader grows stronger with practice.

3. Spicy foods make me very thirsty. Believe it or not, ice cream affects me _____*in the same way*_____.

4. The Amish people farm their land _____*as*_____ their 18th-century relatives did, without benefit of gasoline-powered tractors or other modern equipment.

5. _____*Just as*_____ rats become hostile when they live in a crowded cage, humans become aggressive in crowded conditions.

Words That Show Contrast

Put a check (✓) beside the item that is easier to understand:

____ A roller coaster scares many people. They love riding on it.

_✓_ Even though a roller coaster scares many people, they love riding on it.

In the first item, the two sentences seem to contradict each other. We want to ask, "Do people like a roller coaster or don't they?" In the second item, the phrase *even though* makes clear the relationship between the two ideas: In spite of the fact that a roller coaster is scary, people still love riding on it. *Even though* and other words and phrases like it are contrast words.

Contrast words show that things *differ* in one or more ways. Here are some common words that show contrast:

Contrast Words

but	instead	still	even though
yet	in contrast	as opposed to	different (ly)
however	on the other hand	in spite of	differs from
although	on the contrary	despite	unlike
nevertheless	converse (ly)	rather than	while

Examples:

The sentences below contain contrast words. Notice how these words signal that one idea is *different from* another idea.

People used to think that getting chilled would lead to catching a cold. *However,* getting chilled has nothing to do with getting sick.

Skunks are unpopular creatures, *yet* they eat lots of mice and bugs and don't spray unless they feel threatened.

Some people look upon eating as something to be done quickly so they can get on to better things. *In contrast,* others think eating *is* one of the better things.

➤ **Practice 4**

Comment: Remind students to use the hint on page 212 as they complete these sentences.

Complete each sentence with a suitable contrast word or phrase from the above box. Try to use a variety of transitions.

Answers may vary.

1. Most of us could live without food for a month; _____*however*_____, we need two quarts of water a day to survive.

2. _____*Although*_____ going up a ladder is easy, looking down can be difficult.

3. At first we were planning on spending our vacation at a campground, _____*but*_____ now we've decided to save money by relaxing at home.

4. Paula was not satisfied with her paper _____*despite*_____ the fact that she had already written five drafts.

5. We use seventeen muscles to smile. _____*In contrast*_____, we have to use forty-three muscles to frown.

Comparison and contrast transitions are often used in paragraphs organized in the comparison and/or contrast pattern.

The Comparison and/or Contrast Pattern

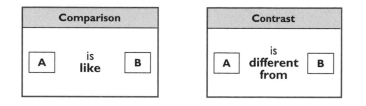

To get a sense of the comparison and/or contrast pattern, try to arrange the following sentences in an order that makes sense. Put a *1* in front of the sentence that should come first, a *2* in front of the sentence that comes next, and a *3* in front of the sentence that should be last. The result will be a short paragraph.

_3_ Yet the large, hairy tarantula is relatively harmless, while the small brown recluse is dangerously poisonous.

_1_ The tarantula and the brown recluse are more different than they are similar.

_2_ It's true, both spiders are alike in inspiring a great deal of fear.

The first sentence of this paragraph is the general one, the one with the main idea: "The tarantula and the brown recluse are more different than they are similar." The words *similar* and *different* suggest a comparison and/or contrast pattern of organization. The comparison word *alike* and the contrast words *yet* and *while* in the other two sentences show that the spiders are indeed being compared and contrasted: "It's true, both spiders are alike in inspiring a great deal of fear. Yet the large, hairy tarantula is relatively harmless, while the small brown recluse is dangerously poisonous."

The comparison-contrast pattern shows how two things are alike or how they are different, or both. When things are compared, their similarities are pointed out; when they are contrasted, their differences are discussed. (The tarantula and the brown recluse spider are alike in the fear they inspire; they are different in the effects of their bites, as well as in their appearance.)

Authors frequently find it useful to compare and contrast. The author of a child-development textbook, for example, compares and contrasts the ways in which boys and girls develop. Although they experience a similar growth spurt at the beginning of adolescence, the spurt begins about a year or so earlier in girls. Also, while boys gain proportionately more muscle, girls gain proportionately more fat, giving them more of the look of an adult woman. The authors of a sociology text contrast American cities with those in underdeveloped nations. They point out, for instance, that although the populations of American cities are leveling off, the populations of most third-world cities are exploding.

☑ *Check Your Understanding*

In the following paragraph, the main idea is stated in the first sentence. As is often the case, the main idea suggests a paragraph's pattern of organization. Here the transition *differently* is a hint that the paragraph may be organized in a comparison and/or contrast pattern. Read the paragraph and answer the questions below. Then read the explanation that follows.

> [1]In middle age, men and women often view life very differently, especially if they are couples who have led traditional lives. [2]By middle age, the husband is often comfortable in his position at work and has given up any dreams of advancing further. [3]He may then become more family-oriented. [4]In contrast, once the children are grown, the wife may find herself free to explore interests and develop abilities she has had no time for in the previous fifteen or twenty years. [5]Unlike her husband, she may be more interested in non-family activities than ever.

1. Is this paragraph comparing, contrasting, or both?   *contrasting*

2. What two things are being compared and/or contrasted? _____
   _____ *Views of traditional middle-aged men and women* _____

3. What three comparison or contrast transition words or phrases are used in the paragraph?   *differently, in contrast, unlike*

Explanation:

This paragraph is only contrasting, not comparing—it discusses only differences, not similarities. The two things being contrasted are the views of traditional middle-aged men and women. The transition words or phrases that show contrast are *differently, in contrast,* and *unlike*.

➤ *Practice 5*

A. The following passage uses the pattern of either comparison or contrast. Read the passage and answer the questions that follow.

> [1]Employment policies are quite different in Japan and the United States. [2]In Japan teamwork is an essential part of hiring and promotion. [3]College graduates who join a corporation are all paid about the same starting salary. [4]To learn about the company's various departments, they are rotated as a team through the organization. [5]They are also promoted as a team. [6]Only in later years are individuals singled out for recognition. [7]When there is an opening in the firm, outsiders are not even considered.

⁸In the United States, on the other hand, an employee is hired on the basis of what the firm thinks that individual can contribute. ⁹Employees try to outperform others, and they strive for raises and promotions as signs of personal success. ¹⁰The individual's loyalty is to himself or herself, not to the company. ¹¹Outsiders are considered for openings in U.S. firms.

Check (✓) the pattern which is used in this passage:

___ Comparison

_✓_ Contrast

What two things are being compared or contrasted?

1. _Japanese employment practices_   2. _U.S. employment practices_

B. The following paragraph uses the pattern of either comparison or contrast. Read the passage and then answer the questions and complete the outline that follows.

¹Among the school experiences new to young children is the regimented environment. ²At home children may have been able to do what they wanted when they wanted to do it. ³But in school, they are given a set time for talking, working, playing, eating, and even going to the toilet. ⁴Another source of anxiety may be the public method of discipline that some teachers use. ⁵Whereas at home children are scolded in private, in school they may be held up to embarrassment in front of their peers. ⁶"Mandy," the teacher may say, "why are you the only one in the class who didn't do your homework?" ⁷Or, "Scott, why are you the only one who can't work quietly at your seat?" ⁸Last, a child may be scared by the competitive atmosphere of the school. ⁹At home, one hopes, such competition for attention is minimal. ¹⁰In school, however, children may vie for the teacher's approving glance or tone of voice, or for stars on a paper, or for favored seats in the front row.

Check (✓) the pattern which is used in this passage:

___ Comparison

_✓_ Contrast

Complete the following map of the paragraph:

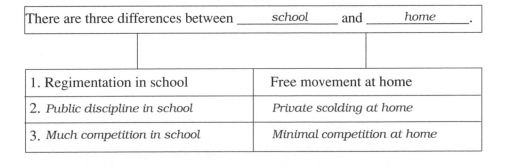

There are three differences between _____school_____ and _____home_____.	
1. Regimentation in school	Free movement at home
2. _Public discipline in school_	_Private scolding at home_
3. _Much competition in school_	_Minimal competition at home_

3   CAUSE AND EFFECT

Words That Show Cause and Effect

Put a check (✓) beside the item that is easier to understand:

_____ The paint has worn off the wooden siding. Fungus has begun to grow on it.

__✓__ Because the paint has worn off the wooden siding, fungus has begun to grow on it.

In the first item, it seems the author is simply listing two things that have happened to the wooden siding. The word *because* in the second item makes clear the relationship between the two ideas—the protective paint wore off, and for this reason, the fungus was able to grow. *Because* and words like it are cause and effect words.

Cause and effect words signal that the author is explaining *the reason why* something happened or *the result* of something happening. Here are some common words that show cause and effect:

Cause and Effect Words

therefore	so	result	because (of)
thus	as a result	effect	reason
as a consequence	results in	cause	explanation
consequently	leads to	if . . . then	accordingly
due to	since	affect	

Examples:

The following examples contain cause and effect words. Notice how these words introduce a *reason* for something or the *results* of something.

My sister became a vegetarian *because* she doesn't want to eat anything that had a mother.

If the weather gets too humid, *then* the wooden doors in our house swell up and begin to stick.

At one time in history, birth records were not kept for ordinary people. *As a result,* the only birthday parties were for kings, queens, and other royalty.

➤ *Practice 6*   ***Comment:*** Remind students to use the hint on
                                            page 212 as they complete these sentences.

Complete each sentence with a suitable cause and effect word or phrase from the
box on the previous page. Try to use a variety of transitions.   *Answers may vary.*

1. _____*Because*_____ property taxes in the city have gone sky high,
   many corporations are moving to the suburbs.

2. Maria's resumé is impressive; _____*as a result*_____, she has
   already had several job interviews.

3. My family is full of great Italian cooks, _____*so*_____ canned
   ravioli tastes like cardboard to me.

4. _____*Since*_____ car dealers have a monthly quota of cars to sell,
   they are more likely to offer good deals near the end of a month.

5. Some zoo animals have not learned how to be good parents.
   _____*Therefore*_____, baby animals are sometimes brought up in
   zoo nurseries and even in private homes.

Cause and effect transitions often signal the cause and effect pattern of
organization.

The Cause and Effect Pattern

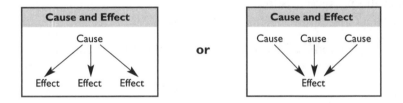

To get a sense of the cause and effect pattern, try to arrange the following
sentences in an order that makes sense. Put a *1* in front of the sentence that should
come first, a *2* in front of the sentence that comes next, and a *3* in front of the
sentence that should be last. The result will be a short paragraph.

_2_ Growing up without parents around resulted in the monkeys drinking
   enormous amounts of alcohol.

_1_ A study of monkeys suggests two factors may lead to alcoholism.

_3_ Low levels of serotonin in the brain also caused the monkeys to drink more.

As the words *resulted in, lead to,* and *caused* suggest, this paragraph is organized in a cause and effect pattern. The paragraph begins with the general idea: "A study of monkeys suggests two factors may lead to alcoholism." Next come two causes: "Growing up without parents around resulted in the monkeys drinking enormous amounts of alcohol. Low levels of serotonin in the brain also caused the monkeys to drink more."

Note that even in the cause and effect pattern—or any other pattern—addition words may be used to introduce points and show their order. The last sentence of the above paragraph, for example, includes the word *also,* showing that a second point is being added to the first: "Low levels of serotonin in the brain also caused the monkeys to drink more."

Information in a cause and effect pattern addresses the questions "Why does a behavior or event happen?" and/or "What are the results of a behavior or event?" An author may then discuss causes, or effects, or both causes and effects.

Authors usually don't just tell what happened; they try to explain both what happened and why. A textbook section on the sinking of the ship *Titanic,* for example, would be incomplete if it did not include the cause of the disaster—going at a high speed, the ship collided with an iceberg. Or if the number of homeless families in the country increases, journalists will not simply report the increase. They would also explore the reasons for and effects of that increase.

☑ Check Your Understanding

Read the paragraph below and see if you can answer the questions about cause and effect that follow. Then read the explanation to see how you did.

> [1]Even the best listeners are unable to listen carefully to everything they hear. [2]One reason is the overload of messages we encounter each day. [3]Besides the numerous hours we spend hearing others speak, we may spend several more hours listening to the radio or television. [4]It just isn't possible to avoid having our attention wander at least part of this time. [5]Another cause of poor listening is a preoccupation with personal concerns. [6]A romance gone sour or a good grade on a test may take prominence in our mind even as someone is speaking to us. [7]In addition, being surrounded by noise may result in poor listening. [8]For example, many voices at a noisy party or the sound of traffic may make it difficult for us to hear everything that is being said.

1. What are the three causes described in this paragraph?

     A. *Message overload*

     B. *Preoccupation with personal concerns*

     C. *Being surrounded by noise*

2. The three causes lead to what result or effect? _____

Poor listening
_____

3. What three cause and effect signal words or phrases are used?

reason, cause, result in
_____

Explanation:

The paragraph begins with the main idea: "The best listeners are unable to listen carefully to everything they hear." That point is then supported by three reasons, or causes. The first is the overload of messages we hear each day. The second reason is our preoccupation with personal concerns. The third cause given is that we are at times surrounded by interfering noise. The effect is stated in the main idea—our inability to listen carefully to everything we hear. The cause and effect signals used are *reason, cause,* and *result in.*

➤ *Practice 7*

A. Read the paragraph below, looking for one cause and three main effects (the three major details). Then complete the diagram that follows.

> [1]Chronic stress can lead to many serious health problems. [2]One effect of stress is painful muscle tension. [3]Headaches, backaches and sore shoulders are direct consequences of this tension. [4]Another result of long-term exposure to stress is a weakening of the body's immune system. [5]The body is then more vulnerable to infection and diseases, and normal colds or minor infections are more likely to develop into serious illnesses. [6]Third, stress can result in psychological disorders including depression, anxiety, phobias, and addictions. [7]In one way or another, our bodies will eventually protest a prolonged exposure to stressful situations.

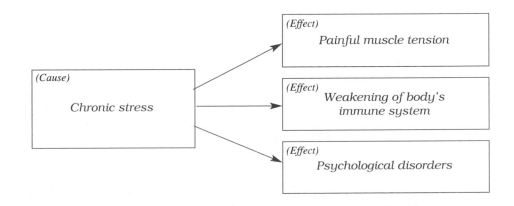

(Cause)
Chronic stress

(Effect)
Painful muscle tension

(Effect)
Weakening of body's immune system

(Effect)
Psychological disorders

B. Read the paragraph below, looking for the one effect and the four causes. Then complete the outline that follows.

> [1]Why do people daydream? [2]One reason is boring jobs that are tolerable only when workers imagine themselves doing something else. [3]Deprivation also leads to daydreaming. [4]During World War II, conscientious objectors who volunteered to go on semistarvation diets for six months fantasized about food. [5]Some even hung enticing pictures of foods on their walls to give themselves something to dream about. [6]Another reason people daydream is to discharge hostile feelings. [7]For example, an angry student may imagine dropping his instructor out of a classroom window, helping him to laugh at and dismiss his annoyance with her. [8]Last, some people fantasize as a way to plan for the future so that by the time they face future situations, they will know what to say and how to act.   *Wording of answers may vary.*

Main idea *(the effect):*   <u>*There are several reasons that people daydream.*</u>

Major supporting details *(the causes):*

1. <u>*To tolerate boring jobs*</u>

2. <u>*To endure deprivation*</u>

3. <u>*To discharge hostile feelings*</u>

4. <u>*To plan for the future*</u>

A Note on Main Ideas and Patterns of Organization

Remember that a paragraph's main idea often indicates its pattern of organization. For example, here is the main idea of a paragraph you worked on earlier:

> In middle age, men and women often view life very differently, especially if they are couples who have led traditional lives.

This sentence may have made you expect that the paragraph would go on to contrast the views of middle-aged men and women. If so, the paragraph would be organized according to the comparison and/or contrast pattern.

☑ *Check Your Understanding*

Finding the main idea of a paragraph may help you decide on its pattern of organization. Try, for instance, to guess the pattern of paragraphs with these main ideas:

> The development of the automobile in the early twentieth century resulted in a number of changes in U.S. society.

Pattern: <u>   *cause and effect*   </u>

A franchise is a business arrangement in which an individual obtains rights from a larger company to sell a well-known product or service.

Pattern: _____ *definition and example* _____

Explanation:

In the first sentence, the words *resulted in* suggest that the paragraph will have a cause and effect pattern, discussing the social effects of the introduction of the automobile. In the second sentence, the word *franchise* is defined, suggesting that the paragraph will follow a definition and example pattern, with examples of various franchises to follow.

➤ Practice 8

Most of the main ideas below come from college textbooks. In the space provided, write the letter of the pattern of organization that each suggests.

___A___ 1. A communicable disease is one in which an infectious organism is usually passed from person to person.
  A. Definition and   B. Comparison and/or   C. Cause and effect
     example   contrast

___C___ 2. Following are three reasons for the existence of stereotypes.
  A. Definition and   B. Comparison and/or   C. Cause and effect
     example   contrast

___B___ 3. College students in their thirties and forties face many of the same pressures as younger students, but they are often better equipped to withstand these pressures.
  A. Definition and   B. Comparison and/or   C. Cause and effect
     example   contrast

___C___ 4. A growing concern with health has affected the way that many Americans eat.
  A. Definition and   B. Comparison and/or   C. Cause and effect
     example   contrast

___A___ 5. A mission statement is an organization's declaration of how it will achieve its purpose.
  A. Definition and   B. Comparison and/or   C. Cause and effect
     example   contrast

___B___ 6. Americans typically think of men as naturally better suited to perform the most strenuous physical labor, but not all peoples of the world hold the same view.
- A. Definition and example
- B. Comparison and/or contrast
- C. Cause and effect

___C___ 7. Because of economic pressures, increasing numbers of people are seeking housing assistance.
- A. Definition and example
- B. Comparison and/or contrast
- C. Cause and effect

___A___ 8. Nonverbal communication behaviors are those bodily actions and vocal qualities that accompany a verbal message and have agreed-upon interpretations within a culture.
- A. Definition and example
- B. Comparison and/or contrast
- C. Cause and effect

___C___ 9. There are several possible explanations for why retail prices often end on certain numbers.
- A. Definition and example
- B. Comparison and/or contrast
- C. Cause and effect

___B___ 10. First-year college students who expect to do well in school need to learn quickly the right and wrong ways of preparing for exams.
- A. Definition and example
- B. Comparison and/or contrast
- C. Cause and effect

The right way to prepare for exams and the wrong way to prepare for exams will be contrasted.

A Final Point

Keep in mind that a passage may often be made up of more than one pattern of organization. For instance, the paragraph in this chapter about acrophobia (the unreasonable fear of high places) uses the definition and example pattern. But the example itself—a series of events on one evening in Sally Maxwell's life—uses a time order pattern.

Or consider the following passage:

> ¹Have you ever had the experience of recognizing someone's face but not being able to recall his or her name? ²The reason is that the information about that person is split up and stored in the two different sides of your brain, and each side has its own way of thinking and remembering. ³Recalling someone's face is the task of the right side of your brain, which understands whole things at once and is responsible for visualizing, recognizing similarities, and supplying intuitions. ⁴This side of your brain provides insights that are hard to put into words. ⁵The left side of your brain deals with language and stores words themselves, including the person's name that you have temporarily forgotten. ⁶This is the side responsible for speaking, reading, writing, and listening.

The paragraph uses in part a cause and effect pattern, explaining the reason why we may recognize a face but not recall a name. It also uses a contrast pattern, explaining the different functions of the two sides of the brain. Pages 257–258 offer practice on passages with more than one pattern of organization.

CHAPTER REVIEW

In this chapter, you learned about three kinds of relationships that authors use to make their ideas clear:

- **Definitions and examples**

  — To help readers understand the important ideas and terms in a subject, textbook authors often take time to include key definitions (often setting them off in *italic* or **boldface**) and examples of those definitions. When reading a textbook, it is usually a good idea to mark off both definitions and examples. (Underline each definition, and put *Ex* in the margin next to each example.)

  — Transition words that signal the definition and example pattern include *for example, for instance, to illustrate,* and *such as.*

- **Comparison and/or contrast**

  — Authors often discuss how two things are alike or how they are different, or both.

  — Transition words that signal comparisons include *alike* and *similar.*

  — Transition words that signal contrasts include *but, however,* and *in contrast.*

- **Cause and effect**

  — Authors often discuss the reasons why something happens or the effects of something that has happened.

  — Transition words that signal causes include *reason* and *because.*

  — Transition words that signal effects include *therefore, consequently,* and *as a result.*

Note that pages 251–258 list and offer practice in all the transitions and patterns of organization you have studied in "Relationships I" and "Relationships II."

The next chapter—Chapter 7—will be devoted to helping you distinguish between fact and opinion in writing.

On the Web: If you are using this book in class, you can visit our website for additional practice in understanding relationships that involve examples, comparison or contrast, and cause and effect. Go to **www.townsendpress.com** and click on "Online Exercises."

➤ Review Test 1

To review what you've learned in this chapter, fill in the blanks or choose the best answer for the following items.

1. When textbook authors provide a definition of a term, they are also likely to provide one or more _____*examples*_____ to help make that definition clear.

2. A(n) _____*comparison*_____ transition signals that two things are alike in some way.

3. A(n) _____*contrast*_____ transition signals that two things are different in some way.

__C__ 4. A cause and effect paragraph might be about
  A. reasons.
  B. results.
  C. reasons and/or results.

__C__ 5. The pattern of organization of a paragraph may be suggested by
  A. the transitions it contains.
  B. its topic sentence.
  C. both A and B.

➤ Review Test 2

A. Fill in each blank with one of the words in the box. Use each word once. Then write the letter of the word in the space provided.

A. because	B. effects	C. just like
D. such as	E. however	

__B__ 1. Strong emotions can have negative _____*effects*_____ on digestion.

__C__ 2. Mariah claims her teenage brother is _____*just like*_____ a cockroach—he enjoys going out at night and eating junk food.

_E_   3. An adult elephant weighs about 12,000 pounds. _____However_____, its eyes are almost exactly the size of a human's.

_A_   4. _____Because_____ Ray's father and grandfather have both become bald, Ray expects to lose his hair, too.

_D_   5. For people who wish to work with children, there are many career choices, _____such as_____ teaching, school counseling, and working at a day-care center.

B. Below are the beginnings of five passages. Label each one with the letter of its pattern of organization. (You may find it helpful to underline the transition or transitions in each item.)

    A Definition and example
    B Comparison and/or contrast
    C Cause and effect

_B_   6. [1]Television news stories resemble newspaper articles in being timely and appealing to a wide audience. [2]However, TV coverage tends to be more superficial, emphasizing the visual aspects of a story rather than important background issues. . . .   *However* is a contrast word.

_C_   7. [1]Many drivers take to the roads in July and August, when families traditionally go on vacation. [2]As a result, oil companies often raise the price of gasoline during the summer months. . . .   *As a result* is a cause and effect transition.

_A_   8. [1]In a mystery story, the term *red herring* refers to a false or misleading clue meant to deceive the reader. [2]One famous red herring is Sherlock Holmes's farewell note to Dr. Watson in "The Final Problem," which leads the reader to believe Holmes has fallen to his death. . . .
The format clearly indicates a definition: *red herring* is being defined.

_C_   9. [1]One type of hearing loss is caused by damage to the nerve cells in the inner ear. [2]The damage may be the result of loud noises, allergic reactions to medicines, or a hard blow to the ear or skull. [3]Certain diseases can also cause damage to the nerve cells of the inner ear. . . .
Caused, result and *cause* are cause and effect words.

_A_   10. [1]A complementary relationship is one in which the distribution of power is unequal. [2]One partner says, "Let's go to a movie tonight," and the other says, "Sure." [3]The boss asks several employees to work overtime, and they all agree. . . .   The format clearly indicates a definition: *complementary relationship* is being defined.

➤ Review Test 3

Read each paragraph and answer the questions that follow.

A. [1]Pessimists have long had a poor image as sourpusses and doomsayers, but a concept called "defensive pessimism" is beginning to be recognized as a useful, helpful attitude. [2]Defensive pessimism means acting positively—taking specific steps—to reduce the anxiety and stress of expecting the worst. [3]For instance, taking the time to back up important files eliminates worries about computer crashes, viruses, and mistakes that can wipe out days or months of work. [4]Diversifying one's savings and investments eliminates the fear of being financially ruined if a company in which one holds too much stock goes bankrupt. [5]And rather than worry about being arrested for speeding or jailed for tax evasion, for example, the defensive pessimist drives within the speed limit and pays taxes honestly.

_____A_____ 1. The main pattern of organization of the paragraph is
   A. definition and example.   The format clearly indicates a definition:
   B. cause and effect.   *defensive pessimism* is being defined.
   C. comparison and/or contrast.

2. The transition that signals the pattern of organization of this paragraph
   is _____*for instance*_____.

B. [1]The three most common non-prescription pain relievers are aspirin, acetaminophen, and ibuprofen. [2]They are alike in inhibiting the production of prostaglandins in the body, which are hormone-like substances that trigger pain, inflammation, and fever. [3]But while aspirin and ibuprofen can reduce all three symptoms, acetaminophen does not reduce inflammation. [4]Aspirin is considered to have the greatest number of uses but also has the greatest number of side effects, including allergic reactions, stomach upset, and bleeding. [5]In contrast, ibuprofen generally has fewer side effects than aspirin. [6]Acetaminophen has the fewest side effects; its only drawback is that it is probably the least effective of the three pain killers.

_____C_____ 3. The main pattern of organization of the paragraph is
   A. definition and example.   Aspirin, acetaminophen, and ibuprofen are
   B. cause and effect.   being compared and contrasted.
   C. comparison and/or contrast.

4. One transition that signals the pattern of organization of this paragraph
   is _____*Any of the following: alike, but, while, in contrast*_____.

C. [1]Alternate freezing and thawing is one of the most important processes of mechanical weathering. [2]Water has the unique property of expanding about 9 percent as it freezes. [3]This increase in volume occurs because as water solidifies, the water molecules arrange themselves into a very open crystalline structure. ⁴As a result, when water freezes, it exerts a tremendous outward force. ⁵In nature, water works its way into cracks or voids in rock. ⁶When the water then freezes and expands, the effect is to break the rock into angular fragments.

_B_   5. The main pattern of organization of the paragraph is
   A. definition and example.
   B. cause and effect.
   C. comparison and/or contrast.

   6. One transition that signals the pattern of organization of this paragraph
      is _____*Any of the following: because, as a result, effect*_____.

D.   ¹Corporate welfare refers to financial aid given by the government to corporations, especially when the handout is considered unjust. ²The government aid to Borden Chemicals in Louisiana is a good example. ³The company buried hazardous wastes without a permit and released hazardous chemicals so thick that to protect drivers, the police sometimes shut down the highway that runs near the plant. ⁴Borden even contaminated the groundwater beneath its plant, threatening the aquifer that provides drinking water for residents of Louisiana and Texas. ⁵Borden's pollution has cost the company a hefty $7 million, but thanks to corporate welfare, the company didn't make out so badly. ⁶With $15 million in reduced and canceled property taxes, Borden has enjoyed a net gain of $8 million.

_A_   7. The main pattern of organization of the paragraph is
   A. definition and example.   *Corporate welfare* is being defined.
   B. cause and effect.
   C. comparison and/or contrast.

   8. The transition that signals the pattern of organization of this paragraph
      is _____*example*_____.

E.   ¹The use of fire by prehistoric people probably affected wildlife both intentionally and unintentionally. ²In all likelihood, early people used fire to drive game toward waiting hunters. ³Later, new plant growth in the burned areas would attract more wild animals. ⁴In addition, accidental fires must have occurred frequently. ⁵Because prehistoric people had trouble starting fires, they would have kept burning embers on hand. ⁶The result must have been widespread accidental fires, especially in dry areas. ⁷Certainly, these fires also would have greatly altered the habitat for wildlife.

_B_   9. The main pattern of organization of the paragraph is
   A. definition and example.
   B. cause and effect.
   C. comparison and/or contrast.

10. One transition that signals the pattern of organization of this paragraph is _____*Any of the following: affected, because, result*_____.

➤ Review Test 4

Here is a chance to apply your understanding of relationships to a full-length article. The reading, from *Newsday Magazine*, is a firsthand account of what it was like for one boy to be the first black student in a midwestern school.

To help you continue to strengthen your skills, the reading is followed by questions not only on what you've learned in this chapter but also on what you've learned in previous chapters.

Words to Watch

Below are some words in the reading that do not have strong context support. Each word is followed by the number of the paragraph in which it appears and its meaning there. These words are indicated in the article by a small circle (°).

pristine (2): still pure
prevailing (2): common
deplored (4): disapproved of
incipient (6): in the early stages of being
derivative (7): not original
tentatively (9): with uncertainty
groused (11): complained
ventured (11): dared
mortified (12): humiliated

I BECAME HER TARGET

Roger Wilkins

1   My favorite teacher's name was "Deadeye" Bean. Her real name was Dorothy. She taught American history to eighth graders in the junior high section of Creston, the high school that served the north end of Grand Rapids, Michigan. It was the fall of 1944. Franklin D. Roosevelt was president; American troops were battling their way across France; Joe DiMaggio was still in the service; the Montgomery bus boycott was more than a decade away, and I was a twelve-year-old black newcomer in a school that was otherwise all white.

2   My mother, who had been a widow in New York, had married my stepfather, a Grand Rapids physician, the year before, and he had bought the best house he could afford for his new family. The problem for our new neighbors was that their neighborhood had previously been pristine° (in their terms) and that they were ignorant about black people. The prevailing° wisdom in the neighborhood was that we were spoiling it and that we ought to go back where we belonged (or alternatively, ought not intrude where we were not wanted). There was a lot of

angry talk among the adults, but nothing much came of it.

3   But some of the kids, those first few weeks, were quite nasty. They threw stones at me, chased me home when I was on foot, and spat on my bike seat while I was in class. For a time, I was a pretty lonely, friendless and sometimes frightened kid. I was just transplanted from Harlem, and here in Grand Rapids, the dominant culture was speaking to me insistently. I can see now that those youngsters were bullying and culturally disadvantaged. I knew then that they were bigoted, but the culture spoke to me more powerfully than my mind, and I felt ashamed for being different—a non-standard person.

4   I now know that Dorothy Bean understood most of that and deplored° it. So things began to change when I walked into her classroom. She was a pleasant-looking single woman, who looked old and wrinkled to me at the time, but who was probably about 40. Whereas my other teachers approached the problem of easing in their new black pupil by ignoring him for the first few weeks, Miss Bean went right at me. On the morning after having read our first assignment, she asked me the first question. I later came to know that in Grand Rapids, she was viewed as a very liberal person who believed, among other things, that Negroes were equal.

5   I gulped and answered her question and the follow-up. They weren't brilliant answers, but they did establish the facts that I had read the assignment and that I could speak English. Later in the hour, when one of my classmates had bungled an answer, Miss Bean came back to me with a question that required me to clean up the girl's mess and established me as a smart person.

6   Thus, the teacher began to give me human dimensions, though not perfect ones for an eighth grader. It was somewhat better to be an incipient° teacher's pet than merely a dark presence in the back of the room onto whose silent form my classmates could fit all the stereotypes they carried in their heads.

7   A few days later, Miss Bean became the first teacher ever to require me to think. She asked my opinion about something Jefferson had done. In those days, all my opinions were derivative°. I was for Roosevelt because my parents were and I was for the Yankees because my older buddy from Harlem was a Yankee fan. Besides, we didn't have opinions about historical figures like Jefferson. Like our high school building or old Mayor Welch, he just was.

8   After I had stared at her for a few seconds, she said: "Well, should he have bought Louisiana or not?"

9   "I guess so," I replied tentatively°.

10   "Why?" she asked.

11   Why! What kind of question was that, I groused° silently. But I ventured° an answer. Day after day, she kept doing that to me, and my answers became stronger and more confident. She was the first teacher to give me the sense that thinking was part of education and that I could form opinions that had some value.

12   Her final service to me came on a day when my mind was wandering and I was idly digging my pencil into the writing surface on the arm of my chair. Miss Bean impulsively threw a hunk of gum eraser at me. By amazing chance, it hit my hand and sent the pencil flying. She gasped, and I crept mortified° after my pencil as the class roared. That was the ice breaker. Afterward, kids came up to me to laugh about "Old Deadeye Bean." The incident became a legend, and I, a part of that story, became a person to talk to. So that's how I became just another kid in school and Dorothy Bean became "Old Deadeye."

Reading Comprehension Questions

Vocabulary in Context

___B___ 1. In the sentence below, the word *bungled* (bŭng′gəld) means
- A. improved.
- B. handled poorly.
- C. whispered.
- D. corrected.

The words "clean up the girl's mess" are a context clue.

"Later in the hour, when one of my classmates had bungled an answer, Miss Bean came back to me with a question that required me to clean up the girl's mess and established me as a smart person." (Paragraph 5)

___C___ 2. In the excerpt below, the word *establish* (ĭ-stăb′lĭsh) means
- A. challenge.
- B. hide.
- C. demonstrate.
- D. exaggerate.

"I gulped and answered her question and the follow-up. They weren't brilliant answers, but they did establish the facts that I had read the assignment and that I could speak English." (Paragraph 5)

Central Point and Main Ideas

___C___ 3. Which sentence best expresses the central point of the article?
- A. A boy used to Harlem schools had to go to a previously all-white school in Grand Rapids.   Too narrow.
- B. The author was a lot smarter than the other kids thought he would be.   Too narrow.
- C. A teacher helped the first black student in school to grow intellectually and to be welcomed as an individual.
- D. Teachers are the most important influences in a person's life.   Too broad.

___B___ 4. Which sentence best expresses the main idea of paragraph 7?
- A. Miss Bean asked the author for his opinion about something Thomas Jefferson had done.
- B. Miss Bean was the first teacher to ask the author to have his own opinion about something.
- C. The author had been in favor of Franklin D. Roosevelt because his parents had been in favor of Roosevelt.
- D. It seemed odd to the author to have opinions about historical figures like Thomas Jefferson.

The significant idea of paragraph 7 is stated in its first sentence.

Supporting Details

____A____ 5. At first, the teachers at the school other than Miss Bean

  A. ignored the author.

  B. challenged the author.

  C. praised the author.

  D. protected the author.

See paragraph 4.

Transitions

____B____ 6. The sentence below expresses a relationship of

  A. addition.

  B. contrast.

  C. comparison.

  D. cause and effect.

But is a contrast word.

"They weren't brilliant answers, but they did establish the facts that I had read the assignment and that I could speak English." (Paragraph 5)

____C____ 7. The sentence below expresses a relationship of

  A. time.

  B. illustration.

  C. comparison.

  D. contrast.

Like is a comparison word.

"Like our high school building or old Mayor Welch, [Jefferson] just was." (Paragraph 7)

____A____ 8. The sentence below expresses two relationships of

  A. cause and effect.

  B. illustration.

  C. comparison.

  D. contrast.

Because is a cause and effect word.

"I was for Roosevelt because my parents were and I was for the Yankees because my older buddy from Harlem was a Yankee fan." (Paragraph 7)

Patterns of Organization

____B____ 9. Paragraph 3 is organized as a list of

  A. contrasts between the author and his new schoolmates.

  B. effects of being the first black kid in the neighborhood.

  C. comparisons between the author's old and new schoolmates.

  D. examples of the word *transplanted*.

_D_ 10. The patterns of organization of paragraph 12 are time order and
 A. list of items.
 B. comparison and contrast.
 C. definition and example.
 D. cause and effect.

> The *cause* in the paragraph is the incident involving the thrown eraser; the *effect* is stated in the last sentence of the paragraph. The incident itself involves a series of events, told in the order in which they happened.

Discussion Questions

1. Why do you suppose the incident in which Miss Bean threw an eraser at the author was such an "ice breaker"?

2. Have you ever experienced being in a school or class in which you were the only one of a certain group—the only student who was African American, white, Hispanic, older / younger, or different in some other way? What was it like? Did things get better or worse? Why?

3. Did you have any teachers that required you to think on your own? How did they get you to do so?

4. "Deadeye" Bean is Wilkins's favorite teacher. Who was your favorite high-school teacher, and why? Give an example of something special that teacher did, either for you or for the class.

Note: Writing assignments for this selection appear on page 588.

Check Your Performance   **RELATIONSHIPS II**

Activity	Number Right	Points	Score
Review Test 1 (5 items)	_____	× 2 =	_____
Review Test 2 (10 items)	_____	× 3 =	_____
Review Test 3 (10 items)	_____	× 3 =	_____
Review Test 4 (10 items)	_____	× 3 =	_____
	TOTAL SCORE	=	_____%

Enter your total score into the **Reading Performance Chart: Review Tests** on the inside back cover.

RELATIONSHIPS II: Mastery Test 1

A. Fill in each blank with an appropriate transition from the box. Use each transition once. Then, in the spaces provided, write the letter of the transition you have chosen.

A. therefore	B. for example	C. just as
D. because	E. in contrast	

Hint: Make sure that each word or phrase that you choose fits smoothly into the flow of the sentence. Test your choices by reading each sentence to yourself.

___B___ 1. ¹Some thieves read the newspapers to find out good times to rob houses. ²___*For example*___, after reading the obituaries, such thieves may "clean out" a home while the family is at a loved one's funeral.

___C___ 2. ¹Whenever something bad happens to me, my grandmother tries to help me through it. ²When I was depressed after breaking up with my boyfriend, she told me, "___*Just as*___ we must go through the storm before seeing the rainbow, we often must experience sorrow before joy."

___A___ 3. ¹Honeybees attack just to protect their hives. ²___*Therefore*___, if you run away from the hive when attacked, the bees will eventually lose interest in you.

___D___ 4. ¹___*Because*___ there are no clocks in gambling casinos, gamblers can easily lose all sense of time. ²That is clearly what the casino management wants to happen. ³The longer people stay at the tables or in front of the slot machines, the better.

___E___ 5. ¹Most birds are born in either of two very different states. ²Some are born weak, blind, and usually naked. ³About all they can do for themselves is open their mouths for food. ⁴___*In contrast*___, other newborn baby birds are bright-eyed and covered with down. ⁵As soon as their down is dry, they are able to peck at things and run after their parents.

(Continues on next page)

B. Label each item with the letter of its main pattern of organization.

A Definition and example
B Comparison and/or contrast
C Cause and effect

___A___ 6. [1]Phobias are intense, irrational fears that are out of proportion to the actual danger in a situation. [2]For example, people with the fear of open places (agoraphobia) are often reluctant to leave their homes.   The illustration transition is *for example.*

___C___ 7. [1]Bread made with whole-wheat flour is brown, but not all brown bread is whole-wheat bread. [2]Some manufacturers add molasses or honey to white-flour dough to give it a brown color, and they are allowed to label the product "wheat bread." [3]For this reason, it is important to read the package label before buying.   The cause and effect transition is *for this reason.*

___A___ 8. [1]Climate is the average weather experienced in a given geographic area. [2]Areas fall into climate categories according to their year-round temperature and rainfall. [3]An oppressively hot and humid region, for instance, would be said to have a tropical climate.   The illustration transition is *for instance.*

___B___ 9. [1]In the 1890s, most Americans were struggling to reach a middle-class lifestyle. [2]By the 1990s, in contrast, an overwhelming majority had achieved the middle class but were either losing it or struggling to hold on to it. [3]In the 1890s, government responded to the prodding of reform-minded citizens and began to create a framework of rules to control the excesses of giant businesses and to protect the interests of the average citizen. [4]But in the 1990s, that framework of controls on large corporations was being dismantled.   Contrast of the 1890s and the 1990s, with two contrast phrases: *in contrast* and *on the other hand.*

___C___ 10. [1]Prison overcrowding is dangerous because it increases unrest among inmates and produces a climate in which violence is more likely. [2]Riots, escapes, and hostage taking become more of a problem. [3]Prison overcrowding also makes it more difficult for correctional officers and prison administrators to manage the prison. [4]The result is that prisons are more costly to run.   Cause and effect words are *because* and *result.*

RELATIONSHIPS II: Mastery Test 2

Read each paragraph and answer the questions that follow in the spaces provided.

A. ¹The incomes of middle- and working-class Americans was dealt a severe blow during the 1980s. ²A major reason was a decline in industrial jobs. ³The economy became less devoted to manufacturing goods and more focused on providing services. ⁴Many manufacturing jobs, especially in the steel and auto industries, were transferred from the United States to Third World countries. ⁵As a result, millions of blue-collar workers in the Midwest and Northeast were stranded. ⁶They were forced into much lower-paying jobs with fewer benefits and opportunities for advancement.

    B   1. The main pattern of organization of the paragraph is
   A. definition and example.   Paragraph A discusses the *reasons* why
   B. cause and effect.   the incomes of middle- and working-class
   C. comparison and/or contrast.   Americans suffered during the 1980s.

    2. One transition that signals the pattern of organization of this paragraph

    is _____*reason* or *as a result*_____.

B. ¹Boys who mature early physically have a decided advantage over their more slowly maturing peers. ²Early maturers become heroes in sports and leaders in both formal and informal activities. ³Other boys look up to them; girls have crushes on them. ⁴Even adults tend to trust them. ⁵They are more self-confident and independent than other boys. ⁶In contrast, their less mature male peers, with their high-pitched voices and underdeveloped physiques, feel inadequate. ⁷They are weaker at sports and more awkward with girls.

    C   3. The main pattern of organization of the paragraph is
   A. definition and example.   Paragraph B *contrasts* boys who
   B. cause and effect.   physically mature early with their more
   C. comparison and/or contrast.   slowly maturing peers.

    4. The transition that signals the pattern of organization of this paragraph

    is _____*in contrast*_____.

C. ¹There are often more than two sides to a question, and offering only two choices when more actually exist is called an either-or fallacy. ²For example, the statement "You are either with us or against us" assumes that there is no middle ground. ³Or consider the following conclusion: People opposed to total freedom of speech are really in favor of censorship. ⁴This argument ignores the fact that a person could believe in free speech as well as in laws

(Continues on next page)

241

that prohibit slander or that punish someone for falsely yelling "Fire!" in a crowded theater.

<u>_A_</u> 5. The main pattern of organization of the paragraph is
     A. definition and example.   *Paragraph C defines and*
     B. cause and effect.   *illustrates the either-or fallacy.*
     C. comparison and/or contrast.

     6. The transition that signals the pattern of organization of this paragraph
     is _____*for example*_____.

D. ¹Why does lightning make such a loud sound? ²The answer has to do with the electrical energy it gives off. ³A single bolt may produce as much as 3,750 million kilowatts of electrical energy. ⁴Most of this energy—75 percent—turns into heat, causing the temperature of the surrounding air to rise greatly. ⁵Since heated air expands, the sudden increase in temperature leads to a rapid expansion of the air around the lightning. ⁶And that air expansion causes sound waves—thunder—which can be heard up to eighteen miles away.

<u>_B_</u> 7. The main pattern of organization of the paragraph is
     A. definition and example.   *Paragraph D discusses the reasons*
     B. cause and effect.   *lightning makes such a loud sound.*
     C. comparison and/or contrast.

     8. One transition that signals the pattern of organization of this paragraph
     is _____*Any of the following: causing, since, leads to, causes*_____.

E. ¹People are different from other primates, but not as different as they might like to think. ²It's true that that there are significant contrasts in size and proportion between humans and other primates. ³And, of course, humans are by far the more intelligent. ⁴Nevertheless, to use chimpanzees as an example, both they and humans have the same muscles and bones, located in almost the same places and working in nearly the same ways. ⁵The internal organs of both animals are also very much alike, as are their blood and other body fluids. ⁶Seen under a microscope, even their genes are strikingly similar.

<u>_C_</u> 9. The main pattern of organization of the paragraph is
     A. definition and example.   *Paragraph E compares and contrasts*
     B. cause and effect.   *people and other primates.*
     C. comparison and/or contrast.

     10. One transition that signals the pattern of organization of this paragraph
     is ___*Any of the following: different, contrasts, nevertheless, same, alike,*___.
                                     similar

RELATIONSHIPS II: Mastery Test 3

A. (1–4.) Arrange the scrambled sentences below into a logical paragraph by numbering them *1, 2, 3,* and *4* in an order that makes sense. Then, in the space provided, write the letter of the main pattern of organization used.

Note that transitions will help you by clarifying the relationships between sentences.

___3___ Also, high tuitions affect the amount of time available for studying; because loans and scholarships are hard to get, many students have to put in numerous hours at work in order to afford school.

___2___ For one thing, it undoubtedly prevents some students from attending college in the first place.

___4___ Finally, those who do manage to get loans know that they must begin their careers with large debts.

___1___ The high cost of college today causes problems for many students in more ways than one.

___C___ 5. The main pattern of organization is
   A. contrast.
   B. comparison.
   C. cause and effect.
   D. definition and example.

> The paragraph discusses the problems that *result from* the high cost of college.

B. Read each paragraph and answer the questions that follow.

[1]Men and women may interpret women's actions on a date very differently. [2]One study found that acts such as speaking in a low voice or smiling were interpreted by men as indicating that the woman was interested in sex. [3]Women, in contrast, tended to see the same behaviors as simply friendly. [4]Drinking with a man, going to the man's apartment, or wearing sexy clothes were all seen by men as indicating a desire for sex, while women regarded these behaviors as appropriate or fashionable.

___C___ 6. The main pattern of organization of the paragraph is
   A. definition and example.
   B. cause and effect.
   C. comparison and/or contrast.

> The paragraph *contrasts* men's and women's interpretations of women's actions on a date.

7. One transition that signals the main pattern of organization of this paragraph is _____*Any of the following: differently, in contrast, while*_____.

(Continues on next page)

243

¹Mass hysteria is a type of group behavior that involves a widely held and contagious anxiety, usually as a result of a false belief. ²The reaction in part of the country to the 1938 radio broadcast of *The War of the Worlds* is one example. ³This dramatization of Martians landing on Earth was so realistic that people began to panic and flee before the realization set in that they were reacting to a radio play. ⁴The medieval witch-hunts are another good example of mass hysteria. ⁵They were based on the belief that witches were the cause of many problems in late medieval society, including natural disasters and illness. ⁶Those accused of being witches (mainly old women) were tortured until they confessed or they died. ⁷As many as 500,000 people were burned to death by the clergy between the fifteenth and seventeenth centuries.

_D_ 8. The major supporting details of the selection are
   A. definitions.
   B. causes.
   C. comparisons.
   D. examples.

   The paragraph provides two *examples* of the term *defined*, "mass hysteria."

_A_ 9. The main pattern of organization of the paragraph is
   A. definition and example.
   B. cause and effect.
   C. comparison and/or contrast.

10. The transition that signals the main pattern of organization of this paragraph is _____ *example* _____.

RELATIONSHIPS II: Mastery Test 4

A. (1–4.) Arrange the scrambled sentences below into a logical paragraph by numbering them *1, 2, 3,* and *4* in an order that makes sense. Then, in the space provided, write the letter of the main pattern of organization used.

Note that transitions will help you by clarifying the relationships between sentences.

 4 In contrast, the original Italian story is the gruesome tale of the Princess Talia, who falls into a deep magical sleep in the woods, where she is raped by a nobleman and, later on, gives birth to twins, whom the nobleman's wife tries to have killed and cooked for dinner.

 1 It is often said that fairy tales, with their heavy doses of terror and violence, are too scary for young children.

 3 Consider the story of Sleeping Beauty that today's children know, which involves a princess who is put to sleep by a wicked witch and then awakened by the kiss of her true love.

 2 But today's versions of fairy tales are actually less frightening than the original stories.

 A 5. The main pattern of organization is
    A. contrast.
    B. comparison.
    C. cause and effect.
    D. definition and example.

> The paragraph *contrasts* today's versions of fairy tales with the original stories.

B. Read each paragraph and answer the questions that follow.

[1]A long sausage in a bun received the name "hot dog" in 1906 as the result of a cartoonist's poor spelling ability. [2]A sausage vendor, Harry Stevens, sold what he called "dachshund sausages" (named after the short-legged dog) at New York City baseball games. [3]During one of those games, newspaper cartoonist Tad Dorgan was in the audience. [4]He sketched a cartoon of a live dachshund, smeared with mustard and folded into a bun. [5]Not knowing how to spell "dachshund," however, he settled on "dog," giving the cartoon the caption "Get your hot dogs!" [6]Once the cartoon was published in newspapers, readers began demanding their own "hot dogs."

 A 6. The main idea is expressed in the
    A. first sentence.
    B. second sentence.
    C. last sentence.

(Continues on next page)

___B___ 7. The selection mainly

    A. defines and illustrates the term "hot dog."

    B. gives the reason small sausages are now called hot dogs.

    C. contrasts "dachshund sausage" with "hot dog."

8. The transition that signals the main pattern of organization of this paragraph is _____*as the result*_____.

[1]When a crowd is watching as someone threatens to jump from a building, its behavior seems affected by the time of day. [2]In daylight, the crowd is usually quite quiet, but under the cover of darkness, many individual members will shout encouragement to the person to kill himself or herself. [3]A similar reaction was seen when women college students took part in an experiment where they were asked to press a button to shock other volunteers. [4]When the women pushing the buttons were visible to the victims, they administered only brief shocks. [5]However, when they were allowed to wear gowns and masks that hid their identity, they shocked the volunteers twice as much. [6]Clearly the feeling of being anonymous causes people to engage in antisocial behavior.

___B___ 9. *(Write two answers.)* Two patterns of organization of the selection are

___C___ 10. A. definition and example.

    B. cause and effect.

    C. comparison and/or contrast.

The paragraph discusses the *effects* of anonymity on people's behavior and *contrasts* the way people behave when they are not anonymous with the way they behave when they are. Cause-effect words are *affected* and *causes*; comparison-contrast words are *similar* and *however*.

RELATIONSHIPS II: Mastery Test 5

A. Read the textbook paragraph below. Then answer the question and complete the outline that follows.

> ¹There are several reasons why middle-aged adults are returning to school. ²Some want to learn to do their jobs better. ³College courses can help them improve their job skills and keep up in their fields. ⁴Others return to school because more credits may mean a raise or promotion. ⁵Teachers, for instance, get raises for reaching certain levels of education. ⁶Also, some adults return to the classroom because of interest in a new field, such as telecommunications or computer programming. ⁷Finally, others want to study subjects such as foreign languages, history, or literature for the sake of learning. ⁸Such classes help adults spend their time in more productive and interesting ways and deepen their understanding of themselves and their world.

  _B_   1. The organizational patterns of the paragraph are list of items and
          A. definition and example.   The paragraph *lists* the *reasons* why
          B. cause and effect.   middle-aged adults are returning to school.
          C. comparison and/or contrast.   Cause and effect words are *reasons*,
                                                  because, and *because of*.

2–5. Complete the outline of the paragraph by writing in the four major supporting details.

Main idea: There are several reasons why middle-aged adults are returning to school.

Wording of answers may vary.

Major supporting details:

1. _To learn to do their jobs better_

2. _To earn credits for a raise or promotion_

3. _To learn a new field_

4. _To learn for the sake of learning_

(Continues on next page)

B. Read the textbook paragraph below. Then answer the question and complete the map that follows.

> [1]While management styles vary, there are certain factors that separate the good administrator from the poor one. [2]A good manager anticipates problems and prepares for them, but a poor manager is often taken by surprise. [3]The effective administrator makes changes to eliminate repeated problems; the less effective boss deals with one crisis at a time, never seeing patterns of problems. [4]In addition, a good boss delegates work to others, while the poor one prefers to take on one extra task after another rather than train employees to do the work right. [5]The effective administrator is also flexible enough to adapt to changing situations. [6]In contrast, the poor one often clings to the old rules whether or not they apply.

_B_   6. The organizational patterns of the paragraph are list of items and

  A. definition and example.   The paragraph *lists* the *contrasting* factors that
  B. comparison and/or contrast.   separate the good administrator from the
  C. cause and effect.   poor one. Contrast words are *while, but,*
                                        and *in contrast.*

7–10. Complete the map of the paragraph by writing in the missing supporting details.

Wording of answers may vary.

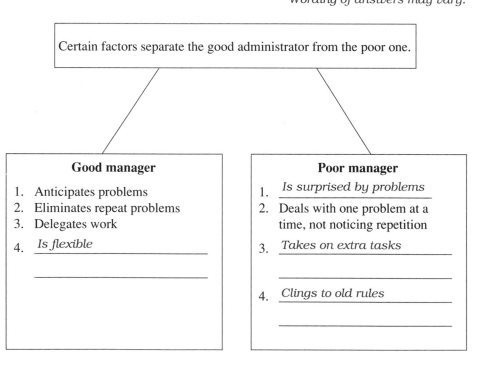

Certain factors separate the good administrator from the poor one.

Good manager

1. Anticipates problems
2. Eliminates repeat problems
3. Delegates work
4. *Is flexible*
   _____

Poor manager

1. *Is surprised by problems*
2. Deals with one problem at a time, not noticing repetition
3. *Takes on extra tasks*
   _____
4. *Clings to old rules*
   _____

RELATIONSHIPS II: Mastery Test 6

A. Read the textbook paragraph below. Then answer the question and complete the outline that follows.

> ¹One researcher has identified five basic causes of frustration above and beyond daily hassles. ²To begin with, delays are hard for us to accept because our culture stresses the value of time. ³Anyone who has been caught in a traffic jam is familiar with the frustration of delay. ⁴Lack of resources is another cause of frustration, especially to low-income Americans, who cannot afford the new cars or vacations that TV programs and magazine articles would have us believe everyone must have. ⁵Losses, such as the end of a love affair or a cherished friendship, are frustrating because they often make us feel helpless, unimportant, and worthless. ⁶Failure is a frequent source of frustration in our competitive society. ⁷The aspect of failure that is hardest to cope with is guilt. ⁸We imagine that if we had done certain things differently, we might have succeeded, and so we feel responsible for our own or someone else's pain and disappointment. ⁹Discrimination can also be a source of frustration. ¹⁰Being denied opportunities or recognition simply because of one's sex, age, religion, or skin color, regardless of one's personal qualifications or accomplishments, is immensely frustrating.

_C_ 1. The organizational patterns of the paragraph are list of items and
  A. definition and example.
  B. comparison and/or contrast.
  C. cause and effect.

Cause and effect words are *causes* and *because*.

2–6. Complete the outline of the paragraph by writing in the five major supporting details.

Main idea: There are five causes of frustration above and beyond daily hassles.

Major supporting details:

1. _Delays_

2. _Lack of resources_

3. _Losses_

4. _Failure_

5. _Discrimination_

Comment: Paragraph A *lists* five basic causes of frustration above and beyond daily hassles.

(Continues on next page)

B. Read the textbook paragraph below. Then answer the question and complete the map that follows.

> ¹Role conflict is a situation in which the different roles an individual is expected to play make incompatible demands. ²A working mother provides one example. ³In meeting the requirements of a full-time job, she automatically violates the expectation that a mother will put her children's needs before everything else. ⁴In meeting the cultural demands of motherhood (staying home if the child is sick, attending school plays), she automatically violates the requirements of a nine-to-five job. ⁵A priest provides another example. ⁶He is expected to treat confessions as strictly confidential. ⁷But a priest, like any other citizen, has responsibilities toward the community. ⁸What should he do if a parishioner confesses that he has committed several rapes and cannot control his behavior? ⁹In living up to one role expectation (confidentiality), the priest violates another (community responsibility). ¹⁰The key point here is that the difficulties the individuals in these positions experience—the feelings of conflict, inadequacy, and anguish—are not of their own making. ¹¹They are built into their roles.

_B_   7. The main pattern of organization of the passage is
   A. cause and effect.
   B. definition and example.   The format clearly indicates a definition.
   C. comparison.   The paragraph *defines* and *illustrates* the
   D. contrast.   term "role conflict."

8–10. Complete the map of the passage. In doing so, you will need to summarize the main idea and the two supporting details.

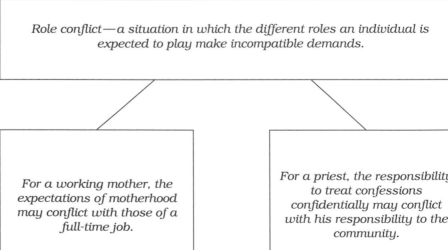

Role conflict—a situation in which the different roles an individual is expected to play make incompatible demands.

For a working mother, the expectations of motherhood may conflict with those of a full-time job.

For a priest, the responsibility to treat confessions confidentially may conflict with his responsibility to the community.

TO THE STUDENT

The pages that follow contain three mastery tests that offer additional practice in the skills covered in Chapters 5 and 6:

- Relationships that involve **addition**
- Relationships that involve **time**
- Relationships that involve **illustration**
- Relationships that involve **comparison and/or contrast**
- Relationships that involve **cause and effect**

For ease in reference, the lists of words that show these relationships have been reprinted on the next page.

Addition Words

one	to begin with	in addition	last
first	another	next	last of all
first of all	second	moreover	finally
for one thing	also	furthermore	

Time Words

before	during	while	later
previously	now	next	eventually
first	as	soon	finally
then	when	after	last
following			

Illustration Words

(for) example	(for) instance	illustration
including	such as	once

Comparison Words

(just) as	likewise	in a similar manner
(just) like	in like manner	in the same way
alike	similar(ly)	resemble

Contrast Words

but	instead	still	even though
yet	in contrast	as opposed to	different(ly)
however	on the other hand	in spite of	differs from
although	on the contrary	despite	unlike
nevertheless	converse(ly)	rather than	while

Cause and Effect Words

therefore	so	result	because (of)
thus	as a result	effect	reason
as a consequence	results in	cause	explanation
consequently	leads to	if . . . then	accordingly
due to	since	affect	

RELATIONSHIPS I AND II: Mastery Test 1

A. Fill in each blank with an appropriate transition from the box. Use each transition once. Then, in the spaces provided, write the letter of the transition you have chosen.

A. unlike	B. then	C. for example
D. first	E. cause	

_B_ 1. [1]If you are approached by a vicious neighborhood or stray dog, you have a good chance of avoiding being attacked or bitten if you do the following. [2]First of all, stand still. [3]Secondly, do not look the dog directly in the eyes; instead, look just over the top of its head. [4]Next, talk in as soft and unconcerned a way as you can to the dog, saying "Hey, what's up, pal?" [5]_____Then_____ slowly back away while facing the dog.

_C_ 2. [1]Public opinion can be defined as those opinions held by ordinary citizens that they are willing to express openly. [2]This expression need not be verbal. [3]It could also take the form, _____for example_____, of a protest demonstration or a vote for one candidate rather than another.

_D_ 3. [1]The opossum reacts to danger in one of several ways. [2]_____First_____, some varieties of opossum can spray an unpleasant odor. [3]A second reaction to danger used by opossums is to bluff their way out of a tight spot by hissing and baring their teeth. [4]Finally, the best-known of possum defenses is to "play dead" by entering into a coma-like state brought on by fear.

_E_ 4. [1]Swollen glands can be uncomfortable, but they are a welcome sign that your body is working to defend itself. [2]They are often associated with an illness such as mumps, German measles, a cold, or flu; but an insect bite or infected cut can also result in swelling. [3]A blocked duct in a salivary gland is another possible _____cause_____ of a swollen gland. [4]Still, if swollen glands last more than a few days, they can be a sign of a serious illness, such as Hodgkin's disease.

_A_ 5. [1]The feeling of awe is similar to fear in some ways. [2]With both, we have a sense of being overwhelmed, of confronting someone or something much more powerful than we are. [3]But _____unlike_____ fear, awe is a positive feeling, an expansive feeling. [4]While fear makes us want to run away, awe makes us want to draw closer even as we hesitate to get too close.

(Continues on next page)

B. Fill in each blank with an appropriate transition from the box. Use each transition once. Then, in the spaces provided, write the letter of the transition you have chosen.

A. for instance	B. next	C. after
D. however	E. as a result	

_____D_____ 6. [1]There are more than a few similarities between the ancient Egyptian religion and our modern religions of today. [2]_____*However*_____, a belief that you "could take it with you" is a prime difference. [3]In fact, the Egyptians thought the dead could take a considerable number of items with them. [4]In many cases, Egyptian royalty and high officials began stocking their tombs with goods long before their death.

_____C_____ 7. [1]Scotch tape is not wound up in the factory in the little rolls found in stores. [2]During the manufacturing process, sheets of cellophane several feet wide are first run through a machine that coats them with adhesive. [3]_____*After*_____ that, a machine winds the sticky film around tubes that are also several feet wide. [4]Next, this wide roll of Scotch tape is fed through a slicing machine, which produces the thin rolls of tape sold to consumers.

_____E_____ 8. [1]For two decades, the Chinese government tried to control population by limiting most rural families to one child. [2]Because boys are prized in rural areas—they can work the land and give more support to their families—many couples aborted female fetuses, killed newborn daughters, or neglected them to death. [3]_____*As a result*_____, China in 2002 was short 50 million females. [4]With so few brides to go around, desperate bachelors have taken to marrying relatives.

_____A_____ 9. [1]Communicators who want to set themselves apart from others adopt the strategy of divergence, speaking in a way that emphasizes their differences from others. [2]_____*For instance*_____, an attorney who wants to impress a client might speak formally and use professional jargon to create a sense of distance. [3]The implicit message here is, "I'm different (and more knowledgeable) than you."

_____B_____ 10. [1]Almost all good writing begins with terrible first efforts. [2]You need to start somewhere. [3]Start by getting something—anything—down on paper. [4]A friend of mine says that the first draft is the down draft—you just get it down. [5]The _____*next*_____ draft is the up draft—you fix it up. [6]You try to say what you have to say more accurately. [7]And the third draft is the dental draft, where you check every tooth, to see if it's loose or cramped or decayed, or even, God help us, healthy.

RELATIONSHIPS I AND II: Mastery Test 2

Read each selection and answer the questions that follow.

A. ¹The conflict over secrecy between the federal government and journalists arises from the different roles they play in society. ²The government has the job of conducting foreign policy. ³To do so effectively, government officials sometimes prefer to distort or withhold information. ⁴Journalists, however, see their role as digging up and giving information to the public. ⁵If they always sought government permission before publishing information, they would be able to print or broadcast only what the government wanted to appear in the media.

_____C_____ 1. The main pattern of organization of the selection is
   A. time order.
   B. list of items.
   C. comparison and/or contrast.

2. One transition that signals the pattern of organization of this paragraph is
   _____*Either of the following: different, however*_____.

B. ¹Pictures of starving Africans leave the impression that Africa is overpopulated. ²Why else would all those people be starving? ³But the truth is far different. ⁴Africa has 22 percent of the earth's land, but only 10.5 percent of the earth's population. ⁵The reason for famines in Africa, then, cannot be too many people living on too little land. ⁶In fact, Africa contains some of the world's largest untapped lands suitable for agriculture. ⁷The reality is that famines are due to three primary causes: drought, inefficient farming techniques, and wars that disrupt harvests and food distribution.

_____C_____ 3. The main pattern of organization of the selection is
   A. time order.
   B. definition and example.
   C. cause and effect.

4. One transition that signals the pattern of organization of this paragraph is
   _____*Any of the following: reason, due to, causes*_____.

C. ¹A conflict of interest exists when a businessperson is faced with a situation in which an action benefiting one person or group has the potential to harm another. ²For instance, lawyers, business consultants, or advertising agencies would face a conflict of interest if they represented two competing companies: A strategy that would most benefit one of the client companies might harm the other client. ³Another example would be a real estate agent who faces an ethical conflict if he or she represents both the buyer and seller in a transaction. ⁴In general, the buyer benefits from a low price, and the seller benefits from a high price. ⁵Handling the situation responsibly may be possible, but it would also be difficult.

(Continues on next page)

255

_B_   5. The main pattern of organization of the selection is
   A. time order.
   B. definition and example.
   C. list of items.

6. One transition that signals the pattern of organization of this paragraph is
   _____ *Either of the following: for instance, example* _____.

D. [1]Sawing a woman in half is an easy illusion for magicians. [2]The trick begins when a table holding a coffin-like box is rolled onstage. [3]A female assistant is hiding inside that table. [4]When the magician displays the box to the audience, it is, of course, empty. [5]Then the magician asks a female assistant on stage to climb into the box. [6]As she does this, the hidden woman enters the box through a trapdoor in the table, sticks her feet out one end, and curls up with her head between her knees. [7]The other woman, drawing her knees up to her chin, puts her head out the other end of the box. [8]Now the box appears to be holding one woman, and the magician can saw right through. [9]After he does so, the woman at the foot end slides back into the table as the magician reopens the box.

_A_   7. The main pattern of organization of the selection is
   A. time order.
   B. definition-example.
   C. comparison and/or contrast.

8. One transition that signals the pattern of organization of this paragraph is
   _____ *Any of the following: when, then, as, now, after* _____.

E. [1]Three musical instruments played an important role in eighteenth-century warfare. [2]One of the most important was the snare drum. [3]Often played by boys between 12 and 16 years old, snare drums were used to set the marching rhythm for soldiers. [4]With a skilled drummer playing 96 beats per minute, a commander could march his troops three miles in fifty minutes, allowing ten minutes each hour for a breather and a drink. [5]Another important instrument was a small flute called a fife. [6]The fife's role in an army was to entertain soldiers and communicate orders. [7]For example, the song "Pioneer's March" was the signal for road-clearing crews to get started ahead of the infantry. [8]Fifes were also used to give orders to soldiers during battle since they could be heard above the roar of firearms. [9]A third instrument used in warfare was the trumpet. [10]Requiring just one hand to play, it was used by soldiers on horseback to send messages to soldiers in battle and on the march.

_B_   9. The main pattern of organization of the selection is
   A. time order.
   B. list of items.
   C. comparison and/or contrast.

10. One transition that signals the pattern of organization of this paragraph is
   _____ *Any of the following: one, another, third* _____.

RELATIONSHIPS I AND II: Mastery Test 3

Each of the following selections uses **two** patterns of organization. Read each selection and then, in the spaces provided, write the letter of the two patterns of organization.

A. [1]A boycott is an expression of protest consisting of an organized refusal by a group of people to deal with another person or group. [2]An illustration is the famous boycott that began in 1955 when Mrs. Rosa Parks of Montgomery, Alabama, refused to obey a local ordinance requiring black people to sit at the back of city buses. [3]Mrs. Parks was arrested, which resulted in a boycott of the Montgomery bus system by blacks. [4]The boycott was organized and led by Dr. Martin Luther King, Jr. [5]Rather than continue to lose revenue needed to run the bus system, the city repealed the ordinance.

___C___ 1. The main patterns of organization of the selection are
   A. definition-example and list of items.
   B. cause-effect and contrast.
   C. definition-example and cause-effect.

   The term *boycott* is being defined.

B. [1]On May 18, 1980, Mt. St. Helens in the state of Washington erupted violently, killing nearly one hundred people and leveling thousands of acres of timber. [2]By contrast, many volcanoes in Hawaii never explode, but simply have lava flowing out of them. [3]The difference between volcanic eruptions and simple lava flows is the result of the differing composition of the molten rock that comes to the surface as lava. [4]The lava from Mt. St. Helens is a type that cools more quickly, which causes it to build a lava dome that plugs up the flow. [5]Eventually the pressure becomes so intense that a tremendous explosion blows the lava dome off and sends a massive cloud of ash into the air. [6]By contrast, the lava from Hawaiian volcanoes contains enough iron to keep it from hardening to rock when it reaches the air, but flows down the side of the cone until it hits an obstacle or eventually cools and becomes solid. [7]It never plugs the volcano; therefore, there is no explosion.

___B___ 2. The main patterns of organization of the selection are
   A. definition-example and time order.
   B. contrast and cause-effect.
   C. list of items and comparison.

   Contrast words—*contrast, difference, contrast*; cause-effect words—*result* and *causes*.

C. [1]The United States ranks near the bottom among the world's democracies in the percentage of eligible citizens who participate in national elections. [2]One reason for the low voter turnout is that individual Americans are responsible for registering to vote, whereas in most other democracies, voters are automatically registered by government officials. [3]In addition, unlike some

(Continues on next page)

other democracies, the United States does not encourage voting by holding elections on the weekend or by imposing penalties, such as fines, on those who do not participate.

___A___ 3. The main patterns of organization of the selection are
- A. cause-effect and contrast.
- B. time order and comparison.
- C. definition-example and time order.

Cause-effect word—*reason*; contrast words—*whereas* and *unlike*.

D. [1]What caused our distant ancestors to move from walking on all fours to standing upright? [2]First, and probably most important, it freed the forelimbs to carry things. [3]With dangerous animals around more than willing to make a meal out of a small primate, the ability to search for food while possibly carrying one's offspring and to carry the food back to a safe location would certainly be a benefit. [4]Second, by elevating the head, walking upright provided better views of food and danger. [5]In addition, the vertical orientation helped cool the body by presenting a smaller target to the intense equatorial rays of the sun and by placing more of the body above the ground to catch cooling air currents. [6]Finally, standing upright, while using a great deal of energy for running, was very efficient for walking. [7]Long periods of steady walking in search of food required less energy if done in an upright position.

___A___ 4. The main patterns of organization of the selection are
- A. cause-effect and list of items.
- B. definition-example and time order.
- C. list of items and time order.

Cause-effect word—*caused*; list words—*first, second, in addition, finally*.

E. [1]When a honeybee finds a new source of food—flower pollen and nectar—she flies back to the hive. [2]Within minutes, more bees emerge and, amazingly, fly straight to the food. [3]Their ability to do this is a result of what goes on in the hive after that first bee flies in. [4]Inside the hive, that bee does a dance, called a waggling dance, to communicate to the other bees the direction, distance, and identity of the food. [5]First, because it's usually dark in the hive, she emits sound signals that help the other bees determine where she is and how she's moving. [6]She then dances in a figure-eight pattern, waggling only when she is facing the direction of the food source in relation to the sun. [7]The pace of her dancing tells how far away the food is; the faster she dances, the closer the food. [8]At some point, the bees observing the dance emit sounds that vibrate the honeycomb. [9]This causes the dancer to stop, and she gives the watchers small samples of the food so they know its taste, smell, and quality. [10]After receiving the necessary information, the other bees then fly out to find the food.

___B___ 5. The main patterns of organization of the selection are
- A. definition-example and list of items.
- B. cause-effect and time order.
- C. comparison and time order.

Cause-effect word—*result*; time words—*when, after, first, then, after*.

7
Fact and Opinion

Look at the photograph below of my great-grandmother's gravestone and the information that it provides. In the spaces provided, do the following:

1. Write what you think are the **facts** on the gravestone.
2. Write what you think is the **opinion** it contains.

Facts: _____

_____

Opinion: _____

FACT

A **fact** is information that can be proved true through objective evidence. This evidence may be physical proof or the spoken or written testimony of witnesses. The photograph on the previous page presents mostly facts: Elizabeth L. Miller was born on December 4, 1828, and died (at the age of 60) on July 21, 1889.

Following are some more facts—they can be checked for accuracy and thus proved true.

Fact: The Quad Tower is the tallest building in this city.

(A researcher could go out and, through inspection, confirm that the building is the tallest.)

Fact: Albert Einstein willed his violin to his grandson.

(This statement can be checked in historical publications or with Einstein's estate.)

Fact: On September 11, 2001, terrorists destroyed the New York World Trade Center, killing thousands.
(This event was witnessed in person or on television by millions, and it's firmly in records worldwide.)

OPINION

An **opinion** is a belief, judgment, or conclusion that cannot be objectively proved true. As a result, it is open to question. For instance, on my great-grandmother's gravestone, we are told that she is "sweetly sleeping." Of course I certainly *hope* that she is sleeping sweetly, but I have no way of knowing for sure. The statement is an opinion.

Or consider this example: after watching a movie, someone might state that the film was too sentimental. The statement is an opinion because it cannot be objectively proved. Another person might see the same movie and find it realistic. Neither statement can be proved; both are opinions.

Here are some more opinions:

Opinion: The Quad Tower is the ugliest building in the city.

(There's no way to prove this statement because two people can look at the same building and come to different conclusions about its beauty. *Ugly* is a **value word**, a word we use to express a value judgment. Value or judgment words are signals that an opinion is being expressed. By their very nature, these words represent opinions, not facts.)

Opinion: Einstein should have willed his violin to a museum.

(Who says? Not his grandson. This is an opinion.)

Opinion: The attack on the World Trade Center was the worst act of terrorism in the history of humankind.

(Whether something is "worst" is always debatable. *Worst* is another value word.)

Writing Facts and Opinions

To get a better sense of fact and opinion, take a few minutes to write three facts about yourself and then to write three of your opinions. Here, for example, are three facts about me and three of my opinions.

Three facts about me:

- I am six feet tall.
- I do my writing on a Macintosh computer.
- I have two sisters and one wife.

Three of my opinions:

- Schools should encourage students to do a great deal of reading.
- Macintosh computers are much easier to use than PC's.
- People should not get special treatment just because they are rich.

Now write your facts and opinions in the space below.

Three facts about you:

- _____
  _____

- _____
  _____

- _____
  _____

Three of your opinions:

Hint: To make sure that these are opinions, do not begin them with "I." For example, do not write "I think handguns should be banned." Simply write, "Handguns should be banned."

- _____
  _____

- _____
  _____

- _____
  _____

Fact and Opinion in Reading

The amount of fact and opinion in a piece of writing varies, depending on the author's purpose. For example, news articles and scientific reports, which are written to inform readers, are supposed to be as factual as possible. On the other hand, the main points of editorials, political speeches, and advertisements—materials written to persuade readers—are opinions. Such writings may contain facts, but, in general, they are facts carefully selected to back up the authors' opinions.

Both facts and opinions can be valuable to readers. However, it is important to recognize the difference between the two.

☑ *Check Your Understanding*

To sharpen your understanding of fact and opinion, read the following statements and decide whether each is fact or opinion. Put an **F** (for "fact") or an **O** (for "opinion") beside each statement. Put **F+O** beside the **one** statement that is a mixture of fact *and* opinion. Then read the explanation that follows.

> *Hint:* Remember that opinions are signaled by value words—words such as *great* or *hard* or *beautiful* or *terrible* that express a value judgment. Take care to note such words in your reading.

   _F_   1. Last night, a tree outside our house was struck by lightning.

   _O_   2. The waiters at that restaurant are rude, and the food costs twice as much as it's worth.

   _F_   3. Ostriches do not hide their heads in the sand.

   _O_   4. Tom Cruise and Halle Berry are the most gorgeous movie stars in Hollywood today.

   _O_   5. It's a fact that the best of the fifty states to live in is Hawaii.

   _O_   6. Installing a new sink is an easy job for the do-it-yourselfer.

   _F_   7. The Grimm brothers collected their fairy tales from other storytellers.

   _O_   8. There is nothing like a bottle of Coca-Cola to satisfy thirst.

   _F_   9. In the late 1890s, when Coke was first sold, it included a small amount of cocaine, which was then legal.

  _F+O_ 10. One of the most delicious of soft drinks, Coca-Cola was first intended to cure various ills, including headaches.

Explanation:

1. This is a statement of fact. You and your family might have seen or heard the lightning strike, or you could go outside later and see the type of damage done to the tree.

2. This is an opinion. Not every customer is likely to agree that all the waiters are rude and that the food is overpriced. The word *rude* is a value word.

3. This is a fact (contrary to popular belief) which can be checked through observation and scientific reports.

4. This is an opinion. Not everyone would regard Tom Cruise and Halle Berry in this way. Here the value word *gorgeous* shows us that a judgment is being expressed.

5. This is an opinion. Just saying that something is a fact doesn't make it so. Different people will judge locations very differently.

6. This is an opinion. The word *easy* suggests that a judgment is being made. What might be an easy job for one person might be an impossible challenge for another. The word *easy* is a value word.

7. This is a fact. It can be confirmed through the Grimms' writings and through research on the background of their stories.

8. This is an opinion. Many people might prefer cold water or some other drink as a thirst-quencher.

9. All the details here are facts that can be looked up and confirmed in historical records.

10. The first part of the statement is an opinion—not everyone would consider Coke to be one of the most delicious of soft drinks. (*Delicious* is another value word.) The second part of the statement is a fact that could be confirmed by researching historical records of the time.

➤ Practice 1

Some of the statements below are facts, and some are opinions. Label facts with an **F** and opinions with an **O**. Remember that facts can be proved, but opinions give personal views.

__F__ 1. Novels by Dean R. Koontz include *Watchers, Intensity*, and *The Bad Place*.

__O__ 2. *Watchers,* by Dean R. Koontz, is a terrifying story that is bound to keep you awake at night.

__O__ 3. Butterflies are the most beautiful of all insects.

__F__ 4. The taste sensors in butterflies are located in their feet, so that by standing on food, they can taste it.

__F__ 5. Depression is most common among persons between the ages of 25 and 44.

Judgment words and opinions are underlined.

   _O_   6. There's no illness <u>harder to cope with</u> than depression.

   _O_   7. The <u>best</u> exercise for a healthy heart is walking.

   _F_   8. The heart pumps slightly more than a gallon of blood per minute through approximately 60,000 miles of blood vessels in the body.

   _F_   9. More Bibles have been printed than any other book in history.

   _O_ 10. The Roman Catholic concept of God is <u>more correct</u> than the Protestant or the Jewish view.

➤ *Practice 2: Using the Internet*   *Answers will vary.*

If a computer with an online service is easily available to you, do the following exercises. If not, use a Sunday edition of a newspaper to do the A and B exercises.

A. Look up a recent newspaper. For example, you might go to the current issue of the national newspaper *USA Today* on the Internet by typing in **www.usatoday.com**. After recording the name and date of the paper, write down one fact and one opinion from the paper.

Name and date of the newspaper: _____

_____

One fact in the paper: _____

_____

One opinion in the paper: _____

_____

B. Look up a movie review site. For example, you might go the popular movie site **www.rottentomatoes.com**. Look up reviews of a movie that has come out recently and record the following:

Name of the movie and of the reviewer: _____

_____

One fact the reviewer includes about the movie: _____

_____

One opinion the reviewer expresses about the movie: _____

_____

C. Go to a book site. For example, you might go the well-known book site **www.amazon.com**. Look up a review of one of the following books: 1) *Dracula*; 2) *Charlotte's Web*; or 3) *I Know Why the Caged Bird Sings*. Record the following:

Name of the book and of the reviewer: _____

One fact the reviewer includes about the book: _____

_____

One opinion the reviewer expresses about the book: _____

_____

Comment: Students may need to be "walked through" the steps of finding a book review online.

Other Points About Fact and Opinion

There are several added points to keep in mind when separating fact from opinion.

1 Statements of fact may be found to be untrue.

Suppose you discovered that the Quad Tower is only the second-tallest building in the city. The statement would then be an error, not a fact. It is not unusual for evidence to show that a "fact" is not really true. It was once considered to be a fact that the world was flat, for example, but that "fact" turned out to be an error.

2 Opinions may be masked as facts.

People sometimes present their opinions as facts, as shown in sentence 5 on page 262. Here are two more examples:

In point of fact, neither candidate for the mayor's office is well-qualified.

The truth of the matter is that frozen foods taste as good as fresh foods.

Despite the words to the contrary, the above are not statements of fact but statements of opinion.

3 Remember that value (or judgment) words often represent opinions. Here are examples of these words:

Value Words

best	great	beautiful
worst	terrible	bad
better	lovely	good
worse	disgusting	wonderful

Value words often express judgments—they are generally subjective, not objective. While factual statements report on observed reality, subjective statements interpret reality. For example, the observation that it is raining outside is an objective one. The statement that the weather is bad, however, is subjective, an interpretation of reality. (Some people consider rain to be good weather.)

4   The words *should* and *ought to* often signal opinions. Those words introduce what people think should, or ought to, be done. Other people will disagree.

> Couples should definitely not live together before marriage.

> Couples ought to live together before getting married to be sure they are compatible.

5   Finally, remember that much of what we read and hear is a mixture of fact and opinion.

Recognizing facts and opinions is important because much information that sounds factual is really opinion. A political candidate, for example, may say, "My record is outstanding." Voters would be wise to wonder what the value word *outstanding* means to this candidate. Or an advertisement may claim that a particular automobile is "the most economical car on the road today," a statement that at first seems factual. But what is meant by *economical*? If the car offers the most miles per gallon but the worst record for expensive repairs, you might not agree that it's economical.

It is also worth noting that some opinions are more widespread than others— and may seem like facts. If 90 percent of those who see a movie think it's terrible, then many people will take it as a fact that the movie is a poor one. Nevertheless, this widespread belief is still opinion; it's possible that another generation of moviegoers will disagree with the popular opinion of the moment. Similarly, if many people believe the rumor that a particular politician has cheated on his taxes, it doesn't mean the rumor is a fact. Fair-minded people will base their own conclusion on more than widespread belief; they will want facts.

> ## Practice 3

Some of the statements below are facts, and some are opinions; in addition, **three** include fact and opinion. Label facts with an **F**, opinions with an **O**, and statements of fact *and* opinion with an **F+O**.

___O___   1. German shepherds are the <u>scariest</u> dogs alive.

___F___   2. The dog that bites people the most often, according to one twenty-seven-year study, is the German shepherd.

Judgment words and opinions are underlined.

_F+O_ 3. German shepherds, <u>which always make poor pets</u>, are used in police work and as guide dogs for the blind.

_F+O_ 4. Because many studies have concluded that smoking is a health hazard, cigarettes <u>should be banned.</u>

_F_ 5. Scientists predict that one-third of people who begin smoking under the age of 18 will die prematurely because of their habit.

_F_ 6. Smoking has been found to be one cause of lung cancer.

_O_ 7. Executives of corporations that pollute the environment <u>should be jailed.</u>

_F_ 8. According to scientists, all the water on Earth has been recycled for millions of years, and we drink the same water as the dinosaurs did.

_F+O_ 9. Low-flow shower heads save water, so all homeowners <u>should be required</u> to buy and install them in their showers.

_O_ 10. Homeowners <u>ought to plant</u> water-conserving ground covers such as periwinkle instead of grass.

➤ Practice 4

A. Here are short descriptions taken from a restaurant guide. Some descriptions present only factual information; others contain opinions as well. Identify the three factual descriptions with an **F** and the two descriptions that include both fact *and* opinion with an **F+O**.

_F_ 1. **Dunkin Donuts.** 480 Hamilton Street. Coffee, donuts, soup, and more. Eat in or take out.

_F+O_ 2. **Mocha's.** 735 North Front Street. Area's <u>best</u> place for coffee and dessert. <u>Tempting</u> homemade cakes, pies, ice cream, and pastries. Rare coffees and herbal teas. Imported chocolates.

_F_ 3. **Country Club Diner.** Railroad Place and Exchange Street. Sandwiches to full meals. Soups and desserts made daily. Private room for small parties.

_F_ 4. **Wing Tai Oriental Restaurant.** 284 Bishop Street. Chinese cuisine. Full service restaurant and lunch buffet. Take-out also.

_F+O_ 5. **Mel's Bar and Grill.** Route 14 South. <u>Impressive</u> menu features steak, lobster, pasta, chicken, and brick-oven pizza. Free valet parking, live entertainment. <u>Upscale</u> but <u>affordable.</u> Selection of 35 fine wines.

Judgment words and opinions are underlined.

B. Here are short reviews taken from a newspaper movie guide. Some reviews present only facts; others contain opinions about the movie as well. Identify the two factual reviews with an **F** and the three reviews that include both fact *and* the reviewer's opinion with an **F+O**.

___F___ 6. *Enough,* **2002.** Jennifer Lopez, Bill Campbell. A diner waitress meets and marries a rich man who becomes a cheating wife-beater. When the police cannot help her, she takes martial-arts classes to face his physical threats.

___F+O___ 7. *Psycho,* **1960.** Anthony Perkins, Janet Leigh. <u>The godfather of today's slasher films.</u> A blonde <u>impulsively</u> steals $40,000 from her employer. She has the <u>bad luck</u> to choose the Bates Motel as her hideout. Hotel manager Norman Bates just knows that Mother wouldn't approve of the blonde, so he makes sure she checks out early. <u>Still scary after all these years.</u>

___F___ 8. *Unforgiven,* **1992.** Clint Eastwood, Gene Hackman. In the Old West, a former hired killer (Eastwood) is lured out of retirement by the promise of a $1,000 reward. The film won the Academy Awards for Best Picture and Best Director and earned Hackman a Best Supporting Actor award for his role as a small-town sheriff.

___F+O___ 9. *Citizen Kane,* **1941.** Orson Welles, Joseph Cotten. <u>A classic that is as fresh today as the year it was released</u>. A poor boy is taken from his mother and raised by a rich businessman. The boy becomes a newspaper tycoon, but at his life's end is <u>a lonely and bitter man</u>. <u>On everyone's top 10 list.</u>

___F+O___ 10. *Shakespeare in Love,* **1998.** Gwyneth Paltrow, Joseph Fiennes. Will Shakespeare (Joseph Fiennes) needs inspiration to break <u>a bad case</u> of writer's block. A secret romance with the <u>beautiful</u> Lady Viola (Paltrow) ends up providing the spark he needs—and much more. A <u>can't-miss</u> motion picture with an <u>impressive</u> collection of awards.

Judgment words and opinions are underlined.

Facts and Opinions in Passages

People tend to accept what they read as fact, but much of what is written is actually opinion. Keeping an eye out for opinion will help you to think for yourself and to question what you read.

☑ *Check Your Understanding*

Two sentences in the following passage are facts, two are opinions, and one combines fact and opinion. Read the passage, and identify facts with an **F**, opinions with an **O**, and the statement of fact *and* opinion with an **F+O**. Then read the explanation that follows.

[1]It is time for educators to assume the responsibility for children's unhealthy lunch menus. [2]There is little value in teaching academics to children only to damage their minds and bodies with the wrong foods at lunch time. [3]About 13 percent of our nation's schools have sold fast-food restaurants the right to put their food items on the lunch menu. [4]A number of schools also allow snack and soft-drink vending machines in their buildings. [5]With the many high-sodium, high-fat, and low-fiber foods on school lunch menus, there is a major public-health disaster in the making.

1. __O__   2. __O__   · 3. __F__   4. __F__   5. __F+O__

Explanation:

Sentence 1 contains an opinion: some people may feel that not only educators but also parents and the larger school community should be responsible for children's lunch menus. Sentence 2 is also an opinion; others may feel there is considerable value in teaching academics to children even with poor meal choices. Sentences 3 and 4 contain researchable facts. The last sentence is a mixture of fact and opinion: the first half of the sentence contains facts, and the second half is clearly an opinion. Many people might agree there is cause for alarm but not that there is a "major public-health disaster in the making." There may even be some who feel there is no cause for alarm.

➤ *Practice 5*   Judgment words and opinions are underlined.

A. The following passage contains five sentences. Two sentences are facts, two are opinions, and one combines fact and opinion. Identify the facts with an **F**, the opinions with an **O**, and the statement of fact *and* opinion with an **F+O**.

[1]There were several queens of Egypt by the name of Cleopatra, including the one who ruled in the days of Antony and Caesar. [2]She remains to this day the most fascinating figure in Egyptian history. [3]History records that she was born in 69 B.C. and killed herself almost forty years later. [4]The story of how she killed herself is very easy to believe. [5]Reports say she killed herself with an asp, the Egyptian cobra—a symbol of Egyptian royalty, so there could have been no better way for the queen to end her life.

1. __F__   2. __O__   3. __F__   4. __O__   5. __F+O__

B. The following newspaper editorial contains five sentences. Three sentences are facts, and two combine fact and opinion. Identify the facts with an **F** and the statements of fact *and* opinion with an **F+O**.

> [1]Currently, about half of all three- to five-year-olds in the United States are enrolled in preschool programs, including Head Start, school-based prekindergarten programs, nursery schools, and child care. [2]A task force of the Carnegie Corporation has now recommended that almost all children be enrolled in a preschool program at age 3 to improve their prospects for success in school. [3]The task force estimates that 75 percent of the funding for existing early-education services can be provided by families. [4]It is most regrettable that the task force did not provide in the report any suggestions about who should pay the rest of the bill. [5]As a result, while the task force calls for immediate action, its proposal should be seen as a long-term goal that deserves serious study by policymakers and parents.

1. _F_   2. _F_   3. _F_   4. _F+O_   5. _F+O_

➤ Practice 6

Here are excerpts from four book reviews. Identify the two factual descriptions with an **F** and the two descriptions that include both fact *and* the reviewer's opinion with an **F+O**.

_F_ 1. [1]From June 1942 to August 1944, Anne Frank, a young Jewish girl, lived every day in fear of arrest by the German Nazis. [2]All Jews in Nazi-occupied lands, and anyone else the Nazis considered inferior, were being arrested and sent to concentration camps. [3]Anne went into hiding with her sister and parents in Amsterdam two days after her thirteenth birthday. [4]They were concealed upstairs behind a folding bookcase and aided by Dutch men and women. [5]Soon they were joined by a second family and a bachelor who were also avoiding arrest. [6]In *The Diary of a Young Girl,* Anne describes her hopes, secrets and feelings during over two years in hiding.

_F+O_ 2. [1]*Charlotte's Web,* one of the best-known books in children's literature, is loved by adults as well as children. [2]This imaginative story by E. B. White centers on the barnyard life of a young pig who is to be butchered in the fall. [3]The animals of the yard (especially a haughty gray spider named Charlotte) plan with the farmer's daughter to save the pig's life. [4]While the author incorporates much humor into his story, he also skillfully blends a wise sadness into his themes of friendship and the cycle of life. [5]This is a book that should not be missed.

Judgment words and opinions are underlined.

_F_   3. ¹In George Orwell's *Animal Farm,* the horses, sheep, pigs, cows, and other animals of Manor Farm rebel against Mr. Jones, the hard-drinking farmer who owns them. ²They don't want to be treated like slaves anymore. ³The pigs lead all the farm's animals in the revolution, driving away all humans and leaving the animals in charge of the farm and their own destiny. ⁴With their newly improved conditions, the animals turn for leadership to the pig Napoleon. ⁵However, whether Napoleon and his fellow pigs will transform the farm into a paradise for all animals—or just for pigs—only time will tell.

_F+O_   4. ¹In his book *Amazing Grace,* Jonathan Kozol brings us face to face with the daily lives and seemingly endless struggles of the people who live in Mott Haven, a desperately poor neighborhood in the South Bronx. ²The book reminds us that the residents, like those in poor communities throughout the country, are not a breed apart but human beings like the rest of us, with feelings and needs and hopes and dreams for their children. ³As human beings they have the right in this wealthy country to adequate shelter and food. ⁴They have the right to accessible health care and education that will enable them to survive in the twenty-first century. ⁵This is a painful and necessary book to read at an increasingly cold hour of our nation's history.

A Note on Informed Opinion

In much of what we read, the distinction between fact and opinion is not nearly as clear-cut as in the practice materials in this chapter. But the chapter has helped you to begin looking at information with the questioning eye necessary to being a critical reader.

As you question what you read, remember that just because something is an opinion doesn't mean it isn't valid. Opinions are fundamental to much of our lives (democracy is the best form of government, everyone should receive basic health care, etc.). However, look for realistic, meaningful support for opinions. Solid support is often made up of facts based on direct observation, expert opinion, and research. Textbook authors, in particular, work very hard to back up their opinions with such factual support.

The textbook passage on the next page is an example. One sentence represents an opinion. The rest of the passage is made up of facts used in support of that opinion. Somebody with an opposite view would choose very different information to support his or her opinion. Which sentence presents the author's opinion? Write its number in the space provided.

Sentence with the opinion: ___1___

¹Crime is probably one of the urban problems that the average citizen thinks most about. ²Although crime can be found in suburbs and rural areas, it is more common in cities. ³The rate of violent crime is eight times greater in our largest cities than it is in rural areas; the rate of property crimes is four times greater. ⁴The greatest disparity is for robbery, which is at least forty-five times greater in large cities than in rural areas! ⁵Also, the larger the city, the higher the crime rate. ⁶And suburban areas have lower crime rates than all but the smallest cities.

Explanation:

Sentences 2–6 present facts that are based on statistics. The first sentence, however, represents the author's opinion (as suggested by the word *probably*). He assumes that since crime is common in cities, it is likely to be one of the urban problems that the average citizen thinks most about. You may agree with that opinion, or you may feel that the average citizen, while cautious about crime, tries not to think about it much.

CHAPTER REVIEW

In this chapter, you learned the difference between fact and opinion:

- A **fact** is information that can be proved true through objective evidence. This evidence may be physical proof or the spoken or written testimony of witnesses.

- An **opinion** is a belief, judgment, or conclusion that cannot be objectively proved true. As a result, it is open to question.

Both facts and opinions can be valuable. However, it is important to distinguish between the two, and you should look at information with the questioning eye of a critical reader.

The next chapter—Chapter 8—will sharpen your ability to make inferences in reading.

On the Web: If you are using this book in class, you can visit our website for additional practice in distinguishing facts from opinions. Go to **www.townsendpress.com** and click on "Online Exercises."

➤ Review Test 1

To review what you've learned in this chapter, complete each of the following sentences about facts and opinions.

1. *(A fact, An opinion)* _____*A fact*_____ can be proved true through objective evidence.

2. *(An editorial, A political speech, A news report)* ____*A news report*____ is likely to be totally factual.

3. Most of what we read is *(fact, opinion, a mixture of fact and opinion)* _____*a mixture of fact and opinion*_____ .

4. *(Facts, Opinions)* _____*Opinions*_____ often include words that express judgments.

5. An example of a value word is *(rectangular, objective, enjoyable, tall, wet, full, rounded)* _____*enjoyable*_____ .

➤ Review Test 2

A. Two of the statements below are facts, and two are opinions. Identify facts with an **F** and opinions with an **O**.

__*F*__ 1. Falling coconuts kill about 150 worldwide each year, and sharks kill about 10 people.

__*O*__ 2. The <u>greatest</u> danger in swimming in the ocean is of being attacked by a shark.

__*F*__ 3. At the turn of the century, only one of ten married women held a paying job.

__*O*__ 4. For self-fulfillment, any mother in today's world <u>should hold down an outside job</u> as well as care for her children.

B. Here are short reviews taken from a movie guide. Identify the factual review with an **F** and the reviews that include both a factual report *and* an opinion with an **F+O**.

__*F+O*__ 5. ***Training Day*, 2001.** Denzel Washington, Ethan Hawke. A <u>disturbing</u> suspense tale about a veteran Los Angeles Police Department lieutenant who escorts a new officer on his first day on the job. <u>Dark and violent.</u>

Judgment words and opinions are underlined.

F+O 6. ***Braveheart*, 1995.** Mel Gibson. Big, booming epic tale of the thirteenth-century Scottish rebel warrior William Wallace. Manages to tell a <u>gripping</u> personal story that grows in scale through a series of <u>eye-popping</u> and bloody battle scenes. A <u>powerful, passionate</u> film.

F 7. ***Spider-Man*, 2002.** Tobey McGuire, Kirsten Dunst. After being bitten by a genetically altered spider, high-school student Peter Parker develops unusual powers. He uses his ability to fight crime while he pursues Mary Jane, the girl next door.

F+O 8. ***101 Dalmatians*, 1996.** Glenn Close. It's supposed to be *about* dogs; it's not supposed to *be* a dog. <u>Disappointing</u> live-action remake of the Disney animated classic.

C. Here are excerpts from two book reviews. Identify the factual description with an **F** and the description that includes both fact *and* opinion with an **F+O**.

F 9. [1]Frank McCourt, who taught writing for many years in the public school system, waited more than forty years to tell the story of his childhood in his book *Angela's Ashes*. [2]McCourt had a father who drank away the family's food money, and a mother who thus felt she had to beg to feed her family. [3]The McCourts were too poor to afford sheets or blankets for their flea-infested bed, too poor to buy new shoes for the children, too poor to get milk for the new baby. [4]By 11, Frank was the chief breadwinner of the family, stealing bread and milk so the family would have something to eat. [5]By 15, he lost his first girlfriend to tuberculosis. [6]By 19, he saved enough money to go to the United States.

F+O 10. [1]*The Fellowship of the Ring* is the first book in J.R.R. Tolkien's <u>remarkable</u> fantasy trilogy *The Lord of the Rings*. [2]This <u>gripping</u> novel begins with Middle Earth in danger of being enslaved by Sauron, an evil lord. [3]What Sauron needs to complete his destruction is the One Ring, an all-powerful magic ring which is owned by Frodo Baggins, hobbit of the Shire. [4]To prevent Sauron from getting the ring, Frodo agrees to take it to the one place it can be destroyed—the fires of Mount Doom. [5]Waiting to stop Frodo are armies of orcs, goblins, the Dark Riders and other more powerful and evil enemies. [6]Frodo's journey, begun in this book, is one of the <u>most exciting and entertaining</u> tales written in the English language.

Judgment words and opinions are underlined.

> **Review Test 3**

A. Some of the statements below are facts, and some are opinions; in addition, **three** include both fact and opinion. Identify facts with an **F**, opinions with an **O**, and statements of fact *and* opinion with an **F+O**.

___O___ 1. My son is the most considerate person in our family.

___F___ 2. My son once left half a sandwich under his bed for more than a week.

___F+O___ 3. Although my son got a B in English this semester, he deserved an A.

___F___ 4. New York City is not the capital of New York State.

___F+O___ 5. New York City, where visitors can see Broadway plays, museums, and sights such as the Statue of Liberty, is an ideal place for a summer vacation.

___O___ 6. The Empire State Building is the most memorable of all the sights in New York City.

___F___ 7. Elephants are the largest of all land animals.

___F___ 8. Researchers have found that elephants react nervously to rabbits and dachshunds, but not to mice.

___O___ 9. The lively scampering of the rabbits and dachshunds is always fun to watch.

___F+O___ 10. Because they use their trunks both to clean themselves and to eat, elephants are the most fascinating animals in the zoo.

B. (11–20.) Each passage below contains five sentences. Two are facts, two are opinions, and one combines fact and opinion. Identify facts with an **F**, opinions with an **O**, and the statement of fact *and* opinion with an **F+O**.

1.   [1]There are few problems more annoying than hiccups, which can last for hours or even days. [2]According to one doctor who has studied them, hiccups are usually caused by eating or drinking too quickly. [3]People do some pretty strange things to remedy this ridiculous problem. [4]Some common remedies include holding your breath, eating a teaspoon of sugar, and putting a paper bag over your head. [5]Undoubtedly, that last one is the strangest one of all.

   1. __F+O__   2. __F__   3. __O__   4. __F__   5. __O__

Judgment words and opinions are underlined.

2.   [1]The Lincoln Memorial is surely America's <u>best loved</u> public monument. [2]Designed by Henry Beacon, it was dedicated on Memorial Day, 1922, more than fifty years after a memorial to Lincoln was first proposed. [3]Built to resemble a Greek temple, it contains a seated figure of Lincoln by sculptor Daniel Chester French. [4]Many people <u>probably</u> learn to admire the monument long before they visit it in person through seeing its picture, which is on the penny and the five-dollar bill. [5]<u>All Americans must feel pride mingled with sorrow</u> when they come to Washington in person and look up at the <u>kindly, mournful</u> face of Abraham Lincoln.

1. __O__   2. __F__   3. __F__   4. __F+O__   5. __O__

➤ **Review Test 4**

Here is a chance to apply your understanding of facts and opinions to a full article. The selection presents new information about a topic many people already know something about—the importance of napping.

To help you continue to strengthen your skills, the reading is followed by questions not only on what you've learned in this chapter but also on what you've learned in previous chapters.

Words to Watch

in vogue (4): in favor; in general practice
tactic (4): method
restorative (5): energizing
chronically (5): continuously
accommodations (5): arrangements
scintillating (6): lively and interesting
susceptible to (6): likely to have
prophylactic (7) protective
cumulative (7): collective
nocturnal (9): nighttime
lethargy (12): state of extreme tiredness and inactivity

NEW RESPECT FOR THE NAP,
A PAUSE THAT REFRESHES

Jane E. Brody

1   *"You must sleep sometime between lunch and dinner, and no halfway measures. Take off your clothes and get into bed. That's what I always do. Don't think you will be doing less work because you sleep during the day. That's a foolish notion held by people who have no imaginations. You will be able to accomplish more. You get two days in one—well, at least one and a half."*

—Winston Churchill

2   As a short sleeper who is rarely in bed for more than six hours a night, I'm a strong believer in naps for recharging my batteries. Sir Winston and I are in good company. Napping enthusiasts have included Albert Einstein, Napoleon Bonaparte, Thomas Edison and at least three presidents: John F. Kennedy, Ronald Reagan and Bill Clinton. Besides, sleep researchers have shown that regardless of how long one sleeps at night, the human body is programmed to become sleepy in the early afternoon, even without a big lunch.

3   "Napping should not be frowned upon at the office or make you feel guilty at home," writes Dr. James B. Maas, a psychologist and sleep expert at Cornell. "It should have the status of daily exercise."

4   In the old days, people would doze for an hour or so after the midday meal, and in some Latin American and European countries siestas are still in vogue°. But in most industrialized nations, the usual response to the afternoon sag in energy is to try to jump-start the system with caffeine. But sleep experts say that tactic° is actually counterproductive, creating only the illusion of efficiency and alertness and depriving the body and brain of much-needed sleep.

How Naps Help

5   Now, however, there is growing evidence that restorative° naps are making a comeback. Recognizing that most of their employees are chronically° sleep-deprived, some companies have set up nap rooms with reclining chairs, blankets and alarm clocks. If unions are truly interested in worker welfare, they should make such accommodations° a standard item in contract negotiations.

6   Workers who take advantage of the opportunity to sleep for twenty minutes or so during the workday report that they can go back to work with renewed enthusiasm and energy. My college roommate, Dr. Linda Himot, a psychiatrist in Pittsburgh, who has a talent for ten-minute catnaps between patients, says these respites help her focus better on each patient's problems, which are not always scintillating°. And companies that encourage napping report that it reduces accidents and errors and increases productivity, even if it shortens the workday a bit. Studies have shown that sleepy workers make more mistakes and cause more accidents, and are more susceptible to° heart attacks and gastrointestinal disorders.

7   A NASA scientist's study showed that twenty-four-minute naps significantly improved a pilot's alertness and performance on transatlantic flights. (The copilot remained awake.) Dr. David Dinges, a sleep researcher at the University of Pennsylvania, is a strong advocate of prophylactic° napping—taking what he and others call a "power nap" during the day to head off the cumulative° effects of sleep loss. He explained that the brain "sort of sputters" when it is deprived of sufficient sleep, causing slips in performance and attentiveness and often resulting in "microsleeps"—involuntary lapses into sleep, in which accidents can occur.

8   A brief afternoon nap typically leaves people feeling more energized than if they had tried to muddle through without sleeping. Studies have shown that the brain is more active in people who nap during the day.

9   Dr. Maas, the Cornell psychologist and author of *Power Sleep,* points out that naps "greatly strengthen the ability to pay close attention to details and to make critical decisions." He also states that "naps taken about eight hours after you wake have been proved to do much more for you than if you added those twenty minutes onto already adequate nocturnal° sleep."

10   There are two kinds of naps: brief ones taken to revive the brain and long ones taken to compensate for significant sleep loss. The reviving workday nap should not be longer than thirty minutes; any more and the body lapses into a deep sleep, from which it is difficult to awake.

How and When to Nap

11   Long naps help when you've accumulated a considerable sleep debt—for example, when the previous night's sleep was much shorter than usual, or when you know you will have to be alert and awake considerably later than your usual bedtime. I usually try to nap for an hour or more before attending a play, concert or late party. But long naps have a temporary disadvantage: they cause what researchers call sleep inertia, a grogginess upon awakening that can last about half an hour. Also, long naps can affect the body's clock, making it more difficult to wake up at the proper time in the morning.

12   As Dr. Maas maintains, "Brief naps taken daily are far healthier than sleeping in or taking very long naps on the weekend." They are also far better than caffeine as a pick-me-up. "Consumption of caffeine will be followed by feelings of lethargy° and reduced R.E.M. (or dream) sleep that night," Dr. Maas writes. "A debt in your sleep bank account is not reduced by artificial stimulants."

13   He suggests that naps be scheduled for midday because late-afternoon naps can cause a shift in your biological clock, making it harder to fall asleep at night and get up the next morning. To keep naps short—fifteen to thirty minutes, set an alarm clock or timer. Westclox makes a device called Napmate, a power-nap alarm clock that allows you to program your nap to last for a specific number of minutes. If you can lie down on a couch or bed, all the better. If not, use a reclining chair. You need not follow Churchill's advice to get undressed, but make yourself as comfortable as possible. Lap robes are very popular and inexpensive; if a blanket helps you to doze off, use one.

14   Try to take your nap about the same time each day. Dr. Maas recommends a nap eight hours after you wake up (in the middle of your day, about eight hours

before you go to bed at night). Even on days when you don't feel particularly sleepy, he suggests taking a rest rather than a coffee break at your usual nap time.

15   There are special cases. People who have trouble falling asleep at night might be wise to avoid daytime naps. Parents of newborns should nap when the baby does, rather than using all the baby's sleep time to do chores.

Finally, naps are often essential for 16 people trying to work through illness, injury or chemotherapy, even if they get adequate sleep at night. A woman I know who continued working while receiving cancer therapy napped each day on the floor under her desk. Like so many workplaces, hers had no suitable place to rest.

Reading Comprehension Questions

Vocabulary in Context

____D____ 1. In the sentence below, the word *counterproductive* (koun′tər-prə-dŭk′tĭv) means
   A. truthful.
   B. practical and easy.
   C. overly helpful.
   D. having the opposite effect of what is intended.

   "But . . . the usual response to the afternoon sag in energy is to try to jump-start the system with caffeine, a tactic that . . . is actually counterproductive, creating only the illusion of efficiency and alertness and depriving the body and brain of much-needed sleep." (Paragraph 4)

____B____ 2. In the sentence below, the word *respites* (rĕs′pĭtz) means
   A. problems.
   B. breaks.
   C. workouts.
   D. examinations.

   "Dr. Linda Himot, a psychiatrist in Pittsburgh, who has a talent for ten-minute catnaps between patients, says these respites help her focus better on each patient's problems . . ." (Paragraph 6)

Central Point and Main Ideas

___D___ 3. Which sentence best expresses the central point of the selection?

    A. Naps of an hour or so after the midday meal were once popular and are still in favor in Latin American and European countries.

    B. There are two types of naps: short ones that energize body and brain and long ones that make up for great sleep loss.

    C. According to sleep researchers, the human body is programmed to become sleepy in the early afternoon.

    D. Naps, generally short ones about eight hours after waking, energize people mentally and physically.   Answers A, B, and C are too narrow.
           Only answer D includes all the ideas in the selection.

___C___ 4. At times, a main idea may cover more than one paragraph. Which sentence best expresses the main idea of paragraphs 13 and 14?

    A. It is important to schedule naps at midday instead of late afternoon, says Dr. Maas.   Too narrow.

    B. People who take naps should be sure they are as comfortable as possible.   Too narrow.

    C. Dr. Maas suggests simple steps people can take in order to have a good nap.

    D. For many reasons, says Dr. Maas, taking a nap is superior to taking a coffee break.   Not stated in the paragraph. (See the comment below.)

Supporting Details

___C___ 5. According to the selection, napping

    A. is generally best done in the late afternoon.

    B. reduces conflict among workers.   See paragraph 9.

    C. improves workers' concentration and performance.

    D. can help most people sleep better in the evening.

Transitions

___D___ 6. The relationship expressed in the sentence below is one of

    A. comparison.

    B. addition.

    C. contrast.

    D. cause and effect.

        ". . . long naps can <u>affect</u> the body's clock, making it more difficult to wake up at the proper time in the morning." (Paragraph 11)

Comment: Item 4: The paragraphs list a number of steps: midday naps, short naps, reclining, being as comfortable as possible, napping at the same time each day. Note that in this *New York Times* article, the author does not include any transitions; a textbook author probably would.

Patterns of Organization

   7. *(Complete the sentence:)* Paragraphs 6–9 discuss some effects of
_____ *short naps* _____.

Fact and Opinion

___C___ 8. The word that makes the excerpt below an opinion is
   A. *because.*
   B. *sleep.*
   C. *foolish.*
   D. *people.*

   "Don't think you will be doing less work because you sleep during the day. That's a foolish notion held by people who have no imaginations." (Paragraph 1)

___A___ 9. The sentence below is mainly
   A. fact.
   B. opinion.

   "A NASA scientist's study showed that twenty-four-minute naps significantly improved a pilot's alertness and performance on transatlantic flights." (Paragraph 7)

___A___ 10. The sentence below is
   A. a fact.
   B. an opinion.
   C. a mix of fact and opinion.

   "Westclox makes a device called Napmate, a power-nap alarm clock that allows you to program your nap to last for a specific number of minutes." (Paragraph 13)

DISCUSSION QUESTIONS

1. Are you a "napping enthusiast"? If so, when and where do you generally nap? How does napping affect you? After reading this article, do you agree that napping should, as Dr. Maas suggests, "have the status of daily exercise"?

2. According to Brody, companies recognize "that most of their employees are chronically sleep-deprived." Why do you think so many people get inadequate sleep? Do you or does anybody you know fail to get enough sleep? If so, how does it affect you or the other person?

3. Brody argues that employers should promote napping at the workplace. How do you feel about such a proposal? What objections do you think employers might have to such a suggestion?

4. The NASA scientist's research showed that napping can improve a pilot's alertness and performance. What else (besides napping) do you think people could do to boost their alertness and performance, either in school or in the workplace?

Note: Writing assignments for this selection appear on pages 588–589.

Check Your Performance			**FACT AND OPINION**
Activity	*Number Right*	*Points*	*Score*
Review Test 1 (5 items)	_____	× 2 =	_____
Review Test 2 (10 items)	_____	× 3 =	_____
Review Test 3 (20 items)	_____	× 1.5 =	_____
Review Test 4 (10 items)	_____	× 3 =	_____
		TOTAL SCORE =	_____ %

Enter your total score into the **Reading Performance Chart: Review Tests** on the inside back cover.

FACT AND OPINION: Mastery Test 1

A. Five of the statements below are facts, and five are opinions. Identify statements of fact with an **F** and statements of opinion with an **O**.

_F_ 1. In 1924, the Model T Ford could be purchased for $290.

_O_ 2. The Model T Ford was the <u>most significant</u> invention of the twentieth century.

_F_ 3. The core of a pencil is made out of graphite and clay, not lead.

_O_ 4. It is always <u>better</u> to use a ball-point pen rather than a pencil when taking notes <u>in class</u>.

_O_ 5. Finding a double yolk in an egg is a <u>sure sign</u> of good luck in the future.

_F_ 6. A hen in Russia once laid an egg that had nine double yolks.

_F_ 7. Jay Leno became official host of *The Tonight Show* in 1992.

_O_ 8. Jay Leno is the <u>greatest</u> talk-show host of them all.

_F_ 9. Baltimore's traffic lights were designed with colorblind people in mind—green lights have a vertical shape, and red ones are horizontal.

_O_ 10. People that disregard traffic lights and stop signs <u>should be sentenced</u> to a few days in jail.

B. Here are short movie reviews taken from a newspaper guide. Some reviews provide only factual reports; others contain opinions about the movie as well. Identify the factual reviews with an **F**; identify reviews that also contain the reviewer's opinion with an **F+O**.

_F+O_ 11. ***Pearl Harbor, 2001.*** Ben Affleck, Josh Hartnett. <u>Terrific</u> battle sequence can't save this war movie from its <u>laughably bad</u> dialogue and <u>who-cares</u> romance.

_F_ 12. ***My Mom's a Werewolf, 1989.*** Susan Blakely, John Saxon. Bitten on the toe by a pet-shop owner, a woman turns into a werewolf.

_F+O_ 13. ***Good Will Hunting, 1997.*** Matt Damon, Robin Williams. <u>Good</u>, though <u>predictable</u>, story about a troubled young university janitor who also happens to be an undiscovered mathematical genius.

In Tests 1–6, judgment words and opinions are underlined.

(Continues on next page)

_F_ 14. *John Q, 2002.* Denzel Washington, Robert Duvall. When a working man learns his son needs a heart transplant, he discovers his health insurance won't cover the operation. In a gamble to save his son's life, he takes the hospital's emergency room hostage.

_F+O_ 15. *I Am Sam, 2002.* Sean Penn, Michelle Pfeiffer. Drama about a mentally challenged father struggling to keep custody of his young daughter. <u>Fine</u> performances, but the movie is a <u>sugary tearjerker</u> instead of a serious look at a complicated issue.

C. (16–20.) The passage below contains five sentences. Identify each sentence with an **F** (for fact), an **O** (for opinion), or **F+O** (for a combination of fact *and* opinion). Note that **one** sentence combines fact and opinion.

[1]The first bathing suits for women were created in the mid-1800s. [2]Invented by a man, they were <u>ridiculous-looking</u>, high-necked costumes that included knee-length skirts, elbow-length sleeves, black stockings, and shoes. [3]Once such suits became wet, they could weigh as much as the bather, and they are actually thought to have caused drowning on more than one occasion. [4]It is <u>incredible</u> that women ever agreed to wear such clothing. [5]<u>Only a man could have invented</u> something quite so <u>impractical</u> for women.

1. _F_   2. _F+O_   3. _F_   4. _O_   5. _O_

FACT AND OPINION: Mastery Test 2

A. Five of the statements below are facts, and five are opinions. Identify statements of fact with an **F** and statements of opinion with an **O**.

___O___ 1. It would be nice to have more than 24 hours in a day.

___F___ 2. Earth makes a complete rotation on its axis every 23 hours, 56 minutes and 4.09 seconds.

___O___ 3. Cats are much easier to care for than dogs.

___F___ 4. A cat once fell from a building's twentieth floor and suffered only a pelvic fracture.

___F___ 5 Fishing is ranked as the fourth most popular outdoor activity in the United States, following walking, swimming, and camping.

___O___ 6. Families who participate in outdoor activities together are happier than those who do not.

___O___ 7. Organ transplantation is the most important medical achievement of the twentieth century.

___F___ 8. Through transplants, more than two thousand people each year receive a heart that once belonged to someone else.

___O___ 9. The globefish is nature's strangest creature.

___F___ 10. The globefish keeps from being eaten by gulping so much water that it becomes too large to be swallowed by its enemies.

B. Here are five short book reviews. Identify a factual review with an **F**; identify a review that includes both facts about the book *and* the reviewer's opinion with an **F+O**.

___F+O___ 11. *Good Night, Mr. Tom* takes place while England was being bombed during World War II. City children were sent to live with country families who would keep them safe. Soon Willie Beech, a badly abused boy, is brought to the home of a gruff but kind older man, Tom Oakley. An incredibly heartwarming story then follows, making this a wonderful book for young people and adults alike.

(Continues on next page)

285

_F_ 12. Bram Stoker's *Dracula* begins with the story of Jonathan Harker, a young English lawyer hired by Count Dracula. After he arrives in Dracula's castle in Transylvania, Jonathan finds himself the prisoner of the Count, who he slowly realizes is a monstrous vampire. Back in England, Harker's fiancée, Mina, watches helplessly as her best friend falls victim to a mysterious illness that is draining her life, and blood, away. When Jonathan and Mina realize that Dracula is on the loose in England, they join with a small group of friends to destroy the bloodthirsty Count forever. Their story is told in the form of their letters, notes, and diaries.

_F+O_ 13. Any reader who thrives on terror and suspense <u>must read</u> Mary Higgins Clark's novel *The Cradle Will Fall*. In it, a country prosecutor uncovers evidence that proves a famous doctor is killing women, not realizing that she herself is his next target. Higgins <u>squeezes every possible bit of tension</u> into this story.

_F+O_ 14. What is the definition of human evil? In *People of the Lie*, psychiatrist M. Scott Peck makes an <u>impressive</u> attempt to answer that question. Drawing from everyday experiences, Dr. Peck shows how evil people attack others rather than risk looking at their own failures. As <u>hard to put down</u> as a suspense novel, *People of the Lie* <u>is sure to fascinate and trouble you.</u>

_F_ 15. *Harry Potter and the Sorcerer's Stone* concerns a young boy, Harry Potter, who has been orphaned as an infant. He is raised by his aunt and uncle, the Dursleys. They don't like or want him, and their son Dudley bullies him. But Harry's life changes when he is called to attend Hogwarts—a school for young wizards and witches.

C. (16–20.) The passage below contains five sentences. Identify each sentence with an **F** (for fact), an **O** (for opinion), or **F+O** (for a combination of fact *and* opinion). Note that **one** sentence combines fact and opinion.

[1]According to a recent study, about 1.7 percent (850,000) of American students are homeschooled. [2]Many parents make that choice for a <u>very understandable</u> reason: concern about the influence of peer pressure, drugs, and alcohol in public schools. [3]But other parents choose to homeschool because public schools do not support their particular religious beliefs. [4]Those parents <u>should be concerned</u> about how their children will ever learn to think for themselves. [5]A <u>narrow</u> religious point of view can be just as <u>bad</u> as no religious training.

1. _F_   2. _F+O_   3. _F_   4. _O_   5. _O_

FACT AND OPINION: Mastery Test 3

A. Identify facts with an **F**, opinions with an **O**, and the **two** combinations of fact *and* opinion with an **F+O**.

   F   1. Rice grows in a warm, wet climate.

   O   2. Rice is far <u>better</u> with stir-fried vegetables than noodles are.

   F   3. Brown rice provides more B vitamins than white rice does.

  F+O 4. White rice is the result of milling that removes much of the grain's nutrients; thus people <u>should eat</u> only brown rice.

   O   5. Comic strips are <u>never suitable</u> reading for young children.

   F   6. In 1907, the San Francisco Chronicle began publishing the first daily comic strip—"Mr. Mutt," later named "Mutt and Jeff."

   F   7. Before Popeye the Sailor became a children's cartoon character, he was a freely swearing character in an adult comic strip.

   O   8. Fighting during hockey games <u>should be outlawed</u>.

   F   9. Basketball was invented in 1891 when a YMCA instructor created a game using two peach baskets and a soccer ball.

 F+O 10. Baseball players have been known to do some really <u>ridiculous</u> things; for example, some players break in a new glove by <u>rubbing</u> it with shaving cream.

B. Here are five short book reviews. Identify a factual review with an **F**; identify a review that includes both facts about the book *and* the reviewer's opinion with an **F+O**.

 F+O 11. Richard Adams's *Watership Down* is a <u>wonderfully entertaining</u> novel about rabbits who act a great deal like people. The plot may sound <u>unlikely</u>, but <u>it will grab your attention and not let go</u>.

  F 12. *The Silence of the Lambs*, a novel by Thomas Harris, is about an intelligent mentally ill killer who is on the loose. In trying to find him, the FBI relies upon the clues provided by the killer himself. This story was made into a movie.

(Continues on next page)

_F+O_ 13. *In Cold Blood* by Truman Capote is a frightening true story about the murder of a family and also an examination of what made their killers tick. Many books today tell gripping stories of real-life crimes. *In Cold Blood* was the first book of this type and may be the best.

_F_ 14. In *Cry of the Kalahari*, Mark and Delia Owens tell about going to Africa to study wildlife and to save some animals from destruction. This husband and wife team describe their encounters with hyenas, lions, and a predator they consider even more dangerous: man.

_F+O_ 15. In his inspiring book *Man's Search for Meaning*, Viktor Frankl answers the question "How do people go on when they have been stripped of everything, including human dignity?" The author describes his time in a concentration camp and what he learned there about survival. This real-life story is simply told but unforgettable.

C. (16–20.) The passage below contains five sentences. Identify each sentence with an **F** (for fact), an **O** (for opinion), or **F+O** (for a combination of fact *and* opinion). Note that **one** sentence combines fact and opinion.

[1]Americans have become much too concerned about success and about owning things. [2]According to a recent study, as many as 80 percent of job resumés contain false or misleading information. [3]Also, studies show that Americans use as much as 50 percent of their paycheck to pay back consumer loans. [4]For their wardrobes alone, consumers each year pay out millions of dollars, dollars that should have ended up in such worthy projects as health research and housing for the homeless. [5]It's time for Americans to become less selfish and to contribute more to the community.

1. _O_   2. _F_   3. _F_   4. _F+O_   5. _O_

FACT AND OPINION: Mastery Test 4

A. Identify facts with an **F**, opinions with an **O**, and the two combinations of fact *and* opinion with an **F+O**.

___O___ 1. Adults <u>shouldn't consume</u> dairy products.

___F+O___ 2. Goat's milk is more easily digested by some people who are allergic to cow's milk, and goat's milk <u>tastes better</u>, too.

___O___ 3. Watching sports events in person is <u>more exciting</u> than watching them on TV.

___O___ 4. Children <u>should not be allowed</u> to watch more than one hour of television a day.

___F___ 5. In the Middle Ages it was commonly believed that the seat of human intelligence was the heart.

___F+O___ 6. The Middle Ages was the <u>worst</u> time to be alive; for example, in the mid-fourteenth century, bubonic plague killed millions of people.

___F___ 7. During the Middle Ages it was mainly the clergy that could read and write; most other people—including royalty—did not have these skills.

___F___ 8. Rubber was at first made only from the sap of certain tropical plants and now is often made synthetically.

___F___ 9. Joseph Priestley, an eighteenth-century scientist, named the substance rubber because it could rub away pencil marks.

___F___ 10. Bessie Smith, known as the "empress of the blues," was killed in a car accident in 1937.

___F___ 11. A week after the stock-market crash of 1929, Columbia released Smith's recording of "Nobody Knows You When You're Down and Out."

___O___ 12. No singer alive today can sing that song <u>better</u> than Smith did.

(Continues on next page)

B. (13–17.) The passage below contains five sentences. Identify each sentence with an **F** (for fact), an **O** (for opinion), or **F+O** (for a combination of fact *and* opinion). Note that **one** sentence combines fact and opinion.

¹A common definition of retirement includes the idea of leaving the labor force, but that notion of retirement is <u>too narrow</u>. ²After retiring, it is much <u>better</u> to remain involved in the work world part-time. ³Some companies have recently supported this type of involvement for the retired by hiring two or three older part-timers in place of one full-time employee. ⁴The Travelers Corporation, for example, has employed six hundred retired employees for three hundred shared jobs. ⁵Other retirees have continued to work part-time by volunteering for organizations such as hospitals and museums.

1. <u>*F+O*</u>   2. <u>*O*</u>   3. <u>*F*</u>   4. <u>*F*</u>   5. <u>*F*</u>

C. The following passage is from a newspaper editorial page. One of the excerpts listed below it is fact, one is opinion, and one combines fact and opinion. Identify the fact with an **F**, the opinion with an **O**, and the combination of fact *and* opinion with **F+O**.

¹Even casual observers of school reform know that one of the most frequently heard topics revolves around the length of the school year. . . .

²We hear endlessly about the 240-plus days put in by Japanese students, and, by implication, we assume that most of the rest of the world is a lot closer to their standard than to ours.

³Actually, the great majority of the world's countries are closer to our standard than to that of the Japanese. ⁴Almost all of them have more than our 180 days, but most do not have many more. ⁵The international average is 190 days. ⁶Of some twenty-seven countries and provinces, only six exceed 200 days. . . .

⁷All of this suggests a couple of things. ⁸First, the length of the school day may be a bigger issue than the length of the school year, since students in other countries tend to spend more hours in the classroom than American students. ⁹Second, the broader issue of the quality of time in school is probably much more significant than the issue of the quantity of time.

<u>*F*</u> 18. The international average is 190 days. Of some twenty-seven countries and provinces, only six exceed 200 days.

<u>*F+O*</u> 19. First, the length of the school day <u>may be</u> a <u>bigger</u> issue than the length of the school year, since students in other countries tend to spend more hours in the classroom than American students.

<u>*O*</u> 20. Second, the broader issue of the quality of time in school is <u>probably</u> much more <u>significant</u> than the issue of the quantity of time.

FACT AND OPINION: Mastery Test 5

A. Read the following textbook excerpts, and identify facts with an **F**, opinions with an **O**, and the **two** combinations of fact *and* opinion with an **F+O**.

_O_   1. Your attitude about college work is even more <u>crucial</u> than any reading or study skill.

_F_   2. Most newborns sleep two-thirds of the time, on the average of sixteen hours a day.

_F+O_   3. Some tycoons built their fortunes by <u>ruthlessly</u> destroying the competition. A classic example was John D. Rockefeller. He organized Standard Oil in 1870.

_O_   4. Many instructors working with older adults are <u>insensitive</u> to their students' feelings of discouragement.

_F_   5. Canaries were found on the Canary Islands, before Columbus and his crew found America, and were taken home by the sailors and kept for their singing.

_F_   6. Permanent precautions against frozen pipes include wrapping them in fiberglass insulation or heat tape.

_O_   7. Single fathers do a <u>better</u> job of balancing the demands of work and child care than do single mothers.

_F_   8. Surveys show that in the United States, the majority of children under eighteen years old live in a household with their mother and father.

_F_   9. Apple trees generally do not begin to bloom and bear fruit until they are five to eight years old.

_F_ 10. In Belgium, where elections are held on Sunday, as many as 90% of the people vote.

_O_ 11. As a general, George Washington was not a <u>brilliant</u> strategist like Napoleon.

_F+O_ 12. Alfred Stieglitz published fifty-four volumes of *Camera Work* between 1903 and 1917, giving us the <u>finest</u> record ever made of the art of photography.

(Continues on next page)

B. (13–15.) The following paragraph contains three sentences. One expresses facts, one expresses an opinion, and one sentence combines fact and opinion. Identify the factual sentence with an **F**, the opinion with an **O**, and the combination of fact *and* opinion with an **F+O**.

> [1]The flashing of fireflies is one of the most delightful sights of a summer night. [2]These charming little insects blink their lights as part of their fascinating mating ritual. [3]Although many different varieties of firefly may be blinking in one area, males and females of the same type find one another through the pattern of flashes.

1. __O__   2. _F+O_   3. __F__

C. Read the following textbook passage, and then identify each of the listed excerpts from the passage as fact (**F**), opinion (**O**), or both fact *and* opinion (**F+O**). (**Two** of the excerpts are both fact and opinion.)

> [1]Frederick Douglass, a former slave who had escaped from Maryland, was one of the most remarkable Americans of his generation. [2]While a slave, he had received a full portion of beatings and other indignities. [3]But he had been allowed to learn to read and write and to learn a trade. [4](Such opportunities were denied to the vast majority of slaves.) [5]Settling in Boston, he became an agent of the Massachusetts Anti-Slavery Society and a featured speaker at its public meetings.
>
> [6]Douglass was a majestically handsome man who radiated determination and indignation. [7]In 1845 he published his *Narrative of the Life of Frederick Douglass*, one of the most spellbinding accounts of a slave's life ever written. [8]Douglass insisted that emancipation alone would not provide the slaves with freedom. [9]He demanded full equality, social and economic and well as political. [10]Few white northerners accepted his reasoning. [11]But fewer still who heard him or read his works could afterward maintain that all blacks were dull-witted or resigned to inferior status.

_F+O_ 16. Frederick Douglass, a former slave who had escaped from Maryland, was one of the most remarkable Americans of his generation.

__F__ 17. But he had been allowed to learn to read and write and to learn a trade.

__F__ 18. Settling in Boston, he became an agent of the Massachusetts Anti-Slavery Society and a featured speaker at its public meetings.

__O__ 19. Douglass was a majestically handsome man who radiated determination and indignation.

_F+O_ 20. In 1845 he published his *Narrative of the Life of Frederick Douglass*, one of the most spellbinding accounts of a slave's life ever written.

FACT AND OPINION: Mastery Test 6

A. Read the following textbook excerpts, and identify facts with an **F**, opinions with an **O**, and the **two** combinations of fact *and* opinion with an **F+O**.

_F_ 1. During the late 1700s, doctors used a technique called blistering, the creation of second-degree burns on the skin, to draw out infection through the formation of pus.

_F_ 2. Until the late 1800s, Americans were unaware that most deadly diseases were caused by microorganisms.

_O_ 3. Given the views that 19th century Americans had about diseases, there is no way it would have been good to live in that century.

_F_ 4. Alcohol was first discovered and drunk during the Stone Age.

_F+O_ 5. The Parthenon was built in Athens in the fifth century B.C. and dedicated to the goddess Athena. It remains an example of near-perfect architectural design.

_F_ 6. Infertility rates have been rising over the past twenty years: 10 to 15 percent of couples who want a baby cannot conceive.

_F_ 7. Cells in the stomach secrete gastric juice, which is a mixture of water, enzymes, and hydrochloric acid.

_O_ 8. Beethoven came on the scene at a favorable moment in history.

_F+O_ 9. One truly outstanding contributor to the area of motivational research is Abraham Maslow, who developed the concept of the hierarchy of needs.

_O_ 10. McDonalds is more than a restaurant—it is a symbol of our way of life, an institution that dominates U.S. society.

B. (11–15.) The passage below contains five sentences. Identify each sentence with an **F** (for fact), an **O** (for opinion), or **F+O** (for a combination of fact *and* opinion). Note that **one** sentence combines fact and opinion.

[1]Legally, a check doesn't have to come from a checkbook; it can be written on any material. [2]For instance, a man in Iowa painted a check for $30 on a door and delivered it to a neighbor to whom he owed the money. [3]An Englishman named Albert Haddock paid his taxes in the strangest possible way: he painted a check on the side of a cow. [4]Although such unusual checks

(Continues on next page)

are legal, the law allows the persons being paid to refuse to accept them. [5]The government <u>ought to outlaw</u> such unconventional checks altogether.

1. __F__   2. __F__   3. __F+O__   4. __F__   5. __F+O__

C. Read the following textbook passage, and then identify each listed excerpt as either fact (**F**), opinion (**O**), or fact *and* opinion (**F+O**). (Only **one** of the excerpts combines fact and opinion.)

> [1]The educational system of the United States has long been characterized by discriminatory treatment of women. [2]In 1833, Oberlin College became the first institution of higher learning to admit female students—some 200 years after the first men's college was established. [3]But Oberlin treated its female students like future wives and mothers, not like future lawyers and intellectuals. [4]Female students washed men's clothing, cared for their rooms, and served them at meals. [5]In the 1840s Lucy Stone, an Oberlin undergraduate and later one of the nation's most outstanding feminist leaders, refused to write a commencement address because it would have been read to the audience by a male student. [6]In the twentieth century, sexism in education was manifested in many ways. [7]Textbooks contained negative stereotypes of women, counselors put pressure on female students to prepare for "women's work," and women's recreation programs received less money than men's. [8]But nowhere has educational discrimination been more evident than in the employment of teachers. [9]The positions of university professor and college administrator have generally been reserved for men. [10]Yet public school teachers, who earn much lower salaries, are largely female.

__F__ 16. In 1833, Oberlin College became the first institution of higher learning to admit female students—some 200 years after the first men's college was established.

__F__ 17. But Oberlin treated its female students like future wives and mothers, not like future lawyers and intellectuals. Female students washed men's clothing, cared for their rooms, and served them at meals.

__F+O__ 18. In the 1840s Lucy Stone, an Oberlin undergraduate and later one of the nation's most <u>outstanding</u> feminist leaders, refused to write a commencement address because it would have been read to the audience by a male student.

__O__ 19. But nowhere has educational discrimination been more <u>evident</u> than in the employment of teachers.

__F__ 20. The positions of university professor and college administrator have generally been reserved for men. Yet public school teachers, who earn much lower salaries, are largely female.

8

Inferences

You have probably heard the expression "to read between the lines." When you "read between the lines," you pick up ideas that are not directly stated in what you are reading. These implied ideas are often important for a full understanding of what an author means. Discovering the ideas that are not stated directly in writing is called **making inferences**, or **drawing conclusions**.

AN INTRODUCTION TO INFERENCES

Consider first some inferences you might make in everyday life.

- You drive into a small town that has two diners. There are two cars at one diner and many cars at the other. Which diner may have better food and prices?

  The one with many cars

- You come upon a dog in the park and it cringes when you try to pet it. What might you infer?

  The dog has been mistreated.

- You look in the newspaper for a movie to see. One film has a full-page ad with favorable comments from well-known film reviewers. Another movie has a full-page ad with favorable comments from radio stations and newspapers you never heard of. Which may be the better movie?

  The one whose comments are from well-known reviewers

You probably inferred that the diner with many cars may be the better choice, the dog you tried to pet has been mistreated, and the movie with the well-known reviewers' comments may be more enjoyable. In each case, you made a reasonable guess based on the evidence presented.

You have already practiced making inferences in this book. Do you remember the following sentence from Chapter 1?

Many of us have *ambivalent* feelings about our politicians, admiring but also distrusting them.

That sentence does not tell the meaning of *ambivalent*, but it does suggest that *ambivalent* involves both positive and negative feelings. Thus you can infer from this sentence that *ambivalent feelings* probably means "mixed feelings," and you'd be correct.

You also made inferences in the chapter on implied main ideas. Implied ideas are ones that are not stated directly. Instead, you must use the evidence in a selection to find them through inference.

In this chapter, you will get more practice in drawing inferences. Read the following passage, and then check (✓) the **two** inferences that are most firmly based on the information given.

[1]A sociology professor wrote on the board, "A woman without her man is nothing" and, with a smile, asked students to punctuate the sentence correctly. [2]The men all wrote, "A woman, without her man, is nothing." [3]However, the women wrote, "A woman: Without her, man is nothing."

____ 1. The professor was definitely a man.

____ 2. The professor did not believe students could punctuate the words correctly.

✓ 3. The professor knew there was more than one way to punctuate the words correctly.

____ 4. The professor is not a good teacher.

✓ 5. Gender differences caused students to read and punctuate the professor's words differently.

Explanation:

1. There is no indication of the professor's gender in the passage. You should not have checked this item.

2. Nothing in the passage implies that the professor doubted students' ability to punctuate the words correctly. You should not have checked this item.

3. Since the professor chose the particular sentence and smiled while writing the words, we can conclude that the professor was aware of more than one punctuation possibility. Therefore, you should have checked this item.

4. There is no suggestion in the passage that the professor is a poor teacher. In fact, the professor has chosen a dramatic way to suggest that each sex sees the world from its own point of view. You should not have checked this item.

5. Male and female students had very different responses to the sentence. Gender was the only apparent difference among the students, so we can conclude that it caused the different responses. You should have checked this item.

☑ *Check Your Understanding*

Take a minute now to look at the following *New Yorker* cartoon. What do you think is the artist's point?

"Dad, can you read?"

Drawing by Peter Steiner; © 1990 The New Yorker Magazine, Inc.

Put a check (✓) by the **two** inferences that are most logically based on the information given in the cartoon. Then read the explanation that follows.

✓ 1. The boy enjoys reading.

___ 2. The boy is doing his homework.

✓ 3. The man must watch a great deal of television.

___ 4. The father cannot read.

___ 5. The father prefers a good novel to watching TV.

Explanation:

1. This inference is supported by the fact that the boy is reading instead of playing or watching TV.

2. This is not a logical inference. The cartoonist would have given us more clues if he wanted us to think that the boy was doing schoolwork. For instance, he might have shown him at a table with a book and worksheets.

3. This is a logical inference. The boy's question and the father's activity in the picture lead us to believe that the boy never sees his father reading, only watching a great deal of TV.

4. This inference is not well supported. The father doesn't seem to read much, but that doesn't mean he cannot; in fact, the magazine on the television set suggests that he can read.

5. This is not a logical inference. The boy's question tells us that he never sees his father reading.

➤ Practice 1

Put a check (✓) by the inference most logically based on the information provided. Look first at the example.

Example

A student always sits in the back of the classroom.

_____ A. The student dislikes the course.

_____ B. The student is unprepared for class.

__✓__ C. The student feels uncomfortable in the front of the room.

_____ D. The student is farsighted.

The correct answer is C. On the basis of the information we are given, we can conclude only that the student—for some reason—does not like sitting in the front. We are not given enough information to know why the student feels this way.

1. A pencil has teeth marks on it.

_____ A. The person who used the pencil was nervous.

_____ B. The pencil was chewed up by a toddler or pet.

__✓__ C. Someone or something chewed the pencil.

_____ D. The pencil belongs to someone who is trying to quit smoking.

2. People are crowding around the entrance to a toy store, which won't open for another hour.

   _____ A. The store is the only toy store in the entire state.

   _____ B. There is always a crowd like this an hour before opening.

   _____ C. The store has paid a crowd to show up.

   ✓ D. The store is having a well-publicized sale.

3. Inside a car with an out-of-state license are several maps, suitcases, and bags of snacks.

   _____ A. The driver of the car is on vacation.

   _____ B. The driver of the car is on a business trip.

   _____ C. The driver of the car has children.

   ✓ D. The driver of the car is on a trip of some kind.

INFERENCES IN READING

In reading, too, we make logical leaps from the information given in a straightforward way to ideas that are not stated directly. As one scholar has said, inferences are "statements about the unknown made on the basis of the known." To draw inferences, we use all the clues provided by the writer, our own experience, and logic.

☑ *Check Your Understanding*

Read the following passage and check (✓) the **three** inferences that can most logically be drawn from it. Then read the explanation that follows.

> [1]A famous psychology experiment conducted by Dr. John B. Watson demonstrates that people, like animals, can be conditioned—trained to respond in a particular way to certain stimulations. [2]Watson gave an eleven-month-old baby named Albert a soft, furry white rat. [3]Each time Albert tried to stroke the rat, Dr. Watson hit a metal bar with a hammer. [4]Before long, Albert was afraid not only of white rats but also of white rabbits, white dogs, and white fur coats. [5]He even screamed at the sight of a Santa Claus mask.

   _____ 1. Dr. Watson did not like small children.

   ✓ 2. Before the experiment, Albert was not afraid of white rats.

   _____ 3. Albert had been familiar with rats before the experiment.

   _____ 4. If he had seen a black fur coat, Albert would have screamed.

   ✓ 5. Albert connected the loud noise of the hammer striking the metal bar with the white rat.

   ✓ 6. Albert was afraid of unexpected loud noises.

Explanation:

1. This is not a logical inference. We might certainly question the way the baby was used, but the passage doesn't give enough information for us to infer logically that Watson did not like small children.

2. This is a logical inference. Because Albert tried to pet the rat, it is fair to assume that he wasn't frightened of the animal.

3. This is not a logical inference. The passage gives no clues about Albert's having previous experience with rats.

4. This is not a logical inference. The passage makes no mention of Albert's response to any color but white.

5. This is a logical inference. Because the noise appears to have changed Albert's attitude toward the rat, we can assume he associated the noise with the rat.

6. This is a logical inference. Since the noise is what made Albert afraid of the rat, we have to infer that he was afraid of the noise. In addition, experience tells us that babies are likely to be frightened of unexpected loud noises.

Guidelines for Making Inferences in Reading

The exercises in this chapter provide practice in making careful inferences when you read. Here are three guidelines to that process:

1 **Never lose sight of the available information.** As much as possible, base your inferences on the facts. For instance, in the paragraph about Watson's experiment, we are told, "Albert tried to stroke the rat." On the basis of that fact, we can readily conclude that the baby had no fear of rats.

   It's also important to note when a conclusion lacks support. For instance, the idea that Albert would have screamed at the sight of a black fur coat has no support in the paragraph. We are told only that Albert was frightened by white furry things.

2 **Use your background information and experience to help you in making inferences.** Our understanding and experience with babies, for example, help us realize that Albert was frightened of unexpected loud noises.

   The more you know about a subject, the better your inferences are likely to be. So keep in mind that if your background in an area is weak, your inferences may be shaky. A doctor's inferences about your rash and fever are likely to be more helpful than those of your car mechanic.

3 **Consider the alternatives.** Don't simply accept the first inference that comes to mind. Instead, consider all of the facts of a case and all the possible explanations. For example, the doctor analyzing your rash and fever may first think of and then eliminate several possibilities before coming to the right conclusion.

➤ *Practice 2*

Read the following passages. Then, in the space provided, write the letter of the most logical answer to each question, based on the information given in the passage.

A.   [1]A corporate president recently made a visit to a nearby Native American reservation as part of his firm's public relations program. [2]"We realize that we have not hired any Indians in the five years our company has been located in this area," he told the assembled tribespeople, "but we are looking into the matter very carefully." [3]"*Hora, hora*," said some of the audience. [4]"We would like to eventually hire 5 percent of our total work force from this reservation," he said. [5]"*Hora, hora*," shouted more of the audience. [6]Encouraged by their enthusiasm, the president closed his short address by telling them that he hoped his firm would be able to take some hiring action within the next couple of years. [7]"*Hora, hora, hora*," cried the total group. [8]With a feeling of satisfaction, the president left the hall and was taken on a tour of the reservation. [9]Stopping in a field to admire some of the horses grazing there, the president asked if he could walk up closer to the animals. [10]"Certainly," said his guide, "but be careful not to step in the *hora*."

___C___   1. To get the main point of this passage, the reader must infer
   A. the location of the reservation.
   B. what kind of company the president headed.
   C. the meaning of the word *hora*.

___B___   2. From the passage, we can infer that the audience
   A. believed the president's speech.   The more he promised,
   B. did not believe the president's speech.   the louder they shouted.
   C. was confused by the president's speech.

___C___   3. From the passage, we can infer that the president
   A. thought the Native Americans deserved to be hired.
   B. thought his company should not hire the Native Americans.
   C. misinterpreted the Native Americans' reaction to his speech.

___B___   4. From the passage, we can infer that the main reason the president spoke to the Native Americans about jobs was that
   A. they needed the jobs.
   B. he thought promising jobs to Native Americans would make his company look good.
   C. he thought hiring Native Americans would be good for his company. If he thought so, why has he not hired any Indians in five years?

B.   [1]Parents bewildered by their teen alien can take comfort from one sign that Junior may be from the same species as they are: High-school status ladders look just as they did when Corvettes were the hot cars of choice.

[2]A new study of social systems at eighteen high schools in various states reveals some familiar patterns, reports sociologist Murray Milner, Jr. [3]Still tops in popularity: male athletes and attractive girls. [4]Just beneath them stand well-dressed "preppies" who try to act indifferent to school and snag the "right" party invitations.

[5]"Nerds" cluster near the bottom. [6]Their sin? [7]Open preoccupation with academic success. [8]But they're not lowest. [9]The "dorks," Milner says, "were hopelessly inept" about clothes and social events. [10]They often had low grades and poor athletic ability, too.

[11]Kids typically date only within their status level, which is set in stone by the first year and seldom can be upgraded. [12]Downgrading is a danger, though. [13]A girl dating a star athlete who later got injured and couldn't play found his status—and hers—suddenly declining. [14]And being seen talking to classmates "beneath" one's status can pull students down very fast.

[15]"High school is a very scary place," Milner says.

[16]It often is, agrees San Diego psychiatrist Martin Greenberg. [17]To take the pressure off at home, consider cutting teens some slack on minor disputes, he advises. [18]"Try to be flexible because a lot of them are having a hard time. [19]No matter how it looks," he says, "they're desperate for love."

___C___ 5. From the beginning of the passage, we can conclude that a generation ago
    A. teens became popular for very different reasons than they do today.
    B. social status was not very important in high schools.
    C. good-looking girls and athletic boys were the most popular kids.
    D. only "dorks" drove Corvettes.   Sentence 3 supports answer C
                                      as a logical inference.

___B___ 6. We can infer from the passage that
    A. teenagers generally don't care about their social status.
    B. the high-school years are stressful ones for many teens.
    C. most teens admire students who openly care about school.
    D. teens typically behave lovingly when they are home.

___A___ 7. The passage suggests that in high school,
    A. boys are most valued for their athletic ability and girls for their appearance.
    B. female athletes are generally as popular as male athletes.
    C. a nonathletic boy can be very popular as long as he is a good student.
    D. athletes don't care about getting invited to parties.   Sentence 3
                       supports answer A as a logical inference.

___C___ 8. The passage suggests that
    A. teenagers are independent thinkers who aren't bothered by other people's opinions.   Sentence 4 supports answer C as a logical
    B. popular teens often make friends with less popular kids.   inference.
    C. outward appearance is an important factor in determining high schoolers' status.
    D. a teenager's social status often changes from year to year.

C. [1]During World War II, the troop ship *SS Dorchester* steamed out of New York harbor with 904 men headed for Greenland. [2]Among those leaving anxious families behind were four chaplains, Methodist preacher George Fox, Rabbi Alexander Goode, Catholic priest John Washington, and Reformed Church minister Clark Poling. [3]Some 150 miles from their destination, a Nazi submarine sighted the *Dorchester* in its cross hairs. [4]Within moments of a torpedo's impact, reports a survivor, stunned men were pouring out from their bunks as the ship began tilting. [5]With power cut off, the escort vessels, unaware of the unfolding tragedy, pushed on in the darkness. [6]Onboard, chaos ruled as panicky men came up from the hold without life jackets and leaped into overcrowded lifeboats.

[7]When the four chaplains made it up to the steeply sloping deck, they began guiding the men to their boat stations. [8]They opened a storage locker, distributed life jackets, and coaxed the men over the side. [9]In the icy, oil-smeared water, Private William Bednar heard the chaplains preaching courage and found the strength to swim until he reached a life raft. [10]Still onboard, Grady Clark watched in awe as the chaplains handed out the last life jackets, and then, with ultimate selflessness, gave away their own. [11]As Clark slipped into the water he saw the chaplains standing—their arms linked—praying, in Latin, Hebrew, and English. [12]Other men, now calm, joined them in a huddle as the *Dorchester* slid beneath the sea.

_B_ 9. We can infer from this passage that
   A. the Nazis had been hunting for the *Dorchester* for a long time.
   B. the *Dorchester's* passengers and their families knew that because the ship carried soldiers, it might be attacked.   Sentence 2 (anxious
   C. the Nazi submarine was eventually found and destroyed.   families)
   supports answer B. Answers A and C are not mentioned in the passage at all.

_A_ 10. We can infer that the chaplains and others remaining on the boat didn't jump off because
   A. there was no more room in the lifeboats, and they knew they could not survive in the icy sea without a life jacket. "Icy" in Sentence 9 and
   B. they couldn't swim.   "handed out the last life jackets" in Sentence 10
   C. they assumed a friendly ship would soon pass by and save them.
        make A the logical answer.

_B_ 11. We can infer from the passage that Grady Clark
   A. was one of the men who died in the *Dorchester* tragedy.
   B. survived the attack and reported what the chaplains had done.
   C. was the sole survivor of the attack on the *Dorchester*.   Sentence 11
        supports answer B as a logical inference.

_B_ 12. The passage suggests that
   A. the chaplains had known each other for many years.
   B. religious faith may strengthen courage.   Sentence 9 supports answer B
   C. the chaplains had no fear of death.   as a logical inference.

➤ *Practice 3*

Read the following textbook passages. Then put a check (✓) by the **three** inferences that are most logically based on the given facts in each passage.

A.   ¹George Washington's honesty is a trait that has been well publicized. ²The famous story of how little George chopped down his father's favorite cherry tree, then bravely admitted to the deed, has an honored place in American presidential history. ³The cherry tree story was first recorded in 1806 by Parson Mason Weems, a Maryland preacher and storyteller. ⁴Unfortunately, Parson Weems was none too honest himself, and it appears that he invented the story of George and the cherry tree. ⁵There is no record of the cherry tree incident anywhere until it appears in Weems's book. ⁶The parson, it seems, thought it acceptable to teach the virtue of honesty through a made-up story. ⁷We can judge Weems's own truthfulness by the fact that he describes himself in the book as "formerly rector of Mount Vernon Parish." Such a parish never existed.

___ 1. The passage suggests that George Washington was not so honest after all.

___ 2. We can conclude that Parson Weems knew George Washington well.

✓ 3. Widely accepted stories about history are not necessarily true.

✓ 4. Parson Weems wrote about a virtue he didn't have himself.

___ 5. The author of this passage doubts that George Washington was a great leader and president.

✓ 6. In his stories and sermons, Weems may well have told other false stories.   Item 3 is supported by sentences 4–5; Item 4 is supported by sentences 4, 7–8; Item 6 is supported by sentences 6–8.

B.   ¹The *Chicago Tribune* once wrote that Henry Ford, the founder of the Ford Motor Company, was an ignorant man. ²Ford sued, challenging the paper to "prove it." ³During the trial, Ford was asked dozens of simple, general information questions: "When was the Civil War?" "Name the presidents of the United States," and so on. ⁴Ford, who had little formal education, could answer very few. ⁵Finally, exasperated, he said, "I don't know the answers to those questions, but I could find a man in five minutes who does. ⁶I use my brain to think, not store up a lot of useless facts."

✓ 1. Henry Ford was probably angered by the article in the *Chicago Tribune*.

___ 2. Ford frequently sued people.   Item 1 is supported by sentence 2 ("Ford sued"); item 4 is supported by sentence 5;

___ 3. The Tribune won the case in court.   item 6 is supported by sentence 6.

✓ 4. Ford believed that knowing where to find a fact is good enough.

___ 5. Ford would have been even more successful in his career had he had a formal education.

✓ 6. Ford believed that knowing how to think is more important than knowing facts.

C. [1]Most people would like to think that they choose their friends solely on the basis of personal characteristics. [2]A classic study of a housing complex for married students at the Massachusetts Institute of Technology (MIT) suggests that proximity—nearness and availability—can be an important factor. [3]Researchers asked couples to list their friends in the complex. [4]They found that residents were far more likely to list the couple in the next apartment than one that lived two doors away, and more likely to visit with a couple two doors away than with one three or four doors away. [5]A distance of thirty feet or a short elevator ride made the difference between friends and strangers! [6]More recent studies have confirmed the importance of proximity. [7]One possible explanation is that whenever people encounter strangers, they feel tense. [8]The more they see a person, the more they come to think of that person as predictable and safe, and hence the more likely they are to strike up a conversation that leads to friendship. [9]This would explain why the most popular couples in the MIT housing complex were those who lived at the bottom of the stairs near the garbage cans that everyone used.

   ✓   1. Most people probably think their personal preferences determine whom they choose for friends.

   ____   2. In fact, our personal preferences have no effect on who our friends are.

   ____   3. A person who lives in a big country is more likely to be have more friends than someone who lives in a small country.

   ✓   4. Someone living in an apartment house is likely to have more friends than someone who lives on a farm.

   ____   5. A garbage collector is likely to have more friends than a letter carrier.

   ✓   6. Someone who works in a busy office is likely to have more friends than someone who works at home.   Item 1 is supported by Sentence 1; Items 4 and 6 are supported by Sentence 2 ("nearness and availability").

INFERENCES IN LITERATURE

Inference is very important in reading literature. While writers of factual material usually state directly much of what they mean, creative writers often provide verbal pictures that show us what they mean. It is up to the reader to infer the point of what the creative writer has said. For instance, a nonfiction author might write the following:

A man got angry at the person using a cell phone in the theater.

But a novelist might write this:

Thomas turned to face the laughing red-haired girl sitting behind him in the theater. A vein on his forehead was throbbing. "Would you mind very much turning off that cell phone?" he hissed. "A few of us are here to actually see the movie."

Rather than merely stating that Thomas was angry, the author *shows* the anger with vivid details. To get the most out of literature, you must often infer meanings—just as you do in everyday life. Your may have inferred, for example, that the laughing girl is insensitive to the rights of others in the theater. You could also have concluded that Thomas has probably been waiting a while for her to quiet down, but she has not, and his temper is now boiling.

Now look at the following statement that a nonfiction writer might produce:

A farmer is about to kill a small pig but his daughter objects, so the farmer decides to let his daughter learn for herself that a small pig can be a problem.

Compare the above line with the following scene from *Charlotte's Web*, a literary classic that is beloved by young and old alike:

[1]"Fern," said Mr. Arable, "I know more about raising a litter of pigs than you do. [2]A weakling makes trouble. [3]Now run along!"

[4]"But it's unfair," cried Fern. [5]"The pig couldn't help being born small, could it? [6]If I had been very small at birth, would you have killed me?"

[7]Mr. Arable smiled. [8]"Certainly not," he said, looking down at his daughter with love. [9]"But this is different. [10]A little girl is one thing, a little runty pig is another."

[11]"I see no difference," replied Fern, still hanging on to the ax. [12]"This is the most terrible case of injustice I ever heard of."

[13]A queer look came over John Arable's face. [14]He seemed almost ready to cry himself.

[15]"All right," he said. [16]"You go back to the house and I will bring the runt when I come in. [17]I'll let you start it on a bottle, like a baby. [18]Then you'll see what trouble a pig can be."

☑ *Check Your Understanding*

See if you can answer the following inference questions about the excerpt.

__C__ 1. Fern and Mr. Arable probably live
   A. in a city.
   B. in a small town.
   C. on a farm.

__A__ 2. We can infer from the excerpt that Mr. Arable
   A. has probably raised many pigs in his lifetime.
   B. has had little experience raising pigs.
   C. does not like pigs.

_C_ 3. Mr. Arable appears almost ready to cry because he
  A. gets worried about how difficult it would be to raise the pig.
  B. does not like to lose an argument with his daughter.
  C. is touched by his daughter's willingness to stand up for the runt pig.

_B_ 4. We can conclude that Mr. Arable agrees to spare the pig because
  A. Fern has convinced him that it is unfair to kill pigs, no matter what their size.
  B. He believes that raising a pig will teach Fern some lessons.
  C. He realizes that taking care of a runt pig is not that difficult.

_B_ 5. By the end of this passage, we can infer that Mr. Arable is
  A. a cruel man.
  B. a reasonable man.
  C. not a very patient man.

Explanation:

1. Fern and Mr. Arable live in a place where pigs are born and raised. That strongly suggests that they live on a farm. The correct answer, then, is C.

2. Mr. Arable mentions that he knows about "raising a litter of pigs." He also tells Fern how to begin feeding the pig. These details suggest that he has raised pigs before. Therefore, the answer is A.

3. Mr. Arable seems near crying after Fern insists there's no difference between killing a runt pig and killing a small daughter. And the passage has already described Mr. Arable looking at his daughter with love. So we can conclude the plea for justice from the young daughter he adores is what touched him so. Thus the answer is C.

4. When Mr. Arable agrees to let his daughter raise the pig, he says "you'll see what trouble a pig can be." His words suggest that he expects Fern to learn a lesson. Therefore B is the answer.

5. Mr. Arable talks to Fern, listens to her opinions, and agrees to allow her to do something he does not fully support. These actions suggest he is a fair and reasonable man. So answer B is correct.

The excerpt from *Charlotte's Web* is a small example of how inference skills can increase your appreciation of literary forms—fiction, poetry, autobiographies, and other imaginative literature. Poetry, especially, by its nature implies much of its meaning. Authors often imply their meanings through comparisons. For example, Emily Dickinson begins one of her poems with the lines on the following page:

> Hope is the thing with feathers
> That perches in the soul
> And sings the tune without the words,
> And never stops at all.

Here, Dickinson uses a figure of speech known as metaphor, comparing hope to a singing bird. The comparison implies, among other things, that hope is a sweet and welcome thing.

A Note on Figures of Speech

Creative writers often use figures of speech to give us a fresh way of looking at something. The two most common figures of speech are similes and metaphors.

- **simile**—a stated comparison, introduced with the word *like* or *as*.

  Instead of saying, "The window shade snapped up," you could express it more vividly by saying, "The window shade snapped up like a gunshot." The simile shows that the noise of the window shade was loud and startling.

Here are some other similes:

- The school bus stopped at the corner, and children scattered *like brightly-colored leaves in the wind.*
- That Halloween night was *as dark as the inside of a witch's hat.*
- After you've broken up with a boyfriend or girlfriend, every day feels *like a cloudy, cold Monday morning.*
- If he senses you don't know the material, our math teacher attacks *like a shark.*
- That runner moves *as gracefully as a gazelle.*

- **metaphor**—an implied comparison, with *like* or *as* omitted.

  The thought "No person can be self-sufficient" was expressed vividly in a metaphor by the poet John Donne, who wrote: "No man is an island." His comparison says no one can be long disconnected from the mainland—the rest of humanity.

Here are some other metaphors:

- The grade on the paper was *a dash of ice water in my face.*
- When Nate got up to speak, he was *a mass of quivering Jell-O.*
- *The warm honey* of her voice melted my anger.
- Watching TV for hours, the children were *glassy-eyed statues.*
- The dancer's head was *a rose* on *the slender stem* of her neck.

➤ *Practice 4*

Use a check (✓) to identify each figure of speech as a simile or a metaphor. Then, in the space provided, answer each inference question that follows.

___B___ 1. His friendship is as genuine <u>as</u> a plastic Christmas tree.

✓ simile   ___ metaphor

You can infer that the friendship is
A. easy to maintain.
B. fake and cheap.   The words indicating that items 1
c seasonal and glittery.   and 2 are similes are underlined.

___C___ 2. A gang of teenaged boys moved through the mall <u>like</u> a pack of wild dogs.

✓ simile   ___ metaphor

You can infer that the boys were
A. polite and friendly.
B. sneaky and quiet.
C. loud and disruptive.

___B___ 3. The executives did not admit that the company was a sinking ship until after they had taken millions of dollars for themselves.

___ simile   ✓ metaphor

You can infer that the company
A. was well-managed.
B. was failing.
C. was going in more than one direction.

___C___ 4. Everyone at work thinks that Jasmine is a real gem.

___ simile   ✓ metaphor

You can infer that Jasmine is
A. disliked and unfriendly.
B. shy and quiet.
C. admired and valued.

___C___ 5. I'm writing a family history so that my grandparents' stories do not go up in ashes and smoke.

___ simile   ✓ metaphor

You can infer that the grandparents' stories are
A. full of fire and passion.
B. uneventful and unimportant.
C. in danger of being lost forever.

➤ *Practice 5*

George Orwell is famous for his novels *Animal Farm* and *1984* as well as his classic literary essays. Following is an excerpt from "A Hanging," an essay Orwell wrote about an execution he witnessed while he was an English police officer stationed in Burma. Read the excerpt and then answer the inference questions that follow.

Note that the meanings of a few words in the excerpt are given below.

reiterated: repeated
Ram: Hindu god
abominable: hateful
timorously: timidly
oscillated: swung back and forth

¹We stood waiting, five yards away. ²The warders had formed in a rough circle round the gallows. ³And then, when the noose was fixed, the prisoner began crying out to his god. ⁴It was a high, reiterated° cry of "Ram°! Ram! Ram! Ram!" not urgent and fearful like a prayer or a cry for help, but steady, rhythmical almost like the tolling of a bell. ⁵The dog answered the sound with a whine. ⁶The hangman, still standing on the gallows, produced a small cotton bag like a flour bag and drew it down over the prisoner's face. ⁷But the sound, muffled by the cloth, still persisted, over and over again: "Ram! Ram! Ram! Ram!"

⁸The hangman climbed down and stood ready, holding the lever. ⁹Minutes seemed to pass. ¹⁰The steady, muffled crying from the prisoner went on and on, "Ram! Ram! Ram!" never faltering for an instant. ¹¹The superintendent, his head on his chest, was slowly poking the ground with his stick; perhaps he was counting the cries, allowing the prisoner a fixed number—fifty, perhaps, or a hundred. ¹²Everyone had changed color. ¹³The Indians had gone grey like bad coffee, and one or two of the bayonets were wavering. ¹⁴We looked at the lashed, hooded man on the drop, and listened to his cries—each cry another second of life; the same thought was in all our minds: oh, kill him quickly, get it over, stop that abominable° noise!

¹⁵Suddenly the superintendent made up his mind. ¹⁶Throwing up his head he made a swift motion with his stick. ¹⁷"Chalo!" he shouted almost fiercely.

¹⁸There was a clanking noise, and then dead silence. ¹⁹The prisoner had vanished, and the rope was twisting on itself. ²⁰I let go of the dog, and it galloped immediately to the back of the gallows; but when it got there it stopped short, barked, and then retreated into a corner of the yard, where it stood among the weeds, looking timorously° out at us. ²¹We went round the gallows to inspect the prisoner's body. ²²He was dangling with his toes pointed straight downward, very slowly revolving, as dead as a stone.

²³The superintendent reached out with his stick and poked the bare body; it oscillated°, slightly. ²⁴"*He's* all right," said the superintendent. ²⁵He

backed out from under the gallows, and blew out a deep breath. [26]The moody look had gone out of his face quite suddenly. [27]He glanced at his wristwatch. [28]"Eight minutes past eight. [29]Well, that's all for this morning, thank God."

_B_   1. We can infer from the simile below that the prisoner's cry was like
    A. wedding bells.
    B. a funeral bell.
    C. a doorbell.

       "It was a high…cry…steady, rhythmical…like the tolling of a bell."

_B_   2. The reaction of the Indian spectators, described in the simile below, suggests they are
    A. sympathetic to the superintendent's duty.
    B. disturbed by the prisoner's hanging.
    C. relieved that the prisoner was about to die.

       "Everyone had changed color. The Indians had gone grey like bad coffee . . ."

_C_   3. In the second paragraph, we can conclude that the superintendent waited for the prisoner to say his prayers because he
    A. had the same religious beliefs as the prisoner.
    B. was distracted by something on the ground.
    C. understood the prisoner's fear and showed him respect.

_C_   4. We can infer from the passage that the word *chalo* was a
    A. word of protest against the hanging.
    B. cheer in support of the hanging.
    C. command used to begin the hanging.

_A_   5. Orwell's description of the prisoner being as "dead as a stone" is a simile that suggests the prisoner was
    A. still and lifeless.
    B. dirty and round.
    C. solid and strong.

_B_   6. The author implies that the dog
    A. belonged to the superintendent.
    B. sensed that something terrible had happened.
    C. has no understanding of what's going on around him.

_A_   7. When the superintendent says, "Well, that's all for this morning," he implies that
    A. there may be more executions in the afternoon.
    B. there has been only one execution that morning.
    C. there will be no other work to do in the morning.

Since it's only a little past 8 a.m., there will probably be other kinds of work to do in the morning, but no more executions.

_____A_____ 8. When the superintendent says, "*He's* all right," he means that
    A. while the prisoner is at peace, everyone else is still shaken.
    B. the prisoner got the punishment that he deserved.
    C. the prisoner had wanted to die and got his wish.

_____C_____ 9. We can infer from the superintendent's behavior that he
    A. was a cruel man who enjoyed seeing others executed.
    B. refused to attend any more executions after this one.
    C. considered executions an unpleasant part of his duty.

_____B_____ 10. We can infer from the details in this passage and another excerpt from
the essay, shown below, that the author probably was
    A. in favor of capital punishment.
    B. troubled by capital punishment.
    C. not interested in the issue of capital punishment.

> "He [the prisoner] and we were a party of men, walking together, seeing, hearing, feeling, understanding the same world; and in two minutes, with a sudden snap, one of us would be gone—one mind less, one world less."

INFERENCES IN GRAPHS AND TABLES

You have already tried your hand at making inferences from a picture, the cartoon about the father who watches more TV than he reads. Many of the cartoons in newspapers and magazines depend on your inference skills. Other "pictures" that require inferences are graphs and tables, which combine words with visual representations. Authors of textbooks, professional and newspaper articles, and other materials often organize large amounts of material into graphs and tables. Very often, the graphs and tables are used to show comparisons and changes that take place over time.

As with other reading material, to infer the ideas presented in graphs and tables, you must consider all the information presented.

Steps in Reading a Graph or Table

To find and make sense of the information in a graph or table, follow a few steps.

1 Read the title. It will tell you what the table or graph is about in general.

• What is the title of the graph on the next page? _____
        Changes in the U. S. Work Force, 1900–2010
_____

2 Check the source. At the bottom of a table or graph, you will usually find the source of the information, an indication of the reliability of its material.

• What is the source of the graph on the next page? _____
        Statistical Abstract, 1999; James M. Henslin, 2002

Changes in the U.S. Work Force, 1900–2010

Source: Statistical Abstract, 1999; James M. Henslin, 2002

3 Read any labels or captions at the top, the side, or underneath that tell exactly what each column, line, bar, number, or other item represents. This information includes such things as quantities, percentages, and years.

- What is the span of years covered in the graph? _____1900–2010_____

- Which types of work does the graph cover? _____
_____White-collar, blue-collar, and farming_____

4 Once you have taken the above steps, you are ready to infer from the graph or table whatever information you seek from it.

☑ *Check Your Understanding*

See if you can put a check (✓) by the **three** inferences that are most logically based on the graph.

   ✓   1. The work force of 1900 was very different from the work force of today.

   ___   2. Before 1900, farmers made up the smallest percentage of workers.

   ___   3. In 1940, the percentages of farm workers and white-collar workers were about equal.

   ✓   4. In general, as the number of farming and blue-collar workers has decreased, the number of white-collar workers has increased.

   ___   5. In 1940, blue-collar workers made up about 25 percent of the U.S. work force.

   ✓   6. In the future, most U.S. workers are likely to be white-collar workers.

Explanation:

1. The movement of the three horizontal lines across the graph shows a significant change in the U.S. work force since 1900, with farmers and blue-collar workers decreasing sharply and white-collar workers rising strongly. You should have checked this item.

2. At the extreme left side of the graph, which represents 1900, the lowest of the three horizontal lines is for white-collar workers, not farmers. So we can infer that for at least a short time before 1900, white-collar workers probably also made up the smallest percentage of the work force.

3. The graph shows that in 1940 the number of farm workers was far below that of white-collar workers.

4. The graph shows the decline of farmers and blue-collar workers accompanied by the steady rise of white-collar workers. You should have checked this item.

5. The graph shows that in 1940 over 50 percent of U.S. workers were blue-collar.

6. Given the trends shown on the graph, estimated through 2010, it seems a reasonable assumption that most U.S. workers will be white-collar workers. You should have checked this item.

➤ Practice 6

Read the table on the next page, following the steps for reading graphs and tables on pages 312–313. Then put a check (✓) by the **three** inferences that are most logically based on the table.

     ____ 1. Most jobs which require short-term training pay about the same as those which require associate's degrees.

     ✓ 2. In general, as the education requirement of a job rises, so does the pay.

     ____ 3. There will be almost no need in the years ahead for new teachers and teaching assistants in United States classrooms.

     ____ 4. Employment growth for retail salespeople is greater than that of security guards.

     ✓ 5. Registered nursing pays well yet requires less education than other high-paying jobs.

     ✓ 6. There will be many opportunities in the years ahead in the computer, health, education, and food service areas.

Occupations with the largest job growth, 2000–2010
(Numbers in thousands of jobs)

Occupation	Employment		Change		Salary Ranking	Education and training category
	2000	2010	Number	%		
Food preparation and serving workers, including fast food	2,206	2,879	673	30	4	Short-term on-the-job-training
Customer service representatives	1.946	2,577	631	32	3	Moderate-term on-the-job-training
Registered nurses	2,194	2,755	561	26	1	Associate degree
Retail salespersons	4,109	4,619	510	12	4	Short-term on-the-job-training
Computer support specialists	506	996	490	97	2	Associate degree
Cashiers, except gaming	3,325	3,799	474	14	4	Short-term on-the-job-training
Office clerks, general	2,705	3,135	430	16	3	Short-term on-the-job-training
Security guards	1.106	1,497	391	35	4	Short-term on-the-job-training
Computer software engineers, applications, systems software	697	1,361	664	190	1	Bachelor's degree
Waiters and waitresses	1,983	2,347	364	18	4	Short-term on-the-job-training
Truck drivers, heavy and tractor-trailer	1,749	2,095	346	20	2	Moderate-term on-the-job-training
Nursing aides, orderlies, and attendants	1,373	1,697	323	24	3	Short-term on-the-job-training
Janitors and cleaners, except maids and housekeeping cleaners	2,348	2,665	317	13	4	Short-term on-the-job-training
Postsecondary teachers	1,344	1,659	315	23	1	Doctoral degree
Teacher assistants	1,262	1,562	301	24	4	Short-term on-the-job-training
Home health aides	615	907	291	47	4	Short-term on-the-job-training
Laborers & freight, stock & material movers, hand	2,084	2,373	289	14	3	Short-term on-the-job-training
Landscaping and groundskeeping workers	894	1,154	260	29	4	Short-term on-the-job-training
Personal and home care aides	414	672	258	62	4	Short-term on-the-job-training
Analysts and administrators, network and computer systems	660	1,105	445	142	1	Bachelor's degree
Receptionists and information clerks	1,078	1,334	256	24	3	Short-term on-the-job-training
Truck drivers, light or delivery services	1,117	1,331	215	19	4	Short-term on-the-job-training
Packers and packagers, hand	1,091	1,300	210	19	4	Short-term on-the-job-training
Elementary school teachers, except special ed	1,532	1,734	202	13	1	Bachelor's degree
Medical assistants	329	516	187	57	3	Moderate-term on-the-job-training
Secondary school teachers, except special and vocational education	1,004	1,190	187	19	1	Bachelor's degree
Accountants and auditors	976	1,157	181	19	1	Bachelor's degree

Salary rankings: 1 = very high ($39,700 and over), 2 = high ($25,760 to $39,660), 3 = low ($18,500 to $25,760), and 4 = very low (up to $18,490).

Source: Bureau of Labor Statistics, 2002.

Comments: Item 2 — The jobs with a salary ranking of "1" require an associate's degree, a bachelor's degree, etc.

Item 5 — Registered nursing requires only an associate's degree.

Item 6 — As the heading indicates, the table contains "occupations with the largest job growth." Many of these jobs are in the computer, health, education, and food service areas.

CHAPTER REVIEW

In this chapter, you learned the following:

- Many important ideas in reading are not stated directly, but must be inferred. To make inferences about implied ideas, use the information provided as well as your own experience and logic.
- Inferences are also a key part of reading literature and such visual materials as cartoons, tables, and graphs.

The next chapter—Chapter 9—will help make you aware of an author's purpose and tone.

On the Web: If you are using this book in class, you can visit our website for additional practice in making inferences. Go to **www.townsendpress.com** and click on "Online Exercises."

➤ *Review Test 1*

To review what you've learned in this chapter, answer each of the following questions about inferences.

1. An inference is an idea that is *(directly stated, suggested)* _____ _____suggested_____ by the author.

2. When making inferences, it is *(a mistake, useful)* _____useful_____ to use our own experience as well as the author's clues.

3. When making inferences, it is *(a mistake, useful)* _____useful_____ to use our sense of logic as well as the author's clues.

4. __T__ TRUE OR FALSE? A reader must make inferences when finding the meaning of words through context and when finding implied main ideas.

5. Making inferences is a key skill in reading literature because writers of fiction do not so much *(tell, show)* _____tell_____ us what they mean as *(tell, show)* _____show_____ us with vivid specific details.

▶ **Review Test 2**

A. (1–4.) Put a check (✓) by the **four** inferences that are most logically based on the information given in the cartoon.

DILBERT reproduced by permission of United Feature Syndicate, Inc.

Item 1 is supported when the man with glasses says, "The dumpster seems a bit inappropriate."

Item 3 is supported with "no employee benefits."

Item 5 is supported with "I just love hiring . . ."

Item 7 is supported with "no union."

✓ 1. The man with glasses thinks the boss is unfair to temporary workers.

___ 2. The man with glasses agrees with the boss's behavior.

✓ 3. The boss values saving money more than he values caring for workers.

___ 4. The boss feels a bit guilty about his treatment of temporary workers.

✓ 5. The boss has probably hired and fired other temporary workers.

___ 6. The worker in the boss's arms is about to be promoted.

✓ 7. The cartoonist implies that temporary workers have no power in the workplace.

___ 8. The cartoonist implies that companies should not hire temporary workers.

B. (5–8.) Read the following textbook passage and then put a check (✓) by the **four** inferences that are most logically supported by the information given.

¹Your sister has a new boyfriend. ²The first time you meet him, he corners you and talks to you for an hour about football, a subject in which you have no interest at all. ³You come away with the impression that he is an inconsiderate bore. ⁴The next two times you see him, however, he says not a word about football; instead, he participates in the general conversation and makes some witty and intelligent remarks. ⁵What is your impression of him now? ⁶Do you find him likable and interesting on the basis of the last two encounters? ⁷Do you average out the early minus and the later plus and come out with a neutral zero? ⁸Neither is likely. ⁹What is likely is that you still think of him as an inconsiderate bore, for research suggests that first impressions, as our mothers and fathers told us, are quite lasting.

___ 1. First impressions are usually negative.

✓ 2. It is useful to make good first impressions.

___ 3. It's a bad idea to discuss football when you first meet someone.

Sentence 9 supports item 2.

✓ 4. To make a good impression, it helps to notice what interests the other person.

___ 5. A "neutral zero" impression of someone would be negative.

✓ 6. A "neutral zero" impression of someone would be neither positive nor negative.

Sentences 2–3 support Item 4.

✓ 7. It's not so easy to be objective about others.   Sentence 7 supports Item 6.

___ 8. Second impressions can be even more powerful than first impressions.

Item 7—Being objective would require us to change first opinions, but we don't do that.

C. (9–10.) After reading the following passage, put a check (✓) by the **two** inferences that are most firmly based on the given facts.

[1]A man is talking to the Lord, trying to understand His eternal nature. [2]"Lord," he asks, "what's a million years to you?" [3]"A million years is but a second to me," the Lord explains. [4]"And a million dollars?" [5]"A penny," the Lord replies. [6]The man feels bold and now proceeds to ask, "Lord, would you give me a million dollars?" [7]"Sure," the Lord replies. [8]"Just a second."

✓ 1. In comparison with eternity, a million years is a short time.

✓ 2. The man will not live long enough to collect his million dollars.

___ 3. The Lord knows the man would just waste the money.

___ 4. The man is poor.

Sentence 3 is the key to the punchline at the end.

➤ Review Test 3

A. (1–4.) Read the graph on the next page. Then put a check (✓) by the **four** statements that are most logically supported by the graph.

Comments:

Item 1—
Over 60% loss in twenty minutes

Item 2—People remember only 20%

Item 3—
Almost 70%

Item 4—80%

Item 5—As the graph makes clear

Item 6—
Common-sense ways to offset the speed of forgetting

✓ 1. The most memory loss takes place in the first twenty minutes after exposure to new material.

___ 2. After one month, most people remember only half of the new material they've learned.

✓ 3. In a single day, people are likely to forget over half of the new material they've learned.

___ 4. By the end of a month, people tend to forget 100 percent of new material learned.

✓ 5. After two days, the rate of forgetting slows down greatly.

✓ 6. Since people rapidly forget new material, taking notes in classes and reviewing them regularly are useful study techniques.

___ 7. A student who sits in class and listens carefully but does not take notes can often do just as well as a student who takes notes.

Classic study on forgetting and memory loss

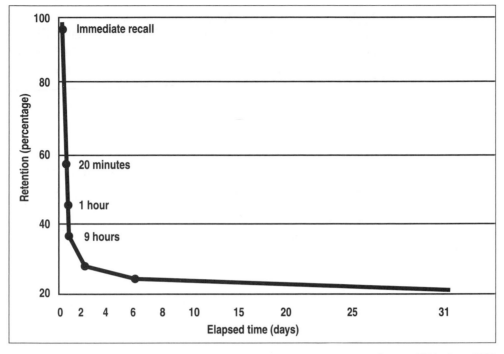

Source: Ebbinghaus, 1885

B. Identify each figure of speech as a simile or a metaphor. Then answer each inference question that follows.

___A___ 5. My mother's angry gaze bored into me <u>like</u> twin laser beams.
   A. simile   B. metaphor

___A___ 6. You can infer that the mother's gaze was
   A. intense   B. exciting and   C. unfocused and
      and cutting.   adventurous.   bored.

___B___ 7. A tidal wave of bad events overtook the family.
   A. simile   B. metaphor

___A___ 8. You can infer that the bad events were
   A. overwhelming.   B. unexpected.   C. bearable.

___A___ 9. His kind words were as welcome <u>as</u> a flash of sunlight on a cloudy day.
   A. simile   B. metaphor

___C___ 10. You can infer that the words were
   A. depressing and   B. disorienting.   C. warm and
      sad.   unexpected.

➤ *Review Test 4*

Here is a chance to apply your understanding of inferences to a passage from a college textbook: *Essentials of Sociology*, Fourth Edition, by James M. Henslin. To help you continue to strengthen your skills, the reading is followed by questions not only on what you've learned in this chapter but also on what you've learned in previous chapters.

Words to Watch

Below are some words in the reading that do not have strong context support. Each word is followed by the number of the paragraph in which it appears and its meaning there. These words are indicated in the article by a small circle (°).

resident (6): a doctor receiving specialized training
clinch (6): make sure of getting
implications (8): effects
profound (8): great
pinpoints (10): identifies with exactness
industrialized (11): developed in the manufacturing and sales of goods

GENDER INEQUALITY IN HEALTH CARE AND IN THE WORKPLACE

James M. Henslin

Gender Inequality in Health Care

1   Medical researchers were puzzled. Reports were coming in from all over the country: Women were twice as likely as men to die after coronary bypass surgery. Researchers at Cedars-Sinai Medical Center in Los Angeles checked their own records. They found that of 2,300 coronary bypass patients, 4.6 percent of the women died as a result of the surgery, compared with 2.6 percent of the men.

2   These findings presented a sociological puzzle. To solve it, researchers first turned to biology (Bishop 1990). In coronary bypass surgery, a blood vessel is taken from one part of the body and stitched to a coronary artery on the surface of the heart. Perhaps this operation was more difficult to perform on women because of their smaller coronary arteries. To find out, researchers measured the amount of time that surgeons kept patients on the heart-lung machine while they operated. They were surprised to learn that women spent less time on the machine than men. This indicated that the operation was not more difficult to perform on women.

3   As the researchers probed, a surprising answer unfolded—unintended sexual discrimination. Physicians had not taken the chest pains of their women patients as seriously as they took the complaints of their male patients. They were *ten* times more likely to give men exercise stress tests and radioactive heart scans. They also sent men to surgery on the basis of abnormal stress tests, but waited until women showed clear-cut

symptoms of coronary heart disease before sending them to surgery. Having surgery after the disease is further along reduces the chances of survival.

4   You obviously are also more likely to die if you are sent home from a hospital emergency room when you are having a heart attack. Researchers have also found that when people with heart pain go to emergency rooms, doctors are more likely to admit the men and to send the women home (Seiker and Pope 2000).

Women's Organs as Causes of Disease—and Sources of Profit

5   Sociologist Sue Fisher (1986), who did participant observation in a hospital, was surprised to hear surgeons recommend total hysterectomy (removal of both the uterus and the ovaries) when no cancer was present. When she asked why, the men doctors explained that the uterus and ovaries are "potentially disease producing." They also said that they are unnecessary after the childbearing years, so why not remove them?

6   Surgical sexism is reinforced by another powerful motive—greed.

Surgeons make money by performing this surgery. But they have to "sell" the operation, for women, to understate the matter, are reluctant to part with these organs. Here is how one resident° explained the "hard sell" to sociologist Diana Scully (1994):

> You have to look for your surgical procedures; you have to go after patients. Because no one is crazy enough to come and say, "Hey, here I am. I want you to operate on me." You have to sometimes convince the patient that she is really sick—if she is, of course [laughs], and that she is better off with a surgical procedure.

To "convince" a woman to have this surgery, the doctor tells her that, unfortunately, the examination has turned up fibroids in her uterus—and they might turn into cancer. This statement is often sufficient, for it frightens women, who picture themselves dying from cancer. To clinch° the sale, the surgeon withholds the rest of the truth—that the fibroids probably will not turn into cancer and that she has several nonsurgical alternatives.

Gender Inequality in the Workplace

7   One of the chief characteristics of the U.S. work force is a steady growth in the numbers of women who work outside the home for wages. Figure 1 shows that in 1930 one of five U.S. workers was a woman. By 1940, this ratio had grown to one of four, by 1960 to one of three, and today it is almost one of two.

8   Because the changes have been so gradual and the implications° so profound°, sociologists use the term **quiet revolution** to refer to the many women who have joined the ranks of paid labor. This trend, shown in Figure 1, has led to a dramatic transformation in consumer patterns, relations at work, self-concepts,

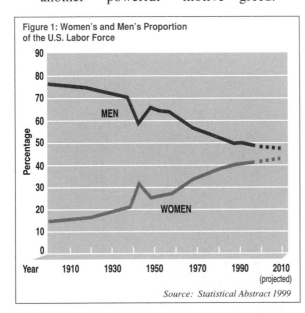

Figure 1: Women's and Men's Proportion of the U.S. Labor Force

MEN

WOMEN

Percentage

Year   1910   1930   1950   1970   1990   2010 (projected)

Source: Statistical Abstract 1999

and relationships with boyfriends, husbands, and children. One of the most significant consequences of the quiet revolution is that since 1960 the percentage of married women who have preschool children and work for wages has tripled. It now equals the average percentage of all U.S. women.

The Gender Pay Gap

9   Chances are, you are going to go to work after you complete college. How would you like to earn an extra $950,000 on your job? If this sounds appealing, read on. I'm going to reveal how you can make an extra $2,000 a month between the ages of 25 and 65.

10   Is this hard to do? Actually, it is simple for some, but impossible for others. All you have to do is be born a male and graduate from college. As Figure 2 shows, if we compare full-time workers, this is how much more the average male college graduate earns over the course of his career. Hardly any single factor pinpoints° gender discrimination better than this total. From this figure, you can also see that the pay gap shows up at all levels of education.

11   The pay gap is so great that women who work full time average only two-thirds (67 percent) of what men are paid. As Figure 3 shows, the pay gap used to be even worse. This gap does not occur only in the United States. All industrialized° nations have it, although only in Japan is the gap larger than in the United States (Blau and Kahn 1992).

12   What logic can underlie the gender pay gap? Earlier we saw that college degrees are gender-linked, so perhaps this gap is due to career choices. Maybe women are more likely to choose lower-paying jobs, such as teaching grade school, whereas men are more likely to go into better-paying fields, such as business, law, and engineering. Actually, this is true, and researchers have found that about *half* the pay gap is due to such factors. The balance, however, is due to gender discrimination (Kemp 1990).

13   Depending on your sex, then, you are likely either to benefit from gender discrimination—or to be its victim. Because the pay gap will be so important

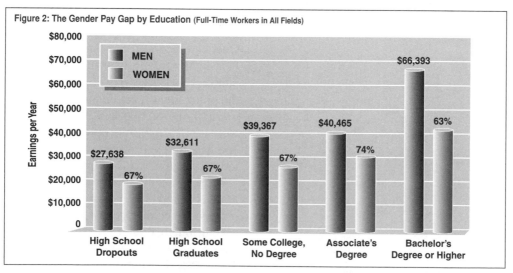

Figure 2: The Gender Pay Gap by Education (Full-Time Workers in All Fields)

MEN
WOMEN

High School Dropouts: $27,638 / 67%
High School Graduates: $32,611 / 67%
Some College, No Degree: $39,367 / 67%
Associate's Degree: $40,465 / 74%
Bachelor's Degree or Higher: $66,393 / 63%

Earnings per Year

Source: Statistical Abstract 1999

in your own work life, let's follow some college graduates to see how it actually comes about. Economists Rex Fuller and Richard Schoenberger (1991) examined the starting salaries of the business majors at the University of Wisconsin, of whom 47 percent were women. They found that the women's starting salaries averaged 11 percent ($1,737) less than the men's.

14   You might be able to think of valid reasons for this initial pay gap. For example, the women might have been less qualified. Perhaps their grades were lower. Or maybe they completed fewer internships. If so, they would deserve lower salaries. To find out, Fuller and Schoenberger reviewed the students'

college records. To their surprise, they found that the women had higher grades and more internships. In other words, if women were equally qualified, they were offered lower salaries—and if they were more qualified, they were offered lower salaries—a classic lose-lose situation.

What happened after these   15 graduates had been on the job awhile? Did things tend to even out, so that after a few years the women and men earned about the same? Fuller and Schoenberger checked their salaries five years later. Instead of narrowing, the pay gap had grown even wider. By this time, the women earned 14 percent ($3,615) less than the men.

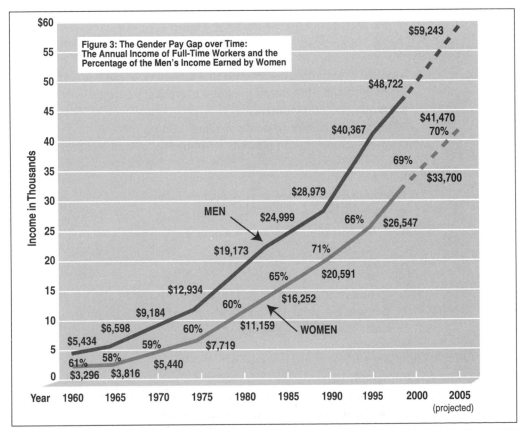

Figure 3: The Gender Pay Gap over Time: The Annual Income of Full-Time Workers and the Percentage of the Men's Income Earned by Women

Source: Statistical Abstract 1999

Reading Comprehension Questions

Vocabulary in Context

   B   1. In the excerpt below, the word *probed* (prōbd) means:
      A. decided.
      B. investigated.
      C. knew all along.
      D. gave up.

> "As the researchers probed, a surprising answer unfolded—
> unintended sexual discrimination." (Paragraph 3)

Central Point and Main Ideas

   D   2. Which sentence best expresses the central point of the selection?
      A. Among a group of business graduates, women who were as qualified as the men were offered lower salaries than the men.
      B. Doctors have given better care to men than to women.
      C. An excellent way to improve your lifetime earnings is to graduate from college.
      D. Discrimination against women exists in the country's health care systems and workplaces.   Answers A and B are too narrow. Answer C is not discussed in the selection.

Supporting Details

   C   3. Medical researchers discovered that coronary bypass surgery is
      A. more difficult to do on people with smaller coronary arteries.
      B. rarely done on women.   See paragraph 2.
      C. no more difficult to do on women than on men.
      D. more successful on patients with greatly advanced heart disease.

Transitions

   C   4. The sentence below expresses a relationship of
      A. addition.   The transition *but* is a contrast word. The basis for
      B. comparison.   doing surgery on men is being contrasted to the
      C. contrast.   basis for doing surgery on women.
      D. time.

> "They . . . sent men to surgery on the basis of abnormal stress tests,
> but waited until women showed clear-cut symptoms of coronary
> heart disease. . . ." (Paragraph 3)

Patterns of Organization

   A   5. Paragraph 12
      A. looks at the possible causes of the gender pay gap.
      B. lists instances of the pay gap according to profession.
      C. defines and illustrates the pay gap in the U.S. work force.
      D. compares men's and women's similar salary expectations.

Fact and Opinion

___A___ 6. Paragraph 1 is made up of
   A. facts.
   B. opinions.

Inferences

___B___ 7. The author put the words *sell, hard sell,* and *convince* in quotation marks (in paragraph 6) to imply that some surgeons
   A. must convince themselves of the need to remove a woman's uterus and ovaries.
   B. consider the total hysterectomy to be a money-making procedure for which good salesmanship is required.
   C. do not realize that fibroids will probably not turn into cancer and thus may not require any surgery.
   D. are not qualified or sufficiently experienced to do a total hysterectomy safely.

___D___ 8. Figure 1 suggests that
   A. in a few years, women are likely to make up half of the U.S. work force.
   B. the proportion of women in the work force has increased almost continuously since the early 1900s.
   C. in the early part of the twentieth century, a working mother would have been considered unusual.
   D. all of the above.

___D___ 9. Figure 2 suggests that
   A. women with a college degree makes less than men with a high school degree.
   B. women are better off not working for a college degree.
   C. more education decreases the gap between men's and women's pay.
   D. men and women are paid unequally at all educational levels.

___B___ 10. From Figure 3, we can infer that
   A. there has not been much change in men's salaries between 1960 and 2000.
   B. the gender gap actually increased from about 1990 to 1995.
   C. in the near future, women's salaries are likely to catch up with men's.
   D. in the near future, men's salaries are likely to stay the same.

Discussion Questions

1. Medical researchers discovered that men and women receive different health care because of "unintended sexual discrimination." How might such clear-cut discrimination be "unintended"? Do you know of any cases of gender health discrimination? Tell what happened.

2. According to Henslin, women suffer and men benefit from gender discrimination in the U.S. work force. Have you ever experienced or witnessed gender discrimination at work? Tell what happened.

3. Henslin states that a "quiet revolution" has taken place over the past century. Tell what you think are some of the changes he refers to when mentioning "a transformation in consumer patterns, relations at work, self-concepts, and relationships with boyfriends, husbands, and children." Also, describe any benefits or problems you feel may have been caused by the changes.

4. Did it surprise you to learn that in modern U.S. society, women earn significantly less than men? Explain. In your opinion, what are the causes of the gender gap, and what do you think would have to happen for it to end?

Note: Writing assignments for this selection appear on page 589.

Check Your Performance **INFERENCES**

Activity	Number Right	Points	Score
Review Test 1 (5 items)	_____	× 2 =	_____
Review Test 2 (10 items)	_____	× 3 =	_____
Review Test 3 (10 items)	_____	× 3 =	_____
Review Test 4 (10 items)	_____	× 3 =	_____
	TOTAL SCORE	=	_____%

Enter your total score into the **Reading Performance Chart: Review Tests** on the inside back cover.

INFERENCES: Mastery Test 1

A. Put a check (✓) by the **three** inferences that are most logically based on the information suggested by the cartoon.

PEANUTS reproduced by permission of United Feature Syndicate, Inc.

    ✓   1. Lucy has just criticized the boy, Linus.

         2. Linus feels Lucy's criticism is valid.

         3. Lucy feels very guilty that Linus has taken her criticism badly.

    ✓   4. Lucy doesn't seem to realize that people may accept constructive criticism but not destructive criticism.

         5. The cartoonist believes we should never criticize others.

    ✓   6. The cartoonist believes it's best to criticize others in a constructive way.

B. Read the passage below. Then check the **three** inferences that are most logically supported by the information given.

    [1]Shortly after the young woman sat down in the bus, she lit a cigarette. [2]The man next to her waved some smoke away, nudged her, and pointed to the sign at the front of the bus.

    [3]The woman did not turn to look at the man and continued smoking calmly. [4]The man got up and spoke to the bus driver, who continued driving and shook his head. [5]At the next stop, the man, looking disgusted, got off the bus.

         1. The man had never smoked.

    ✓   2. The smoke was bothering the man.

    ✓   3. The man pointed to a no-smoking sign.

    ✓   4. The driver refused to get involved.

         5. The man got off the bus because it was his stop.

         6. The driver was related to the woman.

Sentence 2 ("waved smoke away") supports item 2.
Sentence 2 supports item 3.
Sentence 4 supports item 4.

(Continues on next page)

327

C. Read each passage below. Then check the **two** inferences after each passage which are most logically supported by the information given.

1.   [1]My day has not ended. [2]When I get home I suddenly realize that I have between thirty and forty pounds of fish to clean—rockfish yet, all full of spines and pricklers and razor-sharp teeth. [3]When I'm finished, I have so many holes in me I look like a composite of George Custer, Saint Sebastian, and Bonnie and Clyde, but my family comes out to view the catch and restore my faith in the whole enterprise.

   [4]"Yuk," says my daughter.

   [5]"That's a lot of rockfish for people who aren't all that into rockfish," says my wife.

   [6]"I wouldn't eat that on a bet," says my son.

> Sentence 2 ("When I get home") eliminates Item 1.
> Sentences 2–3 support Item 2.
> Sentences 4, 5, and 6 eliminate Item 3.
> Sentence 2 eliminates Item 4.
> Sentences 4, 5, and 6 support Item 5.

   ____ 1. The family is on vacation.

   ✓ 2. Rockfish are difficult to clean.

   ____ 3. The author's family appreciates his hard work to feed them.

   ____ 4. The man enjoys the challenge of cleaning rockfish.

   ✓ 5. When he praises his family for restoring his faith, the author is being sarcastic.

2.   [1]I guess I did it because I hadn't studied very much. [2]And it seemed so easy—everybody knows that Mr. Wagner keeps his office door unlocked. [3]It's just too bad things didn't work out for me. [4]Now my classmates are mad at me because they must re-study for the new test Mr. Wagner is making up. [5]My parents have taken away my car keys. [6]And even worse, I'll have to go to summer school for biology.

   ✓ 1. The speaker stole a test.

   ____ 2. The speaker had been failing the course.

   ____ 3. The speaker deeply regrets not studying more.

   ____ 4. The speaker will never cheat again.

   ✓ 5. The speaker does not seem to have a guilty conscience about what he did.

   Passage 2: Item 1 — This inference is supported by sentences 1 and 2.

   Item 2 — This inference is eliminated by sentence 6.

   Item 3 — The speaker deeply regrets getting caught, but there is no evidence that he deeply regrets not studying more.

   Item 4 — There is no evidence to support this inference.

   Item 5 — Sentences 3–6 suggest that the speaker is sorry that he got caught and is not happy with the consequences, but nothing he says suggests remorse.

INFERENCES: Mastery Test 2

A. Read the following passage. Then, in the spaces provided, write the letter of the most logical answer to each question, based on the information given in the passage.

> [1]My friends have no friends. [2]They are men. [3]They think they have friends, and if you ask them whether they have friends they will say yes, but they don't really. [4]They think, for instance, that I'm their friend, but I'm not. [5]It's OK. [6]They're not my friends either.
>
> [7]The reason for that is that we are all men—and men, I have come to believe, cannot or will not have real friends. [8]They have something else—companions, buddies, pals, chums, someone to drink with and someone to lunch with, but no one when it comes to saying how they feel—especially how they hurt.
>
> [9]Women know this. [10]They talk about it among themselves. [11]To women, this inability of men to say what they feel is a source of amazement and then anguish and then, finally, betrayal. [12]Women will tell you all the time that they don't know the men they live with. [13]They talk of long silences and of drifting off and of keeping feelings hidden and never letting on about troubles or bothers or whatever.

___C___ 1. We can infer that the author of this passage
  A. has genuine friends himself.   Sentence 7 supports C.
  B. believes men have no need of genuine friends.
  C. feels something prevents men from having genuine friends.

___B___ 2. We can infer that the author
  A. is proud he is able to share his feelings better than other men.
  B. believes women want the men in their lives to share their feelings.
  C. believes men have more hurt feelings than women do.   Sentence 11 supports B.

___A___ 3. We can infer that the author believes women
  A. have genuine friends.
  B. prefer "strong, silent" men.   Sentence 7 supports A.
  C. understand why men do not talk about their feelings.

___C___ 4. We can conclude that the author thinks
  A. men realize they don't have friends.   Sentence 8 supports C.
  B. women should try to be more like men when it comes to friendship.
  C. men's relationships aren't deep enough to be genuine friendships.

(Continues on next page)

B. Read the passage below, taken from an essay titled "Darkness at Noon" by Harold Krents, an attorney who was born blind. Then check the **six** statements which are most logically supported by the information given.

Note that the meanings of two words in the passage are given below.

narcissistic: self-admiring
cum laude: with honor

[1]Blind from birth, I have never had the opportunity to see myself and have been completely dependent on the image I create in the eye of the observer. [2]To date it has not been narcissistic°.

[3]There are those who assume that since I can't see, I obviously also cannot hear. [4]Very often people will converse with me at the top of their lungs, enunciating each word very carefully. [5]Conversely, people will also often whisper, assuming that since my eyes don't work, my ears don't either.

[6]For example, when I go to the airport and ask the ticket agent for assistance to the plane, he or she will invariably pick up the phone, call a ground hostess and whisper: "Hi, Jane, we've got a 76 here." [7]I have concluded that the word "blind" is not used for one of two reasons: Either they fear that if the dread word is spoken, the ticket agent's retina will immediately detach, or they are reluctant to inform me of my condition, of which I may not have been previously aware.

[8]On the other hand, others know that of course I can hear but believe that I can't talk. [9]Often, therefore, when my wife and I go out to dinner, a waiter or waitress will ask Kit if "he would like a drink," to which I respond that "indeed he would.". . .

[10]The toughest misconception of all is the view that because I can't see, I can't work. [11]I was turned down by over forty law firms because of my blindness, even though my qualifications included a *cum laude*° degree from Harvard College and a good ranking in my Harvard Law School class.

____ 1. It would offend Krents if people were to use the word "blind" in reference to him.

✓ 2. The airline's code for a blind passenger was "76."

____ 3. It is better to whisper to blind people than to speak to them loudly.

✓ 4. Krents prefers that people speak to him in a normal tone of voice.

✓ 5. Sighted persons are sometimes uncomfortable directing conversation toward a blind person.

Sentence 6 supports Item 2.

Sentence 4 supports Item 4.

✓ 6. Krents's wife is not blind.

Sentence 9 supports Items 5 and 6.

____ 7. Blindness seems to harm a person's intelligence.

Sentence 11 supports Item 8.

✓ 8. Some employers are biased against blind workers.

____ 9. Harvard is apparently biased against blind students.

The entire passage supports Item 10.

✓ 10. Krents speaks frankly about his blindness.

INFERENCES: Mastery Test 3

A. Read the passage below, taken from the autobiographical book *Move On* by the television journalist Linda Ellerbee. Then, in the spaces provided, write the letter of the most logical answer to each question, based on the information given in the passage.

[1]Television changed my family forever. [2]We stopped eating dinner at the dining-room table after my mother found out about TV trays. [3]We kept the TV trays behind the kitchen door and served ourselves from pots on the stove. [4]Setting and clearing the dining-room table used to be my job; now, setting and clearing meant unfolding and wiping our TV trays, then, when we'd finished, wiping and folding our TV trays. [5]Dinner was served in time for one program and finished in time for another. [6]During dinner we used to talk to one another. [7]Now television talked to us. [8]If you had something you absolutely had to say, you waited until the commercial, which is, I suspect, where I learned to speak in thirty-second bursts. [9]As a future writer, it was good practice in editing my thoughts. [10]As a little girl, it was lonely as hell. [11]Once in a while, I'd pass our dining-room table and stop, thinking I heard our ghosts sitting around talking to one another, saying stuff.

_____A_____ 1. We can infer that as a child, Ellerbee
    A. preferred eating at the dining-room table to eating in front of TV.
    B. was glad that she no longer had to clean and set the dining room table.
    C. wished that her parents watched TV programs that she enjoyed.   Sentences 10–11 support A.

_____B_____ 2. Ellerbee suggests that
    A. TV can help people feel less lonely.
    B. it's possible to feel lonely even when others are around.   Sentence
    C. talking with others does not help to reduce loneliness.   10 supports B.

_____C_____ 3. We can infer that in Ellerbee's home
    A. her mother was aware that Ellerbee was unhappy with TV.   Sentence
    B. there were no other children for Ellerbee to talk to.   8 supports C.
    C. watching TV became more important than talking and listening to family members.

_____A_____ 4. We can infer that when Ellerbee imagined ghosts, she
    A. was remembering better times with her family.
    B. was scared of passing by the dining room.
    C. realized her childhood home was haunted.

B. (5–6.) Read the following textbook passage. Then check the **two** statements which are most logically supported by the information given.

[1]The swim team at the University of California at Berkeley was having a practice. [2]After a race, the coach told each swimmer his time—but it wasn't his real time. [3]The coach falsified the time, making it slower than it really was. [4]During the next race, the coach watched what happened. [5]Some of his swimmers swam significantly faster than before, while others swam considerably slower than their usual pace.

(Continues on next page)

_____ 1. The swim coach at Berkeley expected his swimmers to react exactly the way they did.

_____ 2. Some of the Berkeley swimmers probably knew about their coach's experiment before it took place.

_____ 3. Giving disappointing news to athletes is the best way to increase their performance.

✓ 4. Disappointing news about performance can make some athletes try harder and perform better.

✓ 5. People's ability to perform certain tasks is often related to their thoughts and attitudes.

C. (7–10.) Read the paragraph below. Then check the **four** statements which are most logically supported by the information given.

> [1]In 1995, the American Academy of Pediatrics declared that "advertising directed at children is inherently deceptive and exploits children under eight years of age." [2]The academy did not recommend a ban on such advertising because it seemed impractical and would infringe upon advertisers' freedom of speech. [3]Today the health risks faced by the nation's children far outweigh the needs of its mass marketers. [4]Congress should immediately ban all advertisements aimed at children that promote foods high in fat and sugar. [5]Thirty years ago Congress banned cigarette ads from radio and television as a public health measure—and those ads were directed at adults. [6]Smoking has declined ever since. [7]A ban on advertising unhealthy foods to children would discourage eating habits that are not only hard to break, but potentially life-threatening. [8]Moreover, such a ban would encourage the fast-food chains to alter the recipes for their children's meals. [9]Greatly reducing the fat content of McDonald's Happy Meals, for example, could have an immediate effect on the diet of the nation's kids. [10]Every month more than 90 percent of the children in the United States eat at McDonald's.

Comments:
Sentence 6
supports Item 1.
Sentence 10
supports Item 3.
Sentence 4
supports Item 5.
Sentences 5–7
support Item 8.

✓ 1. Cigarette advertisements were effective in encouraging people to continue smoking.

_____ 2. The author values advertisers' freedom of speech, especially as it relates to commercials targeting children.

✓ 3. The author believes the number of children at risk of health problems due to poor diets has increased since 1995.

_____ 4. Banning fast-food ads is unlikely to have any lasting effect on children's diets, according to the author.

✓ 5. The author feels that the advertisers' right to free speech is less important than the health of the nation's children.

_____ 6. TV commercials and other ads probably have little effect on children's behaviors.

_____ 7. The author believes fast-food chains can be convinced to voluntarily refrain from advertising unhealthy foods for young children.

✓ 8. The author suggests that children's poor eating habits are as serious a health problem as adults' smoking.

INFERENCES: Mastery Test 4

A. After reading the following textbook passage, write the letter of the best answer to each question.

> [1]Suppose a man works six or seven days a week in a factory, trying to support his family, but never seems to be able to make ends meet. [2]If he analyzed his situation rationally, he would probably blame the well-to-do generally, and his employers specifically, for failing to pay him an adequate wage. [3]But these people have the power to cut off his income; to oppose them openly would be self-destructive. [4]He could also blame himself for his financial problems, but this too makes him uncomfortable. [5]Instead, he looks to the immigrants who have begun working in his factory. [6]He doesn't really know them, but he suspects they're willing to work for low wages and that many other immigrants are eager to take his job. [7]By a process of twisted logic, he blames these people for his poverty. [8]Soon he is exchanging rumors about "them" with his cronies and supporting efforts to close the border. [9]Hating immigrants makes the man and his friends feel a little better.

___C___ 1. We can infer that the author of the passage thinks
  A. factory workers are not good at managing money.
  B. all factory workers are underpaid.
  c. the man in the example is underpaid.

___C___ 2. We can infer that the author
  A. agrees with what the man in the example thinks.
  B. feels that employers and other well-to-do's should hire only immigrants.
  c. is critical of both the man in the example and his well-to-do employers.

___C___ 3. We can infer that the man in the example probably
  A. has many friends and neighbors who are immigrants.
  B. understands what immigrants think and is aware of their problems.
  c. has no understanding of or meaningful contact with immigrants.

___B___ 4. We can infer from the passage that
  A. immigrants are eager to take other people's jobs.
  B. the man in the example would probably oppose hiring immigrants.
  c. most immigrants don't do their jobs as well as domestic workers.

___A___ 5. The passage suggests that
  A. some people make themselves feel better by thinking less of others.
  B. immigration should be limited or reduced to protect workers' jobs.
  c. employers are wrong to hire immigrants when domestic workers are available.

(Continues on next page)

B. Read the following textbook passage. Then, in the space provided, write the letter of the best answer to each question.

[1]People interrupt for various reasons. [2]One is believing that what they have to say is more important than what the other person is saying. [3]Another reason people interrupt is that they believe they know what the other person is going to say and want the person to know that they already know. [4]People may also interrupt when they are not paying close attention. [5]The interruption communicates a lack of sensitivity, a superior attitude, or both. [6]People need to be able to verbalize their ideas and feelings fully; inappropriate interruptions are bound to damage their self-concepts or make them hostile—and possibly both. [7]Simply stated, whatever you have to say is seldom so important that it requires you to interrupt a person. [8]When you do interrupt, you should realize that you may be perceived as putting a person down. [9]The more frequent the interruptions, the greater the potential harm.

_A___ 6. The author of the above passage suggests that people   Sentence 6
    A. feel good if others listen carefully to their ideas.   supports A.
    B. who interrupt don't mind being interrupted themselves.
    C. should learn not to feel insulted when they are interrupted.

_A___ 7. The author suggests that people may interrupt because they
    A. don't realize that the speaker is in the middle of a point.
    B. are nervous and want the speaker to like and respect them.
    C. are angry at the speaker.   Sentence 4 supports A.

_C___ 8. The author suggests that
    A. it is okay to interrupt others if you feel you are superior to them.
    B. you will never be interrupted if you don't interrupt others.
    C. interruptions can make people feel that their ideas are not worth listening to.   Sentence 8 supports C.

_B___ 9. We can conclude from this paragraph that   Sentences 6 and 8
    A. it is okay for a parent to interrupt a child.   support B.
    B. a boss will gain more cooperation by not interrupting workers.
    C. the author of the passage has never been interrupted in a conversation.

_B___ 10. The passage suggests that people who interrupt
    A. usually are able to predict what others will think about their behavior.
    B. don't always realize how the other person will view the interruption.
    C. should not worry about trying to guess what others are thinking about them.

INFERENCES: Mastery Test 5

A. (1–4.) Read the table below. Then put a check by the **four** statements that are most logically based on the table.

Voter Turnout Among the World's Democracies

Country	Approximate Voter Turnout	Automatic Registration	Election Day a Holiday or Weekend Day?
Belgium	90%	Yes	Yes
Italy	90%	Yes	Yes
Denmark	85%	Yes	No
Austria	80%	Yes	Yes
France	80%	No	Yes
Germany	80%	Yes	Yes
Great Britain	70%	Yes	No
Canada	65%	Yes	No
Japan	60%	Yes	Yes
United States	50%	No	No

Source: Thomas E. Patterson, The American Democracy, *2001.*

____ 1. About a third of voters in the United States do not vote.

✓ 2. Election Day holidays tend to increase voter turnout rates.

✓ 3. Voter turnout might increase if the United States had automatic voter registration and an Election Day holiday.

____ 4. Low voter turnout in the United States probably has little to do with automatic voter registration or Election Day holidays.

✓ 5. Factors that have increased voter participation in other countries have not worked as well in Japan.   Japan's voter turnout is only 60%.

✓ 6. Compared to the United States, other countries make it easier for voters to participate in elections.

____ 7. Voter turnout would be better if elections were held on weekend days rather than on holidays.

____ 8. Voter turnout would be better if elections were held on holidays rather than on weekend days.

(Continues on next page)

B. (5–10.) In the spaces provided, write the letter of the answer to each inference question.

____A____ 5. My mother gave me a river of love, which is inside me still.

You can infer that the mother's love was

A. abundant and never-ending.
B. unexpected and uncertain.
C. suffocating and dangerous.

____B____ 6. The assembly instructions for the table saw were as useful as a camel in the Arctic.

You can infer that the instructions were

A. not in English.
B. not very helpful.
C. extremely useful.

____C____ 7. The detective had a mind like a computer.

You can infer that the detective was

A. cold and impersonal.
B. brilliantly playful.
C. logical and quick.

____C____ 8. Some people say television is bubble gum for the mind.

You can infer that those people consider television to be

A. educational.
B. highly sophisticated entertainment.
C. as good for the mind as junk food is for the body.

____A____ 9. The new phone system looked to me as if it could launch a nuclear missile.

You can infer that the new phone system is

A. frighteningly complicated.
B. inexpensive.
C. simple to use.

____B____ 10. "What a surprise to see you here," she said, icicles dripping from every syllable.

You can infer that the speaker

A. feels uncomfortably cold.
B. dislikes the person she's speaking to.
C. is pleased to meet the other person unexpectedly.

INFERENCES: Mastery Test 6

A. Shown below is a well-known poem by the American poet Carl Sandburg. Read the poem and then choose the inferences which are most logically supported by the information given. Note that Sandburg refers in the poem to five battlefields where many died (Austerlitz, Waterloo, Gettysburg, Ypres, and Verdun).

Grass

Pile the bodies high at Austerlitz and Waterloo.
Shovel them under and let me work—
    I am the grass; I cover all.
And pile them high at Gettysburg
And pile them high at Ypres and Verdun.
Shovel them under and let me work.
Two years, ten years, and passengers ask the conductor:
    What place is this?
    Where are we now?
I am the grass.
Let me work.

_C_ 1. The poem refers to the bodies of
    A. the living.
    B. all those who have died.
    C. those who have died in wars.

    Austerlitz, Waterloo, Gettysburg, Ypres, and Verdun are battlefields.

_B_ 2. The poet suggests that
    A. the war dead were never found.
    B. there were numerous deaths during the wars.
    C. there were fewer deaths than one would suppose.

    Line 1, "Pile the bodies high. . . ."

_B_ 3. The supposed speaker of the poem is
    A. a train passenger.
    B. the grass.
    C. a conductor.

    Lines 3 and 10, "I am the grass."

_C_ 4. The poet implies that
    A. time passes too slowly.
    B. wars scar the land forever.
    C. even bloody battlefields can be cleansed by time and nature.

    Lines 3 ("I cover all") and 7–9 ("Two years, ten years, and passengers ask the conductor: What place is this? Where are we now?")

_A_ 5. The poet implies that
    A. nature's work outlasts humans' work.
    B. humans and nature are equal partners.
    C. humans' work will outlast anything nature does.

    Grass is "nature's work"; the tragedy of war is "humans' work."

(Continues on next page)

B. Following is a passage from *A Hole in the World*, an autobiographical account by the Pulitzer Prize-winning author Richard Rhodes. Read the passage, and then choose the inferences which are most logically supported by the information given.

> [1]We played dodgeball at recess. [2]Dodgeball was my sport. [3]I was light and quick and often managed to escape being picked off until I was the last of my team inside the circle, the winner of the round. [4]My friend was usually my competition. [5]One day I kidded him too sharply when he lost and I won. [6]He gathered a knot of classmates afterward, the girl I dreamed about among them. [7]They strolled over and surrounded me. [8]They were smiling and I thought they were friendly; it didn't occur to me to dodge. [9]The boys grabbed me. [10]My friend led them. [11]"You stink," he told me happily. [12]"We think you're dirty. [13]We want to see." [14]They jerked down the straps on my bib overalls, held my arms high, peeled off my ragged shirt. [15]They exposed my filth, my black armpits, my dirty neck for everyone to see. [16]The faces of those children, the girl well forward among them, filled with horror perverted with glee. [17]I went the only way I could go, down, dropping to the asphalt of the playground. [18]They formed a circle around me, laughing and pointing. [19]I couldn't get away. [20]I covered my head and drew up my knees. [21]I knew how to make myself invisible. [22]I'd learned to make myself invisible when my stepmother attacked. [23]It worked because I couldn't see her even if she could still see me. [24]I made myself invisible. [25]They couldn't hear me crying.

_B_   6. We can infer from the passage that the author's friend
  A. felt sorry for him.
  B. meant to embarrass him.
  C. did not expect the other kids to laugh.

_A_   7. We can infer from the passage that the girl in the crowd   The fact that
  A. made the author's humiliation greater.   she was the girl of his dreams
  B. had strong feelings for the author.   (Sentence 6) would make his
  C. was against teasing the author.   humiliation even greater.

_C_   8. The author implies that his stepmother
  A. was very fond of him.
  B. worried about him.
  C. abused him.

_A_   9. We can infer from the passage that the author
  A. probably wasn't very well cared for at home.
  B. was usually clean, but just happened to be dirty that day.
  C. expected kids to tease him about his dirtiness.

_A_ 10. We can infer that when the author made himself "invisible,"
  A. he was really putting others out of sight.   Sentence 25
  B. he was free from the hurt caused by the other kids.   implies that
  C. the other kids stopped teasing him.   the author was still feeling pain.

9

Purpose
and Tone

There is an author—a person with thoughts, feelings, and opinions—behind everything you read. Whether this person is a sports writer, a newspaper columnist, a novelist, or a friend sending you a letter, he or she works from a personal point of view. That point of view is reflected in (1) the *purpose* of a piece of writing as well as (2) its *tone*—the expression of the author's attitude and feeling. Both purpose and tone are discussed in this chapter.

PURPOSE

Authors write with a reason in mind, and you can better evaluate their ideas by determining what that reason is. The author's reason for writing is also called the **purpose** of a selection. Three common purposes are as follows:

- To **inform**—to give information about a subject. Authors with this purpose wish to provide facts that will explain or teach something to readers.

  For example, the author of an informative paragraph about sandwiches might begin, "Eating food between two slices of bread—a sandwich—is a practice that has its origins in eighteenth-century England."

- To **persuade**—to convince the reader to agree with the author's point of view on a subject. Authors with this purpose may give facts, but their main goal is to argue or prove a point to readers.

  The author of a persuasive paragraph about sandwiches might begin, "There are good reasons why every sandwich should be made with whole grain bread."

- To **entertain**—to amuse and delight; to appeal to the reader's senses and imagination. Authors with this purpose entertain in various ways, through fiction and nonfiction.

  The author of an entertaining paragraph about sandwiches might begin, "What I wanted was a midnight snack, but what I got was better—the biggest, most magical sandwich in the entire world."

While the cover and title of anything you read—books, articles, and so on—don't necessarily suggest the author's main purpose, often they do. Here are the covers of three books. See if you can guess the primary purpose of each of these books.

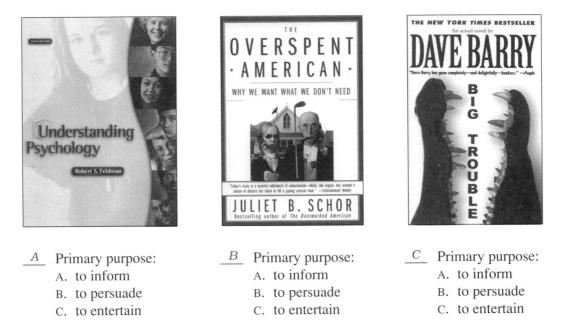

A   Primary purpose:
A. to inform
B. to persuade
C. to entertain

B   Primary purpose:
A. to inform
B. to persuade
C. to entertain

C   Primary purpose:
A. to inform
B. to persuade
C. to entertain

As you probably concluded, the main purpose of the textbook is to inform; the main purpose of *The Overspent American* is to persuade; and the main purpose of the novel by Dave Barry is to entertain.

☑ *Check Your Understanding*

Read each of the three paragraphs below and decide whether the author's purpose is to inform, to persuade, or to entertain. Write in your answers, and then read the explanations that follow.

1.   Each Saturday morning, TV commercials advertise fast foods and high-calorie cereals directly to children. These ads teach children unhealthy eating habits and have been linked to childhood obesity. Parents must realize how harmful such commercials are and should pressure companies to stop marketing unhealthy products to children.

Purpose: _____ *To persuade*

2. About 113 billion people have lived and died in the history of our planet, according to scientific estimates. Of all these people, the names of about 7 billion, or approximately 6 percent, are recorded in some way—on monuments or in books, manuscripts, and public records. The other 106 billion people are gone without a trace.

    Purpose: _____ *To inform* _____

3. Because of the war between his medium-size shirts and pants and his extra-large-size body, my brother has made a commitment to only three meals a day. His definition of a meal, however, is as broad as his belly. If we spot a pretzel salesman or a hot-dog stand on our way to a restaurant, for example, he is not beyond suggesting that we stop. "It'll make a good appetizer," he says.

    Purpose: _____ *To entertain* _____

Explanation:

In the first paragraph, the writer's purpose is to persuade the audience that parents should protest the marketing of unhealthy products to children. Words such as *must* in "must realize" and *should* in "should pressure" are meant to convince us rather than to inform us.

The purpose of the second paragraph is to inform. The author is simply providing readers with information about the people who have lived and died on Earth.

In paragraph 3, the playful and exaggerated details tell us the author's main goal is to entertain with humor.

A Note about Writing with More Than One Purpose

At times, writing may combine two or even all three purposes. A persuasive letter to an editor, for example, may contain factual information, or an informative article on losing weight may include comic touches and some implied persuasion.

*   What would you say is the main purpose of this book?

        A. To inform   B. To persuade   C. To entertain

If you chose answer A, you're correct—my main purpose is to inform and provide practice. But I also have two other purposes at times. For example, on the first page (page 10) of an earlier section, "Reading for Pleasure and Power," what is my main purpose?

        A. To inform   B. To persuade   C. To entertain

My main purpose on page 10 was to persuade you about the importance of becoming a regular reader.

You'll notice, too, that I have included in this book high-interest readings such as the story of Lizzie Borden (page 483) or amusing passages such as the one about not stepping in the *hora* (page 301). What is my purpose in choosing such content?

A. To inform   B. To persuade   <u>C. To entertain</u>

While my main purpose is to inform, I do at times have a second and even third purpose—to persuade and to entertain. And that is the case for other authors as well. What you need to remember when trying to determine purpose is to ask yourself, "What is the author's *main* purpose here?"

➤ Practice 1

Label each item according to its main purpose: to inform (**I**), to persuade (**P**), or to entertain (**E**).

   P   1. Professional athletes do not deserve their inflated salaries, nor does their behavior merit so much media attention.

   I   2. The career of a professional athlete is usually quite short.

   P   3. Nurses assigned to intensive-care units should be given shorter shifts and higher pay because the work is unusually demanding and stressful.

   I   4. On average, women dream more than men, and children dream more than adults.

   E   5. The best approach to take when you feel the urge to exercise is to lie down quickly in a darkened room until the feeling goes away.

   E   6. It's easy to quit smoking; I've done it hundreds of times.

   P   7. More women should get involved in local politics and support the growing number of female candidates for public office.

   I   8. An artificial odor is added to natural gas so that people can tell whether or not gas is leaking.

   E   9. Once football season begins, Matt starts jogging every night—to the refrigerator during commercial breaks.

   I 10. The first person to die of radiation poisoning was a co-discoverer of radium, Marie Curie.

➤ *Practice 2*

Following are three passages, one each from a textbook, a humor book, and a collection of essays. In the spaces provided, write the letter of the best description of the purpose of each passage.

___B___ 1. ¹We have all heard the story of how the young, impoverished Abraham Lincoln trekked miles to borrow books from a neighbor and then read them by firelight. ²We know that nineteenth-century readers would rush to the wharf to greet the ship carrying the latest chapters of a Dickens novel. ³Today, reading seems less urgent and less exciting to many of us. ⁴Worse, few people impart a passion for books to their children. ⁵Instead, they leave the children in front of the television and hope, weakly, that too much watching won't be bad for them. ⁶But we cannot afford to stop reading. ⁷Books shed a light that illuminates our problems and crises. ⁸They are also mirrors that reflect the truest image of ourselves.   Impassioned phrases such as "we cannot afford to stop reading" are intended to persuade.

The main purpose of this passage is to
A. explain something about Abraham Lincoln and Dickens to readers.
B. convince readers of the importance of books.
C. delight readers with entertaining material from books.

___C___ 2. ¹Most of what I know about carpentry, which is almost nothing, I learned in Shop. ²You should know that I took Shop during the Eisenhower administration, when boys took Shop and girls took Home Economics—a code name for "cooking." ³Schools are not allowed to separate boys and girls like that anymore. ⁴They're also not allowed to put students' heads in vises and tighten them, which is what our Shop teacher, Mr. Schmidt, did to Ronnie Miller in the fifth grade when Ronnie used a chisel when he should have used a screwdriver. ⁵(Mr. Schmidt had strong feelings about how to use tools properly.) ⁶I guess he shouldn't have put Ronnie's head in the vise, but it (Ronnie's head) was no great prize to begin with, and you can bet Ronnie never confused chisels and screwdrivers in later life—assuming he made it to later life.   The exaggerated details—for example, "put students' heads in vises"—are meant to entertain.

The main purpose of this passage is to
A. inform readers about the nature of shop classes.
B. argue that shop classes should be eliminated from public schools.
C. amuse readers with humorous details about shop classes.

___A___ 3. ¹Studies of job satisfaction indicate that the vast majority of workers are at least somewhat satisfied with their jobs and would continue to work even if they didn't have to. ²The meaning of work varies from person to person. ³To some, it is a source of self-respect and life purpose. ⁴For others, work is a means of passing time. ⁵To still others, it is primarily a source of financial independence. ⁶Among women, available work is often less satisfying than home management. ⁷Yet most women report increases in self-esteem when employed, especially if they experience support from their families.

The main purpose of this passage is to
A. report on what has been learned through studies of job satisfaction.
B. convince readers of the importance of job satisfaction.
C. entertain readers with rich, sensual descriptions of job satisfaction.

> The straightforward, factual language of this passage
> indicates that its purpose is informational.

TONE

A writer's **tone** reveals the attitude that he or she has toward a subject. Tone is expressed through the words and details the writer selects. Just as a speaker's voice can project a range of feelings, a writer's voice can project one or more tones, or feelings: anger, sympathy, hopefulness, sadness, respect, dislike, and so on. Understanding tone is, then, an important part of understanding what an author has written.

To appreciate the differences in tone that writers can employ, look at the following versions of a murder confession. Then read them aloud—in the tone of voice appropriate in each case.

"I just shot my husband five times in the chest with this .357 Magnum." (*Tone:* matter-of-fact, objective.)

"How could I ever have killed him? I just can't believe I did that!" (*Tone:* shocked, disbelieving.)

"Oh, my God. I've murdered my husband. How can I ever be forgiven for this dreadful deed?" (*Tone:* guilty, regretful)

"That dirty rat. He's had it coming for years. I'm glad I finally had the nerve to do it." (*Tone:* revengeful, self-satisfied.)

➤ Practice 3

Following are five reactions to a fender-bender accident (in which one car hits and slightly damages the rear fender of another car). Label each statement with the tone of voice that you think is present. Choose each tone from the following box, and use each tone only once.

| A. apologetic | B. defensive | C. concerned |
| D. calm | E. angry | |

___C___ 1. "Are you hurt? Are you sure you're okay? Don't move too quickly. Take your time getting out of the car."

___A___ 2. "I am really sorry. I was daydreaming a bit, which is no excuse. I should have been more careful."

___E___ 3. "You idiot! If you hadn't stopped short, I would never have hit you. You should be tossed in jail. You could have gotten us both killed. "

___D___ 4. "It's no big deal. Neither of us was hurt, which is all that counts. The damage is slight. Don't worry about it."

___B___ 5. "Hey, this wasn't my fault. Don't even think about blaming me. You're the one that stopped too quickly, not me. I did nothing wrong here."

Words That Describe Tone

Below and on the next page are two lists of words commonly used to describe tone. With the exception of the words *matter-of-fact* and *objective*, the words reflect a feeling or judgment. The words on this page are more familiar ones. Brief meanings are given in parentheses for the words on the next page. Refer to these meanings as needed to learn any words you don't know yet.

Some Words That Describe Tone

admiring	cruel	loving
affectionate	curious	playful
amused	defensive	praising
angry	doubtful	respectful
apologetic	encouraging	self-pitying
ashamed	excited	serious
calming	forgiving	sorrowful
caring	frightened	sympathetic
cheerful	grateful	threatening
conceited	humorous	tragic
concerned	insulting	warm
critical	joyous	worried

More Words That Describe Tone—with Their Meanings

ambivalent	(*uncertain about a choice*)
arrogant	(*full of self-importance; conceited*)
bewildered	(*confused; puzzled*)
bitter	(*angry; full of hate*)
compassionate	(*deeply sympathetic*))
depressed	(*very sad or discouraged*)
detached	(*emotionally uninvolved*)
disbelieving	(*unbelieving*)
distressed	(*suffering sorrow, misery, or pain*)
hypocritical	(*false*)
impassioned	(*filled with strong feeling*)
indignant	(*angry about something unfair or mean*)
instructive	(*teaching*)
ironic	(*meaning the opposite of what is expressed*)
lighthearted	(*happy and carefree*)
matter-of-fact	(*sticking to facts; unemotional*)
mocking	(*making fun of and/or looking down upon something*)
nostalgic	(*longing for something or someone in the past*)
objective	(*not influenced by feelings or personal prejudices*)
optimistic	(*looking on the bright side of things*)
pessimistic	(*looking on the gloomy, unfavorable side of things*)
pleading	(*begging*)
prideful	(*full of pride or exaggerated self-esteem*)
remorseful	(*guilty over a wrong one has done*)
revengeful	(*wanting to hurt someone in return for an injury*)
sarcastic	(*sharp or wounding; ironic*)
scheming	(*tricky*)
scornful	(*looking down on someone or something*)
self-mocking	(*making fun of or looking down on oneself*)
sentimental	(*showing tender feelings; romantic; overly emotional*)
solemn	(*involved with serious concerns*)
straightforward	(*direct and honest*)
superior	(*looking down on others*)
tolerant	(*respectful of other views and behavior; patient about problems*)
uncertain	(*doubting*)

☑ *Check Your Understanding*

Below are five statements expressing different attitudes about a shabby apartment. Five different tones are used:

optimistic	tolerant	humorous
bitter	sentimental	

Feel free to check the lists on pages 345–346 for the meaning of any unfamiliar tone words. Label each statement with the tone you think is present. Use each tone once. Then read the explanation that follows.

___*sentimental*___ 1. This place may be shabby, but since both of my children were born while we lived here, it has a special place in my heart.

___*tolerant*___ 2. This isn't the greatest apartment in the world, but it's not really that bad.

___*bitter*___ 3. If only there were some decent jobs out there, I wouldn't be reduced to living in this miserable dump.

___*optimistic*___ 4. This place does need some repairs, but I'm sure the landlord will be making improvements sometime soon.

___*humorous*___ 5. When we move away, we're planning to release three hundred cockroaches and two mice so we can leave the place exactly as we found it.

Explanation:

The tone of item 1 is sentimental. "It has a special place in my heart" expresses tender emotions. In item 2, the words "not really that bad" show that the writer is tolerant, accepting the situation while recognizing that it could be better. We could describe the tone of item 3 as bitter. The writer resents a situation that forces him or her to live in a "miserable dump." Item 4 is optimistic since the writer is expecting the apartment to be improved soon. Finally, the tone of item 5 is humorous. Its writer claims to be planning a comic revenge on the landlord by returning the apartment to the terrible condition it was in when the tenants moved in.

A Note on Irony

One commonly used tone is irony. When writing has an **ironic** tone, it says one thing but means the opposite. Irony is found in everyday conversation as well as in writing. Following are a few examples; notice that the quotation in each says the opposite of what is meant.

- If at the beginning of a semester you discover that one of your instructors is particularly demanding, you might comment, "This class is sure going to be a piece of cake."
- After seeing a terrible performance in a movie, someone might say about the actor involved, "Now there's a person with a great chance for an Oscar."
- While standing in a long slow line at a supermarket or bank, you might say to people in line with you, "My, this is exciting."
- If a friend arrives at your place two hours late, you might say, "Well, thanks for showing up on time."
- If you're suffering from the flu and someone asks how you feel, you might say: "I feel terrific today."

Irony also refers to situations in which what happens is the opposite of what we might expect. We would call it ironic, for example, if a young woman who failed English in high school went on to become a well-known writer, or if a young man who was cut from his Little League baseball team went on to star in the major leagues. Here are a few more examples of this type of irony:

- Security cameras installed to stop crime were stolen during a robbery.
- A new computer purchased to help a small business crashes, causing the business to lose many of its customers.
- An instructor at a health club smokes a cigarette during lunch break.
- Albert Einstein, one of the century's most brilliant scientists, did poorly in school.
- Beethoven's music teacher once said of him, "As a composer, he is hopeless."
- A newspaper editor fired Walt Disney because he "lacked imagination and had no good ideas."

As you can see, irony is a useful tone for humor and can be used to imply exactly the opposite of what is said or what is done.

☑ *Check Your Understanding*

Look now at the cartoon below. See if you can explain the irony.

GRAND AVENUE reproduced by permission of United Feature Syndicate, Inc.

The irony in the little girl's comment "People are so self-absorbed" is that _____
the little girl herself is self-absorbed
.

Explanation:

The irony is that the little girl herself is completely self-absorbed. She shows no interest in the people around her and is concerned only about their paying attention to her new hair style.

➤ *Practice 4*

In items 1, 2, 3, and 5, the words indicating each tone are underlined.

A. Below are five statements expressing different attitudes about a boss. Five different tones are used:

admiring	sympathetic	objective
ironic	critical	

For each statement, write the tone that you think is present. Use each tone once.

_____*admiring*_____ 1. Tony is an <u>excellent</u> manager—the <u>best</u> one I've ever had.

_____*sympathetic*_____ 2. I know Tony's daughter has been sick. Naturally it's <u>hard for him to concentrate</u> on work right now.

4. The lack _____*critical*_____ of emotion in this sentence demonstrates an objective _____*objective*_____ tone.

3. Tony's <u>too ambitious for his own good</u>. That ambition <u>may destroy</u> both him and the company.

4. Since Tony Roberts became manager, sales in the appliance division have increased 30 percent.

_____*ironic*_____ 5. These words suggest that Tony is actually *not* wonderful at all.

5. Tony's wonderful, all right. <u>He's gotten as far as he has without the slightest idea of how to manage a division.</u>

B. The following conversation between a mother and son involves five of the tones shown in the box below. For each statement, write the tone that you think is present. Five tones will be left over.

threatening	joyful	solemn	straightforward
sympathetic	pessimistic	self-pitying	sarcastic
nostalgic	disbelieving		

_____*straightforward*_____ 6. "Please take the garbage out on your way to school this morning."   No emotion is expressed in this sentence.

_____*sarcastic*_____ 7. "Sure, Mom. I've been looking forward to that chore all morning."   He has most assuredly *not* been looking forward to taking the garbage out all morning—or any morning.

_____*threatening*_____ 8. "Listen, young man, if you don't start fulfilling your responsibilities around this house, your father and I will start asking you to pay rent or find your own place."   The expression "if you don't . . . , your father and I will . . . ." is a threat.

_____*self-pitying*_____ 9. "Okay, I'll take the garbage out. But you know it's not easy going to school full-time and working twenty hours a week when I'm just getting over a bad case of the flu."   The underlined expressions suggest that the young man is feeling sorry for himself.

_____*sympathetic*_____ 10. "I know, honey, this semester has been an especially difficult one for you."   Expressions like "I know, honey" and "especially difficult for you" suggest sympathy.

➤ Practice 5

Each passage illustrates one of the tones in the box below. In each space, put the letter of the tone that best applies. Don't use any letter more than once. Five tones will be left over.

A. affectionate	B. ambivalent	C. accepting	D. ashamed
E. bitter	F. revengeful	G. forgiving	H. playful
I. alarmed	J. grateful		

Remember that the tone of a selection reflects the author's attitude. To find the tone of a paragraph, ask yourself what attitude is revealed by its words and phrases.

_F_ 1. ¹In my fantasies I have ways of dealing with drivers who irritate the heck out of me. ²At times I have 50-caliber machine guns instead of headlights on the front of my car. ³That way, I can send several hundred rounds of burning lead into the slow-moving gas guzzler car in front of me. ⁴I also have a fantasy to deal with another driver I really despise—the truck driver who tailgates just inches from my rear bumper. ⁵In his case, I have flame throwers that rise up out of the trunk of my car and melt down his front tires; that gets him out of my life fast. ⁶I also have a way to deal at night with the guy behind me who has his high beams on. ⁷It feels like a spotlight is shining into my car. ⁸In this case, I'm driving a rented car, so I suddenly slam on my brakes, causing him to plow into me. ⁹That puts his lights out in a hurry. ¹⁰Then I drive on, leaving him to find his way home in the dark. ¹¹My motto is, "Don't just get mad, get even."

_I_ 2. ¹The percentage of children who are classified as overweight has more than doubled in the last thirty years. ²A lack of exercise and increasingly unhealthy, junk-food-filled diets are making kids heavier and heavier. ³More than 22 percent—that's close to one in four—are classified as dangerously obese. ⁴One in four! ⁵This is an urgent public health crisis that people need to wake up to and recognize. ⁶Most overweight children become overweight adults, and overweight adults are at risk for developing heart disease, cancer, diabetes, and stroke. ⁷The costs of dealing with those health problems—from work-hours lost to medical costs—are going to be immense. ⁸If we don't start dealing with this problem immediately, we're going to be in big trouble. ⁹Parents, schools, the government, and the media need to join forces to do something about this problem before it's too late.

_C_ 3. ¹I'm at peace now with my husband's death. ²I had been out shopping when a sudden intuition prompted me to call him. ³My husband had been diagnosed six months before his death with a rare cancer of the body's soft tissues that had since spread to his lungs. ⁴"Are you all right?" I asked him. ⁵"No," he replied. ⁶"I'm having trouble breathing here." ⁷I rushed home and drove him to the ER. ⁸That's where the deck of cards came tumbling down. ⁹During the week that followed, my husband developed serious complications. ¹⁰In his final hours, he told me he wanted everything done for him because he wanted to live so much. ¹¹But as I watched his condition deteriorate, I made the most difficult decision of my life. ¹²It had gotten to the point that life support wasn't the right thing to do. ¹³I went in and held him. ¹⁴And I said, "I want you to let go and come into my heart because it's safe there." ¹⁵He stopped breathing. ¹⁶And now he's in my heart. ¹⁷I can feel his arms around me.

Comments: Item 1 — Expressions like "I have ways of dealing with" and "get even" suggest revenge.

Item 2 — Expressions like "that's one in four," "urgent health crisis," "health problems . . . immense," and "we're going to be in big trouble" suggest alarm.

Item 3 — Expressions like "I'm at peace now" and "come into my heart because it's safe there" show that the writer accepted the situation.

_B_   4. ¹The proposal has been made that students in our schools be required to wear uniforms. ²In some ways, this sounds good. ³It is true that shopping for fashionable clothing and deciding what to wear in the morning take up a lot of money and time. ⁴But kids need to learn to deal with social pressure about things like clothing, and school might be as good a place as any for that lesson. ⁵Also, the way people dress is one way they express themselves, and maybe students should have that avenue of expression open to them too. ⁶However, it is a shame if they constantly worry about their appearance and waste valuable class time by wishing they could have the name-brand shirt across the room. ⁷So uniforms might be helpful in keeping students' minds on their education. ⁸Uniforms could save students and their parents money, too, which is certainly a good thing. ⁹On the other hand, those uniforms are not cheap, and most students will want to have several sets, so the savings might not be all that significant. ¹⁰It's really hard to say whether uniforms are a good idea or not.

Comments:

Item 4—
Expressions like "In some ways . . . But," "Also . . . However," "might be . . . On the other hand," and "It's really hard to say" demonstrate ambivalence.

Item 5—
Expressions like "turned their backs," "rug pulled out from under their feet," "greedy employers," and "unscrupulous managers" suggest bitterness.

_E_   5. ¹After twenty-two years of business in this community, Acme Supplies closed its doors for the final time today. ²Ninety-seven people lost their jobs. ³Many of them had worked for Acme since it opened. ⁴You might think the management of Acme would feel it owed those loyal workers something, but you would be wrong. ⁵Despite the factory's record of efficiency and high production, Acme executives leapt at the chance to make more money by moving the plant to Mexico, where wages are lower. ⁶In doing so, they turned their backs on the men and women who have made their company so successful over the years. ⁷Some of those employees were only months away from retirement. ⁸Instead of looking forward to some well-deserved rest, those employees are frantically trying to adjust to having had the rug pulled out from under their feet by their greedy employers. ⁹Although Acme always claimed to treat its workers "like family," the reality is that those workers were never more than tools used to fatten the bank accounts of the company's unscrupulous managers.

➤ Practice 6

Read the following letter to the late Ann Landers along with her response. Then answer the questions about purpose and tone that follow.

Dear Ann Landers: When our daughter won a scholarship to a very fine university in the East last year, we were thrilled and proud of her.   1

"Mary" does not drink or smoke and has high moral standards. We   2 were not the least bit uneasy about her moving so far from home to go to school, and we didn't worry about peer pressure. ⁴She has always been a leader, not a follower.

Mary's letters, however, are depressing. She says so many people who live in her dorm (it's mixed, both men and women) get drunk at least four nights a week, and they make so much noise she can't study. She also has spent several nights taking care of sick, hung-over friends. Her roommate, she says, often stays out until 3 or 4 in the morning, comes in dead drunk, and throws up. Mary resents having to clean up after her, but she has no choice. 3

We did not anticipate this sort of thing when we sent our daughter away to college. We asked Mary if she would consider changing schools next year (we would be willing to forgo the scholarship and pay her tuition). She said, "No, an Ivy League school has always been my dream, and these problems exist all over." 4

What on Earth is going on? Can you tell us? 5

Dear Parents: You ask, "What's going on?" You just described it, according to the information I receive regularly from the National Clearinghouse for Alcohol and Drug Information. College students spend $5.5 billion a year on alcohol. Harvard School of Public Health researchers have reported that excessive use of alcohol on college campuses may be hazardous not only to the health of drinkers but to nondrinkers as well. Nondrinkers suffer from loss of sleep and study time, vandalism, physical assault, unwanted sexual advances, and rape. 6

Dr. Henry Wechsler, director of college alcohol studies at the Harvard School of Public Health, was the lead author of a report that studied the drinking habits of 17,592 students from 140 colleges. The study found that alcohol on college campuses poses a serious hazard to the physical health and emotional well-being of students. One student said she was fed up with people urinating in the elevators, vomiting in the halls, wrecking the bathroom, and pounding holes in the walls. 7

Wechsler's research revealed that nearly half the college students are binge drinkers who cause most of the trouble by depriving others of study time and sleep and by attacking classmates. College security officers and administrators report that alcohol is involved in the majority of rapes and almost all violent incidents on campus. 8

Wechsler urges students who do not drink to speak up and demand their rights. *Time* magazine quoted Wechsler as saying, "If your roommate gets drunk every night, either insist on a new roommate or demand that you be moved." He urges people who are bothered by excessive drinking to complain. He said, "I want students to complain. I want parents to complain. That's the only way we will get change." 9

Although Wechsler does not beat the drum for total abstinence (he says it is not "realistic"), I disagree. If you don't drink at all, you will never have to worry about how much is too much. 10

_B_ 1. The first paragraph of the parents' letter has a
   A. tragic tone.
   B. prideful tone.
   C. pleading tone.

The paragraph lists positive achievements and qualities.

_A_ 2. In its third paragraph, the parents' letter takes on a
   A. distressed tone.
   B. revengeful tone.
   C. doubtful tone.

The details in the paragraph express distressing events.

_B_ 3. The parents' letter ends in a(n)
   A. instructive tone.
   B. bewildered tone.
   C. sentimental tone.

The expression "What on Earth is going on?" shows bewilderment.

_A_ 4. The purpose of much of the parents' letter is to
   A. inform Ann Landers of their daughter's situation.
   B. persuade Ann Landers to convince their daughter to leave her school.
   C. amuse Ann Landers with the ridiculous behavior of today's college students.

None of the details support answer B or C.

_B_ 5. On the basis of the facts she has chosen to include and her last paragraph, we can conclude that Landers's main purpose is
   A. simply to inform people about various views of alcohol.
   B. to persuade readers that it is best to drink little or no alcohol.
   C. to entertain readers with colorful views about alcohol.

See paragraph 10.

CHAPTER REVIEW

In this chapter, you learned that part of reading critically is to do the following:

- Be aware of an author's **purpose**: the reason why he or she writes. Three common purposes are to inform, to persuade, and to entertain.

- Be aware of **tone**—the expression of the author's attitude and feeling about a subject. A writer's tone might be objective—the case in most textbook writing—or it might be lighthearted, sympathetic, angry, affectionate, respectful, or any of many other tones shown on pages 345–346.

   One important tone to recognize is **irony**: saying one thing but meaning the opposite.

The final chapter in Part One—Chapter 10—will explain another part of reading critically: recognizing an author's point and evaluating the support for that point.

On the Web: If you are using this book in class, you can visit our website for additional practice in identifying an author's purpose and tone. Go to **www.townsendpress.com** and click on "Online Exercises."

➤ Review Test 1

To review what you've learned in this chapter, fill in the blank(s) or write, in the space provided, the letter of the correct answer for each question.

1. The author's reason for writing something is called the ___*purpose*___ of a selection.

2–4. What is the purpose of each of the types of writing below? Label each according to its usual main purpose: to inform, to persuade, or to entertain.

A news report: _____*inform*_____

A mystery novel: _____*entertain*_____

An editorial: _____*persuade*_____

5. The tone of a selection reveals the author's _____*attitude*_____ toward his or her subject.

6. An ironic comment is one that means the _____*opposite*_____ of what is said.

___*B*___ 7. Imagine a bad morning when everything goes wrong—there is no hot water for the shower, milk for the cereal is sour, a pool of oil is under the car, and so on. Which of the following would be an ironic comment on the situation?
A. "What a lousy start to the day."
B. "What a great day this is going to be."
C. "Good grief. What did I do to deserve this?"

___*C*___ 8. A (A. forgiving; B. critical; C. matter-of-fact) tone reveals no personal feeling.

___*C*___ 9. An arrogant tone suggests that the speaker or writer
A. is angry.
B. looks on the unfavorable side of things.
C. thinks a lot of himself or herself.

_B_ 10. An objective tone indicates that the speaker or writer is telling something
   A. dishonestly.
   B. without personal prejudice.
   C. with a longing for something in the past.

➤ **Review Test 2: Purpose**

In the space provided, indicate whether the primary purpose of each passage is to inform (**I**), to persuade (**P**), or to entertain (**E**).

_P_ 1. ¹Let's pretend for a moment. ²Suppose that in the hospital room where your mother lies dying with terminal cancer there is a button. ³You have the power by pushing that button to quickly and painlessly end the life of this person you dearly love. ⁴You know your mother will be confined to that hospital room for her remaining days. ⁵Would you push the button for her? ⁶You watch as she is hooked up to a life-support machine, and you also watch and listen as her pain increases and she pleads for you to help. ⁷You watch her worsen day after day until she reaches a point where she can no longer talk or hear, and she is only alive because of that machine. ⁸Now would you push that button? ⁹If you can imagine the horror of what I have described, then you may agree our country should reconsider its laws against mercy killing.

Should in sentence 9 indicates a persuasive purpose.

_I_ 2. ¹Traditionally, English grammar called for the use of the masculine pronoun *he* to stand for the entire class of humans regardless of sex. ²Thus in the past, the following sentence would have been considered proper English: "Everyone in class must hand in his paper tomorrow." ³Today, many language experts would consider that sentence sexist because it excludes females. ⁴They say that one way to avoid the problem is to recast a sentence using plurals: "All students in the class must hand in their papers tomorrow." ⁵Alternately, they advise using *both* male and female singular pronouns: "Everyone in class must hand in his or her paper tomorrow."

This passage offers facts, not judgments, in a straightforward way.

_E_   3. [1]An elderly woman in a Cadillac was preparing to back into a parking space. [2]Suddenly a small red sports car appeared and pulled into the space. [3]"That's what you can do when you're young and fast," the young man in the car yelled to the old woman. [4]As he strolled away, laughing, he heard a terrible crunching sound. [5]"What's that noise?" he asked. [6]Turning around, he saw the old woman backing repeatedly into his small car and crushing it. [7]"You can't do that, old lady!" he yelled.

[8]"What do you mean, I can't?" she yelled back, as metal grated against metal. [9]"This is what you can do when you're old and rich."

This passage is obviously meant to amuse.

_I_   4. [1]College students who contract mononucleosis ("mono") can be forced into a long period of bed rest during a semester when they can least afford it. [2]Other common diseases can be managed with minimal disruption, but the overall weakness and fatigue seen in many people with mono sometimes requires a month or two of rest and recuperation. [3]Mono is a viral infection in which the body produces an excess of one type of white blood cells. [4]After an uncertain, perhaps long, incubation, the acute symptoms of mono can appear, including weakness, headache, low-grade fever, swollen lymph glands (especially in the neck), and sore throat. [5]Mental fatigue and depression are sometimes reported as side effects of mono. [6]After the acute symptoms disappear, the weakness and fatigue usually persist, sometimes for a few months.

This passage offers facts in a straightforward way.

_P_   5. [1]Americans love parks and wildlife refuges, but the crowding they find there is a national disgrace. [2]Parking lots are packed, and roadways through parks and refuges are often so jammed that they might as well be the parking lots. [3]Playing fields and barbecue grills are claimed early in the day, and even on remote trails voices can be heard from every direction. [4]Americans badly need more land devoted to open space where nature walks, picnics, and camping can take place in uncrowded tranquillity. [5]Communities across the nation should establish parks and trails that provide free access to open space for everyone.   *Should* in sentence 5 indicates a persuasive purpose.

➤ *Review Test 3: Tone*

Each of the following five passages illustrates one of the tones in the box below. In the space provided, put the letter of the tone that best applies to each passage. Don't use any letter more than once. Three tones will be left over.

Remember that the tone of a selection reflects the author's attitude. To find the tone of a paragraph, ask yourself what attitude is revealed by its words and phrases.

A. tolerant	B. pessimistic	C. objective	D. ironic
E. indignant	F. sentimental	G. forgiving	H. ashamed

___C___ 1. [1]Most animals have a "sweet tooth," and humans are no exception. [2]That's why food manufacturers often add sugars and other sweeteners to their products. [3]Indeed, many commercial breakfast cereals are 40% sugar by weight. [4]Because added sugar provides calories but no essential nutrients, sugar is usually described as contributing "empty calories" to the diet. [5]Excess calories from added sugar are converted to fat, which in some cases may contribute to overweight problems. [6]Populations that consume large amounts of sugar exhibit high rates of heart disease, obesity, diabetes, and tooth decay. [7]Sugar consumption in the United States averages about 133 pounds per person per year.

The passage is not judgmental but gives objective information.

___E___ 2. [1]Relentless greed and horrifying dishonesty characterized the treatment of Indians in the 1860s and 1870s, when massacres of Native Americans were commonplace. [2]The massacre at Sand Creek in Colorado in 1864 was sadly typical. [3]The territorial governor had persuaded the Indians to gather there and had promised them protection. [4]Despite this pledge, Colonel J. M. Chivington's militia attacked the defenseless Indian camp. [5]They disregarded that sacred symbol, the American flag, and the white flag of truce that the Indians were flying at Sand Creek. [6]Four hundred fifty peaceful Indians—men, women, and children—were slaughtered in what has been called "the foulest and most unjustified crime in the annals of America." [7]This was only one of the heartless massacres of Native Americans recorded by history.

Expressions like "Relentless greed and horrifying dishonesty," "sadly typical," "disregarded that sacred symbol," "slaughtered," and "heartless massacres" show indignation.

___B___ 3. [1]During my last physical, the doctor found a little lump in my throat. [2]I'm going into the hospital tomorrow so they can check out what it is. [3]The doctor said it was most likely a harmless cyst, but of course he would say that. [4]What's he going to say: "Sorry—looks like cancer to me"? [5]He also said that if it is cancer, it's probably of a kind that is easily treated. ⁶Right, I thought. ⁷He's trying to be nice, I know, but I also know how these things go. ⁸First he'll say it's nothing; then he'll say it's cancer but no big deal; and finally he'll tell me the truth. ⁹I'm done for.   All the details right down to "I'm done for" show pessimism.

   _D_   4. ¹Gregory Jenkins would make an ideal candidate for governor. ²A governor needs experience with a large organization, and in our state, there are fewer organizations bigger than the mob. ³Jenkins's connections statewide with that distinguished group of business people ensure him a plentiful supply of cash to support a long and difficult campaign. ⁴In addition, he is an inspiring speaker and civic activist. ⁵In a recent comment to the press, he noted, "Ain't no stronger supporter of our education system than me." ⁶And nobody has a more loving approach to his friends and colleagues than Jenkins. ⁷In fact, he's well known for loving his best pal's wife for several years.   The details suggest that Jenkins would be the opposite of an ideal candidate.

   _H_   5. ¹I can't look my best friend in the eye. ²He doesn't know what happened last weekend, and I hope he never will. ³We were all at a party at a friend's house. ⁴It was pretty loud and wild, and I was having a good time. ⁵I found myself in the corner of a crowded room with the girl he's been dating all year. ⁶We were joking around and then we started dancing. ⁷I don't even know how it began, but somehow we ended up alone in a bathroom. ⁸I started kissing her and she kissed me back. ⁹We stayed in there until somebody started pounding on the door. ¹⁰That night it didn't seem like a big deal, but the next day I couldn't believe I had done it. ¹¹This is a girl he really cares for a lot, and she doesn't mean a thing to me. ¹²Now everything is a mess. ¹³I'm so uncomfortable around her I don't know what to do. ¹⁴And I know he considers me one of his best friends. ¹⁵I feel like such a jerk for betraying him.   Sentences 1–2 and 10–15 indicate that the writer feels ashamed of his behavior.

➤ Review Test 4

Here is a chance to apply your understanding of purpose and tone to a full-length selection. In "The Scholarship Jacket," Marta Salinas writes about a moment of disappointment in her childhood in southern Texas. By focusing on an award that school authorities decided she should not receive, Salinas shows us the pain of discrimination as well as the need for inner strength.

To help you continue to strengthen your skills, the reading is followed by questions not only on what you've learned in this chapter but also on what you've learned in previous chapters.

Words to Watch

Below are some words in the reading that do not have strong context support. Each word is followed by the number of the paragraph in which it appears and its meaning there. These words are indicated in the article by a small circle (°).

agile (2): able to move quickly
P.E. (3): the abbreviation for physical-education class
eavesdrop (4): secretly listen
filtered through (7): passed through
fidgeted (8): fussed
muster (12): call forth
mesquite (15): a sweet-smelling thorny tree
clod (15): lump of earth
gaunt (25): thin and bony
vile (29): very unpleasant
adrenaline (31): a hormone that responds to emotion, raising blood pressure and
　　　　stimulating the heart

THE SCHOLARSHIP JACKET

Marta Salinas

1　　The small Texas school that I attended carried out a tradition every year during the eighth grade graduation: a beautiful gold and green jacket, the school colors, was awarded to the class valedictorian, the student who had maintained the highest grades for eight years. The scholarship jacket had a big gold S on the left front side, and the winner's name was written in gold letters on the pocket.

2　　My oldest sister, Rosie, had won the jacket a few years back, and I fully expected to win also. I was fourteen and in the eighth grade. I had been a straight-A student since the first grade, and the last year I had looked forward to owning that jacket. My father was a farm laborer who couldn't earn enough money to feed eight children, so when I was six I was given to my grandparents to raise. We couldn't participate in sports at school because there were registration fees, uniform costs, and trips out of town; so even though we were quite agile° and athletic, there would never be a sports school jacket for us. This one, the scholarship jacket, was our only chance.

3　　In May, close to graduation, spring fever struck, and no one paid any attention to class; instead we stared out the windows and at each other, wanting to speed up the last few weeks of school. I despaired every time I looked in the mirror. Pencil thin, not a curve anywhere, I was called "Beanpole" and "String Bean," and I knew that's what I looked like. A flat chest, no hips, and a brain, that's what I had. That really isn't much for a fourteen-year-old to work with, I thought, as I absentmindedly wandered from my history class to the gym. Another hour of sweating during basketball and displaying my toothpick legs was coming up. Then I remembered my P.E.° shorts were still in a bag under my desk where I'd forgotten them. I had to walk all the way back and get them. Coach Thompson was a real bear if anyone wasn't dressed for P.E. She had said I was a good forward and once she even tried to talk Grandma into letting me join the team. Grandma, of course, said no.

4   I was almost back at my classroom door when I heard angry voices and arguing. I stopped. I didn't mean to eavesdrop°; I just hesitated, not knowing what to do. I needed those shorts and I was going to be late, but I didn't want to interrupt an argument between my teachers. I recognized the voices: Mr. Schmidt, my history teacher, and Mr. Boone, my math teacher. They seemed to be arguing about me. I couldn't believe it. I still remember the shock that rooted me flat against the wall as if I were trying to blend in with the graffiti written there.

5   "I refuse to do it! I don't care who her father is, her grades don't even begin to compare to Martha's. I won't lie or falsify records. Martha has a straight-A-plus average and you know it." That was Mr. Schmidt, and he sounded very angry. Mr. Boone's voice sounded calm and quiet.

6   "Look, Joann's father is not only on the Board, he owns the only store in town; we could say it was a close tie and—"

7   The pounding in my ears drowned out the rest of the words, only a word here and there filtered through°. "Martha is Mexican . . . resign . . . won't do it. . . ." Mr. Schmidt came rushing out, and luckily for me went down the opposite way toward the auditorium, so he didn't see me. Shaking, I waited a few minutes and then went in and grabbed my bag and fled from the room. Mr. Boone looked up when I came in but didn't say anything. To this day I don't remember if I got in trouble in P.E. for being late or how I made it through the rest of the afternoon. I went home very sad and cried into my pillow that night so Grandmother wouldn't hear me. It seemed a cruel coincidence that I had overheard that conversation.

8   The next day when the principal called me into his office, I knew what it would be about. He looked uncomfortable and unhappy. I decided I wasn't going to make it any easier for him, so I looked him straight in the eye. He looked away and fidgeted° with the papers on his desk.

9   "Martha," he said, "there's been a change in policy this year regarding the scholarship jacket. As you know, it has always been free." He cleared his throat and continued. "This year the Board decided to charge fifteen dollars—which still won't cover the complete cost of the jacket."

10   I stared at him in shock and a small sound of dismay escaped my throat. I hadn't expected this. He still avoided looking in my eyes.

11   "So if you are unable to pay the fifteen dollars for the jacket, it will be given to the next one in line."

12   Standing with all the dignity I could muster°, I said, "I'll speak to my grandfather about it, sir, and let you know tomorrow." I cried on the walk home from the bus stop. The dirt road was a quarter of a mile from the highway, so by the time I got home, my eyes were red and puffy.

13   "Where's Grandpa?" I asked Grandma, looking down at the floor so she wouldn't ask me why I'd been crying. She was sewing on a quilt and didn't look up.

14   "I think he's out back working in the bean field."

15   I went outside and looked out at the fields. There he was. I could see him walking between the rows, his body bent over the little plants, hoe in hand. I walked slowly out to him, trying to think how I could best ask him for the money. There was a cool breeze blowing and a sweet smell of mesquite° in the air, but I didn't appreciate it. I kicked at a dirt clod°. I wanted that jacket so much. It was more than just being a valedictorian and giving a little thank-you speech for the jacket on graduation night. It represented eight years of hard work and expectation. I knew I had to be honest with Grandpa; it was my only chance. He saw me and looked up.

16   He waited for me to speak. I cleared my throat nervously and clasped my hands behind my back so he wouldn't see them shaking. "Grandpa, I have a big favor to ask you," I said in Spanish, the only language he knew. He still waited silently. I tried again. "Grandpa, this year the principal said the scholarship jacket is not going to be free. It's going to cost fifteen dollars and I have to take the money in tomorrow, otherwise it'll be given to someone else." The last words came out in an eager rush. Grandpa straightened up tiredly and leaned his chin on the hoe handle. He looked out over the field that was filled with the tiny green bean plants. I waited, desperately hoping he'd say I could have the money.

17   He turned to me and asked quietly, "What does a scholarship jacket mean?"

18   I answered quickly; maybe there was a chance. "It means you've earned it by having the highest grades for eight years and that's why they're giving it to you." Too late I realized the significance of my words. Grandpa knew that I understood it was not a matter of money.

It wasn't that. He went back to hoeing the weeds that sprang up between the delicate little bean plants. It was a time-consuming job; sometimes the small shoots were right next to each other. Finally he spoke again.

19   "Then if you pay for it, Marta, it's not a scholarship jacket, is it? Tell your principal I will not pay the fifteen dollars."

20   I walked back to the house and locked myself in the bathroom for a long time. I was angry with Grandfather even though I knew he was right, and I was angry with the Board, whoever they were. Why did they have to change the rules just when it was my turn to win the jacket?

21   It was a very sad and withdrawn girl who dragged into the principal's office the next day. This time he did look me in the eyes.

22   "What did your grandfather say?"

23   I sat very straight in my chair.

24   "He said to tell you he won't pay the fifteen dollars."

25   The principal muttered something I couldn't understand under his breath, and walked over to the window. He stood looking out at something outside. He looked bigger than usual when he stood up; he was a tall, gaunt° man with gray hair, and I watched the back of his head while I waited for him to speak.

26   "Why?" he finally asked. "Your grandfather has the money. Doesn't he own a small bean farm?"

27   I looked at him, forcing my eyes to stay dry. "He said if I had to pay for it, then it wouldn't be a scholarship jacket," I said and stood up to leave. "I guess you'll just have to give it to Joann." I hadn't meant to say that; it had just slipped out. I was almost to the door when he stopped me.

28   "Martha—wait."

29   I turned and looked at him, waiting. What did he want now? I could feel my heart pounding. Something bitter and vile° tasting was coming up in my mouth; I was afraid I was going to be sick. I didn't need any sympathy speeches. He sighed loudly and went back to his big desk. He looked at me, biting his lip, as if thinking.

30   "Okay, damn it. We'll make an exception in your case. I'll tell the Board, you'll get your jacket."

31   I could hardly believe it. I spoke in a trembling rush. "Oh, thank you, sir!" Suddenly I felt great. I didn't know about adrenaline° in those days, but I knew something was pumping through me, making me feel as tall as the sky. I wanted to yell, jump, run the mile, do something. I ran out so I could cry in the hall where there was no one to see me. At the end of the day, Mr. Schmidt winked at me and said, "I hear you're getting a scholarship jacket this year."

32   His face looked as happy and innocent as a baby's, but I knew better. Without answering I gave him a quick hug and ran to the bus. I cried on the walk home again, but this time because I was so happy. I couldn't wait to tell Grandpa and ran straight to the field. I joined him in the row where he was working and without saying anything I crouched down and started pulling up the weeds with my hands. Grandpa worked alongside me for a few minutes, but he didn't ask what had happened. After I had a little pile of weeds between the rows, I stood up and faced him.

33   "The principal said he's making an exception for me, Grandpa, and I'm getting the jacket after all. That's after I told him what you said."

34   Grandpa didn't say anything; he just gave me a pat on the shoulder and a smile. He pulled out the crumpled red handkerchief that he always carried in his back pocket and wiped the sweat off his forehead.

35   "Better go see if your grandmother needs any help with supper."

36   I gave him a big grin. He didn't fool me. I skipped and ran back to the house whistling some silly tune.

Reading Comprehension Questions

Vocabulary in Context

   _D_   1. In the sentences below, the word *dismay* (dĭs-mā′) means
      A. joy.
      B. comfort.
      C. surprise and relief.
      D. sudden discouragement.

      "I stared at him in shock and a small sound of dismay escaped my throat. I hadn't expected this." (Paragraph 10)

Central Point and Main Ideas

___C___ 2. Which sentence best expresses the main idea of this selection?
   A. When she went to pick up her gym clothes, Marta overheard a conversation between two teachers that shocked and saddened her.
   B. At Marta's school, it was a tradition to award a beautiful gold and green jacket to the eighth-grade valedictorian.
   C. Although fourteen-year-old Marta had earned a school jacket awarded for scholarship, she almost lost this award because of discrimination.
   D. Marta's sister had won the scholarship jacket, and Marta deeply wanted to win it as well.   Answers A, B, and D are too narrow.

___B___ 3. Which sentence best expresses the main idea of paragraph 7?
   A. Marta was unable to hear every word of Mr. Schmidt's and Mr. Boone's conversation.
   B. Marta was shocked and saddened when she overheard two teachers arguing about her.
   C. Mr. Schmidt didn't see Marta when he rushed out of the room.
   D. Marta didn't want her grandmother to know she was crying.

Expressions like "ears pounded," "shaking," "fled from the room,"
Supporting Details   and "don't remember" show that Marta was shocked and saddened.

___A___ 4. Which of the following statements is false?
   A. Marta was being raised by her grandparents because her parents were dead.
   B. Mr. Schmidt was angry at the attempt to give the scholarship jacket to someone less deserving than Marta.
   C. Marta's grandfather refused to give her the money for the scholarship jacket.   See paragraph 2.
   D. Marta was called by a different name at school.   (Marta's father was poor.)

Transitions

___D___ 5. The relationship between the two parts of the sentence below is one of
   A. time.
   B. contrast.
   C. comparison.
   D. cause and effect.

   "I decided I wasn't going to make it any easier for him, so I looked him straight in the eye." (Paragraph 8)   *So* is a cause-effect word.
   The *cause* is the decision;
   the *effect* is looking him straight in the eye.

Patterns of Organization

___B___   6. The overall pattern of organization of the selection is
     A. cause and effect.
     B. time order.
     C. comparison.
     D. contrast.

> Narrations such as this passage
> are usually in time order.

Fact and Opinion

___B___   7. The word that adds an element of opinion in the factual sentence below is
     A. *tradition.*
     B. *beautiful.*
     C. *valedictorian.*
     D. *highest.*

> "The small Texas school that I attended carried out a tradition every year during the eighth-grade graduation: a beautiful gold and green jacket, the school colors, was awarded to the class valedictorian, the student who had maintained the highest grades for eight years." (Paragraph 1)

Inferences

___B___   8. By saying, "if you pay for it, Marta, it's not a scholarship jacket, is it?" Marta's grandfather was implying that
     A. the jacket was not worth fifteen dollars.
     B. a real award should not have to be bought with money.
     C. Marta did not deserve to win the scholarship jacket.
     D. he did not understand the purpose of the scholarship jacket.

Purpose and Tone

___A___   9. The author's purpose in this selection is to
     A. inform and engage readers with an interesting and meaningful anecdote.
     B. persuade schools not to charge students for academic awards.
     C. entertain with an amusing, light-hearted story about a young girl in school.

___C___ 10. The tone of paragraph 31 can be described as
     A. contented.
     B. angry.
     C. joyous.
     D. conceited.

> Expressions like "felt great," "adrenaline pumping," and "tall as the sky" describe an attitude of joy.

Discussion Questions

1. In her first meeting with the principal, Marta could have challenged him by telling what she had overheard the two teachers saying. Why do you think she stayed silent? What do you think the principal would have said or done if she'd told him she knew the real reason she wasn't being given the jacket?

2. Why do you think the principal gave in during his second meeting with Marta? What do you think that shows about Marta's grandfather's decision? What do you think might happen when the principal has to face the Board again? If you were the principal, what would you have said to the Board?

3. Marta implies that she was discriminated against because of her racial background (she was Mexican) and her family's economic condition (they were poor). Have you ever experienced discrimination, or do you know of a friend who has experienced it? Explain.

4. Marta stresses again and again how important the scholarship jacket was to her and how hard she worked to win it. Is there something you worked hard to achieve when you were younger? How long did you work toward that goal? How did you feel when you finally succeeded— or did not succeed? What lessons, if any, did you learn from the experience?

Note: Writing assignments for this selection appear on pages 589–590.

Check Your Performance   **PURPOSE AND TONE**

Activity	Number Right	Points		Score
Review Test 1 (10 items)	_____	× 1	=	_____
Review Test 2 (5 items)	_____	× 6	=	_____
Review Test 3 (5 items)	_____	× 6	=	_____
Review Test 4 (10 items)	_____	× 3	=	_____
	TOTAL SCORE		=	_____%

Enter your total score into the **Reading Performance Chart: Review Tests** on the inside back cover.

PURPOSE AND TONE: Mastery Test 1

A. In the space provided, indicate whether the primary purpose of each item is to inform (**I**), to persuade (**P**), or to entertain (**E**).

_____I_____ 1. Every month more than 90 percent of the children in the United States eat at McDonald's.

_____P_____ 2. Fast-food chains must be encouraged to offer meals that are healthier for our children.   *Must* is a word used to persuade.

_____E_____ 3. Fred's idea of healthy eating is to have a double cheeseburger without putting any salt on it.

_____P_____ 4. The federal government needs to hire more inspectors to insure the safety of the meals served to our schoolchildren.   *Needs to* is a phrase used to persuade.

_____E_____ 5. Rachel says she eats a balanced diet by choosing items from the four major food groups: chips, soda, candy, and pastries.

B. Each of the following passages illustrates one of the five tones in the box below. In the space provided, write the letter of the tone that applies to each passage.

A. caring	B. critical	C. pessimistic
D. humorous	E. self-mocking	

_____D_____ 6. ¹Recently, my sister asked me to baby-sit her two sons for the evening. ²I figured I would get them dinner, let them watch a little TV, and then put them to bed early. ³The rest of the night I planned to watch TV and collect an easy twenty dollars. ⁴Well, right before we sat down for a pizza dinner, Rickie let the parakeet out of its cage. ⁵The dog started chasing the bird as it flew around the house, so I decided to catch it before the dog did. ⁶The boys and I had the bird cornered by the fireplace when Rickie jumped for it and knocked over the hamster cage. ⁷The hamsters took off under the sofa while the bird flew away. ⁸Fortunately, the dog had disappeared at this point. ⁹I took care of the hamsters while the boys caught the parakeet and put it back in its cage. ¹⁰When we returned to the kitchen to eat cold pizza, I discovered why the dog had lost interest in the bird chase. ¹¹What was left of the pizza was lying on the floor, and tomato sauce was dripping like blood from the dog's chin. ¹²Later, when my sister returned, I took the twenty dollars and told her to get someone else next time.

All the examples are humorous ones.

(Continues on next page)

_B_   7. [1]Whatever happened to the practice of saving up for what you want? [2]It seems nobody has that kind of patience any more. [3]Many Americans buy what they want when they want it and worry about paying for it later. [4]The average American spends significantly more than he or she earns, much to the enjoyment of the credit-card companies. [5]Apparently people need to reach a financial crisis before they realize that it's downright stupid to neglect balancing their budgets and saving for a rainy day.   "Downright stupid" is a critical remark.

_E_   8. [1]Machines are complete mysteries to me, and this has resulted in some embarrassing service calls at my home. [2]For example, there was the time I called in a repairman because our refrigerator was too warm. [3]Imagine my humiliation when he told me that the cause of the problem was a dirty filter, which I didn't know existed and therefore hadn't cleaned even once in the two years we owned the refrigerator. [4]The best example of my brilliance with machines, however, has to be the time I called for someone to fix my washing machine. [5]The repairman's solution was simply to put the plug back in the outlet, from which it had been jarred loose by the constant vibration of the washer.

The writer makes fun of her own lack of expertise.

_C_   9. [1]Research on rats shows that when animals live in crowded conditions, they live disorderly, violent lives. [2]Humans are no different. [3]Crowded inner cities are models of lawlessness; the crowded highways of Los Angeles encourage aggression by drivers, and even shootings. [4]As our urban areas continue to grow in population density, these types of problems will surely also grow. [5]That means more family violence and more fighting over available resources. [6]The American dream will become just that—only a dream.

The writer sees only the negative side.

_A_   10. [1]Those addicted to drugs and alcohol probably feel terrible about themselves—even if they don't show it—and harsh judgments only worsen their self-image. [2]What these people need are programs to help rid themselves of their addictions. [3]It is also important that we all open our hearts and minds to these troubled people. [4]Their addiction does not make them any less "children of God"; nor does it mean that they deserve to be stripped of the dignity that is the birthright of every human being. [5]We must strive to create an environment of hope and help for those who so desperately need it.

All the details show that the writer cares about these people.

Name _____

Section _____ Date _____

SCORE: (Number correct) _____ × 10 = _____%

PURPOSE AND TONE: Mastery Test 2

A. In the space provided, indicate whether the primary purpose of each item is to inform (**I**), to persuade (**P**), or to entertain (**E**).

_I_ 1. The world's first ads were neither printed nor broadcast electronically; they were vocal, called out by street peddlers promoting their wares.

_P_ 2. Billboard advertising is a form of visual pollution and should be banned.

_E_ 3. Instead of nagging my father to lose weight, my mother bought him an extra-large T-shirt imprinted with the message "This space for rent."

_I_ 4. For television, the top advertising spenders are manufacturers of cars and light trucks; automobile dealers spend the most on newspaper ads.

_P_ 5. Advertisers should not be allowed to continue misleading consumers by lying or exaggerating.

_I_ 6. On average, each person in the United States and Canada uses more than 300 gigajoules (GJ) (equivalent to about 60 barrels) of oil per year. By contrast, in some of the poorest countries of the world, such as Ethiopia, Nepal, and Bhutan, each person generally consumes less than 1 GJ per year.

_P_ 7. The foundation of public education has always been reading, writing, and arithmetic—the "three R's." Yet the schools insist that students who have not mastered these fundamentals continue to take all the other subjects as well. What good does it do for young people to sit in on a history or science class if they can't read or calculate well? Schools ought to require students who are very far behind in the fundamentals to devote all their time to the three R's until they are at or near grade level.

Comment: Items 2, 5, and 7 contain persuasive signals—*should* and *ought to*.

(Continues on next page)

B. Each of the following passages illustrates one of the tones identified in the box below. In each space provided, put the letter of the tone that applies to the passage. (Three tone choices will be left over.)

A. objective	B. amused	C. depressed
D. optimistic	E. critical	F. arrogant

___C___ 8. [1]When I was younger I thought that by this age, I would be pretty well set for life. [2]I imagined that I would have a nice house, some money in the bank, and a decent job. [3]But things haven't worked out that way at all. [4]I'm living a one-bedroom apartment with shabby furniture and a view of a parking lot. [5]My office job is dull and unrewarding, and I bring home hardly enough to cover my rent and expenses, much less put anything away. [6]My place is so unattractive that I don't want to invite anyone over, so I'm alone most of the time. [7]Whatever dreams I had in my youth are pretty well gone now. [8]Sometimes I think about going back to school and trying to prepare for a different career, but at my age there doesn't seem to be much point in doing that. [9]I guess this is just what life had in store for me. *The passage lists dreary details that are depressing.*

___E___ 9. [1]Parents who do not read to their children often excuse themselves by claiming a lack of time. [2]But with few exceptions, their failure to read is a matter of priorities. [3]Most parents find the time to put in a full workday, take several coffee breaks, eat lunch and dinner, read the newspaper, watch the nightly newscast or ball game, do the dishes, talk on the phone for thirty minutes (mostly about nothing), run to the store for a pack of cigarettes or a lottery ticket, drive to the mall, and never miss that favorite prime-time show. [4]Somehow they find the time for those things—important or unimportant as they are—but can't find time to read to a child, which is much more important than all the other items on a leisure priority list. *The writer of the passage is criticizing parents who will not make time to read to their children.*

___A___ 10. [1]Scientists say grilling meat creates cancer-causing substances that affect the meat in two ways. [2]First, when fat drips onto the source of heat, the substances are formed and then carried up to the food by smoke. [3]They are also formed when flames touch the meat. [4]There are, however, a few ways that experts say will minimize the risk of grilling meat: (1) Use low-fat meats and nonfat sauces. [5](2) Partially cook meat before grilling. [6](3) Cover the grill with foil; punch holes in the foil to let fat drip down. [7](4) Avoid fire flare-ups, which cause harmful smoke. [8](5) Scrape off blackened material on the surface of meat before eating it. [9](6) Don't cook out every day. *The author presents facts about grilling meat and cancer.*

PURPOSE AND TONE: Mastery Test 3

A. Seven quotations in the story below are preceded by a blank space. Identify the tone of each italicized quotation by writing in the letter of one of these tones. (Three tone choices will be left over.)

A. sympathetic	B. straightforward	C. pleading	D. angry
E. superior	F. excited	G. depressed	H. scheming
I. curious	J. frightened		

The television reporter knocked on the door of the small row home. A woman opened the door.

__B__ 1.   *"My name is Tod Hunter,"* the reporter said. *"I'm with* Action News, *and I'd like to talk to the woman who lost her daughter in the school fire last night."*

"Oh, I'm sorry, but she's not much in the mood for visitors."

"I understand," the reporter said. "Please tell her that we only want a moment of her time."

While the woman was gone, the reporter turned to his crew.

__H__ 2.   *"You could shoot from this angle,"* he whispered, *"but let's try to get inside. If she's at all responsive to my questions, let's gradually move in through the doorway."*

Children in the neighborhood crowded around the TV crew.

__F__ 3.   *"Those are TV cameras!"* some shouted, laughing. *"Wow, real TV cameras!"*

__I__ 4.   Pausing to look at the crew standing outside the house, passersby asked, *"What do you suppose happened there?"*

Then the mother of the fire victim appeared at the door, looking drawn and exhausted. "What do you want?"

"I'm really very sorry for your great loss, Ma'am." Hunter continued, "I'm here for *Action News.* Do you know what caused the terrible fire?"

"Please, no interviews."

"Our viewers want to know about this awful fire."

__D__ 5.   *"I don't care about your viewers!"* she shouted. *"It's none of their business. It's none of your business, either, young man."*

__J__ 6.   *"Run! She's mad!"* shouted the children as they raced away.

__C__ 7.   *"All I want is two minutes,"* the reporter said. *"Please, just two minutes of your time."*

But the door had already slammed in his face.

"Let's get out of here," the frustrated reporter said to his crew. "I'm starved."

(Continues on next page)

B. In the space provided, indicate whether the primary purpose of each passage is to inform (**I**), to persuade (**P**), or to entertain (**E**).

_____I_____ 8. [1]Why do people swear and engage in coarse language? [2]One researcher suggests that swearing is a way of asserting independence by breaking adult taboos. [3]In a society that prizes adulthood and independence, the increasing use of vulgar and profane language at younger and younger ages is not surprising. [4]When used infrequently, profanity and vulgar expressions communicate strong emotions for which there may be no other appropriate words. [5]They are meant to shock and to communicate one's deep disgust or contempt.

_____P_____ 9. [1]Advertising aimed at children is not just annoying—it is destructive and should be controlled. [2]Especially around the holiday season, children are hammered with media messages intended to make them want the latest toy, game, computer, sneakers, doll, music, and clothing on the market. [3]While manufacturers are busy sucking money from the pockets of children and their families, they are contributing to a growing sense of dissatisfaction and greed. [4]That serves the manufacturers' purpose—after all, if children were ever satisfied, they would not ask their parents to buy more merchandise. [5]But the effect is to produce a nation of selfish men and women whose lives are ruled by the need to have more, more, more. [6]It is frightening to see a generation being trained from childhood to be greedy consumers. [7]What chance do they have to ever become contented adults whose values extend beyond a price tag?

_____E_____ 10. [1]While I was watching a cartoon with my daughter, she said, "Dad, why does Bugs Bunny wear gloves?" [2]The question has bothered me ever since. [3]Why do Mickey Mouse, Bugs and Woody Woodpecker all wear gloves? [4]And who decides which characters get pants? [5]Mickey always wears them, yet Donald Duck just wears that sailor shirt. [6]Porky has a jacket and a bow tie, but no shirt or pants, and Daffy just has his feathers. [7]And, come to think of it, how did Goofy, a dog, make the evolutionary leap to stand up on his hind legs, put on pants, a shirt, and a vest, and talk? [8]Yet Pluto is content to hang out in the doghouse getting his butt kicked by the chipmunks Chip 'n Dale.

PURPOSE AND TONE: Mastery Test 4

A. Seven quotations in the story below are preceded by a blank space. Identify the tone of each italicized quotation by writing in the letter of one of these tones. (Three tone choices will be left over.)

A. disgusted	B. ashamed	C. outraged	D. amused
E. cheerful	F. understanding	G. straightforward	H. sorrowful
I. joyous	J. vengeful		

The scene is a busy restaurant on a Saturday evening.

_E_ 1.   *"Good evening!"* a young waitress chirped to a table of diners. *"It's so nice to see you here tonight! My name is Annette, and I'll be your server this evening."*

_A_ 2.   Meanwhile, across the room, a man stared at his food as he pushed it around with his fork. *"Yuk! They call this 'ocean-fresh fish,'"* he said, *"but it sure doesn't smell all that fresh. It's making me gag!"*

    But at the next table, a young man said to his friend, "This great spaghetti really hits the spot. I was starved."

_I_ 3.   Nearby, in a dimly lit corner of the restaurant, a young man and woman sat close together, smiling at the diamond ring on the woman's finger. *"Oh, darling,"* sighed the woman. *"This is the happiest night of my life. This restaurant will always be my favorite because this is where you asked me to marry you."*

_C_ 4.   A conversation of a different sort was taking place at another table: *"I cannot believe you would do this!"* a woman hissed at her husband. *"What kind of man takes his wife into a public place to tell her he's having an affair with her best friend? What am I supposed to do now—order an appetizer?"*

_G_ 5.   Back in the kitchen, the restaurant manager was instructing the staff. *"Annette, you cover tables one through four. Ben, you're responsible for five through eight. A party of sixteen people is coming in at eight o'clock; Lisa and Suzette will take care of them."*

    "Well, we got passed over again, didn't we?" Ben remarked to Annette after the manager was gone. "Lisa and Suzette always get the big groups and the big tips. It makes me wonder why I try to do a good job here."

_F_ 6.   *"Oh, I don't mind,"* Annette said. *"Lisa and Suzette do work a lot more hours than you or I do. I can see why the manager thinks they deserve the best assignments."* Then Annette walked out of the kitchen.

_J_ 7.   *"Well, it's not okay with me,"* Ben muttered to himself. *"When I quit this lousy job, they're going to pay for the way they've treated me. I'll get back at them somehow."*

(Continues on next page)

B. (8.) In the space provided, indicate whether the primary purpose of each passage is to inform (**I**), to persuade (**P**), or to entertain (**E**).

___*I*___   ¹Eye contact, also referred to as gaze, is how and how much we look at people with whom we are communicating. ²By maintaining our eye contact, we can tell when or whether people are paying attention to us, when people are involved in what we are saying, and whether what we are saying is eliciting feelings. ³The amount of eye contact differs from person to person and from situation to situation. ⁴Studies show that talkers hold eye contact about 40 percent of the time and listeners nearly 70 percent of the time. ⁵We generally maintain better eye contact when we are discussing topics with which we are comfortable, when we are genuinely interested in a person's comments or reactions, or when we are trying to influence the other person. ⁶On the other hand, we tend to avoid eye contact when we are discussing topics that make us uncomfortable, when we lack interest in the topic or person, or when we are embarrassed, ashamed, or trying to hide something.

C. Read the paragraph below. Then carefully consider the questions that follow, and write the letters of the best responses.

¹There are certain types of people you should not trust. ²One type is people who tell you that God told them to ask you to send them money. ³You know the guys I mean. ⁴They get on television and say: "God told me He wants you to send me some money, say $100, or even just $10, if that's all you can afford, but in all honesty I must point out that God is less likely to give you some horrible disease if your gift is in the $100 range." ⁵The theory here seems to be that God talks only to the guys on television. ⁶I always thought that if God needed money all that badly, He would get in touch with us directly.

___*C*___ 9. The purpose of this paragraph is
    A. to persuade readers that they should not send money to television evangelists.
    B. to entertain readers by exaggerating points.
    C. both of the above.

___*B*___ 10. The tone of this paragraph can be described as
    A. straightforward and serious.
    B. humorous and mocking.
    C. prayerful and respectful.
    D. sentimental and warm.

PURPOSE AND TONE: Mastery Test 5

Read the paragraphs below. Then carefully consider the questions that follow, and, in the spaces provided, write the letters of the best responses.

A. [1]A successful doctor is scheduled to operate on a patient at 8 a.m., but it has snowed during the night, and driving is difficult. [2]Do you think the doctor will stay home in bed? [3]Not if he or she is professional. [4]This attitude of professionalism is the key to being a successful college student, too. [5]And it is within your reach, no matter how well or how poorly you have done in school up until now. [6]You cannot undo the past, but you can adopt an attitude of professionalism from now on. [7]All you have to do is intend to take school seriously, and the rest will follow. [8]By attending classes, turning in assignments on time, and coming prepared for tests, you will gradually build your skills.

_____B_____ 1. The primary purpose of this paragraph is to
     A. present facts on student behavior.
     B. inspire students to be conscientious.
     C. entertain students with a dramatic story about professionalism.

_____C_____ 2. In general, the tone of this paragraph can be described as
     A. critical.
     B. pessimistic.
     C. encouraging.
     D. praising.

B. [1]According to memory experts, there are ways you can improve your chances of remembering the names of people you meet. [2]One way is to make associations between a person's name and looks. [3]For example, if you meet a man named Baker, you might picture him wearing a baker's hat. [4]If the name is a difficult one, ask for the spelling and visualize the letters mentally. [5]It's also useful to repeat the person's name as you converse, keeping your mental images in mind. [6]And when your conversation ends, repeat the person's name as you say goodbye.

_____A_____ 3. The primary purpose of this paragraph is to
     A. inform.
     B. persuade.
     C. entertain.

_____D_____ 4. The overall tone of this paragraph can be described as
     A. critical and angry.
     B. obviously humorous.
     C. doubtful.
     D. straightforward and instructive.   *(Continues on next page)*

C. [1]I was sitting on a beach one summer day, watching two children, a boy and a girl, playing in the sand. [2]They were hard at work building an elaborate sandcastle by the water's edge, with gates and towers and moats and internal passages. [3]Just when they had nearly finished their project, a big wave came along and knocked it down, reducing it to a heap of wet sand. [4]I expected the children to burst into tears, devastated by what had happened to all their hard work. [5]But they surprised me. [6]Instead, they ran up the shore away from the water, laughing and holding hands, and sat down to build another castle. [7]I realized that they had taught me an important lesson. [8]All the things in our lives, all the complicated structures we spend so much time and energy creating, are built on sand. [9]Only our relationships with other people endure. [10]Sooner or later, a wave will come along and knock down what we have worked so hard to build up. [11]When that happens, only the person who has somebody's hand to hold will be able to laugh.

_B_   5. The primary purpose of this paragraph is to
    A. inform readers about how children behave.
    B. persuade readers of the importance of relationships.
    C. delight readers with a story of childhood playfulness.

_D_   6. The tone of this paragraph can be described as
    A. forgiving.
    B. humorous.
    C. self-pitying.
    D. instructive.

D. [1]My best school report was in first grade from Mrs. Varulo. [2]First, she told my parents about my amazing physical energy: "Lisa never tires of chasing and punching her classmates." [3]Next, she praised my class participation and active, questioning mind: "After every instruction—even one as simple as 'Please take out your pencils'—Lisa asks 'Why?'" [4]Mrs. Varulo was so impressed with my vocabulary that she commented, "I don't know where Lisa has picked up some of the words she uses—certainly not in my classroom." [5]Somehow she even knew I would become a famous fiction writer. [6]"More than any other student I have ever taught," she wrote, "Lisa is a born liar."

_C_   7. The primary purpose of this paragraph is to
    A. inform.
    B. persuade.
    C. entertain.

_D_   8. The tone of this paragraph can best be described as
    A. enthusiastic and cheerful.
    B. annoyed and bitter.
    C. cheerful and nostalgic.
    D. ironic and humorous.

PURPOSE AND TONE: Mastery Test 6

Read the paragraphs below. Then carefully consider the questions that follow, and, in the spaces provided, write the letters of the best responses.

A. ¹Throughout history, people have suffered from ailments that could have been easily avoided if they had only been understood. ²For instance, it used to be common for hat makers to be tortured by uncontrollable trembling, slurred speech, and mental confusion. ³The condition led to Lewis Carroll's creation of the Mad Hatter in his book *Alice's Adventures in Wonderland.* ⁴Sadly, the hatters did not know that the mercury they used in creating felt hats was poisoning them, leading to their strange symptoms. ⁵Similarly, many of the world's greatest artists suffered from terrible depression. ⁶Today we know that the lead in the paint they used probably affected their mental state. ⁷How tragic that so many lives were destroyed for want of a little knowledge.

___A___ 1. The primary purpose of the passage is
    A. to tell readers about formerly misunderstood ailments.
    B. to persuade readers to protect themselves against easily avoidable ailments.
    C. both of the above.

___A___ 2. The tone of the passage can be described as
    A. regretful.
    B. angry.
    C. alarmed.
    D. pessimistic.

B. ¹Al Smith, the Democratic candidate for President in 1928, was known for his ready wit and quick comebacks. ²Once he was heckled while making a campaign speech. ³"Tell 'em everything you know, Al," yelled the heckler. ⁴"It won't take very long."

⁵Al Smith answered with a grin, "I'll tell 'em everything we both know—it won't take any longer."

___A___ 3. The primary purpose of this passage is to
    A. inform students about a humorous aspect of a historical figure.
    B. persuade people to support the Democrats.
    C. argue that Al Smith should have won the 1928 presidential campaign.

___B___ 4. The tone of the paragraph can be described as
    A. forgiving.
    B. amused.
    C. bitter.
    D. disbelieving.

(Continues on next page)

C. ¹Three people were killed because a man was angry that his girlfriend wanted to break up with him. ²Now the state is planning to kill him, and that's as it should be. ³Some may argue that taking a life is always wrong, that two wrongs don't make a right. ⁴But there is nothing right about making taxpayers give free room and board to a person who killed innocent people. ⁵And there's nothing right about putting such a dangerous person in prison, from which he will probably one day be released to again threaten society.

_B_ 5. The primary purpose of this paragraph is to
   A. report on facts about the death penalty.
   B. persuade readers that the death penalty has merit.
   C. entertain readers with a description of an interesting problem.

_A_ 6. The overall tone of this paragraph can be described as
   A. impassioned.
   B. insulting.
   C. compassionate and sentimental.
   D. excited and joyous.

D. ¹When people are unemployed, two major sources of stress come into play. ²One is the loss of income, with all the financial hardships that this brings. ³Suddenly there are the difficulties of paying the monthly rent or mortgage, of making the car payment and paying credit-card bills, of dealing with utility costs, and the fundamental matter of putting enough food to eat on the table. ⁴The other source of stress is the effect of the loss of income on workers' feelings about themselves. ⁵Workers who derive their identity from their work, men who define manhood as supporting a family, and people who define their worth in terms of their work's dollar value lose more than their paychecks when they lose their jobs. ⁶They lose a piece of themselves; they lose their self-esteem.

_A_ 7. The primary purpose of this paragraph is
   A. to inform readers about the major sources of stress for the unemployed.
   B. to persuade readers that unemployment should be eliminated.
   C. to amuse readers with observations about human nature.

_D_ 8. The tone of this paragraph can be described as
   A. depressed and sorrowful.
   B. angry and desperate.
   C. surprised but optimistic.
   D. serious and sympathetic.

10
Argument

"I shall now punch a huge hole in your argument."

Many of us enjoy a good argument. A good argument is not an emotional experience in which people's feelings get out of control, leaving them ready to start throwing things. Instead, it is a rational discussion in which each person advances and supports a point of view about some matter. We might argue with a friend, for example, about where to eat or what movie to go to. We might argue about whether a boss or a parent or an instructor is acting in a fair or an unfair manner. We might argue about whether certain performers or sports stars deserve to get paid as much as they do. In a good argument (such as the one that appears to be going on in the above cartoon), the other person listens carefully as we state our case, waiting to see if we really have solid evidence to support our point of view.

Argumentation is, then, a part of our everyday dealings with other people. It is also an important part of much of what we read. Authors often try to convince us of their opinions and interpretations. Very often there are three important things we must do as critical readers:

1 Recognize the **point** the author is making.

2 Decide if the author's support is **relevant**.

3 Decide if the author's support is **adequate**.

This chapter will give you practice in doing the above, first in everyday arguments and then in textbook material.

THE BASICS OF ARGUMENT: POINT AND SUPPORT

A good **argument** is one in which you make a point and then provide persuasive and logical evidence to back it up. Here is a point:

Point: The Beef and Burger Shop is a poor fast-food restaurant.

This statement hardly discourages us from visiting the Beef and Burger Shop. "Why do you say that?" we might legitimately say. "Give your reasons." Support is needed so we can decide for ourselves whether a valid point has been made. Suppose the point is followed by these three reasons:

1. The burgers are full of gristle.

2. The roast beef sandwiches have a chemical taste.

3. The fries are lukewarm and soggy.

Clearly, the details provide solid support for the point. They give us a basis for understanding and agreeing with the point. In light of these details, our mouths are not watering for lunch at the Beef and Burger Shop.

We see here, then, a small example of what clear thinking in an argument is about: making a point and providing support that truly backs up that point. A valid argument may also be described as a conclusion supported by logical reasons, facts, examples, and other evidence.

Let's look at another example:

Point: There are certain creatures in particular that you would never want to bite you.

Of course, we would not want *any* creature to bite us. But in this statement we're told that certain creatures in particular can be nasty biters. We'd like to get supporting details so we can see and judge for ourselves. Here are details:

1. A bite from the venomous king cobra can cause muscle paralysis and lead to respiratory failure in a matter of minutes.

2. A lion's bite is powerful enough to rip off your arm or take large chunks out of your body.

3. A crocodile's jaws will snap closed like a steel trap and if the crocodile then decides to roll, you can usually say goodbye to your arm, leg, or whatever is in its mouth.

With such solid support, you're likely to agree that the king cobra, lion, and crocodile are especially scary biters and that a logical point has been made.

The Point and Support of an Argument

In everyday life, of course, people don't simply say, "Here is my point" and "Here is my support." Nor do writers state their ideas so directly. Even so, the basic structure of point and support is still at work beneath the surface, and to evaluate an argument, you need to recognize that point.

The following activity will help you distinguish between a point and its support.

➤ *Practice 1*

In each group of statements, one statement is the point, and the other statement or statements are support for the point. Identify each point with a **P** and each statement of support with an **S**.

> *Hint:* If it sounds right to insert the word *because* in front of a sentence, you probably have a statement of support. For example, we could say, "Because the burgers are full of gristle, because the roast beef sandwiches have a chemical taste, and because the fries are lukewarm and soggy, I've come to the conclusion that the Beef and Burger Shop is a poor fast-food restaurant."

1. _*S*_ A. You have constant headaches and blurred vision.

   _*P*_ B. You should see a doctor.

2. _*S*_ A. A number of accidents have now occurred at that intersection.

   _*P*_ B. A traffic light is needed at the intersection.

3. _*S*_ A. A television is always blaring in one corner of the lounge.

   _*P*_ B. The student lounge is not a place for quiet study.

   _*S*_ C. There are always people there talking loudly to each other.

4. _P_ A. High schools need to teach personal finance skills.

   _S_ B. Many young people do not know how to budget their money.

   _S_ C. More and more people are getting into serious credit-card debt.

5. _S_ A. Cats refuse to learn silly tricks just to amuse people.

   _P_ B. Cats are more sensible than dogs.

   _S_ C. Dogs will accept cruel mistreatment, but if a cat is mistreated, it will run away.

6. _S_ A. Scientists have proved that acid rain harms trees and bodies of water.

   _P_ B. Laws should be passed to reduce acid rain.

   _S_ C. The damage done by acid rain is hard or impossible to undo.

7. _S_ A. Fewer companies are offering health plans and retirement benefits.

   _P_ B. Conditions in the workplace are tougher than they used to be.

   _S_ C. In many industries, workers have had to take wage cuts.

8. _S_ A. The people upstairs make a lot of noise.

   _P_ B. We'd better look for another apartment.

   _S_ C. Roaches seem to be taking over this apartment.

   _S_ D. The landlord does nothing but promise to fix the leaky faucets.

9. _P_ A. The library should be kept open on Sundays and holidays.

   _S_ B. Many students save their studying for days when they do not have classes.

   _S_ C. Library facilities are overcrowded on weekdays.

   _S_ D. During the week, other students are often using needed books and other research materials.

10. _S_ A. Almost half of the stores in the shopping center are empty.

    _S_ B. A deathly hush fills the building.

    _P_ C. That shopping center is a depressing place.

    _S_ D. Unhappy-looking store owners stare out at the few passing shoppers.

Relevant Support

Once you identify the point and support of an argument, you need to decide if each piece of evidence is **relevant**—in other words, if it really applies to the point. The critical reader must ask, "Is this reason relevant support for the argument?" In their enthusiasm for making an argument, people often bring up irrelevant support. For example, in trying to persuade you to lend him some money this week, a friend might say, "You didn't lend me money last week when I needed it." But last week is beside the point; the question is whether or not you should lend him money *this* week.

An excellent way to develop your skill in recognizing relevant support is to work on simple point-support outlines of arguments. By isolating the reasons of an argument, such outlines help you think about whether each reason is truly relevant. Paying close attention to the relevance of support will help your writing as well as your reading.

☑ *Check Your Understanding*

Consider the following outline. The point is followed by six "facts," only three of which are relevant support for the point. See if you can check (✓) the numbers of the **three** relevant statements of support.

> **Point:** My dog Otis is not very bright.
>
> ✓ 1. He's five years old and doesn't respond to his name yet.
>
> ___ 2. He cries when I leave for work every day.
>
> ___ 3. He always gets excited when visitors arrive.
>
> ✓ 4. He often attacks the back-yard hedge as if it's a hostile animal.
>
> ___ 5. He gets along very well with my neighbor's cat.
>
> ✓ 6. I often have to put food in front of him because he can't find it by himself.

Now read the following comments on the six items to see which ones you should have checked and why.

Explanation:

1. Most dogs know their names, so Otis's unfamiliarity with his own name reveals a weak memory, and memory is one aspect of intelligence. You should have checked the number of this item.

2. Even an intelligent dog might be sad when its companions leave the house.

3. Both bright and not-so-bright dogs are happy to see old and new human friends.

4. The inability to distinguish between a bush and an animal—friendly or hostile—suggests a lack of analytical skills. This is the second item whose number you should have checked.

5. Dogs of all degrees of intelligence have been known to be friendly with cats.

6. Since most dogs recognize food much more often than their owners would like them to, Otis's inability to find food clearly indicates poor problem-solving skills. You should also have checked the number of this item.

➤ Practice 2

Each point is followed by three statements that provide relevant support and three that do not. In the spaces, write the letters of the **three** relevant statements of support.

> *Hint*: To help you decide if a sentence is irrelevant or not, ask yourself, "Does this provide logical support for the point being argued?"

1. **Point:** Wildlife can be found even in the middle of the city.
   A. Raccoons sometimes raid the garbage containers near urban apartments.
   B. Many animals have been pushed out of their homes by building development.
   C. Squirrels, chipmunks, and rabbits make their home in city parks.
   D. Heavy traffic makes it dangerous for animals in the city.
   E. Many city dwellers own a cat or a dog.
   F. Hawks build their nests on the window ledges of skyscrapers.

   Items that logically support the point: ___A___   ___C___   ___F___

2. **Point:** Singapore is a society with strict controls on people's behavior.
   A. There are four official languages spoken in Singapore.
   B. Singapore declared its independence from Malaysia in 1965.
   C. Chewing gum on the street is prohibited by law.
   D. Most Singaporeans are of Chinese, Malay, or Indian descent.
   E. Persons convicted of vandalism are whipped with a long rattan cane.
   F. There is a $95 fine for failing to flush a public toilet.

   Items that logically support the point: ___C___   ___E___   ___F___

Comments: Item 1 — Answers A, C, and F are examples of wildlife found in the middle of the city. Answers B and D do not support the point; answer E concerns domesticated animals, not wildlife.

Item 2 — Answers C, E, and F explain in what way Singapore has strict controls on behavior of its people. Answers A, B and D do not address control issues.

3. **Point:** In general, deeply-colored fruits and vegetables are more nutritious than ones with little color.   Answers A, D, and F state how nutritious the foods are.
   A. Broccoli, spinach, kale, and chard are highly nutritious. Answers B, C, and E do not address nutrition issues.
   B. Bananas are the best-selling fruit in the United States.
   C. More adults than children like strong-flavored vegetables like spinach.
   D. Dark orange sweet potatoes are richer in nutrients than ordinary white potatoes.
   E. Many vegetables are delicious in both cooked and raw forms.
   F. Pale green iceberg lettuce is mostly water and provides few vitamins.

   Items that logically support the point: ____*A*____   ____*D*____   ____*F*____

4. **Point:** Alcohol and tobacco are among the most dangerous drugs that Americans use today.
   A. Cancer from cigarette smoking kills numerous Americans every year.
   B. During Prohibition, liquor bootleggers fought one another as drug dealers do today.   Answers A, C, and F explain in what ways the drugs are dangerous today.
   C. About half of all fatal traffic accidents are due to drunk driving.
   D. Nothing is more annoying than trying to enjoy a restaurant meal when the people at nearby tables are smoking and drinking heavily.
   E. We often don't think of alcohol and tobacco as "drugs" because they are legal.   Answers B, D, and E do not address the danger today issue.
   F. Alcohol abuse causes many people to become more aggressive and violent.

   Items that logically support the point: ____*A*____   ____*C*____   ____*F*____

5. **Point:** Psychologically healthy people have some general characteristics in common.
   A. Depression, stress, or fatigue can interfere with a person's normal functioning.
   B. A person who is psychologically healthy is productive, doing tasks without making a big deal of them.
   C. The culture we live in has a great deal to do with what we consider "normal" behavior.
   D. People who are well-balanced psychologically get along well with most other people.
   E. Psychologically healthy persons can focus their attention on people or things outside of themselves.
   F. Consistently inappropriate behavior can be a symptom of mental illness.

   Items that logically support the point: ____*B*____   ____*D*____   ____*E*____

   Answers B, D, and E explain the characteristics of psychologically healthy people.
   Answers A, C, and F do not address issues of good health.

Relevant Support in Paragraphs

The point, or main idea, of the argument in the paragraph below is stated in the first sentence. One of the other sentences is not relevant support for that point.

☑ *Check Your Understanding*

Read the paragraph and see if you can find the statement that does **not** support the point of the argument.

> [1]Every high-school student should be required to take a class in parenting skills. [2]The absence of such classes shows how little our schools do for young people. [3]Numerous young people today are bearing children without having the least idea of how to be a good parent. [4]Many of them have grown up in families where poor parenting was the norm, and so they have no good parenting models. [5]Well-planned parenting classes could give future parents at least an idea of what responsible parenting is all about. [6]The classes might then reduce future problems, including child abuse.

The number of the irrelevant sentence: ___2___

Explanation:

The point of this argument is stated in the first sentence: "Every high-school student should be required to take a class in parenting skills." Any statement that doesn't help prove this point is irrelevant. Sentences 3–6 support that argument: Sentences 5–6 tell the benefits of parenting classes. Sentences 3–4 explain why students need those benefits. Sentence 2, however, is about something else altogether—it complains about the little that is being done for young people by schools. Whether that is true or not doesn't change the point and support of the argument. Even if the schools did much for young people, parenting classes could still be useful. Thus sentence 2 is irrelevant to the argument.

➤ *Practice 3*

The point of the argument in each paragraph that follows is stated in the first sentence. One sentence in the paragraph does not support that point. Read each paragraph, and decide which sentence is **not** relevant evidence. Then write its letter in the space provided.

> *Hint:* To decide if a sentence is irrelevant, ask yourself, "Does this provide logical support for the point being argued?"

_B_ 1. ¹Nobody in this neighborhood will miss the Martins when they move. ²They keep their poor dog chained to a tree 24 hours a day, and it howls for most of that time. ³When the neighborhood kids play ball anywhere near their house, Mr. Martin yells at them, "Don't you dare get that ball in my yard!" ⁴Of course he has had a lot of illness, so you can understand his being short-tempered. ⁵In addition, the Martins refuse to come to neighborhood block parties, and then they complain about the noise. ⁶And they mow their lawn at 6 a.m. on Saturday morning, when other people are trying to get a little extra sleep.

Which of the following statements does **not** support the author's argument that no one will miss the Martins when they move?

A. Sentence 3   C. Sentence 5
B. Sentence 4   D. Sentence 6

_B_ 2. ¹National health insurance is entirely possible, as many industrialized countries have proven. ²The National Health Service in Great Britain provides free health care to all citizens. ³The Health Service is almost completely tax-supported. ⁴That doesn't help the immigrants living in Britain, however. ⁵In Sweden, medical care is provided by publicly funded hospitals and clinics. ⁶A national health insurance system reimburses the providers. ⁷Canadians rely on private physicians and hospitals for day-to-day care, but health care is guaranteed as a right for all citizens. ⁸Income taxes are used to finance Canada's public medical insurance.

Which of the following statements does **not** support the author's argument that providing national health insurance is entirely possible?

A. Sentence 3   C. Sentence 5
B. Sentence 4   D. Sentence 6

Adequate Support

A valid argument must include not only relevant support but also an **adequate** amount of support—enough to prove the point. For example, it would not be valid to argue "Abortion is wrong" if one's only support was "My sister had an abortion and has regretted it ever since." Such an important issue would require more support than the attitude and experience of a single relative. Arguing a point that doesn't have adequate support is called "jumping to a conclusion."

☑ *Check Your Understanding*

In the argument below, three supporting items are given, followed by four possible points. The evidence adequately supports only one of the points; it is insufficient to support the other three. Choose the **one** point you think is adequately supported, and put a check mark (✓) beside it.

Support:

- The first time I went to that beach, I got a bad case of sunburn.
- The second time I went to that beach, I couldn't go in the water because of the pollution.
- The third time I went to that beach, I stepped on a starfish and had to go to the emergency room to have the spikes removed from my foot.

Which **point** is adequately supported by all the evidence above?

___ A. That beach is unsafe and should be closed.

_✓_ B. I've had a string of bad experiences at that beach.

___ C. Beaches are not safe places.

___ D. We're never going to get this planet cleaned up.

Explanation:

The correct answer is B. Answer A is not adequately supported by three isolated instances; we'd need many more reports of dangerous conditions before considering having the beach closed. Answer C is even more poorly supported. We'd need many, many reports of dangerous conditions at beaches worldwide to come to the conclusion stated in C. Answer D is supported in part by the reference to pollution in the second statement of support, but the other two statements (about sunburn and starfish) are not examples of pollution.

➤ *Practice 4*

For each group, read the three items of support (the evidence). Then check (✓) the **one** point that is adequately supported by that evidence.

Group 1

Support:

> • Many credit cards do not carry an annual fee.
> • You can earn cash back, frequent-flyer miles, or other benefits.
> • If you pay your balance monthly, no interest is charged.

Point: Which of the following conclusions is best supported by all the evidence above?

____ A. You need to shop around for the right credit card.

____ B. Credit cards charge high interest rates on unpaid balances.

✓ C. When used wisely, credit cards can be helpful. Answer C is supported by only the second

____ D. Many people get into trouble by overusing credit cards. bulleted item.

Group 2

Support:

> • Some people put off writing or calling a friend because they feel they do not have time to do it right, but a quick note or call is often better than nothing.
> • Sometimes it makes sense to do a routine chore quickly rather than perfectly in order to save time for something more important.
> • Even a desk and office need not be perfectly neat; sometimes cleaning them up is just an excuse for putting off more important work.

Point: Which of the following conclusions is best supported by all the evidence above?

✓ A. Perfection is not always a worthwhile goal.

____ B. Striving for perfection always pays off in the end.

____ C. You can be better organized if you plan each day more carefully.

____ D. Getting things done haphazardly is always better than not getting them done at all.

ARGUMENT IN TEXTBOOK WRITING

In most textbook writing, argument takes the form of well-developed ideas or theories presented with experiments, surveys, studies, reasons, examples, or other evidence of support. Textbook arguments generally have solid support, but recognizing the author's point and watching for relevant and adequate support will help you become a more involved and critical reader. Following are two exercises that will give you practice in thinking through the arguments in textbooks.

➤ *Practice 5*

The point of the argument in each of the textbook paragraphs below is stated in the first sentence. One sentence in each paragraph does not support the point. Read each paragraph, and then decide which sentence is **not** relevant to the argument. Then, in the space provided, write the letter of that sentence.

To help you decide if a sentence is irrelevant or not, ask yourself, "Does this provide logical support for the point being argued?"

___B___ 1. ¹Short-term goals encourage self-discipline better than distant aims. ²For instance, dieters lose more weight by attempting to shed two pounds a week than by worrying about a total of twenty pounds or more. ³Low-fat diets are another help for dieters. ⁴Also, students who try to increase study time by a half hour each day do better than those who think only about compiling straight A averages. ⁵And alcoholics and drug addicts achieve more lasting recovery when they deal with their problems one day at a time.

Which sentence is **not** relevant support for the argument that short-term goals are better for will power than long-term goals?

A. Sentence 2   C. Sentence 4   Sentence 3 does not
B. Sentence 3   D. Sentence 5   support the point
                                              about goals.

___C___ 2. ¹The wish for acceptance by the dominant culture sometimes causes people to turn their backs on their own cultural tradition. ²In Australia, Aborigines who have become part of the dominant society may refuse to acknowledge their darker-skinned grandparents on the street. ³In India, the well-off Indians who dominate the culture copy the traditions and prejudices of the British, leaving many Hindus unhappy about their behavior. ⁴India won its independence from Britain after Mahatma Gandhi led a campaign of peaceful resistance. ⁵And in the United States, many descendants of immigrants have changed their ethnic-sounding family names to names like those of white Protestants. ⁶Also, children of U.S. immigrants are sometimes ashamed to let their school friends see that their parents speak another language.   Sentence 4
does not support the point about turning their backs on cultural tradition.

Which sentence is **not** relevant support for the argument that people at times turn their backs on their own cultural tradition?

A. Sentence 2   C. Sentence 4
B. Sentence 3   D. Sentence 5

➤ Practice 6

In each group, the support is from a study reported on in a textbook. Check (✓) the point in each case that is adequately supported by that evidence.

Group 1

Support:

- Some thieves who are sent to jail steal again as soon as they are released.
- A dog that has been hit for eating food off the table will often continue to gobble what it can find when the owner is not around.
- A teenage girl who is "grounded" because she sneaked out of the house may try to come up with a more creative plan to get out without being caught.

Which **point** is adequately supported by all the evidence above?

_____ A. Many studies have found advantages and problems with punishment.

_✓_ B. Punishment does not always have the intended effects.

_____ C. Punishment is rarely effective.

_____ D. Punishment can be effective in some cases.

Group 2

Support:

- Elderly nursing-home patients who have little control over their activities tend to decline faster and die sooner than do those given more control over their activities.
- If two rats receive simultaneous shocks, but only one of them can turn a wheel to stop the shocks, the helpless rat becomes more vulnerable to ulcers and has lower immunity to disease.
- When allowed to adjust office furnishings and control interruptions and distractions, workers experience less stress and illness.

Which **point** is adequately supported by all the evidence above?

____ A. It is possible to gain full control over our lives.

____ b. Many negative life events are uncontrollable.

____ c. Loss of control is a major problem in our society.

_✓_ D. A loss of control is stressful and makes one more vulnerable to ill health.

A Final Note

This chapter has dealt with the basics of argument, including the need for relevant and adequate support. If time permits, you may want to turn to pages 571–582 to consider common errors in reasoning—also known as **logical fallacies**—that people may make when advancing an argument.

CHAPTER REVIEW

In this chapter, you learned the following:

- A good argument is made up of a point, or a conclusion, and logical evidence to back it up.

- To critically read an argument, you must recognize the **point** the author is making.

- To think through an argument, you need to decide if each piece of evidence is **relevant**.

- To think through an argument, you also need to decide if the author's support is **adequate**.

- Textbook arguments generally have solid support, but recognizing the author's point and watching for relevant and adequate support will help you become a more involved and critical reader.

On the Web: If you are using this book in class, you can visit our website for additional practice in evaluating arguments. Go to **www.townsendpress.com** and click on "Online Exercises."

➤ Review Test 1

To review what you've learned in this chapter, complete each sentence or write the letter of the correct answer in the space provided.

_C_ 1. The point of an argument can also be called its
A. relevance.   B. evidence.   C. conclusion.

_A_ 2. The support for an argument can be referred to as the (A. evidence; B. conclusion) that backs up the point.

_C_ 3. Relevant support for an argument is information that (A. enthusiastically; B. partially; C. logically) supports the point.

_B_ 4. If there is too little information to support a point, we say the support is
A. dull.   B. inadequate.   C. irrelevant.

_D_ 5. Textbook authors may support their arguments with
A. experiments.   C. studies.
B. surveys.   D. all of the above and more.

➤ Review Test 2

A. In each group, one statement is the point, and the other statement or statements are support for that point. Write the letter of the point in the space provided.

> **Hint:** If it sounds right to insert the word *because* in front of a sentence, you probably have a statement of support.

_B_ 1. A. Chemicals in dark chocolate help protect arteries from heart disease.
B. Dark chocolate can be good for the human body.
C. Dark chocolate contains ingredients that fight depression.

_B_ 2. A. A healthy adult tree can produce 5 pounds of pure oxygen per day.
B. People should plant more trees around their homes.
C. Mature trees can increase property value by 10 percent.
D. Trees planted properly around buildings provide shade that cuts air conditioning costs by 20 percent.

Comments: Item 1 — You can insert the word *because* in front of A and C to explain why dark chocolate can be good for the human body.

Item 2 — The word *should* in B is a clue to the point. You can insert the word *because* in front of answers A, C, and D to explain why people should plant more trees around their homes.

_____D_____ 3. A. Teaching is a great way to learn because one needs to know the material well enough to explain it.

Comments:
Item 3—You can insert the word *because* in front of answers A, B, and C to explain why students should be required to teach a class for a day.

Item 4—Answers A, B, and D explain how training for doctors has changed dramatically in the past two centuries.

   B. By teaching a class, students will better appreciate their teachers' efforts.

   C. Some students may pay more attention when another student teaches, out of curiosity if nothing else.

   D. All students should be required to teach a class for a day.

_____C_____ 4. A. In the 1700s, doctors in the American colonies were not required to attend college.

   B. In the mid-1800s, most doctors completed just two years of medical school.

   C. The training for doctors has changed dramatically in the past two centuries.

   D. Today, doctors receive about 10 years of education after high school.

B. Each point is followed by three statements that provide relevant support and three that do not. In the spaces, write the letters of the **three** relevant statements of support.

5–7. **Point:** Drinking coffee can have unpleasant effects.

   A. Some people don't like the taste of decaffeinated coffees.

   B. Coffee in the evening can interfere with sleep at night.

   C. As addictions go, coffee is less dangerous than tobacco.

   D. Too much coffee can cause the hands to shake.

   E. Drinking too much coffee can lead to a faster heartbeat and light-headedness.

   F. Most coffees cost under five dollars a pound.

Items that logically support the point: ___B___   ___D___   ___E___

   Only B, D, and E support the point about unpleasant effects of drinking coffee.

8–10. **Point:** Some people have very poor telephone manners.

   A. They never identify themselves, but just begin the conversation.

   B. They often make their calls on cordless phones.

   C. They have an unlisted telephone number.

   D. They conduct conversations with people around them at the same time they're talking on the phone.

   E. Some people don't like to talk on the phone.

   F. They often call around 6 p.m., which is most people's dinner hour.

Items that logically support the point: ___A___   ___D___   ___F___

   Only A, D, and F support the point about poor telephone manners.

➤ Review Test 3

A. In the space provided, write the letter of the irrelevant sentence in each paragraph—the sentence that changes the subject.

___C___ 1. [1]Most people who have trouble with schoolwork don't lack intelligence—instead, they are tripped up by their own attitudes toward the work. [2]For example, the "I can't do it" state of mind gets in many students' way. [3]Instead of making an honest effort to do the work, the "I can't do it" type gives up before he or she begins. [4]This type often also has trouble on the job. [5]Then there's the "I'm too tired" attitude. [6]Students with this problem give in to the temptation to nap whenever there is work to be done. [7]Another view that leads to low achievement is "The instructor is boring." [8]Students with that attitude expect every course to be highly entertaining and claim they can't be expected to learn anything otherwise.

Which sentence does **not** support the argument that people who have trouble with school work are tripped up by their own attitudes rather than a lack of intelligence?

A. Sentence 2	C. Sentence 4
B. Sentence 3	D. Sentence 7

Sentence 4 changes the subject from school problems to job problems.

___A___ 2. [1]Sigmund Freud was one of the most important scientists of the twentieth century. [2]A loving father, he had three sons and three daughters. [3]He was among the first to study mental disorders, such as hysteria and neurosis, in a systematic way. [4]He developed the theory of the unconscious and showed how people's behavior is greatly affected by forgotten childhood events. [5]His discoveries are the basis of psychoanalysis, a method of treating mental illness that is still important today.

Which sentence is **not** relevant support for the argument that Freud is one of the most important scientists of the twentieth century?

A. Sentence 2	C. Sentence 4
B. Sentence 3	D. Sentence 5

Sentence 2 changes the subject from Freud's scientific contributions to his family.

___D___ 3. [1]People's ability to remember what they see is less dependable than they think. [2]In a famous experiment performed at Harvard, researchers showed people a videotape of a basketball game and asked them to count how many times players passed the ball. [3]After about 45 seconds, a man dressed in a gorilla suit walked slowly across the scene, passing between the players. [4]Although he was visible for five seconds, 40 per cent of the viewers did not notice him at all. [5]When the tape was played again, and they were asked simply to watch it, they saw him easily. [6]Not surprisingly, some insisted that it could not be the same tape. [7]They simply could not believe they had "tuned out" something as bizarre as a gorilla on the basketball floor. [8]At least they had a good story to tell when they got home.

Which of the following statements does **not** support the author's argument that people's ability to remember what they see is less dependable than they think?

A. Sentence 5

B. Sentence 6

C. Sentence 7

D. Sentence 8

> Sentence 8 changes the subject from the experiments being discussed.

B. (4–5.) For each group, read the three items of support (the evidence). Then, in the space provided, write the letter of the **one** point that is adequately supported by that evidence.

Remember that the point, or conclusion, should follow logically from the evidence. Do not jump to a conclusion that is not well supported.

Group 1

Support:

- Many day-care facilities have health and safety standards that are barely satisfactory.
- Long waiting lists exist at most good day-care centers.
- Day-care centers can't get enough qualified help.

_D_ 4. Which **point** is adequately supported by all the evidence above?

A. Day care is unreasonably expensive.

B. Mothers with young children should not work.

C. Our present birthrate must be drastically reduced.

D. Our present day-care system is inadequate.

Group 2

Support:

- Nearly all of those accused during the Salem, Massachusetts witch trials of 1692 had little political power or legal protection.
- On the basis of rumor and hearsay, innocent people in Salem were accused, tried, convicted and executed for the crime of witchcraft.
- The trial and execution of alleged witches in the Salem area ended suddenly when the wife of a "witch judge" found herself accused of practicing witchcraft.

___C___ 5. Which **point** is adequately supported by all the evidence above?
    A. Many innocent people have been persecuted with charges of witchcraft over the centuries.
    B. People in positions of power were less likely to be charged with witchcraft.
    C. The Salem witch trials of 1692 were a shameful episode in American colonial history.
    D. Some of the people executed during the Salem witch trials were guilty of serious crimes.   All three items listed are shameful.

➤ *Review Test 4*

Can failing a course be good for students? Here is a chance to apply your understanding of argument to an essay that addresses that question.

To help you continue to strengthen your skills, the reading is followed by questions not only on what you've learned in this chapter but also on what you've learned in previous chapters.

Words to Watch

Below are some words in the reading that do not have strong context support. Each word is followed by the number of the paragraph in which it appears and its meaning there. These words are indicated in the article by a small circle (°).

validity (1): soundness or worth
trump card (4): a tactic that gives one an advantage (like a trump suit in card games)
flustered (6): nervously confused
composure (6): calmness and self-control
radical (6): extreme
conspiracy (11): plot

IN PRAISE OF THE F WORD

Mary Sherry

1   Tens of thousands of eighteen-year-olds will graduate this year and be handed meaningless diplomas. These diplomas won't look any different from those awarded their luckier classmates. Their validity° will be questioned only when their employers discover that these graduates are semiliterate.

2   Eventually a fortunate few will find their way into educational-repair shops—adult-literacy programs, such as the one where I teach basic grammar and writing. There, high-school graduates and high-school dropouts pursuing graduate-equivalency certificates will learn the skills they should have learned in school.

They will also discover they have been cheated by our educational system.

3   As I teach, I learn a lot about our schools. Early in each session I ask my students to write about an unpleasant experience they had in school. No writers' block here! "I wish someone had made me stop doing drugs and made me study." "I liked to party and no one seemed to care." "I was a good kid and didn't cause any trouble, so they just passed me along even though I didn't read well and couldn't write." And so on.

4   I am your basic do-gooder, and prior to teaching this class I blamed the poor academic skills our kids have today on drugs, divorce, and other impediments to concentration necessary for doing well in school. But, as I rediscover each time I walk into the classroom, before a teacher can expect students to concentrate, he has to get their attention, no matter what distractions may be at hand. There are many ways to do this, and they have much to do with teaching style. However, if style alone won't do it, there is another way to show who holds the winning hand in the classroom. That is to reveal the trump card° of failure.

5   I will never forget a teacher who played that card to get the attention of one of my children. Our youngest, a world-class charmer, did little to develop his intellectual talents but always got by. Until Mrs. Stifter.

6   Our son was a high-school senior when he had her for English. "He sits in the back of the room talking to his friends," she told me. "Why don't you move him to the front row?" I urged, believing the embarrassment would get him to settle down. Mrs. Stifter looked at me steely-eyed over her glasses. "I don't move seniors," she said. "I flunk them." I was flustered°. Our son's academic life flashed before my eyes. No teacher had ever threatened him with that before. I regained my composure° and managed to say that I thought she was right. By the time I got home I was feeling pretty good about this. It was a radical° approach for these times, but, well, why not? "She's going to flunk you," I told my son. I did not discuss it any further. Suddenly English became a priority in his life. He finished out the semester with an A.

7   I know one example doesn't make a case, but at night I see a parade of students who are angry and resentful for having been passed along until they could no longer even pretend to keep up. Of average intelligence or better, they eventually quit school, concluding they were too dumb to finish. "I should have been held back," is a comment I hear frequently. Even sadder are those students who are high-school graduates who say to me after a few weeks of class, "I don't know how I ever got a high-school diploma."

8   Passing students who have not mastered the work cheats them and the employers who expect graduates to have basic skills. We excuse this dishonest behavior by saying kids can't learn if they come from terrible environments. No one seems to stop to think that—no matter what environments they come from—most kids don't put school first on their list unless they perceive something is at stake. They'd rather be sailing.

9   Many students I see at night could give expert testimony on unemployment, chemical dependency, abusive relationships. In spite of these difficulties, they have decided to make education a priority. They are motivated by the desire for a better job or the need to hang on to the one they've got. They have a healthy fear of failure.

10   People of all ages can rise above their problems, but they need to have a reason to do so. Young people generally don't have the maturity to value education in the same way my adult students value it. But fear of failure, whether economic or academic, can motivate both.

11   Flunking as a regular policy has just as much merit today as it did two generations ago. We must review the threat of flunking and see it as it really is—a positive teaching tool. It is an expression of confidence by both teachers and parents that the students have the ability to learn the material presented to them. However, making it work again would take a dedicated, caring conspiracy° between teachers and parents. It would mean facing the tough reality that passing kids who haven't learned the material—while it might save them grief for the short term—dooms them to long-term illiteracy. It would mean that teachers would have to follow through on their threats, and parents would have to stand behind them, knowing their children's best interests are indeed at stake. This means no more doing Scott's assignments for him because he might fail. No more passing Jodi because she's such a nice kid.

12   This is a policy that worked in the past and can work today. A wise teacher, with my husband's and my support, gave our son the opportunity to succeed—or fail. It's time we return this choice to all students.

Reading Comprehension Questions

Vocabulary in Context

   C   1. In the excerpt below, the word *impediments* (ĭm-pĕd′ə-mənts) means
      A. questions.
      B. skills.
      C. obstacles.
      D. paths.

> "I blamed the poor academic skills our kids have today on drugs, divorce and other impediments to concentration. . . . " (Paragraph 4)

Central Point and Main Ideas

   D   2. Which sentence best expresses the central point of the selection?
      A. Before students will concentrate, the teacher must get their attention.
      B. Many adults cannot read or write well.
      C. English skills can be learned through adult literacy programs.
      D. The threat of failure should be returned to our classrooms.

___C___ 3. Which sentence best expresses the main idea of paragraph 6?
- A. According to his teacher, Sherry's son sat at the back of the room, talking to his friends.
- B. Mrs. Stifter said that she didn't move seniors, she flunked them.
- C. The fear of failure motivated Sherry's son to do well in English.
- D. Sherry was at first nervous and confused to learn that her son might fail English.   *Answers A, B, and D are too narrow.*

Supporting Details

___C___ 4. According to the author, many students who get "passed along"
- A. are lucky.   *See paragraph 7.*
- B. don't get into trouble.
- C. eventually feel angry and resentful.
- D. will never learn basic grammar and writing skills.

Transitions

___D___ 5. The relationship between the two sentences below is one of
- A. time.   *In spite of is a contrast expression.*
- B. addition.
- C. comparison.
- D. contrast.

> "Many students I see at night could give expert testimony on unemployment, chemical dependency, abusive relationships. In spite of these difficulties, they have decided to make education a priority." (Paragraph 9)

Patterns of Organization

___A___ 6. The main pattern of organization of paragraph 6 is
- A. time order.
- B. list of items.
- C. definition and example.
- D. comparison.

Fact and Opinion

___A___ 7. Paragraph 6 is primarily
- A. fact.
- B. opinion.

Inferences

  C   8. The author implies that our present educational system is
- A. doing the best that it can.
- B. the best in the world.
- C. not demanding enough of students.
- D. very short of teachers.

Purpose

  B   9. The author's primary purpose in this article is
- A. to inform.
- B. to persuade.
- C. to entertain.

The author doesn't simply *explain* the advantages and disadvantages of failing students—she *supports* the practice. (See the statement of the central point in item 2.)

Argument

10. Label the point of the following argument from the reading with a **P**; label the two statements of support for the point with an **S**. Label with an **X** the one statement that is neither the point nor the support of the argument.

  S   A. Fear of failure motivated the author's son to do well in English.

  P   B. Fear of failure is a good motivator.

  X   C. Some people learn skills after high school in adult literacy programs.

  S   D. Some kids won't put school first unless they know they might fail.

Discussion Questions

1. Do you know anyone who has failed or almost failed a course? What effect did the experience have on that person?

2. Most people think of failing a course as a negative experience. Why, then, does Sherry consider the threat of failure to be a positive teaching tool? Do you agree?

3. Besides the threat of failure, what are some other ways that teachers can motivate students? What have teachers done to make you want to work harder for a class?

4. People often look back on their education and realize that some of the teachers they learned the most from were their strictest teachers. Who do you think you learned more from, strict teachers or lenient ones? Give examples to support your point.

Note: Writing assignments for this selection appear on page 590.

Check Your Performance ARGUMENT

Activity	Number Right	Points		Score
Review Test 1 (5 items)	_____	× 2	=	_____
Review Test 2 (10 items)	_____	× 3	=	_____
Review Test 3 (5 items)	_____	× 6	=	_____
Review Test 4 (10 items)	_____	× 3	=	_____
		TOTAL SCORE	=	_____%

Enter your total score into the **Reading Performance Chart: Review Tests** on the inside back cover.

ARGUMENT: Mastery Test 1

A. In each group, one statement is the point of an argument, and the other statements are support for that point. In the space provided, write the letter of the point of each group.

_A_ 1. A. I'm a good example of someone who has "math anxiety."
 B. I feel dread every time I sit down to take our Friday math quiz.
 C. During the math midterm, I "froze" and didn't even try to answer most of the questions.
 D. I turned down a job as a salesclerk because I would have had to figure out how much change customers should get back.

_D_ 2. A. Often you'll wait half an hour for a Route 27 bus, and then three will show up at once.
 B. Sometimes Route 27 buses will roar right past you at a bus stop, even though they aren't full.
 C. Route 27 seems to be assigned the oldest buses, ones that rattle and have broken seats.
 D. It is wise to avoid the Route 27 bus whenever possible.

_B_ 3. A. Elected officials could spend more time on their jobs and less on raising money.
 B. There should be a limit on how much can be spent for political campaigns.
 C. Candidates with less money would have a fairer chance of competing.
 D. Elected officials would be less likely to be influenced by rich contributors to their campaigns.

_A_ 4. A. Congress should enact a comprehensive highway program.
 B. Some of the numerous accidents, injuries, and fatalities on our nation's roads are the result of poor highway design.
 C. There is an urgent need for bridge construction and maintenance throughout this country.
 D. This nation needs programs to alleviate traffic jams.

Comments:

Item 1 — You can insert the word *because* in front of answers B, C, and D to explain why I'm a good example of someone who has "math anxiety."

Item 2 — Insert *because* in front of answers A, B, and C to explain why it is wise to avoid the Route 27 bus.

Item 3 — Insert *because* in front of answers A, C, and D to explain why political campaigns should have a spending limit.

Item 4 — Insert *because* in front of answers B, C, and D to explain why Congress should enact a comprehensive highway program.

(Continues on next page)

B. Each point is followed by three statements that provide relevant support and three that do not. In the spaces, write the letters of the **three** relevant statements of support.

5–7. **Point:** My boss is a very unpleasant man to work for.

A. He barks orders and never asks for an employee's opinion.

B. His fashion-plate wife is said to be even nastier than he is.

C. His office is decorated in dull browns and grays.

D. Even when he invites employees out to lunch, he expects them to pick up their own checks.

E. He changes his mind so often than an employee who pleased him on Friday can be in the doghouse by Monday.

F. He once accumulated so many parking tickets that the police actually came to his home to arrest him.

Items that logically support the point: ____A____   ____D____   ____E____

8–10. **Point:** Stress has a negative effect on health.

A. Stress triggers a person's "flight or fight" response, which can save him or her from danger.

B. Stress can cause an irregular heartbeat, which can lead to a heart attack.

C. Stress can be caused by scary events or by pleasant ones, such as a romantic encounter.

D. Stress depresses the immune system, making people more vulnerable to illness.

E. Stress raises blood pressure, increasing the chance of stroke.

F. Yoga, meditation, and breathing exercises can all be used to reduce stress.

Items that logically support the point: ____B____   ____D____   ____E____

Comments: Items 5–7— Only answers A, D, and E support the point that my boss is unpleasant to work for. Answer B is about the boss's wife, not the boss. Answer C is about the boss's office decorations. Answer F indicates that the boss is not law-abiding, but this quality would not necessarily make him unpleasant to work for.

Items 8–10 — Only answers B, D, and E support the point that stress has a negative effect on health. Answer A is a *positive* effect of stress; Answer C is about the *causes* of stress; and answer F is about ways to *reduce* stress.

ARGUMENT: Mastery Test 2

A. In each group, one statement is the point of an argument, and the other statements are support for that point. In the space provided, write the letter of the point of each group.

  C 1. A. The school has been vandalized twice this year.
     B. Two weeks ago, someone stole a computer from a classroom.
     C. The school needs better security.   *Insert because in front of answers*
     D. A stranger got into the school and threatened a student.   *A, B, and D*
                to explain how we know that the school needs better security.

  C 2. A. Profits Unlimited has been the target of many complaints to the Better Business Bureau.
     B. The company's advertising tells you that you can learn the secrets of getting rich quickly by buying its guidebook and audio tapes for two hundred dollars.   *Insert because in front of answers*
     C. Profits Unlimited is very likely a dishonest business.   *A, B, and D*
     D. The owner has served time for fraud in state prison.   *to explain how*
                we know that Profits Unlimited is very likely dishonest.

  B 3. A. Most fur products are made from animals bred for that purpose, so few endangered species are threatened by the fur industry.
     B. Animal-rights activists should not attack others for using animals for fur and medical experiments.
     C. Many treatments that save human lives were developed through animal testing programs.   *The word should in B is a clue to the point.*
     D. Animals bred for fur coats are generally well cared for because breeders want a healthy coat.   *Insert because in front of answers*
                A, C, and D to explain why animal-rights activists should not attack others
                for using animals for fur and medical experiments.

B. Each point is followed by three statements that provide relevant support and three that do not. In the spaces, write the letters of the **three** relevant statements of support.

  4–6. **Point:** Convenience stores live up to their name.

     A. Convenience stores are close to home.

     B. Small local businesses should be supported by the community.

     C. Some convenience store chains sell products under their own brand name.

     D. Convenience stores are open till late or all night.

     E. Parking is right outside the convenience store's door.

     F. The produce at most of our supermarkets is usually terrible.

     Items that logically support the point: __*A*__   __*D*__   __*E*__

  Comment: Items 4–6— Only A, D, and E support the point
       that convenience stores *are* convenient.   *(Continues on next page)*

7–9. **Point:** Eating yogurt is healthful.

   A. Yogurt contains natural antibiotics that can prevent certain kinds of infection.

   B. Yogurt is available in nearly all food stores.

   C. Yogurt kills the bacteria that can cause diarrhea.

   D. You can substitute yogurt in many recipes calling for milk or sour cream.

   E. Yogurt is a staple of the diet in many Middle Eastern countries.

   F. Eating yogurt has been shown to lower cholesterol levels.

   Items that logically support the point: ___A___   ___C___   ___F___

   > Only A, C, and F support the point that yogurt is healthful.

C. Read the following paragraph and then answer the question that follows.

> [1]Sexual harassment in the workplace must be recognized for the serious problem it is. [2]Too many people make light of the problem, believing sexual harassment to be nothing more than pleasant flirtation between coworkers. [3]However, many women, and even some men, have been driven to quit their jobs because of unwanted sexual attention from their supervisors. [4]An employer can more or less subtly pressure employees to grant sexual favors in order to keep their jobs. [5]Even employers who do not demand sex can make their employees miserable through unwelcome remarks about their bodies or dress. [6]Supervisors who sexually harass their employees must have a need to feel important or powerful. [7]All degrees of sexual harassment have the effect of creating a hostile and degrading atmosphere in the workplace. [8]To protect people from having to work in such an environment should be the aim of laws against sexual harassment.

___D___ 10. Which sentence is **not** relevant to the argument that laws should protect people from unwanted sexual attention?

   A. Sentence 3

   B. Sentence 4

   C. Sentence 5

   D. Sentence 6

   > The paragraph's main idea is that workers must be protected against sexual harassment.
   > Sentence 6 suggests a possible reason for the sexual harassment; this is a separate question entirely.

ARGUMENT: Mastery Test 3

A. In the space provided, write the letter of the statement that is **not** logical support for the argument in each paragraph.

___C___ 1. ¹Proms are one traditional part of the high-school experience that should be discontinued. ²For one thing, proms are just too expensive. ³Between the girl's dress, the guy's tuxedo, flowers, tickets, and probably dinner in a restaurant, it's way too much money for an average high-school couple to spend. ⁴Rich parents, however, are glad to show off their wealth by supporting such expensive occasions. ⁵Secondly, proms encourage destructive forms of social competition. ⁶Teenagers get caught up in worrying about who has the best-looking date, who spends most on a dress, or who arrives in a rented limousine. ⁷And finally, proms often turn into excuses for underage drinking-and-driving excursions.

Which sentence is **not** relevant support for the argument that high-school proms should be discontinued?　Sentence 4 changes the subject from why proms should be discontinued.

   A. Sentence 2　　　　　　　　　C. Sentence 4
   B. Sentence 3　　　　　　　　　D. Sentence 5

___B___ 2. ¹Non-human animals, even highly intelligent ones, are not capable of using language. ²In the 1930s, a husband and wife research team raised a young chimpanzee along with their human baby, treating the two youngsters exactly alike. ³The chimp didn't learn any language at all. ⁴It wasn't reported how the human baby was affected. ⁵In the 1950s, another team of married researchers gave a young chimp extensive language lessons. ⁶She finally learned to make sounds resembling "papa," "mama," and "cup," but nothing more. ⁷More recently, several chimps and gorillas have been taught to use some American Sign Language. ⁸But they use ASL only to request food or social reward, not to communicate complex ideas or feelings.

Which sentence is **not** relevant support for the argument that non-human animals cannot use language?　Sentence 4 changes the subject from non-human animals to human ones.

   A. Sentence 3　　　　　　　　　C. Sentence 5
   B. Sentence 4　　　　　　　　　D. Sentence 6

___D___ 3. ¹Society, not biology, gives meaning to the idea of "race." ²A scientist looking at a drop of blood under a microscope can't tell if the person it came from is Irish, Ethiopian, Hawaiian, or Apache. ³In the United States, people of African ancestry who run the color spectrum from the

(Continues on next page)

palest tan to the deepest ebony are all considered "black." [4]But many Central and South American societies would divide those "black" people into a number of smaller categories, based on differences in their skin tone. [5]Brazilians, for example, have about 40 color groupings to describe people. [6]Brazilians of all colors speak Portuguese, while Spanish is spoken in most of the rest of Central and South America.

Which sentence is **not** relevant to the author's conclusion that society, not biology, gives meaning to the idea of "race"?

A. Sentence 3   C. Sentence 5

B. Sentence 4   D. Sentence 6

Sentence 6 changes the subject from the idea of "race" to languages spoken.

B. For each group, read the three items of support (the evidence). Then, in the space provided, write the letter of the point that is adequately supported by that evidence.

Group 1

Support:

- A growing number of Japanese women are choosing to stay single, viewing their traditional marriage role as a "raw deal."
- The cost of living and raising a child in Japan is very high.
- Long work days and lengthy commutes leave many Japanese working people too exhausted to deal with children.

_D_ 4. Which **point** is adequately supported by all the evidence above?

A. Japanese women are demanding changes in their society.

B. Japanese people work longer hours than workers in any other country.

C. Japanese families have traditionally been large.

D. There are a number of reasons why the birthrate in Japan is falling.

Group 2

Support:

- Dolphins appear to be able to talk to one another through a language of squeals and grunts.
- There have been reports of dolphins helping people who were lost at sea.
- Dolphins in captivity have learned to perform sophisticated tasks, such as fetching objects in a particular order.

_B_ 5. Which **point** is adequately supported by the evidence above?

A. There are no other animals as intelligent as dolphins.

B. Dolphins appear to be highly intelligent animals.

C. Dolphins are better off in captivity.

D. Dolphins are good parents.

ARGUMENT: Mastery Test 4

A. In the space provided, write the letter of the statement that is **not** logical support for the argument in each paragraph.

____A____ 1. ¹Much of America's drug problem could actually be eliminated by legalizing narcotics. ²Harsh drug laws have not ended illegal drug use. ³We already sell many drugs over the counter as cold and flu medicines. ⁴If all drugs were legal, illegal street dealers would swiftly go out of business. ⁵Actually, most drug-related crimes are not due to the drugs themselves, but to the need for money to buy drugs (which would be affordable if legal) or to turf battles between dealers. ⁶Legalized drugs would also positively affect the problem of addiction because profits from drug sales could be taxed to support drug treatment and education programs.

Which sentence is **not** relevant to the author's conclusion that drugs should be legalized?

    A. Sentence 3   C. Sentence 5

    B. Sentence 4   D. Sentence 6

Sentence 3 changes the subject from illegal drugs to legal ones.

____D____ 2. ¹Statistics show that people travel more safely in airplanes than in cars. ²For that reason, it seems foolish to be afraid of flying and not be concerned about safety in a car. ³The figures are clear—planes, per passenger mile, are safer than cars. ⁴But statistics do not tell the whole story. ⁵Automobile accidents usually involve only a few people per occurrence and kill or injure only some of the victims. ⁶They involve situations which drivers believe they can avoid through skill or caution. ⁷On the other hand, airplane accidents usually involve large numbers of people and high death rates. ⁸One hundred percent is not uncommon. ⁹Surviving an airplane accident requires luck, not skill or caution, and passengers are totally dependent upon their crew. ¹⁰And to add insult to injury, passengers have paid unreasonably high amounts for tickets for this unsafe type of transportation. ¹¹There's no question about it: when driven by a safe and sober driver, a car is a safer bet than an airplane.

Which sentence is **not** relevant support for the argument that when a car is driven by a safe and sober driver, it is a safer bet than an airplane?

    A. Sentence 5   C. Sentence 9

    B. Sentence 8   D. Sentence 10

Sentence 10 changes the subject from safety to the cost of a ticket.

____A____ 3. ¹The level of personal service in the American marketplace is quite low. ²Catalog phone clerks have snapped at me in exasperation when I can't find the customer identification number on my catalog. ³Even

(Continues on next page)

worse, returning a catalog item is highly inconvenient—it must be rewrapped and mailed back to the company. ⁴Service in local stores is no better. ⁵Yesterday I waited for nearly five minutes at a cash register while two clerks complained bitterly to one another about how much they hated their jobs. ⁶I have heard workers in restaurants groan loudly when customers walked in too close to quitting time. ⁷Even when I ask for assistance in finding a product in a store, clerks sometimes shrug their shoulders and walk away.

Which sentence is **not** relevant support for the argument that the level of personal service in the American marketplace is low?

A. Sentence 3   C. Sentence 5   Sentence 3 changes the subject
B. Sentence 4   D. Sentence 6   from personal service

by company salespeople to personal inconvenience that would occur anyway.

B. For each group, read the three items of support (the evidence). Then, in the space provided, write the letter of the point that is adequately supported by that evidence.

Group 1   All four items in the box below are examples of new vocabulary that Internet use has created (C). Note that although *should* in answer D is often used in a

Support: point, in this particular case answer D does not cover the details listed.

> • The term *cyberspace* was invented in 1984 by a science-fiction writer.
> • A "hacker" is a person who breaks into a computer network without permission.
> • *Spam* is the term now given to unwanted junk e-mail.
> • To "flame" someone means to insult him or her online.

___C___ 4. Which **point** is adequately supported by all the evidence above?
  A. Illegal or annoying behavior is common on the Internet.
  B. More people are using computers today than ever before.
  C. Internet use has created a whole new vocabulary.
  D. Steps should be taken to control the sending of unwanted e-mail.

Group 2   All three items in the box below tell why music is a useful treatment for physical and emotional ailments.

Support: Try inserting *because* in front of each of them.

> • Music is often quite effective in helping emotionally disturbed children communicate.
> • Music can help relieve anxiety in patients about to undergo surgery.
> • Music can help relieve persistent arthritis pain.

___D___ 5. Which **point** is adequately supported by the evidence above?
  A. Everyone should listen to music each day.
  B. Music is one of our most effective medical tools.
  C. More people should enter thc field of music therapy.
  D. Music is a useful treatment for physical and emotional ailments.

ARGUMENT: Mastery Test 5

A. Each point is followed by three statements that provide relevant support and three that do not. In the spaces, write the letters of the **three** relevant statements of support.

1–3. Point: Professional boxing should be banned.

Only A, D, and F are reasons why boxing should be banned. Answer B changes the subject to broadcasting; answer C is about women's boxing; answer E states a positive effect of boxing.

A. Too many boxers have been critically injured and even killed in the ring.

B. Most important boxing matches are broadcast on a pay-per-view basis.

C. Women's boxing is becoming increasingly popular.

D. Boxing encourages people's cruelest, most savage instincts.

E. Boxing has given many young at-risk men a source of self-discipline and pride.

F. Boxers who survive their careers are often left with permanent brain damage.

Items that logically support the point: ___A___ ___D___ ___F___

4–6. Point: Feeling guilty is not all bad.

Only B, C, and F support the point that feeling guilty is not all bad. Answer A explains one reason for feeling guilty; answers D and E state that some people feel guilty even when they themselves have done nothing wrong.

A. Some people feel guilty because they can't do everything others ask of them.

B. Feelings of guilt can encourage a person to think about his or her behavior and act differently the next time.

C. People who feel guilt are less likely to commit a crime than those who feel no guilt for their wrongdoings.

D. People often feel guilty even when they have done nothing wrong.

E. Parents often feel guilty when their children, even their adult children, do something wrong.

F. People who feel guilt have more understanding of and compassion for other people's imperfections.

Items that logically support the point: ___B___ ___C___ ___F___

B. Read the following three items of support (the evidence). Then write the letter of the point that is adequately supported by that evidence.

Support:

- During two months at the peak of their popularity, 25 million hula hoops were sold.
- Sales of Davy Crockett coonskin caps grossed more than 100 million dollars in the late 1950s.
- During several Christmas-shopping seasons in the early 1980s, police had to control crowds waiting at toy stores to buy Cabbage Patch Dolls.

(Continues on next page)

_C_ 7. Which **point** is adequately supported by the evidence above?

The items listed (hula hoops, Davy Crockett coonskin caps, and Cabbage Patch Dolls) are proof that fad toys capture the imagination of a huge number of consumers.

A. It is easy to produce a successful toy.

B. It is possible to predict what toys will be popular and which ones will not.

C. Every so often, a fad toy captures the imagination of a huge number of consumers.

D. People should not get so caught in up materialism.

C. Read the paragraphs below, and then answer the questions that follow.

[1]In addition to highways and airlines, America should have a high-speed rail system. [2]Democrats and Republicans are equally to blame for our failure to develop such a system. [3]High-speed trains are good time-savers. [4]Over distances up to several hundred miles, they would actually get you there faster than jetliners, which have to fly to and from outlying airports. [5]In addition, trains powered by electricity produce less pollution than airplanes and also save oil. [6]Developing a high-speed rail system would also be a boost to American industry by providing a highly reliable, speedy method of transportation.

_A_ 8. Which sentence is **not** relevant to the author's argument that the United States should build high-speed trains?

Sentence 2 changes the subject from why we should have a high-speed rail system to one possible reason that we don't have one.

A. Sentence 2   C. Sentence 4
B. Sentence 3   D. Sentence 5

[1]The death penalty is popular with voters, who are frightened of violent crime, but it is not very effective in reducing the murder rate. [2]In the 1960s and 1970s, when murder rates were lower than today, the death penalty was hardly ever used. [3]Even today, the states that use the death penalty most also often have the highest murder rates. [4]In addition, every death sentence costs taxpayers hundreds of thousands of dollars in appeals and lawyers' fees. [5]The number of executions that take place in a state doesn't seem to matter either. [6]There have actually been some years in which states that had many executions experienced higher homicide rates than states with fewer executions.

_B_ 9. Which statement is the point of the argument?

A. The death penalty is popular with voters, who are frightened of violent crime.

B. The death penalty is not very effective in reducing the murder rate.

C. The murder rate has gone up in this country since the 1960s and 1970s.

All the details in the passage (except Sentence 4) prove that the death penalty has not reduced the murder rate.

D. Executions cost more than they are worth.

_B_ 10. Which sentence is **not** relevant support for the point of the argument?

A. Sentence 3   C. Sentence 5
B. Sentence 4   D. Sentence 6

Sentence 4 changes the subject from the reduction of the murder rate to the cost of a death sentence.

ARGUMENT: Mastery Test 6

A. Each point is followed by three statements that provide relevant support and three that do not. In the spaces, write the letters of the **three** relevant statements of support.

1–3. **Point:** It makes sense to give alternative sentences, not jail, to some nonviolent offenders.   Only B, D, and F stick to the subject of alternative sentences for nonviolent offenders.

A. Everyone is entitled to legal representation.
B. Alternative sentences cost less than jail.
C. The crime rate goes up every year.
D. Prisons are overcrowded.
E. The courts always have a backlog of cases.
F. Evidence suggests that alternative sentences offer a better chance of rehabilitating the offender.

The other answers do not tell why alternative sentences make sense.

Items that logically support the point: ___B___   ___D___   ___F___

4–6. **Point:** Religion is a powerful force in modern American life.

Only B, C, and F explain how we know that religion is a powerful force in modern American life. The other answers change the subject to different aspects of religion in modern American life.

A. The main religion in America is Christianity.
B. Television evangelists can collect millions of dollars from contributors.
C. Religious leaders are often influential voices on public issues in America.
D. In America, there is no state religion.
E. The Pilgrims came to America seeking religious freedom.
F. Public opinion polls show that a majority of Americans consider religion personally important to them.

Items that logically support the point: ___B___   ___C___   ___F___

B. Read the following three items of support (the evidence). Then write the letter of the point that is adequately supported by that evidence.

Support:

- Vitamin C, unlike some other vitamins, is not stored in the body fat.
- Any vitamin C not used by the body is excreted within a few hours.
- In addition, vitamin C is an acid, and thus it's best not to take large doses of it on an empty stomach.

___C___ 7. Which **point** is adequately supported by the evidence above?
A. Everyone should take supplemental doses of vitamin C.
B. For people who take vitamin C pills, it is more efficient to take one pill a day.

(Continues on next page)

413

c. People should spread their vitamin C intake throughout the day.

d. It is not necessary to include vitamin C in one's diet if vitamin C pills are taken.   All three items in the list explain why people should spread their vitamin C intake throughout the day.

C. Read the paragraphs below, and then answer the questions that follow.

> [1]America's top corporate executives are often greatly overpaid. [2]They use their enormous incomes to support an overly lavish lifestyle. [3]Some corporate bosses make nearly a hundred million dollars a year—thousands of times more than what some of their employees are making. [4]Such wide discrepancies in pay lower the morale of employees, especially when the executives aren't performing well. [5]Some corporate executives have gotten multi-million-dollar bonuses even though their companies lost money.

_A_ 8. Which sentence is **not** relevant to the author's point that corporate executives are often overpaid?   How the executives spend their money doesn't determine whether or not they are overpaid.

    A. Sentence 2   c. Sentence 4

    B. Sentence 3   D. Sentence 5

> [1]Schizophrenia, a serious type of mental illness, involves delusions, hallucinations, and inappropriate emotional states. [2]Other types of diseases, such as brain tumors, may cause those symptoms as well. [3]There is reason to believe that schizophrenia is genetically linked—that is, it runs in families. [4]One piece of evidence that supports this theory is that schizophrenia occurs at a similar rate around the world. [5]For example, one study showed that about one-half of one percent of people in Chandigarh, India; Nottingham, England; and Moscow, Russia, will become schizophrenic at some point in their lives. [6]If schizophrenia were caused by some sort of environmental factor, we would expect it to occur at different rates in different cultures.

_B_ 9. Which statement is the point of the argument?

    A. Schizophrenia is a serious type of mental illness.

    B. There is reason to believe that schizophrenia is genetically linked.

    c. Schizophrenia is probably caused by environmental factors.

    D. Schizophrenia occurs at a similar rate around the world.

_A_ 10. Which sentence is **not** relevant support for the point of the argument?

    A. Sentence 2   c. Sentence 4

    B. Sentence 3   D. Sentence 5

Part II

TEN READING SELECTIONS

1

The Yellow Ribbon
Pete Hamill

Preview

When is a yellow handkerchief like a pair of open arms? For the answer, read this selection, which first appeared in a *New York Post* newspaper column by Pete Hamill. The story became the inspiration for the popular song "Tie a Yellow Ribbon 'Round the Old Oak Tree." This moving article probably also suggests the origin of using yellow ribbons as a symbol of America's wish to see her troops return home safely.

Words to Watch

cocoon (2): protective covering
bluntness (13): abruptness
exaltation (22): joy

1   They were going to Fort Lauderdale, the girl remembered later. There were six of them, three boys and three girls, and they picked up the bus at the old terminal on 34th Street, carrying sandwiches and wine in paper bags, dreaming of golden beaches and the tides of the sea as the gray cold spring of New York vanished behind them. Vingo was on board from the beginning.

2   As the bus passed through Jersey and into Philly, they began to notice that Vingo never moved. He sat in front of the young people, his dusty face masking his age, dressed in a plain brown ill-fitting suit. His fingers were stained from cigarettes and he chewed the inside of his lip a lot, frozen into some personal cocoon° of silence.

3   Somewhere outside of Washington, deep into the night, the bus pulled into a Howard Johnson's, and everybody got off except Vingo. He sat rooted in his seat, and the young people began to

wonder about him, trying to imagine his life: Perhaps he was a sea captain, maybe he had run away from his wife, he could be an old soldier going home. When they went back to the bus, the girl sat beside him and introduced herself.

4   "We're going to Florida," the girl said brightly. "You going that far?"

5   "I don't know." Vingo said.

6   "I've never been there," she said. "I hear it's beautiful."

7   "It is," he said quietly, as if remembering something he had tried to forget.

8   "You live there?"

9   "I did some time there in the Navy. Jacksonville."

10   "Want some wine?" she said. He smiled and took the bottle of Chianti and took a swig. He thanked her and retreated again into his silence. After a while, she went back to the others, as Vingo nodded in sleep.

11   In the morning they awoke outside another Howard Johnson's, and this time Vingo went in. The girl insisted that he join them. He seemed very shy and ordered black coffee and smoked nervously, as the young people chattered about sleeping on the beaches. When they went back on the bus, the girl sat with Vingo again, and after a while, slowly and painfully and with great hesitation, he began to tell his story. He had been in jail in New York for the last four years, and now he was going home.

12   "Four years!" the girl said. "What did you do?"

13   "It doesn't matter," he said with quiet bluntness°. "I did it and I went to jail. If you can't do the time, don't do the crime. That's what they say and they're right."

14   "Are you married?"

15   "I don't know."

16   "You don't know?" she said.

17   "Well, when I was in the can I wrote to my wife," he said. "I told her, I said, Martha, I understand if you can't stay married to me. I told her that. I said I was gonna be away a long time, and that if she couldn't stand it, if the kids kept askin' questions, if it hurt her too much, well, she could just forget me. Get a new guy—she's a wonderful woman, really something—and forget about me. I told her she didn't have to write me or nothing. And she didn't. Not for three and a half years."

18   "And you're going home now, not knowing?"

19   "Yeah," he said shyly. "Well, last week, when I was sure the parole was coming through I wrote her. I told her that if she had a new guy, I understood. But if she didn't, if she would take me back, she should let me know. We used to live in this town, Brunswick, just before Jacksonville, and there's a great big oak tree just as you come into town, a very famous tree, huge. I told her if she would take me back, she should put a yellow handkerchief on the tree, and I would get off and come home. If she didn't want me, forget it, no handkerchief, and I'd keep going on through."

20   "Wow," the girl said. "Wow."

21   She told the others, and soon all of them were in it, caught up in the approach of Brunswick, looking at the pictures Vingo showed them of his wife and three children, the woman handsome in a plain way, the children still unformed in a cracked, much-handled snapshot. Now they were twenty miles from Brunswick and the young people took over window seats on the right side, waiting for the approach of the great oak tree. Vingo stopped looking, tightening his face into the ex-con's mask, as if fortifying himself against still another disappointment. Then it was ten miles,

and then five and the bus acquired a dark hushed mood, full of silence, of absence, of lost years, of the woman's plain face, of the sudden letter on the breakfast table, of the wonder of children, of the iron bars of solitude.

22   Then suddenly all of the young people were up out of their seats, screaming and shouting and crying, doing small dances, shaking clenched fists in triumph and exaltation°. All except Vingo.

Vingo sat there stunned, looking at   23 the oak tree. It was covered with yellow handkerchiefs, twenty of them, thirty of them, maybe hundreds, a tree that stood like a banner of welcome blowing and billowing in the wind, turned into a gorgeous yellow blur by the passing bus. As the young people shouted, the old con slowly rose from his seat, holding himself tightly, and made his way to the front of the bus to go home.

BASIC SKILL QUESTIONS

Vocabulary in Context

   _A_   1. In the sentence below, the word *fortifying* (fôr′tə-fī′ĭng) means
      A. strengthening.
      B. watching.
      C. hurrying.
      D. losing.

   "Vingo stopped looking, tightening his face into the ex-con's mask, as if fortifying himself against still another disappointment." (Paragraph 21)

   _B_   2. In the sentence below, the word *acquired* (ə-kwīrd′) means
      A. needed.
      B. took on.
      C. stopped.
      D. lost.

   "Then it was ten miles, and then five and the bus acquired a dark hushed mood. . . ." (Paragraph 21)

Central Point and Main Ideas

   _D_   3. Which sentence best expresses the main idea of this selection?
      A. Prison sentences can ruin marriages.   The main idea of a narrative
      B. If you commit a crime, you must pay for it.   will be a summary
      C. Vingo did not know what to expect.   of its events.
      D. Vingo returned from prison to find that his wife still loved him.

_B_   4. Which sentence best expresses the main idea of paragraph 3?
    A. The bus stopped at a Howard Johnson's.   Too narrow.
    B. The young people began to be curious about Vingo.
    C. Vingo might have been a sea captain.   Too narrow.
    D. Everyone got off the bus except Vingo.   Too narrow.

Supporting Details

_F_   5. TRUE OR FALSE? Vingo felt he should not have been put in prison.

See paragraph 13.

Transitions

_B_   6. The relationship between the two sentences below is one of
    A. time.
    B. contrast.   Vingo is contrasting two possible reactions by his wife.
    C. comparison.
    D. illustration.

> ". . . I told her that if she had a new guy, I understood. **But** if she didn't, if she would take me back, she should let me know." (Paragraph 19)

_D_   7. The transition words *as, when, after, now,* and *then,* which Hamill uses throughout this selection, all signal
    A. cause and effect.   Because narratives tell about events in the
    B. examples.   order in which they happened, they use
    C. contrast.   many time signals.
    D. time.

_B_   8. The relationship expressed in the phrase "a tree that stood <u>like</u> a banner of welcome" (paragraph 23) is one of
    A. contrast.   The tree with handkerchiefs is being compared to
    B. comparison.   a banner. *Like* is a comparison word.
    C. cause and effect.
    D. time.

Patterns of Organization

_C_   9. The main pattern of organization of paragraph 2 is
    A. cause and effect.   The "items" listed are details that
    B. comparison and/or contrast.   describe Vingo, so they can be
    C. list of items.   presented in any order.
    D. time order.

_D_   10. The main pattern of organization of the entire selection is
    A. cause and effect.
    B. comparison and/or contrast.   Narratives tell about events
    C. list of items.   in a time order.
    D. time order.

ADVANCED SKILL QUESTIONS

Fact and Opinion

____D____ 11. In telling this narrative, Hamill
   A. stresses his own opinions.   See paragraphs 20–22.
   B. leaves out any of Vingo's opinions.
   C. reveals the bus driver's opinions.
   D. reveals through the young people's actions how they feel about Vingo.

____C____ 12. Judging by the first sentence of the selection, Hamill got some facts for this nonfiction narrative by
   A. observing everything as a passenger on the bus ride.
   B. only imagining what might have happened on such a ride.
   C. interviewing at least one passenger.   The words "the girl remembered
   D. using a tape recording of the bus ride.   later" (paragraph 1) suggest
                   that Hamill got his information by interviewing one of the girls on the bus.

Inferences

____C____ 13. We can infer that the young people were going to Florida
   A. on business.   Hamill states that the young people were
   B. to visit relatives.   "dreaming of golden beaches and the tides of
   C. on vacation.   the sea" (paragraph 1).
   D. to get married.

____B____ 14. The author implies that Vingo thought   Vingo's nervousness and the
   A. he would someday be in prison again.   fact that his wife hadn't
   B. there might be no yellow handkerchief on the tree.   written imply the
   C. his wife was wrong for not writing to him in prison.   possibility that
   D. his wife was sure to want him back.   she might not
                                                    want him back.

____T____ 15. TRUE OR FALSE? The statement that Vingo "rose from his seat, holding himself tightly" (last paragraph) implies that Vingo was trying to contain his emotions.   We can make this inference based on the
                                        "message" Vingo just received.

____C____ 16. By telling us that the picture of Vingo's family was a "cracked, much-handled snapshot," the author implies that
   A. Vingo didn't know how to take good care of photos.
   B. the pictures were not really of Vingo's family.
   C. Vingo had looked at the snapshot a great deal while in jail.
   D. the photo was relatively new.   For the four years that Vingo was in jail,
                                    the photo may have been his only
                                    concrete connection with his family.

Purpose and Tone

  C 17. The main purpose of "The Yellow Ribbon" is to
- A. inform readers that a convict's life can be rebuilt after prison.
- B. persuade readers to avoid a life of crime.
- C. entertain readers with a heartwarming story.

  C 18. In paragraphs 17 through 21, the author's tone becomes increasingly
- A. bitter.
- B. amused.
- C. suspenseful.
- D. disbelieving.

> The author chooses details that increase suspense about what the oak tree will look like.

Argument

  A 19. Which of the following points is well supported by the evidence below?
- A. Vingo was nervous about something.
- B. Vingo was on the verge of a nervous breakdown.
- C. Vingo had a hostile personality.
- D. Vingo disliked young people.

> Nothing in the sentence suggests the points in B, C, and D.

"[Vingo's] fingers were stained from cigarettes and he chewed the inside of his lip a lot, frozen into some personal cocoon of silence." (Paragraph 2)

  C 20. Which statement does *not* support the following point?

Point: Vingo deserved the yellow handkerchiefs.

- A. He admitted his mistake.
- B. He paid for his crime by serving four years in jail.
- C. He probably caused his wife and children a lot of pain and embarrassment.
- D. He seemed to regret causing his wife pain.

> Point C would be a reason for Vingo's family to reject him.

Comment: Item 17—If the author's *main* purpose had been to show that a convict's life can be rebuilt after prison, he would have told us more about Vingo's life after the bus ride. If *B* were his purpose, he would have focused more on Vingo's punishment.

SUMMARIZING

Following is an incomplete summary of "The Yellow Ribbon." In the space provided, write the letter (A, B, or C) of the item below that best completes the summary.

_B_   A man named Vingo had just been released from prison and was on a bus headed home. Some young people were also on the bus, and they got Vingo to tell his story. He said he had written to his wife when he went to prison to explain he would understand if she found another man. He hadn't heard from her since but still loved her very much. So he recently wrote to her, telling her to put a yellow handkerchief on a well-known oak tree in town if she wanted him to come home. If the handkerchief wasn't on the tree, he wouldn't get off the bus there. . . .

A. Vingo showed pictures of his wife and children to the young people, who got caught up in waiting to see the oak tree. As the bus got closer to Vingo's hometown, the bus became quiet and filled with suspense.

B. The young people got caught up in Vingo's situation. After a tense ride to his hometown, he and his fellow travelers finally got his wife's answer: not one, but scores of handkerchiefs fluttering on the tree.

C. Vingo would just continue on the bus to Florida, which is where the young people were going. He understood that while he was in prison, his wife might have started a new life for herself and their children.

DISCUSSION QUESTIONS

1. According to the information in the selection, what is Vingo's attitude toward his wife?

2. Has Vingo assumed responsibility for his crime, in your opinion?

3. While there is much we don't learn about Vingo in this very short narrative, Hamill does provide us with clues to some important aspects of his personality. What evidence is there that he is a decent man, a person who we could feel deserves a second chance?

4. Many people are thrilled, some even to tears, by this story. What makes "The Yellow Ribbon" have such a powerful effect on readers?

Note: Writing assignments for this selection appear on page 591.

Check Your Performance   **THE YELLOW RIBBON**

Activity   *Number Right*   *Points*   *Score*

BASIC SKILL QUESTIONS

   Vocabulary in Context (2 items)   _____   × 4 =   _____

   Central Point and Main Ideas (2 items)   _____   × 4 =   _____

   Supporting Details (1 item)   _____   × 4 =   _____

   Transitions (3 items)   _____   × 4 =   _____

   Patterns of Organization (2 items)   _____   × 4 =   _____

ADVANCED SKILL QUESTIONS

   Fact and Opinion (2 items)   _____   × 4 =   _____

   Inferences (4 items)   _____   × 4 =   _____

   Purpose and Tone (2 items)   _____   × 4 =   _____

   Argument (2 items)   _____   × 4 =   _____

SUMMARIZING (1 item)   _____   × 20 =   _____

                           TOTAL SCORE = _____%

Enter your total score into the **Reading Performance Chart: Ten Reading Selections** on the inside back cover.

2

Urban Legends
Beth Johnson

Preview

Did you hear the one about a woman who was looking through some Asian carpets and was bitten by a poisonous snake? Or was the story that the woman tried on a coat from Mexico, put her hand in the pocket, and found the snake there? These are just two versions of what folklorists call an urban legend. This selection explains what urban legends are and gives more examples of them.

Words to Watch

homicidal (3): murderous
legend (8): a story that can't be proven true
sophisticated (9): knowledgeable about the world
mint (15): brand-new
agonizing (18): painful

1   A group of college freshmen were sitting around in a friend's dorm room one night, eating popcorn and comparing notes on classes. Eventually the talk drifted away from academics and into the area of spooky stories. Tales of haunted houses were being giggled and shivered over when a girl from a small town in Michigan broke in. "I know a scarier story than any of those!" she announced.

"And the scariest thing is, this one is true. It happened to a girl my sister knew."

She began her story.   2

"This girl went to baby-sit at a   3
house way out in the country one evening. It was a stormy night, and she was feeling a little nervous anyway when the phone rang. When she answered, a man said, 'Have you checked the children?' and laughed weirdly. She was

scared to death and ran to check the kids. They were all right, but a few minutes later the guy called again and said again, 'Have you checked the children?' and laughed like crazy. She called the operator to see if she could get the calls traced. A few minutes later, the operator called back to say, 'Get out of the house! He's in the house with you!' So she hurried and grabbed the kids and ran out into the rain just as the police pulled up. They found this escaped homicidal° maniac in the parents' upstairs bedroom. She was lucky to get out alive."

4 "Wow! What an awful story!" the girl's roommate exclaimed.

5 "But wait a minute!" called out another friend, this one from Iowa. "That didn't happen in Michigan. It happened near my home town, back when my mother was in high school. The guy had escaped from an asylum in Cedar Rapids."

6 "Well, it sounds an awful lot like something that happened a few years ago to a friend of my cousin's in Colorado," said another freshman. "Only the guy actually caught the babysitter."

7 What's going on here? How could the same event have happened to three different babysitters in three different parts of the country at three different times?

8 Urban legend° is what's going on.

9 Urban legend is the modern-day equivalent of the Paul Bunyan story. We're too sophisticated° these days to believe in Babe the blue ox or men who use pine trees to comb their beards. But we haven't quite given up our need for scary stories that are a little too good to be true. So we've developed our own type of slightly more believable tall tales. They're modern. They sound real. They include a humorous, unexpected, or frightening twist. And they probably never happened.

10 The deadly hairdo. Kentucky fried rats. The nude surprise party.

11 Do any of those ring a bell? Have you heard them told as true? Have you told them as true? If you've believed them, don't be embarrassed. You've got lots of company. And if you've helped spread them, well, you're just continuing a great American folk tradition.

12 Urban legends have come in for some serious attention in the last couple of decades. Their biggest fan is a University of Utah professor of English named Jan Harold Brunvand. Professor Brunvand has devoted years to collecting, researching, and analyzing urban legends all across the United States and even in other countries. He's written two books, *The Vanishing Hitchhiker* and *The Mexican Pet*. These books are jam-packed with the stories we love to tell and will swear are true—despite all evidence to the contrary.

13 Americans love their automobiles, and so some of the most familiar urban legends involve cars. One of the best-known is the classic story of teenagers parked late at night in a lovers' lane. The couple are listening to music on a car radio when a news bulletin comes on: a dangerous maniac has escaped from a nearby mental asylum. (Escaped madmen are common characters in urban legends.) Frightened, the girl demands to be taken home. But when the boy tries to start the car, it won't run. The boy gets out, locks the girl in the car, and walks off to find help.

14 The girl huddles in the cold car, becoming more and more frightened as minutes and then hours go by with no sign of her boyfriend. Her fright turns to terror when she begins to hear a soft "click, click" noise on top of the car. Finally, just as dawn breaks, police cars arrive at the scene. Cops surround the

car, help the girl out, and tell her, "Just walk to the police car and get in. Don't look back." Naturally, though, she does look back. Her boyfriend's body, suspended from a rope, is hanging upside down from a tree. As he sways back and forth in the breeze, his class ring scrapes—"click, click"—against the roof of the car.

15   But not all "car" urban legends are so horrible. "The Playboy's Car" tells of a man who is in the market for a luxury sports car. He sees an ad in the newspaper for a nearly new Porsche for $29.95. He figures the price is a mistake but goes to check it out anyway. A woman greets him at the house, assures him that the price is correct, and invites him to test-drive the Porsche. He drives a few miles. The car is in mint° condition. Hardly believing his luck, he hurries back to the house to close the deal. As the ownership papers are changing hands, he blurts out, "I can't stand not knowing. Why are you selling this car so cheap?" The woman smiles and answers, "My husband left me and moved in with his secretary last week. He asked me to sell his Porsche and send him the money."

16   How do these stories spread from coast to coast—and sometimes beyond? They probably begin wherever people gather: slumber parties, bowling nights, breaks at the office water cooler, transcontinental airplane flights. Eventually, they make their way into our modern communications network: telephones, television, radio, and newspapers. They sometimes even slip into local and national publications as true events. The fact that the stories have shown up in the media convinces the public that they must be true. People clip the articles and send them to friends and family and also to columnists and radio and television talk-show hosts, who give them further

publicity. And the more the stories travel, the more realistic-sounding details they pick up, and the more variations develop.

Another category of urban legends 17 demonstrates, Brunvand believes, the great American concern with cleanliness and health. "The Spider in the Hairdo," popular in the 1950s and 1960s, told of the girl with a fashionable "beehive" hairdo. She rarely washed her highly teased and sprayed hair. So—wouldn't you know it—a black widow spider got in there, bit her, and she died. A subcategory of the "cleanliness" stories is the set of "dreadful contamination" stories. These include tales about people finding pieces of mice in their bottled soft drinks, or the poor girl who bit into an oddly shaped piece of restaurant chicken, only to discover that it was a batter-fried rat.

And then there are the stories 18 concerning nudity. They sound familiar to any of us who've ever had the agonizing° dream of being at work or on stage with no clothes on. There's the man left naked by the roadside when his wife (not knowing he'd stepped out) drove off with their trailer. Or the crafty host who gave his female guests bathing suits that fell apart when they got wet. Or the poor woman who, feeling playful on her birthday, came downstairs naked to surprise her husband—and walked into her own birthday party.

What purpose do these stories 19 serve? Why have they developed? They're part of a long tradition that includes Aesop's fables—remember the hare and the tortoise?—and the morality plays of the Middle Ages, where "Truth" and "Virtue" were actual characters. They are stories that touch some of our deepest fears and concerns. And they teach us lessons. Don't park on lonely lovers' lanes. Don't pick up strangers. Don't fool around on your spouse. Don't eat food you're not sure of. Bathe regularly. It's all the same stuff your parents told you, but it's told in a far more entertaining way.

20   One more story? Well, have you heard about the cement-truck driver who stopped in to say hello to his wife during the day? When he got to his house, he found a brand-new Cadillac in his driveway. Becoming suspicious, he looked in the window and saw his wife and a strange man drinking coffee in the kitchen and laughing. Aha, he thought. So this is what she does all day. He could think of only one appropriate response. He backed his truck up to the Caddy, filled it full of cement, and then drove away.

21   When the truck driver got home that night, he found his wife hysterical. "Honey," she sobbed. "I've been saving my money for twenty years to buy you a wonderful present. It came today, and when the man that delivered it left the house—well, just go *look* at your car!"

BASIC SKILL QUESTIONS

Vocabulary in Context

___D___ 1. In the sentence below, the word *equivalent* (ĭ-kwĭv′ə-lənt) means
A. explanation.
B. cost.
C. storyteller.
D. equal.

"Urban legend is the modern-day equivalent of the Paul Bunyan story." (Paragraph 9)

___A___ 2. In the excerpt below, the word *contamination* (kən-tăm′ə-nā′shən) means
A. impurity.   The context clues are examples.
B. disease.
C. restaurant.
D. bottling.

"'dreadful contamination' stories. . . . include tales about people finding pieces of mice in their bottled soft drinks, or the poor girl who bit into an oddly shaped piece of restaurant chicken, only to discover that it was a batter-fried rat." (Paragraph 17)

Central Point and Main Ideas

___D___ 3. Which sentence best expresses the central point of the selection?
A. Urban legends begin in unknown ways and then travel throughout the country.   Too narrow.
B. Urban legends are scary stories based on old superstitions.   Incorrect.
C. Urban legends are very interesting to scholars.   Too narrow.
D. Urban legends are modern tales that touch upon deep fears and concerns and that teach lessons.

_C_ 4. Which sentence best expresses the main idea of paragraph 16?   Too
     A. Urban legends are believed because they sound so realistic. narrow.
     B. Urban legends are often published in newspapers. Too narrow.
     C. Urban legends spread in various ways, gaining more realism and variations.
     D. Because of our modern communications network, information of all kinds can be spread over a wide area relatively quickly. Too broad.

_A_ 5. The main idea of paragraph 17 is best expressed in its
     A. first sentence.
     B. second sentence.
     C. third sentence.
     D. last sentence.

The "cleanliness and health" referred to only generally in the first sentence is illustrated by the specific examples in the rest of the paragraph.

Supporting Details

_D_ 6. According to the article, urban legends are
     A. always horrible and scary.
     B. very difficult to believe.   See paragraph 9.
     C. usually started by college students.
     D. part of a long tradition of folk tales.

_A_ 7. The author specifically mentions urban legends that are concerned with
     A. cars.
     B. sports.   See paragraph 13.
     C. twins.
     D. none of the above.

Transitions

_B_ 8. The relationship of the second sentence below to the first is one of
     A. addition.
     B. time.   One topic of conversation followed another.
     C. illustration.
     D. cause and effect.

    "A group of college freshmen were sitting around in a friend's dorm room one night, eating popcorn and comparing notes on classes. Eventually the talk drifted away from academics and into the area of spooky stories." (Paragraph 1)

_C_ 9. The relationship between the two parts of the sentence below is one of
     A. time.
     B. comparison.   Urban legends contrast with "the stuff your parents told you" in how entertaining they are.
     C. contrast.
     D. illustration.

    "It's all the same stuff your parents told you, but it's told in a far more entertaining way." (Paragraph 19)

Patterns of Organization

_D_ 10. The main pattern of organization of the selection is a version of
    A. time order.
    B. comparison and/or contrast.
    C. cause and effect.
    D. definition and example.

> The reading defines, discusses, and gives examples of "urban legends."

_A_ 11. The main pattern of organization of paragraph 3 is
    A. time order.
    B. comparison.
    C. cause and effect.
    D. illustration.

> Anecdotes are mini-narratives.

ADVANCED SKILL QUESTIONS

Fact and Opinion

_A_ 12. The word that makes the sentence below an opinion is
    A. *biggest.*
    B. *fan.*
    C. *Utah.*
    D. *named.*

> There's no way to *prove* who the biggest fan is.

"Their biggest fan is a University of Utah professor of English named Jan Harold Brunvand." (Paragraph 12)

_A_ 13. The statement below is
    A. fact.
    B. opinion.
    C. fact and opinion.

> The statement can be verified by checking programs and articles and by interviewing people.

"[Urban legends] make their way into our modern communications network: telephones, television, radio, and newspapers." (Paragraph 16)

Inferences

_C_ 14. The author implies that
    A. people should always check their food before eating.
    B. husbands should never be suspicious of their wives.
    C. throughout history people have told stories with morals.
    D. urban legends lack meaning and purpose.

> See paragraph 19.

__*B*__ 15. From the selection we might conclude that urban legends are
      A. based upon European superstitions.
      B. worthy of serious study.   See paragraph 12.
      C. not interesting to the average American.
      D. usually about true events.

__*D*__ 16. We can infer that the lesson of the story about the cement-truck driver
and the Cadillac is   The cement-truck driver
      A. some cars cost too much.   jumped to the conclusion
      B. women should not have coffee with strange men. that his wife was
      C. don't save money for something unimportant. having an affair
      D. don't jump to conclusions.   (see paragraph 20).

Purpose and Tone

__*A*__ 17. The author (A. informs; B. persuades) the reader about urban legends
and illustrates with entertaining examples.

__*B*__ 18. In general, the author's tone is
      A. formal.   Examples of informal wording: "What's going on here?"
      B. conversational.   (paragraph 7); "The deadly hairdo . . . " (10).

__*C*__ 19. The tone of the urban legend about the babysitter (paragraph 3) is
      A. playful.
      B. forgiving.   The author emphasizes the sense of a growing threat
                    to the babysitter and the children.
      C. threatening.
      D. mocking.

Argument

__*B*__ 20. Write the letter of the statement that is the point of the following
argument. The other statements are support for that point.
      A. The baby-sitting legend relates to our desire for the safety of our
         children.
      B. Urban legends are about some of our deepest fears and concerns.
      C. "The Spider in the Hairdo" story has to do with our interest in
         cleanliness and health.
      D. Our fear of making fools of ourselves gives power to the legends
         about nudity.   Answers A, C, and D are specific examples of
                        "our deepest fears and concerns."

MAPPING

The map below divides the selection into three main parts. Complete the map by filling in the following four missing items.

- Gather more realistic details and variations as they travel
- The cement-truck driver's revenge
- What they are
- The playboy's car

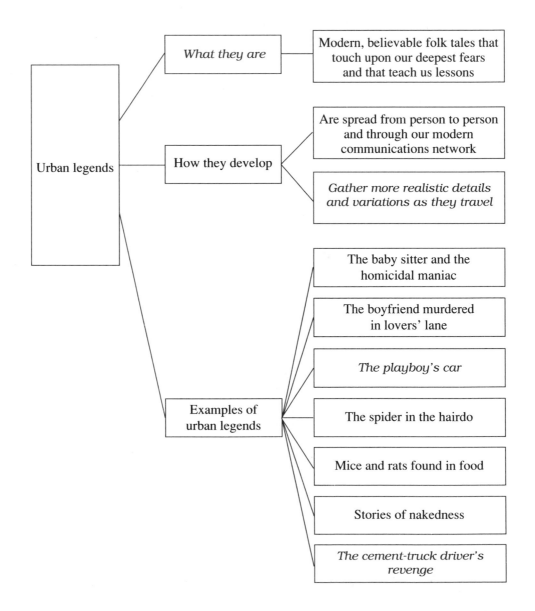

DISCUSSION QUESTIONS

1. Johnson writes that urban legends "teach us lessons." Which of the stories in the article do you think teaches the most effective lesson?

2. Have you ever heard any of the stories described, but in slightly different form? Or have you heard any story that is so dramatic that you wonder if it is true or not? Retell any such story you have heard, as best as you can remember it.

3. Johnson claims that "we haven't quite given up our need for scary stories that are a little too good to be true." In our culture, where else besides urban legends do we find such stories?

4. Frightening stories, whether in movies or in novels such as those by Stephen King, are a large part of our entertainment. In your opinion, why might people so enjoy being scared?

Note: Writing assignments for this selection appear on page 591–592.

Check Your Performance   **URBAN LEGENDS**

Activity	Number Right	Points	Score
BASIC SKILL QUESTIONS			
Vocabulary in Context (2 items)	_____	× 4 =	_____
Central Point and Main Ideas (3 items)	_____	× 4 =	_____
Supporting Details (2 items)	_____	× 4 =	_____
Transitions (2 items)	_____	× 4 =	_____
Patterns of Organization (2 items)	_____	× 4 =	_____
ADVANCED SKILL QUESTIONS			
Fact and Opinion (2 items)	_____	× 4 =	_____
Inferences (3 items)	_____	× 4 =	_____
Purpose and Tone (3 items)	_____	× 4 =	_____
Argument (1 item)	_____	× 4 =	_____
MAPPING (4 items)	_____	× 5 =	_____
	TOTAL SCORE =		_____ %

Enter your total score into the **Reading Performance Chart: Ten Reading Selections** on the inside back cover.

3

Shame
Dick Gregory

Preview

When we receive help, most of us feel grateful. But what if the help is given in an inconsiderate way? In this autobiographical piece, the comedian and social activist Dick Gregory shows that the good intentions of a giver are not enough if they don't take the recipient's pride into account.

Words to Watch

complected (1): complexioned
stoop (2): an outside stairway, porch, or platform at the entrance to a house
mackinaw (28): a short, plaid coat or jacket
googobs (29): Gregory's slang for *gobs*, a large amount

1   I never learned hate at home, or shame. I had to go to school for that. I was about seven years old when I got my first big lesson. I was in love with a little girl named Helene Tucker, a light-complected° little girl with pigtails and nice manners. She was always clean and she was smart in school. I think I went to school then mostly to look at her. I brushed my hair and even got me a little old handkerchief. It was a lady's handkerchief, but I didn't want Helene to see me wipe my nose on my hand. The pipes were frozen again, there was no water in the house, but I washed my socks and shirt every night. I'd get a pot, and go over to Mister Ben's grocery store, and stick my pot down into his soda machine. Scoop out some chopped ice. By evening the ice melted to water for washing. I got sick a lot that winter because the fire would go out at night before the clothes were dry. In the morning I'd put them on, wet or dry, because they were the only clothes I had.

2   Everybody's got a Helene Tucker, a symbol of everything you want. I loved her for her goodness, her cleanness, her popularity. She'd walk down my street and my brothers and sisters would yell, "Here comes Helene," and I'd rub my tennis sneakers on the back of my pants and wish my hair wasn't so nappy and the white folks' shirt fit me better. I'd run out on the street. If I knew my place and didn't come too close, she'd wink at me and say hello. That was a good feeling. Sometimes I'd follow her all the way home, and shovel the snow off her walk and try to make friends with her Momma and her aunts. I'd drop money on her stoop° late at night on my way back from shining shoes in the taverns. And she had a Daddy, and he had a good job. He was a paper hanger.

3   I guess I would have gotten over Helene by summertime, but something happened in that classroom that made her face hang in front of me for the next twenty-two years. When I played the drums in high school it was for Helene and when I broke track records in college it was for Helene and when I started standing behind microphones and heard applause I wished Helene could hear it, too. It wasn't until I was twenty-nine years old and married and making money that I finally got her out of my system. Helene was sitting in that classroom when I learned to be ashamed of myself.

4   It was on a Thursday. I was sitting in the back of the room, in a seat with a chalk circle drawn around it. The idiot's seat, the troublemaker's seat.

5   The teacher thought I was stupid. Couldn't spell, couldn't read, couldn't do arithmetic. Just stupid. Teachers were never interested in finding out that you couldn't concentrate because you were so hungry, because you hadn't had any breakfast. All you could think about was noontime, would it ever come? Maybe you could sneak into the cloakroom and steal a bite of some kid's lunch out of a coat pocket. A bite of something. Paste. You can't really make a meal of paste, or put it on bread for a sandwich, but sometimes I'd scoop a few spoonfuls out of the big paste jar in the back of the room. Pregnant people get strange tastes. I was pregnant with poverty. Pregnant with dirt and pregnant with smells that made people turn away, pregnant with cold and pregnant with shoes that were never bought for me, pregnant with five other people in my bed and no Daddy in the next room, and pregnant with hunger. Paste doesn't taste too bad when you're hungry.

6   The teacher thought I was a troublemaker. All she saw from the front of the room was a little black boy who squirmed in his idiot's seat and made noises and poked the kids around him. I guess she couldn't see a kid who made noises because he wanted someone to know he was there.

7   It was on a Thursday, the day before the Negro payday. The eagle always flew on Friday. The teacher was asking each student how much his father would give to the Community Chest. On Friday night, each kid would get the money from his father, and on Monday he would bring it to the school. I decided I was going to buy a Daddy right then. I had money in my pocket from shining shoes and selling papers, and whatever Helene Tucker pledged for her Daddy I was going to top it. And I'd hand the money right in. I wasn't going to wait until Monday to buy me a Daddy.

8   I was shaking, scared to death. The teacher opened her book and started calling out names alphabetically.

9   "Helene Tucker?"

10   "My Daddy said he'd give two dollars and fifty cents."

11   "That's very nice, Helene. Very, very nice indeed."

12   That made me feel pretty good. It wouldn't take too much to top that. I had almost three dollars in dimes and quarters in my pocket. I stuck my hand in my pocket and held onto the money, waiting for her to call my name. But the teacher closed her book after she called everybody else in the class.

13   I stood up and raised my hand.

14   "What is it now?"

15   "You forgot me."

16   She turned toward the blackboard. "I don't have time to be playing with you, Richard."

17   "My Daddy said he'd . . . ."

18   "Sit down, Richard, you're disturbing the class."

19   "My Daddy said he'd give . . . fifteen dollars."

20   She turned around and looked mad. "We are collecting this money for you and your kind, Richard Gregory. If your Daddy can give fifteen dollars you have no business being on relief."

21   "I got it right now, I got it right now, my Daddy gave it to me to turn in today, my Daddy said . . . ."

22   "And furthermore," she said, looking right at me, her nostrils getting big and her lips getting thin and her eyes opening wide, "we know you don't have a Daddy."

23   Helene Tucker turned around, her eyes full of tears. She felt sorry for me. Then I couldn't see her too well because I was crying, too.

24   "Sit down, Richard."

25   And I always thought the teacher kind of liked me. She always picked me to wash the blackboard on Friday, after school. That was a big thrill, it made me feel important. If I didn't wash it, come Monday the school might not function right.

26   "Where are you going, Richard?"

27   I walked out of school that day, and for a long time I didn't go back very often. There was shame there.

28   Now there was shame everywhere. It seemed like the whole world had been inside that classroom, everyone had heard what the teacher had said, everyone had turned around and felt sorry for me. There was shame in going to the Worthy Boys Annual Christmas Dinner for you and your kind, because everybody knew what a worthy boy was. Why couldn't they just call it the Boys Annual Dinner, why'd they have to give it a name? There was shame in wearing the brown and orange and white plaid mackinaw° the welfare gave to three thousand boys. Why'd it have to be the same for everybody so when you walked down the street the people could see you were on relief? It was a nice warm mackinaw and it had a hood, and my Momma beat me and called me a little rat when she found out I stuffed it in the bottom of a pail full of garbage way over on Cottage Street. There was shame in running over to Mister Ben's at the end of the day and asking for his rotten peaches, there was shame in asking Mrs. Simmons for a spoonful of sugar, there was shame in running out to meet the relief truck. I hated that truck, full of food for you and your kind. I ran into the house and hid when it came. And then I started to sneak through alleys, to take the long way home so the people going into White's Eat Shop wouldn't see me. Yeah, the whole world heard the teacher that day, we all know you don't have a Daddy.

29   It lasted for a while, this kind of numbness. I spent a lot of time feeling sorry for myself. And then one day I met this wino in a restaurant. I'd been out hustling all day, shining shoes, selling

newspapers, and I had googobs° of money in my pocket. Bought me a bowl of chili for fifteen cents, and a cheeseburger for fifteen cents, and a Pepsi for five cents, and a piece of chocolate cake for ten cents. That was a good meal. I was eating when this old wino came in. I love winos because they never hurt anyone but themselves.

30   The old wino sat down at the counter and ordered twenty-six cents worth of food. He ate it like he really enjoyed it. When the owner, Mister Williams, asked him to pay the check, the old wino didn't lie or go through his pocket like he suddenly found a hole.

31   He just said: "Don't have no money."

32   The owner yelled: "Why in hell you come in here and eat my food if you don't have no money? That food cost me money."

33   Mister Williams jumped over the counter and knocked the wino off his stool and beat him over the head with a pop bottle. Then he stepped back and watched the wino bleed. Then he kicked him. And he kicked him again.

34   I looked at the wino with blood all over his face and I went over. "Leave him alone, Mister Williams. I'll pay the twenty-six cents."

35   The wino got up, slowly, pulling himself up to the stool, then up to the counter, holding on for a minute until his legs stopped shaking so bad. He looked at me with pure hate. "Keep your twenty-six cents. You don't have to pay, not now. I just finished paying for it."

36   He started to walk out, and as he passed me, he reached down and touched my shoulder. "Thanks, sonny, but it's too late now. Why didn't you pay it before?"

37   I was pretty sick about that. I waited too long to help another man.

BASIC SKILL QUESTIONS

Vocabulary in Context

__C__ 1. In the excerpt below, the word *pledged* (plĕjd) means
   A. repeated.
   B. studied.
   C. promised to give.
   D. brought home.

   Context clue: "The teacher was asking each student how much his father would give to the Community Chest."

   "I had money in my pocket . . . and whatever Helene Tucker pledged for her Daddy, I was going to top it." (Paragraph 7)

__D__ 2. In the sentence below, the word *hustling* (hŭs′lĭng) means
   A. complaining.
   B. relaxing.
   C. studying hard.
   D. working energetically.

   The context clues are the examples: "shining shoes" and "selling newspapers" [all day].

   "I'd been out hustling all day, shining shoes, selling newspapers, and I had googobs of money in my pocket." (Paragraph 29)

Central Point and Main Ideas

___C___ 3. Which sentence best expresses the central point of this selection?
    A. Dick Gregory had a long-standing crush on a girl named Helene Tucker.   Answers A, B, and D are too narrow.
    B. The charity Gregory received was given in a way that labeled him as poor, which made him ashamed.
    C. As both a receiver and a giver, young Gregory learned that how some-thing is given is as important as what is given.
    D. Gregory grew up in a fatherless, poor family.

___A___ 4. Which sentence best expresses the main idea of paragraph 2?
    A. The author adored Helene Tucker, a symbol of everything he wanted.   Answers B, C, and D are too narrow.
    B. Everybody has a symbol of everything he or she wants.
    C. Helene Tucker made the author feel ashamed of his looks.
    D. Unlike the author, Helene Tucker had a father.

___D___ 5. Which sentence best expresses the main idea of paragraph 5?
    A. Gregory liked to eat paste.   Answers A, B, and C are too narrow.
    B. The teacher assumed that Gregory was stupid.
    C. The teacher never realized that Gregory was hungry all the time.
    D. The teacher assumed that Gregory was stupid and never realized that his poor work was the result of hunger.

Supporting Details

___T___ 6. TRUE OR FALSE? Helene Tucker represented a way of life that Gregory wished he had.   See the first two sentences of paragraph 2.

___B___ 7. After the teacher told him he was the type of person the Community Chest helped and that he was fatherless, Gregory
    A. never went back to school.   See the first two sentences of paragraph 29.
    B. felt sorry for himself for a while.
    C. stopped working.
    D. felt that Helene Tucker did not feel sorry for him.

___C___ 8. As support for his central point, the author uses several
    A. statistics.   Gregory relates his early experiences in feeling shame.
    B. expert opinions.
    C. personal experiences.
    D. famous quotations.

Transitions

___D___ 9. The sentence below contains a(n)
   A. contrast signal.
   B. comparison signal.
   C. illustration signal.
   D. cause-effect signal.

   "I got sick a lot that winter <u>because</u> the fire would go out at night before the clothes were dry." (Paragraph 1)

___C___ 10. The relationship of the second sentence below to the first is one of
   A. addition.
   B. comparison.
   C. contrast.
   D. illustration.

   The teacher's action contrasted with Gregory's expectation.

   "I stuck my hand in my pocket and held onto the money, waiting for her to call my name. <u>But</u> the teacher closed her book after she called everybody else in the class." (Paragraph 12)

Patterns of Organization

___B___ 11. The main pattern of organization of paragraph 28 is
   A. time order.
   B. list of items.
   C. definition and example.
   D. contrast.

   Gregory lists some of the places where he felt shame. (The first sentence of paragraph 28 is the topic sentence.)

___B___ 12. The pattern of organization used in paragraphs 30–36 is
   A. list of items.
   B. time order.
   C. cause and effect.
   D. comparison.

   In these paragraphs, the author narrates a series of events.

ADVANCED SKILL QUESTIONS

Fact and Opinion

___B___ 13. Which of the following is a statement of opinion?
   A. "I was sitting in the back of the room, in a seat with a chalk circle drawn around it."
   B. "Paste doesn't taste too bad when you're hungry."
   C. "She turned toward the blackboard."
   D. "Helene Tucker turned around, her eyes full of tears."

   How something tastes is a matter of opinion.

Inferences

___F___ 14. TRUE OR FALSE? In the classroom scene, the author implies that Helene is not sensitive.   See paragraph 23.

___C___ 15. In paragraph 5, the author implies that   Gregory writes that teachers "weren't interested in finding out that you couldn't concentrate because you were so hungry. . . ."
   A. he is stupid.
   B. teachers understood him well.
   C. it was difficult for him to concentrate in school.
   D. the only way he ever got food was to steal it.

___T___ 16. TRUE OR FALSE? The author implies that the wino taught him a valuable lesson.   Gregory implies this by including the wino story in his essay on shame and stating, in the last sentence, the lesson he learned.

Purpose and Tone

___T___ 17. TRUE OR FALSE? One of the author's purposes is to inform readers of how he learned the meaning of shame.   Gregory suggests this purpose in the first two sentences of the selection.

___D___ 18. The word that best describes the tone of the last paragraph of the selection is   In the last two sentences, Gregory clearly expresses his sense of shame.
   A. angry.
   B. objective.
   C. sentimental.
   D. ashamed.

Argument

___T___ 19. TRUE OR FALSE? The teacher's conclusion that Gregory was stupid did not take into account all the relevant evidence.   See paragraph 5.

___A___ 20. Which evidence from the selection supports Gregory's statement that, after the school incident, he felt shame everywhere?
   A. Gregory stuffed the plaid mackinaw into a garbage can.
   B. Gregory was always chosen to wash the blackboards on Fridays.
   C. Helene Tucker's eyes were full of tears.   See paragraph 28.
   D. Gregory wanted to pay for the wino's dinner.

OUTLINING

The following outline of "Shame" is missing two major supporting details and three minor supporting details. Complete the outline by filling in the missing details, which are listed after the outline.

Central point: Young Gregory learned both the shame of being let down by those who were supposed to help him and the shame of letting down another person.

1. *Becomes ashamed of his poverty* _____

    a. Intends to impress Helene Tucker by pledging to Community Chest

    b. *Is humiliated by teacher* _____

    c. *Leaves school and avoids it in the future* _____

2. *Becomes ashamed of his own failure to help another* _____

    a. Earns a lot of money one day and goes to a restaurant for a good meal

    b. Sees wino being beaten for not being able to pay for his meal

    c. *Offers to pay for meal, but too late* _____

Items Missing from the Outline

- Offers to pay for meal, but too late
- Becomes ashamed of his own failure to help another
- Is humiliated by teacher
- Becomes ashamed of his poverty
- Leaves school and avoids it in the future

DISCUSSION QUESTIONS

1. Why did Gregory include both the classroom and the restaurant anecdotes in one selection? What is the difference between the shame he felt in the first incident and the shame he felt in the second? What are the similarities between the two incidents?

2. What could Gregory mean by the sentence "The eagle always flew on Friday" (paragraph 7)? What does this fact reveal about his world?

3. One type of irony is an event or an effect that is the opposite of what might be expected. In what ways are the following parts of "Shame" ironic?

   - I never learned hate at home, or shame. I had to go to school for that.

   - If I knew my place and didn't come too close, she'd wink at me and say hello. That was a good feeling.

   - I looked at the wino with blood all over his face and I went over. "Leave him alone, Mister Williams. I'll pay the twenty-six cents."
     The wino got up. . . . He looked at me with pure hate.

4. Has anyone ever tried to help you in a way that didn't take all your needs into account? If so, how did you feel toward that person? In what ways might activities that are meant to help people also hurt them?

Note: Writing assignments for this selection appear on page 592.

Check Your Performance   SHAME

Activity	Number Right	Points	Score
BASIC SKILL QUESTIONS			
Vocabulary in Context (2 items)	_____	× 4 =	_____
Central Point and Main Ideas (3 items)	_____	× 4 =	_____
Supporting Details (3 items)	_____	× 4 =	_____
Transitions (2 items)	_____	× 4 =	_____
Patterns of Organization (2 items)	_____	× 4 =	_____
ADVANCED SKILL QUESTIONS			
Fact and Opinion (1 item)	_____	× 4 =	_____
Inferences (3 items)	_____	× 4 =	_____
Purpose and Tone (2 items)	_____	× 4 =	_____
Argument (2 items)	_____	× 4 =	_____
OUTLINING (5 items)	_____	× 4 =	_____
		TOTAL SCORE =	_____%

Enter your total score into the **Reading Performance Chart: Ten Reading Selections** on the inside back cover.

4

The Bystander Effect
Dorothy Barkin

Preview

A few years ago, thirty-eight people witnessed a brutal attack—and hardly raised a finger to stop it. That kind of unwillingness to get involved is the topic of this article by Dorothy Barkin, who analyzes the confusion and lack of responsibility bystanders often feel when witnessing a crime or medical emergency. She begins by describing four crisis situations—and placing you right there at the scene. How would you react?

Words to Watch

intervene (2): interfere
phenomena (4): facts
apathy (23): indifference
diffusion (32): spreading thin
paralysis (32): inability to act

1   It is a pleasant fall afternoon. The sun is shining. You are heading toward the parking lot after your last class of the day. All of a sudden, you come across the following situations. What do you think you'd do in each case?

> *Situation One:* A man in his early twenties dressed in jeans and a T-shirt is using a coat hanger to pry open a door of a late-model Ford sedan. An overcoat and a camera are visible on the back seat of the car. You're the only one who sees this.

> *Situation Two:* A man and woman are wrestling with each other. The woman is in tears. Attempting to fight the man off, she screams, "Who are you? Get away from me!" You're the only one who witnesses this.

Situation Three: Imagine the same scenario as in Situation Two except that this time the woman screams, "Get away from me! I don't know why I ever married you!"

Situation Four: Again imagine Situation Three. This time, however, there are a few other people (strangers to you and each other) who also observe the incident.

2   Many people would choose not to get involved in situations like these. Bystanders are often reluctant to intervene° in criminal or medical emergencies for reasons they are well aware of. They fear possible danger to themselves or getting caught up in a situation that could lead to complicated and time-consuming legal proceedings.

3   There are, however, other, less obvious factors which influence the decision to get involved in emergency situations. Complex psychological factors, which many people are unaware of, play an important part in the behavior of bystanders; knowing about these factors can help people to act more responsibly when faced with emergencies.

4   To understand these psychological phenomena°, it is helpful to look at what researchers have learned about behavior in the situations mentioned at the beginning of this article.

Situation One: Research reveals a remarkably low rate of bystander intervention to protect property. In one study, more than 3,000 people walked past 214 staged car break-ins like the one described in this situation. The vast majority of passers-by completely ignored what appeared to be a crime in progress.

Not one of the 3,000 bothered to report the incident to the police.

Situation Two: Another experiment involved staging scenarios like this and the next situation. In Situation Two, bystanders offered some sort of assistance to the young woman 65 percent of the time.

Situation Three: Here the rate of bystander assistance dropped down to 19 percent. This demonstrates that bystanders are more reluctant to help a woman when they believe she's fighting with her husband. Not only do they consider a wife in less need of help; they think interfering with a married couple may be more dangerous. The husband, unlike a stranger, will not flee the situation.

Situation Four: The important idea in this situation is being a member of a group of bystanders. In more than fifty studies involving many different conditions, one outcome has been consistent: bystanders are much less likely to get involved when other witnesses are present than when they are alone.

5   Thus, membership in a group of bystanders lowers the likelihood that each member of the group will become involved. This finding may seem surprising. You might think there would be safety in numbers and that being a member of a group would increase the likelihood of intervention. How can we explain this aspect of group behavior?

6   A flood of research has tried to answer this and other questions about bystanders in emergencies ever since the infamous case of the murder of Kitty Genovese.

7   In 1964 in the borough of Queens in New York City, Catherine "Kitty" Genovese, twenty-eight, was brutally murdered in a shocking crime that outraged the nation.

8   The crime began at 3 a.m. Kitty Genovese was coming home from her job as manager of a bar. After parking her car in a parking lot, she began the hundred-foot walk to the entrance of her apartment. But she soon noticed a man in the lot and decided instead to walk toward a police call box. As she walked by a bookstore on her way there, the man grabbed her. She screamed.

9   Lights went on and windows opened in the ten-story apartment building.

10   Next, the attacker stabbed Genovese. She shrieked, "Oh, my God, he stabbed me! Please help me! Please help me!"

11   From an upper window in the apartment house, a man shouted, "Let that girl alone!"

12   The assailant, alarmed by the man's shout, started toward his car, which was parked nearby. However, the lights in the building soon went out, and the man returned. He found Genovese struggling to reach her apartment—and stabbed her again.

13   She screamed, "I'm dying! I'm dying!"

14   Once more lights went on and windows opened in the apartment building. The attacker then went to his car and drove off. Struggling, Genovese made her way inside the building.

15   But the assailant returned to attack Genovese yet a third time. He found her slumped on the floor at the foot of the stairs and stabbed her again, this time fatally.

16   The murder took over a half hour, and Kitty Genovese's desperate cries for help were heard by at least thirty-eight people. Not a single one of the thirty-eight who later admitted to having witnessed the murder bothered to pick up the phone during the attack and call the police. One man called after Genovese was dead.

17   Comments made by bystanders after this murder provide important insight into what group members think when they consider intervening in an emergency.

18   These are some of the comments:

19   "I didn't want my husband to get involved."

20   "Frankly, we were afraid."

21   "We thought it was a lovers' quarrel."

22   "I was tired."

23   The Genovese murder sparked a national debate on the questions of public apathy° and fear and became the basis for thousands of sermons, editorials, classroom discussions, and even a made-for-television movie. The same question was on everybody's mind—how could thirty-eight people have done so little?

24   Nine years later, another well-publicized incident provided additional information about the psychology of a group witnessing a crime.

25   On a summer afternoon in Trenton, New Jersey, a twenty-year-old woman was brutally raped in a parking lot in full view of twenty-five employees of a nearby roofing company. Though the workers witnessed the entire incident and the woman repeatedly screamed for help, no one came to her assistance.

26   Comments made by witnesses to the rape were remarkably similar to those made by the bystanders to the Genovese

murder. For example, one witness said, "We thought, well, it might turn out to be her boyfriend or something like that."

27 It's not surprising to find similar excuses for not helping in cases involving a group of bystanders. The same psychological principles apply to each. Research conducted since the Genovese murder indicates that the failure of bystanders to get involved can't be simply dismissed as a symptom of an uncaring society. Rather, the bystander effect, as it is called by social scientists, is the product of a complex set of psychological factors.

28 Two factors appear to be most important in understanding the reactions of bystanders to emergencies.

29 First is the level of ambiguity involved in the situation. Bystanders are afraid to endanger themselves or look foolish if they take the wrong action in a situation they're not sure how to interpret. A person lying face down on the floor of a subway train may have just suffered a heart attack and be in need of immediate medical assistance—or he may be a dangerous drunk.

30 Determining what is happening is especially difficult when a man is attacking a woman. Many times lovers do quarrel, sometimes violently. But they may strongly resent an outsider, no matter how well-meaning, intruding into their affairs.

31 When a group of bystanders is around, interpreting an event can be even more difficult than when one is alone. Bystanders look to others for cues as to what is happening. Frequently other witnesses, just as confused, try to look calm. Thus bystanders can mislead each other about the seriousness of an incident.

32 The second factor in determining the reactions of bystanders to emergencies is what psychologists call the principle of moral diffusion°. Moral diffusion is the lessening of a sense of individual responsibility when someone is a member of a group. Responsibility to act diffuses throughout the crowd. When a member of the group is able to escape the collective paralysis° and take action, others in the group tend to act as well. But the larger the crowd, the greater the diffusion of responsibility, and the less likely someone is to intervene.

33 The more social scientists are able to teach us about how bystanders react to an emergency, the better the chances that we will take appropriate action when faced with one. Knowing about moral diffusion, for example, makes it easier for us to escape it. If you find yourself witnessing an emergency with a group, remember that everybody is waiting for someone else to do something first. If you take action, others may also help.

34 Also realize that any one of us could at some time be in desperate need of help. Imagine what it feels like to need help and have a crowd watching you suffer and do nothing. Remember Kitty Genovese.

BASIC SKILL QUESTIONS

Vocabulary in Context

__C__ 1. In the sentence below, the word *scenario* (sĭ-nâr′ē-ō′) means
  A. fight.
  B. relationship.
  C. suggested scene.
  D. quotation.

  "Imagine the same scenario as in Situation Two except that this time the woman screams, 'Get away from me! I don't know why I ever married you!'" (Paragraph l)

__D__ 2. In the excerpt below, the word *assailant* (ə-sā′lənt) means
  A. observer.
  B. bystander.   *Assailant* is a synonym for *attacker*.
  C. victim.
  D. attacker.

  "Next, the attacker stabbed Genovese. . . . From an upper window in the apartment house, a man shouted, 'Let that girl alone!'
    "The assailant, alarmed by the man's shout, started toward his car . . . ." (Paragraphs 10–12)

__B__ 3. In the excerpt below, the word *ambiguity* (ăm′bĭ-gyoō′ĭ-tē) means
  A. argument.
  B. uncertainty.
  C. lack of interest.
  D. crowding.

  "First is the level of ambiguity involved . . . . Bystanders are afraid to endanger themselves or look foolish . . . in a situation they're not sure how to interpret." (Paragraph 29)

Central Point and Main Ideas

__D__ 4. Which sentence best expresses the central point of this selection?
  A. People don't want to get involved in emergencies.
  B. Kitty Genovese was murdered because no one helped enough.
  C. People don't care what happens to others.
  D. Understanding why bystanders react as they do in a crisis can help people act more responsibly.   Answers A and B are too narrow; answer C is incorrect.

_D_ 5. Which sentence best expresses the main idea of paragraph 27?
  A. Bystanders always have the same excuses for not helping.
  B. There has been research on bystanders since the Genovese murder.
  C. The "bystander effect" is a symptom of an uncaring society.
  D. Research shows that a number of psychological factors, not a simple lack of caring, keeps bystanders from getting involved.

> Answers A and B are too narrow; answer C is incorrect.

_D_ 6. The sentence that makes up paragraph 28 states the main idea of
  A. paragraph 29.
  B. paragraphs 29–30.
  C. paragraphs 29–31.
  D. paragraphs 29–32.

> The two factors mentioned in paragraph 28 are introduced by the addition transitions *first* and *second*.

Supporting Details

_C_ 7. Bystanders are most likely to help
  A. a woman being attacked by her husband.
  B. in any emergency when others are around.
  C. a woman being attacked by a stranger.
  D. when property is being stolen.

> See "Situation Two" in paragraphs 1 and 2.

_D_ 8. According to the author, when there is a group of bystanders,
  A. everyone is more likely to help.
  B. it is easier to understand what is happening.
  C. they are not influenced at all by each other.
  D. each is more likely to act after someone else takes action.

> See paragraph 32.

_C_ 9. The author supports her statement that "bystanders are much less likely to get involved when other witnesses are present" with
  A. opinions.
  B. quotations from experts.
  C. research and examples.
  D. no evidence.

> The examples: The Genovese murder and the Trenton rape; the research-based information precedes and follows the examples.

Transitions

_D_ 10. In the excerpt below, *thus* serves as
  A. an addition signal.
  B. an illustration signal.
  C. a contrast signal.
  D. a cause and effect signal.

> The *cause*: confused witnesses try to look calm. The *effect*: bystanders mislead each other about how serious an incident is.

Frequently other witnesses, just as confused, try to look calm. Thus bystanders can mislead each other about the seriousness of an incident. (Paragraph 31)

_____A_____ 11. The relationship between the two parts of the sentence below is one of
- A. cause and effect.
- B. comparison.
- C. contrast.
- D. illustration.

The *cause:* you take action.
The *effect:* others may help.

"If you take action, others may also help." (Paragraph 33)

Patterns of Organization

_____D_____ 12. The pattern of organization of paragraphs 7–16 is
- A. comparison and/or contrast.
- B. list of items.
- C. definition and example.
- D. time order.

A series of events is narrated in the order in which the events happened.

ADVANCED SKILL QUESTIONS

Fact and Opinion

_____D_____ 13. Which sentence is a statement of opinion?
- A. "The crime began at 3 a.m."
- B. "From an upper window in the apartment house, a man shouted, 'Let that girl alone!'"
- C. "Though the workers witnessed the entire incident and the woman repeatedly screamed for help, no one came to her assistance."
- D. "Two factors appear to be most important in understanding the reactions of bystanders to emergencies."

The words "appear to be" tell us that the author feels it is not a proven fact that the two factors are the most important.

_____A_____ 14. The following sentence is a statement of
- A. fact.
- B. opinion.
- C. fact and opinion.

The number and outcome of the studies are factual.

"In more than fifty studies involving many different conditions, one outcome has been consistent: bystanders are much less likely to get involved when other witnesses are present than when they are alone." (Paragraph 4)

Inferences

_____C_____ 15. The reading suggests that people tend to believe
- A. theft is okay.
- B. loss of property is worse than bodily harm.
- C. bodily harm is worse than loss of property.
- D. rape is worse than murder.

See "Situation One" and "Situation Two" in paragraph 4.

_D_ 16. From the article, we can conclude that Kitty Genovese's killer
- A. knew his victim.
- B. was unaware of the witnesses.   See paragraphs 12–15.
- C. stabbed her too quickly for her to get help.
- D. kept attacking when he realized no one was coming to help her.

_B_ 17. From the article, we can conclude that of the following situations, the bystander is most likely to get involved when
- A. a man passes a clothing store from which people are carrying away clothes.
- B. a college student sees a man collapsing on a street where no one else is present.   The article suggests that bystanders tend not to help
- C. a neighbor sees a father and son fighting in their yard.   in cases of
- D. a softball team sees the coach angrily chasing his wife.   loss of property or family feuds, and when others are around.

Purpose and Tone

_C_ 18. The main purpose of this article is to
- A. inform readers about the bystander effect and the factors that contribute to it.
- B. persuade people to be more helpful in emergency situations.
- C. both of the above.   See paragraphs 33–34, in which the author appeals directly to readers.

_C_ 19. The tone of the last paragraph of this article can be described as
- A. surprised.
- B. confused.
- C. pleading.
- D. lighthearted.

Argument

_B_ 20. Write the letter of the statement that is the point of the following argument. The other statements are support for that point.
- A. "When a member of the group is able to escape the collective paralysis and take action, others in the group tend to act as well."
- B. "If you take action [in an emergency], others may also help."
- C. "Bystanders are afraid to endanger themselves or look foolish if they take the wrong action in a situation they're not sure how to interpret."   Statements A and C explain statement B.

SUMMARIZING

Wording of answers may vary.

Add the ideas needed to complete the following summary of "The Bystander Effect."

Witnesses to crisis situations are less likely to help when only property is at risk and when a woman is being attacked by a man who may be her husband. Numerous studies have shown that witnesses' resistance to helping is also increased when there are other ___*witnesses*___ ___*present*___. A famous example is the case of Kitty Genovese, who was stabbed to death at 3 a.m. while returning to her apartment. The attack went on for over half an hour. Thirty-eight people listened to her cries for help, but ___*no one called the police*___ ___*during the attack*___. In another example, employees of a roofing company ignored a rape taking place on a nearby parking lot. Two psychological factors seem to explain ___*the reactions*___ ___*of bystanders to emergencies*___. One is the level of uncertainty in the situation. If the bystanders don't know how to ___*interpret*___ a situation, they don't want to take action. The other factor is the principle of moral diffusion. The larger the crowd that is watching, the less responsibility ___*is felt by*___ ___*each member of the crowd*___. Understanding these factors can help people be more useful in emergency situations.

DISCUSSION QUESTIONS

1. Have you ever been in a situation where the bystander effect played a part? Would your behavior be any different in light of what you have learned from this article?

2. The author states in paragraph 31, "Bystanders look to others for cues as to what is happening. Frequently other witnesses, just as confused, try to look calm." Why do you think witnesses would try to look calm during an emergency?

3. In paragraph 33, the author suggests that if you understand what causes "the bystander effect," you can act appropriately in an emergency: "If you take action, others may also help." If, say, you were in a group of onlookers while a fight was in progress, what could you do that would encourage others to intervene?

4. How does the conclusion of this article clarify the author's purpose for the reader? How does the article's beginning fit in with that purpose?

Note: Writing assignments for this selection appear on pages 592–593.

Check Your Performance   **THE BYSTANDER EFFECT**

Activity	Number Right	Points	Score
BASIC SKILL QUESTIONS			
Vocabulary in Context (3 items)	_____	× 4 =	_____
Central Point and Main Ideas (3 items)	_____	× 4 =	_____
Supporting Details (3 items)	_____	× 4 =	_____
Transitions (2 items)	_____	× 4 =	_____
Patterns of Organization (1 item)	_____	× 4 =	_____
ADVANCED SKILL QUESTIONS			
Fact and Opinion (2 items)	_____	× 4 =	_____
Inferences (3 items)	_____	× 4 =	_____
Purpose and Tone (2 items)	_____	× 4 =	_____
Argument (1 item)	_____	× 4 =	_____
SUMMARIZING (5 items)	_____	× 4 =	_____
	TOTAL SCORE =		_____%

Enter your total score into the **Reading Performance Chart: Ten Reading Selections** on the inside back cover.

5

The Real Story of Flight 93

Karen Breslau, Eleanor Clift, and Evan Thomas

Preview

The terrorists had years to plan their hijacking. The passengers had just minutes to respond. But a band of patriots came together to defy death and save a symbol of freedom. Here's their story, taken from *Newsweek* magazine.

Words to Watch

chronically (5): continuously
sparsely (6): thinly
muffled (9): unable to be heard clearly
speculate (11): think
derision (17): ridicule
submission (19): nonresistance
subdue (21): control
lurching (21): moving suddenly up, down, or to the side
valiantly (32): courageously

1   In the first few days after September 11, 2001, Lisa Beamer could not sleep for more than an hour. Then she would wake up and cry. She worried about the boys, David, 3, and Drew, 19 months, and the new baby due in January. David wanted to know why, if their father loved them so much, he had gone to be with Jesus. And there was that one nagging question. Why had her husband not called her from the plane? Other passengers had called home from Flight 93 to say goodbye and talk to their loved ones. Why not Todd?

2   Then on Friday night, September 14, she got a call from her crisis counselor at United Airlines. Todd Beamer, it turned out, had made a call; it had been routed to an Airfone operator in Chicago. The counselor said she had a message for Lisa, but she was worried it might be too much to handle. "Read it to me right now," said Lisa. The letter recounted a conversation between Todd and an Airfone supervisor, Lisa Jefferson, and some last words that will never be forgotten. The next morning the two Lisas had a tearful conversation. Jefferson told Beamer that her husband had been calm and matter-of-fact. Lisa Beamer was relieved; she had not wanted her husband to die in terror.

3   Actually, Todd had been afraid. They all had been deathly afraid. But Beamer, like so many others aboard Flight 93, did not wait to die. The passengers and crew of Flight 93 went out bravely and heroically, and by doing so they may have saved countless others and spared a symbol of democracy and freedom in our nation's capitol from destruction.

4   The terrorist Osama bin Laden is said to have thought that the United States has become soft and weak. He might have been wise to have learned more about the historical willingness of Americans to die for liberty. The first American flag flown by the patriots of the early Revolutionary War was not the Stars and Stripes but a banner showing a coiled snake, with the inscription "Don't tread on me." America's latest war for freedom did not begin with a cruise-missile attack on a terrorist-training camp in Afghanistan. It began with a group of citizen soldiers on Flight 93 who rose up, like their forefathers, to defy tyranny. And when they came storming down the aisle, it wasn't the Americans who were afraid. It was the terrorists.

5   The four hijackers who took over Flight 93 were not supermen by any means. From the outset their timing was off. Flight 93 was delayed at chronically° clogged Newark International Airport for nearly 45 minutes. It did not take off until 8:42. Aboard the other planes, the hijackers moved quickly to seize control. But on Flight 93 the four terrorists waited for breakfast to be served.

6   At about 9:25 a.m., in the sparsely° filled main cabin, passengers were settling back for a snooze or popping open their laptops or picking up a novel for the long coast-to-coast flight. But passengers up front in first class may have observed something unsettling: four Middle Eastern-looking passengers tying red bandannas around their heads.

7   In the cockpit, the captain and his first officer had already been warned to be on the alert for trouble. A message had flashed on the cockpit computer screen, sent out to all United Airlines pilots by the home office. American Flight 11 had already crashed into the first World Trade Center tower, and United 175 had just plowed into the second tower. American Flight 77 had been hijacked and was headed for Washington, D.C. Flight 93's pilots,

Captain Jason Dahl and First Officer LeRoy Homer, were not told these details, just given a general warning: "Beware, cockpit intrusion." One of the two pilots simply typed, "Confirmed."

8   At about 9:25 the pilots checked in with Cleveland air-traffic control. Suddenly the air-traffic controller could hear the sound of screaming and scuffling over the open mike. "Did somebody call Cleveland?" the controller asked.

9   No answer. Just the muffled° sounds of struggle. Then silence.

10   It's not clear what was happening in the passenger cabin. After 40 seconds of silence, one of the pilots turned on the microphone again, allowing Cleveland air control to hear more muffled clamor and someone frantically shouting, "Get out of here! Get out of here!" The mike went dead again.

11   The tape of the automatic cockpit voice recorder of Flight 93 begins shortly after 9:30 a.m. The sounds it picked up were grim. Someone is crying and moaning, pleading not to be hurt, not to be killed. Some investigators speculate° that the hijackers may have slashed the throats of the pilots as the two men were still strapped into their seats.

12   In San Ramon, California, a prosperous suburb in the hills of the East Bay across from San Francisco, Deena Burnett was preparing breakfast for her three girls. The phone rang. It was her husband, Tom. "Are you OK?" she asked. "No," he said. "I'm on a plane, and we've been hijacked. They've knifed a guy, and there's a bomb onboard. Call the authorities, Deena." Then he hung up.

13   At Cleveland Center, the air-traffic controllers furiously tried to contact Flight 93. A thickly accented voice came back on the air: "Hi, this is the captain. We'd like you all to remain seated. There is a bomb onboard. We are going to turn

back to the airport. And they have our demands, so please be quiet." Investigators think the hijacker had flipped the wrong switch, thinking he was addressing the passengers over the PA system when he was calling Cleveland control instead.

14   In upstate Windham, New York, where Lyz Glick had taken her 12-week-old baby to visit her parents, the phone rang. Her husband, Jeremy, was calling from Flight 93, pouring out an incredible story. He described "three Iranian-looking men" wearing red headbands and saying they had a bomb.

15   Jeremy Glick was a 6-foot-1, 220-pound former NCAA judo champion. He told his wife that there were some other big men on the plane. Herded into the back by the hijackers, the passengers were beginning to whisper among themselves. They were talking about "rushing the hijackers."

16   United flight attendant Sandy Bradshaw called her husband, Phil, in Greensboro, North Carolina. "Have you heard what happened?" she began. "We've been hijacked." There was talk of doing something, she said. She and several of the other flight attendants were filling coffeepots with boiling water—to throw at the hijackers.

17   Back in rows 30 to 34, where most of the passengers had been confined, a rebellion was in the works. No one seems to have paid too much heed to the guard who had a red box strapped around his waist. He said it was a bomb, but he seems to have inspired more derision° than fear. If the hijackers had hoped for a timorous group of passengers, they picked the wrong plane. In addition to judo expert Glick and Tom Burnett, a take-charge type who had been a quarterback in college, there was Todd Beamer, who had never been the biggest

or fastest guy on the court but who was known as a "gamer," the team member who makes the winning play. Mark Bingham, 6 feet 5, had played rugby at Cal on a national-championship team. A risk taker, he had once been arrested for tackling the Stanford mascot at a football game. Lou Nacke, at 5 feet 3 and 200 pounds, was a weight lifter with a Superman tattoo on his shoulder. Rich Guadagno, an enforcement officer with California Fish and Wildlife, had been trained in hand-to-hand combat. Flight attendant CeeCee Lyles had been a police detective. William Cashman was a former paratrooper. Linda Gronlund, a lawyer, had a brown belt in karate. Lauren Grandcolas had organized a sky-diving expedition. Alan Beaven was a rock climber and former Scotland Yard prosecutor. The hijackers had been training for two years; the passengers came together in a few minutes. But the odds were not hopeless. There was even a pilot among them: Don Greene, the vice president of a company that made safety devices for airlines, had flown single-engine aircraft.

18   At about 9:45 a.m., Tom Burnett called Deena again. He told her that the hijackers claimed to have a bomb, but he was skeptical. "I think they're bluffing," he said. "We're going to do something," he went on. "I've got to go."

19   Todd Beamer may have been having trouble with his credit card, or he may just have punched 0 into the Airfone. In any case, his call at 9:45 was routed to the GTE Customer Center in Oakbrook, Illinois. An operator told supervisor Lisa Jefferson that she had a call from a man who said his plane was being hijacked. "This is Mrs. Jefferson," said the GTE supervisor, in her calmest, most professional voice. "What is your situation?" In an equally calm and businesslike way, Beamer told her. In the cabin, the hijackers must have realized that the passengers were stirring against them. One of the hijackers begins praying. Another suggests using an ax—there is one hanging in the back of the cockpit, to break out in case of fire—to scare the passengers into submission°.

20   In the back of the plane, knots of passengers were talking to each other, debating how to strike. At one point Jeremy Glick told Lyz that the passengers were taking a vote. "What do you think we should do?" he asked. "Go for it," answered Lyz. She was no longer panicked. "Do what you have to do." Jeremy took heart. There was some discussion, he said, among the passengers about what they could use for weapons. "I've got my butter knife from breakfast," he joked.

21   In the cockpit, the hijackers apparently decided to try to subdue° the restless passengers by knocking them off their feet. Switching off the autopilot, the hijacker pilot sent the plane lurching° and bobbing.

22   For a moment Todd Beamer's composure cracked. "Jesus, we're going down," he said, his voice rising. Then he steadied. "We're coming back up," he told Lisa Jefferson. "No, I think we're just turning around. We're heading north. I don't know where we're heading."

23   Up to this moment, Beamer had been all business. "Lisa," he said suddenly. "Yes?" responded Jefferson. "That's my wife," said Beamer. "Well, that's my name, too, Todd," said Jefferson. "Oh, my God," said Beamer. "I don't think we're going to get out of this thing. I'm going to have to go out on faith." Beamer asked her to promise to call his wife if he didn't make it home. He told her about his little boys and the new baby on the way. Then he said that

the passengers were going to try to jump the hijackers. He asked her to pray with him. He began to recite the ancient litany, and she joined him:

Our Father which art in heaven, Hallowed be thy name.
Thy kingdom come. Thy will be done in earth, as it is in heaven.
Give us this day our daily bread.
And forgive us our trespasses, as we forgive those who trespass against us.
And lead us not into temptation, but deliver us from evil: For thine is the kingdom, and the power, and the glory, for ever. Amen.

24 "Jesus help me," Beamer said. He recited the 23rd Psalm. Then Jefferson heard him say:

25 "Are you guys ready? Let's roll."

26 In the minutes before they fought to save their dignity and honor, if not their lives, the passengers of Flight 93 showed small acts of kindness and grace. They said goodbye to their families and to each other. Lauren Grandcolas left a message for her husband, Jack, on the answering machine, telling him how much she loved him and her family. Elizabeth Wainio, 28, reached her stepmother, Esther, in Catonsville, Maryland. She said she had been frightened, but that a nice woman next to her had comforted her and told her to call home.

27 In Greensboro, North Carolina, as he talked to his wife, flight attendant Sandy, Phil Bradshaw could hear a group of men reciting the 23rd Psalm: "Yea, though I walk through the valley of the shadow of death, I will fear no evil . . ."

28 Sandy told him it was time to go. "We're running to first class now," she said. CeeCee Lyles called her husband, Lorne. "Babe," she said, "my plane's been hijacked." They talked about their love and their four boys. Suddenly Lorne heard screaming, and CeeCee yelled, "They're doing it! They're doing it!" Elizabeth Wainio ended her phone call with her stepmother, saying, "I've got to go, they're breaking into the cockpit. I love you. Goodbye."

29 The distance on a Boeing 757 from the rear galley to the cockpit door is 110 feet. It's not known who led the charge, or how many followed. When *Newsweek* interviewed the families and friends of the passengers of Flight 93, they all imagined their loved one in the hero's role—whether it was a grandmother whacking away at a hijacker with her purse or a disabled sister tripping a hijacker with her cane. In a sense they were all right; resistance—fierce, unyielding resistance—was the spirit of Flight 93.

30 Beginning at 9:57, the cockpit voice recorder began to pick up the sounds of a death struggle. There is the crash of galley dishes and trays being hurled, a man's voice screaming loudly. One of the passengers cries out, "Let's get them!" The end is near. The hijackers can be heard talking about finishing off the plane, which has begun to dive. The cockpit voice recorder picks up shouting by one of the male passengers. It is unclear whether the passengers have broken into the cockpit or are just outside the door. The hijackers apparently begin to fight among themselves for the controls, demanding, "Give it to me."

31 In the hilly country of Somerset County, Pennsylvania, eyewitnesses saw a plane rocking from side to side, like a seesaw, as it plunged toward the earth. The crater in the field was 50 feet deep after it hit, but nothing compared with what the Capitol or the White House might have looked like if Flight 93 had kept on its course.

32   Amid her sorrow, Lisa Beamer can laugh a little now about her strange celebrity as the Hero Widow, about the time she asked the CNN limo to stop at Macy's so she could get a new maternity dress on the way to *Larry King Live*. She still goes from time to time to Todd's den. It was on his desk that she found, on a folded piece of paper at the bottom of his in-box, a passage quoting Teddy Roosevelt:

> *The credit belongs to the man who is actually in the arena . . . who strives valiantly°, who knows the great enthusiasms, the great devotions, and spends himself in worthy causes. Who, at best, knows the triumph of high achievement and who, at worst, if he fails, fails while daring greatly so that his place shall never be with those cold and timid souls who know neither victory nor defeat.*

33   In daring and dying, the passengers and crew of Flight 93 found victory for us all.

BASIC SKILL QUESTIONS

Vocabulary in Context

__D__ 1. In the sentence below, the word *clamor* (klăm′ər) means
   A. celebration.
   B. silence.
   C. music.
   D. noise.

The general sense of the sentence indicates that Cleveland air control most likely did not hear sounds of celebration, silence, or music. They'd have heard just undistinguishable noises.

"After 40 seconds of silence, one of the pilots turned on the microphone again, allowing Cleveland air control to hear more muffled clamor and someone frantically shouting, 'Get out of here! Get out of here!'" (Paragraph 10)

__B__ 2. In the sentence below, the word *timorous* (tĭm′ər-əs) means
   A. bold.
   B. timid.
   C. knowledgeable.
   D. young.

The words "they picked the wrong plane" are an antonym clue. "Timid" is the opposite of how the passengers are described and of what the hijackers had hoped for.

"If the hijackers had hoped for a timorous group of passengers, they picked the wrong plane. In addition to judo expert Glick and Tom Burnett, a take-charge type who had been a quarterback in college, there was Todd Beamer, . . . who was known as . . . the team member who makes the winning play." (Paragraph 17)

Central Point and Main Ideas

__B__ 3. The central point of the article is best expressed in the
   A. first sentence of the selection.
   B. last sentence of paragraph 3.
   C. first sentence of paragraph 28.
   D. last sentence of paragraph 31.

The details of the selection strongly indicate that the bravery of the Flight 93 passengers might have prevented a horrible disaster. Answers A, C, and D are too narrow.

_A_ 4. The main idea of paragraph 26 is best expressed in its
  A. first sentence.
  B. second sentence.
  C. third sentence.
  D. fourth sentence.

> The first sentence of Paragraph 26 promises to tell the reader how the passengers of Flight 93 showed "small acts of kindness and grace." The remaining sentences describe such acts.

Supporting Details

_F_ 5. TRUE OR FALSE? When Jeremy Glick asked his wife Lyz whether she thought the passengers should challenge the hijackers, she begged him to quietly remain in his seat.   See paragraph 20.

Transitions

_C_ 6. The relationship of the second sentence to the first one is one of
  A. time.
  B. addition.
  C. contrast.
  D. illustration.

> The behavior of the other hijackers is being contrasted to that of the four terrorists on Flight 93.

> "Aboard the other planes, the hijackers moved quickly to seize control. <u>But</u> on Flight 93, the four terrorists waited for breakfast to be served." (Paragraph 5)

_A_ 7. The relationship of the second sentence below to the first is one of
  A. time.
  B. addition.
  C. contrast.
  D. illustration.

> "He told her about his little boys and the new baby on the way. <u>Then</u> he said that the passengers were going to try to jump the hijackers." (Paragraph 23)

Patterns of Organization

_A_ 8. Paragraph 4 (A. compares; B. contrasts; C. defines; D. illustrates) the passengers on Flight 93 and the heroes of the American Revolution.

> Both groups were willing "to die for liberty." The comparison word *like* in paragraph 4 is a clue to the relationship.

_D_ 9. The main pattern of organization of paragraph 17 is
  A. definition and example.
  B. cause and effect.
  C. comparison.
  D. list of items.

> Most of the details in paragraph 17 list the passengers and describe the attributes of each.

___C___ 10. The main overall pattern of organization of the selection is
  A. definition.
  B. contrast.
  C. time order.
  D. comparison.

> The selection mostly chronicles what happened during the last flight of Flight 93 on the morning of September 11, 2001.

ADVANCED SKILL QUESTIONS

Fact and Opinion

___B___ 11. The sentence below is
  A. a fact.
  B. an opinion.

> *Wise* is a value word.

"[Osama bin Laden] might have been wise to have learned more about the historical willingness of Americans to die for liberty." (Paragraph 4)

___A___ 12. The sentence below is
  A. a fact.
  B. an opinion.

> The sentence provides verifiable details about Jeremy Glick.

"Jeremy Glick was a 6 foot 1, 220-pound former NCAA judo champion." (Paragraph 15)

Inferences

___B___ 13. In paragraph 5, the authors imply that
  A. various political conditions justified the actions of the Flight 93 hijackers.
  B. the hijackers of Flight 93 were less competent than the other September 11th hijackers.
  C. if Flight 93 had departed on time, it would never have been hijacked.
  D. officials at Newark International Airport could have prevented the hijacking of Flight 93.

13. Expressions such as "not supermen," "their timing was off," "Aboard the other planes, the hijackers moved quickly.... But on Flight 93 the four terrorists waited for breakfast. ..." show that the hijackers of Flight 93 were not as organized and single-minded as those on the other planes.

___D___ 14. We can infer from paragraph 29 that
  A. the families and friends of the Flight 93 victims all have unhealthy imaginations.
  B. there is evidence that a grandmother and a disabled woman led the attack against the hijackers.
  C. the hijackers admired the bravery and resolve of the passengers.
  D. the surviving families and friends find comfort in the idea of the passengers' heroism.

> The words "they all imagined their loved one in the hero's role" show that families and friends believe in the heroism of those lost in the crash of Flight 93.

_D_ 15. The authors imply that the note Lisa Beamer found on her late husband's desk illustrates
See paragraph 32.
   A. that Todd was an expert on Teddy Roosevelt.
   B. Todd's belief that people should avoid violence at all costs.
   C. that Todd liked to keep secrets from his wife.
   D. Todd's belief that heroism comes through decisive action.

_D_ 16. We can infer that the authors got information for their article from
   A. interviews with friends and family of the passengers and Phil Bradshaw.
Answer A has supporting details in many paragraphs.
   B. the cockpit voice recorder.
Answer B has supporting details in paragraphs 10, 11, 13, and 30.
   C. eyewitnesses of the crash.
Answer C has supporting details in paragraph 31.
   D. all of the above.

Purpose and Tone

The article makes no attempt to persuade readers to think

_A_ 17. The main purpose of this selection is to   or act differently, nor is it meant
   A. inform and inspire.   merely to entertain. It simply informs us
   B. persuade readers to act.   of the events on that September morning—
   C. entertain.   and at the same time shows us the heroism
of which ordinary Americans are capable.

_C_ 18. In general, the authors' tone in the selection is
   A. lighthearted and optimistic.   Adjectives used to describe the
   B. objective and scientific.   character and actions of passengers
   C. serious and respectful.   show the authors' respect for them.
   D. angry and scornful.   Details are presented in a serious manner.

_B_ 19. The tone of paragraph 4 can be described as being
   A. sorrowful.
   B. prideful.   Adjectives used in paragraph 4
   C. bitter.   convey pride in both the
   D. forgiving.   forefathers and the passengers.

Argument

_D_ 20. Write the letter of the statement that is the point of the following argument. The other statements are support for that point.
   A. Several of the Flight 93 passengers were athletes or had been trained in combat.
   B. Todd Beamer told Lisa Jefferson that the passengers would try to "jump" the hijackers.
   C. Beginning at 9:57, the cockpit voice recorder picked up the sounds of a struggle between the passengers and the hijackers.
   D. Osama bin Laden was wrong to think Americans were soft and weak.
Answers, A, B, and C give evidence that these Americans were strong, not soft and weak.

OUTLINING

Complete the following general outline of "The Real Story of Flight 93" by filling in the missing paragraph numbers and missing topics.

1. Introduction—paragraphs 1 to __4__

   a. _Lisa Beamer's conversations with counselor and Airfone supervisor_

   b. Fighting of Flight 93 passengers despite fear

   c. Americans' willingness to die for liberty

2. _Narrative of the events of Flight 93_ _____—paragraphs

   __5__ to __31__

3. Conclusion—paragraphs __32__ to 33

   a. _Lisa Beamer as hero's widow_

   b. _Teddy Roosevelt's words_

   c. Final statement of admiration and gratitude

   Items Missing from the Outline

   • Narrative of the events of Flight 93

   • Teddy Roosevelt's words

   • Lisa Beamer as hero's widow

   • Lisa Beamer's conversations with counselor and Airfone supervisor

DISCUSSION QUESTIONS

1. Where were you on the terrible day of September 11th, 2001, and what were your reactions to the events of that day?

2. How did reading this selection affect you? For example, as you were reading, did you feel pity, anger, horror, surprise, admiration, pride, or a combination of the above? Explain.

3. While the selection focuses mainly on the struggle between a group of passengers and the hijackers, we are also given specific details about individual passengers. Which details would you say are particularly effective in making you see these people as individuals? If you could interview any of the passengers, whom would you choose, and what questions would you want to ask?

4. The authors of this selection—and people throughout the world—have celebrated the passengers of Flight 93 as true heroes. Do you agree with this view? Why or why not? In stating your case, compare your personal definition of the word *hero* with the behaviors of the passengers.

Note: Writing assignments for this selection appear on page 593.

Check Your Performance	THE REAL STORY OF FLIGHT 93		
Activity	*Number Right*	*Points*	*Score*
BASIC SKILL QUESTIONS			
Vocabulary in Context (2 items)	_____	× 4 =	_____
Central Point and Main Ideas (2 items)	_____	× 4 =	_____
Supporting Details (1 item)	_____	× 4 =	_____
Transitions (2 items)	_____	× 4 =	_____
Patterns of Organization (3 items)	_____	× 4 =	_____
ADVANCED SKILL QUESTIONS			
Fact and Opinion (2 items)	_____	× 4 =	_____
Inferences (4 items)	_____	× 4 =	_____
Purpose and Tone (3 items)	_____	× 4 =	_____
Argument (1 item)	_____	× 4 =	_____
OUTLINING (4 items)	_____	× 20 =	_____
	TOTAL SCORE =		_____ %

Enter your total score into the **Reading Performance Chart: Ten Reading Selections** on the inside back cover.

6

Coping with Nervousness
Rudolph F. Verderber

Preview

Do you have trouble relaxing when you speak in front of a group? Do your legs tremble, does your heart pound, is your mouth dry? For many people, public speaking can be a nerve-racking experience. However, there are ways to deal with the nervousness. In this selection from his widely used college textbook *Communicate!* (Seventh Edition, Wadsworth), Rudolph F. Verderber provides information that may make your future speaking assignments less painful.

Words to Watch

virtually (2): almost
channel (3): direct
adrenaline (4): a hormone that stimulates and strengthens parts of the body
flabbergasted (5): amazed
eliciting (5): drawing out
psyching . . . up (9): preparing (oneself) psychologically
initial (10): first

1   Most people confess to extreme nervousness at even the thought of giving a speech. Yet you must learn to cope with nervousness because speaking is important. Through speaking, we gain the power to share what we are thinking with others. Each of us has vital information to share: we may have the data needed to solve a problem; we may have an idea for a procedure that will save money for our company or group; we may have insights that will influence

the way people see an issue. We can only imagine the tremendous loss to business, governmental, educational, professional, and fraternal groups because anxiety prevents people from speaking up.

2   Let's start with the assumption that you are indeed nervous—you may in fact be scared to death. Now what? Experience has proved that virtually° anyone can learn to cope with the fear of public speaking. Consider the following points:

3   *1. You are in good company.* Not only do most beginning speakers suffer anxiety at the thought of speaking in public, but many experienced speakers confess to nervousness when they speak as well. Now, you may think, "Don't give me that line—you can't tell me that [fill in the name of a good speaker you know] is nervous when speaking in public!" Ask the person. He or she will tell you. Even powerful speakers like Abraham Lincoln and Franklin D. Roosevelt were nervous before speaking. The difference in nervousness among people is a matter of degree. Some people tremble, perspire, and experience shortness of breath and increased heartbeat. As they go through their speech, they may be so preoccupied with themselves that they lose contact with the audience, jump back and forth from point to point, and on occasion forget what they had planned to say. Others, however, may get butterflies in their stomachs and feel weak in the knees—and still go on to deliver a strong speech. The secret is not to get rid of all of your feelings but to learn to channel° and control your nervousness.

2. Despite nervousness, you can make it through a speech. Very few people are so bothered by anxiety that they are unable to proceed with the speech. You may not enjoy the experience—especially the first time—but you can do it. In fact, it would be detrimental if you were not nervous. Why? Because you must be a little more aroused than usual to do your best. A bit of nervousness gets the adrenaline° flowing—and that brings you to speaking readiness.   4

3. Your listeners aren't nearly as likely to recognize your fear as you might think. "The only thing we have to fear," Franklin Roosevelt said, "is fear itself." Many speakers worry that others will notice how nervous they are—and that makes them even more self-conscious and nervous. The fact is that people, even speech instructors, will greatly underrate the amount of stage fright they believe a person has. Recently, a young woman reported that she broke out in hives before each speech. She was flabbergasted° when other students said to her, "You seem so calm when you speak." Try eliciting° feedback from your listeners after a speech. Once you realize that your audience does not perceive your nervousness to the degree that you imagine, you will remove one unnecessary source of anxiety.   5

4. The more experience you get in speaking, the better you become at coping with nervousness. As you gain experience, you learn to think more about the audience and the message and less about yourself.   6

Moreover, you come to realize that audiences, your classmates especially, are very supportive, especially in informative speech situations. After all, most people are in the audience because they want to hear you. As time goes on, you will come to find that having a group of people listening to you alone is a very satisfying experience.

7   Now let's consider what you can do about your nervousness. Coping with nervousness begins during the preparation process and extends to the time you actually begin the speech.

8   The best way to control nervousness is to pick a topic you know something about and are interested in. Public speakers cannot allow themselves to be saddled with a topic they don't care about. An unsatisfactory topic lays the groundwork for a psychological mindset that almost guarantees nervousness at the time of the speech. By the same token, selecting a topic you are truly interested in will help you focus on what you want to communicate and so lay the groundwork for a satisfying speech experience.

9   A second key to controlling nervousness is to prepare adequately for your speech. If you feel in command of your material and delivery, you'll be far more confident. During the preparation period, you can also be "psyching yourself up°" for the speech. Even in your classroom speeches, if you have a suitable topic, and if you are well prepared, your audience will feel they profited from listening to you. Before you say, "Come on, who are you trying to kid!" think of lectures, talks, and speeches you have heard. When the speaker seemed knowledgeable and conveyed enthusiasm, weren't you

impressed? The fact is that some of the speeches you hear in class are likely to be among the best and most informative or moving speeches you are ever going to hear. Public speaking students learn to put time and effort into their speeches, and many classroom speeches turn out to be surprisingly interesting and valuable. If you work at your speech, you will probably sense that your class looks forward to listening to you.

10   Perhaps the most important time for coping with nervousness is shortly before you give your speech. Research indicates that it is during the period right before you walk up to give your speech and the time when you have your initial° contact with the audience that your fear is most likely to be at its greatest.

11   When speeches are being scheduled, you may be able to control when you speak. Are you better off "getting it over with," that is, being the first person to speak that day? If so, you may be able to volunteer to go first. But regardless of when you are scheduled to speak, try not to spend your time thinking about yourself or your speech. At the moment the class begins, you have done all you can to be prepared. This is the time to focus your mind on something else. Try to listen to each of the speeches that come before yours. Get involved with what each speaker is saying. When your turn comes, you will be far more relaxed than if you had spent the time worrying about your own speech.

12   As you walk to the speaker's stand, remind yourself that you have ideas you want to convey, that you are well prepared, and that your audience is going to want to hear what you have to say. Even if you make mistakes, the audience will be focusing on your ideas and will profit from your speech.

13   When you reach the stand, pause a few seconds before you start and establish eye contact with the audience. Take a deep breath to help get your breathing in order. Try to move about a little during the first few sentences— sometimes, a few gestures or a step one way or another is enough to break some of the tension. Above all, concentrate on communicating with your audience— your goal is to share your ideas, not to give a performance.

BASIC SKILL QUESTIONS

Vocabulary in Context

_C_   1. In the excerpt below, the word *detrimental* (dĕt′rə-mĕn′tl) means
    A. helpful.
    B. expensive.
    C. harmful.
    D. funny.

> "Despite nervousness, you can make it through a speech. . . . In fact, it would be detrimental if you were not nervous. Why? Because you must be a little more aroused than usual to do your best." (Paragraph 4)

_B_   2. In the excerpt below, the word *conveyed* (kən-vād′) means
    A. prevented.
    B. communicated.
    C. forgot.
    D. delayed.

> "When the speaker seemed knowledgeable and conveyed enthusiasm, weren't you impressed?" (Paragraph 9)

Central Point and Main Ideas

_B_   3. Which sentence best expresses the central point of the selection?
    A. Nearly everyone feels nervous about speaking in public.
    B. It is possible to control the fear of public speaking.
    C. You can control your nervousness about speaking by picking a topic that interests you.   Answers A, C, and D are too narrow.
    D. Even famous speakers report feeling nervous before giving speeches.

_A_   4. Which sentence best expresses the main idea of paragraph 3?
    A. Nearly everyone gets nervous before giving a speech, but good speakers are able to channel and control their nervousness.
    B. Franklin D. Roosevelt and Abraham Lincoln were nervous before speaking.   Answers B, C, and D are too narrow.
    C. Giving a speech can be a stressful experience.
    D. Speakers who tremble, perspire, and experience shortness of breath and increased heartbeat may lose contact with the audience.

__C__ 5. Which sentence best expresses the main idea of paragraphs 7–13?
  A. When preparing a speech, choose a topic you know something about and are interested in.
  B. You will feel far more confident about a speech if you prepare adequately for it.   Answers A, B, and D are too narrow.
  C. There are various things you can do to cope with nervousness during the preparation for and beginning of a speech.
  D. According to research, it is just before you walk up to give your speech and the time of your first contact with the audience that your fear is likely to be at its greatest.

Supporting Details

__C__ 6. The supporting details in paragraphs 3–6 are
  A. reasons public speaking is important.
  B. suggestions for avoiding the fear of public speaking.
  C. evidence that people learn to deal with the fear of public speaking.
  D. steps in the process of public speaking.   See paragraph 2.

__B__ 7. Nervousness
  A. is rarely experienced by people who give speeches on a regular basis.
  B. can actually help a speaker to do his or her best.
  C. cannot be effectively controlled.   See paragraph 4.
  D. always interferes with the effectiveness of a speech.

__C__ 8. The audience
  A. is usually able to tell how nervous a speaker is.
  B. should never be allowed to make direct eye contact with the speaker.   See paragraph 5.
  C. usually underestimates the nervousness of a speaker.
  D. rarely is interested in classroom speeches.

__B__ 9. One way to control being nervous about a speech is to
  A. speak loudly.
  B. prepare adequately.   See paragraph 9.
  C. avoid eye contact.
  D. all of the above.

Transitions

__D__ 10. The sentence below expresses a relationship of
  A. addition.
  B. time.
  C. cause and effect.   How you feel is contrasted with
  D. contrast.   what you can achieve.

    "Despite nervousness, you can make it through a speech." (Paragraph 4)

_A_ 11. The relationship of the second sentence below to the first is one of
- A. addition.
- B. illustration.
- C. contrast.
- D. cause and effect.

> A second thing learned from experience is being added to a first one.

"As you gain experience, you learn to think more about the audience and the message and less about yourself. <u>Moreover,</u> you come to realize that audiences, your classmates especially, are very supportive, especially in informative speech situations." (Paragraph 6)

Patterns of Organization

_A_ 12. The main pattern of organization of paragraphs 3–6 is
- A. list of items.
- B. time order.
- C. contrast.
- D. definition and example.

> The paragraphs list points that prove that "anyone can learn to cope with the fear of public speaking."

_A_ 13. The main pattern of organization of paragraphs 7–13 is
- A. time order.
- B. contrast.
- C. comparison.
- D. definition and example.

> These paragraphs present steps that take place "during the preparation process" and "the time you actually begin the speech."

ADVANCED SKILL QUESTIONS

Fact and Opinion

_A_ 14. The sentence below is
- A. a fact.
- B. an opinion.
- C. both fact and opinion.

> While fear is subjective, it is real and can be studied factually.

"Research indicates that it is during the period right before you walk up to give your speech and the time when you have your initial contact with the audience that your fear is most likely to be at its greatest." (Paragraph 10)

Inferences

_A_ 15. The author suggests that
- A. thinking about your speech shortly before giving it is likely to make you more nervous.
- B. you should revise your speech up until the last possible moment.
- C. it is always best to try to be the first speaker of the day.
- D. with proper preparation, you will certainly not be nervous once your speech begins.

See paragraph 11.

___D___ 16. The author suggests that with practice, you
  A. can completely get over all fear of speaking in public.
  B. will find it is no longer so necessary to be in command of your speech material.
  C. will choose better and better topics for your speeches.
  D. will experience less fear.   See, for example, the end of paragraph 5 and the end of paragraph 11.

___D___ 17. The author implies that
  A. it is possible to think about your speech too much.   See paragraph 11.
  B. everyone has worthwhile ideas to share in a speech.   See paragraph 1.
  C. making mistakes in a speech doesn't ruin it.   See paragraph 12.
  D. all of the above.

Purpose and Tone

___C___ 18. The purpose of this reading is
  A. to inform.
  B. to persuade.
  C. both of the above.

  The author wishes to *persuade* us "to cope with nervousness because speaking is important" and to *inform* us about how to do so.

___A___ 19. The tone of this reading is
  A. optimistic and helpful.
  B. outspoken and critical.
  C. sympathetic and forgiving.
  D. excited and joyous.

  The author stresses the positive aspects of speaking and the likelihood of success and provides encouraging advice.

Argument

___A___ 20. One of the following statements is the point of the author's argument in paragraph 1. The other statements are support for that point. Write the letter of the point of the argument.   Answers B, C, and D are reasons why speaking is important.
  A. Speaking is important.
  b. Speaking gives us the power to share our thoughts with others.
  c. Through speaking, we can provide the data needed to solve a problem.
  D. We may be able to share a money-saving idea for our company.

OUTLINING

Complete the outline by filling in the missing major and minor details. The missing items are listed in random order below the outline.

Central point: You can cope with the nervousness of public speaking.

  A. Introduction: Since speaking is important, it's important to learn to cope with nervousness.

B. _People can learn to cope with the fear of public speaking._

1. Even good speakers get nervous; they just learn to channel and control their nervousness.
2. Nervousness won't stop you from completing a speech, and it will even help you.
3. Your nervousness during a speech won't show nearly as much as you might think it will.
4. The more experience you get in speaking, the better you become at coping with nervousness.

C. _There are various ways to cope with your nervousness about public speaking._

1. Pick a topic you know something about and are interested in.
2. _Prepare adequately for your speech._

3. Try to control your nervousness just before you walk up to give your speech.
   a. Try to schedule your speech at a comfortable time.
   b. Focus your mind on something other than your speech.
4. _Use coping methods for walking to the speaker's stand and just after._

   a. As you walk to the speaker's stand, focus on your ideas and the fact that you're well prepared.
   b. When you reach the stand, do a few things to break some of the tension.
      1) Pause a few seconds and establish eye contact with the audience.
      2) Take a deep breath.
      3) Move about a little during your first few sentences.
      4) Concentrate on communicating with your audience.

Items Missing from the Outline

- There are various ways to cope with your nervousness about public speaking.
- Prepare adequately for your speech.
- Use coping methods for walking to the speaker's stand and just after.
- People can learn to cope with the fear of public speaking.

DISCUSSION QUESTIONS

1. What have your public speaking experiences been like? Have some speeches gone better than others? If so, what were the differences, and what do you think were the reasons for those differences? What did you find helpful in preparing and giving speeches?

2. Why might it be a good idea to speak on a topic you know a great deal about and are interested in? Can you think of any examples from the speeches you've given or heard?

3. You may need to give speeches in your classes, but do you think you will have to speak in public after you graduate from school? In what situations might you have to give a speech or even a presentation to a small group?

4. Obviously, Verderber feels that nervousness is no reason to avoid speaking in public. What other activities have you willingly done despite the fact that they made you nervous in some way? Was being nervous in these situations helpful in some ways? If so, how?

Note: Writing assignments for this selection appear on page 594.

Check Your Performance	**COPING WITH NERVOUSNESS**		
Activity	*Number Right*	*Points*	*Score*
BASIC SKILL QUESTIONS			
Vocabulary in Context (2 items)	_____	× 4 =	_____
Central Point and Main Ideas (3 items)	_____	× 4 =	_____
Supporting Details (4 items)	_____	× 4 =	_____
Transitions (2 items)	_____	× 4 =	_____
Patterns of Organization (2 items)	_____	× 4 =	_____
ADVANCED SKILL QUESTIONS			
Fact and Opinion (1 item)	_____	× 4 =	_____
Inferences (3 items)	_____	× 4 =	_____
Purpose and Tone (2 items)	_____	× 4 =	_____
Argument (1 item)	_____	× 4 =	_____
OUTLINING (4 items)	_____	× 20 =	_____
		TOTAL SCORE =	_____%

Enter your total score into the **Reading Performance Chart: Ten Reading Selections** on the inside back cover.

7

Compliance Techniques: Getting People to Say Yes
Shelley E. Taylor, Letitia Anne Peplau, and David O. Sears

Preview

People who make a living selling products or ideas do not rely on mere chance as they make their pitch. They use time-proven techniques to convince buyers that they are getting a good deal. This selection from *Social Psychology*, Eighth Edition, reveals some widely used compliance techniques. See if you recognize any of them.

Words to Watch

compliance (1): going along with someone else's wishes
induce (2): persuade
explicitly (2): in a clear way
implicitly (2): in a way that is not obvious
replicated (4): duplicated
self-perception (5): how one views oneself
proposition (10): suggested plan
unscrupulous (10): without moral standards

1   Research has investigated the specific techniques that people use to gain compliance°. Robert Cialdini has studied car salesmen, con artists, and other professionals who earn a living by getting people to buy their products or go along with their schemes. He and other social psychology researchers have identified several important compliance techniques.

2   **The Foot-in-the-Door Technique.** One way of increasing compliance is to induce° a person to agree first to a small request. Once someone has agreed to the small action, he or she is more likely to agree to a larger request. This is the so-called foot-in-the-door technique. It is used explicitly° or implicitly° in many advertising campaigns. Advertisers often concentrate on getting consumers to do something connected with the product—even sending back a card saying that they do not want it. The advertisers apparently think that any act connected with the product increases the likelihood that the consumer will buy it in the future.

3   A classic study by Freedman and Fraser demonstrated this effect. Experimenters went from door to door and told homemakers they were working for the Committee for Safe Driving. They said they wanted the women's support for this campaign and asked them to sign a petition that was to be sent to the state's senators. The petition requested the senators to work for legislation to encourage safe driving. Almost all the women agreed to sign. Several weeks later, different experimenters contacted the same women and also other women who had not been approached before. At this time, all the women were asked to put in their front yards a large, unattractive sign that read "Drive Carefully."

4   The results were striking. Over 55 percent of the women who had previously endorsed the petition (a small request) also agreed to post the sign (a relatively large request). In contrast, less than 17 percent of the other women agreed to post the sign. Getting the women to agree to the initial small request tripled the amount of compliance to the large request. This effect has been replicated° in several studies.

5   Why this technique works is not entirely clear. One explanation is that people who agree to a small request get involved and committed to the issue itself, to the behavior they perform, or perhaps simply to the idea of taking some kind of action. Another explanation is based on self-perception° theory. The idea here is that in some ways the individual's self-image changes as a result of the initial act of compliance. In the safe-driving experiment, for example, a woman may have thought of herself as the kind of person who does not take social action, who does not sign petitions, who does not post signs, or, perhaps, who does not agree to things that are asked of her by someone at the door. Once she has agreed to the small request, which was actually difficult to refuse, she may have changed her perception of herself slightly. Once she has agreed to sign a petition, she may come to think of herself as the kind of person who does this sort of thing. Then, when the second request was made, she was more likely to comply than she would have been otherwise.

6   **The Door-in-the-Face Technique.** Sometimes a technique opposite to the foot-in-the-door also works. First asking for a very large request and then making a smaller request can increase compliance to the small request. This is sometimes called the door-in-the-face technique, since the first request is typically so outrageously large that people might be tempted to slam the door in the requester's face. In one study, subjects were asked to volunteer time for a good cause. Some were asked first to give a huge amount of time. When they refused, as almost all did, the experimenter immediately said then perhaps they might agree to a much smaller commitment of time. Other

subjects were asked only the smaller request, while a third group was given a choice between the two. The results were striking. In the small-request-only condition, 17 percent of subjects agreed. In the choice condition, 25 percent of subjects complied with the smaller request. But in the condition where subjects had first turned down a big request, 50 percent agreed to the smaller request.

7   This effect is familiar to anyone who has ever bargained about the price of a used car or been involved in negotiations between a labor union and management. The tactic is to ask for the moon and then settle for less. The more you ask for at first, the more you expect to end up with eventually. The idea is that when you reduce your demands, the other person thinks you are compromising and the amount seems smaller. In a compliance situation, such as asking for money for charity, the same might apply. Five dollars doesn't seem like so much when the organization initially asked for a hundred dollars.

8   Clearly, both the foot-in-the-door and the reverse tactic work at times, but we do not yet know when each of them will operate. Both seem to work best when the behavior involved is prosocial, that is, when the request is to give money or help a worthwhile cause. One difference seems to be that the door-in-the-face technique works when the smaller request follows the larger request immediately and is obviously connected. The foot-in-the-door technique works even when the two requests are seemingly unconnected.

9   **The Low-Ball Technique.** Consider how likely you would be to agree to the following requests. In one case, a researcher calls you on the phone and asks you to participate in an experiment scheduled for 7:00 in the morning. In a second case, a researcher calls and asks you to participate in a study. Only after you initially agree to participate does the researcher inform you that the study will be scheduled at 7:00 a.m. When Robert Cialdini and his associates compared these two procedures, they found that the second approach was much more effective. When students were told from the outset that an experiment would be conducted early in the morning, only 25 percent agreed to participate and showed up on time. In contrast, using the second approach of initially concealing the time of the study, 55 percent of students agreed to the request and almost all of them actually showed up for the early morning appointment. Once having agreed to participate, few people backed out of their agreement when they were informed about the time of day.

10   This tactic, in which a person is asked to agree to something on the basis of incomplete information and is later told the full story, is called the low-ball technique. Essentially, the person is tricked into agreeing to a relatively attractive proposition°, only to discover later that the terms are actually different from those expected. This technique appears to work because once an individual has made an initial commitment to a course of action, he or she is reluctant to withdraw, even when the ground rules are changed. Although this technique can be effective (Burger & Petty, 1981), it is clearly deceptive. To protect consumers from unscrupulous° salespersons, laws have been enacted to make low-balling illegal for several industries, such as automobile dealerships.

11   Our discussion of the foot-in-the-door, door-in-the-face, and low-ball

techniques by no means exhausts the possible tactics people use to gain compliance. Research by Jerry Burger has begun to explore another strategy that he calls the **that's-not-all technique**. Consider this situation: A salesperson describes a new microwave oven to a potential customer and quotes a price. Then, while the customer is mulling over the decision, the salesperson adds, "But that's not all. Today only, we're having a special deal. If you buy the microwave now, we'll give you a five-piece set of microwave dishes at no additional cost." In actuality, the dishes always come with the oven, but by presenting the dishes as a "special deal" or something "just for you," the salesperson hopes to make the purchase even more attractive. The essence of this technique is to present a product at a high price, allow the customer to think about the price, and then improve the deal either by adding an additional product or by lowering the price.

In a series of seven experiments, 12 Burger has demonstrated the potential effectiveness of the "that's-not-all" approach. In one illustrative study, experimenters held a psychology club bake sale on campus. At random, half the people who stopped at the table and asked about the cupcakes were told that they could buy a prepackaged set including one cupcake and two cookies for 75 cents. In this control condition, 40 percent of those who inquired actually purchased a cupcake. In the "that's-not-all condition," people who inquired were first told that the cupcakes were 75 cents each. A moment later, they were told that actually, they would get not only the cupcake but also 2 cookies for the 75-cent price. In this "that's-not-all" condition, 73 percent of people bought a cupcake, a substantially higher proportion than in the control condition.

BASIC SKILL QUESTIONS

Vocabulary in Context

____C____ 1. In the sentence below, the word *endorsed* (ĕn-dôrst′ *or* ĭn-dôrst′) means
    A. rejected.
    B. asked for.
    C. supported.
    D. ignored.

    "Over 55 percent of the women who had previously endorsed the petition (a small request) also agreed to post the sign (a relatively large request)." (Paragraph 4)

____D____ 2. In the excerpt below, the words *mulling over* (mŭl′ĭng ō′vər) mean
    A. regretting.
    B. paying for.
    C. agreeing to.
    D. thinking about.

    "A salesperson describes a new microwave oven to a potential customer and quotes a price. Then, while the customer is mulling over the decision, the salesperson adds, 'But that's not all. Today only, we're having a special deal.'" (Paragraph 11)

Central Point and Main Ideas

   A   3. Which sentence best expresses the central point of the selection?

      A. Certain techniques are widely used to persuade consumers to buy a product or go along with a plan.

      B. The "foot in the door" technique relies on people's tendency to agree to a larger request after they have agreed to a small one.

      C. Anyone who has bargained to buy a car will recognize the "door in the face" technique.

      D. Social psychologists study why people are influenced by certain kinds of sales techniques.   Answers B, C, and D are too narrow.

   A   4. Which sentence best expresses the main idea of paragraph 5?

      A. While it is not certain why the "foot in the door" technique works, there are some likely explanations.

      B. People adjust their actions based on changes in their self-perception.

      C. It is difficult to refuse a small, reasonable request.

      D. A woman may not have considered herself to be the sort of person who takes social action.   Answers B, C, and D are too narrow.

   B   5. Which sentence best expresses the main idea of paragraph 7?

      A. The "door in the face" technique is commonly used when one bargains for a used car.

      B. When someone starts out making a large request and then replaces it with a smaller one, the second request seems reasonable by contrast.

      C. Compared with one hundred dollars, five dollars does not seem like much.

      D. People often begin negotiations by asking for more than they expect.   Answers A, C, and D are too narrow.

Supporting Details

   C   6. The major supporting details of the reading are a series of

      A. questions.

      B. events.   See paragraph 1.

      C. techniques.

      D. steps.

   D   7. One explanation given for why the foot-in-the-door technique works is that agreeing to a small task

      A. makes the person feel he or she has done enough.

      B. angers the person.   See paragraph 5.

      C. improves a person's opinion of the requester.

      D. changes the person's self-image.

Transitions

___D___   8. The relationship of the second sentence below to the first one is one of
        A. cause and effect.
        B. comparison.   The two events happened in sequence.
        C. illustration.
        D. time.

> "Almost all the women agreed to sign. Several weeks later, different experimenters contacted the same women and also other women who had not been approached before." (Paragraph 3)

___C___   9. The relationship of the second sentence below to the first one is one of
        A. time.
        B. addition.   The degree of compliance in the first condition
        C. contrast.   contrasts with that in the second condition.
        D. comparison.

> "In the choice condition, 25 percent of subjects complied with the smaller request. But in the condition where subjects had first turned down a big request, 50 percent agreed to the smaller request." (Paragraph 6)

Patterns of Organization

___A___ 10. Paragraph 5
                        The explanations are introduced with
        A. lists two explanations.   the words "one explanation" and
        B. describes two events.   "another explanation." The second
        C. defines and illustrates a term. explanation includes
        D. compares and contrasts two events. a detailed example.

___C___ 11. The main pattern of organization of paragraph 6 is
        A. list of items.
        B. time order.   The door-in-the-face technique is
        C. definition and example. defined and then illustrated in the
        D. comparison.   context of a study.

___D___ 12. The main pattern of organization of paragraph 8 is
        A. list of items.
        B. time order.   The foot-in-the-door and the door-in-the-
        C. definition and example. face techniques are compared in the
        D. comparison and/or contrast. second sentence and contrasted in the
                                next two sentences.

ADVANCED SKILL QUESTIONS

Fact and Opinion

___C___ 13. In the sentence below, the word that represents the authors' opinion is
   A. *researchers*.
   B. *several*.   The word *important* places a value on something
   C. *important*.   and thus represents an opinion.
   D. *techniques*.

> "He and other social psychology researchers have identified several important compliance techniques." (Paragraph 1)

___A___ 14. The sentence below is
   A. all factual.   While people might argue about what
   B. all opinion.   "unscrupulous salespersons" are,
   C. a mix of fact and opinion.   it is a fact that the laws have been
                                    passed for the reason stated.

> "To protect consumers from unscrupulous salespersons, laws have been enacted to make low-balling illegal for several industries, such as automobile dealerships." (Paragraph 10)

Inferences

Since the report characterizes the signs as unattractive, that feature must have been part of the study, and it conforms with the requirement that the second request should be something people would think twice about doing.

___C___ 15. We can infer from paragraph 3 that
   A. women are more likely to be concerned about safe driving than men.
   B. the experimenters were aggressive and pushy in their dealings with the homemakers.
   C. the "Safe Driving" signs were deliberately made unattractive.
   D. the researchers were truly employees of the Committee for Safe Driving.

___B___ 16. We can conclude from paragraph 5 that
   A. experiments often reveal very little.
   B. even though an experiment proves something, that doesn't mean it is fully understood.   See the first sentence of paragraph 5.
   C. human behavior is generally easy to explain.
   D. we will never know why the foot-in-the-door technique works.

___D___ 17. We can conclude that the "that's-not-all" technique works because
   A. people like to buy things.
   B. microwave ovens are especially popular these days.
   C. people buy what they need or want.   See the end of paragraph 11.
   D. people like to feel that they are getting more for their money.

Purpose and Tone

___F___ 18. TRUE OR FALSE? The main purpose of this selection is to persuade people to stop using the techniques that are described. The authors suggest that the techniques are widely used (paragraph 1) without indicating that they should not be.

___B___ 19. The tone of the reading can be identified as
   A. upbeat and positive.
   B. scholarly and matter-of-fact.
   C. concerned and angry.
   D. forgiving and understanding.

In general, the authors simply report on the relevant facts.

Argument

___C___ 20. Which of the statements does *not* support the point of the argument?

   Point: There are ways to make it more likely that people will do what you want them to do.

   A. Experiments have shown that some compliance techniques work.
   B. Salespeople find that certain techniques work better than others.
   C. There is nothing wrong with trying to influence people.
   D. People are more likely to buy something if they are made to feel it's a great bargain.

SUMMARIZING

Wording of answers may vary.

Study notes on this reading might be made up of a summary of each compliance technique, including 1) a definition, 2) an example, and 3) an explanation of why the technique works. Complete the summary below by filling in the incomplete or missing items.

Compliance Techniques

1. Foot-in-the-door technique—getting a person to agree first to a small request so that he or she is more likely to agree to a larger one. This technique may work either because people become more committed or because they change their self-image. It works even when the requests appear unconnected.

   Example: Women were more likely to agree to put a large, unattractive "Drive Carefully" sign in their front yards if they had first signed a petition asking senators to work for legislation encouraging safe driving.

2. Door-in-the-face technique—first asking for a very large request and then

   making a smaller request. The first request is so outrageously large that

   people might be tempted to slam the door in the requester's face.

   This works when the smaller request follows the larger one immediately and is obviously connected to it.

Example: Study subjects were more likely to volunteer a small amount of time for a good cause if they were first asked *to give a great deal of time.*

3. Low-ball technique— *asking a person to agree to something on the basis of incomplete information and then later telling the full story.*

This may work because people are reluctant to withdraw after making a commitment.

Example: Students were more likely to take part in an experiment at 7 a.m. if they weren't told about the time until after agreeing to participate.

4. That's-not-all technique — presenting a product at a high price, allowing the customer to think about the price, and then improving the deal either by adding an additional product or by lowering the price.

Example: *At a bake sale, customers were more likely to buy cupcakes for 75 cents if they were told they would also get two free cookies.*

DISCUSSION QUESTIONS

1. While reading this selection, did you recognize techniques that have been used to influence you to make a purchase or support someone's plan? How were the techniques used?

2. Which of the compliance techniques do you feel is most clearly deceptive? Why?

3. The authors state that no one is really sure why the "foot in the door" technique is effective, but they offer two possible explanations. Does either of these theories seem to you to adequately explain why the technique works? Can you think of an alternative explanation?

4. Imagine that you are in the business of selling home computers. Describe how you would use the foot-in-the-door technique, the door-in-the-face technique, and the low-ball technique to try to make a sale.

Note: Writing assignments for this selection appear on page 594.

Check Your Performance

COMPLIANCE TECHNIQUES

Activity	Number Right	Points	Score

BASIC SKILL QUESTIONS

Activity	Number Right	Points	Score
Vocabulary in Context (2 items)	_____	× 4 =	_____
Central Point and Main Ideas (3 items)	_____	× 4 =	_____
Supporting Details (2 items)	_____	× 4 =	_____
Transitions (2 items)	_____	× 4 =	_____
Patterns of Organization (3 items)	_____	× 4 =	_____

ADVANCED SKILL QUESTIONS

Activity	Number Right	Points	Score
Fact and Opinion (2 items)	_____	× 4 =	_____
Inferences (3 items)	_____	× 4 =	_____
Purpose and Tone (2 items)	_____	× 4 =	_____
Argument (1 item)	_____	× 4 =	_____
SUMMARIZING (4 items)	_____	× 20 =	_____

TOTAL SCORE = _____ %

Enter your total score into the **Reading Performance Chart: Ten Reading Selections** on the inside back cover.

8

Lizzie Borden
James Kirby Martin and others

Preview

A prosperous businessman and his wife lay dead, murdered with an ax. Their unhappy daughter had the motive and opportunity to kill. Modern experts strongly believe that Lizzie Borden was guilty of her parents' murder. Yet she was swiftly found innocent. In this selection taken from the history textbook *America and Its People*, Second Edition, Lizzie's acquittal is examined in light of the social views of the late nineteenth century.

Words to Watch

maintained (1): claimed
alienated (3): set apart from
grisly (5): causing horror
preponderance (7): great amount
unanimous (7): agreed upon by everyone
affirmed (7): stated
preconceived (9): decided before knowing all the facts
docile (9): obedient
frivolous (9): silly

1   Andrew Borden had, as the old Scottish saying goes, short arms and long pockets. He was cheap, not because he had to be frugal but because he hated to spend money. He had dedicated his entire life to making and saving money, and tales of his unethical and parsimonious business behavior were legendary in his hometown of Fall River, Massachusetts. Local gossips maintained° that as an

undertaker he cut off the feet of corpses so that he could fit them into undersized coffins that he had purchased at a very good price. Andrew, however, was not interested in rumors or the opinions of other people; he was concerned with his own rising fortunes. By 1892 he had amassed over half a million dollars, and he controlled the Fall River Union Savings Bank as well as serving as the director of the Globe Yard Mill Company, the First National Bank, the Troy Cotton and Manufacturing Company, and the Merchants Manufacturing Company.

2   Andrew was rich, but he did not live like a wealthy man. Instead of living alongside the other prosperous Fall River citizens in the elite neighborhood known as The Hill, Andrew resided in an area near the business district called the flats. He liked to save time as well as money, and from the flats he could conveniently walk to work. For his daughters Lizzie and Emma, whose eyes and dreams focused on The Hill, life in the flats was an intolerable embarrassment. Their house was a grim, boxlike structure that lacked comfort and privacy. Since Andrew believed that running water on each floor was a wasteful luxury, the only washing facilities were a cold-water faucet in the kitchen and a laundry-room water tap in the cellar. Also in the cellar was the only toilet in the house. To make matters worse, the house was not connected to the Fall River gas main. Andrew preferred to use kerosene to light his house. Although it did not provide as good light or burn as cleanly as gas, it was less expensive. To save even more money, he and his family frequently sat in the dark.

3   The Borden home was far from happy. Lizzie and Emma, ages 32 and 42 in 1892, strongly disliked their stepmother, Abby, and resented Andrew's penny-pinching ways. Lizzie especially felt alienated° from the world around her. Although Fall River was the largest cotton-manufacturing town in America, it offered few opportunities for the unmarried daughter of a prosperous man. Society expected a woman of social position to marry, and while she waited for a proper suitor, her only respectable social outlets were church and community service. So Lizzie taught a Sunday school class and was active in the Women's Christian Temperance Union, the Ladies' Fruit and Flower Mission, and other organizations. She kept herself busy, but she was not happy.

4   In August, 1892, strange things started to happen in the Borden home. They began after Lizzie and Emma learned that Andrew had secretly changed his will. Abby became violently ill. In time so did the Bordens' maid Bridget Sullivan and Andrew himself. Abby told a neighborhood doctor that she had been poisoned, but Andrew refused to listen to her wild ideas. Shortly thereafter, Lizzie went shopping for prussic acid, a deadly poison she said she needed to clean her sealskin cape. When a Fall River druggist refused her request, she left the store in an agitated state. Later in the day, she told a friend that she feared an unknown enemy of her father's was after him. "I'm afraid somebody will do something," she said.

5   On August 4, 1892, Bridget awoke early and ill, but she still managed to prepare a large breakfast of johnnycakes, fresh-baked bread, ginger and oatmeal cookies and raisins, and some three-day-old mutton and hot mutton soup. After eating a hearty meal, Andrew left for work. Bridget also left to do some work outside. This left Abby and Lizzie in the house alone. Then somebody did something very specific and very grisly°. As Abby was bent over making the bed in the guest

room, someone moved into the room unobserved and killed her with an ax.

6   Andrew came home for lunch earlier than usual. He asked Lizzie where Abby was, and she said she did not know. Unconcerned, Andrew, who was not feeling well, lay down on the parlor sofa for a nap. He never awoke. Like Abby, he was slaughtered by someone with an ax. Lizzie "discovered" his body, still lying on the sofa. She called Bridget, who had taken the back stairs to her attic room. "Come down quick; father's dead; somebody came in and killed him."

7   Experts have examined and reexamined the crime, and most have reached the same conclusion: Lizzie killed her father and stepmother. In fact, Lizzie was tried for the gruesome murders. Despite a preponderance° of evidence, however, an all-male jury found her not guilty. Their verdict was unanimous° and was arrived at without debate or disagreement. A woman of Lizzie's social position, they affirmed°, simply could not have committed such a terrible crime.

8   Even before the trial began, newspaper and magazine writers had judged Lizzie innocent for the same reasons. As historian Kathryn Allamong Jacob, an expert on the case, noted, "Americans were certain that well-brought up daughters could not commit murder with a hatchet on sunny summer mornings." Criminal women, they believed, originated in the lower classes and even looked evil. They did not look like round-faced Lizzie, and did not belong to the Ladies' Fruit and Flower Mission.

9   Jurors and editorialists alike judged Lizzie according to their preconceived° notions of Victorian womanhood. They believed that such a woman was gentle, docile°, and physically frail, short on analytical ability but long on nurturing instincts. "Women," wrote an editorialist for *Scribner's*, "are merely large babies. They are shortsighted, frivolous°, and occupy an intermediate stage between children and men." Too uncoordinated and weak to accurately swing an ax and too gentle and unintelligent to coldly plan a double murder, women of Lizzie's background simply had to be innocent because of their basic innocence.

BASIC SKILL QUESTIONS

Vocabulary in Context

____C____ 1. In the excerpt below, the word *parsimonious* (pär′sə-mō′nē-əs) means
   A. generous.
   B. lazy.
   C. stingy.
   D. deadly.

> ". . . tales of his unethical and parsimonious business behavior were legendary in his hometown . . . . Local gossips maintained that as an undertaker he cut off the feet of corpses so that he could fit them into under-sized coffins that he had purchased at a very good price." (Paragraph 1)

___C___ 2. In the excerpt below, the word *amassed* (ə-măst′) means
    A. spent.
    B. found.
    C. accumulated.
    D. donated.

> "By 1892 [Andrew Borden] had amassed over half a million dollars . . . . " (Paragraph 1)

Central Point and Main Ideas

___C___ 3. Which sentence best expresses the central point of the selection?
    A. Andrew Borden's unpleasant personality and cheap ways probably led to his murder.
    B. The case of Lizzie Borden should be reopened and reexamined to determine if she was truly guilty.
    C. Despite much evidence of her guilt, Lizzie Borden was found innocent of murder because of society's beliefs about women of her social class.
    D. In the late 1800s, Americans assumed that middle-class women who were well brought up were silly people who could not possibly commit a murder.   Answer A is incorrect; answer B is not addressed by the authors; answer D is too narrow.

___A___ 4. The main idea of paragraph 2 is expressed in its
    A. first sentence.
    B. second sentence.   The rest of the paragraph illustrates the fact that
    C. third sentence.   Andrew "did not live like a wealthy man."
    D. last sentence.

___B___ 5. Which sentence best expresses the main idea of paragraph 8?
    A. Lizzie had a round face and belonged to the Ladies' Fruit and Flower Mission.
    B. Americans couldn't believe a pleasant-looking, respectable woman like Lizzie could be a killer.
    C. Trials in the late 1800s were widely covered in newspapers and magazines.   Answer C is not stated; answers A and D are too narrow.
    D. Americans of Lizzie's day believed that killers looked evil.

Supporting Details

___A___ 6. The supporting details of paragraph 2 are mainly about
    A. ways in which Andrew Borden saved money.
    B. Lizzie's and Emma's embarrassment with their home.
    C. the reason the Bordens often sat in the dark.
    D. the fact that the Bordens used kerosene rather than gas for light.

The ways Borden saved money are the supporting details for the main idea. (See question 4.)

_C_   7. The odd occurrences in the Borden home began after
  A. Bridget Sullivan was hired to be the maid.
  B. Andrew Borden brought Abby home to be Lizzie and Emma's stepmother.
  C. Andrew Borden changed his will.
  D. Lizzie joined the church's Fruit and Flower Mission.

See paragraph 4.

_D_   8. When she tried to buy prussic acid, Lizzie told the druggist
  A. it was not his business why she needed it.
  B. that she needed it to poison rats.
  C. that Emma had asked her to buy it.
  D. that she needed it to clean an article of clothing.

See paragraph 4.

Transitions

_B_   9. The relationship between the two parts of the sentence below is one of
  A. cause and effect.
  B. contrast.
  C. time order.
  D. addition.

The sentence contrasts two neighborhoods.

"<u>Instead of</u> living alongside the other prosperous Fall River citizens in the elite neighborhood known as The Hill, Andrew resided in an area near the business district called the flats." (Paragraph 2)

_C_   10. The relationship of the second sentence below to the first is one of
  A. time.
  B. contrast.
  C. cause and effect.
  D. addition.

The first sentence presents the cause. The second gives the effect.

"Society expected a woman of social position to marry, and while she waited for a proper suitor, her only respectable social outlets were church and community service. <u>So</u> Lizzie taught a Sunday school class and was active in the the Women's Christian Temperance Union, the Ladies' Fruit and Flower Mission, and other organizations." (Paragraph 3)

Patterns of Organization

_B_   11. Paragraph 2 is organized as a
  A. series of events in the Borden household.
  B. list of ways in which the Bordens lived very thriftily.
  C. comparison and contrast between the members of the Borden household.
  D. definition of *wealthy* followed by examples.

The ways the Bordens saved money are listed.

_A_ 12. The pattern of organization of paragraphs 4–6 is
    A. time order.
    B. list of items.
    C. comparison and contrast.
    D. definition and example.

> The author narrates events at the time of the murder in the order in which they occurred.

ADVANCED SKILL QUESTIONS

Fact and Opinion

_A_ 13. The sentence below contains
    A. only facts.
    B. only opinions.
    C. a mixture of both fact and opinion.

> Everything in the sentence can be proved in historical records.

> "By 1892 he had amassed over half a million dollars, and he controlled the Fall River Union Savings Bank as well as serving as the director of the Globe Yard Mill Company, the First National Bank, the Troy Cotton and Manufacturing Company, and the Merchants Manufacturing Company." (Paragraph 1)

Inferences

_C_ 14. We can infer from the mention of Andrew Borden's changing his will that
    A. he had decided to leave all of his money to his daughters.
    B. he was a lawyer.
    C. his new will was unfavorable to Lizzie.
    D. his new wife was not going to inherit any of his money.

> Lizzie apparently took action because the will was changed (see paragraph 4).

_C_ 15. The authors imply that Bridget, Andrew, and Abby all became ill at about the same time because
    A. they became sick from living in the cold, dark house.
    B. they suffered from food poisoning as a result of eating three-day-old mutton.
    C. Lizzie poisoned them.
    D. Bridget poisoned them, but pretended to be ill herself to hide her actions.

> See paragraph 4.

_C_ 16. Which of the following statements is a valid conclusion based on the information in paragraph 9?
    A. The editorialist for Scribner's expressed opinions that were unusual for the day.
    B. Lizzie Borden was an exceptionally unintelligent, gentle person.
    C. Men were thought to be more competent, mature, and intelligent than women.
    D. The ax used in the Borden murders was very heavy.

> See paragraph 9.

Purpose and Tone

___A___ 17. The main purpose of this selection is to

    A. persuade the reader that society's views about women led to Lizzie Borden's being found innocent of two murders that she probably committed.

    B. inform the reader about the everyday life of a well-known nineteenth- century family and about a famous trial of the time.

    C. entertain the reader with a crime story.

> The authors show why they feel the jury was wrong.

___B___ 18. In general, the authors' tone is

    A. sad and hopeless.

    B. objective and analytical.

    C. light and amusing.

    D. bitterly critical.

> The authors present facts and reason out their meaning.

Argument

___D___ 19. Which statement does *not* support the following point?

Point: Lizzie Borden was probably guilty.

    A. She had attempted to buy poison shortly before the killings.

    B. She was miserable living with her stingy father and disliked her stepmother.

    C. She was alone in the house with her parents when the killings occurred.

> Answer D is irrelevant to the point.

    D. She was active in church and community organizations.

___B___ 20. One of the following statements is the point of an argument. The other statements support that point. Write the letter of the point.

    A. The common belief that upper-class women were unable to swing an ax well was false.

    B. The jurors' reasoning in finding Lizzie Borden innocent was faulty.

    C. The jurors' idea that criminals looked a certain way was mistaken.

    D. The jurors' belief that women were too gentle and unintelligent to plan a murder was false.

> Statements A, C, and D are reasons for the conclusion in B.

SUMMARIZING

In the space provided, write the letter of the paragraph (A, B, or C) that best summarizes the reading "Lizzie Borden."

As you read the three choices, keep in mind that a good summary will include general statements that sum up the selection. It will cover the key elements of the reading. Some specific details may be included as well.

___B___ is the best summary of the reading.

A. Lizzie Borden lived the respectable life expected of a woman of social position. One day she and her sister discovered that their father, Andrew, had secretly changed his will. Strange things then began to happen in the Borden household. First of all, their stepmother, Abby, became violently ill. After that, the Borden's maid, Bridget Sullivan, and Andrew himself became ill too. Then Lizzie went shopping for a deadly poison, prussic acid. She said she needed it to clean her sealskin cape. However, the local druggist refused to sell the poison to her. Lizzie later told a friend that she feared an enemy would do something to her father. On August 4, Lizzie was alone in the house with her stepmother. As Abby was making a bed in the guest room, someone came into the room unobserved and killed her with an ax. Later that day, Andrew came home for lunch and, feeling unwell, lay down on the parlor sofa and napped. He never woke up. Like Abby, he was axed to death. Although there is strong evidence that Lizzie was the murderer, she was found innocent in a trial.

B. Lizzie Borden lived the respectable life expected of unmarried women of her social class, but she wasn't happy. Although her father, Andrew, was rich, he was miserly, and the Borden home was grim. In addition, Lizzie disliked her stepmother, Abby. In 1892, she and her sister learned their father had changed his will. Soon after, Abby and then the maid and Andrew became very ill. After that, Lizzie tried unsuccessfully to buy a deadly poison. Then, on August 4, both Abby and Andrew were found axed to death. Lizzie was tried for the crimes. Although experts today conclude she was guilty, the jury found her innocent. Like others of their day, they believed that upper-class women were too gentle, weak, and stupid to plan and carry out a murder. Also, they believed that criminal women came from the lower classes and looked evil.

c. Andrew Borden was rich but miserly. The Borden home therefore lacked comforts. It had no running water on each floor, and the only toilet in the house was in the cellar. To save money, since kerosene was cheaper than gas, the house was not connected to the town gas main. And to save yet more money, the Bordens often sat in the dark. Furthermore, the house was in a neighborhood near the business district, not the elite neighborhood that his daughters, Lizzie and Emma, felt was equal to their social class. The sisters also disliked their stepmother, Abby. Women of the time were expected to marry, and while waiting for the proper man, to do volunteer work for the church and community. So Lizzie taught a Sunday school class and was active in such organizations as the Women's Christian Temperance Union and the Ladies' Fruit and Flower Mission. One day she discovered her father had changed his will; not longer after that, he and Abby were found axed to death.

DISCUSSION QUESTIONS

1. Based on the information in the reading, do you agree or disagree with the experts who say Lizzie was guilty? Explain your answer.

2. As you read this selection, what impression did you form of life in the Borden household? What particular details helped you form that opinion?

3. The authors imply that the story about Andrew Borden's cutting off the feet of corpses to make them fit undersized coffins was a rumor, not a proved fact. Why, then, do you think they include the story in this piece?

4. Do you believe that any of the notions about women that existed in Lizzie Borden's day are still at work in some ways today? Explain your answer.

Note: Writing assignments for this selection appear on page 595.

Check Your Performance **LIZZIE BORDEN**

Activity	Number Right	Points	Score
BASIC SKILL QUESTIONS			
Vocabulary in Context (2 items)	_____	× 4 =	_____
Central Point and Main Ideas (3 items)	_____	× 4 =	_____
Supporting Details (3 items)	_____	× 4 =	_____
Transitions (2 items)	_____	× 4 =	_____
Patterns of Organization (2 items)	_____	× 4 =	_____
ADVANCED SKILL QUESTIONS			
Fact and Opinion (1 item)	_____	× 4 =	_____
Inferences (3 items)	_____	× 4 =	_____
Purpose and Tone (2 items)	_____	× 4 =	_____
Argument (2 items)	_____	× 4 =	_____
SUMMARIZING (1 item)	_____	× 20 =	_____
		TOTAL SCORE =	_____%

Enter your total score into the **Reading Performance Chart: Ten Reading Selections** on the inside back cover.

9
Nonverbal Communication
Anthony F. Grasha

Preview

When we think of communication, we usually think of language. But a great deal of human communication takes place without speaking. When we are angry, we may make a fist. When we are happy, our faces give us away. The extent to which we reveal our feelings without words, however, goes much further than we are often aware of. In this excerpt from a college textbook titled *Practical Applications of Psychology*, Third Edition (Scott, Foresman/Little, Brown), Anthony F. Grasha provides an overview of just how much we really say without words.

Words to Watch

norms (2): normal standards
culprit (6): guilty one
manipulate (7): use
utterances (7): expressions
quivering (8): trembling

1   The way we dress, our mannerisms, how close we stand to people, eye contact, touching, and the ways we mark our personal spaces convey certain messages. *Such nonverbal behaviors communicate certain messages by themselves and also enhance the meaning of our verbal* *communications.* Pounding your fist on a table, for example, suggests anger without anything being spoken. Holding someone close to you conveys the message that you care. To say "I don't like you" with a loud voice or waving fists increases the intensity of the verbal message. Let us

examine the concepts of *personal space* and *body language* to gain additional insights into the nonverbal side of interpersonal communication.

NONVERBAL MESSAGES: THE USE OF PERSONAL SPACE

2   Edward Hall notes that we have personal spatial territories or zones that allow certain types of behaviors and communications. We allow only certain people to enter or events to occur within a zone. Let us look at how some nonverbal messages can be triggered by behaviors that violate the norms° of each zone. The four personal zones identified by Hall are as follows:

3   **1. Intimate distance.** This personal zone covers a range of distance from body contact to one foot. Relationships between a parent and child, lovers, and close friends occur within this zone. As a general rule, we allow only people we know and have some affection for to enter this zone. When people try to enter without our permission, they are strongly repelled by our telling them to stay away from us or by our pushing them away. Why do you think we allow a doctor to easily violate our intimate distance zone?

4   **2. Personal distance.** The spatial range covered by this zone extends from one to four feet. Activities like eating in a restaurant with two or three other people, sitting on chairs or on the floor in small groups at parties, or playing cards occur within this zone. Violations of the zone make people feel uneasy and act nervously. When you are eating at a restaurant, the amount of table space that is considered yours is usually divided equally by the number of people present. I can remember becoming angry and

generally irritated when a friend of mine placed a plate and glass in my space. As we talked I was visibly irritated, but my anger had nothing to do with the topic we discussed. Has this ever happened to you?

5   **3. Social distance.** Four to twelve feet is the social distance zone. Business meetings, large formal dinners, and small classroom seminars occur within the boundaries of the social distance zone. Discussions concerning everyday topics like the weather, politics, or a best seller are considered acceptable. For a husband and wife to launch into a heated argument during a party in front of ten other people would violate the accepted norms for behavior in the social zone. This once happened at a formal party I attended. The nonverbal behaviors that resulted consisted of several people leaving the room, others looking angry or uncomfortable, and a few standing and watching quietly with an occasional upward glance and a rolling of their eyeballs. What would violate the social distance norms in a classroom?

6   **4. Public distance.** This zone includes the area beyond twelve feet. Addressing a crowd, watching a sports event, and sitting in a large lecture section are behaviors we engage in within this zone. As is true for the other zones, behaviors unacceptable for this zone can trigger nonverbal messages. At a recent World Series game a young male took his clothes off and ran around the outfield. Some watched with amusement on their faces, others looked away, and a few waved their fists at the culprit°. The respective messages were "That's funny," "I'm afraid or ashamed to look," and "How dare you interrupt the game." What would your reaction be in this situation?

NONVERBAL MESSAGES: THE USE OF BODY LANGUAGE

7   *Body language* refers to the various arm and hand gestures, facial expressions, tones of voice, postures, and body movements we use to convey certain messages. According to Erving Goffman, they are the things we "give off" when talking to other people. Goffman notes that our body language is generally difficult to manipulate° at will. Unlike our verbal utterances°, we have less conscious control over the specific body gestures or expressions we might make while talking. Unless we are acting on a stage or purposely trying to create a certain effect, they occur automatically without much thought on our part.

8   Michael Argyle notes that body language serves several functions for us. *It helps us to communicate certain emotions, attitudes, and preferences.* A hug by someone close to us lets us know we are appreciated. A friendly wave and smile as someone we know passes us lets us know we are recognized. A quivering° lip tells us that someone is upset. Each of us has become quite sensitive to the meaning of various body gestures and expressions. Robert Rosenthal has demonstrated that this sensitivity is rather remarkable. When shown films of people expressing various emotions, individuals were able to identify the emotion correctly 66 percent of the time even when each frame was exposed for one twenty-fourth of a second. *Body language also supports our verbal communications.* Vocal signals of timing, pitch, voice stress, and various gestures add meaning to our verbal utterances. Argyle suggests that we may speak with our vocal organs, but we converse with our whole body. *Body language helps to control our conversations.* It helps us to decide when it is time to stop talking, to interrupt the other person, and to know when to shift topics or elaborate on something because our listeners are bored, do not understand us, or are not paying attention.

BASIC SKILL QUESTIONS

Vocabulary in Context

___B___ 1. In the excerpt below, the word *enhance* (ĕn-hăns′) means
   A. replace.
   B. reinforce.
   C. contradict.
   D. delay.

   "The way we dress, our mannerisms . . . convey certain messages. Such nonverbal behaviors communicate certain messages by themselves and also enhance the meaning of our verbal communications." (Paragraph 1)

___B___ 2. In the excerpt below, the word *repelled* (rĭ-pĕld′) means
    A. greeted.
    B. turned away.
    C. encouraged.
    D. ignored.

    Context clue: Being told "to stay away" would tend to turn someone away.

> "When people try to enter without our permission, they are strongly repelled by our telling them to stay away from us. . . ." (Paragraph 3)

Central Point and Main Ideas

___C___ 3. Which sentence best expresses the central point of the selection?
    A. It is possible to express anger without words.   Incorrect.
    B. People communicate with each other in various ways.   Too broad.
    C. We can convey nonverbal messages and emphasize verbal messages through the use of personal space and body language.
    D. According to Michael Argyle, body language has several functions.
    Too narrow.

___D___ 4. Which sentence best expresses the main idea of paragraph 7?
    A. We must plan our body language.   Contradicted in the paragraph.
    B. It is hard to control body language.   Too narrow.
    C. Actors use body language to create an effect.   Too narrow.
    D. *Body language* refers to the nonverbal ways we communicate, usually without conscious control.

___A___ 5. The main idea of paragraph 8 is expressed in the
    A. first sentence.
    B. second sentence.
    C. next-to-last sentence.
    D. last sentence.

    The first sentence states that body language serves several functions, according to Argyle. The paragraph goes on to name and discuss three functions, highlighted by italics.

Supporting Details

___A___ 6. According to Rosenthal's work, we
    A. frequently understand body language.
    B. rarely understand body language.
    C. always understand body language.
    D. never understand body language.

    See paragraph 8.

___D___ 7. To support his central point, the author uses
    A. examples.   See paragraphs 3–6.
    B. research.   See paragraph 8, for example.
    C. opinions of other experts.
    D. all of the above.

    The four categories of personal space, for instance, represent Hall's opinions on how to categorize personal space.

Comment: Item 3—The central point is clearly stated (and italicized) in paragraph 1.

_B_   8. Playing cards occurs within
      A. an intimate distance.
      B. a personal distance.   See paragraph 4.
      C. a social distance.
      D. a public distance.

_D_   9. The major supporting details of the reading are
      A. nonverbal messages and verbal messages.   See the headings
      B. communicating well and communicating poorly.   of the reading.
      C. intimate distance and body language.
      D. communicating through personal space and through body language.

Transitions

_C_   10. The signal word at the beginning of the sentence below shows
      A. addition.
      B. comparison.   The sentence contrasts the control we have over "verbal
      C. contrast.   utterances" and over body gestures and expressions.
      D. time.

    "<u>Unlike</u> our verbal utterances, we have less conscious control over the specific body gestures or expressions we might make while talking." (Paragraph 7)

Patterns of Organization

_C_   11. The pattern of organization of paragraph 3 (as well as 4, 5, and 6) is
      A. time order.
      B. cause and effect.   Each of these paragraphs begins
      C. definition and example.   with a boldfaced term which is
      D. list of items.   then defined and illustrated.

_B_   12. On the whole, paragraph 8
      A. compares and contrasts body language and verbal expression.
      B. lists the functions of body language.
      C. defines body language and gives examples of it.   See question 5.
      D. uses time order to narrate an incident about body language.

ADVANCED SKILL QUESTIONS

Fact and Opinion

_____A____ 13. The sentence below is
   A. totally factual.
   B. only opinion.
   C. both fact and opinion.

> This information can be verified in records of Rosenthal's study.

> "When shown films of people expressing various emotions, individuals were able to identify the emotion correctly 66 percent of the time even when each frame was exposed for one twenty-fourth of a second." (Paragraph 8)

Inferences

_____T____ 14. TRUE OR FALSE? Just as body language generally occurs automatically, so does the use of personal space.

_____B____ 15. Goffman's ideas on body language (paragraph 7) imply that
   A. we usually are aware of our own body language.
   B. our body language might reveal emotions we wish to hide.
   C. we can never manipulate our body language.
   D. we should learn to manipulate our body language.

_____A____ 16. We can conclude from the reading and our own experience that body language
   A. communicates positive and negative messages of all sorts.
   B. is best at communicating friendly messages.
   C. communicates poorly.
   D. communicates rarely.

_____B____ 17. Two students reviewing together for a test would be working within
   A. an intimate distance.
   B. a personal distance.
   C. a social distance.
   D. a public distance.

> See paragraph 4.

Purpose and Tone

_____A____ 18. The author's primary purpose in this selection is to
   A. inform.
   B. persuade.
   C. entertain.

> The author is simply passing along information.

Comments: Item 14 — Personal experience tells us that when people react to personal space in the ways Hall suggests, they are usually unaware of the issue of personal space.

Item 15—If our body language occurs "automatically without much thought on our part," we can conclude that we sometimes unknowingly move in ways that reveal our true feelings.

   B   19. On the whole, the author's tone is
- A. humorous.
- B. objective.
- C. scornful.
- D. enthusiastic.

> The author presents the information in a straightforward, factual manner.

Argument

   D   20. Write the letter of the statement that is the point of the following argument. Note that two other statements support the point, and that one statement expresses another point.
- A. I became angry and generally irritated when a friend of mine placed a plate and glass in my space.
- B. As we talked I was visibly irritated, but my anger had nothing to do with the topic we discussed.
- C. Business meetings take place within the boundaries of the social distance zone.
- D. Violations of the personal zone make people feel uneasy and act nervously.

> Statement C is about the social distance zone, not the personal zone.

OUTLINING

Complete the following outline of "Nonverbal Communication" by using the information in the boldface headings, italics, and numbers in the selection. (Five items need to be added to the outline.)

Central point: Our use of personal space and body language communicates meaning and emphasizes verbal communication.

A. *Nonverbal messages: the use of personal space* _____

  1. Intimate distance
  2. Personal distance
  3. *Social distance* _____
  4. *Public distance* _____

B. Nonverbal messages: the use of body language

  1. Definition and explanation of body language
  2. Functions of body language
    a. *Helps communicate certain emotions, attitudes, and preferences* _____

    _____

    b. *Supports our verbal communications* _____

    c. Helps control our conversations

DISCUSSION QUESTIONS

1. What are your answers to the following questions from the selection? Why do you think the author included these questions?

   - Why do you think we allow a doctor to easily violate our intimate distance zone?

   - I can remember becoming angry and generally irritated when a friend of mine placed a plate and glass in my space. . . . Has this ever happened to you?

   - What would violate the social distance norms in a classroom?

2. This selection includes headings, italics, labels, and numbered items. How are these related to the author's purpose?

3. What are some examples of a dating or business situation in which someone's body language might contradict his or her verbal communication?

4. Give examples from your own experience of all four types of personal space.

   Note: Writing assignments for this selection appear on pages 595–596.

Check Your Performance   **NONVERBAL COMMUNICATION**

Activity	Number Right	Points	Score
BASIC SKILL QUESTIONS			
Vocabulary in Context (2 items)	_____	× 4 =	_____
Central Point and Main Ideas (3 items)	_____	× 4 =	_____
Supporting Details (4 items)	_____	× 4 =	_____
Transitions (1 item)	_____	× 4 =	_____
Patterns of Organization (2 items)	_____	× 4 =	_____
ADVANCED SKILL QUESTIONS			
Fact and Opinion (1 item)	_____	× 4 =	_____
Inferences (4 items)	_____	× 4 =	_____
Purpose and Tone (2 items)	_____	× 4 =	_____
Argument (1 item)	_____	× 4 =	_____
OUTLINING (5 items)	_____	× 4 =	_____
	TOTAL SCORE =		_____%

Enter your total score into the **Reading Performance Chart: Ten Reading Selections** on the inside back cover.

10
Preindustrial Cities
Rodney Stark

Preview

"What was it like in London and Paris when they had only 40,000 to 50,000 residents and before they had factories or freeways, subways or suburbs?" asks Rodney Stark in his popular college textbook (*Sociology*, Fifth Edition, Wadsworth). If you think problems in big cities are modern "inventions," this excerpt from Stark's book may surprise you. In it, he discusses the uncleanliness, crowding, and crime that existed in "big" cities before machines and electricity changed society.

Words to Watch

densely (2): closely
virtually (5): for all practical purposes
ravaged (7): violently destroyed
trenches (8): ditches
strewn (9): scattered
radius (14): a line from the center of a circle to its edge
lurked (16): hid, ready to attack
incentive (18): motivation
vital (18): essential
innovations (19): things that are newly introduced
enticed (20): tempted
rampant (20): widespread
condoning (20): forgiving or overlooking
exalted (21): high
replenished (22): resupplied

1   Let us go back into history and examine what life was like in the famous cities of preindustrial times. What was it really like in ancient Athens and Rome? What was it like in London and Paris when they had only 40,000 to 50,000 residents and before they had factories or freeways, subways or suburbs?

PREINDUSTRIAL CITIES

2   Until very recently, cities were small, filthy, disease-ridden, densely° packed with people, and disorderly, and they were dark and very dangerous at night. If that description is unlike your image of Athens during the Golden Age of Greek civilization, that is because history so often leaves out the mud, manure, and misery.

3   Typically, preindustrial cities contained no more than 5,000 to 10,000 inhabitants. Large national capitals were usually smaller than 40,000 and rarely larger than 60,000. Few preindustrial cities, such as ancient Rome, grew as large as 500,000 and then only under special circumstances. Moreover, these cities rapidly shrank back to a much smaller size as slight changes in circumstance made it impossible to support them.

Limits on City Style

4   A major reason why cities remained small was poor transportation; food had to be brought to feed a city. With only animal and human power to bring it, however, food could not be transported very far. Therefore, cities were limited to the population that could be fed by farmers nearby. The few large cities of preindustrial times appeared only where food could be brought long distances by water transport. Ancient Rome, for example, was able to reach the size of present-day Denver (and only briefly) because it controlled the whole Mediterranean area. Surplus food from this vast region was shipped by sea to feed the city's masses.

5   However, as the power of the empire weakened, Rome's population declined as the sources of food supplies dwindled. By the ninth century, the sea-power of Islam had driven nearly all European shipping from the Mediterranean, and the cities of southern Europe, including Rome, were virtually° abandoned. In fact, Europe had practically no cities during the ninth and tenth centuries.

6   Disease also checked the size of cities. Even early in the twentieth century, cities had such high mortality rates that they required a large and constant influx of newcomers from the countryside just to maintain their populations. As recently as 1900, the death rate in English cities was 33 percent higher than that in rural areas (Davis, 1965). A major reason for the high mortality in cities was the high incidence of infectious diseases, which are spread by physical contact or by breathing in germs emitted by coughs and sneezes. Disease spreads much more slowly among less dense rural populations.

7   Disease in cities was also caused by filth, especially by the contamination of water and food. Kingsley Davis (1965) pointed out that even as late as the 1850s, London's water "came mainly from wells and rivers that drained cesspools, graveyards, and tidal areas. The city was regularly ravaged° by cholera."

8   Sewage treatment was unknown in preindustrial cities. Even sewers were uncommon and what sewers there were consisted of open trenches° running along the streets into which sewage, including human waste, was poured from buckets and chamber pots. Indeed, sewage was often poured out of second-story windows without any warning to pedestrians below.

9   Garbage was not collected and was strewn° everywhere. It was hailed as a major step forward when cities began to keep a municipal herd of pigs, which were guided through the streets at night

to eat the garbage dumped during the day. Of course, the pigs did considerable recycling as they went. Still, major cities in the eastern United States depended on the pigs for their sanitation services until the end of the nineteenth century.

10   Today we are greatly concerned about pollution, especially that produced by automobile exhausts and factories. But the car and the factory cannot match the horse and the home fireplace when it comes to pollution. It is estimated that in 1900 horses deposited 26 million pounds of manure and 10 million gallons of urine on the streets of New York City every week.

11   London's famous and deadly "fogs" of previous centuries were actually smogs caused by thousands of smoking home chimneys during atmospheric inversions, which trapped the polluted air. Indeed, the first known air-quality law was decreed in 1273 by England's King Edward I. It forbade the use of a particularly smoky coal. The poet Shelley wrote early in the nineteenth century that "Hell is a city much like London, a populous and smokey city." In 1911, coal smoke during an atmospheric inversion killed more than a thousand people in London, and this incident led to the coining of the word *smog*.

12   Pedestrians in preindustrial cities often held perfume-soaked handkerchiefs over their noses because the streets stank so. They kept alert for garbage and sewage droppings from above. They wore high boots because they had to wade through muck, manure, and garbage. And the people themselves were dirty because they seldom bathed. Not surprisingly, they died at a rapid rate.

13   Population density also contributed to the unhealthiness of preindustrial cities. People were packed closely together. As we saw in Chapter 13, whole families lived in one small room. The houses stood wall to wall, and few streets were more than ten to twelve feet wide.

14   Why was there such density when the population was so small? First of all, for most of its history, the city was also a fortress surrounded by massive walls for defense. Once the walls were up, the area of the city was fixed (at least until the walls were rebuilt), and if the population grew, people had to crowd ever closer. Even cities without walls were confined. Travel was by foot or by hoof. Cities did not spread beyond the radius° that could be covered by these slow means of transportation, and thus the city limit was usually no more than three miles from the center.

15   Second, preindustrial cities could not expand upward. Not until the nineteenth century, when structural steel and reinforced concrete were developed, could very tall structures be erected. Moreover, until elevators were invented, it was impractical to build very high. By expanding upward, people could have much greater living and working space in a building taking up no greater area at ground level. This could, of course, have meant that cities would become even more crowded at street level. They did not, however, because even modern high-rise cities have much more open space than did preindustrial cities, and, as we shall see, newer cities have expanded primarily outward rather than upward.

16   Preindustrial cities were not only dirty, disease-ridden, and dense but also dark and dangerous. Today we some-times say people move to the city because they are attracted by the bright lights, and we joke about small towns where they "roll up the sidewalks by 9 p.m." The preindustrial city had no sidewalks to roll up and no electricity to light up the night. If lighted at all,

homes were badly and expensively illuminated by candles and oil lamps. Until the introduction of gas lamps in the nineteenth century, streets were not lighted at all. Out in the dark, dangerous people lurked°, waiting for victims. To venture forth at night in many of these cities was so dangerous that people did so only in groups accompanied by armed men bearing torches. Many people today fear to walk in cities at night. Still, it is much safer to do so now than it used to be.

Why Live in Such Cities?

17   Knowing what preindustrial cities were like, one must ask why anyone willingly lived there and why a large number of newcomers were attracted to cities each year from rural areas.

18   One reason was economic incentive°. Cities offered many people a chance to increase their incomes. For example, the development of an extensive division of labor, of occupational specialization, virtually required cities. Specialists must depend upon one another for the many goods and services they do not provide for themselves. Such exchanges are hard to manage when people live far apart. Thus skilled craftsmen, merchants, physicians, and the like gathered in cities. Indeed, cities are vital° to trade and commerce, and most early cities developed at intersections of major trade routes.

19   In addition to economic attractions, cities drew people because they offered the prospect of a more interesting and stimulating life. As Gideon Sjoberg (1965) noted, "new ideas and innovations° flowed into [cities] quite naturally," as travelers along the trade routes brought ideas as well as goods from afar. Moreover, simply by concentrating

specialists in an area, cities stimulated innovation not just in technology but also in religion, philosophy, science, and the arts. The density of cities encouraged public performances, from plays and concerts to organized sporting events.

20   Cities undoubtedly also enticed° some to migrate from rural areas in pursuit of "vice." The earliest writing we have about cities includes complaints about rampant° wickedness and sin, and through the centuries cities have maintained the reputation for condoning° behavior that would not be tolerated in rural communities (Fischer, 1975). In part, this may be because from the beginning cities have been relatively anonymous places. Preindustrial cities may have been even more anonymous, given their size, than modern cities.

21   Consider that cities relied on large numbers of newcomers each year just to replace the population lost through mortality. As a result, cities tended to abound in people who were recent arrivals and who had not known one another previously. Before modern identification systems, many people in cities were not even who they claimed to be—runaway sons and daughters of peasants could claim more exalted° social origins. The possibility of escaping one's past and starting anew must have drawn many to the cities. But this also meant that cities then were even less integrated by long-standing interpersonal attachments than modern cities.

22   In any event, it was primarily adventuresome, single, young adults who constantly replenished° city populations. E. A. Wrigley (1969) has computed that in the years from 1650 to 1750, London needed eight thousand newcomers each year to maintain its population. The newcomers averaged twenty years of age, were unmarried, and came from

farms. Most of these newcomers came from more than fifty miles away—at least a two-day trip at that time.

23   For all our complaints about modern cities, industrialization did not ruin city life. Preindustrial cities were horrid. Yet for many young people on farms, the prospect of heading off to one of these miserable cities seemed far superior to a life of dull toil. Then as the Industrial Revolution began, the idea of going off to the city suddenly appealed not just to restless young people but also to whole families. Soon the countryside virtually emptied, as people flocked to town.

BASIC SKILL QUESTIONS

Vocabulary in Context

___C___ 1. In the excerpt below, the word *checked* (chĕkt) means
    A. encouraged.
    B. predicted.
    C. limited.
    D. increased.

    "A major reason why cities remained small was poor transportation. . . . Disease also checked the size of cities." (Paragraphs 4 and 6)

___B___ 2. In the sentence below, the word *dwindled* (dwĭn'dld) means
    A. increased.
    B. decreased.   A synonym-like context clue.
    C. remained the same.
    D. became less expensive.

    "Rome's population declined as the sources of food supplies dwindled." (Paragraph 5)

___B___ 3. In the sentence below, the word *coining* (koin'ĭng) means
    A. paying for.
    B. invention.   Context clue: New words are invented.
    C. denial.
    D. pronunciation.

    "In 1911, coal smoke during an atmospheric inversion killed more than a thousand people in London, and this incident led to the coining of the word *smog*." (Paragraph 11)

Central Point and Main Ideas

<u>B</u>   4. Which sentence best expresses the central point of the selection?
  A. Poor transportation and fortress walls kept cities from becoming too large.   Too narrow.
  B. Preindustrial cities had major disadvantages, but they still attracted people.
  C. Until structural steel, reinforced concrete and elevators were invented, it wasn't possible or practical to build high buildings.   Too narrow.
  D. Life in earlier times was very different from life today.   Too broad.

<u>A</u>   5. The main idea of paragraph 6 is best expressed in its
  A. first sentence.
  B. second sentence.
  C. third sentence.
  D. fourth sentence.

The rest of the paragraph discusses how and why disease affected the size of cities.

<u>B</u>   6. Which sentence best expresses the main idea of paragraphs 17–21?
  A. Despite the great disadvantages of preindustrial cities, people were drawn to the cities for economic reasons.
  B. Despite the great disadvantages of preindustrial cities, people were drawn to the cities for several reasons.
  C. Preindustrial cities allowed people to escape their past and start anew.
  D. Our earliest knowledge of cities includes complaints about widespread vice, and cities have kept the reputation for allowing behavior that would not be tolerated in rural communities.

Paragraphs 18–21 discuss, in turn, each of the reasons.

Supporting Details

<u>T</u>   7. TRUE OR FALSE? According to the author, preindustrial cities, on the whole, were more crowded and dangerous than modern cities.

See paragraphs 13 and 16.

<u>C</u>   8. The major supporting details of paragraphs 14 and 15 are
  A. 1) travel by foot or horse and 2) elevators.
  B. crowding of 1) preindustrial cities and 2) modern-day cities.
  C. the limits on city size caused by 1) city walls and 2) lack of construction technology.
  D. 1) cities with walls and 2) cities without walls.

Transitions

<u>A</u>   9. The relationship between the two sentences below is one of
  A. addition.
  B. time.
  C. contrast.
  D. definition and example.

The second sentence gives another reason for the small size of preindustrial cities.

  "A major reason why cities remained small was poor transportation
  . . . . Disease also checked the size of cities." (Paragraphs 4 and 6)

_C_ 10. The relationship between the two sentences below is one of

    A. comparison.

    B. time.

    C. cause and effect.

    D. illustration.

> *The cause:* Many newcomers entered the cities each year.
> *The effect:* Cities were filled with people who were strangers to each other.

"Consider that cities relied on large numbers of newcomers each year just to replace the population lost through mortality. As a result, cities tended to abound in people who were recent arrivals and who had not known one another previously." (Paragraph 21)

Patterns of Organization

_C_ 11. The main pattern of organization of paragraph 4 is

    A. time order.

    B. list of items.

    C. cause and effect.

    D. definition and example.

> The cause-effect signals are *reason, therefore, because.*

ADVANCED SKILL QUESTIONS

Fact and Opinion

_A_ 12. Paragraph 6 is made up of

    A. facts.

    B. opinions.

    C. both facts and opinions.

> All the information in this paragraph can be verified in historical and medical publications.

Inferences

_B_ 13. From paragraph 4, we can conclude that cities probably grew significantly larger after the invention of

    A. elevators.

    B. trains.

    C. bicycles.

    D. antibiotics.

> Trains enable food to be shipped to distant points.

_B_ 14. The author implies that today's cities

    A. are as dirty as preindustrial cities were.

    B. are better places to live than preindustrial cities.

    C. shouldn't have so many tall buildings.

    D. are very safe places at night.

> See, for example, paragraphs 16 and 23.

_D_ 15. From paragraph 11, we can deduce that the word *smog*

    A. comes from another language.

    B. is a shortening of a longer word.

    C. has no real meaning.

    D. is a combination of the words *smoke* and *fog*.

> The paragraph tells us that the "deadly *fogs*" in London were caused by "*smoking* home chimneys."

_A_ 16. Reread paragraph 21; from that paragraph, we can conclude
   A. people's social class influenced how others treated them.
   B. it was easy in preindustrial times to check on people's pasts.
   C. both of the above.   Statement A explains why people would
   D. neither A nor B.   claim "more exalted social origins."

Purpose and Tone

_A_ 17. The author's main purpose is to
   A. inform readers of what life in preindustrial cities was like.
   B. persuade readers to appreciate the countryside.
   C. entertain readers with amusing details about preindustrial cities.

                                      This purpose is suggested by
_D_ 18. In paragraph 2, the author's tone is   the first sentence of the selection.
   A. amused.
   B. disappointed.
   C. objective.   The author uses negative words ("filthy," "disease-ridden")
   D. critical.   and then criticizes "history" for omitting "the mud,
                              manure, and misery" of preindustrial cities.

Argument

_B_ 19. To support the statement that "the car and the factory cannot match the
        horse and the home fireplace when it comes to pollution," the author
        provides in paragraphs 10 and 11
   A. facts about how cars and factories pollute.
   B. facts about how horses and home fireplaces pollute.
   C. both of the above.

20. Complete the following argument by adding a statement of support.

   Point: Preindustrial cities were not better than our cities.

   Support: Preindustrial cities had worse environmental pollution.

   Support: *Preindustrial cities were more crowded (or dangerous*
                or disease-ridden).

MAPPING

Complete the map of the selection by filling in the five missing major and minor
details scrambled in the following list.

   • Population density
   • Opportunity to start a new life
   • Disease limited size of city
   • Reasons people were attracted to them
   • Not being able to expand upward

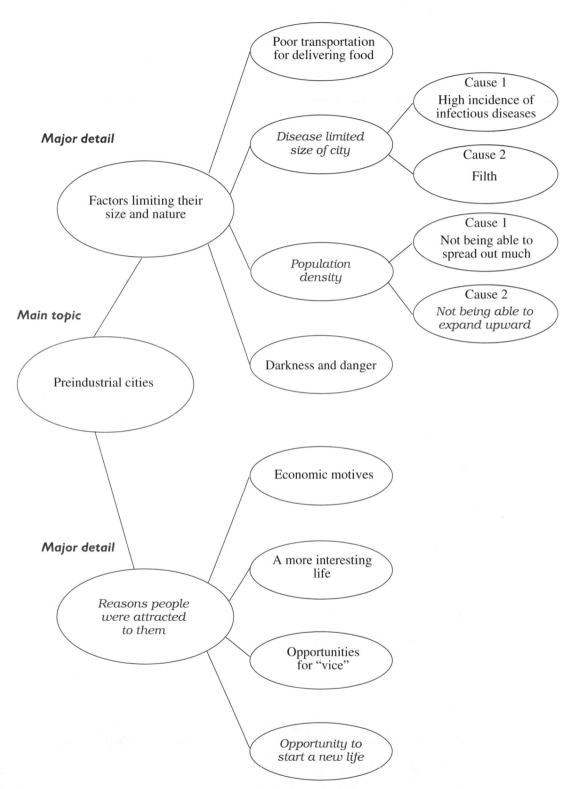

Poor transportation for delivering food

Cause 1
High incidence of infectious diseases

Major detail

Disease limited size of city

Cause 2
Filth

Factors limiting their size and nature

Cause 1
Not being able to spread out much

Population density

Cause 2
Not being able to expand upward

Main topic

Darkness and danger

Preindustrial cities

Economic motives

A more interesting life

Major detail

Reasons people were attracted to them

Opportunities for "vice"

Opportunity to start a new life

DISCUSSION QUESTIONS

1. If you had lived in preindustrial days, do you think you would have chosen to live in a city or in a rural area? Why?

2. What draws people to or keeps them in big cities today? Compare these reasons with those which attracted newcomers to preindustrial cities.

3. The radius of preindustrial cities was "usually no more than three miles from the center." What factors have allowed today's huge cities and their suburbs to exist?

4. According to the reading, preindustrial city dwellers had to protect themselves from the filth and crime in big cities. How are problems of city dwellers today the same or different?

Note: Writing assignments for this selection appear on page 596.

Check Your Performance	PREINDUSTRIAL CITIES		
Activity	*Number Right*	*Points*	*Score*
BASIC SKILL QUESTIONS			
Vocabulary in Context (3 items)	_____	× 4 =	_____
Central Point and Main Ideas (3 items)	_____	× 4 =	_____
Supporting Details (2 items)	_____	× 4 =	_____
Transitions (2 items)	_____	× 4 =	_____
Patterns of Organization (1 item)	_____	× 4 =	_____
ADVANCED SKILL QUESTIONS			
Fact and Opinion (1 item)	_____	× 4 =	_____
Inferences (4 items)	_____	× 4 =	_____
Purpose and Tone (2 items)	_____	× 4 =	_____
Argument (2 items)	_____	× 4 =	_____
MAPPING (5 items)	_____	× 4 =	_____
	TOTAL SCORE =		_____ %

Enter your total score into the **Reading Performance Chart: Ten Reading Selections** on the inside back cover.

Part III

FOR FURTHER STUDY

1

Combined-Skills Tests

Following are fifteen tests that cover the skills taught in Part I of this book. Each test consists of a short reading passage followed by questions on any of the following: vocabulary in context, main ideas, supporting details, relationships, fact and opinion, inferences, purpose and tone, and argument.

Notes:

1. In the comments on test questions, the term "too narrow" describes an item that is only a detail within the selection. "Too broad" describes an item that covers a great deal more than is in the selection.

2. Because these combined-skills tests are on facing pages, you might not want to ask students to remove them from the book. In that case, one option would be to pass out copies of the model answer sheet that is on page 544. Alternatively, you could ask students to put their answers to a given test on a piece of notebook paper; you would then collect the answers at the end of class.

COMBINED SKILLS: Test 1

Read the passage below. Then write the letter of the best answer to each question that follows.

> ¹Johnny Appleseed, one of the gentlest and most beloved of American folk heroes, was born in 1774 in Leominster, Massachusetts. ²His real name was John Chapman. ³Chapman's early life was full of misfortune. ⁴First, his father left home to fight in the Revolutionary War. ⁵Then John's mother and baby brother died before John's second birthday. ⁶However, John's fortunes improved when his father returned and remarried, and by the time John was in his teens, he had ten brothers and sisters.
>
> ⁷As a young man, John began traveling west on foot, stopping to clear land and plant the apple seeds he always carried with him. ⁸Settlers who followed John's path were delighted to find young apple orchards dotting the landscape.
>
> ⁹John was a friendly fellow who often stopped to visit with families along his way, entertaining them with stories of his travels. ¹⁰Tales of his exploits followed him through Pennsylvania, Ohio, and Indiana. ¹¹Many of the stories were true. ¹²For instance, John really did travel barefoot through the snow, lived on the friendliest of terms with Indian tribes, and refused to shoot any animal. ¹³Other tales about John, however, were exaggerations. ¹⁴Settlers said, for example, that he slept in the treetops and talked to the birds or that he had once been carried off by a giant eagle. ¹⁵Johnny Appleseed never stopped traveling until his death in Fort Wayne, Indiana, in 1845.

___C___ 1. As used in sentence 6, the word *fortunes* means
  A. wealth.
  B. possessions.
  C. luck.
  D. health.

___C___ 2. The details in sentences 4 and 5 support the point or points in
  A. sentence 1.
  B. sentence 2.
  C. sentence 3.
  D. sentence 6.

___A___ 3. The relationship between sentences 3 and 6 is one of
  A. contrast.
  B. addition.
  C. cause and effect.
  D. comparison.

_A_   4. We can conclude that Johnny Appleseed
      A. provided apples for numerous settlers.
      B. was quickly forgotten by the settlers.
      C. grew wealthy from selling his apple trees.
      D. left home because of problems with his family.

_B_   5. The passage suggests that Johnny Appleseed
      A. grew weary of traveling.
      B. had great respect for other people and animals.
      C. lived a very short but rich life.
      D. planted many trees other than apple trees.

_C_   6. Sentence 1 is a statement of
      A. fact.
      B. opinion.
      C. fact and opinion.

_D_   7. The tone of the passage is
      A. pessimistic.
      B. bitter and impassioned.
      C. amused and excited.
      D. straightforward with a touch of admiration.

_D_   8. Which is the most appropriate title for this selection?
      A. The Planting of American Apple Orchards
      B. Folk Heroes of America
      C. Settlers Recall Johnny Appleseed
      D. The Life and Legends of John Chapman

Comments: Item 1—The paragraph shows no evidence of wealth (answer A) or possessions (answer B) and does not mention health (answer D). The antonym *misfortune* ("bad luck") in sentence 3 suggests that *fortunes* means "luck" *(answer C).*

Item 2—Sentences 4 and 5 detail the misfortune mentioned in sentence 3.

Item 3—The contrast transition *however* signals a change in Chapman's fortunes.

Item 4—See sentence 8.

Item 5—See sentence 12.

Item 6—The part of the sentence between commas is opinion. "Gentlest" and "most beloved" are value expressions.

Item 7—The author's admiration comes through in the value words in sentence 1.

Item 8—Answer A is incorrect (while apple orchards are mentioned, the selection isn't about apple orchards in general). Answer B is too broad, and answer C is too narrow, mentioned only in sentence 14.

COMBINED SKILLS: Test 2

Read the passage below. Then write the letter of the best answer to each question that follows.

[1]Little League baseball in its present form should be abolished. [2]For one thing, the pressure that children are put under to succeed may harm them more than help them. [3]One mother discovered her son taking Maalox tablets from the medicine chest whenever a game approached. [4]He explained that they helped relieve the stomach burn he would feel during the game. [5]Other children have been found taking tranquilizers. [6]Another drawback to today's Little League baseball is that some parents take the game too seriously and set a bad example for their children. [7]Recently, a disillusioned coach said, "At our field, we put the bleachers way back from the dugout where the players are. [8]That way, parents can't be hissing down advice to their children all the time and getting them upset." [9]A final reason Little League should be abolished is that it doesn't offer enough success to most players. [10]Instead, the game revolves around the more developed kids who are able to hit and throw the ball harder than the smaller children. [11]In one recent game, most of the batters were clearly afraid of the speed of the hardball, which was pitched by a boy bigger than many of the other players.

[12]A workable alternative to Little League hardball would be lob-pitch softball. [13]The ball is pitched slowly and underhand, which offers a high level of success to kids without a high level of ability. [14]Lob-pitch softball would get more children involved in the game, and help people remember that it is a game—not an adult arena where one is branded with success or failure.

_B_ 1. In sentences 1 and 9, the word *abolished* means
 A. supported.
 B. eliminated.
 C. expanded.
 D. imitated.

_D_ 2. According to the author, one advantage of lob-pitch softball is the
 A. weight of the ball.
 B. age of the players.
 C. size of the field.
 D. lesser degree of skill required.

_B_ 3. The relationship of sentence 6 to the sentences that come before it is one of
 A. time.
 B. addition.
 C. contrast.
 D. comparison.

___B___ 4. Sentence 1 is a statement of
      A. fact.
      B. opinion.
      C. fact and opinion.

___A___ 5. From the passage, you can conclude the author would agree with the idea that
      A. it's not whether you win or lose; it's how you play the game.
      B. competition in baseball helps prepare people for competition in life.
      C. children's games should imitate adults' games.
      D. sports should help children learn that there are winners and losers in life.

___B___ 6. The author's main purpose is to
      A. inform.
      B. persuade.
      C. entertain.
      D. predict.

___A___ 7. The main idea of paragraph 1 is best stated in
      A. sentence 1.
      B. sentence 2.
      C. sentence 9.
      D. sentence 11.

___C___ 8. What is the most appropriate title for this selection?
      A. The Pressures on Today's Children
      B. Lob-Pitch Softball
      C. Let's Reform Little League
      D. Sportsmanship in Baseball

Comments: Item 1—Sentence 2 suggests that *abolished* means "eliminated." We would want to get rid of anything that harms children.

Item 2—See sentence 13.

Item 3—*Another* is an addition word.

Item 4—*Should be* is a definite signal that the sentence is an opinion.

Item 5—See sentence 14.

Item 6—Note the main idea in the next question. *Should* in the main idea shows the author's intent to persuade.

Item 7—Sentence 1 states that we should abolish Little League baseball in its present form; the details tell why the author thinks so.

Item 8—Answer A is too broad, and answers B and C are too narrow.

COMBINED SKILLS: Test 3

Read the passage below. Then write the letter of the best answer to each question that follows.

¹Most people dislike bats, and surely the most feared of all the species is the dreaded vampire bat. ²Vampires live up to their horror-story reputation as greedy and efficient stealers of blood.

³Depending upon its type, the vampire bat may prefer to dine on the blood of mammals (including humans) or birds. ⁴The bat begins its meal by circling above its usually sleeping target for several minutes, probably to allow heat-sensitive patches on its face to determine where best to bite. ⁵It then inflicts a small wound with its teeth, which are so razor-sharp as to make the incision virtually painless. ⁶The wound bleeds freely as long as the bat continues feeding, thanks to a substance in the bat's saliva that prevents clotting. ⁷As many as half a dozen of the bat's fellows may join it to feed from one wound.

⁸Vampire bats have such great appetites for blood that they may drink more than their own weight at one feeding, thus making it briefly impossible for them to fly. ⁹A single vampire drinks about twenty-five gallons of blood in its lifetime. ¹⁰Although vampire bats are sometimes responsible for the death of humans or animals, those deaths are not due to loss of blood. ¹¹Rather, the deaths are the result of rabies or other diseases spread by the bats.

_____B_____ 1. In sentence 5, *incision* means
    A. heat-sensitive patch.
    B. cut.
    C. blood.
    D. saliva.

_____D_____ 2. Sentences 10 and 11
    A. narrate events.
    B. define a term.
    C. compare two things.
    D. discuss a cause and effect relationship.

_____C_____ 3. The main patterns of organization of the second paragraph are cause-effect and
    A. contrast.
    B. comparison.
    C. time order.
    D. definition and example.

____B____ 4. We can conclude that vampire bats use their heat-sensitive patches
        A. for personal temperature control.
        B. to find where blood is close to their victims' skin.
        C. to find sleeping victims.
        D. to find out which potential victims have the best blood.

____D____ 5. The passage suggests that
        A. bats are usually solitary feeders.
        B. all vampire bats have rabies.
        C. vampire bats intend to kill their victims.
        D. vampire bats prefer victims that lie still.

____A____ 6. The author's main purpose is to
        A. inform.
        B. persuade.
        C. entertain.
        D. predict.

____B____ 7. On the whole, the tone of the passage is
        A. fearful.
        B. objective.
        C. disbelieving.
        D. playful.

____A____ 8. Which is the most appropriate title for this passage?
        A. Vampire Bats' Feeding Habits
        B. Bats and Disease
        C. Bats in Social Groups
        D. How Bats Live

Comments: Item 1—"Wound with its teeth" in sentence 5 suggests that *incision* means "cut."

Item 2—Sentences 10 and 11 tell why people and animals sometimes die from vampire bat bites. The *cause* is the disease of the bats; the *effect* is the death of humans or animals from the disease transmitted by the bite.

Item 3—Words like *begin*s (sentence 4) and *then* (sentence 5) signal time order.

Item 4—Heat-sensitive patches must show where blood is. Bats are seeking blood.

Item 5—Sentence 4 mentions that bats seek "sleeping targets," who would be still.

Item 6—The author gives information without value judgments or evaluations.

Item 7—The passage is mostly facts and is presented without value words or opinions.

Item 8—Answers B and D are too broad. Although the passage does mention a group of bats in sentence 7, it does not focus on bats in social groups (answer C).

COMBINED SKILLS: Test 4

Read the passage below. Then write the letter of the best answer to each question that follows.

¹The social psychologist Philip Zimbardo set out to test a theory that the anonymity of city life encourages crime. ²He arranged to have automobiles abandoned in two different locations: New York City and Palo Alto, California, a medium-sized suburban community. ³The cars' license plates were removed and their hoods were raised to signal that the autos were abandoned. ⁴Then each car was secretly watched for sixty-four hours.

⁵The person assigned to watch the New York car did not have long to wait. ⁶Within ten minutes the car received its first auto strippers—a father, mother, and eight-year-old son. ⁷The mother appeared to be a lookout, while the son aided the father's search of the trunk, glove compartment, and motor. ⁸He then handed his father the tools necessary to remove the battery and radiator. ⁹Total time of destructive contact: seven minutes.

¹⁰This, however, was only the first "contact." ¹¹By the end of the sixty-four hours, the car had been vandalized twenty-four times, often by well-dressed, seemingly middle-class adults. ¹²What remained when the experiment was over was a useless hunk of metal. ¹³In contrast, the Palo Alto car was approached only once: when it started to rain, a passerby stopped to lower the hood.

¹⁴According to Zimbardo, the crucial factor in the different fates of the two cars was anonymity. ¹⁵In a large city, where the chances of being recognized outside one's own neighborhood are extremely slim, even "upstanding citizens" can afford a temporary turn at thievery. ¹⁶In a smaller community, on the other hand, the higher probability of being recognized and caught keeps people honest.

_B_ 1. In sentence 14, *crucial* means
  A. least interesting.
  B. most important.
  C. most unlikely.
  D. most helpful.

_B_ 2. According to the passage, Zimbardo's main purpose in doing the experiment was to
  A. illustrate a point.
  B. test a theory.
  C. catch thieves.
  D. teach honesty.

_A_   3. The pattern of organization in sentences 5 through 9 is one of
   A. time order.
   B. list of items.
   C. comparison.
   D. contrast.

_C_   4. The relationship between sentences 15 and 16 is one of
   A. time.
   B. comparison.
   C. contrast.
   D. cause and effect.

_A_   5. Sentence 13 is a statement of
   A. fact.
   B. opinion.
   C. fact and opinion.

_C_   6. The passage suggests that
   A. people who vandalize cars always travel in groups.
   B. New Yorkers are more dishonest than people in most other big cities.
   C. social pressure promotes honesty.
   D. the car used in Palo Alto was probably in better condition than the car in New York City.

_A_   7. The tone of the passage can be described as mainly
   A. objective.
   B. doubtful.
   C. alarmed.
   D. scornful.

_D_   8. Which statement best states the main idea of the passage?
   A. Philip Zimbardo is a creative social psychologist.
   B. People are now more dishonest than ever.
   C. In big cities, ordinary people's chances of being recognized outside of their neighborhood are quite slim.
   D. Zimbardo's experiment suggests that the anonymity of city life encourages crime.

Comments: Item 1—*Crucial* must mean "most important." Sentence 15 tells us that if a criminal hopes not to be caught then anonymity would be an important factor (sentence 14).

Item 2—See sentence 1—"Zimbardo set out to test a theory."

Item 3—Sentences 5–9 cover activities during about seventeen minutes.

Item 4—*On the other hand* (sentence 16) signals a contrast relationship.

Item 5—Sentence 4 offers verification for sentence 13.

Item 6—See sentence 16.

Item 7—The passage describes the experiment and results without being judgmental.

Item 8—A is too narrow; B is not addressed at all; C is stated in sentence 15 but is too narrow to include all the details in the selection.

COMBINED SKILLS: Test 5

Read the passage below. Then write the letter of the best answer to each question that follows.

¹We live in an era in which more women are entering formerly male-dominated professions, demanding equal pay for equal work, and generally rejecting the societal double standard which has held them back from reaching their full potential. ²Yet many women are still bound by old-fashioned and harmful ideas about sexuality. ³An epidemic of "date rapes" on college campuses is evidence that warped beliefs about sexuality are barriers that women—as well as men—need to break in order to achieve a full human partnership. ⁴As many as 25 percent of all college women may become victims of rape or attempted rape. ⁵Women at the beginning of their college careers are especially vulnerable to date rape. ⁶They may be living in coed dorms with men whom they assume they can trust. ⁷They are eager to appear cool, sophisticated, not paranoid or uptight. ⁸Most destructively of all, many women still subscribe at least subconsciously to the belief that they "owe" sexual favors to a man they date. ⁹After a sexual attack by a date, many women are racked with guilt rather than anger. ¹⁰Were they to blame, they ask themselves, because they drank too much? ¹¹Because they wore a short skirt? ¹²Similarly, men have grown up in a culture which suggests that once they have spent "good money" entertaining a date, they are owed sex in return.

_B_ 1. In sentence 8, the words *subscribe . . . to* mean
    A. describe.
    B. agree with.
    C. ignore.
    D. argue with.

_C_ 2. The relationship of sentence 2 to sentence 1 is one of
    A. addition.
    B. illustration.
    C. contrast.
    D. comparison.

_C_ 3. The relationship of sentence 12 to sentences 9–11 is one of
    A. time.
    B. contrast.
    C. comparison.
    D. cause and effect.

___D___ 4. You can conclude that the author believes
  A. many men and women should change their attitudes about sexuality.
  B. attitudes about rights in the workplace have changed more than attitudes about sexuality.
  C. victims of date rape often feel responsible for having been attacked.
  D. all of the above.

___B___ 5. The main purpose of this passage is to
  A. inform readers about interesting sexual attitudes.
  B. use facts to argue that sexual attitudes need improving.
  C. entertain readers with dramatic sexual images.
  D. predict the future of the American sex scene.

___D___ 6. The author's tone can be described as
  A. sarcastic.
  B. optimistic.
  C. arrogant.
  D. concerned.

___C___ 7. The point made in sentence 2 is best supported by
  A. sentence 1.
  B. sentence 4.
  C. sentence 8.
  D. sentence 12.

___B___ 8. The main idea of the passage is that
  A. women are now close to reaching their full potential.
  B. societal attitudes toward sexuality are old-fashioned and harmful.
  C. colleges should provide better security in coed dorms.
  D. men's sexual attitudes are strongly in need of change.

Comments: Item 1—The fact that women go along with the idea that they "owe" sexual favors suggests that they agree with that notion.

Item 2—*Yet* in sentence 2 is a contrast word. The idea of equality is being contrasted with the actual behavior.

Item 3—*Similarly* in sentence 12 is a comparison word. Women's beliefs are being compared to men's beliefs about sexual "owing."

Item 4—Answer A is supported by sentences 2 and 3. Answer B is supported by sentence 1. Answer C is supported by sentences 9–11.

Item 5—Sentence 3 suggests a purpose of persuading (argument) with the use of the words "need to." The author's purpose goes beyond informing but does not attempt to entertain readers about such a serious subject. Predictions are not evident in the passage, which discusses the present and mentions the past but does not predict the future.

Item 6—See, especially, sentences 2–4.

Item 7—The words "Most destructively of all . . . still subscribe . . . to the belief" in sentence 8 suggest that the belief is an old-fashioned and harmful one.

Item 8—See sentences 2 and 3.

COMBINED SKILLS: Test 6

Read the passage below. Then write the letter of the best answer to each question that follows.

> [1]The concept of adopting a child to raise as one's own is a relatively modern phenomenon. [2]While there have always been instances of families taking in unrelated children to raise for a variety of reasons, most had more to do with helping the children of a dead or disabled relative or securing cheap labor than adding a new member to the family.
>
> [3]A remarkable chapter in American history that began in 1853 helped to sow the seeds of modern adoption practices. [4]The story began when Charles Loring Brace, a wealthy Connecticut man, visited New York City. [5]He was appalled by the number of orphans and abandoned children he found living in the streets there. [6]In response, Brace organized the Children's Aid Society, dedicated to finding loving homes for such children. [7]Its method was to send trainloads of orphaned children into Western states, where community leaders would encourage friends and neighbors to adopt a child "to treat in every way as a member of the family."
>
> [8]The Children's Aid Society was a remarkable success. [9]By the time its program ended in 1929, "orphan trains" had carried almost 100,000 children to new homes. [10]The orphans grew up to make solid contributions to their communities; many became respected farmers, while others went on to practice law or medicine. [11]One of the orphans became governor of North Dakota; another became governor of Alaska.

___D___ 1. In sentence 5, the word *appalled* means
- A. annoyed.
- B. unmoved.
- C. excited.
- D. horrified.

___A___ 2. The relationship between sentences 5 and 6 is one of
- A. cause and effect.
- B. addition.
- C. comparison.
- D. general idea and illustration.

___A___ 3. Sentence 11 expresses
- A. fact.
- B. opinion.
- C. fact and opinion.

Comments: Item 1—General sense. How would most people have felt about seeing children abandoned by their parents to live in the streets without adult care?

Item 2—*In response* is a cause-effect signal. The *cause*—finding the children in the streets. The *effect*—founding the Children's Aid Society.

Item 3—Both items in sentence 11 can be verified in public documents.

_B_   4. The passage suggests that the success of the Children's Aid Society
      was due in part to
      A. the attractiveness of the children.
      B. the participation of leaders in the communities that the trains went
         through.
      C. the national reputation of Charles Loring Brace.
      D. none of the above.

_B_   5. The author's main purpose in writing this selection is to
      A. predict future adoption practices.
      B. inform readers about a significant chapter in American history.
      C. persuade readers to consider adopting orphans or abandoned
         children.
      D. entertain readers with stories of the "orphan train."

_A_   6. The author's tone in this passage is largely
      A. approving.
      B. critical.
      C. regretful.
      D. pessimistic.

_A_   7. The main idea of the third paragraph is stated in
      A. sentence 8.
      B. sentence 9.
      C. sentence 10.
      D. sentence 11.

_C_   8. Which sentence best states the main idea of the selection?
      A. Charles Loring Brace was appalled by the number of orphans and
         abandoned children he found living in the streets of New York City.
      B. Individuals can make a great impact on society, for both good and
         bad.
      C. Modern adoption practices began with the successful Children's
         Aid Society's orphan-trains program.
      D. The orphans placed by the Children's Aid Society made numerous
         worthwhile contributions to their communities.

Comments: Item 4—See sentence 7.

Item 5—The passage informs in a mostly objective way. It does not predict, persuade, or
entertain.

Item 6—Sentences 3 and 8 use the word *remarkable*. Sentence 10 indicates approval with
"went on to make solid contributions."

Item 7—The signal words "remarkable success" announce the supporting details in the
rest of the paragraph.

Item 8—Answers A and D are too narrow. Answer B is too broad.

COMBINED SKILLS: Test 7

Read the passage below. Then write the letter of the best answer to each question that follows.

[1]Perception is strongly influenced by attention. [2]Unfortunately, if you daydream during a lecture, little or nothing will reach your brain. [3]Attending is not always easy, so so you take notes and make conscious efforts to remain alert. [4]Did you notice an error in the previous sentence? [5]You probably were concentrating on the content and although your eyes saw the word *so* repeated, you ignored it. [6]Similarly, you were probably not focusing any attention on your thumb until you read this sentence. [7]You simply cannot attend to every stimulus around you, so only certain things are selected. [8]Have you ever driven down a highway with your gas needle nearing "empty"? [9]Chances are you become preoccupied with the location of gas stations. [10]Another day when your tank was full but your stomach was empty, the gas stations might have been overlooked, but every diner and restaurant would have caught your eye. [11]Attention is usually focused on needed things. [12]If you are hungry or thirsty right now, you might have a problem keeping your attention focused on the reading rather than on the refrigerator.

_____B_____ 1. As used in sentence 3, the word *attending* means
    A. showing up.
    B. paying attention.
    C. taking care.
    D. waiting.

_____A_____ 2. In sentence 9, the words *preoccupied with* mean
    A. fully interested in.
    B. forgetful about.
    C. expert in.
    D. confident about.

_____D_____ 3. According to the author, we usually concentrate on
    A. what we are expected to pay attention to.
    B. random things.
    C. daydreaming.
    D. needed things.

_____C_____ 4. The relationship between sentences 5 and 6 is one of
    A. time.
    B. contrast.
    C. comparison.
    D. general point and example.

___D___ 5. Sentence 12 discusses a
      A. series of events.
      B. contrast.
      C. comparison.
      D. cause and effect.

___B___ 6. You might conclude from the paragraph that it would be a good idea to
      A. forget about taking notes in classes.
      B. avoid being hungry when you go to your classes.
      C. take a difficult class just before lunchtime.
      D. eat less.

___C___ 7. What is the best title for this selection?
      A. Daydreaming
      B. Perception
      C. The Relationship Between Perception and Attention
      D. How Hunger Influences Attention

___D___ 8. Which statement best expresses the main idea of the paragraph?
      A. You are unlikely to notice an error in writing if you are concentrating on its content.
      B. If you are hungry, you will focus on eating.
      C. Unfortunately, when students daydream during lectures, nothing will reach their brains.
      D. Perception is strongly influenced by attention, which is usually focused on needed things.

Comments: Item 1—The general sense of the sentence tells you that you take notes and make efforts to remain alert in order to pay attention.

Item 2—General sense: What would you do if your gas tank were nearing "empty"?

Item 3—See sentence 11.

Item 4—*Similarly* (sentence 6*)* is a comparison transition.

Item 5—*Cause:* being hungry or thirsty. *Effect:* thinking about the refrigerator.

Item 6—Sentences 10–12 suggest that going to class hungry would cause us not to pay attention to class.

Item 7—Answers A and D are too narrow. Answer B is too broad.

Item 8—Answers A, B, and C are too narrow.

COMBINED SKILLS: Test 8

Read the passage below. Then write the letter of the best answer to each question that follows.

[1]In 1948, during the re-election campaign of Senator Claude Pepper of Florida, large numbers of leaflets with an unsigned message were circulated throughout the state just before election day. [2]The message was as follows:

[3]Are you aware that Claude Pepper is known all over Washington as a shameless extrovert? [4]Not only that, but this man is reliably reported to practice nepotism with his sister-in-law, and he has a sister who was a thespian in wicked New York City. [5]Worst of all, it is an established fact that Mr. Pepper, before his marriage, habitually practiced celibacy.

[6]In a literal sense, the statements were not false. [7]However, the words *extrovert* (a person who is active and expressive), *nepotism* (favoritism to relatives), *thespian* (an actor or actress) and *celibacy* (not being sexually active) were used in contexts that seemed threatening to people who did not know the meanings of these uncommon words.

[8]A very clever and dishonest writer had purposely selected words that gave the impression that Senator Pepper was a very immoral person. [9]The effect was very damaging. [10]Senator Pepper was defeated at the polls by George Smathers, who denied that he was involved in this political "dirty trick." [11]However, the damage could not be undone.

_D_ 1. In sentence 6, *literal* means
    A. based on imagination.
    B. marital.
    C. not understood.
    D. according to actual meanings of words.

_D_ 2. The relationship of sentence 7 to sentence 6 is one of
    A. addition.
    B. cause and effect.
    C. comparison.
    D. contrast.

_B_ 3. The pattern of organization of sentences 3 through 5 is
    A. time order.
    B. list of items.
    C. comparison and/or contrast.
    D. cause and effect.

Comments: Item 1—Using the actual meanings of the words, the statements could actually be true without being critical of Pepper.

Item 2—*However* in sentence 7 is a contrast word.

Item 3—The sentences list accusations.

_D_   4. The passage
  A. defines and illustrates the term "dirty trick."
  B. lists a series of dirty tricks.
  C. compares and contrasts dirty tricks.
  D. explains a dirty trick and its effect.

_C_   5. The passage implies that Senator Pepper
  A. probably did not deserve to be elected.
  B. was in reality a very shy person who never practiced celibacy.
  C. may have lost the election because of a "dirty trick."
  D. had been an excellent senator.

_A_   6. You could conclude from the passage that
  A. the writer of the leaflet assumed many readers would not know some uncommon words.
  B. Claude Pepper never showed favoritism to his sister-in-law nor had a sister who was an actress.
  C. the writer of the leaflet did not understand the psychology of the average voter.
  D. George Smathers was defeated in his next election.

_D_   7. The author of this passage would probably agree with which of the following statements?
  A. Honest political campaigns don't succeed.
  B. Political tricks have ruined Florida's politics.
  C. Senator Pepper should not have been a candidate for senator.
  D. When the truth is told deceitfully, it can do as much damage as a lie.

_C_   8. Which of the following statements best expresses the main idea of the passage?
  A. Dishonesty is a major problem in Florida's political campaigns.
  B. Florida's citizens are easily fooled.
  C. A "dirty trick" that twisted the truth affected the outcome of a political campaign.
  D. Claude Pepper should have run a better senatorial campaign.

Comments: Item 4—Answer A is incorrect because "dirty trick" is not defined. Answers B and C are incorrect because only one dirty trick (not a series of them) is described, and it is not compared to or contrasted with any other dirty trick.

Item 5—See sentences 10 and 11.

Item 6—Answer B is incorrect; we have no reason to doubt these statements. Answer C is incorrect because the writer of the leaflet *did* understand the average voter—as proved by Pepper's defeat. Answer D is incorrect; we are not told about Smathers's next election.

Item 7—Answer A cannot be chosen because the passage isn't about honest campaigns. Answer B cannot be chosen because the only information we have about Florida's politics is this one incident. Answer C is not discussed in the passage.

Item 8—Answers A and B are incorrect because one incident does not provide adequate support. Answer D is not covered in the passage.

COMBINED SKILLS: Test 9

Read the passage below. Then write the letter of the best answer to each question that follows.

[1]Mary was watching a mystery on television. [2]The end of the movie was near, and she was totally engrossed. [3]Then her baby started crying. [4]She shouted at him to shut up. [5]His response was intensified crying. [6]Mary got angry and shook him. [7]The baby cried even louder. [8]In the meanwhile, the mystery's conclusion took place, and Mary missed it. [9]Angrily, she slapped her son's face. [10]In this situation, someone was pursuing a goal—seeing the end of a suspenseful television show. [11]But something happened to block the achievement of that goal. [12]The person thus became frustrated, anger built up, and direct aggression occurred.

[13]Aggression is not always aimed at the original frustrater. [14]For example, consider a businessman who had a hard day at the office. [15]He was about to close a deal with a client when his boss clumsily interfered and lost the sale. [16]On the way home in his car, the frustrated businessman blew his horn angrily at a car ahead when it didn't immediately pull away from a stoplight. [17]As he entered his home, his dog jumped up on him, only to receive a quick kick. [18]He then shouted at his wife during supper. [19]All these aggressive behaviors are examples of displaced aggression. [20]Aggression against the person who caused the original frustration can often be harmful. [21]In this case, assaulting or swearing at the boss could cost the businessman his job. [22]When the original frustrater has status and power over the frustrated person, aggression may be displaced onto a less threatening target, who may have nothing at all to do with the original frustration.

_____A_____ 1. In sentence 2, the word *engrossed* means
  A. involved.
  B. disgusted.
  C. disappointed.
  D. bored.

_____B_____ 2. The topic of the first paragraph is
  A. parent-child relationships.
  B. direct aggression.
  C. displaced aggression.
  D. suspense.

_____B_____ 3. Aggression is more likely to be displaced if the original frustrater
  A. is a family member.
  B. has power over the frustrated person.
  C. is angry at the frustrated person.
  D. is unfair to the frustrated person.

___D___ 4. The relationship between sentences 11 and 12 is one of
   A. definition and example.
   B. comparison.
   C. contrast.
   D. cause and effect.

___C___ 5. The organizational pattern of each paragraph is
   A. a series of steps in a process.
   B. a contrast of events.
   C. illustration and explanation of a general concept.
   D. a comparison of two or more events.

___B___ 6. The writer's main purpose in writing this selection is to
   A. predict how aggression influences relationships.
   B. inform readers about two types of aggression.
   C. persuade readers to be careful not to take out their aggression on the wrong people.
   D. entertain readers with dramatic anecdotes about aggressive behavior.

___C___ 7. What is the best title for the selection?
   A. Family Relationships
   B. The Causes of Aggression
   C. Direct and Displaced Aggression
   D. Displaced Aggression

___B___ 8. Which sentence best states the main idea of the selection?
   A. A great deal of frustration is aimed against family members.
   B. When frustration and anger build up, direct or displaced aggression may occur.
   C. Sometimes a frustrater may have a great deal more power or status than the person who is frustrated.
   D. Direct aggression is more satisfying than indirect aggression.

Comments: Item 1—Mary's actions show that she was completely involved.

Item 2—See sentence 12.

Item 3—See sentence 22.

Item 4—*Thus* in sentence 12 is a cause-effect word.

Item 5—The general concept (aggression) is explained (two types of responses to aggression) and illustrated with an example for each type: Mary and her baby; the businessman and his wife.

Item 6—The first paragraph explains and illustrates direct aggression; the second paragraph explains and illustrates displaced aggression.

Item 7—Answer A is too broad. Answer B is too narrow because the passage discusses both the cause and types of aggression. Answer D is too narrow, discussing only one of the two types.

Item 8—Answers A and C are too narrow. Answer D is incorrect because the passage does not discuss the degrees of satisfaction with either type of aggression.

COMBINED SKILLS: Test 10

Read the passage below. Then write the letter of the best answer to each question that follows.

> [1]It would be a mistake to assume that primitive societies are mentally backward—unable to benefit from their environment or understand how to cope effectively with it. [2]Given the general level of technology available, they do adapt to and manipulate their environment in a sophisticated and understanding manner. [3]Countless examples can be cited to illustrate this point. [4]Among some Eskimo groups, wolves are a menace—a dangerous environmental feature that must be dealt with. [5]They could perhaps be hunted down and killed, but this involves danger as well as considerable expenditure in time and energy. [6]So a simple yet clever device is employed. [7]A sharp sliver of bone is curled into a springlike shape, and seal blubber is molded around it and permitted to freeze. [8]This is then placed where it can be discovered by a hungry wolf, which, living up to its reputation, "wolfs it down." [9]Later, as this "time bomb" is digested and the blubber disappears, the bone uncurls and its sharp ends pierce the stomach of the wolf, causing internal bleeding and death. [10]This method, though harsh, is undeniably practical. [11]It is a simple yet fairly safe technique that involves an understanding of the environment as well as wolf psychology and habits.

_____C_____ 1. As used in sentence 6, the word *employed* means
   A. hired.
   B. recognized.
   C. used.
   D. known.

_____C_____ 2. The relationship between the two parts of sentence 5 is one of
   A. time.
   B. comparison.
   C. contrast.
   D. addition.

_____B_____ 3. The author implies that among primitive societies, the Eskimos' cleverness is
   A. superior.
   B. typical.
   C. rare.
   D. inferior.

Comments: Item 1—Answer A is incorrect because people, not objects, are hired. Answers B and D are incorrect because the Eskimos did more than just recognize or know the device—they *used* it.

Item 2—*But* in sentence 5 is a contrast word.

Item 3—Sentence 2 implies that Eskimos are typically clever, and sentence 3 mentions that "countless examples" can illustrate the point.

___B___ 4. The author implies that certain societies are considered "primitive" because of their
   A. attitude toward animals.
   B. level of technology.
   C. creative ability.
   D. understanding of their environment.

___C___ 5. The author's attitude toward the Eskimos who created the weapon appears to be
   A. accusing.
   B. disgusted.
   C. objective.
   D. puzzled.

___C___ 6. Which is an appropriate title for this selection?
   A. Mentally Backward Societies
   B. Dangerous Environmental Features
   C. Intelligence in Primitive Societies
   D. Land of the Eskimos

___D___ 7. Which sentence best expresses the main idea of the passage?
   A. There are no greater challenges to a society than that of controlling the environment.
   B. Eskimos are able to control wolves.
   C. With increased technology, primitive societies should be able to cope even more effectively with their environment.
   D. Primitive societies can deal shrewdly and effectively with the demands of their environment.

___D___ 8. The author supports the main idea with a
   A. list of several reasons.
   B. comparison of two things.
   C. contrast between two things.
   D. detailed example.

Comments: Item 4—See sentences 1, 2, 10, and 11.

Item 5—The author never accuses, sounds disgusted, or seems puzzled; therefore, the tone is generally objective. Reference to the method (sentence 10) as harsh does not imply disapproval of Eskimos.

Item 6—Answer A is too narrow. Answers B and D are too broad.

Item 7—Answers A and C are not addressed in the selection. Answer B is too narrow.

Item 8—Answers A, B, and C are not accurate. A detailed example of the Eskimo and the wolf supports the main idea.

COMBINED SKILLS: Test 11

Read the passage below. Then write the letter of the best answer to each question that follows.

> [1]The Hawthorne experiment was conducted in the late 1920s and early 1930s. [2]The management of Western Electric's Hawthorne plant, located near Chicago, wanted to find out if environmental factors, such as lighting, could affect workers' productivity and morale. [3]A team of social scientists experimented with a small group of employees who were set apart from their coworkers. [4]The environmental conditions of this group's work area were controlled, and the subjects themselves were closely observed. [5]To the great surprise of the researchers, the productivity of these workers increased in response to any change in their environmental conditions. [6]The rate of work increased even when the changes (such as as sharp decrease in the level of light in the workplace) seemed unlikely to have such an effect.
>
> [7]It was concluded that the presence of the observers had caused the workers in the experimental group to feel special. [8]As a result, the employees came to know and trust one another, and they developed a strong belief in the importance of their job. [9]The researchers believed that this, not the changes in the work environment, accounted for the increased productivity.
>
> [10]A later reanalysis of the study data challenged the Hawthorne conclusions on the grounds that the changes in patterns of human relations, considered so important by the original researchers, were never measured. [11]However, even if the original conclusions must be revised, they nonetheless raise a problem for social scientists: Research subjects who know they are being studied can change their behavior. [12]Throughout the social sciences, this phenomenon has come to be called the Hawthorne effect.

_C_ 1. In sentences 2 and 5, the word *productivity* means
    A. attendance.
    B. human relations.
    C. rate of work.
    D. health.

        Rate of work in sentence 6 is a synonym of *productivity.*

_D_ 2. The pattern of organization of the second paragraph is
    A. list of items.
    B. time order.
    C. definition and example.
    D. cause and effect.

        As a result and *accounted for* are cause-effect words. *Cause:* presence of observers. *Effect:* employees came to know and trust one another, developing a strong belief in the importance of their job.

_C_ 3. The author implies that a sharp decrease in light increased workers' output because the workers
    A. experienced less eyestrain.
    B. had to pay more attention to what they were doing.

        In sentence 9, the pronoun *this* refers to sentence 7.

C. knew they were being observed, and this motivated them.

D. in the experiment were paid more than other workers.

___C___ 4. Employers might conclude from the Hawthorne experiment that they should

See sentences 7–9.

A. keep plant lighting low.

B. constantly change environmental conditions.

C. consistently let workers know that their work is important.

D. keep social scientists away from their workers.

___A___ 5. The Hawthorne experiment suggests that

A. workers' attitudes are more important than their environment.

B. social scientists are good workers.

See sentences 7–9.

C. productivity in electric plants tends to be low.

D. even those Hawthorne workers who were not in the experiment improved their productivity.

___B___ 6. The Hawthorne effect is a problem for social scientists because

A. the researchers did not measure the changes in human relations among workers.

B. the results of a study will be questionable if the subjects were aware that they were being observed.

See sentence 11.

C. the Hawthorne research was done too long ago, when working conditions were quite different.

D. the group of employees who were studied was small.

___A___ 7. The author's main purpose is to

A. explain the Hawthorne effect.

B. prove the importance of research.

C. amuse with a surprising experiment.

D. suggest ideas for future research.

Answers B and D are not addressed in the passage. Answer C is not correct because the passage has no humorous or amusing wording.

___C___ 8. Which sentence best expresses the main idea of the passage?

A. The famous Hawthorne experiment took place in the late 1920s and early 1930s.

B. The Hawthorne experiment took place because the management of an electric plant wanted to find out the impact of environmental factors on workers.

C. An experiment revealed the fact, known as the Hawthorne effect, that research subjects may behave differently if they know they are being studied.

D. A reanalysis of data from an experiment at an electric plant showed that the researchers were careless about how they conducted their study.

Answers A and B are too narrow.
Answer D is not correct; see sentence 10.

COMBINED SKILLS: Test 12

Read the passage below. Then write the letter of the best answer to each question that follows.

[1]We all know deserts are dry places, but just what is meant by the term *dry*? [2]That is, how much rain defines the boundary between humid and dry regions? [3]Sometimes it is defined by a single rainfall figure, for example, twenty-five centimeters (ten inches) of precipitation per year. [4](*Rainfall* refers to the quantity of water that falls in the form of rain, snow, etc. in an area in a given amount of time.) [5]However, the concept of dryness is a relative one that refers to any situation in which a water deficiency exists. [6]Thus, climatologists define *dry climate* as one in which yearly precipitation is less than the potential loss of water by evaporation. [7]Dryness then is related not only to total annual rainfall but also to evaporation. [8]Evaporation, in turn, greatly depends upon temperature. [9]As temperatures climb, potential evaporation also increases. [10]Fifteen to twenty-five centimeters of precipitation can support forests in northern Scandinavia, where evaporation into the cool, humid air is slight and a surplus of water remains in the soil. [11]However, the same amount of rain falling on New Mexico supports only a sparse vegetative cover because evaporation into the hot, dry air is great. [12]So clearly no specific amount of precipitation can serve as a universal boundary for dry climates.

___C___ 1. In sentence 3, the word *precipitation* means
    A. weather conditions.
    B. humidity in the air.
    C. water that falls to the earth in any form.
    D. dry places.

___B___ 2. Scientists who study weather consider a dry climate to be one in which
    A. ten inches of water fall each year.
    B. potential evaporation is greater than the rainfall.
    C. there is no rainfall at all.
    D. it gets very hot.

___C___ 3. The higher the temperature,
    A. the greater the rainfall.
    B. the smaller the rainfall.
    C. the greater the potential evaporation.
    D. the smaller the potential evaporation.

___A___ 4. In the discussion in the passage, temperature is
    A. a cause.
    B. an effect.

_C_   5. The relationship between sentences 10 and 11 is one of
   A. time.
   B. comparison.
   C. contrast.
   D. cause and effect.

_A_   6. The main purpose of the passage is to
   A. explain.
   B. persuade.
   C. amuse.
   D. predict.

_C_   7. The author implies that one reason evaporation in northern Scandinavian forests is slight is that
   A. the rainfall is low there.
   B. there is no rainfall there.
   C. the air there is cool.
   D. a heavy ground cover prevents the moisture from evaporating.

_B_   8. Which sentence best expresses the main idea of the selection?
   A. The lower the temperature, the less the evaporation.
   B. A dry climate is one in which the rainfall is less than the potential evaporation, which depends on temperature.
   C. Evaporation in a northern forest is slight in comparison with the evaporation in a desert region like that of New Mexico.
   D. *Rainfall* is the amount of water that falls to earth as rain, snow, sleet, and hail.

Comments: Item 1—Sentence 4, which mentions rainfall, rain, and snow, suggests the meaning of *precipitation* as used in sentence 3.

Item 2—See sentence 6.

Item 3—See sentence 9.

Item 4—Temperature causes evaporation. See sentences 8–9.

Item 5—*However* in sentence 11 is a contrast word.

Item 6—The passage explains the cause-effect relationship between precipitation and evaporation.

Item 7—See sentence 10.

Item 8—Answers A, C, and D are too narrow.

COMBINED SKILLS: Test 13

Read the passage below. Then write the letter of the best answer to each question that follows.

¹It's Friday afternoon, and you have almost survived another week of classes. ²You are just looking forward dreamily to the weekend when the English instructor says: "For Monday you will turn in a five-hundred-word composition on college football."

³Well, that puts a good big hole in the weekend. ⁴You don't have any strong views on college football one way or the other. ⁵You get rather excited during the season and go to all the home games and find it rather more fun than not. ⁶On the other hand, the class has been reading Robert Hutchins in the anthology and perhaps Shaw's "Eighty-Yard Run," and from the class discussion you have got the idea that the instructor thinks college football is for the birds. ⁷You are no fool, you. ⁸You can figure out what side to take.

⁹After dinner you sit down at the computer that you got for high-school graduation. ¹⁰You might as well get it over with and enjoy Saturday and Sunday. ¹¹Five hundred words is about two double-spaced pages with normal margins. ¹²You open a new document, think up a title, and you're off:

Why College Football Should Be Abolished

¹³College football should be abolished because it's bad for the school and also bad for the players. ¹⁴The players are so busy practicing that they don't have any time for their studies.

¹⁵This, you feel, is a mighty good start. ¹⁶The only trouble is that it's only thirty-two words. ¹⁷You still have four hundred and sixty-eight to go, and you've pretty well exhausted the subject. ¹⁸It comes to you that you do your best thinking in the morning, so you shut down the computer and go to the movies. ¹⁹But the next morning you have to do your washing and some math problems, and in the afternoon you go to the game. ²⁰The English instructor turns up too, and you wonder if you've taken the right side after all. ²¹Saturday night you have a date, and Sunday morning you have to go to church. ²²(You shouldn't let English assignments interfere with your religion.) ²³What with one thing and another, it's ten o'clock Sunday night before you sit down at the computer again.

_____C_____ 1. In sentence 17, the word *exhausted* means
   A. created.
   B. researched.
   C. completely covered.
   D. forgotten.

General-sense clue. Sentences 15–17 imply that you have no other thoughts and have therefore completely covered the subject at this point. Answer A is not correct because the English instructor created the subject. Answer B is incorrect because there is no evidence that you did any research. Answer D is incorrect. If you had forgotten, you would not be planning to do it the next morning.

___B___ 2. The relationship between the first part of sentence 18 (before the comma) to sentence 19 is one of
    A. cause and effect.
    B. contrast.
    C. comparison.
    D. addition.

> *But* is a contrast word.
> What you think is different from what you do.

___A___ 3. The overall pattern of organization is
    A. time order.
    B. list of items.
    C. definition and example.
    D. comparison.

> The passage chronicles the student's actions from Friday through Sunday.

___C___ 4. The author's tone can be described as
    A. angry and worried.
    B. encouraging and respectful.
    C. humorous and sarcastic.
    D. ambivalent and bewildered.

> Humor is implied throughout the passage.
> Sarcasm is detected in sentence 22.

___B___ 5. To make his points, the author has chosen to use a
    A. factual anecdote.
    B. fictional anecdote.

> The fictional "you" represents the typical student.

___A___ 6. The author suggests that the student
    A. is more skilled at putting things off than at writing compositions.
    B. would miss a party in order to attend church on Sunday.
    C. actually enjoys writing compositions.
    D. should have found out his teacher's view on football before writing the composition.

> See sentences 18–23.

___D___ 7. The author implies in the second paragraph that the student
    A. agrees with Robert Hutchins's views on football.
    B. has no interest in football at all.
    C. has paid no attention to class discussions.
    D. feels his composition should defend the instructor's point of view.

> See sentences 6–7.

___B___ 8. Which sentence best expresses the main idea of the passage?
    A. College football should not be abolished.
    B. A college composition assignment requires time and thought.
    C. English instructors should not assign homework for the weekends, when students have little available time.
    D. Composition assignments should be based on class reading assignments and discussion.

> The student spent neither time nor thought, thereby coming up with no composition.

COMBINED SKILLS: Test 14

Read the passage below. Then write the letter of the best answer to each question that follows.

^{1}Why do American schools fail to create lifetime readers? ^{2}There are two basic and related "facts of life" that parents and educators seem to ignore. ^{3}The first fact is that human beings are pleasure-centered. ^{4}We will voluntarily do over and over that which brings us pleasure. ^{5}For example, we go to the restaurants we like, order the foods we like, listen to the radio stations that play the music we like, and visit the in-laws we like. ^{6}Conversely, we avoid the restaurants, foods, music, and in-laws we dislike.

^{7}What does this pleasure principle have to do with reading? ^{8}Children love stories, so every time we read to a child at home or at school, we send a "pleasure" message to the child's brain. ^{9}You could even call it a commercial, conditioning the child to associate books and print with pleasure. ^{10}However, all too often, parents don't read to their children; and, to make matters worse, schools send "unpleasure" messages about reading. ^{11}Endless hours of work-sheets, intensive phonics instruction, and seemingly unconnected test questions can be—to a child—tedious or boring, threatening, and meaningless. ^{12}If a child seldom experiences the "pleasures" of reading at home and meets only the "unpleasures" at school, then the natural reaction will be avoidance.

^{13}The second basic fact is that reading is an accrued skill. ^{14}In other words, reading is like riding a bicycle, driving a car, or sewing: in order to get better at it, you must do it. ^{15}And the more you do it, the better you get at it. ^{16}The last twenty-five years of reading research confirms this simple formula. ^{17}Regardless of sex, race, nationality, or socioeconomic background, the students who read the most are the ones who read the best, achieve the most, and stay in school the longest. ^{18}In contrast, those who don't read much cannot get better at it. ^{19}And most Americans (children and adults) don't read much, and therefore aren't very good at it.

^{20}Why don't Americans read much? ^{21}The reason is that a lack of "pleasure" messages in the home, coupled with the large number of "unpleasure" messages about reading they received throughout their school years, nullify any attraction a book might offer. ^{22}They avoid books and print the same way a cat avoids a rocking chair.

___B___ 1. In sentence 6, the word *conversely* means

    A. in addition.

    B. in contrast.

    C. as a result.

    D. next.

Conversely contrasts things we do like with things we don't like.

_D_   2. The author feels that children are encouraged to read by
    A. doing worksheets.
    B. riding a bicycle.
    C. having phonics instruction.
    D. being read to.

See sentence 8.

_A_   3. Sentence 12 expresses a relationship of
    A. cause and effect.
    B. comparison.
    C. contrast.
    D. addition.

An unpleasant experience (*cause*) produces withdrawal (*effect*).

_C_   4. The passage discusses
    A. stages of reading education.
    B. a list of methods for teaching reading to children.
    C. the causes of Americans' not becoming skillful, lifetime readers.
    D. a definition of the phrase "lifetime readers" with examples.

All the details tell how parents and educators fail to create healthy readers.

_A_   5. Sentences 16 and 17 state
    A. a fact.
    B. an opinion.

The research is documented and can be validated.

_A_   6. The author's tone can be described as
    A. critical and analytical.
    B. joyful and optimistic.
    C. tolerant and amused.
    D. pleading and hopeful.

The writer analyzes the reasons Americans don't read well or much, making critical remarks about how parents neglect to introduce their children to the pleasures of reading and about how educators often make reading an unpleasant experience.

_B_   7. Sentence 22 implies that most Americans
    A. carelessly seek out books and print.
    B. purposely stay away from books and print.
    C. have no opinion about books and print.
    D. are often harmed by books and print.

A cat purposely stays away from a rocking chair to avoid getting his tail mashed.

_A_   8. Which sentence best states the main idea of the passage?
    A. Most Americans don't read much or well because parents and educators often fail to make reading a pleasant experience.
    B. Reading to children sends a message to them to associate books and print with pleasure.
    C. People, being pleasure-centered, will voluntarily avoid activities they dislike and repeatedly do activities that bring them pleasure.
    D. Twenty-five years of reading research has shown that the students who read the most are those that read the best.

Answers B, C, and D are all too narrow.

COMBINED SKILLS: Test 15

Read the passage below. Then write the letter of the best answer to each question that follows.

¹Imagine being on a treadmill, wearing a face mask connected to oxygen-measuring equipment. ²You are walking at a leisurely pace, at the slowest setting, so your oxygen consumption is fairly low. ³As the speed of the treadmill increases, your metabolism increases, and as a result, your oxygen consumption goes up as well. ⁴Your muscle cells are using the extra oxygen to break down carbohydrates, which they use for fuel, and turn them into energy, so their metabolism is said to be *aerobic* (with air). ⁵You are now jogging along at a comfortable speed, still supplying ample oxygen to your muscle cells, so your exercise is still aerobic. ⁶As you increase your speed, your oxygen consumption will continue to rise, but at some point, it will stop rising. ⁷That is because your heart and lungs have reached their maximum capacity for supplying oxygen to the muscles via the bloodstream. ⁸But you can still run a lot faster. ⁹Your speed keeps increasing and eventually you are running as fast as you can, but your oxygen consumption has not changed. ¹⁰Your muscle cells can keep on firing without getting the extra oxygen they need because they are able to break down carbohydrates without using oxygen. ¹¹This is called *anaerobic* (without air) *metabolism*. ¹²Sprinters, who run at top speed, perform most of their hundred-meter race anaerobically; in contrast, long-distance runners, who have time to vary their speed, perform most of their event aerobically.

¹³Anaerobic metabolism is far less efficient than aerobic metabolism but is capable of generating very high quantities of energy for short periods of time. ¹⁴It also generates lactic acid as a byproduct. ¹⁵This accumulates in the muscles and is associated with muscle fatigue and general exhaustion. ¹⁶That is why sprinting cannot be kept up for very long. ¹⁷After sprinting, the lactic acid that has accumulated in the muscles has to be broken down, and this requires oxygen, which explains why we puff and pant after a hard run.

_A_ 1. The body's energy is usually obtained through the breakdown of
  A. carbohydrates.
  B. lactic acid.   See sentence 4.
  C. the bloodstream.
  D. oxygen.

_C_ 2. When you run, your body begins anaerobic metabolism
  A. as you begin to pick up speed.
  B. after sprinting is completed.
  C. when your heart and lungs cannot supply sufficient oxygen.
  D. when the lactic acid in your muscles must be broken down.

Sentences 10–11 explain that *anaerobic* means *without air*.
Sentence 7 mentions the heart and lungs as suppliers of oxygen.

_A_   3. Aerobic metabolism
  A. is more efficient than anaerobic metabolism.
  B. breaks down carbohydrates without oxygen.
  C. generates lactic acid.
  D. happens for only brief periods.

  Sentence 13 supports answer A by explaining the principle in reverse terms.

_C_   4. The main overall patterns of organization of the passage are cause and effect and
  A. list of items.
  B. comparison.
  C. contrast.

  The passage explains how aerobic metabolism is different from anaerobic metabolism. *But* (four occurrences) and *in contrast* are contrast words.

_A_   5. The purpose of this passage is to
  A. inform.
  B. persuade.
  C. entertain.

  No details attempt to persuade or entertain. The passage is concerned with just the facts about the two ways energy is supplied to the muscles.

_D_   6. We can infer that when we feel we are out of breath, we are low on
  A. lactic acid.
  B. carbohydrates.
  C. muscle cells.
  D. oxygen.

  See sentence 17.

_C_   7. The passage implies that during sprinting,
  A. there is a dangerous strain on the heart.
  B. the body's reserve of carbohydrates increases.
  C. the body breaks down carbohydrates both with and without oxygen.
  D. the body needs less energy than usual.

_A_   8. Which statement best expresses the main idea of the passage?
  A. Walking, jogging, and sprinting create different energy demands on the human body and also consume different amounts of oxygen.
  B. Running at top speed cannot be kept up nearly as long as jogging because of the different ways that energy is supplied to the muscles.
  C. Muscle cells can keep on firing in the absence of oxygen because they are able to break down carbohydrates for short periods.
  D. When lactic acid accumulates in someone's muscles, the person experiences muscle fatigue and general exhaustion.

Comments: Item 7—The word *almost* in sentence 12 makes answer A incorrect. Answer B is incorrect because the passage does not mention a reserve of carbohydrates. Details in sentences 12–17 make answer D incorrect.

Item 8—Answers A, C, and D are too narrow.

SAMPLE ANSWER SHEET

Use the form below as a model answer sheet for the fifteen combined-skills tests on the preceding pages.

Name _____

Section _____ Date _____

SCORE: (Number correct) _____ × 12.5 = _____%

COMBINED SKILLS: Test ____

1. _____

2. _____

3. _____

4. _____

5. _____

6. _____

7. _____

8. _____

2

Propaganda

What do you think is the main difference between the following two evaluations of a city?

> The weather isn't bad in Philadelphia, if you don't mind a few months of winter. And the city has wonderful museums and restaurants. But the streets are often dirty there, and state and city taxes keep going up.

> Philadelphia is the place to live! Once you experience its pleasant climate, its museums, and restaurants, you'll agree with Phillies baseball star Ken Greyson when he says, "Home base for me is Philadelphia. Living here is a ball!"

Did you notice that the first evaluation is an attempt to be objective about Philadelphia? It mentions both positive and negative points so the reader will get a balanced picture of the city. The second approach, however, includes only positive points. It was not meant to provide a balanced, objective view of the city. Instead, it was designed to influence people to come and live in Philadelphia. When such biased information is methodically spread in order to promote or oppose a cause—whether the cause is a city, a political view, a product, or an organization—it is **propaganda**.

PROPAGANDA TECHNIQUES

Propaganda may use one or more common techniques for convincing people by appealing to their emotions. Recognizing these techniques will help you separate the substance of a message (if there is any) from its purely emotional appeal. If you are not aware of the propaganda devices, you may make decisions as a result of emotional manipulation. This chapter will introduce you to seven of the more common propaganda techniques:

- Bandwagon
- Testimonial
- Transfer
- Plain Folks

- Name Calling
- Glittering Generalities
- Card Stacking

Once you have learned these techniques, you will recognize one or more of them in just about every advertisement you encounter. Although many of the examples in this chapter and its tests are made up, they were inspired by real ads.

1 Bandwagon

Old-fashioned parades were usually led by a large wagon carrying a brass band. Therefore, to "jump on the bandwagon" means to join a parade, or to do what many others are doing. For example, we are often told to buy a product or vote for a political candidate because, in effect, "everybody else is doing it." An ad for a cereal may claim that "Sugar-O's Is Everybody's Favorite Breakfast." A political commercial may show people from all walks of life saying they will vote for candidate Fred Foghorn. The ads imply that if you don't jump on the bandwagon, the parade will pass you by.

Here are two examples of real TV ads that have used the **bandwagon** appeal:

> With appealing music in the background, flashing scenes show many people wearing the sponsor's jeans.

> On a beautiful day, almost everyone on the beach leaves in a hurry in order to attend the sponsor's sale.

➤ *Practice 1*

Check (✓) the **two** descriptions of ads that use the bandwagon appeal.

_____ 1. Famous actress Margo Lane explains that she loves to use a certain hair coloring.

__✓__ 2. Most of the people in a crowd at the ball game are drinking the sponsor's cola beverage.

_____ 3. A beautiful woman in a slinky red dress is shown driving the sponsor's car.

_____ 4. The tune of "God Bless America" is being played in the background as an announcer asks viewers to support the home baseball team by coming out to games.

__✓__ 5. An ad for a new movie shows people waiting to buy tickets in a line that extends halfway around the block.

2 Testimonial

Famous athletes often appear on television as spokespersons for all sorts of products, from soft drinks to automobiles. Movie and TV stars make commercials endorsing products and political issues. The idea behind this approach is that the testimony of famous people influences the television viewers who admire these people.

What consumers must remember is that famous people get paid to endorse products. In addition, these people are not necessarily experts about the products, or the political issues, they promote. This does not in itself mean that what they say is untrue. But realizing that celebrities receive money to recommend products that they may know little about should help consumers think twice about such messages.

Here are two examples of real ads that have used the appeal of **testimonials**:

> A famous actor promotes a product intended to help people quit smoking.
>
> A popular TV hostess and singer is the spokesperson for a cruise line.

➤ *Practice 2*

Check (✓) the **two** descriptions of ads that use a testimonial.

_____ 1. Numerous people crowd around the department store door, waiting for the store to open.

__✓__ 2. Famous actress Margo Lane explains that she loves to use a certain hair coloring.

_____ 3. A grandmother, serving a canned vegetable soup to her grandson, says, "This has all the simple, healthy, and delicious ingredients I use in my own vegetable soup."

__✓__ 4. A sports star praises the brand of basketball sneakers he is putting on.

_____ 5. An ad says, "We've got plenty of style and color at Sunny Styles, so come see how our fashions can bring out the rainbow in you."

3 Transfer

Ads that use the transfer technique associate a product with a symbol or image that people admire or love. The advertiser hopes that people's positive feelings for the symbol or image will transfer to the product. For example, calling an automobile "The All-American Car" appeals to would-be buyers' patriotism; the "All-American" image calls to mind all that is best in America. Or consider a real-life ad in which several nuns are surprised and impressed that the fresh-brewed coffee they think they are drinking is actually Folger's instant coffee. The qualities people associate with nuns—seeing them as honest, trustworthy, and highly selective in their worldly pleasures—are then associated with the product as well.

There is also a good deal of transfer value in good looks. Consumers **transfer** the positive feelings they have toward a sexy-looking person to the product being advertised. Many ads today use handsome men and beautiful women to pitch their products; more than ever, Madison Avenue seems convinced that "sex sells."

To summarize, the transfer technique depends upon the appeal value of two special categories:

1) admired or beloved symbols and images
2) sex appeal

Here are two examples from real ads that have used transfer:

An American eagle symbolizes the United States Post Office's Express Mail service.

A tanned blonde in a bikini is stretched out on the beach, holding in her hand a can of light beer.

➤ Practice 3

Check (✓) the **two** descriptions of ads that use the transfer approach.

_____ 1. An announcer claims that a competitor's tires don't last as long as the sponsor's tires do.

___✓___ 2. With the tune of "God Bless America" in the background, an announcer asks viewers to support the home baseball team by coming out to games.

___✓___ 3. A beautiful woman in a slinky red dress is shown driving the sponsor's car.

_____ 4. Several ordinary, friendly-looking young men in jeans buy the sponsor's beer.

_____ 5. "My opponent hasn't made up his mind about state taxes," says a candidate for mayor. "Obviously, he's too wishy-washy to be mayor."

4   Plain Folks

Some people distrust political candidates who are rich or well-educated. They feel that these candidates, if elected, will not be able to understand the problems of the average working person. Therefore, candidates often try to show they are just "plain folks" by referring in their speeches to how poor they were when they were growing up or how they had to work their way through school. They also pose for photographs wearing overalls or buying a hot dog from a curbside stand.

Likewise, the presidents of some companies appear in their own ads, trying to show that their giant enterprises are just family businesses. If a corporation can convince potential customers that it is run by people just like them, the customers are more likely to buy the corporation's product than if they felt the company was run by ruthless millionaire executives. In other words, people using the **plain-folks** approach tell their audience, "We are ordinary folks, just like you."

Yet another plain-folks approach is for a company to show us a product being used and enjoyed by everyday types of people—persons just like ourselves. (In contrast, the propaganda technique of testimonial features famous people. Also, while plain-folks ads feature individuals, bandwagon ads emphasize large numbers of people.)

Here are two examples of real ads that have used the appeal of plain folks:

> A president of a fast-food hamburger chain, dressed in shirtsleeves, carries a food tray to a small table in one of his restaurants, all the while pitching his burgers to the viewer.

> Average-looking American kids are shown at home trying and enjoying a cereal.

➤ *Practice 4*

Check (✓) the **two** descriptions of ads that use the plain-folks approach.

_____✓_____ 1. Two ordinary, friendly looking young men in jeans buy the sponsor's beer.

_____ 2. A famous baseball player wears the sponsor's jeans.

_____ 3. After seeing a play, a man leaves a theater with a big smile on his face. Then his chauffeur pulls up in a Cadillac to take him home.

_____ 4. "Drink our soda," says the announcer. "It's the real thing."

_____✓_____ 5. A grandmother, serving a canned vegetable soup to her grandson, says, "This has all the simple, healthy, and delicious ingredients I use in my own vegetable soup."

5   Name Calling

Name calling is the use of emotionally loaded language or negative comments to turn people against a rival product, candidate, or movement. An example of name calling would be a political candidate's labeling an opponent "uncaring," "radical," or "wimpy." Or a manufacturer may say or imply that a competing product is "full of chemicals," even though in reality everything is made up of chemicals of one kind or another.

Here are two examples of name calling taken from real life:

> In the early days of the "cold war" with the Soviet Union, in the 1950s, an exaggerated concern about communism in this country led to charges of un-Americanism against many people.

> A fast-food chain accused a competitor of selling a seaweed burger simply because the competitor used a seaweed extract to keep its burger moist.

➢ *Practice 5*

Check (✓) the **two** descriptions of ads that use name calling.

_____ 1. "Drink our soda," says the announcer. "It's the real thing."

__✓__ 2. "Brand X's spaghetti sauce tastes like the sauce that Mom used to make," says a man to his wife. "And you know what a lousy cook she was." Then he suggests trying the sponsor's brand.

_____ 3. An ad says, "We've got plenty of style and color at Sunny Styles, so come see how our fashions can bring out the rainbow in you."

__✓__ 4. "My opponent has lived in our state for only two years," says a candidate for state senator. "Let's not put an outsider into state office."

_____ 5. An ad for cigarettes shows a beautiful woman in a strapless gown smoking the sponsor's product and being admired by several handsome men.

6   Glittering Generalities

A **glittering generality** is an important-sounding but unspecific claim about some product, candidate, or cause. It cannot be proved true or false because no evidence is offered to support the claim. Such claims use general words that different people would define differently, such as "progress," "great," and "ultimate."

"Simply the best," an ad might say about a certain television set. But no specific evidence of any kind is offered to support such a generality. "Janet Mayer

Has the Right Stuff! Vote for Mayer for Congress," a campaign slogan might claim. But what seems like "the right stuff" to her campaign manager might seem very wrong to you. The point is that the phrase sounds good but says nothing definite.

Here are two examples from real ads that use glittering generalities:

> A car ad claims, "It just feels right."
>
> A canned-food ad boasts of "nutrition that works."

➢ Practice 6

Check (✓) the **two** descriptions of ads that use glittering generalities.

_✓_ 1. "For a forward-looking government," says the announcer, "vote for Ed Dalton for governor."

_____ 2. A well-known astronaut says that he uses the sponsor's aspirin.

_____ 3. "Millions of satisfied customers can't all be wrong," says the announcer of an ad for grass seed.

_____ 4. "My opponent attends Alcoholics Anonymous meetings," says a candidate for city council. "Do you want him to represent you on the council?"

_✓_ 5. An ad says, "We've got plenty of style and color at Sunny Styles, so come see how our fashions can bring out the rainbow in you."

7 Card Stacking

Card stacking refers to stacking the cards in your favor and presenting only the facts and figures that are favorable to your particular side of the issue. It could also be called the "too-good-to-be-true technique" or the "omitted details technique."

In legal language, deliberately leaving out inconvenient facts is called "concealing evidence." In advertising, such evidence may be concealed in the interests of selling a product. For example, past advertisements for the drug Tylenol called it "the pain reliever hospitals use most," and this statement was perfectly true. What these advertisements failed to mention is that the manufacturer of Tylenol offered hospitals large discounts. Since other drug companies may not have offered similar discounts in the past, most hospital administrators chose to buy Tylenol. The advertising campaign depended on people's jumping to the conclusion, "Hospitals use more Tylenol than any other pain reliever. They must consider it the best drug of its kind available." In fact, other drugs with the same pain reliever as Tylenol might have worked just as well.

Read the following ad and then the list of omitted details below it. Then write the letter of the missing detail you think the advertiser deliberately left out of its ad.

For only forty dollars, Credit Information Services will provide a copy of your credit report. Haven't you been wondering what information a potential lender gets when you apply for a loan? Now you will have all the information you desire for a single low yearly fee.

Missing details:
A. Each additional use of this service will cost only thirty-five dollars.
B. Credit Information Services already has 300,000 customers nationwide.
C. Federal law gives you the right to find out what is in your credit report—without charge.

If you chose C, you are right. If you know this detail, you are not likely to send forty dollars to Credit Information Services.

➤ Practice 7

Which missing details does the reader need to know in order to avoid being tricked? In the space provided, write the letter of the important detail that has been purposely omitted from each paragraph.

_B_ 1. Not only is our new fruit punch delicious, but bottle for bottle, it costs less than the leading brand.
A. The punch comes in assorted flavors.
B. The punch is in a 6-ounce bottle; the leading brand is in an 8-ounce bottle.
C. The punch includes a mixture of more fruit juices than the leading brand.

_A_ 2. If your request for a loan has been turned down by your local bank, don't worry—no matter what your credit rating is like, we will lend you money.
A. The lending company charges a far higher interest rate than banks.
B. You can reach the lending company by calling a toll-free number.
C. The lending company has been in business since 1976.

_C_ 3. Congratulations! You have just won an all-expenses-paid three-night vacation to Atlantic City, New Jersey. You will dine at glamorous restaurants, enjoy stage shows, and swim in the beautiful Atlantic Ocean—all free. This free trip has been awarded to only a handful of selected winners in your area.
A. The certificate for your free trip will arrive by registered mail within two weeks of your acceptance of this offer.
B. You may stay at your choice of two casino hotels: Trump's Castle or Resorts International.
C. You must pay $399 to join a travel club before you become eligible for your free trip.

CHAPTER REVIEW

Propaganda is biased information that tries to influence us by appealing to our emotions rather than our common sense. There are seven common propaganda techniques:

- Bandwagon—do what many others are doing.
- Testimonial—do or think what famous people are doing or thinking.
- Transfer—use a product because it's associated with something that is greatly valued.
- Plain folks—vote for a candidate or use a product because average, everyday people are doing so.
- Name calling—don't support a candidate or use a product because of negative comments about that candidate or product.
- Glittering generalities—believe in something because of important-sounding but unspecific claims.
- Card stacking—believe in something because the limited evidence presented favors it.

➤ Review Test 1

To review what you've learned in this chapter, complete each of the following sentences about propaganda by writing the letter of the correct answer.

  _B_   1. Propaganda is intended to (A. inform; B. persuade).

  _A_   2. An important difference between a testimonial and a plain-folks appeal is that testimonials feature (A. famous; B. ordinary) people.

  _A_   3. The (A. transfer; B. plain-folks) technique associates a product with symbols and images that people respect.

  _A_   4. (A. Glittering generalities; B. Card stacking) is the technique of making dramatic but unspecific and unsupported claims.

  _B_   5. The "omitted details technique" would be an appropriate alternative name for (A. transfer; B. card stacking).

➤ Review Test 2

In each pair of sentences below, the first sentence does **not** illustrate a propaganda technique, but the second one does. On the line, write the letter of the propaganda technique used in the **second** sentence.

_D_   1. • Kiddy Kare is the largest day-care center in town.

• Our competitor's day-care center is more concerned about profits than children.

A. Bandwagon	C. Testimonial
B. Transfer	D. Name calling

_A_   2. • Sureguard sunglasses filter out harmful ultraviolet rays.

• "I'm proud to wear Sureguard sunglasses," says actress Judy Winsor. "You'll love them too."

A. Testimonial	C. Plain folks
B. Transfer	D. Name calling

_A_   3. • In a recent election poll, Margo Levy was ahead of the other candidate.

• Add your vote to the landslide victory Margo Levy will win in next week's election.

A. Bandwagon	C. Transfer
B. Testimonial	D. Name calling

_D_   4. • Twin Oaks is a residential development near Des Moines, Iowa.

• There's nothing else quite like Twin Oaks, a great residential community where you will be proud to live.

A. Bandwagon	C. Transfer
B. Testimonial	D. Glittering generalities

_C_   5. • As a young man, candidate Alan Wilson had a variety of jobs working in a department store and in his family's TV station.

• As a young man, candidate Alan Wilson learned what it means to work hard by spending long hours lifting boxes and sweeping floors.

A. Name calling	C. Plain folks
B. Bandwagon	D. Glittering generalities

_C_   6. • A college degree opens up job doors.

      • Comedian Bill Groff says, "A college degree opens up job doors."

        A. Glittering generalities   C. Testimonial
        B. Plain folks   D. Name calling

_B_   7. • I'm voting for Jones because he has had ten years of experience on the Senate's Committee on International Affairs.

      • I'll bet my French poodle and German shepherd know more about foreign affairs than Smith does. My vote goes to Jones.

        A. Bandwagon   C. Transfer
        B. Name calling   D. Glittering generalities

_D_   8. • Markey's Used Cars will be open on the Fourth of July.

      • A patriotic march plays, and a giant American flag waves over a used car lot. "Celebrate your freedom of choice on the Fourth of July!" says the announcer. "At Markey's, we'll honor the holiday by making some star-spangled deals."

        A. Testimonial   C. Bandwagon
        B. Name calling   D. Transfer

_A_   9. • The presidential candidate supports our country's farmers.

      • The presidential candidate has her own small farm, so she knows the farmers' concerns.

        A. Plain folks   C. Glittering generalities
        B. Testimonial   D. Transfer

_A_   10. • At Triple A Technical School, you can learn skills needed to become a plumber, mechanic, or electrician.

      • Set the world on fire with skills you learn at Triple A Technical School!

        A. Glittering generalities   C. Bandwagon
        B. Name calling   D. Transfer

➤ Review Test 3

A. Each of the passages below illustrates a particular propaganda technique. On the line next to the passage, write the letter of the technique being used.

_B_ 1. The most beautiful hair this season has shape, style, and a luxuriant, natural feel. Leslie Langtree, the television actress whose lovely hair is her trademark, reveals that her secret is Flirt. "Flirt softens my hair and gives it great body," Leslie says. "Thanks to Flirt, my hair has never looked better."

  A. Plain folks   C. Name calling
  B. Testimonial   D. Bandwagon

_D_ 2. They say, "When life gives you lemons, make lemonade." But at Ace Autos, we say that if you paid $11,000 for a lemon at Wheelers' Car Dealers, you should demand your money back and come see us.

  A. Glittering generalities   C. Testimonial
  B. Transfer   D. Name calling

_C_ 3. Liberty Bell Airlines flies anywhere in this great land, from sea to shining sea. We proudly hail America's finest: Liberty Bell.

  A. Plain folks   C. Transfer
  B. Testimonial   D. Name calling

_C_ 4. Monroe Archer is a millionaire and the president of a large corporation, yet he has never lost touch with his small-town roots. Despite his power and fame, he still likes returning to his hometown to enjoy a summer band concert and a simple supper at Charley's Diner.

  A. Name calling   C. Plain folks
  B. Bandwagon   D. Testimonial

_C_ 5. "I wear Form Fit jeans—if I wear anything at all," whispers a shapely model in tight jeans and low-cut T-shirt.

  A. Bandwagon   C. Transfer
  B. Name calling   D. Glittering generalities

_B_ 6. Come one! Come all! Everybody's going to Linwood Furniture for the big eighth annual sale, a sale so big we rented a tent to hold the crowds.

    A. Name calling   C. Transfer
    B. Bandwagon   D. Testimonial

_A_ 7. Cast your vote next Tuesday for Larry Lewis. This fine man has much to offer his community and his nation. As your representative, he pledges to do his best to improve conditions and to bring you closer to the fulfillment of your highest dreams.

    A. Glittering generalities   C. Bandwagon
    B. Transfer   D. Name calling

_D_ 8. A small group comes onto a crowded beach carrying buckets of Deep Southern brand fried chicken. Other people nearby notice the group, leave, and come back with buckets of Deep Southern fried chicken. Soon everyone on the beach is either eating Deep Southern or going to get some.

    A. Glittering generalities   C. Transfer
    B. Name calling   D. Bandwagon

B. The following ads use card stacking—in some way, they are too good to be true. In the space provided, write the letter of the important detail that the advertiser has intentionally omitted.

_B_ 9. Our new line of light cakes is made without any fats at all.
    A. The cakes come in six flavors.
    B. The cakes have the same number of calories as the company's cakes that aren't called "light."
    C. The cakes cost a little less than cakes that aren't called "light."

_C_ 10. "As President," says a candidate, "I will do everything in my power to keep income taxes from rising."
    A. The candidate was governor of a large state for two terms.
    B. The candidate played basketball in college.
    C. The candidate is in favor of raising sales taxes.

Check Your Performance   **PROPAGANDA**

Activity   *Number Right*   *Points*   *Score*

Review Test 1   (5 items)   _____   ×   4   =   _____

Review Test 2 (10 items)   _____   ×   4   =   _____

Review Test 3 (10 items)   _____   ×   4   =   _____

                                              TOTAL SCORE   =   _____%

Enter your total score into the **Reading Performance Chart: Review Tests** on the inside back cover.

PROPAGANDA: Mastery Test 1

In each pair of sentences below, the first sentence does not illustrate a propaganda technique, but the second one does. On the line, write the letter of the propaganda technique used in the **second** sentence.

_A_ 1. • Zesty Zip frozen fruit concentrate is made from five tropical fruits.

• "I get each day off to a roaring start with Zesty Zip," says champion car-racer Miles Leonard.

		A "champion
A. Testimonial	C. Bandwagon	car-racer" is a
B. Plain folks	D. Name calling	celebrity.

_D_ 2. • Olsen Paint has rich color and lasts for years.

• A man in painter's overalls is dipping his brush into a can of Olsen Paint. "Most of the week I'm president of Olsen Paint Company," he says. "On Saturdays, I'm a housepainter myself. So I know what people look for in a quality house paint."

		The company president
A. Transfer	C. Bandwagon	is depicted as
B. Name calling	D. Plain folks	an ordinary guy.

_A_ 3. • Frosty Diet Cola has no calories.

• An attractive couple in bathing suits stop at a soda stand. "What are you drinking?" the man asks. "Frosty Diet Cola, of course," she answers as she slips her hand around his waist.

		The cola is
A. Transfer	C. Name calling	associated with
B. Glittering generalities	D. Testimonial	sex appeal.

_B_ 4. • We hope you'll find that Choco-Chip Cookies are the best you've ever tasted.

• Try Choco-Chip Cookies—the cookies with goodness that doesn't quit.

		"Goodness that
		doesn't quit" is a
A. Name calling	C. Testimonial	significant-sounding
B. Glittering generalities	D. Plain folks	but unspecific claim.

_C_ 5. • Sea Fair cruises will be touring the Caribbean this summer.

• Don't miss out on this cruise of a lifetime enjoyed by thousands of travelers. Ask your agent for details about Sea Fair's very popular tour of the Caribbean.

The cruise's popularity is emphasized ("enjoyed by thousands," "very popular").

A. Glittering generalities	C. Bandwagon
B. Transfer	D. Name calling

(Continues on next page)

___C___ 6. • Come to Smith's Carpets' spring sale.

   • We cannot tell a lie—we honor America's presidents with beauty and savings. Come to Cherry Tree Carpets to see the amazing quality and discounts at our Presidents' Day Sale.

   A. Bandwagon   C. Transfer
   B. Name calling   D. Plain folks

___A___ 7. • Wilson's Department Store carries clothing for men, women, and children.

   • "I shop for my family's wardrobe at Wilson's Department Store. I want good values, not necessarily designer labels," says Anna Hendricks, bank clerk and homemaker.

   A. Plain folks   C. Transfer
   B. Testimonial   D. Glittering generalities

___D___ 8. • You can make a deal at Dave's Auto Dealership.

   • Come early to Dave's Auto Dealership so you won't have to stand in line—because everyone knows you can make a deal with Dave and save.

   A. Name calling   c Testimonial
   B. Transfer   D. Bandwagon

___D___ 9. • West's Tall Men's Store sells well-tailored suits in all tall sizes.

   • Buy your next suit at West's Tall Men's Store, and you'll be walking tall.

   A. Plain folks   C. Testimonial
   B. Transfer   D. Glittering generalities

___A___ 10. • We think Cheesy Pizza is delicious.

   • Al's Pizza is like the thick cardboard we use to wrap take-home orders of Cheesy Pizza. Eat Cheesy Pizza if you're a pizza lover; eat Al's if you love cardboard.

   A. Name calling   C. Testimonial
   B. Glittering generalities D. Plain folks

Comments: Item 6—The company associates itself with patriotism.
   Item 7—The speaker is an ordinary person (a "bank clerk and homemaker").
   Item 8—The sale's popularity is emphasized ("stand in line," "everyone knows").
   Item 9—"And you'll be walking tall" sounds good but is unspecific.
   Item 10—The ad makes negative comments about a rival.

PROPAGANDA: Mastery Test 2

A. Each of the passages below illustrates a particular propaganda technique. On the line next to the passage, write the letter of the main technique being used.

_D_ 1. "Out here in farm country I work hard and live simply," says a farmer. "I don't look for fancy, but I do require quality. That's why, for everyday down home toughness, I drive a Wellbilt pickup truck."

    A. Name calling   C. Bandwagon

    B. Testimonial   D. Plain folks

_B_ 2. The U.S. Heritage Committee has selected Bubble-O as the official soft drink of the Heritage Celebration to be held in the nation's capital this summer. Bubble-O: an important part of your heritage.

    A. Plain folks   C. Bandwagon

    B. Transfer   D. Name calling

_D_ 3. After six terms, the incumbent, Representative Snark, is part of the pampered Washington crowd, out of touch with the people who elected him. Vote for Loretta Reese!

    A. Testimonial   C. Transfer

    B. Glittering generalities   D. Name calling

_D_ 4. You can be part of the growing number of people who are saying "no" to drugs and "yes" to achievement. Be part of the crowd that makes a difference.

    A. Glittering generalities   C. Testimonial

    B. Name calling   D. Bandwagon

_B_ 5. A Pacekeeper minitruck is climbing a dirt road in the desert. "Pacekeeper," says the announcer. "The perfect vehicle to drive you into a new century."

    A. Plain folks   C. Bandwagon

    B. Glittering generalities   D. Name calling

(Continues on next page)

_C_ 6. The best way to warm up on those cold winter days? Ask Olympic skier Terry Niles. "There's nothing like a good hot cup of Myer's Soup to take the chill off," says Terry. "Delicious Myer's makes me feel warm all over."

    A. Bandwagon   C. Testimonial
    B. Glittering generalities   D. Plain folks

_A_ 7. Rancher Bob Curren's casual manners and style are sure to bring a fresh spirit to the Senate. Aren't you ready for a down-to-earth senator?

    A. Plain folks   C. Glittering generalities
    B. Name calling   D. Transfer

_B_ 8. An Arnold Autofocus camera is the camera of your dreams. This delightful camera will make all your photography a pleasure. You'll love your new Arnold Autofocus.

    A. Transfer   C. Bandwagon
    B. Glittering generalities   D. Name calling

B. The following ads involve card stacking—in some way, they are too good to be true. In the space provided, write the letter of the important detail that the advertiser has intentionally omitted.

_B_ 9. Congratulations, Ms. Kerr! You are among the finalists for the Magazine Club's Ten Million Dollar Lottery.
    A. The ten million dollars will be split among several winners.
    B. There are several million other people who are also among the finalists.
    C. The company has sponsored lotteries for twenty years.

_C_ 10. For only $25, Employment Education, Inc., will send you complete information on how to earn money stuffing envelopes at home.
    A. It is not difficult to stuff envelopes.
    B. The company also sells information on learning to type.
    C. Very few people are ever hired to stuff envelopes at home.

PROPAGANDA: Mastery Test 3

Read each of the ads below, and then write the letter of the best answer to each question.

A. ¹First America Bank offers a remarkable protection plan for lost or stolen credit cards. ²For only fifteen dollars, you can buy credit card protection that covers your losses up to $10,000. ³Isn't this impressive guarantee worth the small yearly fee? ⁴Losing a credit card naturally causes some anxiety, but First America's protection plan frees you from needless worry. ⁵We notify your credit card company, and we cover your losses, all for one astonishingly low fee. ⁶Remember, First America Bank is as sound as the country it serves so well.

___B___ 1. Which propaganda technique is used in sentence 6?
    A. Plain folks   C. Bandwagon
    B. Transfer   D. Testimonial

___A___ 2. Which of the following missing details has the advertiser intentionally omitted?
    A. Federal law limits a card owner's legal responsibility for lost or stolen credit cards to fifty dollars.
    B. The First America protection plan covers no more than twenty credit cards.
    C. A lost or stolen credit card should be reported within forty-eight hours.
    D. The bank offers its own Red, White, and Blue Bank Card to members in the plan.

B. ¹"The Tri-County Regional Craft Festival is an event our family never misses," says Belinda Groffman, famous folk singer. ²"It's a weekend all of us look forward to all year," adds her singing partner and husband Bob. ³"Not only do we enjoy the best in crafts from all over the region, but the other activities are so much fun—from puppet shows to magicians and jugglers. ⁴This year, join the thousands of families who have already discovered how much fun they can have at the Tri-County Folk Festival."

___D___ 3. Which is the main propaganda technique used in this ad?
    A. Plain folks   C. Name calling
    B. Transfer   D. Testimonial

___B___ 4. Which words are a key to the main propaganda technique in the ad?
    A. "Regional Craft Festival"   C. "so much fun"
    B. "Belinda Groffman, famous   D. "magicians and jugglers"
       folk singer"

(Continues on next page)

_B_   5. Which is the main propaganda technique used in sentence 4?
    A. Name calling   C. Testimonial
    B. Bandwagon   D. Transfer

C.   [1]Wouldn't a hot cup of coffee taste great right now? [2]With a Dr. Zip coffee-maker, a fresh cup like the coffee Mom has always made for Dad will be ready in minutes. [3]You can even set Dr. Zip's automatic timer to prepare a heavenly pot of coffee to greet you first thing in the morning. [4]Dr. Zip has lots of convenient features, like the brew-strength lever that lets you decide how strong you want your coffee to be. [5]And you can make as many as twelve cups of coffee at one time with a Dr. Zip coffeemaker. [6]Follow the lead of Richie Martz, basketball's highest scorer this season, who says, "Every morning, I'm a beast until I get my first delicious cup of coffee from Dr. Zip."

_B_   6. Which propaganda device is used in sentence 2?
    A. Testimonial   C. Name calling
    B. Plain folks   D. Transfer

_B_   7. Which of the following is a glittering generality?
    A. "ready in minutes"   C. "automatic timer"
    B. "heavenly pot of coffee"   D. "brew strength lever"

_C_   8. Which of the following details has the advertiser intentionally omitted?
    A. It takes only four minutes for coffee to brew in a Dr. Zip coffeemaker.
    B. The coffeemaker allows you to make as few as two cups at a time.
    C. The twelve cups made by the coffeemaker equal ten cups of other coffeemakers.
    D. The Dr. Zip company also makes its own brand of coffee.

D.   Read the fictional ad below, and then write the letter of the best answer to each question.

    [1]Get off of that sofa, thunderthighs! [2]Drag your tired, shapeless body to Norman's Sporting Goods in time for our exercise bike and treadmill sale. [3]Join the multitude of former slobs like yourself who are now fit, trim, and energetic, thanks to a regular program of exercise on one of our quality home workout machines. [4]You can be like our customer James Woodall, a plumber, who says, "I shed forty pounds and cut my cholesterol level in half after purchasing one of Norman's affordable exercise bikes."

_A_   9. Which is the main propaganda technique used in sentence 3?
    A. Bandwagon   C. Transfer
    B. Glittering generalities   D. Testimonial

_C_   10. Which is the main propaganda technique used in sentence 4?
    A. Name calling   C. Plain folks
    B. Testimonial   D. Glittering generalities

PROPAGANDA: Mastery Test 4

Read each of the ads below, and then write the letter of the best answer to each question.

A. [1]You are invited to join a new movement based on the belief that the cycle of losing and regaining weight is worse for people than maintaining a stable (yet plump) weight. [2]Thousands of people are joining Roberta Rice, a champion of this splendid new cause, in the pledge, "I'll never diet again." [3]True, Miss Rice weighs much more than the vain models whose thin, sickly thighs are displayed in fashion magazines. [4]But she is attractive, self-confident, and delighted with her role in the new movement.

_____C_____ 1. Which propaganda technique is used in sentence 2?
      A. Name calling   C. Bandwagon
      B. Transfer   D. Plain folks

_____C_____ 2. Which propaganda technique is used in sentence 3?
      A. Bandwagon   C. Name calling
      B. Testimonial   D. Glittering generalities

B. [1]At Build-Rite Furniture, we know that do-it-yourself is the traditional American way. [2]Build-Rite carries a fantastic variety of exceptional home furnishings that await only your finishing touches. [3]Just follow the simple instructions and, in no time, you've assembled a magnificent patio set or charming night table. [4]Join the millions of Americans who take pleasure and pride in creating their own homes with Build-Rite Furniture, the right furniture to buy.

_____D_____ 3. Which propaganda technique is used in the opening sentence?
      A. Testimonial   C. Glittering generalities
      B. Name calling   D. Transfer

_____C_____ 4. Which fact has the advertiser intentionally omitted?
      A. Build-Rite's "do-it-yourself" furniture is cheaper than furniture assembled by a manufacturer.
      B. Build-Rite does not sell electronic equipment.
      C. Build-Rite's furniture does not come with the tools necessary for assembly.
      D. Build-Rite's furniture comes in a variety of woods and plastics.

_____B_____ 5. Which of the following is **not** a glittering generality?
      A. "exceptional home furnishings"   C. "the right furniture to buy"
      B. "millions of Americans"   D. "magnificent patio set"

(Continues on next page)

C.   ¹Are you tired of big impersonal banks that treat you like a number? ²At HomeTown Savings and Loan Bank, you aren't a code in a giant computer somewhere. ³Here, you're a valued customer, a member of the community we're a part of. ⁴As lending officer Janet Morris says, "At HomeTown Savings Bank, I can assist my neighbors, people like me."

_B_   6. Which propaganda technique is used in the first sentence?
    A. Bandwagon   C. Transfer
    B. Name calling   D. Testimonial

_C_   7. Which propaganda technique is used in the last sentence?
    A. Transfer   C. Plain folks
    B. Name calling   D. Glittering generalities

D.   Read the description below of an actual ad, and then write the letter of the best answer to each question.

¹Music plays as television viewers see a man, woman, and dog running through the rain, up some steps, and into a house. ²The man sets down a grocery bag, the woman squeezes out her dripping shirt, and the dog shakes the rain off its coat. ³A voice says, "In over half the homes in America, people come home to Kenmore appliances."

_D_   8. Which propaganda technique is used in the scenes described in sentences 1 and 2?
    A. Testimonial   C. Transfer
    B. Bandwagon   D. Plain folks

_C_   9. Which propaganda technique is used in sentence 3?
    A. Testimonial   C. Bandwagon
    B. Glittering generalities   D. Name calling

_A_   10. Which words are the key to the propaganda technique used in sentence 3?
    A. "over half the homes in America"
    B. "come home"
    C. "Kenmore appliances"

PROPAGANDA: Mastery Test 5

A. Below are descriptions of eight actual ads. On each line, write the letter of the main propaganda technique that applies to the ad.

A Bandwagon   D Plain folks

B Testimonial   E Name calling

C Transfer   F Glittering generalities

_C_ 1. An ad for Mercedes Benz automobiles shows a photograph of a beautiful woman wearing a dress cut down to her navel. The text reads, "You give in to its sensuality. Your heart races as you take in every curve."

_B_ 2. America's Dairy Farmers and Milk Producers "Got Milk?" campaign shows professional football quarterback Tom Brady with a milk moustache.

_F_ 3. An ad for Natural White tooth whitener states, "Your smile isn't white until it's Natural White."

_D_ 4. In an ad for J.C. Penney fashions, a fresh-faced girl, her hair tied back and wearing jeans and a sweatshirt, smiles at the camera as she clutches a football.

_A_ 5. A Ford ad states, "More repeat buyers than anyone, domestic or import" and "The best-selling cars and trucks four years running."

_E_ 6. "For moisturized skin even the leading bar doesn't touch," says an ad for Oil of Olay's soap and moisturizer product.

_C_ 7. For a "Presidents' Weekend" sale, a large picture of George Washington and red, white, and blue streaks accompany pictures of new Toyotas.

_D_ 8. A girl identified as "Shelley, Wal-Mart customer," is shown wearing Almay lipstick. The caption is, "Look like a million for just a few bucks."

(Continues on next page)

B. The following ads involve card stacking—in some way, they are too good to be true. In the space provided, write the letter of the important detail that the advertiser has intentionally omitted.

_____*B*_____ 9. An ad for a shaving gel for women claimed, "New Soft Sense Moisturizing Shave Gel with Vitamin E."

Which detail below do you think has been omitted?
A. What the scent of the gel is like
B. Whether or not vitamin E has been shown to moisturize well or benefit the skin in any other way
C. The percentage of women who have decided not to shave their legs at all

_____*B*_____ 10. A new roll of Bounty paper towels was hailed with the slogan "New! More Absorbent Than Ever."

Which detail below do you think has been omitted?
A. The new towels are 10 percent more absorbent than before.
B. The new roll has fewer sheets of towels than before.
C. The price has remained the same.

PROPAGANDA: Mastery Test 6

A. Below are descriptions of eight actual ads. On each line, write the letter of the main propaganda technique that applies to the ad.

A Bandwagon   D Plain folks
B Testimonial   E Name calling
C Transfer   F Glittering generalities

_B_ 1. Actor James Brolin is shown with a bottle of Flex-A-Min dietary supplement. He says, "I have a pretty active lifestyle and I can't let sore, stiff joints slow me down. So I take Flex-A-Min every day. It works for me."

_D_ 2. An ad shows a grandmother before and after taking Tylenol: first she is suffering from aches and pains, and later she is able to play baseball with her young grandchildren.

_C_ 3. Eddie Bauer introduces its new material, "Seattle Suede," by showing a shirt made of the material photographed against a field of rippling golden wheat.

_E_ 4. An ad for NyQuil Cough Syrup says, "Unlike those cough medicines you take every four hours, NyQuil Cough is made to last through the night."

_F_ 5. A picture of a new-model Jeep simply states, "Jeep: There's only one."

_A_ 6. An Epson printer is shown printing a photograph of kids marching in a line. The caption reads, "Looking for the best digital photos? Follow the leader. . . . many digital camera owners look to Epson for all their printing needs."

_B_ 7. A series of photographs shows Sarah, Duchess of York, over the past four years. She states, "Weight Watchers not only helped me reach my goal, it helps me stay there."

_C_ 8. A picture of beautiful actress Catherine Zeta-Jones shows her wearing a sexy, low-cut dress. The caption reads: "Introducing Arden Beauty Eau de Parfum."

(Continues on next page)

B. The following ads involve card stacking—in some way, they are too good to be true. In the space provided, write the letter of the important detail that the advertiser has intentionally omitted.

___A___ 9. "The California Avocado. It's a rich source of vitamins and minerals—seventeen, to be exact. It also has lots of potassium. And it contains absolutely no cholesterol. So when it comes to adding nutrition to your daily routine, the delicious California Avocado is a natural."
  A. A California avocado is 90 percent fat.
  B. A California avocado has a small amount of sodium.
  C. Half of a California avocado provides a quarter of the Recommended Daily Allowance of vitamin C.

___C___ 10. The Kellogg's Corn Pops box explains that an ounce of Corn Pops (once called Sugar Pops) contains less sugar than an apple, a banana, or two pancakes with syrup. What information has the advertiser intentionally omitted?
  A. Corn Pops contains less sugar than cola drinks.
  B. Corn Pops can be eaten out of the box like a snack.
  C. Many people eat more than an ounce of Corn Pops for breakfast.

3

More About Argument: Errors in Reasoning

Learning about some common errors in reasoning—also known as **fallacies**—will help you to spot weak points in arguments.

You have already learned about two common fallacies in Chapter 10, "Argument." One of those two fallacies is sometimes called **changing the subject**. In Chapter 10, this fallacy was described as irrelevant support. People who use this method of arguing try to divert the audience's attention from the true issue by presenting evidence that actually has nothing to do with the argument.

The second fallacy you worked on in Chapter 10 is sometimes called **hasty generalization**. This fallacy was referred to in that chapter as a point based on inadequate support. To be valid, a point must be based on an adequate amount of evidence. Someone who draws a conclusion on the basis of insufficient evidence is making a hasty generalization.

Below are some other common fallacies that will be explained in this chapter. Exercises throughout will give you practice in recognizing them.

Three Fallacies That Ignore the Issue

- Circular Reasoning
- Personal Attack
- Straw Man

Three Fallacies That Oversimplify the Issue

- False Cause
- False Comparison
- Either-Or

FALLACIES THAT IGNORE THE ISSUE

Circular Reasoning

Part of a point cannot reasonably be used as evidence to support it. The fallacy of including such illogical evidence is called **circular reasoning**; it is also known as **begging the question**. Here is a simple and obvious example of such reasoning: "Mr. Green is a great teacher because he is so wonderful at teaching." The supporting reason ("he is so wonderful at teaching") is really the same as the conclusion ("Mr. Green is a great teacher"). We still do not know why he is a great teacher. No real reasons have been given—the statement has merely been repeated.

Can you spot the circular reasoning in the following arguments?

1. Vitamins are healthful, for they improve your well-being.
2. Since people under 21 are too young to vote, the voting age shouldn't be lowered below age 21.
3. Abortion is an evil practice because it is so wrong.

Let's look more closely at these arguments:

1. The word *healthful*, which is used in the conclusion, conveys the same idea as well-being. We still don't know why vitamins are good for us.
2. The idea that people under 21 are too young to vote is both the conclusion and the reason of the argument. No real reason is given for why people under 21 are too young to vote.
3. The claim that abortion "is so wrong" simply restates the idea that it is an evil practice. No explanation is given for why abortion is evil or wrong.

In all these cases, the reasons merely repeat an important part of the conclusion. The careful reader wants to say, "Tell me something new. You are reasoning in circles. Give me supporting evidence, not a repetition."

➤ Practice 1

Check (✓) the **one** item in each group that contains an example of circular reasoning.

Group 1

_____ 1. Why support Ray O'Donnell's highway safety proposal? He's got the biggest collection of speeding tickets in the district.

__✓__ 2. The government should lower our taxes because taxes are entirely too high.

_____ 3. The people who are in favor of gun control are obviously not concerned about criminals taking control of this fine country.

Comment: Group 1—The statement that "taxes are entirely too high" means essentially the same as "the government should lower our taxes."

Group 2

✓   1. Aretha Franklin is the best soul singer alive because her singing is so great.

_____   2. A local association wants to establish a halfway house for former mental patients in our neighborhood. But the neighbors oppose the idea; they say they don't want dangerous psychopaths roaming our streets.

_____   3. Ms. Jones is an atheist and should not be hired as a math teacher.

Group 3

_____   1. George wants the firm to hire more women and minorities. He doesn't seem to care how qualified our workers are.

✓   2. I feel my salary should be higher because it is too low.

_____   3. Councilman Hawkins is wholly unqualified to be elected mayor. He is a well-known homosexual.

Personal Attack

This fallacy often occurs in political debate. Here's an example:

> Senator Snerd's opinions on public housing are worthless. He can't even manage to hold his own household together, having married and divorced three times already.

Senator Snerd's family life may or may not reflect a weakness in his character, but it has nothing to do with the value of his opinions on public housing. **Personal attack** ignores the issue under discussion and concentrates instead on the character of the opponent.

Sometimes personal attacks take the form of accusing people of taking a stand only because it will benefit them personally. For instance, here's a personal attack on a congressman who is an outspoken member of the National Organization for Women (NOW): "He doesn't care about NOW. He supports it only in order to get more women to vote for him." This argument ignores the congressman's detailed defense of NOW as an organization that promotes equal rights for both men and women. The key to recognizing personal attack is that it always involves an opponent's personal life or character, rather than simply his or her public ideas.

Comments: Group 2—The statement that Franklin's "singing is so great" says almost the same thing as "Aretha Franklin is the best soul singer alive."

Group 3—The statement that one's salary "is too low" means the same as the statement that it "should be higher."

➤ *Practice 2*

Check (✓) the **one** item in each group that contains an example of personal attack.

Group 1

___✓___ 1. Why support Ray O'Donnell's highway safety proposal? He's got the biggest collection of speeding tickets in the district.

_____ 2. The government should lower our taxes because taxes are entirely too high.

_____ 3. The people who are in favor of gun control are obviously not concerned about criminals taking control of this fine country.

> The merit of O'Donnell's proposal has nothing to do with his speeding.

Group 2

_____ 1. Aretha Franklin is the best soul singer alive because her singing is so great.

_____ 2. A local association wants to establish a halfway house for former mental patients in our neighborhood. But the neighbors oppose the idea; they say they don't want dangerous psychopaths roaming our streets.

___✓___ 3. Ms. Jones is an atheist and should not be hired as a math teacher.

> One's religious beliefs have nothing to do with his or her ability to teach math.

Group 3

_____ 1. George wants the firm to hire more women and minorities. He doesn't seem to care how qualified our workers are.

_____ 2. I feel my salary should be higher because it is too low.

___✓___ 3. Councilman Hawkins is wholly unqualified to be elected mayor. He is a well-known homosexual.

> One's sexual orientation is irrelevant to one's professional abilities.

Straw Man

An opponent made of straw can be defeated very easily. Sometimes, if one's real opponent is putting up too good a fight, it can be tempting to build a scarecrow and battle it instead. For example, take the following passage from a debate on the death penalty.

> Ms. Collins opposes capital punishment. But letting murderers out on the street to kill again is a crazy idea. If we did that, no one would be safe.

Ms. Collins, however, never advocated "letting murderers out on the street to kill again." In fact, she wants to keep them in jail for life rather than execute them. The **straw man** fallacy suggests that the opponent favors an obviously unpopular cause—when the opponent really doesn't support anything of the kind. Then that made-up position is opposed.

➤ *Practice 3*

Check (✓) the **one** item in each group that contains an example of straw man.

Group 1

_____ 1. Don't sign Elio's petition for longer library hours. He's never been better than a C student.

_____ 2. The government should lower our taxes because taxes are entirely too high.

__✓__ 3. The people who are in favor of gun control are obviously not concerned about criminals taking control of this fine country.

> People in favor of gun control don't believe that it will allow criminals to take control.

Group 2

_____ 1. Your friends are a bad influence on you; after all, they encourage you to behave terribly.

__✓__ 2. A local association wants to establish a halfway house for former mental patients in our neighborhood. But the neighbors oppose the idea; they say they don't want dangerous psychopaths roaming our streets.

_____ 3. Ms. Jones is an atheist and should not be hired as a math teacher.

> Former mental patients are not psychopaths.

Group 3

__✓__ 1. George wants the firm to hire more women and minorities. He doesn't seem to care how qualified our workers are.

_____ 2. I feel my salary should be higher because it is too low.

_____ 3. Of course Mel supports giving large malpractice awards to patients. As a lawyer specializing in malpractice, his only interest is in big fees.

> George believes that many women and minority workers are qualified.

FALLACIES THAT OVERSIMPLIFY THE ISSUE

False Cause

You have probably heard someone say as a joke, "I know it's going to rain today because I just washed the car." The idea that someone can make it rain by washing a car is funny because the two events obviously have nothing to do with each other. However, with more complicated issues, it is easy to make the mistake known as the fallacy of **false cause**. The mistake is to assume that because event B *follows* event A, event B *was caused by* event A.

Cause-and-effect situations can be difficult to analyze, and people are often tempted to oversimplify them by focusing on one "cause" and ignoring other possible causes. To identify an argument using a false cause, look for alternative causes. Consider this argument:

The Macklin Company was more prosperous before Ms. Williams became president. Clearly, she is the cause of the decline.

> (*Event A:* Ms. Williams became president.
> *Event B:* The Macklin Company's earnings declined.)

However, Ms. Williams has been president for only a few months. What other possible causes could have been responsible for the decline? Perhaps the policies of the previous president are just now affecting the company. Perhaps the market for the company's product has changed. In any case, it's easy but dangerous to assume that just because A *came before* B, A *caused* B.

➤ Practice 4

Check (✓) the **one** item in each group that contains an example of false cause.

Group 1

___✓___ 1. I knew I shouldn't have taken the baby to the park today. Now he's got a cold.

_____ 2. While some people objected to the Vietnam war and didn't serve in the military, others were patriotic and did serve their country.

_____ 3. I don't know why you're so worried about my grades. Albert Einstein had lousy grades in high school, and he did all right.

Group 2

_____ 1. You'll either have to get a good job soon or face the fact that you'll never be successful.

___✓___ 2. After visiting Hal today, I came home with a headache. I must be allergic to his dog.

_____ 3. Of course the legalization of prostitution will work in America. It has worked in European countries, hasn't it?

Group 3

_____ 1. Young people must choose between a career that will help their fellow human beings and one that will earn them a decent living.

_____ 2. Chemicals have made wonderful synthetic fabrics possible, so what's wrong with using plenty of chemicals on our farms?

___✓___ 3. A month after the governor took office, my company fell on hard times, and I got fired. I'll certainly never vote for him again.

Comments: Groups 1 and 2—A single event is insufficient evidence for such generalizations.

Group 3—A complex economic event cannot be attributed to such a recent single event.

False Comparison

When the poet Robert Burns wrote, "My love is like a red, red rose," he meant that both the woman he loved and a rose are beautiful. In other ways—such as having green leaves and thorns, for example—his love did not resemble a rose at all. Comparisons are often a good way to clarify a point. But because two things are not alike in all respects, comparisons (sometimes called analogies) often make poor evidence for arguments. In the error in reasoning known as **false comparison**, the assumption is that two things are more alike than they really are. For example, read the following argument:

> It didn't hurt your grandfather in the old country to get to work without a car, and it won't hurt you either.

To judge whether or not this is a false comparison, consider how the two situations are alike and how they differ. They are similar in that both involve a young person's need to get to work. But the situations are different in that the grandfather didn't have to be at work an hour after his last class. In fact, he didn't go to school at all. In addition, his family didn't own a car he could use. The differences in this case are more important than the similarities, making it a false comparison.

➤ Practice 5

Check (✓) the **one** item in each group that contains an example of false comparison.

Group 1

_____ 1. I knew I shouldn't have taken the baby to the park today. Now he's got a cold.

_____ 2. While some people objected to the Vietnam war and didn't serve in the military, others were patriotic and did serve their country.

__✓__ 3. I don't know why you're so worried about my grades. Albert Einstein had lousy grades in high school, and he did all right.

Group 2

_____ 1. You'll either have to get a good job soon or face the fact that you'll never be successful.

_____ 2. After visiting Hal today, I came home with a headache. I must be allergic to his dog.

__✓__ 3. Of course the legalization of prostitution will work in America. It has worked in European countries, hasn't it?

Comments: Group 1—For most of us, a comparison with Albert Einstein is a false one.

Group 2—Different cultures may react differently to issues.

Group 3

_____ 1. Young people must choose between a career that will help their fellow human beings and one that will earn them a decent living.

__✓__ 2. Chemicals have made wonderful synthetic fabrics possible, so what's wrong with using plenty of chemicals on our farms?

_____ 3. A month after the governor took office, my company fell on hard times, and I got fired. I'll certainly never vote for him again.

Either-Or

It is often wrong to assume that there are only two sides to a question. Offering only two choices when more actually exist is an **either-or** fallacy. For example, the statement "You are either with us or against us" assumes that there is no middle ground. Or consider the following:

> People opposed to unrestricted free speech are really in favor of censorship.

This argument ignores the fact that a person could believe in free speech as well as in laws that prohibit slander or that punish someone for falsely yelling "Fire!" in a crowded theater. Some issues have only two sides (Will you pass the course, or won't you?), but most have several.

➤ Practice 6

Check (✓) the **one** item in each group that contains an example of the either-or fallacy.

Group 1

_____ 1. I knew I shouldn't have taken the baby to the park today. Now he's got a cold.

__✓__ 2. While some people objected to the Vietnam war and didn't serve in the military, others were patriotic and did serve their country.

_____ 3. I don't know why you're so worried about my grades. Albert Einstein had lousy grades in high school, and he did all right.   The speaker assumes that people who objected to the Vietnam war were not patriotic, but many who opposed the war did so on moral grounds and loved their country.

Group 2

__✓__ 1. You'll either have to get a good job soon or face the fact that you'll never be successful.

_____ 2. After visiting Hal today, I came home with a headache. I must be allergic to his dog.

_____ 3. Why can't I just quit school and go to work? Ken quit school and got a great job working at his dad's chain of restaurants.   There's more than one "schedule" for success

Group 3

  ✓   1. Young people must choose between a career that will help their fellow human beings and one that will earn them a decent living.

      2. School prayer is a positive force in parochial schools, so why not try it in our public schools?

      3. A month after the governor took office, my company fell on hard times, and I got fired. I'll certainly never vote for him again.

Some jobs, such as social work or teaching, help others and also pay well.

➤ Review Test 1

Answer each question with a **T** or an **F** (for *true* or *false*) or by writing the letter of the answer you choose.

  T   1. TRUE OR FALSE? The fallacy of personal attack ignores the true issue.

  T   2. TRUE OR FALSE? The fallacy of straw man got its name because an opponent made of straw would be easily defeated.

  F   3. TRUE OR FALSE? A false-cause argument assumes that there are only two sides to the issue.

  C   4. To decide if a statement is a false comparison, you must consider how much two situations
    A. are alike.
    B. are different.
    C. both A and B.

  B   5. In the either-or fallacy, the argument ignores the possibility of an additional
    A. cause for something happening.
    B. side to a question.
    C. comparison.

➤ *Review Test 2*

A. In the space provided, write the letter of the fallacy contained in each argument. Choose from the three fallacies shown in the box below.

> A Circular reasoning (*a statement repeats itself rather than providing a real supporting reason to back up an argument*)
> B Personal attack
> C Straw man (*an argument is made by claiming an opponent holds an extreme position and then opposing that extreme position*)

  C   1. Supporters of state lotteries apparently don't think people should work hard for what they get. They believe it's better to get something for nothing.

  B   2. Earl will make a lousy class treasurer because he's just a conceited jerk.

  A   3. Pollution is wrong because it dirties the environment.

  C   4. Mr. Collins supports sex education in junior high school. Maybe he thinks it's okay for 13-year-olds to be having babies, but I don't agree.

  A   5. Watering new grass is important, since a lot of water is beneficial for new lawns.

B. In the space provided, write the letter of the fallacy contained in each argument. Choose from the three fallacies shown in the box below.

> A False cause (*the argument assumes that the order of events alone shows cause and effect*)
> B False comparison (*the argument assumes that two things being compared are more alike than they really are*)
> C Either-or (*the argument assumes that there are only two sides to a question*)

  A   6. Stay away from Mike's filthy dorm room. After the last time I went there to study, I actually got a rash.

  C   7. Did you tell the boss off, or did you act like a wimp again?

___B___ 8. There's a sign in the dorm lounge saying that excessive alcohol is dangerous. Well, so what? Too much mashed potato can be dangerous, too.

___C___ 9. Do you always tell the truth, or are you a liar?

___A___ 10. Last time there was an eclipse, the stock market went down. I'm going to sell all my stock before next week's eclipse takes place.

➤ Review Test 3

A. In the space provided, write the letter of the fallacy contained in each argument. Choose from the three fallacies shown in the box below.

> **A** Circular reasoning (*a statement repeats itself rather than providing a real supporting reason to back up an argument*)
> **B** Personal attack
> **C** Straw man (*an argument is made by claiming an opponent holds an extreme position and then opposing that extreme position*)

___B___ 1. Congressman Nagel's policy on welfare is nonsense. What do you expect from a man known to cheat on his wife?

___A___ 2. You can always trust an animal lover because people who like animals are more trustworthy than other people.

___C___ 3. The mayor wants to allow liquor stores in town. He may not mind having all those drug pushers around, but I certainly do.

___B___ 4. Who can take Jake Green's argument for raising the sales tax seriously? Judging by the age of his wardrobe and car, the man hasn't paid a sales tax himself in decades.

___A___ 5. Kim Lee is the best choice for city council because she's the best candidate.

B. In the space provided, write the letter of the fallacy contained in each argument. Choose from the three fallacies shown in the box below.

> **A** False cause (*the argument assumes that the order of events alone shows cause and effect*)
>
> **B** False comparison (*the argument assumes that two things being compared are more alike than they really are*)
>
> **C** Either-or (*the argument assumes that there are only two sides to a question*)

_A_ 6. I ate in the company cafeteria yesterday, and today I have the flu. That's the last time I'll eat there.

_C_ 7. There are only two types of citizens in this town: those who support building a new stadium and those who don't care about our town's future.

_B_ 8. Children are like flowers—you only have to feed them and let them have plenty of sunshine, and they'll grow up hardy and beautiful.

_A_ 9. I did well on the finals last semester after having Oreos for breakfast. I'd better remember to buy a bag of Oreos before this semester's finals begin.

_B_ 10. At the grocery, I pay only for what I want, so why should I have to pay taxes that go for welfare and other federal programs I don't support?

Check Your Performance   **MORE ABOUT ARGUMENT**

Activity	Number Right	Points	Score
Review Test 1 (5 items)	_____	× 4 =	_____
Review Test 2 (10 items)	_____	× 4 =	_____
Review Test 3 (10 items)	_____	× 4 =	_____
		TOTAL SCORE =	_____ %

Enter your total score into the **Reading Performance Chart: Review Tests** on the inside back cover.

4

Writing Assignments

A BRIEF GUIDE TO EFFECTIVE WRITING

Here in a nutshell is what you need to do to write effectively.

Step 1: Explore Your Topic Through Informal Writing

To begin with, explore the topic that you want to write about or that you have been assigned to write about. You can examine your topic through **informal writing**, which usually means one of three things.

First, you can **freewrite** about your topic for at least ten minutes. In other words, for ten minutes write whatever comes into your head about your subject. Write without stopping and without worrying at all about spelling or grammar or the like. Simply get down on paper all the information about the topic that occurs to you.

A second thing you can do is to **make a list of ideas and details** that could go into your paper. Simply pile these items up, one after another, like a shopping list, without worrying about putting them in any special order. Try to accumulate as many details as you can think of.

A third way to explore your topic is to **write down a series of questions and answers** about it. Your questions can start with words like *what, why, how, when*, and *where*.

Getting your thoughts and ideas down on paper will help you think more about your topic. With some raw material to look at, you are now in a better position to decide on just how to proceed.

Step 2: Plan Your Paper with an Informal Outline

After exploring your topic, plan your paper using an informal outline. Do two things:

- **Decide on and write out the point of your paper.** It is often a good idea to begin your paragraph with this point, which is known as the topic sentence. If you are writing an essay of several paragraphs, you will probably want to include your main point somewhere in your first paragraph. In a paper of several paragraphs, the main point is called the central point, or thesis.
- **List the supporting reasons, examples, or other details that back up your point.** In many cases, you should have at least two or three items of support.

Step 3: Use Transitions

Once your outline is worked out, you will have a clear "road map" for writing your paper. As you write the early drafts of your paper, use **transitions** to introduce each of the separate supporting items (reasons, examples, or other details) you present to back up your point. For instance, you might introduce your first supporting item with the transitional words *first of all*. You might begin your second supporting item with words such as *another reason* or *another example*. And you might indicate your final supporting detail with such words as *last of all* or *a final reason*.

Step 4: Edit and Proofread Your Paper

After you have a solid draft, edit and proofread the paper. Ask yourself several questions to evaluate your paper:

1 Is the paper **unified**? Does all the material in the paper truly support the opening point?
2 Is the paper **well supported**? Is there plenty of specific evidence to back the opening point?
3 Is the paper **clearly organized**? Does the material proceed in a way that makes sense? Do transitions help connect ideas?
4 Is the paper **well written**? When the paper is read aloud, do the sentences flow smoothly and clearly? Has the paper been checked carefully for grammar, punctuation, and spelling mistakes?

WRITING ASSIGNMENTS FOR THE TWENTY READINGS

Note: The discussion questions accompanying the twenty readings can also make good topics for writing. Some of the writing assignments here are based on them.

"Night Watch"

1. Imagine that you are the son of the old man in the story. The day after your father died, you arrived and heard the story of the other Marine who had been with him in his last hours. How do you think you would feel about the situation? Would you feel primarily grateful, sad, angry, regretful, confused, or something else? Write a paragraph that describes what you think your reaction might be. If your response would be a mix of several emotions, say so. Along with stating your feelings, tell why you feel as you do.

2. The young Marine stayed by the old man's bedside, he said, because "I figured he really needed me." Tell in a paragraph about a time you felt needed. Who was it who needed you, and in what way? How did you respond to that person? Did you feel able to give the person what he or she wanted from you? Was feeling needed a pleasant experience, or did it seem like a burden? Here's a sample topic sentence for this paragraph: "Once my older brother really needed my help, and it felt very good to be able to help him."

3. It's not uncommon to see people reach out to help their loved ones. But the final paragraph of this article states that "in a uniquely human way . . . there are people who care what happens to their fellow human beings"—in other words, they care about people to whom they have no particular obligation. Think of experiences you have had, or heard about, in which people went out of their way to assist someone they do not know well, if at all. Write an essay that tells the stories of two or three such incidents. You might conclude your essay by talking about what, if anything, the "givers" in such situations gain by their actions.

"Here's to Your Health"

1. Few people go through life without being exposed to the negative effects of alcohol. In a paragraph, describe an unpleasant or dangerous incident you have been aware of, or experienced yourself, in which alcohol played a part. Who was involved? What happened? In what way did alcohol contribute to the situation? How did the incident end?

2. The advertising and sale of cigarettes are topics of much debate. There are already some legal restrictions in place—cigarettes are not advertised on television, they are not to be sold to minors, and warning labels on cigarettes inform consumers of health risks associated with smoking. In your opinion, are such restrictions needed or helpful? Should more restrictions be imposed on the tobacco industry, or should cigarettes be advertised and sold like any other product? Write a paragraph that explains your opinions about how or if cigarettes should be regulated and why.

3. As this article shows, alcohol is advertised as something that makes people more successful, sexier, healthier, and happier. The abuse of alcohol, however, often has quite the opposite effect. Write an essay in which you describe what alcohol advertisements would look like if they showed the negative side of drinking. What images would you choose to include in such advertisements? You might organize your essay by addressing several of the positive "myths" about alcohol mentioned in the article and describing an ad that would contradict each myth.

"Child-Rearing Styles"

1. Near the end of the article, the author lists six recommendations to parents who want to raise "competent, socially responsible, independent children." Choose one of those six recommendations and write a paragraph that demonstrates how it was or was not practiced in your own home. Illustrate the paragraph with examples from your childhood. Conclude by stating how you were positively or negatively affected by those examples.

2. Reread the author's descriptions of three parenting style: authoritative, authoritarian, and permissive. Think of a parent you know who is a good example of one of those three styles. Then write a paragraph that describes how that person interacts with his or her child. Provide one or more examples that demonstrate the adult's approach to parenting. You might try using some dialogue to emphasize a point or two. In conclusion, comment on how you think the parent's style is affecting the child.

3. It is not uncommon to hear parents say of their children, "I don't understand—we raised them all just the same, and yet they've turned out so differently." Based on your own experience growing up and your observations of other families, write an essay that comments on several possible explanations for why siblings develop different—sometimes dramatically different—personalities. Provide vivid real-life examples to illustrate your points. A possible central point for this essay might be "Inherited personality, different parental treatment, and birth order account for many of the differences between siblings."

"Rowing the Bus"

1. Logan writes, "In each school, in each classroom, there is a George with a stricken face." Think of a person who filled the role of George in one of your classes. In a paragraph, describe why he or she was the target of teasing, and what form that teasing took. Include a description of your own thoughts and actions regarding the student who was teased.

2. Fearing that his life would be made miserable, the author decided to stop being friends with George. How do you feel about that decision? Do you think it was cruel? Understandable? Were there other options Logan might have tried? Write a paragraph in which you explain what you think of Logan's decision and why. Suggest at least one other way he could have acted, and tell what you think the consequences might have been.

3. In this essay, Logan provides many vivid descriptions of incidents in which bullies attack other students. Reread those descriptions and consider what they teach you about the nature of bullies and bullying. Then write an essay that supports the following main idea: "Evidence in 'Rowing the Bus' suggests that most bullies share certain characteristics." Mention two or three such characteristics and provide evidence from the essay that illustrates how they are present in acts of bullying. In your concluding paragraph, you might talk about what these characteristics tell us about bullies.

"Students in Shock"

1. Students face a good deal of pressure in their new environment, as this essay shows. But they are not the only ones susceptible to "shock." Anyone in a demanding new situation can experience depression, frustration, and hopelessness. For example, someone who is new to a job, to a neighborhood, to marriage, or to parenthood might experience his or her own brand of shock. Write a paragraph that explores the possible causes of shock in a person facing a specific situation. You may choose one of the situations listed here, or another that occurs to you. Suggest ways the person might reduce the pressure he or she feels.

2. When you experience stress, what helps you to relax? Write a paragraph that describes your own favorite stress-reduction technique. Is it exercising, talking with a friend, taking a bath, playing golf, punching a pillow? You might begin with a vivid description of how stress affects you, then contrast that with a description of how your favorite technique changes your mood. Explain in detail how you go about using the technique.

3. *Stress*, *anxiety*, *depression*, *burnout*—these words are common parts of our modern vocabulary. What do you think are some of the main sources of this widespread stress? Write an essay that describes several common causes of stress. You could use as your central point a sentence similar to this: "There are three common reasons why people today are so stressed out." For each cause of stress you mention, provide specific ways in which it affects people. Add interest to your essay by using examples from the lives of people you know or have observed.

"I Became Her Target"

1. Think of a time when you felt like an outsider coming into a group. Perhaps you stood out because of your race, nationality, gender, language, or opinions, or simply because you were new. How did you feel at first—very uncomfortable, nervous, relaxed, angry? How did the group respond to you? As time went on, how did the situation change, for the better or for the worse? Write a paragraph that describes your experience.

2. Wilkins writes that, as a child, his opinions were based upon the opinions of his family and friends. Most children do accept their parents' ideas and ways of doing things as the right way, the normal way. As they get a little older, however, and are exposed to other ways of thinking and doing things, they may change their minds. Write a paragraph about a time when you began to question your family's opinions or way of life. What made you realize that you did not necessarily agree with your parents all of the time? Did you speak up about your opinions? Why or why not?

3. Who stands out in your mind as your most unforgettable—though not necessarily your favorite—teacher? Write an essay that explains who the teacher was. Demonstrate through vivid stories, examples, and dialogue, why he or she was so memorable. You might organize your essay around several incidents involving that teacher or around several of the teacher's characteristics. You might conclude by telling when and under what circumstances that teacher comes into your thoughts.

"New Respect for the Nap, A Pause That Refreshes"

1. When you find yourself feeling groggy in the middle of a school day or workday, what is your best remedy to help restore your energy? A snack? Coffee? Exercise? Write a paragraph about your personal cure for mid-day sleepiness. Make it clear whether you think your remedy is an effective one or not.

2. According to this article, taking a daily nap is an easy way to improve one's overall health. Write a paragraph about one other simple change people can make in their lives that would have a positive impact on their physical or mental health. Your topic sentence could be something like this: "Meditating for just ten minutes each morning can make you a happier, healthier human being."

3. In her article, Brody mentions that some companies provide on-site "nap rooms" as a service to employees. This is an unusual company benefit that many workers would no doubt appreciate. Write an essay in which you describe several other on-site services that you think employers should offer for employees, or that schools should offer for students. For each service, describe how you believe it would help make workers or students happier or more productive.

"Gender Inequality in Health Care and in the Workplace"

1. From your own observations, what group is the most openly discriminated against in the U.S. today? Members of a certain gender? People of a certain sexual orientation? Members of a particular ethnic, social, or religious group? Write a paragraph in which you state your conclusion and back it up by describing what you have witnessed.

2. Describe a time that you (or someone you are acquainted with) have been treated unfairly in school or in the workplace. What happened? What do you think was the reason behind the unfair treatment? How did you (or the other victim) respond? Your topic sentence should explain in a nutshell what occurred. For example, "I once saw a merchant cheat my uncle because he did not speak enough English to complain."

3. All in all, do you think it's preferable to be a man or a woman in today's society? Write an essay in which you defend your choice. Select several points that support your point of view and develop them fully. Your thesis statement might be something like this: "In today's world, there are three very definite advantages to being a man."

"The Scholarship Jacket"

1. Marta remembers herself at 14 as, "Pencil thin, not a curve anywhere, I was called 'Beanpole' and 'String Bean,' and I knew that's what I looked like." Write a paragraph in which you describe yourself at a particular age. You may choose to focus on your appearance or on internal qualities. Here are a couple of sample topic sentences: "The summer I was twelve, I was in a bad mood nearly all of the time." "I went through a growth spurt when I was 15 that left me feeling as gangly and awkward as a baby giraffe."

2. Marta stresses again and again how important the scholarship jacket was to her and how hard she worked to win it. Write a paragraph about something you worked hard to achieve when you were younger. How long did you work toward that goal? How did you feel when you finally succeeded? Or as an alternative, write about not achieving the goal. How did you cope with the disappointment? What lesson, if any, did you learn from the experience.

3. One reason Marta wanted the scholarship jacket so much is that she did not have the chance to participate in school sports. She wanted to make a name for herself somehow, and being a fine scholar was the way that she chose. In your high school, what were (or are) a few ways that people could become well-known? Those ways might be positive, such as being a top scholar or musician, or less so, such as being a class troublemaker. Write an essay in which you identify three categories of well-known students in your school, and describe the kind of people who belong in each category.

"In Praise of the F Word"

1. Has someone you know (or have you) received an F for a course? Write a paragraph describing what happened. What led to the poor performance? What effect did that experience have? Was failing a motivation to work harder? What were the effects, positive and negative, of receiving the failing grade?

2. This article concerns one way of motivating students—the threat of failure. Thinking back on your own classroom experience, what would you say are some other effective ways of motivating students to do their best? Write a paragraph that describes one other method teachers and instructors can use to motivate their students. Provide examples of times you have seen this method put into practice and how effective it seems to be.

3. Sherry believes that giving students F's when they deserve to fail would encourage them to take more responsibility for their performance. Most people agree that individuals truly overcome a problem only when they take responsibility for it, rather than expecting it to magically disappear or to be solved by someone else. In an essay, describe two or three people you know (you might be one) who have accepted responsibility for dealing with a difficult problem. The problems could be an unhappy marriage, an issue at work or school, or a crisis like substance abuse. How did the people demonstrate their willingness to take responsibility for their problems? What action did each take? How was the situation changed by what they did?

"The Yellow Ribbon"

1. Vingo's wife had to decide whether to forgive Vingo and welcome him back into her life. Think of a time when you had to decide whether or not to forgive someone. Write a paragraph that describes that situation. Begin by explaining who the other person was and what your relationship had been like. Then describe what he or she did to hurt or offend you and how you felt about what happened. Continue by explaining how you made the decision whether or not to forgive the person. End your paragraph by saying how you feel about your decision now.

2. In "The Yellow Ribbon," Hamill provides various clues to Vingo's character. His body language, his conversation with his fellow passengers, what he has to say about his past and his family, and his attitude as the bus nears his hometown all contribute to the readers' opinion of what kind of man he is. Write a paragraph that supports the following topic sentence: "Details in the story suggest that Vingo is a decent man who deserves the yellow ribbons." Find specific evidence in the story to back up that statement.

3. Vingo had to wait suspensefully to discover something important about his future. Most people have had the experience of waiting a long time (or what seemed like a long time) to find out something important. Such situations might have involved a job, pregnancy, romance, health, or school. Write an essay about a situation in which you (or someone you know) had to wait for something. Tell the story a little at a time, as Hamill does, in order to keep the reader in suspense until the end. Begin by explaining what was being waited for and why it was important. Continue by describing the wait and the emotions experienced as time went by. Use time transitions (see pages 175–176) to help the reader follow your story. Finish by telling how the wait finally ended and how you (or the person you are writing about) felt once it was over.

"Urban Legends"

1. This article suggests that urban legends, Aesop's fables, and morality plays exist in order to teach us lessons. Familiar children's stories such as "Goldilocks and the Three Bears," "Little Red Riding Hood," and "Beauty and the Beast" could be seen as having a similar purpose. Write a paragraph in which you explain the lesson taught by one well-known children's story. You may select one of the stories mentioned, or another story.

2. Have you ever heard a story that you suspect may have been an urban legend? Write a paragraph in which you tell the story and then explain in what ways it seems similar to an urban legend. Refer to the reading to find common characteristics of urban legends that seem to apply to your story.

3. Johnson writes, "We haven't quite given up our need for scary stories." Write an essay in which you tell why, in your opinion, people get a thrill out of being frightened. Provide examples of two or three ways that people seek out scary experiences and what they gain from those experiences.

"Shame"

1. When have you, like Gregory, regretted the way you acted in a particular situation? Perhaps you didn't speak up when someone was being teased, or perhaps you spoke harshly to someone because you were in a bad mood. Write a paragraph that describes the situation and how you acted. Conclude by explaining why you feel you acted wrongly and what you wish you had done instead.

2. Teachers are powerful figures in the lives of children. At times, because of impatience, poor judgment, a misunderstanding, anger—or some other reason—a teacher may hurt a student's feelings. Write a paragraph about a situation you experienced (or observed) in which you believe a teacher acted inappropriately and made a student feel bad. Be sure to explain not only what the teacher did but also how the student was affected.

3. A dictionary defines a word by briefly explaining its meaning. In this article, Dick Gregory defines the word *shame* in a different manner. He describes two incidents in his life in which shame played a central part. Write an essay in which you define a powerful word by narrating one or more events. Some words to consider include "gratitude," "fear," "jealousy," "pride," "joy," "anger," "kindness," and "disappointment." Your central point might be stated something like this: "Two incidents that happened ten years apart taught me the real meaning of _____." Focus on those parts of the incidents that illustrate the meaning of the word. Your essay will be most powerful if you, like Gregory, include significant bits of description and dialogue.

"The Bystander Effect"

1. This article suggests that people act quite differently when they are alone and when they're in a group, or in public. Write a paragraph that contrasts your own behavior when you're alone and when you're in a specific public setting. Examples of public settings might be a party, football game, dance, family gathering, or workplace. The tone of your paragraph could be serious or humorous. Provide lively examples of your behavior to illustrate your points.

2. "The Bystander Effect" is filled with anecdotes of people who stood back when help was needed, preferring to wait for someone else to act. Think of an individual who has acted in the *opposite* way, someone who perceived a need

and quickly offered assistance. The situation might have involved an emergency like the ones mentioned in the article, or it might have concerned a more long-term need, such as an illness or a financial problem. Be specific in describing what the need was and how the individual reacted. Conclude by stating how the situation might have turned out if the individual had not helped.

3. Barkin defines "moral diffusion" as "the lessening of a sense of individual responsibility when someone is a member of a group." Drawing upon your own experience and knowledge of the world, write an essay that gives two examples of moral diffusion at work. For each example, describe what group is involved, how group members decline to take individual responsibility, and what happens as a result. Examples you might use include soldiers who commit war crimes and then say they were "just following orders," students who allow a classmate to be harassed because they don't want to get involved, or neighborhood people who let a park become overrun with trash because it's not their job to pick it up.

"The Real Story of Flight 93"

1. It is nearly impossible to predict how one will behave in a frightening, unexpected situation. Write a paragraph about a time you suddenly found yourself in a scary situation. Perhaps, for example, you were being bullied, or you found yourself looking on while another student was being physically or verbally harassed. How did you respond? Looking back, are you surprised by your reaction? Do you wish you had done anything differently?

2. The terrorist attacks of September 11, 2001, made the day an unforgettable one for most Americans. Where were you when you first heard about the attacks? What was your first reaction? In looking back at that day, what is your most powerful memory? Write a paragraph about your personal response to that day. Here is a sample topic sentence: "When I think about September 11, I remember the many acts of kindness I saw New Yorkers perform for one another."

3. When the passengers on Flight 93 realized they were likely to die, many of them tried to contact their loved ones to say goodbye. If you knew your life was ending soon, who are two or three people you would want to talk to? What would you want to say to them? Write an essay in which you explain whom you would talk to, why you would choose these people, and what you would want to tell them.

"Coping with Nervousness"

1. What makes you nervous? What is something you occasionally—or often—need to do that makes your mouth go dry and your knees knock? Write a paragraph, in a serious or humorous vein, about a situation that makes you nervous and how you react to it. Some topics to consider include speaking in public, asking someone for a date, and applying for a job. Provide lots of vivid details so the reader can see and feel your nervousness.

2. Imagine that you were required to give a "how-to" speech on a process that you are very familiar with. What would you choose to talk about? Write a paragraph in which you state your topic, then give clear, step-by-step instructions on how to complete the process. Use time transitions (see page 151) to make your instructions easy to follow.

3. Verderber suggests that people who can master their nervousness, rather than allowing it to control them, will enjoy a sense of accomplishment. Think of a problem that you have faced and overcome. It might be a particular fear, like the one described in the article. Or you may have conquered a problem with a difficult person, overcome a bad habit, or figured out a solution to a problem in your life. Write an essay that explains, first, what problem existed and how it affected you; second, how you decided to deal with the problem; and finally, what happened as a result of your actions and how you felt about what you'd done.

"Compliance Techniques: Getting People to Say Yes"

1. Why do you think that compliance techniques are so often effective? What do they appeal to in the mind of the consumer that is lacking in the more straightforward approach of simply making a product available to those who want to buy it? Write a paragraph that explains a few reasons you think people are so easily influenced by compliance techniques.

2. Have you ever agreed to perform a service or to buy something and then later felt you had been persuaded by a clever, manipulative, or deceptive sales technique? Write a paragraph that describes the process that you and the seller engaged in. Use time transitions (pages 175–176) to make the sequence of events clear to the reader. Explain how you believe you were manipulated into the agreement or purchase.

3. Think of a product you might want to sell or service you might want people to agree to perform. Write an essay that tells how you could accomplish your goal by using three of these four compliance techniques: the foot-in-the-door, the door-in-the-face, the low-ball, and the that's-not-all techniques. Give a detailed explanation of the steps you would follow in each case. In conclusion, state which technique you believe would work best and why.

"Lizzie Borden"

1. Based on the information presented in the article, write a paragraph that supports one of the following main ideas: "I believe that Lizzie Borden was guilty of the murder of her parents" or "I think there is reason to doubt that Lizzie Borden killed her parents." Explain your thinking, backing up your opinions with evidence from the text.

2. Think of a time you were wrongly suspected of doing something bad. It might have involved anything from breaking a dish when you were a child to committing a crime. Write a paragraph describing that experience. Tell what you were suspected of and what (if any) evidence pointed to you. Were you able to prove you were innocent? How did you feel about being a target of suspicion?

3. The author suggests that a stereotype that existed in Lizzie's day had a very specific effect—that she was found innocent of murder because of it. What are some stereotypes that exist today? How are people of certain ethnic groups, genders, sexual preferences, or economic groups stereotyped? Write an essay in which you explain how you believe certain groups are stereotyped. What effects might occur because people believe those stereotypes?

"Nonverbal Communication"

1. Write a paragraph that describes a time when you were made uncomfortable by another person's nonverbal communication. Tell where the incident occurred, who else was there, and what the relationship was between you and the person whose communication disturbed you. Then describe specifically what the other person did that made you uncomfortable and how you responded. You may also want to refer to the article and describe what kind of personal space was violated by this person's behavior.

2. As you may know, the "personal space zones" described in the article are not the same worldwide. For example, people from some Middle Eastern countries are accustomed to standing close together as they talk, even if do not know one another well. Based on your reading of this article and your knowledge of human nature, how do you think a person from such a country might be perceived in America? How might an American visiting such a country be viewed? Write a paragraph that describes how people from the two cultures might judge one another based on their nonverbal communication.

3. Think of some people you see often but do not know well—perhaps people like store owners, your mail carrier, school secretaries, a bus driver, or a new neighbor. Based upon their nonverbal communication, what do these people seem to be like? Write an essay in which you introduce each person and tell what impression you have formed of him or her. Be as specific and descriptive as possible as you tell about these people's nonverbal behavior and what it seems to say about them.

"Preindustrial Cities"

1. What do you think would most surprise someone from preindustrial London if he or she could visit a modern city today? Write a paragraph that tells about a few of the changes you think would be most striking to a visitor from preindustrial times. Draw from the article to describe conditions the preindustrial visitor would have been accustomed to, and then contrast those conditions with what the visitor would find today.

2. Are the problems of modern-day city-dwellers significantly different from or pretty much the same as those of people who lived in preindustrial cities? Write a paragraph that supports one of the following main ideas: "The problems of living in cities are basically the same today as in preindustrial times," or "People living in cities today have to deal with problems very different from those of preindustrial people." Use specific examples drawn from the reading and from your knowledge of modern-day city life.

3. What would you consider the biggest attractions of living in a city? What would draw you to live in a small town? What is there about the activities available, the quality of life, economic possibilities, or the like, that makes each attractive? Write an essay that spells out what, for you, would be the best points of city life and small-town life. Use vivid examples of what you could do, see, and experience only in a city, and equally lively examples of what life in a small town would offer. In your final paragraph, tell whether you would choose to live in the city or the town. Be sure to explain why you made the choice you did.

Pronunciation Guide

Each word in Chapter 1, "Vocabulary in Context," is followed by information in parentheses that shows you how to pronounce the word. (There are also pronunciations for the vocabulary items that follow the readings in Parts I and II.) The guide below and on the next page explains how to use that information.

Long Vowel Sounds

ā	pay
ē	she
ī	hi
ō	go
o͞o	cool
yo͞o	use

Short Vowel Sounds

ă	hat
ĕ	ten
ĭ	sit
ŏ	lot
o͝o	look
ŭ	up
yo͝o	cure

Other Vowel Sounds

â	care
ä	card
îr	here
ô	all
oi	oil
ou	out
ûr	fur
ə	ago, item, easily, gallop, circus

Consonant Sounds

b	big
d	do
f	fall
g	dog
h	he

Consonant Sounds

j	jump
k	kiss
l	let
m	meet
n	no
p	put
r	red
s	sell
t	top
v	have
w	way
y	yes
z	zero
ch	church
sh	dish
th	then
th	thick
zh	usual

Note that each pronunciation symbol above is paired with a common word that shows the sound of the symbol. For example, the symbol ā has the sound of the *a* in the common word *pay*. The symbol ă has the sound of the *a* in the common word *hat*. The symbol ə, which looks like an upside-down *e* and is known as the schwa, has the unaccented sound in the common word *ago*. It sounds like the "uh" a speaker often says when hesitating.

Accent marks are small black marks that tell you which syllable to emphasize as you say a word. A bold accent mark (ʹ) shows which syllable should be stressed. A lighter accent mark (ʹ) in some words indicates a secondary stress. Syllables without an accent mark are unstressed.

Limited Answer Key

An important note: To strengthen your reading skills, you must do more than simply find out which of your answers are right and which are wrong. You also need to figure out (with the help of this book, the teacher, or other students) *why* you missed the questions you did. By using each of your wrong answers as a learning opportunity, you will strengthen your understanding of the skills. You will also prepare yourself for the review and mastery tests in Part I and the reading comprehension questions in Part II, for which answers are not given here.

ANSWERS TO THE PRACTICES IN PART I

1 Vocabulary in Context

Practice 1: Examples

1. Examples: *brushing their teeth, washing their hands and faces;* B
2. Examples: *the phones were constantly ringing, people were running back and forth, several offices were being painted;* B
3. Example: *the giant land tortoise can live several hundred years;* B
4. Examples: *going to town concerts and ball games, visiting neighborhood friends, playing board games;* A
5. Examples: *gardening, long-distance bike riding;* A
6. Example: *picking up the language and customs of their new home;* A
7. Examples: *financial help, free medical care;* C
8. Examples: *learning, reasoning, thinking, language;* B
9. Examples: *the TV is talking to them, others can steal their thoughts;* C
10. Examples: *accepting a bribe from a customer, stealing from an employer;* C

Practice 2: Synonyms

1. embarrasses
2. examine
3. practical
4. confusing
5. overlook
6. necessary
7. opponents
8. arrival
9. charitable
10. customary

Practice 3: Antonyms

1. Antonym: *long;* A
2. Antonym: *financial loss;* B
3. Antonym: *openly;* B
4. Antonym: *plainly;* B
5. Antonym: *active;* A
6. Antonym: *clear;* C
7. Antonym: *benefit;* B
8. Antonym: *increase in value;* B
9. Antonym: *careless;* C
10. Antonym: *weak;* C

Practice 4: General Sense

1. B
2. C
3. A
4. B
5. C
6. A
7. C
8. B
9. C
10. B

2 Main Ideas

Practice 1

1. home cooking: S
   take-out: S
   ways to eat dinner: G
   frozen foods: S

2. fot and humid: S
   cold and rainy: S
   cloudy with scattered showers: S
   weather forecasts: G

3. oversleeping: S
   bad habits: G
   overeating: S
   smoking: S

4. traffic delays: S
   head cold: S
   bad coffee: S
   minor problems: G

5. communicating: G
   writing: S
   reading: S
   speaking: S

6. deadbolt locks: S
   alarm system: S
   barking dog: S
   kinds of security: G

7. divorce: S
   failing grades: S
   major problems: G
   eviction: S

8. not taking notes in class: S
   poor study habits: G
   missing classes: S
   cramming for exams: S

9. surprised: S
   tone of voice: G
   enthusiastic: S
   humorous: S

10. hurry up: S
    get to bed: S
    commands: G
    clean up this mess: S

Practice 2

Answers will vary.

Practice 3

1. P	4. P
S	S
S	S
S	S
2. S	5. S
S	P
P	S
S	S
3. S	
S	
S	
P	

Practice 4

1. S	4. S
S	P
P	S
S	S
2. P	5. S
S	S
S	S
S	P
3. S	
P	
S	
S	

Practice 5

1. S	4. S
S	S
P	S
S	P
2. S	5. P
P	S
S	S
S	S
3. P	
S	
S	
S	

Practice 6

Group 1
  A. SD
  B. SD
  C. MI
  D. T

Group 2
  A. MI
  B. SD
  C. SD
  D. T

Group 3
  A. T
  B. SD
  C. SD
  D. MI

Group 4
  A. MI
  B. SD
  C. SD
  D. T

Group 5
  A. MI
  B. SD
  C. T
  D. SD

Practice 7 (*Wording of topics may vary*)

1. *Topic:* Stories
   Main idea: Sentence 1

2. *Topic:* ESP
   Main idea: Sentence 2

3. *Topic:* Hospices vs. hospitals
   Main idea: Sentence 2

4. *Topic:* Driving *or* Poor attitudes about driving
   Main idea: Sentence 10

5. *Topic:* Environment and behavior
   Main idea: Sentence 1

Practice 8

1. 1
2. 4
3. 2
4. 5
5. 1

3   Supporting Details

Practice 1 (*Wording of answers may vary*)

1. *Main idea:* Parents can take several steps to discourage TV watching and encourage reading.

   1. Have only one TV set, and place it in the family room.
   2. Connect reading with eating.
   3. Don't put a TV set in a child's bedroom.

2. *Main idea:* Colleges of the early nineteenth century were distinctly different from today's schools.

   1. Students were mostly white males.
      Minor details: College was considered a final polishing for upper-class gentlemen.

   2. All students had to take the same courses.
      Minor details: They studied ancient languages, literature, natural science, mathematics, and political and moral philosophy.

   3. Colleges were small.
      Minor details: Most had only a few dozen students, three or four professors, and three or four tutors.

   4. Student life was more regulated.
      Minor details: Strict curfews determined when students had to turn off lights, and attendance at religious services was required.

Practice 2 (*Wording of answers may vary*)

1. Introduce yourself
   Refer to physical setting
   Ask a complimentary question
   Seek direct information

2. *Major detail*: Smaller labor force
   Minor detail: Milking machines use only one operator.

   Major detail: Higher milk output
   Minor detail: American cows give 7.5 times more milk than Brazilian cows.

Practice 3

1. C
2. B

Practice 4 *(Examples may vary.)*

1. Passive listening—trying to make sense out of a speaker's remarks without being able to interact with the speaker
   Ex.—Students listen to an instructor's lecture without having the chance to ask questions.

2. Self-serving bias—the practice of judging ourselves leniently
   Ex.—When *he* lashes out angrily, we say he's moody. When *we* lash out angrily, we say we're under pressure.

4   Implied Main Ideas/Central Point

Practice 1

Paragraph 1	Paragraph 3
1. D	5. C
2. A	6. B

Paragraph 2	Paragraph 4
3. C	7. D
4. B	8. B

Practice 2

1. D	3. C
2. B	4. C

Practice 3 *(Wording of answers may vary.)*

1. *Topic:* Reasons for lying
   Implied main idea: People tell lies for several reasons.

2. *Topic:* Being an only child
   Implied main idea: Being an only child has its drawbacks.

3. *Topic:* Opposition to capital punishment
   Implied main idea: People have opposed the death penalty for different reasons.

4. *Topic:* Growing older
   Implied main idea: Growing older can make us better in many ways.

Practice 4

Central point: In fact, the days of a housewife in nineteenth-century America were spent in harsh physical labor. (Sentence 2)

Practice 5

Central point: However, excessive use of alcohol contributes to a number of negative social consequences. (Sentence 2)

5   Relationships I

Practice 1 *(Answers may vary.)*

1. also	4. First
2. For one thing	5. Finally
3. In addition	

Practice 2 *(Answers may vary.)*

1. After	4. before
2. Then	5. while
3. during	

Practice 3 *(Wording of answers may vary.)*

A. Main idea: For several reasons, pork was America's most popular meat a hundred years ago.
1. Pigs grew quickly.
2. Pigs required little attention.
3. Pigs could be preserved cheaply.

B. Main idea: . . . aging process
1. Our bodies simply wear out.
3. Our body chemistry loses its delicate balance.
4. Our bodies, with age, reject some of their own tissues.

Practice 4 *(Wording of answers may vary.)*

Main idea: The 1960s were a time of profound events in America.
1. 1963—the assassination of President Kennedy
2. 1965—urban riots in black ghettos
3. 1968—protests against increasing American presence in Vietnam

Practice 5 *(Wording of answers may vary.)*

Main idea: People pass through three stages in reacting to unemployment.
1. Shock followed by relief
2. Strong efforts to find a new job
3. Self-doubt and anxiety if no job is found

Practice 6 (Wording of answers may vary.)

Main idea: Taking certain steps will help you to remember your dreams.
2. Put a pen and notebook near your bed.
3. Turn off alarm so you can wake up gradually.
4. Write down the dream immediately.

Practice 7

1. B
2. A
3. A
4. B
5. B
6. A
7. A
8. B
9. A
10. B

6 Relationships II

Practice 1 (Answers may vary.)

1. For instance
2. for example
3. such as
4. including
5. illustration

Practice 2

A. *Shaping*; definition—1; example 1—2; example 2—10
B. Irony—saying one thing but meaning another.
   Ex.—To end the famine in Ireland, Swift suggests the Irish should raise babies to be eaten.

Practice 3 (Answers may vary.)

1. Similarly
2. Just like
3. in the same way
4. as
5. Just as

Practice 4 (Answers may vary.)

1. however
2. Although
3. but
4. despite
5. In contrast

Practice 5

A. Contrast: Japanese employment practices and U.S. employment practices
B. Contrast: school and home
   Public discipline   Private scolding
   Much competition   Minimal competition

Practice 6 (Answers may vary.)

1. Because
2. as a result
3. so
4. Since
5. Therefore

Practice 7

A. *Cause:* Chronic stress
   Effect: Painful muscle tension
   Effect: Weakening of body's immune system
   Effect: Psychological disorders

B. *Main idea (effect):* There are several reasons that people daydream.
   Major supporting details (causes):
   1. To tolerate boring jobs
   2. To endure deprivation
   3. To discharge hostile feelings
   4. To plan for the future

Practice 8

1. A
2. C
3. B
4. C
5. A
6. B
7. C
8. A
9. C
10. B

7 Fact and Opinion

Practice 1

1. F
2. O
3. O
4. F
5. F
6. O
7. O
8. F
9. F
10. O

Practice 2

Answers will vary.

Practice 3

1. O
2. F
3. F+O
4. F+O
5. F
6. F
7. O
8. F
9. F+O
10. O

Practice 4

A. 1. F
2. F+O
3. F
4. F
5. F+O

B. 6. F
7. F+O
8. F
9. F+O
10. F+O

Practice 5

A. 1. F
2. O
3. F
4. O
5. F+O

B. 6. F
7. F
8. F
9. F+O
10. F+O

Practice 6

1. F
2. F+O

3. F
4. F+O

8 Inferences

Practice 1

1. C
2. D
3. D

Practice 2

A. 1. C
2. B
3. C
4. B

C. 9. B
10. A
11. B
12. B

B. 5. C
6. B
7. A
8. C

Practice 3

A. 3, 4, 6
B. 1, 4, 6
C. 1, 4, 6

Practice 4

1. Simile, B
2. Simile, C
3. Metaphor, B
4. Metaphor, C
5. Metaphor, C

Practice 5

1. B
2. B
3. C
4. C
5. A

6. B
7. A
8. A
9. C
10. B

Practice 6

2, 5, 6

9 Purpose and Tone

Practice 1

1. P
2. I
3. P
4. I
5. E

6. E
7. P
8. I
9. E
10. I

Practice 2

1. B
2. C
3. A

Practice 3

1. C
2. A
3. E
4. D
5. B

Practice 4

A. 1. admiring
2. sympathetic
3. critical
4. objective
5. ironic

B. 6. straightforward
7. sarcastic
8. threatening
9. self-pitying
10. sympathetic

Practice 5

1. F
2. I
3. C

4. B
5. E

Practice 6

1. B
2. A
3. B

4. A
5. B

10 Argument

Practice 1

1. A. S
   B. P

2. A. S
   B. P

3. A. S
   B. P
   C. S

4. A. P
   B. S
   C. S

5. A. S
   B. P
   C. S

6. A. S
   B. P
   C. S

7. A. S
   B. P
   C. S

8. A. S
   B. P
   C. S
   D. S

9. A. P
   B. S
   C. S
   D. S

10. A. S
    B. S
    C. P
    D. S

Practice 2

1. A, C, F
2. C, E, F
3. A, D, F
4. A, C, F
5. B, D, E

Practice 3

1. B
2. B

Practice 4

1. C
2. A

Practice 5

1. B
2. C

Practice 6

1. B
2. D

ANSWERS TO THE PRACTICES IN PART III

2 Propaganda

Practice 1
2, 5

Practice 2
2, 4

Practice 3
2, 3

Practice 4
1, 5

Practice 5
2, 4

Practice 6
1, 5

Practice 7
1. B
2. A
3. C

3 More About Argument

Practice 1
1. 2
2. 1
3. 2

Practice 2
1. 1
2. 3
3. 3

Practice 3
1. 3
2. 2
3. 1

Practice 4
1. 1
2. 2
3. 3

Practice 5
1. 3
2. 3
3. 2

Practice 6
1. 2
2. 1
3. 1

Acknowledgments

Barkin, Dorothy. "The Bystander Effect." Copyright © 1991 by Trend Publications. Reprinted by permission.

Barry, Dave. Selections on pp. 343 and 374. Reprinted by permission.

Breslau, Karen, Eleanor Clift, and Evan Thomas. "The Real Story of Flight 93." From *Newsweek*, December 3, 2001. Copyright © 2001 by Newsweek, Inc. All rights reserved. Reprinted by permission.

Brody, Jane. "New Respect for the Nap." Copyright © 2001 by the New York Times Company. Reprinted by permission.

Dunayer, Joan. "Here's to Your Health." Reprinted by permission.

Ellerbee, Linda. Excerpt from *Move On*. Reprinted by permission of The Putnam Publishing Group. Copyright © 1991 by Linda Ellerbee.

Grasha, Anthony F. "Nonverbal Communication," from *Practical Applications of Psychology*, 3rd ed., pp. 248-250. Copyright © 1987 by Anthony F. Grasha. Reprinted by permission of Addison-Wesley Educational Publishers.

Gregory, Dick. "Shame," from *Nigger: An Autobiography*. Copyright © 1964 by Dick Gregory Enterprises, Inc. Used by permission of Dutton, a division of Penguin Putnam Inc.

Hamill, Pete. "The Yellow Ribbon." Reprinted by permission of International Creative Management, Inc.

Henslin, James M. "Gender Inequality in Health Care and in the Workplace," and table on page 313 from *Essentials of Sociology: A Down-to-Earth Approach*, 4th ed., pp. 248-252. Published by Allyn and Bacon, Boston, MA. Copyright © 2002 by Pearson Education. Reprinted by permission of the publishers.

Johnson, Beth. "Urban Legends." Reprinted by permission.

Kellmayer, John. "Students in Shock." Reprinted by permission.

Landers, Ann. "College Student Deplores the Drinking Around Her." Permission granted by Ann Landers/Creators Syndicate.

Lamott, Anne. Excerpt on p. 254. Copyright © 1994 by Anne Lamott. Published by Anchor Books.

Logan, Paul. "Rowing the Bus." Reprinted by permission.

Martin, James Kirby, et al. "Lizzie Borden," from *America and Its People*, 2nd ed. Copyright © 1993 by James Kirby Martin, Randy Roberts, Steven Mintz, Linda O. McMurry, and James H. Jones. Reprinted by permission of Addison-Wesley Educational Publishers.

Index